AF557832

THE COMPLETE MAHABHARATA

Drona Parva

THE COMPLETE MAHABHARATA

Volume 6

Drona Parva

S.B. Pillay

RUPA

Published by
Rupa Publications India Pvt. Ltd 2014
7/16, Ansari Road, Daryaganj
New Delhi 110002

Sales centres:
Allahabad Bengaluru Chennai
Hyderabad Jaipur Kathmandu
Kolkata Mumbai

ISBN: 978-81-291-3261-1

First impression 2014

10 9 8 7 6 5 4 3 2 1

Printed at Gopsons Papers Ltd, Noida

To my wife Anita

Contents

A Brief Introduction

The last complete version of the Mahabharata to be written in India in English prose was the translation by Kisari Mohan Ganguli in the late 19th century. He wrote it between 1883 and 1896. To the best of my knowledge, it still remains the only full English prose rendering of the epic by any Indian.

More than a hundred years have passed since Ganguli achieved his monumental task. Despite its closeness to the original Sanskrit and its undeniable power, in more than a hundred years the language and style of the Ganguli translation have inevitably become archaic.

It seemed a shame that this most magnificent of epics, a national treasure, an indisputable classic of world literature, believed by many to be the greatest of all books ever written, is not available in complete form to the Indian (or any) reader in modern, literary and easily accessible English: as retold by Indian writers.

So we, a group of Indian writers and editors, warmly and patiently supported by our publisher Rupa Publications India, undertook a line-by-line retelling of the complete Mahabharata, for the contemporary and future reader. Our aim has not been to write a scholarly translation of the great epic, but an eminently readable one, without vitiating either the spirit or the poetry of the original, and without reducing its length.

This is not a translation from the Sanskrit but based almost entirely on the Ganguli text, and he himself did use more than one Sanskrit version for his work. However, as will be obvious, the style of this new rendering is very much our own, and our hope is to bring as much of the majesty and enchantment of this awesome epic to you as is possible in English.

Ramesh Menon
Series Editor

Acknowledgements

Thanks to my old friend Ramesh Menon, who brought me to this project. And to Kadambari Mishra, who proofread this volume.

CANTO 1

DRONABHISHEKA PARVA

AUM! Having bowed down to Narayana, Nara, the foremost of Purushas, and to Devi Saraswati, I invoke the spirit of *Jaya*!

'Janamejaya said, "O regenerate Rishi, what does the powerful and disconsolate Dhritarashtra, his eyes bathed in tears, do when he hears that Sikhandin, prince of the Panchalas, has felled his sire, the incomparable Bhishma of matchless tejas? His son Duryodhana wants to vanquish the sons of Pandu, mighty bowmen all, through Bhishma, Drona and other maharathas, and have undisputed sovereignty. Tell me, O Tapodhana, you of the wealth of penances, what the scion of the Kurus does after Bhishma, greatest of all bowmen, falls."

'Vaisampayana replied, "When he hears that his sire has fallen, Dhritarashtra is filled with anxiety and sorrow, and has no peace of mind. While he is plunged in grief, Gavalgana's son Sanjaya, who has returned that night to Hastinapura, visits the son of Ambika. With a cheerless heart and anxious for his son's victory, the king in great distress laments and then questions Sanjaya, 'Tell me, Sanjaya, after weeping for the felled mahatman, the invincible Bhishma of terrible prowess, what did the Kauravas do next, sunk as they were in an ocean of grief? Indeed, now that the swelling forces of the Pandavas would strike fear into even the three worlds, what did the assembled kings do after the Bharatarishabha Bhishma's fall?'

Sanjaya says, 'Listen attentively, Rajan, and I will tell you what happened after great Bhishma's fall.

Your warriors and the Pandavas both reflect on the dharma of the Kshatriya and are filled with wonder and joy. Then, following their swadharma, they all bow to the maharatha and make a bed of straight arrows for him, as well as a pillow, and also arrangements for his protection, all the while engaging one another in pleasant converse. The Kshatriyas bid Ganga's son farewell and circumambulate him in pradakshina; looking at one another with angry red eyes and urged by fate, they take the field once more to do battle again.

The best part of the day has passed, when the divisions of your army and those of the enemy, sally forth with a blast of trumpets and the beat of drums. With hearts filled with wrath and touched by fate, they engage each other again, disregarding the wise counsel of Ganga's son Bhishma. Due to your folly and your son's folly and the fall of Bhishma, Death himself seems to summon the Kauravas with all the kings allied to them.

Deprived of Devavrata and filled with great anxiety, the Kurus resemble a herd of goats and sheep without a herdsman lost in a forest teeming with beasts of prey. Indeed, the Kuru army looks like the firmament without its stars, like the sky without the planets, like the earth with her crops all burnt, like an oration flawed by bad grammar, like the ancient Asura sena after Mahabali was struck down, like a beautiful bride deprived of her husband, like a river whose waters have dried up, like a doe who has lost her mate and is surrounded in the vana by wolves, or like a spacious mountain cave with its lion killed by a Sarabha. Indeed, O king, the Bharata army is like a frail boat on the bosom of the ocean, tossed by a tempest blowing from every side.

Hard pressed by the heroic and inexorable Pandavas, the Kaurava host, its steeds, maharathas and elephants are distressed, helpless and panic-stricken. With the frightened kings and the common soldiers no longer relying upon one another, the army deprived of Devavrata seems to sink into the deepest Patala.

Then the Kauravas remember Karna, who, indeed, is equal to Bhishma himself. All hearts turn to the greatest of all wielders of weapons, the one resembling a Guest resplendent with gyana and tapasya, even as the suffering heart of a man turns to a friend who can allay his distress. The kings then cry out, "Karna! Karna! The son of Radha, our friend, the Sutaputra, who is ever prepared to lay down his life in battle! The illustrious Karna, with his followers and friends, did not fight these ten days. O, summon him quickly!"

In the presence of all the Kshatriyas, Bhishma, during the enumeration of valiant and mighty maharathas, called Karna an ardharatha, although that bull among men is equal to two maharathas! Thus did Bhishma slight Karna who is easily the greatest of all rathas and atirathas, he whom all Kshatriyas respect, he who would venture to fight even Yama, Kubera, Varuna and Indra!

In anger at this insult, Rajan, Karna vowed, "As long as you live, O Bhishma, I will never fight! And if you succeed in slaying the sons of Pandu in battle, I will, with Duryodhana's leave, retire to the forest and take sannyasa. But if, Bhishma, the Pandavas kill you and you find swarga, then I will fight from a single chariot, and kill all those whom you regard as great maharathas."

Having said this, and with your son's approval, Karna Mahabaho did not fight for the first ten days of the war. The awesome Bhishma slew a multitude of Yudhishtira's warriors but when he is struck down, your sons think of Karna, like men wanting to cross a river thinking of a boat.

Your warriors and sons, together with all the kings, cry out in unison, "Karna!" And they all say, "This is the time to display your valour."

We look to the invincible Karna, whom Jamadagni's son Parasurama taught the astra shastra! He, Rajan, can save us from great peril, why, even like Govinda always rescues the Devas from the gravest dangers."

To Sanjaya who thus repeatedly lauds Karna, Dhritarashtra sighs like a snake and says, 'I understand that your hearts are all turned towards Vikartana and Radha's son Karna and depend on the hero of the Sutas who is always ready to give his life in battle. I hope that shura will not belie the expectations of the grieving Duryodhana and the Kauravas, all of whom look to him for sanctuary. With Bhishma, the refuge of Kauravas fallen, will Karna, greatest of bowmen, fill the void he left and strike fear into the hearts of the enemy and crown my sons' hopes of victory with success?'"

CANTO 2

Dronabhisheka Parva continued

"Sanjaya says, 'Then Karna, Adhiratha's son of the Suta varna, knowing that Bhishma has fallen, comes like a brother who wants to rescue your son's army from the distress into which it has fallen. Indeed, hearing that Santanu's son, the maharatha of unfading glory, has been struck down from his chariot, Karna, greatest of all wielders of bows, swiftly joins the battle, coming to rescue the Kuru host which is like a boat sunk in the ocean, like a father to save his children.

Karna addresses the soldiers, "When Bhishma parantapa, who possessed firmness, intelligence, prowess, vigour, truth, self-restraint and all the virtues of a Kshatriya, and also devastras, humility, modesty, pleasing speech and freedom from malice, the slayer of the enemies of Brahmanas, in whom these attributes resided as permanently as Lakshmi in the moon, alas, has fallen, I regard all the other Kshatriyas as already slain. Due to the eternal connection of all things with karma, nothing exists in this world that does not perish. When Bhishma Mahavrata has been felled, who can say with certitude that tomorrow's sun will rise? When he, endued with prowess equal to that of the Vasus, born of the tejas of the Vasus, when he, the sovereign of the earth, has fallen, do you grieve then for your possessions, your children, for this very Bhumi, the Kurus and this host?"

Thus does Karna, with a dismal heart and eyes filled with tears, attempt to console your sons. Hearing what he says, your sons and their soldiers, initially wail and weep copious tears. However, when the dreadful battle is rejoined, the Kaurava akshauhinis, urged on by the kings, once more set up loud shouts, and Karna, bull among maharathas, speaks to the great chariot warriors of the Kaurava army, words which bring great joy.

Karna says, "In this transient world, I regard all things as ephemeral for they continually flit towards the jaws of Death. Still, with all of you present, how could Bhishma, bull of the Kurus, immovable as a hill, be struck down from his ratha? The son of Santanu even now lies on the ground like the Sun himself fallen from the firmament and the Kuru kings are scarcely able to face Arjuna, like trees that cannot bear the mountain-wind. Let the burden to protect this helpless and despondent Kuru army, whose greatest warrior the enemy has already cut down, now devolve on me. In this fleeting universe, since the greatest of all Kshatriyas has been laid low, why should I have any fear of battle? Rampaging through this field, I will despatch the Pandavas to Yama. I hold honour and fame as the highest objectives in the world and I will annihilate them in battle, or be slain and sleep on the field of war.

Yudhishtira possesses determination, intelligence, virtue and might; Bhima is equal to a hundred elephants in strength; Arjuna is young and is the son of Indra, the king of the Devas; thus, even the gods cannot easily vanquish the Pandava force. They include in their ranks, the twins, each like Yama himself, Satyaki and Devaki's son Krishna. Approaching them is like entering the jaws of Death from which no coward can return.

As the wise meet growing ascetic power with their own tapasya, so should force be opposed by force. Truly my mind is fixed firmly upon fighting the enemy and protecting my own. O sarathy, today I will defy the enemy's might and vanquish him on this Kurukshetra. I will not allow this feud between cousins to continue. When the troops are broken, he who helps in the endeavour to rally them is truly a friend. I will either achieve this deed of dharma worthy of an honest man, or casting off my life, I will follow Bhishma. I will either slay all my enemies united, or killed by them, find for myself the regions reserved for heroes. O Suta, I know that this is what I must do when women and children cry for help, or when Duryodhana's power sustains a diminution. Therefore will I today vanquish the foe in this terrible war, heedless of my very life; I will protect the Kurus and destroy the sons of Pandu and all my other enemies banded together. And then I will bestow undisputed sovereignty on Dhritarashtra's son.

Let me don my golden kavacha, bright and radiant with jewels and gemstones, and my crown, effulgent as the sun, let me take up my bows, and arrows that resemble fire, poison or serpents. Let also sixteen quivers be tied to my chariot in their proper places and let a number of superior bows be stocked in it as well. Let also shafts, spears, heavy maces and my conch worked with gold, be got ready. Fetch my many-coloured, beautiful and brilliant gold standard, with the lustre of the lotus and bearing the device of an elephant; clean it with a fine cloth and deck it with garlands and cover it with a mesh of wires. O Suta's son, bring me some fleet horses, not lean, of the hue of tawny clouds, bathed in water sanctified with mantras and caparisoned in trappings of bright gold. Quickly bring me such an excellent ratha, decked with garlands of gold, adorned with gems bright as the sun or the moon, stored with every weapon and yoked to superb steeds. Bring me also a number of strong bowstrings for my bows; bring me quivers, large and full of arrows, and armour for my body. Bring me also with haste, every auspicious thing needed before setting out for battle, the brass and gold vessels full of curd. Bring garlands of flowers and tie them to the limbs of my body. Let drums be beaten for victory!

Then fly to where Arjuna Kiritin, Vrikodara, Dharmaputra Yudhishtira and the twins are. I will either kill them, or being killed by them, follow Bhishma. Arjuna, Krishna, Satyaki and the Srinjayas are a force that cannot be conquered by the kings. But even if all-destroying Death himself, with unremitting vigilance, is to protect Arjuna, I will still have his life; or go myself to Yamaloka like Bhishma. Truly I say to you, I will ride into the very midst of those Kshatriyas. The kings that are my allies are not provokers of feuds, or of weak attachment to me, or of unrighteous souls."

And so, riding on a wonderful, rich and mighty chariot, with an excellent flagstaff and to which are yoked the best horses, fast as the wind, decked with gold, auspicious and flying a noble standard, and whose rumble resembles the rumbling of clouds, Karna rides forth fully prepared for battle. Worshipped by the greatest of Kuru maharathas, even like Indra by the Devas, the mahatman and fierce archer, of immeasurable energy like the Sun himself, rides leading a large force to the heart of the battlefield where Bharatarishabha Bhishma has paid his debt to nature.

Handsome and with the splendour of fire, the son of Adhiratha, the matchless bowman and mighty warrior, then mounts his radiant chariot and shines like Indra riding on his celestial vimana.'"

CANTO 3

DRONABHISHEKA PARVA CONTINUED

"Sanjaya says, 'Seeing the Pitamaha, the venerable Bhishma, that destroyer of all the Kshatriyas, the soul of dharma, and of infinite tejas, that matchless archer shot down from his chariot by Arjuna with his devastras and lying on a bed of arrows, looking like the vast ocean dried up by mighty winds, the hope of your sons for victory disappears along with their peace of mind. He was always an island for men sinking in the fathomless ocean in their endeavours to cross it; and that Kshatriya now lies covered with arrows that coursed in a stream as continuous as that of the Yamuna, looking like Mainaka of awesome splendour struck down by Indra. He lies prostrate on the earth like the sun fallen from the firmament, he who looks like the inconceivable Indra himself after his defeat of long ago by Vritra. The depriver of all warriors of their very senses, the greatest of all shuras, the idol and ideal of all bowmen, bull among men, your Pitamaha Bhishma Mahavrata, the grandsire of the Bharatas, has been struck down in battle, covered with Arjuna's terrible shafts, and lies on a Kshatriya's bed.

Adhiratha's son Karna alights from his chariot in great sorrow, numb with grief and in tears. He approaches on foot and with joined palms, says reverentially, "I am Karna. Be you blessed! O Bhaarata, open your eyes and look at me and speak sacred and auspicious words to me. Certainly no man can enjoy in this world the fruits of his pious deeds, when you, venerable in years and devoted to dharma, lie mortally wounded on the ground. O Kurusattama, I do not see that there is anyone else among us who is remotely your equal in filling the treasury, in counsels, in the deploying of troops in the vyuhas of war and in the use of weapons. Alas, you who are endowed with a righteous intellect and have always protected the Kurus from every danger and killed numberless warriors are now on your way to the realm of the Pitris.

From this day, the Pandavas, energised by this success, will slaughter the Kurus like tigers hunting deer. Today the Kauravas, familiar with the force of the twang of the Gandiva, will view Arjuna with complete terror, like the Asuras do Vajradhari Indra. Today, the sound of the arrows shot from the Gandiva, like heaven's thunder, will fill the Kurus and all other kings with absolute fear and like a raging conflagration devours a forest, the shafts of the Kiritin will consume the Dhartarashtras. In the parts of a forest through which fire and wind flare together, they burn all plants, vines and trees. Without doubt, Arjuna is such a surging fire and Krishna is like the wind. The blast of the Panchajanya and the twang of the Gandiva will fill all the Kaurava troops with abject terror and panic.

Without you, when Arjuna rides at them, our kings will hardly bear the thunder of his monkey-bannered chariot. Who among the kings, save you, can match him whose feats in battle the wise say are all superhuman? Superhuman was the battle that he fought with the Mahadeva of three eyes. From Him he obtained a boon that men of unsanctified souls can never attain. Delighted by the duel, Siva blessed the son of Pandu and gave him his own astra. Who is there to vanquish him whom even you could not defeat although you vanquished the fierce destroyer of the very Kshatriya race, Parasurama, whom the Devas and the Danavas worship?

I am skilled and can withstand the son of Pandu, that greatest of

Kshatriyas. With your leave and blessing, I will even kill this valiant and ferocious warrior who is like a snake of virulent poison and who slays his enemies with just the looks from his eyes!"""

CANTO 4

Dronabhisheka Parva continued

"Sanjaya says, 'After listening to Karna, the aged Kuru Pitamaha, with a happy heart, gives this valuable advice, "Like the ocean to rivers, like the Sun to all luminous bodies, like men of dharma to Truth, like fertile soil to seeds, like the clouds to all creatures, be the refuge of your relatives and friends! As the Devas depend on him of a thousand eyes, let your kinsmen look to you. Be the conqueror of your enemies and the enhancer of the joys of your friends. Be to the Kauravas what Vishnu is to the dwellers of swarga.

O Karna, for Dhritarashtra's son you once conquered the Kambojas of Rajapura. In Girivraja, you defeated many kings, among whom Nagnajit was the greatest, as well as all the Ambashtas, the Videhas and the Gandharvas. You forced the Kiratas, so fierce in battle, who dwell in the fastness of Himavat, to accept Duryodhana's sovereignty. You subdued all the Utpalas, the Mekalas, the Paundras, the Kalingas, the Andhras, the Nishadas, the Trigartas and the Balhikas. In many other countries, Karna, driven by just the wish to benefit Duryodhana, you crushed many vamsas and kings of great tejas.

Like Duryodhana, with his kinsmen, relatives and friends, be you also the refuge of all the Kauravas. In words of blessing I command you, go and fight the enemy. Lead the Kurus in battle and bring victory to Duryodhana. You are my grandson just as Duryodhana is. According to the law, all of us also are as much yours as Duryodhana's! The wise say that the companionship of the righteous with other men of dharma is a superior relationship to the one with those born of the same womb. Therefore, regard the Kaurava army as your own and protect it even as Duryodhana would."

Karna reverentially touches Bhishma's feet, bids him farewell and joins the other Kaurava archers. Looking at the vast and matchless Kuru army he encourages and exhorts the well-armed and broad-chested warriors. All the Kauravas led by Duryodhana are overjoyed and seeing the Mahabaho Karna take the field and station himself at the head of their army; eager again for battle, they receive him with loud shouts, slapping of armpits, leonine roars, twanging of bows and diverse other kinds of loud bold sounds.'"

CANTO 5

DRONABHISHEKA PARVA CONTINUED

"Sanjaya says, 'Seeing Karna Purushavyaghra mount his chariot, Duryodhana is filled with joy, and says, "With your protection, this army now has a proper leader. Let us decide our strategy and what we can achieve with our might.'

Karna replies, "Tell us yourself, O Naravyaghra, for you are the wisest of kings. No one can know better what to do than the one who is the most concerned. All these kings want to hear what you have to say. And I am sure that you will say nothing that is amiss."

Duryodhana says, "Bhishma was our commander, our aged and seasoned senapati, mighty, learned and supported by all our warriors. He achieved great glory, massacred vast numbers of my enemies, and served us by fighting with dharma for ten days. He achieved the most difficult feats but now that he is fallen, who, Karna, do you think is fit to be our senapati after him? Without a senapati, an army cannot fight a war for even a short while. You are the greatest warrior among us. An army without a general is like a boat without a helmsman or a chariot without a charioteer. Like a merchant who falls into every kind of distress when he is unacquainted with the ways of the country he visits, an army without a senapati is exposed to every kind of danger and loss. Therefore, look among the noble warriors of our host and identify a commander who can succeed the son of Santanu. All of us, without hesitation, will accept anyone you choose as the one fit to lead us."

Karna says, "All these best of men are mahatmans, and every one of them deserves to be our senapati. There is no need for any minute examination since all of them are highborn and masters of the art of war; they all own prowess and intelligence, and are heedful men who know the shastras. They are all wise and resolute in battle. Yet, since not all of them can at once be the supreme commander of our forces, we must choose just one of them in whom there are special and exceptional merits to be our senapati. All of them regard one another as equals and if you honour one among them, the others will be discontented and will no longer fight wholeheartedly for you.

Drona, however, is the Acharya of all these warriors; he is venerable in years, and worthy of reverence. Therefore, let this greatest of all warriors be made our senapati. Who else is worthy of becoming our supreme leader, when the invincible Drona, foremost of men who know the Brahman, equal to Sukra or Brihaspati, is among us? Among all the kings in your army, Bhaarata, there is not a single warrior who will not gladly follow Drona when he takes the field. Drona is the foremost of all our commanders, our greatest warrior, and the first among all intelligent men. Besides, Rajan, he is your guru. So, Duryodhana, make him the senapati of your forces without hesitation or delay, even as the Devas made Kartikeya theirs in their war against the Asuras."'

CANTO 6

DRONABHISHEKA PARVA CONTINUED

"Sanjaya says, 'Hearing what Karna says, king Duryodhana addresses Drona, who stands amongst the troops. "For the superiority of the varna of your birth, for the nobility of your parentage, for your learning, your age and intelligence, for your prowess, skill, invincibility, knowledge of the world, policy, self-conquest, as well as for your tapasya and your gratitude, superior as you are in every virtue among these kings, there is none who will make a better senapati than you. Protect us, therefore, as Indra did the Devas. With you as our general, we will, O best of Brahmanas, vanquish our enemies.

As Kapali among the Rudras, Pavaka among the Vasus, Kubera among the Yakshas, Vasava among the Maruts, Vasishta among Brahmanas, the sun among light-givers, Yama among the Pitris, Varuna among aquatic beings, as the Moon among the stars, and Usanas among the sons of Diti, so are you the greatest of all lords of armies. Therefore, be you, O Anagha, our lord in war. Let these eleven akshauhinis be obedient to your command. Deploy these men for battle and destroy our enemies like Indra slaying the Danavas. You lead us all, even like Pavaka's son

Kartikeya at the head of the celestial host.

We will follow you into battle, like bulls following the leader of a herd. You are a fierce and great archer, and besides, seeing you stretch your bow at the head of our forces, Arjuna will not strike. Without doubt, Naravyaghra, if you become our senapati, I will vanquish Yudhishtira with all his followers and kinsmen in this war."

After Duryodhana says these words, all the kings in the Kaurava army cry "Jaya! Jaya Drona!" They delight your son with a tremendous shout. The troops, with Duryodhana at their head, filled with joy and eager to win great renown, begin to glorify that best of Brahmanas. Then, Rajan, Drona addresses Duryodhana.'"

CANTO 7

Dronabhisheka Parva continued

'Drona says, "I know the Vedas and their six angas. I am also familiar with the science of human affairs and know the Saivastra and diverse other weapons. I will attempt to display all the virtues that you have attributed to me, while I fight the Pandavas. However, O king, I will not be able to kill Drupada's son Dhrishtadyumna, for he was born to kill me. I will fight the Pandavas who will not fight me with happy hearts and I will raze the Somakas."

Thus permitted by Drona, your son, Rajan, then makes him senapati of his forces with the rites laid down in the shastras. The kings in the Kaurava army led by Duryodhana perform the investiture of Drona as the supreme commander of their forces, even like the Devas led by Indra in the ancient days, performing the investiture of Skanda.

The pounding of drums and the blare of conches follow this ritual—the expression of the Kaurava army's joy. They honour Drona with such cries as greet one's ears on a festive day, with auspicious invocations by Brahmanas, and gratify him with cries of *Jaya!* from the foremost of Brahmanas and with the dance of mimes and other players. The Kaurava warriors regard the Pandavas as already vanquished.

Then maharatha Drona, Bharadwaja's son, now senapati of the Kaurava army, deploys his troops for battle, and goes forth to the field with your sons to engage the enemy. The ruler of the Sindhus, the king of the Kalingas and your son Vikarna, all clad in mail, take up their positions on Drona's right side, supported by Sakuni and a squadron of great horsemen belonging to the Gandhara tribe, bearing bright lances. Kripa, Kritavarman, Chitrasena, and Vivimsati, led by Dusasana, protect the left flank supported by the swift cavalry of Kambojas led by Sudakshina, the Sakas and the Yavanas. The rear guard is comprised of the Madras, the Trigartas the Ambashtas, the westerners, the northerners, the Malavas, the Surasenas, the Sudras the Maladas, the Sauviras, the Kaitavas, the easterners and the southerners with your son Duryodhana at their head.

The Suta's son, Karna, at the head of the bowmen, adds prowess to the advancing force and gladdens the warriors of their army. His blazing, large and tall standard bearing the device of the elephant's girth rope, shines with an effulgence like that of the sun, gladdening his own akshauhinis; seeing Karna, no one anymore regards Bhishma's death as a calamity and the kings, along with the Kurus, are rid of their grief.

Large numbers of warriors huddle together and tell one another, 'Finding Karna on the field, the Pandavas will never be able to face us in battle. When Karna can vanquish the very Devas with Indra at their head, what can the sons of Pandu do, who are of little energy and strength? The Mahabaho Bhishma spared the Parthas in battle, but Karna will kill them with his scorching shafts.' Speaking thus to among themselves and filled with elation, they advance boldly, applauding and worshipping Radha's son Karna.

Drona arrays our legions in a Sakata vyuha, the cart formation, Rajan, while the serene Yudhishtira chooses the vyuha of the Krauncha, the crane, for his army. At the head of their formation are those two greatest of all men, Krishna and Dhananjaya, flying their banner with the device of the great Vanara. The inspiration of the whole army and the refuge of all its bowmen, Partha's banner, imbued with immeasurable tejas as it floats in the sky, seems to illumine the entire host of Yudhishtira Dharmatman. The potent standard of Arjuna seems like the blazing sun that rises at the end of the yuga to consume the world.

Among archers, Arjuna is the best; among bows, the Gandiva is the foremost; among all beings, Krishna is the first; and among all kinds of war chakras, the Sudarshana chakra is the greatest. Bearing these four embodiments of tejas, Swetavahana in his chariot takes up his position at the front of the enemy army, quite like the fierce chakra upraised to strike. Thus, the two greatest warriors stand at the very head of their respective forces—Karna at the head of your army and Dhananjaya at the head of the hostile one. Both excited with wrath and each wanting to kill the other, Karna and Arjuna glower at each other.

When Bharadwaja's son, maharatha Drona rides into battle like a storm, the very earth seems to tremble with a deep, chasmal wailing. The thick dust raised by the wind envelops the sky and the sun like a canopy of tawny silk. Though the firmament is cloudless, a shower of pieces of flesh, bones and blood falls on the earth. Vultures, hawks, cranes, kankas and crows in thousands, incessantly fall upon the Kaurava troops. Jackals howl and many fierce and terrible birds repeatedly wheel to the left of your army, in evil omen, impatient to eat flesh and drink blood; showers of blazing meteors, illuminating the sky and with their tails spread wide, fall on the field echoing with loud and uncanny sounds. And when the senapati of the Kaurava army rides forth, the wide disc of the sun, Rajan, seems to emit flashes of lightning and peals of thunder. One sees these and many other fierce portents, indicating an imminent devastation of Kshatriyas.

Battle erupts again between the armies of the Kurus and the Pandavas, each wanting to annihilate the other. So loud is the din that it seems to fill the whole world; and the Pandavas and the Kauravas, all masters of war, all in the grip of battle's consuming rage, strike each other with every manner of weapon, all determined to win the war.

Drona of blazing glory rides recklessly, furiously at the Pandava host, spraying hundreds of arrows at the enemy every moment. The Pandavas and the Srinjayas reply, O king, with their own searing fusillades. But swiftly routed by Drona, the vast host of the Pandavas and the Panchalas break ranks, like flights of cranes buffeted irresistibly by a dread wind. Invoking a slew of devastras, in moments Drona dreadfully besieges the Pandavas and the Srinjayas, while their blood sprays everywhere. Drona slaughters the Panchala forces led by Dhrishtadyumna, like Indra the Danavas. The Acharya lances terror through the enemy ranks.

Then, spurred to blind rage, Yagnasena's son, maharatha Dhrishtadyumna, master of devastras looses storms of recondite shafts at Drona's troops and rends them savagely all around, hundreds of men falling to his towering archery. He, the Pandava senapati, slaughters as many of Drona's men as the Acharya does his. The mighty-armed Drona quickly rallies his forces around him, and charges Drupada's son ablaze on Kurukshetra. Like an enraged Maghavat attacking the Danavas, Drona assails the Pandava and the Srinjaya ranks, so powerfully and remorselessly that they break ranks and flee before the terrible Brahmana like a herd of small animals set upon by a great lion. The mighty Drona devastates the Pandava force like the fabled ring of fire that protects the chalice of amrita.

It is truly amazing, wondrous, O Rajan, how Drona mounted on his magnificent ratha even like a city coursing through the sky, his horses past superb, his sarathy masterful, his flagstaff like shining crystal, and his banner flapping wide in death's wind, strikes perfect and absolute terror into the hearts of the enemy and wreaks unprecedented carnage among them.'"

CANTO 8

DRONABHISHEKA PARVA CONTINUED

"Sanjaya says, 'Seeing Drona furiously destroy horses, riders, maharathas and elephants, the Pandavas surround him. Yudhishtira tells Dhrishtadyumna and Arjuna, "Carefully surround the pot-born Drona with our men and check the slaughter he brings to us."

The maharathas Arjuna and Dhrishtadyumna, along with their soldiers, challenge Drona's wild onslaught. The Kekaya princes, Bhimasena, Subhadra's son, Ghatotkacha, Yudhishtira, Nakula and Sahadeva, Virata of the Matsyas, Dhrishtadyumna and the five sons of Draupadi, all exhilarated, and Dhrishtaketu, Satyaki, the fierce Chitrasena, the maharatha Yuyutsu, and many other kings who follow the sons of Pandu, all achieve diverse feats in keeping with their lineage and prowess, while now Drona looks on in frustrated rage.

Further inflamed, the invincible Brahmana warrior standing erect in his ratha yet consumes the Pandava host like a tempest dispelling cloud masses. Tilting from all sides at chariot-warriors, horses, foot-soldiers and elephants, Drona, despite his years, careens over the field like a young man. His thoroughbred chestnut horses, fleet as the wind, covered in blood, are beautiful and awesome. Yudhishtira's soldiers flee when they see him razing their ranks like an angry Yama. And as some take flight, others rally, some look at him dazed, and others remain on the field, the noise they make is tumultuous and terrible. The fearful din, which delights the brave and makes the timid tremble, fills all the sky and the earth. And once more Drona, roaring out his own name like a battle cry, makes himself still more awful, scourging his enemies with hundreds of arrows.

Indeed, though old, the mighty Drona even looks half his years as he rides everywhere loosing his tides of arrows at the Pandava legions like Death himself, striking off heads and arms decked with ornaments, emptying chariots in gory blasts, all the while uttering tigerish roars. At his terrifying roars and the force of his shafts, the enemy warriors, my lord, shiver like a herd of cows beset by deep winter's cold.

Kurukshetra resounds with the rumble of Drona's chariot, the twanging of his bow. His shafts fly in thousands from his bow, enveloping all the points of the compass, and fall upon enemy elephants, horses and horsemen, chariots and foot-soldiers.

The Panchalas and the Pandavas unflinchingly advance on Drona, who, with his mighty bow, resembles a dread fire with arrows and astras for its leaping flames. Countless elephants, foot-soldiers and horsemen he despatches to Yama and turns the battleground into bloody mire. Invoking mighty astras and spraying his shafts thickly on every side, Drona soon covers all the points of the compass, so that among millions of foot-soldiers, chariots, horsemen and elephants, one can see nothing save Drona's arrows. The pennant on his chariot is all that one sees, flashing here and there like streak lightning amidst all the other chariots.

The irrepressible Drona attacks the five princes of Kekaya, Drupada of the Panchalas, and then dashes against the akshauhini of Yudhishtira Dharmaraja.

Bhimasena, Arjuna, Satyaki, the sons of Drupada, the ruler of Kasi, the son of Saibya, and Sibi himself, gladly and with loud roars, swathe him with their arrows. Shafts in thousands, with wings of gold, shot from Drona's bow, pierce right through the bodies of the elephants and the young horses of these warriors, and plunge into the earth, their feathers dyed in blood. Strewn with chariots and the prostrate forms of numberless warriors, elephants and horses torn by the Brahmana's shafts, Kurukshetra looks like the sky covered with banks of black clouds.

Ever seeking victory for your sons, Drona rampages to decimate the divisions of Satyaki, Bhima, Dhananjaya, Subhadra's son, Drupada, the king of Kasi, and excoriates many other Kshatriyas as well. Indeed, achieving these and many other terrible feats, that maharathin scorches the world like the sun as he rises apocalyptic at the end of the yuga.

After Drona entirely destroys more than two Pandava akshauhinis of brave and resolute warriors, the canny hero Dhrishtadyumna Mahabuddhi finally slays the Brahmana shura with the golden chariot; and Drona attains mukti, the highest state. Indeed, Rajan, it is only after he has brought the most horrific carnage to the Pandava and Panchala legions with his astras, letting rills of blood on hallowed ground, do they finally kill him.

When the Acharya dies, a loud uproar from all creatures and all the troops fills the sky. Resounding through heaven, earth and the intermediate space and through the cardinal and the subsidiary directions, one hears the loud cry "O Fie!" from all beings; and the Devas, the Pitris, and his friends; all watch that incomparable maharatha, the son of Bharadwaja, slain. With this triumph, the relieved and overjoyed Pandavas give vent to leonine shouts, and the earth trembles with their celebrant roaring.'"

CANTO 9

DRONABHISHEKA PARVA CONTINUED

"Dhritarashtra asks, 'How did the Pandavas and the Srinjayas kill Drona, who was such a matchless warrior? Did his chariot break down in the fight? Did his bow break while he was shooting at the enemy, or was Drona careless at the moment when he was killed? Sanjaya, how could Prishata's son kill the greatest of Brahmanas, that invincible hero gifted with such speed of hand, who could loose torrents of gold-winged shafts to great distances in the twinkling of an eye, who was a master of all the forms of warfare, of astounding skills, self-restrained, and also a master of the devastras?

It is plain to me that destiny is superior to effort and exertion since Dhrishtadyumna has killed the magnificent Drona, maharatha of unfading glory, who was always cautious, who achieved incomparable feats in battle, the Brahmana who verily embodied the four kinds of weapons. Ah, alas, you tell me that the same Drona, Acharya of archery, is slain!

Oh, hearing that the hero who rode his bright ratha covered with tiger skins and adorned with the purest gold is dead, I cannot contain or drive out my burning grief! Undoubtedly, Sanjaya, no one dies of grief from another's end, since, wretch that I am, I am still alive after hearing of Drona's death. Destiny is truly all-powerful and all effort fruitless. Surely, my heart is made of adamant, since it does not break into a hundred pieces after hearing of Drona's death. How can Death take him whom Brahmanas and Kshatriyas alike came and served to acquire instruction in the Vedas and divination and archery? Oh, I cannot brook the killing of Drona; it is even like the ocean drying up, or Meru being uprooted from his place, or the sun falling from the sky.

He restrained the evil, and protected men of dharma, and now he has given up his life for the wretched Duryodhana! He was equal to Brihaspati or Usanas himself in intelligence and upon his ability rested the hope of victory that my evil sons entertained. Alas, how was he slain?

Did his great, strong, keenly-trained, chestnut Sindhu horses, caparisoned in golden mesh, swift as the wind, yoked to his mighty chariot and drawing it so wonderfully, always neighing joyfully and invincible to every weapon, and always protecting him in the midst of war, grow suddenly weak and collapse? How did they overwhelm those Sindhu steeds of wonder that drew Drona's chariot, which could calmly face the sound of elephants trumpeting in war, the blare of conches and the pounding of drums; which were unmoved by the twanging of bows and showers of arrows and other weapons; those steeds that were ominous by their very appearance, never short of breath, exhausted or in pain? When such were the horses that drew his golden ratha, why could he not cross the sea that is the Pandava army?

What feats did Drona achieve in battle, the warrior who always drew tears from other Kshatriyas, and upon whose knowledge of weapons all the best archers of the world rely! What all did this mighty man of dharma do in battle?

Who were the maharathas who challenged that doer of fierce deeds, the best of all the bowmen, first among shuras, who was like Indra himself?

Did the Pandavas flee on seeing him, mighty and strong on the golden chariot, and invoke devastras? Or, did Dharmaraja Yudhishtira and his brothers with Dhrishtadyumna for their binding cord, fall upon Drona after surrounding him with their troops on all sides? Arjuna with his faultless arrows must have checked all the other chariot-warriors, and then, protected by Partha, Dhrishtadyumna must have brought death to the mighty Acharya. Possibly the brave Kekayas, Chedis, Karushas, Matsyas and the other kings surrounded the Acharya, like ants crawling over a snake, even while he was engaged in some difficult feat, and so allowing the wretched Dhrishtadyumna to bring him down.

How could the venerable Brahmana, master of the four Vedas with their angas and the Itihasas the fifth Veda, the refuge of all Brahmanas as the ocean is of rivers, that blazing parantapa, who lived both as a Brahmana and as a Kshatriya, alas, meet his end at the point of a weapon?

A proud spirit, he had yet to often endure humiliation and to suffer much pain on my account. However undeserving, he met his end at the hands of his pupil Arjuna. Such a dharmatman and yuddhavira, whose feats all bowmen in the world looked up to—alas, how could men greedy for riches kill such a one? Foremost in this world, like Indra in swarga, of great might and energy, alas, how could the Parthas kill him, like a whale being killed by smaller fish? He, from whose presence no challenger could ever escape with life, he whom, while he lived, the two sounds of the Vedas being chanted by those learning Vedic lore and the twang of bows, never left; he who was never dispirited or dejected, alas, that Naravyaghra, that shura endowed with prosperity and never vanquished in battle, that warrior of prowess equal to that of the gaja or the simha, has been slain!

Sanjaya, I cannot bear the very thought of his death. How could Dhrishtadyumna, in the sight of all the greatest men in the world, murder the invincible Drona whose might was unequalled and his fame never tarnished?

Who fought in Drona's van, protecting him, and who, riding by his side? Who guarded his rear and who were the maharathas who shielded the right and the left wheels of Drona? Who were before him while he strove in battle? Who were they, who reckless of their lives, met death with him and joined him on his last journey? Did any of these Kshatriyas assigned to protect Drona prove false and abandon him in battle, thus letting the enemy kill him while he was alone? However great the danger, Drona would never turn his back on battle from fear. How then did the enemy kill him? Even in great distress, Sanjaya, an illustrious man should demonstrate his prowess to the full measure of his might. All this was in Drona. Ah, Sanjaya, I am losing my mind! Let us stop this speech a while until I regain my reeling senses.'"

CANTO 10

DRONABHISHEKA PARVA CONTINUED

'Vaisampayana said, "Saying this to Sanjaya, Dhritarashtra, in extreme grief and distressed about the hopelessness of his son, Duryodhana's, victory, falls unconscious onto the ground. His attendants rush forward to fan him and sprinkle him with perfumed cold water, while the royal Bhaarata women surround him, weeping, gently rub him with their soft hands; and slowly lifting him up from the ground, seat him on his throne. He remains insensate and still, until a tremor passes through his body and he slowly regains consciousness.

He begins to question Sanjaya again about the incidents that occurred on the battlefield.

Dhritarashtra asks, 'Ajatasatru Yudhishtira who, like the risen sun, dispels darkness with his own light, who charges an enemy like an inflamed tusker in musth, whom no other herd leader can arrest, rushing eagerly towards a female elephant in heat—which of my warriors keep him at bay when he charged Drona? Who are the Kshatriya heroes that surrounded that best of glorious men, who killed so many of my brave men, that intelligent, courageous king of unbaffled prowess, who, bent on victory, could single-handedly consume the entire host of Duryodhana with just his terrible glances, that resplendent archer, that self-restrained king whom the whole world reveres?

Which valiant men of my army surround the invincible prince, Kunti's son Bhimasena, bowman of unfading glory, Naravyaghra, hero of gigantic fame and untold valour, strong as ten thousand elephants, when he rushed wildly at Drona?

When Arjuna, maharatha of exceeding tejas, came looking like a mass of clouds discharging thunderbolts, loosing showers of arrows like Indra pouring down rain, and making all the points of the compass resound with the slapping of his palms and the rattle of his chariot-wheels; when he whose bow is like the lightning's flash, whose chariot too resembles a cloud with the sound of its wheels its thunder, the hum of whose arrows is so very fierce, whose wrath resembles a dreadful thunderhead and who is as quick as the mind or the tempest; who always strikes an enemy deep in his very vitals, who is terrible to look at, who like Yama himself bathes all the points of the compass with human blood and who, with awful visage and fierce noise, wielding the Gandiva, lashes my warriors led by Duryodhana with arrows whetted on stone and fletched with vultures' feathers—alas, when that hero of great intellect descended upon you, what was your state of mind?

When Arjuna, with Hanuman upon his banner, obstructed the sky with dense swarms of arrows, what was your state of mind? Did Partha advance upon you, slaying your troops at will, with the Gandiva pealing in his hands, accomplishing great feats on the way? Did he take your lives like the tempest destroying gathering cloud-masses or felling forests of reeds by blowing through them? Who is there that can face the Gandivi in battle?

Just hearing that he leads the enemy's forces, the heart of every opponent would seem to be broken. In the war in which the troops tremble and even great Kshatriyas are terrified, who stood firm by Drona and which cowards abandoned him from fear? Who, reckless of their lives, met Death himself, facing them squarely in the shape of Dhananjaya who can vanquish even unworldly adversaries in battle?

My troops cannot withstand the impetus of Swetavahana and the twanging of the Gandiva that is like the thunder of the very clouds. Why, I believe the very Devas and the Asuras united together cannot conquer the chariot that has Vishnu himself for its charioteer and Dhananjaya for its warrior.

When the son of Pandu, Nakula, delicate, young, intrepid and so handsome, gifted with exceptional intelligence, skill, wisdom and prowess, invincible in battle, attacked Drona with loud roars, which shuras of my army contained him?

When Sahadeva, who resembles an angry snake of virulent venom, that invincible hero of the white steeds, who observes laudable vows, is resolute and modest attacked us, which Kshatriyas of our army encircled him?

O Sanjaya, which of my warriors resisted Satyaki who, having crushed the mighty host of the Sauvira king, took for his wife the beautiful, perfect-limbed Bhoja maiden, that bull among men Yuyudhana, gifted with decisiveness, awesome courage and brahmacharya, that maharatha always keeping dharma, never unhappy, never vanquished, who in battle is equal to Krishna and is regarded as Krishna's second self, who, through Arjuna's tutelage has become the greatest of bowmen, why, equal to Partha himself. Who resisted Satyaki, at least trying to keep him away from Drona?

Know, O Sanjaya that Satyaki of the Satwata vamsa, Yuyudhana greatest hero of the Vrishnis, is equal to Parasurama himself in his knowledge and genius in the use of weapons. Ability, fame, truth, determination, intelligence, heroism, the knowledge of Brahman, and of the great astras, are all to be found in him, as the three worlds are in Krishna. Which Kshatriyas of my host confronted this peerless bowman, the indomitable Satyaki whom not the Devas can contain?

Which of my warriors surrounded Uttamaujas, greatest among the heroic Panchalas, ever achieving wondrous feats at arms, high-born, favourite among champion warriors, devoted to Arjuna, born just to destroy my evil, equal to Yama, Vaisravana, Aditya, Mahendra, or Varuna, fearless maharatha always ready to lay down his life?

Who opposed that singular Chedi warrior Dhrishtaketu, ally of the Pandavas, when he charged Drona?

Who resisted the heroic Ketumat, slayer of prince Durjaya, even when Durjaya took refuge in Girivraja? Who kept the predatory Ketumat away from Drona?

Which of my Kshatriyas challenged the Naravyaghra Sikhandin, Yagnasena's son who knows the strengths and weaknesses of his own nature, who is man and also woman, who is always unperturbed in battle, the Kshatriya who became the cause of Mahatman Bhishma's fall? Who kept Sikhandin away from Drona?

O which Kshatriyas of my army defied the greatest hero of the Vrishnis, the noble Abhimanyu, Subhadra's son, that most transcendent of all archers, the intrepid son of Arjuna more accomplished than Dhananjaya himself, in whose weapons truth and brahmacharya dwell, who is equal to Krishna in tejas and Dhananjaya in urjas, who in splendour is equal to Aditya and in intelligence to Brihaspati, who is like Yama himself with yawning maw? Which of my heroes contained the youthful and radiant Abhimanyu when he charged Drona? What was your state of mind when that Parantapa of boundless vigour plunged towards the Acharya?

Which Kshatriyas surrounded the Purushavyaghras, the sons of Draupadi, when like rivers rushing towards the sea they hurtled at Drona? Who tried to keep those children, the heroic sons of Dhrishtadyumna—Kshatranjaya, Kshatradeva, Kshatravarman and Manada, who gave up all boyishness and sport for twelve years to observe stern vratas and to wait upon Bhishma to acquire the astra shastra from him? Who kept those ferocious youths away from the Acharya?

Who defied the great archer Chekitana, whom the Vrishnis regard as superior in battle to a hundred other maharathas, to keep him away from Drona?

O, which of the Kshatriyas of my army attempted to stop the onrush of the five Kekaya brothers, valiant, virtuous, irresistible in fight and of exceptional skills and prowess, who have the hue of the Indragopaka insect, clad always as they are in red coats of mail, with red weapons and red banners, cousins and fervent supporters of the Pandavas? Who faced those heroes when they rode at Drona to have his life?

Which champion from my army withstood Yuyutsu, lord of war, first among great bowmen, of unerring aim and prodigious strength, Naravyaghra whom many vengeful kings battled for six months at Varanavrata but could not quell him, and who, in a swayamvara at Varanasi, overthrew the prince of Kasi with a broad-headed arrow, and seized a young princess for his wife?

Which Kshatriyas of my host confronted the mighty, mighty Dhrishtadyumna, raised almost in Drupada's lap, the fire-born prince who is the chief counsellor and senapati of the Pandavas, who so hates Duryodhana, who was born to kill Drona, when he attacked the Acharya, breaking through my ranks, destroying all my warriors in battle in scarlet tide?

The Maharatha Saibya measured this earth on his chariot as if with a leather belt, and as a substitute for all other sacrifices, performed without hindrance ten Aswamedha yagnas with ample and excellent food, drink and gifts offered in profusion. He rules his subjects as if they are his children, gives away in sacrifices kine as numerous as the grains of sand in the Ganga; he whose feats none among men has or will ever be able to imitate, and after the performance of which, the very Devas once cried out, "We do not see in the three worlds with their mobile and immobile creatures anyone other than Usinara's son, who ever was, is, or will ever be born, who has acquired the rarest realms in the after-life unattainable by other men." O, Sanjaya, who in my army stood firm against this Saibya, Usinara's grandson, while he attacked Drona?

Which heroes of my army encircled the chariot-division of Parantapa Virata, king of the Matsyas, when it neared Drona on the field?

Who kept the gigantic Ghatotkacha away from Drona, that heroic Rakshasa who always puts forth his inhuman strength for the Pandavas' victory, Ghatotkacha who owns great powers of maya, apart from enormous strength and superhuman prowess, he who was born to Bhima in the course of a single day and of whom I entertain such terrible fears?

Who, Sanjaya, can remain unconquered by those who are prepared to lay down their lives in battle? How can the sons of Pritha meet with defeat, when they have the greatest of all beings, Krishna, wielder of Saringa, for their refuge and benefactor? He is, indeed, the Master of all the worlds, the Lord of all, the Eternal One! Narayana Divyatman, of infinite power, is the refuge of men in battle. The wise tell of his unearthly feats. Ah, let me also recite them with devotion, so that I may recover my composure and resolution!'"

CANTO 11

DRONABHISHEKA PARVA CONTINUED

"Sanjaya says, 'Yes, as I saw everything that happened with my own eyes, I will describe how Drona falls, slain by the Pandavas and the Srinjayas.

After he is appointed senapati of the Kaurava army, Bharadwaja's son, Drona maharatha, says to your son in the midst of all the troops, "O Rajan, how can I thank you for honouring me with the command of your legions after the son of Ganga? What desire of yours can I now fulfill? Ask any boon that you wish."

Having consulted with Karna, Dusasana and others, Duryodhana says to the Acharya, "If you will give me a boon, seize Yudhishtira alive and bring him here to me!"

Drona replies, gladdening all the men there, "Praise be to Yudhishtira, Kunti's son, whom you wish only to capture O invincible one. Why do you, Duryodhana, who are a strategist, not seek Yudhishtira's death? It is wonderful that he has no enemy wishing his death. Do you want him to live to preserve your race from extinction, or having vanquished the Pandavas in battle, are you keen to establish brotherly relations with them by giving back their kingdom? Auspicious was the birth of the intelligent prince Yudhishtira Mahabuddhi. He is truly called Ajatasatru—the man with no enemies, for even you have affection for him."

Hearing these words of Drona, the feeling that is ever present in your son's heart is plainly exposed. Not even a Brihaspati can conceal the expressions of his countenance! Your son filled with joy, answers, "By killing Kunti's son in battle, Acharya, victory cannot be mine. The very Devas cannot slay all of them and if Yudhishtira is slain, Arjuna or he among them who survives, will surely annihilate us. Yudhishtira, however, is truthful in his promises. If brought here alive and defeated once more at dice, the Pandavas will again go into the vana, for they are all obedient to their eldest brother. Such a victory will be an enduring one. This is why I do not wish to kill Dharmaraja Yudhishtira but to take him alive."

Ascertaining this crooked purpose of Duryodhana, Drona, conversant with the truths of the science of artha and gifted with great intelligence, reflects a little and gives him the boon, circumscribing it in the following way. Drona says, "If Arjuna does not protect Yudhishtira, you can consider the eldest Pandava as already brought captive to you. As for Arjuna, the very Devas and the Asuras together, led by Indra, cannot face him in battle. It is for him that I dare not do what you ask of me. Without doubt, Arjuna is my sishya and I am his Acharya. He is, however, young, blessed with great good fortune, and set upon achieving his purposes. He has obtained many astras from Indra and Rudra; and, besides, you have provoked him direly. I dare not, therefore, do what you ask.

However, if Arjuna is removed from the battle by whatever means, you may regard Yudhishtira as already taken. Since our victory rests upon his being captured alive, and not upon his death, we can accomplish this by stratagem, O bull among men! Seizing the king devoted to truth and dharma, this very day, I will yield him up to you. But only if he faces me in direct battle for at least a moment, and if you can lure Arjuna away from the field. For otherwise Yudhishtira cannot be captured."

After Drona promises that he would seize Yudhishtira, but if Arjuna is far from him, your foolish sons consider the Dharmaraja as already taken. Duryodhana knows Drona's partiality for the Pandavas and in order to make Drona fulfil his given word, he proclaims Drona's oath before all his troops.'"

CANTO 12

DRONABHISHEKA PARVA CONTINUED

"Sanjaya says, 'When your troops hear of Drona's vow to capture Yudhishtira, they roar their approval, mingling their lusty yells with the whistling of their arrows and the booming of their conches. Dharmaraja Yudhishtira, however, soon learns of Drona's oath and his intention through his spies. He brings together all his brothers and the other kings of his army and tells Arjuna, "You have heard, Naravyaghra, of Drona's plot. Take such measures that will prevent him from capturing me. It is true that Drona has sworn his pledge but its success or failure depends on you. Therefore, stay and fight today in my vicinity so that Drona will not keep his word given to Duryodhana."

Arjuna says, "Just as I can never cause the death of my Acharya, I can never give you up, my brother. O Yudhishtira, I would rather sacrifice my life in battle than fight against my guru. This son of Dhritarashtra wants sovereignty by taking you his captive in battle. He will never succeed. The Sky with its stars may fall down, the Earth herself may split in pieces, but Drona will not take you his captive as long as I am alive, not even if Vajradhari Indra or Vishnu at the head of the Devas comes to help him. As long as I live, Rajan, do not have any fear of Drona, although he is the greatest of all warriors. I further assure you that my word is never broken nor does what I swear ever remain unfulfilled. I do not recollect ever having spoken an untruth, ever being defeated, or leaving the least part of a vow unfulfilled."

Then, Rajan, small and big conches, drums and cymbals are sounded and beaten in the Pandava camp. The noble Pandavas roar and shout, and the awful twanging of their bowstrings and the slaps of palms reach into the high heavens. Hearing the loud booming of conches that arises from the camp of the mighty sons of Pandu, your divisions also sound diverse instruments.

Your legions and the enemy's forces slowly advance against each other in battle order and soon savage, bloodcurdling battle breaks out again between the Pandavas, the Kurus, Drona and the Panchalas. The Srinjayas fight vigorously but cannot make headway as Drona himself shields his forces. So also, your son's best maharathas cannot beat back the Pandava army, for the diademed Arjuna Kiritin protects it. Guarded by Drona and Arjuna, both sides appear as if to stand quite still, like two blossoming forests in the silence of the night.

Then Drona, mounted on his golden chariot, like the magnificent Sun, bursts headlong through the ranks of the Pandavas, smashing them down at will. The Pandavas and the Srinjayas are afraid and feel as if this single mahatejasvin warrior upon his racing ratha has multiplied into many maharathas. Drona's terrible shafts fly in all directions, petrifying his opponents and he is indeed like the Sun himself at mid-day shedding a thousand rays of light all around. Just as once the Danavas could not face Indra, there is no one among the Pandavas who is able to face the raging son of Bharadwaja. After he confounds the hostile troops, Drona swiftly begins to decimate the legion led by Dhrishtadyumna, mowing them down with his incessant volleys of arrows which cover all the points of the compass.'

CANTO 13

DRONABHISHEKA PARVA CONTINUED

"Sanjaya says, 'Seeing Drona, wrathful warrior in his golden chariot, causing great havoc among the Pandava host and destroying their divisions like a forest-fire consuming a vana, the Srinjayas tremble in fear.

In battle, the twang of the maharatha's taut bow resounds like roaring thunder. Fierce arrows that Drona shoots with light like speed decimate chariot-warriors, horsemen, elephant-warriors and foot-soldiers, along with their elephants and horses. Showering down arrows, like roaring clouds helped by the wind raining hailstones at the close of summer, he brings terror to the hearts of the enemy. Raging through the hostile ranks and petrifying the troops, the mighty Drona swells the unnatural fear that his enemies feel. The gold-decked bow on his fleeting ratha is like the streak of lightning in a mass of dark clouds.

The shura, firm in truth, wise and always devoted to dharma, causes an awful river of angry current to flow there, such as seen only at the end of the Yuga. The river has its source in the recklessness of Drona's wrath and is haunted by thronging carnivores. Fighting men are the waves that cover its surface, and great heroes constitute the trees on its banks whose roots the river's current constantly erodes. Its waters are the blood shed in the battle, chariots are its eddies, and elephants and horses form its banks. Coats of mail are its floating lilies, the flesh of men is the mire on its bed, the fat, marrow and bones of fallen animals and men are the sands on its banks, and fallen head-gear is its froth.

The battle itself is the canopy above its surface; lances, the fish with which it abounds, and it is uncrossable for the vast number of slain men, elephants and horses that fall into it. The impetus of shafts loosed constitute its flow, corpses the timber floating on it; chariots its tortoises; heads the stones strewn on its banks and bed; swords and scimitars its fish in profusion; chariots and elephants form its lakes and it is decked with many adornments. Maharathas constitute hundreds of little whirlpools and blood-damp earth its wavelets. Though it can easily be crossed by men of exceptional valour, the timid can never ford the dread river of death. Heaps of bodies pile up on sandbanks, obstructing its navigation, and it is the seething haunt of kankas, vultures and other birds of prey.

It bears away thousands of maharathas to Yama's abode. Long spears are the snakes that infest it in profusion and the living combatants are the fowl frolicking on its waters; torn chatras, parasols, are its swans, and diadems the smaller birds that adorn it. Wheels are its turtles, maces its alligators, and arrows its smaller fish. It is home to frightful swarms of crows, vultures and jackals.

The river carries away hundreds of those that Drona kills in battle to the region of the Pitris. Dammed by these numerous bodies floating upon it, the hair of slain warriors and animals are like its moss and weeds. The inexorable and awesome Drona causes even such a river to flow there, terrifying the timid, magnifying their fears.

While Drona is thus desiccating the enemy army everywhere, the Pandava warriors led by Yudhishtira rush at him from all sides. Seeing this, your brave soldiers counter attack from every direction and a hair-raising battle ensues. Sakuni, full of a hundred kinds of deceit, attacks Sahadeva and pierces his charioteer, standard and chariot, with many keen shafts. Sahadeva, however, remaining unruffled, first cuts down Saubala's standard, breaks his bow, strikes his charioteer and carves splinters from his ratha; and he then pierces Sakuni himself with sixty shafts like thunderbolts.

Seizing up his mace, Sakuni jumps down from his fabulous chariot and fells Sahadeva's charioteer with a blow, so the sarathy falls out of his ratha. Then, Rajan, those two heroic and mighty warriors, both on foot and armed with gadas, battle like the peaks of two mountains.

Drona and Drupada, king of the Panchalas, draw blood from each other with braces of searing arrows. Bhimasena strikes Vivimsati sharply, but Vivimsati remains wonderfully unmoved. Serenely he cuts down Bhimasena's horses, standard and bow winning the worship of all the witnessing troops. The incensed Bhima cannot brook this and in a blur kills Vivimsati's pedigreed horses, at which the mighty Vivimsati, taking up a shield and sword, jumps down and charges Bhimasena and they fight like two demented elephants.

The heroic Salya, laughing the while, pierces, as if in jest, his own beloved nephew Nakula with a flurry of arrows, mainly to annoy him. Nakula, however, in a hot flash shoots down his uncle's horses, royal parasol, standard and charioteer, and blows his conch in echoing triumph.

Dhrishtaketu engages Kripa, wards off diverse kinds of arrows Kripa looses at him, pierces him with seventy fiery barbs and then cuts down the device of his standard with three perfect arrows. Kripa replies with a thick shower of shafts and the fight between the Brahmana and Dhrishtaketu rages on.

An amused Satyaki bloodies Kritavarman squarely through his chest with a special long arrow and then strikes him in a wink with seventy more. The Bhoja replies in kind but like swiftly coursing winds failing to move a mountain, Kritavarman cannot move Satyaki at all or affright him in the least.

The Pandava senapati strikes Susarman deeply in his vitals and is himself stabbed with a lance through his shoulder-joint. Virata, with his energetic Matsya warriors, manfully resists Vikartana's son and this feat of the Matsya king is a deed of great valour for he singly contains an entire legion with his immaculate archery.

King Drupada engages with Bhagadatta, and the combat between these two warriors is quite beautiful to watch. Bhagadatta, bull among men, lacerates Drupada, his sarathy, his standard and whole chariot with a myriad of arrows. The wrathful Drupada swiftly strikes the maharatha squarely through his chest with a flawless shaft. The two great warriors, Somadatta's son Bhurisravas and Sikhandin, masters of every kind of weapon, fight a fierce duel that terrifies all. Bhurisravas covers Yagnasena's son Sikhandin with a heavy downpour of arrows and is in turn pierced with ninety shafts, making him tremble.

Both capable of creating a hundred illusions, and swelling up with pride, Hidimbi's son Ghatotkacha and Alambusha, fierce Rakshasas, battle each other in the most astonishing manner, using their powers of maya, vanishing and reappearing at will—each set on vanquishing the other.

The fierce Chekitana fights Anuvinda, and they range right across the field, causing great amazement. Lakshmana fights Kshatradeva fiercely, even like Vishnu, long ago, against the Asura Hiranyaksha. The mighty Paurava roars at Abhimanyu as he attacks him wildly. Abhimanyu retaliates fiercely but Paurava envelops him in a mantle of arrows. Arjuna's marvellous son fells his antagonist's standard, parasol and rives his bow. He pierces Paurava with seven arrows and with another five strikes deep his charioteer and horses, gladdening his own troops, and then repeatedly roars like a lion.

In a blur, Abhimanyu fits an arrow to his bowstring that is certain to take Paurava's life. Seeing this, Kritavarman, Hridika's son, with two thunderbolt like shafts, breaks both Abhimanyu's bow and arrow. Abhimanyu flings aside his broken bow, takes up a bright sword and a shield decked with many stars, and whirling these at great speed, he careens across the field, putting his prowess on display. Whirling them overhead and then brandishing them fiercely, and leaping high himself, he makes no difference between using blade and shield for defence and vicious attack.

He leaps suddenly onto the axle-shaft of Paurava's ratha, gives a mighty shout and next moment is in the chariot and seizes Paurava by his hair, meanwhile breaking his sarathy's neck with a terrific kick, and cutting down his proud standard with a fluent stroke of his sword. Abhimanyu raises Paurava up high, like Garuda a snake from the bottom of the sea, agitating the waters. All the kings see Paurava helplessly flung down and dragged about on his chariot floor, his hair disheveled, and looking like an ox deprived of its senses and on the point of being killed by a lion. Jayadratha cannot bear to watch Paurava being so roughly mishandled; seizing up a sword and a shield that bears the device of a peacock, decked with a hundred little bells hung in rows, he jumps down from his chariot with a roar. Abhimanyu sees the king of the Sindhus, lets Paurava go and springs like a launching hawk from that warrior's ratha, landing lithely on the ground. Like some dancer, he effortlessly wards off with his sword and shield the javelins, arrows and swords that his enemies aim at him, showing off the strength of his own arms.

Mighty Abhimanyu once more raises his great sword and shield, and now rushes at Vriddhakshatra's son, a sworn enemy of his father, why, like a tiger rushing at an elephant. Both shuras, they joyfully fall on each other, just like a tiger and a lion with claw and tusk. No one finds any difference between them in the swinging strokes and the flashing thrusts and parries of their swords and shields. They circle each other gracefully, quite beautifully, and seem like two winged mountains of old.

Abhimanyu bends low and thrusts out with his sword, and in blink Jayadratha dances aside and swings down mightily from above with own blade but it breaks in shards against the gold-plated shining shield of Arjuna's son. Jayadratha hastily retreats six steps and in the twinkling of an eye, is back on his own chariot. The duel with the sword over, Abhimanyu also climbs back into his own chariot. Ten enemy kings of the Kuru army now unite and surround him, but still eyeing Jayadratha, mighty Abhimanyu continues to whirl his sword and brandish his shield and lets out a deafening roar of triumph.

Having bested Jayadratha, Abhimanyu proceeds to burn the Kaurava legions like the Sun scorching the world at midday. Salya casts a vicious iron spear at him, decked with gold and like a blazing flame. Abhimanyu jumps up high and catches it in flight, as Garuda may a mighty snake in the air. Seeing this, all the kings together give a great howl and in a flash Arjuna's son casts Salya's own spear back at him like a streak of lightning. Looking like, a snake that has recently cast off its slough, the missile kills Salya's charioteer in a burst of blood and fells him from the ratha. Virata, Drupada, Dhrishtaketu, Yudhishtira, Satyaki, Kekaya, Bhima, Dhrishtadyumna, Sikhandin, Nakula and Sahadeva, and the five sons of Draupadi all exclaim, "Uttamam! Excellent!"

Diverse kinds of sounds fill Kurukshetra—the loud hum of arrows, leonine shouts, all exhorting the aggressive son of Arjuna. Your sons cannot bear these sounds and all of them suddenly surround Abhimanyu and cover him with hails of arrows like clouds pouring down rain on a mountain-breast. The parantapa Salya storms up to support your sons and remembering the death of his own charioteer, attacks Abhimanyu furiously.'"

CANTO 14

DRONABHISHEKA PARVA CONTINUED

"Dhritarashtra says, 'O Sanjaya, you have described to me many awesome duels. Hearing about them, I envy those that have eyes. All men will speak of this battle between the Kurus and the Pandavas, which reminds one of the great and wonderful wars of ancient times between the Devas and the Asuras. Ah, I am agog to listen to your narration of this stirring battle. Tell me more about the duel between Salya and Abhimanyu.'

Sanjaya says, 'Seeing his charioteer killed, Salya, with his iron mace upraised, jumps down in rage from his ratha; at which, Bhima hefts his own huge gada and rushes at Salya who looks like the blazing Yuga-fire or the Destroyer Himself, armed with his cudgel. Abhimanyu, too, plucks up a remarkable mace like the Vajra itself, and taunts Salya, crying, "Come! Come on!"

Bhimasena, though, persuades his nephew to stand aside, and advances on Salya who stands immovable as a hill, calmly watching Bhima come towards him like a tiger at an elephant. The blare of trumpets, thousands of conches booming, roars and shouts and the sound of drums then erupt and cries of "Jaya! Jaya!" arise among hundreds of Pandava and Kaurava warriors charging towards each other.

There is no one among all the kings, O Bhaarata, other than the king of the Madras who can bear the might of Bhimasena in single combat; similarly, who else in the world, save Vrikodara, can withstand the illustrious Salya's mighty mace? Grasped by Bhima, his prodigious gada, bound in hempen strings mixed with wires of gold and magnificent to behold, shines so brilliantly. And Salya's mace, adorned with beautiful circles, looks like a blaze of lightning. Both of them bellow like bulls, circle each other, and standing as they do with their maces slightly bent, truly resemble a hillocky pair of horned bulls. The duel between the two lions among men is in every way evenly matched. Bhimasena strikes Salya's formidable mace with his own, and draws a burning cascade of sparks. And Bhima's gada, struck by Salya, is like a beautiful tree covered by fireflies at eventide, during the monsoon.

The mace that Salya hurls at Bhima lights up the sky; likewise, the gada that Bhima flings at his enemy scorches Salya's forces like a meteor falling from the sky. Both wonderful maces strike each other like hissing she-snakes and we see flashes of fire. Like two great tigers mauling each other with their talons, or like two mighty elephants goring each other with their tusks, the titanic warriors circle, striking one another with utmost violence; and soon, covered with blood, they look like a couple of flowering Kinsukas. The sound of the blows of the maces wielded by those two lions among men is as loud as Indra's thunder; and it echoes on all sides. Soon, they are so battered that they can hardly move, like hills stricken by lightning. Yet, both of them are still full of vigour and, moving in smaller circles, quickly fall upon each other again like two bull-elephants, the leaders of their herds, and pound each other with their iron maces, and then fall down at the same moment like a pair of Indra's massive sacrificial stakes!

In a wink, Maharatha Kritavarman darts up to Salya lying breathless and senseless on the field, hauls him up into his chariot and bears him away. Immediately, reeling like a drunk, Bhima gets up and stands ready, gada in hand, for further fight. Seeing Salya of the Madras turn away from the battle demoralizes your sons, along with their elephants, foot soldiers, horsemen and chariot-warriors. Sensing victory, the Pandavas quickly attack the frightened men of your army, who break ranks and flee in all directions, like masses of clouds scattered by the wind.

The triumphant Pandava maharathas are resplendent in that moment, Rajan, like blazing fires. Elated and joyful, they let out loud yells and roars, blow their conchs, beat their drums, large and small, clash cymbals and sound other instruments.'"

CANTO 15

Dronabhisheka Parva continued

"Sanjaya says, 'Seeing your army comprehensively routed, Rajan, Karna's son, the valiant Vrishasena, single-handedly comes to their defence, creating an astounding mayic illusion with his astras. He sends flights of thousands of arrows of blinding effulgence soaring in all directions, like the rays of the sun in mid-summer, and striking men, horses, chariots and elephants, destroying chariot-warriors and horsemen, who fall like trees broken by the wind, in their thousands. Watching this single warrior wheel fearlessly on the field, all the kings of the Pandava army unite to surround him. Nakula's son, Satanika, attacks him and strikes him with ten keen barbs, but in a flash Vrishasena breaks his bow and cuts down his standard.

The other sons of Draupadi, anxious to rescue their brother, charge Vrishasena and shroud him with their arrows. Immediately, many maharathas led by Aswatthama dash up to defend Vrishasena and lash the mighty sons of Draupadi with all kinds of shafts, which fall like rain on mountain breasts. The Pandavas join the fray. The ensuing battle between your troops and those of the Pandavas is fierce and enthralling, indeed like the Devasura yuddha of old.

Having stoked intense enmity between them for past wrongs, in the grip of wrath, the heroic Pandavas and Kauravas fight savagely, even like Garuda and the mighty Nagas battling in the sky. With Bhima, Karna, Kripa, Drona, Aswatthama, Dhrishtadyumna and Satyaki, the battlefield is lustrous, terrible and resplendent as the all-destroying Sun that rises at the end of the Yuga. The brutal and awesome contention is surely like the Devasura yuddha of yore. Roaring like the swollen sea, Yudhishtira's host brings slaughter to your army, and even your maharathas flee the fight. Seeing the debacle, Drona rallies them, crying, "Kshatriyas do not run!"

Drona of the red steeds, now fuming with rage, is like Indra's four-tusked elephant Airavata, and surging forward he scatters the Pandava soldiers, penetrates deep into their host and attacks Yudhishtira. Yudhishtira responds with a fever of arrows fletched with the feathers of the kanka bird, drawing blood on his Acharya. Drona breaks Yudhishtira's bow in his hands and forges ever closer to the Pandava king.

Kumara, renowned prince of the Panchalas, protector of Yudhishtira's chariot-wheels, confronts the advancing Drona, like a continent receiving the surging sea. Seeing Drona, that bull among Brahmanas, contained by Kumara, loud shouts of "Uttamam! Wonderful!" are heard from the Pandava warriors.

Excited and his blood risen, Kumara roars and roars, and pierces Drona deep with an arrow through his chest. Holding up the dangerous Acharya, though tiring, the mighty Kumara shows amazing lightness of hand, and strikes Drona with a thousand shafts. But then, the incensed Drona, bull among men, kills valiant Kumara, Kshatriya of dharma, who knew both mantras and astras well.

The inexorable Brahmana plunges on, loosing firestorms of arrows in every direction, mowing down your legions at his august will. He strikes Sikhandin with twelve arrows, Uttamaujas with twenty, Nakula with five, Sahadeva with seven, Yudhishtira with twelve searing shafts, each of the five sons of Draupadi with three barbs, Satyaki with five, Virata with ten. He attacks each of the Pandavas, one after the other, and beleaguers their entire host. All the while, he is advancing on Yudhishtira, seeking to capture him. Yugandhara looms before the threatening Drona, and holds him up for a while. He only provokes the raging Drona, like the ocean whipped into fury by the tempest. The Acharya strikes him with a fusillade of immaculate arrows in the heart of a moment, and then with a wedge-headed shaft beheads him, and brave Yugandhara falls out of his chariot.

Virata, Drupada, the Kaikeya princes, Satyaki, Sibi, Vyaghradatta, the Panchala princes, the valiant Singhasena and many others rush forward to protect Yudhishtira from the marauding Drona. They surround Drona to slow him down, while he burns on loosing riptides of fire on every side. Vyaghradatta, prince of the Panchalas, strikes Drona with fifty keen barbs, and the Pandava troops shout in exultation. Singhasena also draws blood from the Brahmana; Drona bristles and then, throwing back his head, gives such a dreadful roar that even those Pandava maharathas feel terror touch their hearts. Red-eyed Drona glares, twangs his bowstring like thunder and charges the pair that dares confront him. With two perfect wedge-headed arrows, he decapitates both Singhasena and Vyaghradatta. Flaring on, harrying the other maharathas of the Pandavas with remitless tirades of arrows, he stands before Yudhishtira's chariot, like all-destroying Yama himself.

Then, Rajan, loud cries of *The king is slain!* are heard among Yudhishtira's warriors; seeing Drona's fearsome, ineluctable prowess, many cry in dismay, *Today Dhritarashtra's son will have victory for Drona has captured Yudhishtira!*

But even as black despair grips them, Arjuna Swetavahana thunders up on his chariot of white steeds and suddenly stands implacable between the Brahmana and his brother. He comes bringing carnage with him, leaving a river of blood in his terrible wake, whose eddies are broken chariots and the severed limbs, heads and bodies of brave warriors, whose froth is floating arrows, whose fish are spears and other weapons clutched in the hands of fallen men, river that bore them in swift tide to where spirits of the departed dwell. Driving the enemy before him like wretched animals on a hunt, Arjuna Kiritin breaks like a flash-flood upon Drona's divisions and mantles them in a thick cloud of deadly arrows, every shaft claiming a life.

No one can distinguish when he sets his arrows to his bowstring or looses them; it is a single uninterrupted motion, without pause or let, a fluid blur, a dance, a tandava of slaughtering. Neither the four cardinal directions, nor the firmament above, nor the earth, Rajan, can be distinguished, for the singular darkness of Arjuna's arrows, engulfing all. And then the Sun also sets in a pall of dust, and friend and enemy cannot be told apart. Drona, so close to taking Yudhishtira alive, is frustrated and lets out a howl that reaches into the very sky.

The day's battle ends, and Drona and Duryodhana, Arjuna and the others slowly withdraw their denuded legions. The Pandavas, the Srinjayas and the Panchalas are full of relief and joy, and praise Partha as the Rishis eulogise the Sun. Having thus vanquished his enemies, a happy Arjuna, rides slowly to his tent at the very rear of the rest of the army, with Krishna for his companion. Standing on his beautiful chariot decked with the costliest of sapphires, rubies, gold, silver, diamonds, corals and crystals, the son of Pandu is glorious as the Moon in a firmament spangled with stars.'"

CANTO 16

DRONABHISHEKA PARVA CONTINUED

"Sanjaya says, 'The troops of both the armies retire in disciplined order to their tents, Rajan, according to the divisions and the subdivisions to which they belong.

Having withdrawn the legions, Drona, in great sadness, says to Duryodhana "I told you that when Arjuna is with Yudhishtira, he cannot be captured even by the very Devas. Look how, although all of you fell upon him, Partha frustrated all of you. Do not doubt me when I say that Krishna and Arjuna are invincible. If, however, Swetavahana Arjuna can somehow be lured away from Yudhishtira's side, I say to you that Yudhishtira will be your captive. Let someone challenge Arjuna to a battle and draw him away to a far corner of the field from where he cannot return without vanquishing the challenger. While Arjuna is away, I will penetrate the Pandava host and, in the very sight of Dhrishtadyumna, seize Yudhishtira. This I swear I will do, but only if the son of Dharma stands alone before me for at least a moment in battle. And surely, that single feat of mine will benefit us more than defeating the whole Pandava army!"

Hearing this from Drona, Susarman, king of the Trigartas, who is present there with his brothers, says, "Arjuna constantly wrongs and humiliates us, Rajan, although we have done him no injury. Remembering all those humiliations, we burn in anger and cannot sleep at nights. With some good fortune, Arjuna will confront us on the field and we will have revenge on him, which will not only suit your purpose but also bring us renown. We will lure him out of the very field and kill Arjuna. We solemnly swear that today the Earth will be either without Arjuna or without the Trigartas. Our oath will never prove false."

The five brothers Satyaratha, Satyavarman, Satyavrata, Satyeshu and Satyakarman also endorse what he says. With ten thousand chariots, they come to Duryodhana, having sworn their oath on the battlefield. The Malavas, the Tundikeras with a thousand chariots, and Purushavyaghra Susarman, lord of Prasthala, with the Mavellakas, the Lalithyas, and the Madrakas, also with ten thousand rathas, and his brothers, with another ten thousand chariots from diverse realms, also come.

They bring fire and each prepares for lighting one for himself. They take up ropes of Kusa grass and after they don remarkable coats of mail, they bathe in ghrita, put on robes of Kusa grass and tie their bowstrings as girdles around their waists. These Kshatriyas, who have given away hundreds and thousands of cows and gold nishkas as gifts to Brahmanas, who have performed many yagnas, who have been blessed with children, who have nothing more to achieve in this world, who have earned blessed regions in the hereafter, who are prepared to lay down their lives in battle, who have devoted their souls to the attainment of fame and victory, now only want to reach those unearthly kingdoms through dharma yuddha, those realms attainable by yagnas, with abundant dakshina to Brahmanas and through sacred rites, the chief among which are Brahmacharya and study of the Vedas. Having each gratified Brahmanas by giving them gold, cattle, fine clothes, and having addressed one another in loving discourse, those Kshatriyas kindle their sacred fires and take the solemn vow to either kill or be killed by Arjuna.

In ringing voices they declare in the hearing of all men, "Those realms shall be ours that are reserved for men of mahavratas, worlds which are not for those who drink wine, or have adulterous relations with their guru's wife, steal from Brahmanas, enjoy the king's favour without satisfying its conditions, or who abandon those who seek protection, who slay a rival out of selfish greed. Those exalted worlds are not for those who set fire to homes, who kill kine, who wound others with words or deeds, who harbour malice against Brahmanas, who from folly do not seek the companionship of their wives in their season, who seek the congress with women on the day they are to perform the Sraddha for their ancestors, who harm themselves, who misappropriate what is given to them in trust for safekeeping, who destroy learning, who have battle with eunuchs, who follow mean base men, who are atheists, or those who abandon their sacred fires, their mothers, and who are generally sinners.

May we lose those lofty, sacred worlds if we return from the field without killing Dhananjaya, or if we run from him on the field in fear. While if we do indeed achieve the most difficult feat in the world, of killing Arjuna, we will indeed attain to those most blessed realms of felicity and grace!"

Having said these words, sworn the grave oath for which they are henceforth called the Samsaptakas, Rajan, those Kshatriya shuras go forth into battle, and loudly challenge Arjuna, summoning him to the southernmost part of Kurukshetra. Thus challenged, Arjuna, tiger among men, subjugator of hostile cities, immediately says to Yudhishtira, "I never refuse a challenge. It is a sacred vow I have sworn. These men, Susarman and his brothers, themselves sworn to conquer or die, have challenged me to battle. You must give me leave to kill Susarman with all his followers, O Purusharishabha, for I cannot brook their arrogance and I say to you that these enemies are already dead."

Yudhishtira says, "You know, my child, what Drona has resolved to accomplish. You must not let him succeed in keeping his vile word given to Duryodhana. Drona is endowed with great prowess. He is a shura, accomplished in arms and tireless, and he has vowed to seize me."

Arjuna says, "Rajan, this Satyajit will protect you today in battle. As long as Satyajit lives, the acharya will never succeed in taking you. If, however Satyajit is slain in battle, you must not remain on the field for a moment, even if all our other warriors surround you."

Yudhishtira then gives Arjuna leave to face the Samsaptakas; the king embraces his brother lovingly and chants many mantras of blessing over him. After he makes this arrangement for Yudhishtira's protection, the mighty Partha rides against the Trigartas, like a hungry lion hunting a herd of deer. Filled with joy at Arjuna's absence from Yudhishtira's side, Duryodhana's men are eager to capture Yudhishtira. Both armies plunge furiously at each other, like the Ganga and the Sarayu in spate in the season of rains, when both rivers are swollen with water.'"

CANTO 17

Dronabhisheka Parva continued

"Sanjaya says, 'The Samsaptakas, sworn to kill Arjuna or die, are full of delight as they take their stand on a level part of the field, arraying their chariots in the vyuha of the Half-moon. Seeing Arjuna Kiritin come towards them, they give vent to lusty shouts that fill the sky and all the points of the compass. Because it is an open plain covered only with men, their roars create no echoes.

Seeing them so full of joy, Dhananjaya, with a small smile, tells Krishna, "Look, the Trigarta brothers, who are about to die, are full of delight when they should weep instead. Or, perhaps this is their moment to rejoice, since they will go to those transcendent realms that cowards can never attain."

Arjuna comes upon the arrayed ranks of the Trigartas, takes up his gold embellished conch, the Devadatta, and blows it with great force, filling the place with its blare, suddenly terrifying the Samsaptaka chariot legion, and all their animals, who stand, petrified, with staring eyes, ears, necks and lips paralysed. They urinate helplessly and some even vomit blood.

When they regain composure, they quickly form their ranks and loose their arrows all together in a stream at Arjuna. The mind-swift Pandava invokes fifteen astras and shoots down all those thousands of shafts in flight, before they can reach him. The Samsaptakas strike Arjuna with ten arrows each, and he, them with three. Each of them pierces Arjuna with five shafts; he, with two of storm force.

They shower Arjuna and Kesava with a downpour as thunderclouds do when they open. Thousands of arrows fall upon Arjuna, like swarms of bees on a flowering stand of trees in the forest. Thirty of these gold-winged barbs pierce Arjuna's crown of adamant and stick there, so he seems to wear golden ornaments, and shines like the newly risen sun.

With a wedge-headed arrow, Arjuna shreds Subahu's leathern shield; he covers Sudharman, Sudhanwan and Subahu in searing fire. They find Partha with ten arrows each, and he, the monkey-bannered shura, strikes them all with rashes of arrows, also cutting down their golden standards. He breaks Sudhanwan's bow, kills his horses and then, in a scarlet flash, cuts his turbaned head from his neck.

This terrifies the Samsaptaka troops and, panic-stricken, many break ranks and run headlong back to Duryodhana's main army. The incensed Arjuna inundates the mighty legion with a flood of arrows; he falls upon that host and begins to raze it with a ceaseless torrent of arrows, like the Sun destroying darkness with his rays. The Trigarta forces visibly melt away on all sides. The Samsaptakas are as full of fear as Arjuna is of wrath; they stand transfixed, helpless before him like a terrified herd of deer, and he slaughters them with his supernal archery. And then even their maharathas turn their chariots to flee from the terrible Pandava.

Susarman roars in rage at his maharathas, "Stand and fight, Kshatriyas! It is shameful to flee from battle. You swore such a dread and solemn oath before all the army. What will you say to Duryodhana's great commanders when you go running back to them? The whole world will mock us for such cowardice. Stand and fight!"

Hearing him, Rajan, those shuras roar aloud and blow on their conches to embolden themselves. The Samsaptakas return to the field, along with the fighting Narayana cow-herds, resolved now to face Yama himself.'"

CANTO 18

DRONABHISHEKA PARVA CONTINUED

"Sanjaya says, 'Seeing the Samsaptakas return to the field, Arjuna says to his sarathy, the divine Krishna, "Hrishikesa, ride at the Samsaptakas! They will not yield as long as they are alive. Today you will see the might of my arms and of this Gandiva. Today I will slaughter all these men like Rudra does the creatures at the end of the Yuga."

The invincible Krishna smiles, heartens his warrior with some auspicious words, and sets his chariot towards the enemy. That chariot yoked to white horses is as splendid as a celestial vimana coursing through the sky. And like Indra's ratha, Rajan, in the war between the Devas and the Asuras in olden days, it could fly in every direction.

Armed with diverse weapons, the wrathful Narayanas surround Dhananjaya, and cover him with a thick darkness of arrows. Bharatarishabha, in moments Arjuna and Krishna are entirely shrouded, invisible. His face dark with anger, Arjuna grips the Gandiva more tightly, rubs its bowstring and, his great brow furrowed deep, he blows a reverberant blast on his prodigious conch, the Devadatta. His ire provoked, his greater might summoned, the Pandava invokes and looses the devastating astra called the Tvashtri. Thousands of shining terrible Arjunas and Krishna appear on that field. Confounded and maddened by that sight, the enemy soldiers turn on one another for they see just Arjunas and Krishnas everywhere, and their every comrade one!

"Hah! Arjuna!"

"Krishna!"

"Pandu's son!"

"Yadava!"

Bewildered by the hallucinations of the astra, crying out thus, they hew blindly at one another, and their bodies are quickly like blossoming Kinsukas, sprouted in red flowers and beautiful. The astra consumes all the thousands of arrows they shot at the real Arjuna and Krishna, plunging them in a solid night; the two emerge from darkness glorious as ever. All the while, the occult weapon sends Samsaptaka heroes past counting to Yama's halls. Then, laughing in exhilaration, Arjuna turns to further raze the Lalithya, the Malava, the Mavellaka, and the Trigarta warriors. Arjuna massacres those Kshatriyas in the grip of fate, but they valiantly continue to besiege him with so many different kinds of missiles.

Yet again, the Samsaptaka arrows plunge Arjuna and Krishna in darkness and neither they nor their ratha can be seen. Seeing their arrows find their mark, their enemies roar in joy; they already celebrate, waving bright silks scarves, thinking the two Krishnas are dead. They blow their conches, beat their drums and clash cymbals in thousands, and roar in exultation like some vast pride of lions.

Krishna, bathed in sweat and weak, speaks to Arjuna in the unnatural dark, "Where are you, Partha? I do not see you. Are you alive, O Parantapa?"

At once, Arjuna invokes the Vayavyastra, weapon of the Wind, and blows away the sinister cupola of arrows, and the darkness with it. Illustrious Vayu, god of that mighty astra, blows away whole legions of Samsaptakas, thousands of men, with their horses, elephants, chariots and weapons, as if they are dry leaves. And ah, they look beautiful, like flights of birds taking wing all together from their trees!

Even while they are borne through the air and along the ground, Arjuna cuts off thousands of martial and royal heads; he cuts away weapon-wielding hands from wrists, dissects warriors' thighs like elephants trunks, and strikes others deep and fatally through backs, arms and eyes.

Arjuna dismembers his enemies and shatters their richly adorned chariots that look like cloud palaces in the sky; he kills rathikas, horsemen, elephant-riders and their beasts of war. Ruined chariots lie everywhere in dense profusion, with standards broken, looking like forests of headless palmyra trees. Elephants bearing proud banners, hooks, goads and royal standards, fall like wooded mountains split by Indra's Vajra.

Horses in mail with yak-like tails, roll on the ground with their riders, in death's spasms, their entrails and eyes gouged out, all struck by Partha's shafts. Foot-soldiers lie askew in the final postures of death, their hands no longer grasping the swords that had been their talons, their armour shredded, their bones broken and protruding ghastly, their vitals excoriated, all slain by Arjuna's irresistible arrows.

Kurukshetra, field of war, is dreadful with corpses, with warriors still being killed, the fallen and then falling, standing or being swept away. The showers of blood sprayed copiously all around by Arjuna's indescribable archery wetly clears the air of it dust. The ground strewn with thousands of headless trunks is impassable.

Arjuna's chariot shines fiercely like Rudra's ratha at the end of the Yuga, when the Lord comes as Hara to destroy creation. The warriors, with their holy horses, chariots and elephants, slaughtered by Arjuna become the guests of Indra. Strewn thickly with dead maharathas, Kurukshetra is as macabre as Yama's domains that teem with the spirits of departed creatures.

Meanwhile, as Arjuna is furiously engaged with the Samsaptakas, Drona at the head of his forces in battle array, along with many armed and famous maharathas, hunts Yudhishtira, determined to capture him. The ensuing battle is unimaginably brutal.'"

CANTO 19

DRONABHISHEKA PARVA CONTINUED

"Sanjaya says, 'The next morning, Maharatha Drona tells Suyodhana, "'I am ready! I arranged for Arjuna to be lured away by the Samsaptakas."

When Partha rides after the Samsaptakas, Drona, at the head of his vyuha, sets out to capture Dharmaraja Yudhishtira. Seeing Drona array his forces in a Garuda vyuha, Yudhishtira deploys his troops in an Ardhachakra vyuha.

At the beak of the Garuda is Drona himself while Duryodhana surrounded by his brothers forms the head with Kritavarman and the illustrious Kripa being the two eyes of that Eagle. Bhutasarman, Kshemasarman, the valiant Karakaksha, the Kalingas, the Singhalas, the Easterners, the Sudras, the Abhiras, the Daserakas, the Sakas, the Yavanas, the Kambojas, the Hangsapadas, the Surasenas, the Daradas, the Madras and the Kalikeyas, with hundreds and thousands of elephants, horses, chariots, and foot-soldiers are stationed at its neck. Bhurisravas, Salya, Somadatta, and Balhika, surrounded by a full Akshauhini, take up their position as the right wing, while Vinda, Anuvinda of Avanti and

Sudakshina, king of the Kambojas, station themselves at the left wing with Drona's son Aswatthaman.

At the rear of that Garuda are the Kalingas, the Ambashtas, the Magadhas, the Paundras, the Madrakas, the Gandharas, the Sakunas, the Vasatis, the Easterners and the Mountain-men. At its tail is Vikartana's son Karna, with his sons, kinsmen and friends, leading a large force raised from diverse kingdoms. At the heart of that formation are Jayadratha, Bhimaratha, Sampati, the Jayas, the Bhojas, Bhuminjaya, Vrisha, Kratha, and the mighty king of the Nishadas, all masters of war, surrounded by a large host, keeping Brahmaloka in their hearts and as their goal.

Drona's vyuha with its foot-soldiers, horses, chariots and elephants, heaves like a tempest-tossed ocean, as it advances to engage the enemy. Impatient warriors sally forth from its flanks, like roaring summer clouds charged with lightning, scudding in from all sides. In the midst of that army, the king of the Pragjyotishas, mounted on his war elephant, is magnificent, Rajan, like the rising sun. Decked in garlands of flower and with a royal white chatra held over his head, he is like the full moon when Soma is in conjunction with the Krittika nakshatra. His elephant, blind with the wine-like exudation from its temples rent in musth, looks like a mass of black antimony and shines like a mountain washed by the showers of mighty clouds. Bhagadatta himself, armed with various weapons, riding in the midst of many heroic kings of the hill countries, is like Indra himself surrounded by the Devas.

Yudhishtira sees that superhuman and invincible vyuha and tells Dhrishtadyumna, "O you of the steeds white as doves, do whatever you must to ensure that the Brahmana does not take me his captive."

Dhrishtadyumna replies, "O Punyavrata, Drona will never take you, however he strives to, for I myself will contain him and his forces. As long as I am alive, O Kurusthama, have no fear. Under no circumstances can Drona vanquish me in battle."

With this, Dhrishtadyumna, the mighty son of Drupada, with bow raised and streaming arrows charges Drona. Seeing the fire-born Panchala prince ride straight at him like an evil omen, Drona feels a pang of fear and weakness. Watching this, your son Durmukha, rides between the Acharya and Dhrishtadyumna, and a pitched battle erupts between them, O Bhaarata. Dhrishtadyumna covers Durmukha in a rage of arrows, and looses a scathing volley at Drona as well. Durmukha replies with thick swaths of violent shafts, arrow clouds of every hue and kind.

Even while they are thus engaged, Drona consumes many legions of Yudhishtira's army, like the wind scattering a cloudbank. Only briefly does that battle resemble an ordinary encounter, Rajan, for it swiftly turns into a wild carnage of men of absolute wrath, in the grip of the feral spirit of kali. The men can no longer distinguish their own from the enemy and the battle rages with the warriors guided only by instinct and the crying out of names. Rays of light like those of the Sun seem to fall and play upon the gemstones on their helmets, their necklaces, other ornaments and upon their coats of mail, and turn the chariots, elephants and horses adorned with streaming banners, into clouds with flocks of cranes under them.

Foot soldiers butcher other foot soldiers, cavalrymen riding horses of fiery mettle slay other horsemen, chariot-warriors kill other rathikas, and the elephant-mounted bring down other elephant-riders. Perhaps the most ferocious contention is between the elephant legions with lofty standards on their backs. The mastodons lumber at one another and great bodies collide in thunder; they gore each other deep with curved tusked, while smoke issues from white tusks locking and grinding against other tusks, so that the spectacle is like dark clouds massed in the sky and charged with lighting. The earth, spread over with elephants in mortal combat, dragging along other leviathans, trumpeting shrilly in fury and pain, drawing geysers of blood and then falling with dismal screams, quakes and looks beautiful like the autumn sky covered with clouds. The deep cries of the great beasts cut down by thousands of arrows and savage spears are like the rumble of thunderheads during the monsoon.

Some of the massive beasts, wounded with lance and barb, are panic-stricken and their tails curling run wildly from the field trumpeting in terror even like the roaring of the apocalyptic clouds of the pralaya when a Yuga ends. Some are turned back by their redoubtable riders, to the fray with sharp hooks and goads to charge the enemy again. They come back in renewed frenzy trampling, crushing to bloody pulp all that stand in their way.

Mahouts attack other mahamatras with arrows and lances and fell them from the backs of their beasts, their weapons and hooks falling from dead hands. Many riderless elephants blunder about like clouds torn from greater masses until they encounter one another and then fall to again. Some towering beasts, bearing slain warriors on their backs, or those whose weapons have fallen from their grasps, wander singly, aimlessly in all directions.

In that awful carnage of mammoths, untold numbers of the great animals are killed with spears, arrows, swords and battle-axes, and fall, shaking the earth with their heavy bodies and the sky with their echoing screams. The earth trembles repeatedly, struck all around by the falling creatures heavy as hills. With elephants killed along with their riders lying everywhere with the standards still on their backs, the earth looks eerily beautiful as if strewn with shapely grey hills running streams of red down their sides. The mahamatras on the backs of countless hulking beast, their breasts pierced by broad-headed shafts, collapse, their spears and hooks loosened from nerveless hands. Some elephants, struck through with long shafts, utter crane like cries and bolt in all directions, trampling allies and enemies alike, leaving ghastly patches of crushed bodies in their wake.

Covered with countless corpses of elephants, horses and chariot-warriors, the Earth, Rajan, is sludge of flesh and blood. Large chariots with wheels and many without wheels, shattered by great tusks, are tossed high into the air by the maddened elephants on the rampage, ever cruelly goaded by the warriors perched on their backs. Chariots are seen careering everywhere, their charioteers and warriors slain; and riderless horses and elephants, pouring blood from deep wounds and all crying out pitiably.

On horrible Kurukshetra, father slays son, and son kills father, for the war has turned altogether ghastly; the kali yuga is upon the world and dharma has left the sacred field stalked by unseen demons and every manner of sinister savagery. Men sink ankle-deep in the gory mire and look like tall trees whose lower parts have been swallowed in a forest-fire. Fine Kshatriyas' capes, coats of mail, parasols and standards are all dyed with blood and everything on the yawning field of Yama seems to have turned death's stark crimson. Muscular corpses of slain steeds ripple no more, chariots lie sad and broken, as do brave fighting men beyond count; yet the war rages on and these are further ridden over and truncated by the chariot wheels of those that fight on.

The sea of troops with elephants for its stream, slain men for its floating moss and weeds, and chariots for its fierce eddies, makes a grim and horrific spectacle. Warriors, with horses and elephants for their large craft, seeking victory for their spoil, plunge into that sea, and do not sink but soldier madly on to have their enemies' lives at any cost. When all the warriors, each bearing his particular insignia, are lashed by scathing arrow-storms, none among them loses heart, not though all have lost their proud emblems. In that greatest and most awful battle, Drona flays all the maharathas ranged against him, protecting Yudhishtira, confounding them with archery that defies both imagination and belief. Finally, the Brahmana afire draws near enough to charge Yudhishtira himself.'"

CANTO 20

DRONABHISHEKA PARVA CONTINUED

"Sanjaya continues, 'Seeing Drona near him, Yudhishtira greets him fearlessly with a thick shower of arrows. Yudhishtira's troops receive this like a herd of elephants trumpeting when a lion attacks their leader. Seeing Drona close in on Yudhishtira, the powerful Satyajit rushes at the Acharya; the Panchala prince and the Brahmana come hunting the Pandava king fight lustrously, stirring their troops even like Indra and Bali.

In a blur, Satyajit strikes Drona's charioteer with five barbs smoking like snake-venom, each one looking like Death himself. Drona swoons. Satyajit swiftly kills Drona's horses with ten deadly shafts; incensed, he pierces each of Drona's Parshni charioteers with ten arrows. Flaring around the field in a circle at the head of his troops, wrath of battle high in him, he cuts down Drona's standard.

Recovering himself, seeing his enemy's feats, Drona resolves to dispatch him. The Acharya first breaks Satyajit's bow, even as the prince draws the weapon's string back with an arrow fitted, and then plunges ten more terrible shafts deep into that Kshatriya's body. In a flash, valiant

Satyajit takes up another bow and quick as thinking strikes Drona with thirty barbs winged with the feathers of the Kanka bird. The Pandavas roar in joy and wave their capes to celebrate Satyajit's valour. Now the mighty Vrika amazes all by striking Drona squarely through his chest with a swath of sixty arrows shot in a single moment. Mighty Drona glowers and reaching into his great heart summons all his energy.

He breaks both Satyajit and Vrika's bows, and with six missiles like thunderbolts, in a red flash, he kills Vrika with his charioteer and horses. Satyajit seizes up another stronger bow and again makes Drona, his sarathy and his horses a home burning shafts. Drona cannot bear this ignominy and pounds Satyajit with a hail of shafts, drawing blood from his horses, cleaving the very grip of his new bow, and wounding both his Parshni sarathies. Yet, though his bows are thus repeatedly riven, the Panchala prince, master of the greatest astras, continues to ferociously engage the Brahmana of the red chargers. Seeing Satyajit grow in energy in their pitched duel, Drona strikes off that shining young warrior's handsome head with a crescent-tipped arrow.

When he sees the Panchala prince die, Yudhishtira does not pause a moment but, borne away by his fleet steeds, flees that perilous encounter for fear of the hunting Acharya. The Panchalas, the Kekayas, the Matsyas, the Chedis, the Karushas and the Kosalas dash at Drona from every side to protect Yudhishtira. However, awesome Drona, razer of teeming enemy hosts, calmly begins to consume those legions, like fire consuming some heaps of cotton. Virata's younger brother Satanika leads a sally against Drona, and roaring like a tiger, strikes Drona, his charioteer and horses with six streaks of lightning, polished bright as sunrays. Never pausing, though it is a hard and wild thing he does, for Drona is a Brahmana, Satanika bathes Bharadwaja's maharatha son with arrow showers.

Then, Drona aroused roars back at Satanika and, with an arrow sharp as a razor, dissevers the Matsya hero's head decked with bright earrings. And the Matsya warriors all flee. Having vanquished the Matsyas, the inexorable son of Bharadwaja repeatedly routs the Chedis, the Karushas, the Kaikeyas, the Panchalas, the Srinjayas, and the Pandus.

Seeing the enraged warrior of the golden chariot consuming their akshauhinis like a fire devouring a forest, the Srinjayas tremble with rage and fear. Drona is everywhere massacring the enemy, and we hear the awful twang of his bowstring everywhere. Fierce arrows stream from his bow without pause or let, cutting down elephants, horses, foot-soldiers, chariot-warriors and elephant-riders. As a mighty mass of roaring summer clouds blown by violent winds batters down hailstones, so Drona does arrows and fills fear in the hearts of his enemies. He blows in every direction, seemingly ubiquitous, agitating the enemy sea. We see his gold chased bow in his hands of untold genius, all around us, like streak lighting amidst dark clouds. The beautiful emblem of the Vedi, the altar on his banner resembles a peak of Himavat.

The carnage that Drona fetches to the Pandava troops is like the slaughter that Vishnu, adored by both the Devas and the Asuras, brought to the Daitya army. Heroic, truthful in speech, wise beyond measure, mighty and inexorable, the illustrious Brahmana lets a fierce river of blood, which strikes terror into the timid. Coats of mail are its waves, standards its eddies, and it bears away, as it flows, countless numbers of mortal creatures, elephants and horses its great crocodiles, and swords its fish. Ah, no one can easily cross Drona's river of death.

The bones of heroes form its pebbles; drums and cymbals its tortoises; shields and armour are its boats; the hair of Kshatriyas its floating moss and weeds; arrows are its wavelets and bows its current; the writhing arms of soldiers form its snakes; and that river of fierce tide runs over the battlefield, sweeping away both Kurus and Srinjayas. Human heads, are its grisly stones; their thighs its large fish; maces form the rafts by which many seek to cross it; and floating helmets are the froth that covers its surface and the entrails of animals of war are its reptiles. Terrible in aspect, it bears away numberless heroes to the other world; blood and flesh make up its sludge; elephants its crocodiles and flagstaffs the trees on its banks. Thousands of Kshatriyas sink in it. Fierce corpses clog it and with horse-soldiers and elephant-warriors for its sharks, Drona's blood river is impassable, as it hurtles towards Yamaloka. It abounds with

Rakshasas, wild dogs and jackals and macabre pisachas haunt its banks and drink thirstily from it.

Then, led by Yudhishtira, a host of Pandava warriors attacks Drona, as he burns on Kurukshetra like the Sun beating down on the world and devours their legions greedily like Death himself. The Pandava forces surround Drona from every side, hemming him in. At this, Rajan, the kings and the princes of your army, with weapons raised, all rush to support the Brahmana shura. Meanwhile, Sikhandin strikes Drona with five perfectly straight barbs, Kshatradharman with twenty, and Vasudeva with five; Uttamaujas pierces him with three shafts, and Kshatradeva with five; Satyaki drills him with a hundred thunderbolts, and Yudhamanyu with eight. Yudhishtira shoots the fearsome Brahmana with a dozen shafts, and Dhrishtadyumna with ten and Chekitana with three.

But then Drona, like an elephant with rent temples, routs the chariot-division of the Pandavas and he kills Dridhasena. Attacking king Kshema, who fights without fear, the wild Acharya kills him with nine arrows loosed in the space of a wish and Kshema falls lifeless in his very ratha. Ploughing his way into the very heart of the hostile troop, Drona careening everywhere, Drona bestriding the war, protects his own luminously, while he himself needs no protection at all. He strikes Sikhandin with twelve singing shafts and Uttamaujas with twenty. He despatches Vasudeva with a wedge-tipped arrow that severs his head so very cleanly; Drona savages Kshemavarman with eighty arrows shot quicker than seeing, and Sudakshina with six and twenty. He shoots Kshatradeva down from his chariot with a thick and heavy shaft. Having wounded Yudhamanyu with sixty-four arrows and Satyaki with thirty, Drona of the golden chariot once again rounds on Yudhishtira, that best of kings, who wisely flees like the wind from his Acharya.

Panchala, son of Drupada, attacks Drona feverishly. Drona in his froth breaks his bow, fells his horses and his charioteer and with a single final shaft that plunges through Panchala's armour and blows his noble heart to shreds kills Drupada's son with some satisfaction, and the young hero falls lifeless from his sad chariot like a bright star come loose from the sky.

Upon the fall of the illustrious Panchala, we hear loud cries, "Kill Drona! Kill Drona!"

But the imperturbable and violent Brahmana continues to maim and slaughter the Panchalas, the Matsyas, the Kaikeyas, the Srinjayas and the Pandavas. Supported by your Kurus, Drona then triumphantly quells Satyaki, and Chekitana's son, and Senabindu, and Suvarchas, and many other majestic Kshatriyas. Your warriors, Rajan, are victorious in that fervid encounter, and massacre the Pandava forces as they fly in all directions. The Panchalas, the Kaikeyas and the Matsyas shake with fear as they are butchered on all sides like the Danavas were of old by Indra.'"

CANTO 21

DRONABHISHEKA PARVA CONTINUED

"Dhritarashtra asks, 'When Bharadwaja's son breaks through the Pandavas and the Panchalas is there anybody who challenges him? Alas, seeing Drona standing there at the head of his troops like a tiger or an elephant in musth, such a terror to his enemies, and willing to die for Duryodhana's cause, was there no man who could face him, none of courage to enhance the fame of the Kshatriyas, a spirit that lower men can never have and which is distinctive only of the greatest? Tell me, O Sanjaya, which shuras faced Bharadwaja's son at the head of his forces?'

Sanjaya replies, 'Seeing Drona ravish the Panchalas, the Pandavas, the Matsyas, the Srinjayas, the Chedis, the Kaikeyas with his astras, so they shamefully flee from his unbearable archery, so they are like skiffs by the dreadful waves of a tempested ocean, your sons the Kauravas, roaring like lions, and blowing their conches and beating their drums, suddenly fall recklessly upon the enemy's chariots, elephants and foot-soldiers from all sides. The Pandava fighters break ranks entirely and flee blindly from the fray. At the head of his own forces, surrounded by his brothers and kinsmen, Duryodhana exults, and laughingly says to Karna, "Look Radheya, the Panchalas before Drona are like a herd of the wild deer terrified by a lion. I do not think they will come back to battle for our Acharya has blown them away as a great storm does mighty trees.

Each man for himself, they flee from his golden-winged arrows, no two of them together. They panic as men caught in whirlpools; and look now how they huddle together like elephants in a forest-fire. They are like trees in blossom swarmed by the dark bees that are Drona's arrows. With their blood flowing, they run all together, for they have no answer to the Acharya.

Look there Karna, the sight of the angry Bhima, abandoned by the Pandavas and the Srinjayas and surrounded by my warriors, delights me most of all! Ah today, that evil one see the world full of just Drona! I have no doubt that Pandu's wretched son has lost all hope today of life and kingdom."

Karna replies quietly, "Mahabaho Bhima will not abandon the battle as long as there is life in him. Neither will he brook our triumphant shouts, and nor will the Pandavas be vanquished in battle. They are valiant, resilient, powerful beyond common understanding and hard to resist in war. When they remember how we tried to poison them and burn them alive, and the shame and exile that arose from the game of dice, the Pandavas will not abandon the war.

Look where the mighty-armed Vrikodara of endless tejas has already turned back to the fight. This son of Kunti will certainly kill many of our best maharathas. With sword and bow, with astras, horses, elephants, men, chariots and with his iron gada, he will raze many legions of our soldiers. Other maharathas of the Panchalas, the Kekayas, the Matsyas, and especially the Pandavas themselves, follow him. All of them are intrepid, powerful and skilled. The mighty Bhima leads them again in wrath. Vrikodara surrounded by the bulls of his vamsas, like the clouds around the Sun, engages Drona from all sides.

Intent upon their one object, they will besiege the unprotected Drona, like insects near death flying at a burning flame. They are masters of weapons and equal to facing the Acharya in battle. Heavy is the burden that now rests on Bharadwaja's son. Let us ride quickly to Drona. We must not let them kill him like wolves hunting down a mighty elephant!"

Listening to what Karna says, Duryodhana with his brothers rushes to Drona's rescue. The sound of the Pandava warriors returning to the fight on their chariots drawn by superb horses of diverse colours, all bent upon Drona's death, is deafening.'"

CANTO 22

DRONABHISHEKA PARVA CONTINUED

"Dhritarashtra says, 'Describe for me, Sanjaya, the distinctive marks of their rathas, all those who fight for Bhimasena against Drona.'

Sanjaya says, 'Vrikodara rides a chariot drawn by dappled horses coloured like the antelope, while the brave Satyaki's has a ratha is harnessed to silvery chargers. The furious and irresistible Yudhamanyu rides a ratha with superb horses of variegated hue. Dhrishtadyumna's chariot has fleet horses yoked, in trappings of gold and grey. Red horses draw the ratha of Dhrishtadyumna's son, Kshatradharman of firm vows, who fights to protect his father and ensure his complete success. Sikhandin's son Kshatradeva's finely caparisoned horses are of the colour of lotus-leaves and have pure white eyes.

Beautiful Kamboja chargers, decked with the feathers of the green parrot, bear Nakula towards your army. Horses dark like thunderclouds take Uttamaujas into the battle, against the invincible Drona standing with arrow drawn. Sahadeva, his weapons raised, has horses fleet as the wind and of variegated hues, during that fight encounter.

Yudhishtira Naravyaghra's steeds are ivory coloured with black manes, high-strung and fleet like the wind. He rides at the head of many warriors borne along by equally swift horses, decked in gold trappings. Behind him is Drupada, the king of the Panchalas, with a golden parasol over his head, protected by all these soldiers that follow Yudhishtira. Sautabhi, great archer, has truly beautiful horses that can endure every frightful sound of war, and Virata follows him.

The Kaikeyas, Sikhandin and Dhrishtaketu, surrounded by their respective troops, follow the king of Matsyas. Excellent horses of the pale red tint of trumpet-flowers are most handsome to behold as they bear Virata into the fight, while fleet yellow steeds yellow drawn with chains of gold, carry his son Uttara. Chargers of deep red hue bear the five Kekaya brothers. The aureate Kshatriyas, with red pennants and decked with golden chains, all great heroes, loose arrows like clouds pouring down rain.

Superb steeds of the colour of unbaked earthen pots, the gift of Tumburu pull the chariot of Sikhandin, Panchala prince of great tejas.

Altogether, twelve thousand maharathas of the Panchala race take the field. Of these, six thousand follow Sikhandin. Spirited piebald horses, dappled like the antelope, carry the son of Sisupala into the fray. The bull among the Chedis, the strong and invincible Dhrishtaketu, has Kamboja steeds of variegated complexion, while, fabulous Sindhu horses of beautiful limbs and of the hue of straw smoke draw the Kaikeya prince Brihadkshatra's chariot. Of eyes of pure white their skins the colour of the lotus, horses foaled in the country of the Balhikas and decked with fine ornaments, bear Sikhandin's son, brave Kshatradeva. Senabindu, scourge of his enemies, has quiet horses of the rich hue of red silk, caparisoned in gold. Exceptional stallions of the colour of cranes bring the youthful maharatha, the delicate son of the king of the Kasi, into battle.

White steeds with black necks, swift as the mind, yet always obedient to their sarathy, bear Prince Prativindhya. Arjuna's son Sutasoma has cream-coloured steeds, which he has received from Soma Deva himself. He was born in the Kuru city of Udayendu. Blessed with the brilliance of a thousand moons he came to be called Sutasoma because he also had won great renown in an assembly of the Somakas. Horses of the colour of sala flowers or of the morning sun bear Nakula's praiseworthy son Satanika. Horses of the hue of the peacock's neck, in trappings of gold, carry Draupadi's son by Bhima, the Naravyaghra Srutakarman, her son Srutakirti, who like Arjuna is an ocean of learning, uses marvellous steeds coloured like kingfisher.

The youthful Abhimanyu, who is regarded as one and a half times superior to Krishna or Arjuna in battle, has tawny horses yoked. Horses of gigantic size bear Yuyutsu, the only son of Dhritarashtra who, abandoning his brothers, fights for the Pandavas, into battle. Plump and well-decked horses of the colour of the dried paddy stalk, bear the most energetic Vardhakshemi into the terrible battle while the youthful Sauchitti has obedient horses with black legs, fitted with golden breastplates. Srenimat has well-broken horses, their skins like red silk, whose backs are covered with golden armour and drawn with chains of gold.

Satyadhriti, accomplished in the astra shastra and in the divine Vedas, yokes red horses. Steeds coloured like pigeons draw the ratha of Dhrishtadyumna, senapati of the Pandava army, who always views Drona as his victim by fate. He follows Satyadhriti, the irresistible Sauchitti, Srenimat, Vasudana and Vibhu, son of the Kasi king. They have thought-swift steeds of the best Kamboja breed adorned with chains of gold. Each resembles Yama or Vaisravana as they take the field, striking fear into the hearts of the enemy soldiers.

Six thousand Prabhadrakas of the Kamboja country, with exceptional steeds of different colours yoked to their gold-decked chariots, and resolved to die together, ride into battle, their bows always stretched and loosing tirades of arrows at their enemies, making them tremble. Exceptional warhorses, the shade of tawny silk, decked with shining chains of gold, heartily bear Chekitana into battle.

Arjuna's uncle Purujit, also called Kuntibhoja, has extraordinary rainbow-coloured horses. Steeds the colour of the star-spangled firmament draw king Rochamana's ratha, while stallions the colour of red deer, with white streaks on their bodies, are yoked to the chariot of the Panchala prince Singhasena, son of Gopati.

That tiger among the Panchalas called Janamejaya, has sturdy horses of the hue of mustard flowers. Fleet, massive and dark blue, with golden chains, their backs the colour of curd and faces that of the Moon, are the animals of Drupada himself, which bring him storming into battle. Fearless red steeds with striking white heads, their splendour like that of the sky or the lotus, are Dandadhara's. Vyaghradatta has light brown horses with mouse-coloured backs and their necks proudly drawn up. The Purushavyaghra Sudhanwan, prince of Panchala, yokes dark-spotted horses.

Chitrayudha drives fiercely mettlesome horses of the bright colour of Indragopakas, with variegated patches, and they resemble Indra's very Vajra; while Sukshatra, the son of the king of the Kosalas' horses, draped in golden chains, have bellies the colour of the chakravaka. Stunning tall beasts of many colours and giant bodies, yet exceedingly docile, and draped with chains of gold, fetch the seasoned Satyadhriti to the fight; Sukla's standard, armour, bow and horses are all white.

Magnificent steeds born on the sea-coast and white as the moon, are yoked by Samudrasena's son Chandrasena of burning tejas, while Saiba rides an exotic chariot drawn by horses of the complexion of the blue lotus, lavishly adorned with golden ornaments and bright garlands of flowers. The inexorable Rathasena has superior steeds the colour of kalaya flowers with white and red streaks, while white horses carry that bravest of men Chitrayudha, king who slew the Patachcharas. His chariot is also drawn by other pedigreed horses red as kinsuka flowers, and Chitrayudha himself wears beautiful garlands and wears striking armour, bears diverse marvellous weapons and flies a majestic standard.

King Nila comes to battle with standard, armour, bow, banner and horses all the same colour—blue.

Chitra's chariot-fence, standard and bow are bejewelled and his horses and banner remarkable. Grand steeds of the colour of the lotus carry Hemavarna, the son of Rochamana, into the fight, while bold, strong stallions, which can haul a heavy load of weapons, whose backs are the colour of reeds, and their testicles white as the hen's egg, pull Dandaketu's ratha.

Chargers like the moon's rays wearing kavacha set with stones of lapis lazuli draw the chariot of the mighty Sarangadhwaja, king of the Pandyas, and he advances upon Drona, stretching his tremendous bow into a circle. Krishna had killed his father in battle; his country had been invaded and his kinsmen had fled. Prince Sarangadhwaja learnt and acquired the devastras from Bhishma, Drona, Rama and Kripa, and became the equal of Rukmi, Karna, Arjuna and Krishna in battle. He then wanted to destroy Dwaraka and to subjugate the whole world. Wise friends counselled him against this reckless course. Having given up all thoughts of revenge, he now rules his own dominions. Horses all the colour of the atrusa flower carry a hundred and forty thousand principle mama-rathas that follow Sarangadhwaja into battle.

Chargers of diverse colours and many different kinds of troops follow the heroic Ghatotkacha. Enormous steeds of the Aratta breed are yoked to the golden ratha of Mahabaho Brihanta of the red eyes, prince, who flouted the counsel of all the Bharatas, and singly, from his reverence for Yudhishtira, went over to him, abandoning all his most cherished hopes and desires.

Yudhishtira Dharmaraja yokes the most exceptional steeds shining like gold.

Bhimasena leads a large contingent of Prabhadrakas with horses of various colours, all flying standards of gold and ready to battle with their very lives. Rajan, that force of Bhima's truly resembles the celestial army of Swargavasis, with Indra at their head. This assembled host pleases Dhrishtadyumna no end.

Yet, Drona surpasses all these warriors in splendour. His standard with a black deerskin and the beautiful kamandalu waving in the wind is the most striking. Bhimasena's standard, with the device of a great lion emblazoned in silver, its eyes of lapis lazuli, is also splendid. Yudhishtira's standard of great tejas bears the device of a golden moon with planets around it; it, too, is marvellous. Two large and exquisite kettledrums, called Nanda and Upananda, are fastened to it. Played upon by a yantra, these create wonderful music that delights all who hear it.

We see the tall and fierce standard of Nakula, which strikes terror into the enemy, for it bears the emblem of a golden-backed Sarabha. A graceful silver swan graces Sahadeva's banner, with bells upon; it is somehow terrible, as well, and brings grief to the enemy. The pennants of the five sons of Draupadi bear the marvellous images of Dharma, Maruta, Sakra and the twin Aswins. On youthful Abhimanyu's chariot is a gorgeous flag with a peacock, bright as molten gold. On Ghatotkacha's banner is a vulture which shines brilliantly and his horses can go anywhere at will, like those of Ravana in old days.

In Yudhishtira's hands is the celestial bow Mahendra; Bhimasena has the Vayavya; Phalguni wields the Brahmaa which was created to protect the three worlds; Nakula grasps the Vaishnava, and Sahadeva the Aswina. In Ghatotkacha's hand is the terrible Paulastya.

The jewels among weapons wielded by the five sons of Draupadi are the Raudra, the Agneya, the Kauverya, the Yamya and the Girisa. The great bow called the Raudra, which Rohini's son Baladeva had, he later gave to the noble son of Subhadra, being delighted with Abhimanyu.

We see these and many other standards decked with gold flying on Kurukshetra, all of which belong to brave warriors, all of which strike their enemies with dread. The host that Drona commands does not have a single faint-hearted man in its ranks. Its countless standards flying high together seem to obscure the sky, looking like magic images in a painting. As is the custom, we hear the brave warriors announce their names and lineage as they charge Drona in battle.

Then the royal Drupada takes the field against him at the head of a mighty akshauhini and their encounter is terrible, like that between two aged and mighty tuskers, the leaders of their herds, and yet in musth. Vinda and Anuvinda of Avanti, with their troops, encounter Virata, the Matsya king at the head of his forces, as Indra and Agni did the Asura Bali in days of yore. The dread contention between the Matsyas and the

Kekayas, in which horses, maharathas and elephants fight so savagely, is like the Devasura yuddha of older days. Bhutakarman, also called Sabhapati, keeps away from Drona. However, Nakula's son Satanika attacks this Bhutakarman and with three broad-headed shafts, sharper than razors, hews off both that Kshatriya's arms and then his head.

Vivimsati intercepts the heroic and mighty Sutasoma as he advances towards Drona, spraying him with arrows. Inspired in wrath, Sutasoma drills his uncle with a clutch of line-straight barbs and, cased in mail, stands ready for a duel. Duryodhana's brother Bhimaratha looses six shafts of solid iron at the other Salwa, not the uncle of Madri's twins, and sends him straight to Yama, along with his horses and charioteer.

Chitrasena's son, Rajan, closes with your grandson Srutakarman as Srutakarman rides into battle with horses that are coloured like peacocks. These two grandsons of yours, both invincible in battle, and each determined to kill the other, fight vigorously, each one for his grandsire. Seeing Prativindhya in the van of the thick and heady fray, Aswatthaman attacks him wildly—for the honour of his father. The infuriated Prativindhya looses a rash of arrows, drawing blood from Aswatthaman who flies a lion's tail upon his standard.

Srutakirti, Draupadi's eldest son by Arjuna, sprays Drona's son with his barbs, like a farmer scattering seeds in the sowing season. The son of Dusasana bars the way of maharatha Srutakirti as Draupadi's prince flashes towards Drona. Srutakirti, however, who is equal to Arjuna himself, breaks Dusasana's son's bow in his hands, lacerates his standard and charioteer with three keen wedge-headed missiles, and charges on towards Drona.

Duryodhana's son Lakshmana stands firm against the slayer of the Patachcharas, whom both the armies regard as the bravest of the brave. Srutakirti, however, destroys both Lakshmana's bow and the standard and drawing blood-flowers from his enemy with great swiftness of hand, flares up in splendour. The wise and youthful Vikarna rounds on Sikhandin, son of Drupada, who greets Vikarna with a hot burst of arrows. The mighty Vikarna stands firm against this onslaught and is glorious on darkling Kurukshetra.

Angada confronts the heroic Uttamaujas as that Panchala prince dashes at Drona. Ferocious is the encounter between those two Naravyaghras and it infuses their troops with zeal. The mighty Durmukha covers the valiant Purujit with sizzling arrows as Durmukha also rides towards Drona. Purujit strikes Durmukha between his eyes with a long and slim shaft, so Durmukha's face resembles a lotus on its stalk!

Karna faces the five Kekaya brothers who fly red standards and course at Drona; he burns them with scorching volleys. Scathed by Karna's majestic archery, the five brothers respond with fire of their own, and a running battle erupts. Engulfed by arrows, neither Karna nor the five brothers can be seen, nor their horses, chariots, charioteers and standards.

Your sons Durjaya, Jaya and Vijaya set upon Nila, and the king of the Kasis and Jayatsena; intense is the encounter between these and it enthralls those who watch; it is as if they saw a fight between a lion, a tiger and a wolf, on the one side, and a bear, a buffalo and a bull on the other! The brothers Kshemadhurti and Brihanta harry Satyaki as the Satwata flies at Drona. The battle between these two and Satyaki is breathtaking, like one between a lion and two mighty elephants in musth, in a dim forest.

The king of the Chedis, aflame, kills hundreds of men with wrathful volleys; Ambashta, always delighted by bloody battle, keeps him far from Drona. Ambashta then strikes his antagonist with a long, long arrow that plunges into his very entrails and fells him from his chariot, the bow and arrow loosened from his grasp.

The noble Kripa, son of Saradwata, holds up Vardhakshemi of the Vrishnis, who is fury incarnate on the field, with a storm of short, thick shafts. Those who watch this duel stand riveted; they cannot tear their gazes away from the tremendous contest.

Somadatta's son, fighting of Drona, challenges the vital king Manimat. Manimat breaks his bowstring, flagstaff and sovereign parasol, so they fall out of his chariot. The son of Somadatta, who flies a yupastamba, device of the sacrificial stake, on his banner, leaps down from his ratha and with his great curved sword hacks down his adversary, along with his horses, charioteer, and carves his chariot into shards. Climbing back onto his own ratha, taking up another bow and his horses' reins himself, he begins, Rajan, to consume the Pandava host.

Vrishasena, the gifted son of Karna, looses a thick flock of arrows at the Pandava king, who is rushing into battle like Indra himself after the Asuras. With gadas, spiked cudgels, swords, stones, thick clubs, mallets, discs, short arrows, battle-axes, occult storms of dust and wind, fire and water, ashes, bricks, straw and trees, does Ghatotkacha fall on your forces, smiting and shattering—altogether terrifying as he lets rills of blood flow, also on his careen towards Drona. The fell Rakshasa Alambusha bars Ghatotkacha's way with a myriad of weapons common and strange. The battle between those fiercest and greatest of Rakshasas resembles the one between the Asura Sambara and Indra of long ago.

Thus, with your blessings, O king, hundreds of fervid single battles blaze between the maharathas, elephants, horses and foot-soldiers of your army and theirs in the midst of the dreadful general engagement. Such is the battle, at whose eye is Drona, so bloody and so brutal, that none like it has ever been seen or heard of before. Indeed, O lord, numberless are the pitched encounters that burn across all parts of the field, some of them vile and horrible, some inspired and even beautiful, and some just so fierce.'"

CANTO 23

DRONABHISHEKA PARVA CONTINUED

"Dhritarashtra asks, 'When the troops in separate akshauhinis are thus ferociously engaged, how does Arjuna fight my army, how does he battle the maharathas of the Samsaptakas? And how, O Sanjaya, do the Samsaptakas face Arjuna?'

Sanjaya says, 'As the battle swells all around, your son Duryodhana himself leads his elephant division against Bhimasena. Like one elephant encountering another, like a bull meeting a bull, Bhima, challenged by Suyodhana himself, falls gleefully on the Kauravas' elephant legion. With gales of arrows, awesome Bhima brings bloody havoc to the great beasts of war, big as hills, with blood and ichor trickling from every part of their bodies. Single-handedly, and like a terrific wind scattering clouds massed in it path, Bhima savages the elephant host and the beasts left alive turn tail and flee from him in terror. Bhima is as magnificent as the risen Sun striking everything in the world with his rays swifter than thoughts. Struck by Bhima's bolts of thunder and lightning, the looming, lumbering beasts, bathed in blood, look like cloud masses in the sky painted upon by red rays of the sun.

Duryodhana, livid, looses a wrath of shining arrows at Vayu's son, his detested cousin who mows down his much-vaunted elephant force so joyfully, so disdainfully. He draws blood from Bhima whom, more than any other, Duryodhana would love to kill. Bhima's eyes turn red as plums and he unleashes a lucific volley at your son, whom he hates as much as he is hated by the Kaurava king. Pierced all over by Bhima's manic shafts, stricken with his cousin's warm barbs, but outwardly cool and grinning mockingly, Duryodhana responds with a brace of arrows bright and hot as the sun, piercing Bhima deep.

In a flash Bhima breaks Duryodhana's bow with two flat-headed shafts; he cuts down your son's black banner with the device of the jewelled elephant, unnerving Duryodhana with his ferocity. Seeing Duryodhana violently set upon by Bhima, the king of the Angas quickly thunders up on his loudly trumpeting elephant to rescue your son. Turning on the Anga, Bhimasena shoots a long arrow deep into that great grey beast's head, directly between its temples. The elongated barb drives right through the mastodon's head in a scarlet eruption and plunges into the earth beyond the beast. With an echoing bellow Anga's elephant falls like a hill riven by thunder, and the Mleccha king falls with it. Quicksilver for all his bulk, Vrikodara cuts Anga's head from his neck before that king's body strikes the ground.

When the heroic king of the Angas falls, his akshauhinis panic and flee in all directions. The fleeing chargers, elephants, chariot-warriors trample and run over their own foot-soldiers.

Then the king of the Pragjyotishas, Bhagadatta, riding his elephant, comes to challenge Bhima. Its eyes rolling in rage, it raises its trunk and forelegs and crashes them down on Bhima blazing like a dread fire on Kurukshetra. The great beast pulverises Bhima's chariot and crushes his horses into bloody pulp. Bhima, who has leapt out of his ratha just in time, does not flee but runs under that towering animal's belly. For Bhima knows the Anjalikabedha, the science of fighting the war elephant on foot.

From below Bhima repeatedly strikes Bhagadatta's elephant Supratika with thunderous blows of his mighty fists. The elephant turns and twists in frenzy, desperate to find Bhima and impale him on its tusks. But Vayu's son was born with the strength of ten thousand elephants and he seizes the great pachyderm and begins to whirl it around as potter does his wheel. Having dealt many staggering blows to that colossus, Bhima once more darts out from under its body and stands facing the beast. In a blink, Supratika seizes Bhima in his trunk, by his throat, and lifting him high dashes him down on the ground.

Twisting the elephant's trunk viciously, Bhima frees himself in trice and again gets under the body of the massive creature. Meanwhile, an elephant from the Pandava's side thunders up to face Supratika and now Bhima escapes, running quick as the wind! So swiftly does he go, that believing him dead, a dismal cry goes up from the Pandava army, 'The elephant has killed Bhima!'

Affrighted by the elephant Supratika, the Pandava host breaks and runs, back to a living, waiting Bhima. Meanwhile, Yudhishtira thinks that Bhima has been killed and in fury, riding with the Panchalas, he surrounds Bhagadatta with countless chariots, covering him in gales of vengeful arrows. But Bhagadatta, king of the mountains, strikes aside those arrow showers with his iron goad. Then falling like a natural disaster on the Pandavas and Panchalas, he tramples their legions with his terrible, hulking beast. Rajan, it is wonderful to watch—Bhagadatta and Supratika rampaging among the enemy, crushing them on every side.

The king of Dasarnas, mounted himself on a swift elephant, its temples too rent and the juice of mad musth streaming down, storms at Bhagadatta, attacking him from a flank. The battle that erupts between those two beasts of awful size is as the mythic one of old between two winged mountains covered with forests. Bhagadatta's elephant wheels around in a flash and, with tusks like streaks of lightning, rakes the Dasarna king's animal, tearing open its flank, killing it instantly. Even as that beast totters and falls, Bhagadatta kills the Dasarna king with seven lances cast in the blink of an eye, and bright as sunrays.

Yudhishtira once more surrounds Bhagadatta with a number of

chariots, and makes his body a home for countless arrows. Ah, Bhagadatta seated lordly on Supratika, surrounded by the Pandava maharathas, blazes like a fire on a mountaintop, in a dense forest. He stays fearlessly in the midst of these serried rathas ridden by fierce archers, all of whom rain arrows at him.

The king of the Pragjyotishas presses down on his beast's back, hard with his great toe, urging Supratika to thunder down on Satyaki's chariot. The prodigious beast seizes Satyaki's ratha with his trunk and hurls it like a toy through the air so it shatters on the ground some distance away. Satyaki, however, jumps off in time and escapes. His charioteer, also, abandons the great Sindhu steeds yoked to his chariot and quickly follows his warrior.

Meanwhile, Supratika easily breaks out from the encirclement of Pandava and Panchala chariots, and brings mayhem to the Kshatriyas that stand in his dreadful way. Terrified out of their wits by that singular mastodon attacking them, those bulls among men look up at it in awe as if it has multiplied into a hundred great elephants, why, a thousand. From that indomitable animal's back Bhagadatta razes the Pandava army, even like the king of the Devas mounted on Airavata mowing down the Danavas in ancient times.

Their own elephants trumpeting shrilly and their horses whinnying awfully in fright and panic, the Panchalas flee in all directions. All the while Bhagadatta destroys the Pandava troops. And then wrathful Bhima rushes at the king of the Pragjyotishas. But Supratika terrifies Bhima's horses by spraying thick streams of water over them and the animals bolt from the field with a helpless Bhimasena.

Now Kriti's son, Ruchiparvan, rides at Bhagadatta, spewing arrows like Death himself. The handsome and magnificent Bhagadatta of the mountains shoots just a single shaft and sends Ruchiparvan to Yamaloka.

Upon the fall of the brave Ruchiparvan, Subhadra's son, the sons of Draupadi, Chekitana, Dhrishtaketu and Yuyutsu turn their attention to killing the elephant Supratika. With loud roars, they loose downpours of arrows on the colossal beast, like clouds drenching the earth with rain.

Goaded by the masterful Bhagadatta, with heel, hook and toe, with trunk outstretched and eyes fixed and glittering, Supratika thunders at the enemy. Stamping down Yuyutsu's horses, the elephant kills his charioteer as well; Yuyutsu has to abandon his chariot and flee.

The Pandava warriors continue their combined assault on Supratika, prince of all elephants, inundating him with ceaseless volleys of deadly fire. And now, your son, incensed Duryodhana, wildly attacks Abhimanyu in his chariot.

Bhagadatta on his elephant, loosing arrows in tornadoes over the enemy, is radiant like the Sun himself covering the earth with his rays. Abhimanyu strikes Supratika with a dozen shafts Yuyutsu with ten, and each of the sons of Draupadi and Dhrishtaketu with three feral barbs. Bleeding from these missiles, the grand elephant looks magnificent like a mighty thunderhead wounded by the Sun's rays, bleeding. Impervious to his wounds, Supratika charges ahead tossing enemy warriors, their chariots and horses, around like straws in his mighty path.

Like a cowherd belabouring his cattle in the forest with his staff, Bhagadatta repeatedly strikes the Pandava host. Like the frenzied cawing of scattering crows attacked by hawks, we hear a loud and raucous din among the Pandava troops as they run from the savage elephant and his rider. Prodded repeatedly by Bhagadatta's sharp hook, Rajan, that prince of elephants resembles, an ancient winged mountain; and Supratika fills his enemies' hearts with naked fear, akin to merchants fearful at the sight of a swollen surging sea. As they flee, the elephants, maharathas, horses and kings of the Pandavas, create a resounding commotion, an echoing clamour that fills earth, sky, heaven and all the directions. Mounted on that greatest of elephants, Bhagadatta cleaves the hostile army like the Asura Virochana, who ripped through the celestial host though it was well protected by the Devas.

A violent wind begins to blow; a thick cloud of dust covers the sky and the troops and always the enemy sees that single elephant as multiplied into many, and stampeding murderous across all Kurukshetra.'"

CANTO 24

DRONABHISHEKA PARVA CONTINUED

"Sanjaya says, 'You asked me about the feats of Arjuna in battle. Listen, O Mahabaho to what Partha achieves in the fight. When he sees the rising pall of dust and hears the wail of the troops when Bhagadatta buffets them like a bloody tempest having sway over all the war, Arjuna says to Krishna, "O Madhusudana, it seems that the king of the Pragjyotishas has come to the field on his elephant. This din that we hear must be from his advent. He fights from elephant-back and stamps on all that come in his way. He is no less than Indra himself in battle, why, I believe he is the greatest of all elephant-warriors in the world.

His elephant Supratika, again, has no rival in war. He is amazingly nimble for all his massive bulk; he knows no fatigue, and is impervious to all weapons. Not even fire burns Supratika; by himself, he can destroy the entire Pandava army today. Other than the two of us, no one else can check this giant from the mountains.

Krishna, turn our horses towards Bhagadatta. He is arrogant because of his elephant's strength, and proud of his age. This very day I will send him to be a guest in the halls of Indra."

Krishna turns his chariot to where Bhagadatta continues to devastate the Pandava forces. While Arjuna is riding at Bhagadatta, the mighty Samsaptaka maharathas, numbering fourteen thousand, of which ten thousand are Goals or Narayanas, who once followed Krishna, return to the field and summon him to battle. Seeing the Pandava host broken by Bhagadatta, and challenged on the other hand by the Samsaptakas, Arjuna finds himself in a quandary. He asks himself, "Should I return to fight the Samsaptakas or ride to help Yudhishtira?"

Reflecting on this for a moment, O Kurupravira, Arjuna decides that he would devote himself to extirpating the Samsaptakas.

Wanting only to kill as many maharathas as possible—in their thousands—flying his banner with the image of Hanuman, greatest of Vanaras, Arjuna suddenly turns back. This is exactly as both Duryodhana and Karna had planned. Arjuna's heart wavers for a time, but finally he resolves to face the Samsaptakas and he appears to serve his enemies' purpose.

The excited Samsaptaka maharathas greet Arjuna's return with extravagant salvos, thousands of missiles loosed all together in a moment, shrouding him entirely with a dense locust swarm of arrows so one can no longer see Kunti's son, Krishna, their horses or their shining chariot. So sudden and overwhelming is the onslaught that Krishna briefly breaks into a profuse sweat and even swoons; at least he appears to! Now Arjuna is compelled to summon the Brahmastra and loose it at his enemies. In an apocalyptic flash, with a sound as if the earth broke in two, that astra of the Creator obliterates almost the entire Samsaptaka force in a moment. Thousands of arms with bows, arrows and bowstrings in their grasp, cut clean from their trunks, and thousands of standards, steeds, charioteers and maharathas, fall in the blinding flash of that astra. Elephants big as forested hills, or cloud masses, fall with muffled peals of thunder, their riders dead.

Arjuna does not pause. Countless elephants fall to his supernatural archery, their fine trappings shredded by the Kiritin's arrows, their housings torn, their riders crushed by them. Partha's flat-headed arrows shear countless arms from their shoulders, their hands still clutching spears and swords, clubs and axes. Heads, also, handsome as the morning sun, the lotus or the moon, severed cleanly by Arjuna roll onto the earth. While Phalguni in rage razes the Samsaptakas with storms of diverse missiles, the enemy host seems to be alight. Seeing great Dhananjaya crush the Samsaptaka legion like an elephant trampling some lotus-stalks, all men, why, all creatures applaud him, saying, "Uttamam! Wonderful!"

Krishna marvels seeing Partha's feat which is no less that those of Vasava himself. Indeed Madhava folds his hands to Arjuna and says, "Truly, Partha, I believe that not Sakra, Yama or Kubera can do what you have just done. Ah, in moments you have killed thousands of mighty Samsaptaka warriors."

Having despatched the battling Samsaptakas, Arjuna says to Krishna, "Now let us ride at Bhagadatta.""

CANTO 25

Dronabhisheka Parva continued

"Sanjaya says, 'Krishna turns his white chargers, wearing golden armour and swift as the mind, towards Drona's akshauhini. Even as the Kurusattama courses along toward his brothers beset by Drona, Susarman with his brothers ride after him roaring out a challenge.

The ever-victorious Arjuna says to Krishna, "O you of unfading glory, Susarman and his brothers challenge me again! Towards the north, Drona has broken our army once more. Lord, my heart is full of uncertainty. Shall I kill the Samsaptakas now or save my beleaguered troops from further harm? Which shall I do?"

Without a word, Krishna turns the chariot back towards Susarman, king of the Trigartas. Arjuna stabs Susarman deep with seven visceral shafts and breaks both his bow and standard with two more razor-headed arrows. Never pausing, he sends the Trigarta king's brothers to Yama with another six barbs loosed in the space of a wish. Roaring in shock, Susarman looses a serpentine iron naracha at Arjuna, and casts a thunderbolt of a spear at Krishna. Arjuna cuts both missiles down in flight and with a sizzle of arrows strikes Susarman unconscious in his chariot.

Partha turns back and courses again towards your army, lashing it with his mighty volleys like Vasava pouring down rain. And none among your troops ventures to oppose him. Like a fire consuming bales of straw as he comes, he flares on scorching all the Kaurava maharathas with his flaming missiles. As no living creatures can stand the touch of fire, your troops cannot bear the irresistible Arjuna.

Decimating your legions, Arjuna rides at Bhagadatta, king of the Pragjyotishas, like Garuda swooping down on his prey. Kunti's matchless son grasps the Gandiva in his hands, mighty and mystic bow which protects the Pandavas and is deadly to all enemies. Your son Suyodhana, Rajan, brought destruction down on the race of Kshatriyas when he used deceit in the game of dice to achieve his ends. And now, assailed by Partha, your army shatters like a boat striking a great rock.

The ten thousand archers, all brave and fierce, engage Arjuna and with dauntless hearts those maharathas surround him. Unruffled, mighty Arjuna is upon them like an angry elephant of sixty years in musth among a bed of lotuses; he crushes that legion of your army. Bhagadatta on his elephant charges Arjuna, Naravyaghra, who turns calmly to face him.

Fierce and fervid is the encounter between Arjuna's ratha and Bhagadatta's elephant. These two heroes wheel all over the field, one on his chariot and the other on his elephant. Like the lord Indra from his elephant, looking like a mass of clouds, Bhagadatta rains down arrow showers on Dhananjaya. Intrepid Arjuna fluently cuts all these down in flight before they can reach him. Avoiding Arjuna's fire, the king of the Pragjyotishas now strikes both Partha and Krishna with a veritable cloudburst of arrows, overwhelming them. He prods his Supratika forward to trample the two Krishna in the ratha. Seeing the angry elephant come at them like Death himself, Krishna adroitly maneuvers his chariot out of harm's away, keeping the great beast on his left.

Arjuna has the opportunity to kill both Supratika and Bhagadatta from behind, but always remembering the laws of a dharma yuddha, he has no wish to do this cowardly thing. However, when he sees Supratika wildly slaughtering other elephants and horses, crushing chariots that comes in his way, red rage rises in Arjuna.'"

CANTO 26

DRONABHISHEKA PARVA CONTINUED

"Dhritarashtra asks, 'Tell me all, O Sanjaya, what does the wrathful Partha, the son of Pandu, do to Bhagadatta? And what Bhagadatta to the son of Pandu?'

Sanjaya says, 'While Partha and Krishna are engrossed with the king of the Pragjyotishas, all around them saw them as if in the very jaws of death. From his perch on the neck of his elephant, Bhagadatta looses gales of arrows down on the chariot borne Krishnas. Drawing his bow in a circle, He pierces Devaki's son with many golden-winged arrows of black iron. These sizzling bolts of fire pass right through Krishna into the earth.

Arjuna then breaks Bhagadatta's bow and kills the warrior who protects his flank; why, the inspired Dhananjaya seem to toy with the Pragjyotisha king. Bhagadatta hurls fourteen formidable spears, bright as sunrays, at Arjuna, who with dazzling virtuosity cuts each lance into three slivers. With a thick swath of shafts, he neatly disjoints the armour that encases Supratika, and the kavacha clatters to the ground. Bare without his coat of mail, grievously wounded by Arjuna's arrows, Supratika looks like a naked mountain without any cloud cover, with red streams frothing down its sides.

Once more Bhagadatta flings a vicious iron spear at Krishna, lance streaked with gold that Arjuna neatly bisects in flight. Cutting down the mountain king's standard and parasol, quicker than seeing, Arjuna, smiling, strikes him with a beautiful volley of ten shafts, winged with kanka feathers. Pierced deep, roaring, the incensed Bhagadatta casts a flurry of thick spears down on Arjuna's head, knocking down his crown. Arjuna calmly picks up his kirita, sets it back on his head and cries up to the ruler of the Pragjyotishas, "Look well on this world! For you will not see it long."

Bhagadatta's fury mounts; he seizes up another bright bow and unleashes a torment of arrows down on both, Arjuna and Govinda. Partha, quick as the mind, breaks Bhagadatta's bow, rends his quivers, and then strikes him with a rage of seventy-two shafts, piercing him deep, lancing agony through all his limbs. Roaring still more loudly, Bhagadatta invokes the Vaishnava astra into his goad with mantras, and hurls it straight at Arjuna's chest.

But Krishna sways into the path of that fatal weapon and, shielding Arjuna, receives the Vaishnavastra himself. Striking Krishna's breast, the astra turns into a triumphal garland of flowers!

Arjuna bleakly asks Kesava, "Sinless one, you said that you would only guide my chariot and not fight the war! O lotus-eyed one, why do you break your word? Only if I am helpless and cannot resist an enemy or a weapon, should you intervene; not when I am still standing and able. You know that I can subdue all these worlds of the Devas, Asuras and Manushas with my bow and arrows."

Krishna replies, "Listen, O Partha, to this secret and ancient itihasa! I have four forms, eternally engaged in protecting the worlds. Dividing my own Self, I maintain the weal of the worlds. One form of mine stays on the earth and is engaged in tapasya. Another sees the good and the evil deeds in the world. My third form is in this world of men, engaged in karma. My fourth form lies in sleep for a thousand years and, upon awakening, grants exceptional boons to deserving men. Once, the Earth, knowing that the time had come, asked me for a boon for her son Naraka. The boon, Partha, was for the Vaishnavastra for her son, so that the Devas and the Asuras could not kill him. "You must give me this astra, she pleaded.

Hearing her prayer, I gave of old the supreme Vaishnavastra to the Earth's son. I also said at that time, 'O Bhumidevi, this astra will protect Naraka. No one will be able to kill him, and your son will be invincible in all the worlds and vanquish his enemies.'

Saying, 'Tathaastu!' the Devi went away, her wish fulfilled. And so Naraka became invincible and always destroyed his enemies.

It was from Naraka, O Partha, that the lord of the Pragjyotishas received my weapon. There is no one in the entire world, not even Indra and Rudra, who cannot be killed with this weapon. So, it was for your very life that I received it upon myself. I have divested the great Asura of that supreme astra. Now kill your invincible enemy Bhagadatta, enemy of the Devas, even as, for the good of the worlds, I slew the Asura Naraka."

Hearing this, Arjuna suddenly overwhelms Bhagadatta with a solid swath of jagged arrows. In a blur, Arjuna looses a long arrow straight into the brow of Supratika, missile that rives the elephant like thunder splitting a mountain and pierces its body up to its wings, like a snake flashing into an anthill. Bhagadatta repeatedly prods it with his iron goad, but even as a poor man's wife will not obey her lord, Supratika does not obey him. Its limbs paralysed, the great beast's legs buckle and it falls forward, its tusks goring the earth. With a last dreadful bellow, the mighty elephant dies.

Never pausing, Arjuna looses a deathly shaft straight into Bhagadatta's chest, killing the king of the Pragjyotishas in a crimson explosion. His bow and arrows fall from his lifeless hands; loosened from his head, his rich and precious turban falls off his head like a petal from a lotus whose stalk is violently shaken. Bhagadatta himself, decked with golden garlands, falls from his immense beast's back like a flowering kinsuka uprooted from a mountaintop by a terrific gale.

Having killed the king who resembled Indra himself in power, Bhagadatta who was Indra's friend, Indra's son Arjuna now sweeps unobstructed through your army devastating it like a great storm tearing down a forest of trees.'"

CANTO 27

DRONABHISHEKA PARVA CONTINUED

"Sanjaya says, 'After killing Bhagadatta, who was always Indra's favoured friend and a hero of untold tejas, Arjuna circumambulates the fallen warrior, the Earth's grandson, in solemn pradakshina.

The two sons of the Gandhara king, Sakuni's brothers Vrishaka and Achala, subduers of hostile cities, attack Arjuna feverishly. They ride at him from in front and behind and scourge him with ferocious volleys. Magnificent Arjuna, ablaze after killing Bhagadatta, fairly shreds Vrishaka's horses, charioteer, bow, chatra, standard and chariot. With clouds of arrows and diverse other missiles, Arjuna falls upon the Gandhara army, killing five hundred brave and mighty warriors in moments.

Jumping down from his ruined chariot, its horses dead, Vrishaka swiftly mounts his brother's ratha and takes up another bow. From their single chariot, the Gandhara brothers once more mount a raging attack on Arjuna. They cover him with dark arrow clouds even as Vritra or Bala did Indra in time out of mind. Their aim unerring, the two princes, themselves unhurt, strike Arjuna viciously, tormenting him as the two months of summer do the world.

But then, Rajan, Arjuna kills the two princes, those tigers among men, Vrishaka and Achala, cutting both down as they stand side by side in their chariot—with a single arrow! The splendid brothers, both so alike, both red-eyed, both like lions, both beloved of their kinsmen and their friends, fall onto the earth at the same moment, and lie there, spreading sacred fame all around.

Seeing their heroic uncles cut down by Arjuna, your sons rain a fury of fire down on the Pandava. Sakuni, dark and master sorcerer, sees his brothers die and creates sinister illusions of maya to confound the two Krishnas. Cudgels, iron balls, rocks, sataghnis, darts, gadas, spiked maces, swords, spears, mallets, axes, kampanas, curved scimitars, showers of nails, short clubs, flights of razors, arrows with sharp broad heads, nalikas, calf-tooth tipped shafts, arrows with heads of bone, discs, snake-headed shafts, and diverse other weapons, fall upon Arjuna from everywhere. Donkeys, camels, buffaloes, tigers, lions, deer, leopards, bears, wolves, vultures, monkeys, various reptiles, diverse pisachas and swarms of crows, all ravenous and in frenzy, fly at Arjuna. But Dhananjaya, knower of devastras, greets these occult assailants with mystic weapons of his own; crying out in fear and pain, they either vanish or perish.

Now a turgid darkness appears and covers Arjuna's chariot; from within the gloom, harsh voices rebuke Arjuna. He invokes the Jyotishkastra, which dispels Sakuni's awful night of sorcery. Immediately, cataracts of water rush at Arjuna from every side; he vaporises them with an Adityastra.

Smilingly does Arjuna dispel and destroy the mayic weapons that Sakuni repeatedly creates to assail him. Seeing the ease with which the Pandava negates his most powerful and abstruse spells, fear unmans Sakuni and he flees the duel like some low and vulgar coward, borne by swift horses.

Arjuna, transcendent master of war, puts his unearthly genius on display, and continues to raze the Kaurava forces at will. He is like a mountain that cleaves the very Ganga into two streams, as he faces your legions squarely and massacres your men. One of these panicked streams flows towards Drona and the other, with loud cries, towards Duryodhana.

A thick pall of dust rises and covers all the troops, and we cannot see Arjuna. We only hear the reverberant twanging of the Gandiva, echoing above the blare of conches and the beat of drums and the noise of all the other instruments across the field. Then, on the southern part of the field, a fierce battle breaks out between many great Kuru maharathas and Arjuna. However, I followed Drona.

The various akshauhinis of Yudhishtira's army beset the enemy on every part of the field. Arjuna strikes your son's divisions, O Bhaarata, like the hot wind of summer destroying cloud masses in the sky. Arjuna falls on your legions, loosing clouds of arrows, like Vasava pouring down heavy showers of rain; and there is none in your army who can resist that tiger among men.

Struck by the storm of fear, pain and death that is Partha, your warriors flee, trampling so many of their own as they escape. The arrows Arjuna shoots are fletched with kanka feathers and they pierce every armour, and cover earth and sky like a dire locust swarm. Piercing right through horses, rathikas, elephants and foot-soldiers, the shafts enter the earth like snakes plunging into anthills. Arjuna never shoots twice at any elephant, steed or man; every arrow of his is a killer.

With dead men, elephants and horses lying all around, and echoing with the yowls of dogs and jackals, Kurukshetra presents a strange and horrific sight. Wounded by Arjuna's arrows, fathers abandon sons, friends desert friends and sons leave behind fathers as each one flees for his own life. Struck by Partha's shafts, many warriors abandon the very animals that bear them in war.'"

CANTO 28

DRONABHISHEKA PARVA CONTINUED

"Dhritarashtra asks, 'What is our state of mind when my akshauhinis are routed and all of you flee the field? To rally broken and fleeing men, who find nowhere to make a stand, is always difficult. Tell me all about it, O Sanjaya!'

Sanjaya says, 'Although your general ranks are broken, Rajan, many great kshatriyas of the world, who fight Duryodhana's cause and want to keep their honour and fame, still follow Drona. In the dreadful pass, they fearlessly follow their senapati, achieving great feats against the Pandava troops and Yudhishtira within striking distance.

Taking swift advantage of a careless oversight from Bhimasena, Satyaki and Dhrishtadyumna, the Kuru leaders fall upon the Pandava army. The Panchalas exhort their troops, chanting, "Drona, Drona! Death to Drona!"

Your sons, however, roar to all the Kurus, "Let not Drona be killed! Let Drona not die!"

One side crying, "Kill Drona!", "Kill the Brahmana!" and the other, "Don't let Drona be killed!", "Let not Drona be slain!" the Kurus and the Pandavas seem to gamble again, now with Drona as their stake.

Dhrishtadyumna, fire-prince of the Panchalas, rides up to all the Panchala maharathas whom Drona seeks to annihilate. The kali yuga come and the war turned feral, they no longer observe any law of dharma yuddha about which enemy each warrior could fairly choose to fight. The battle is appalling with Kshatriya fighting Kshatriya with bestial cries and roars. But now maharathas wipe out phalanxes of foot-soldiers with astras; chariot-warriors hack down horsemen; great heroes crucify lesser soldiers. A new darkness falls on sacred Kurukshetra; all nobility melts away.

Their enemies cannot make the Pandavas flinch; while the sons of Pandu remember all their sufferings, and make their enemies tremble with fear. Though humble, yet agitated by rage, and in the grip of the naked spirit of revenge, and they fight as men possessed, reckless of their very lives, to kill Drona. They fight heroes of immense energy, making a sport of horrible war, with life the only stake. The two hosts falling on each other resemble elemental iron colliding with pristine adamant.

And not the oldest men can remember hearing of, let alone seeing, a battle as brutal as this. Carnage spreads in a great stain across the earth; weighed down with those two enormous hosts, Bhumi shudders; the bedlam raised by your army and theirs paralyses blood-drenched holy ground, pierces the firmament, and rings even in Devaloka.

Coming upon the Pandava forces in their thousands, Drona is everywhere on the field in his magnificent ratha, mowing the enemy down at his supreme ease and will. Seeing the awesome Brahmana cover Kurukshetra in blood, Dhrishtadyumna, the Pandava senapati, rides himself to contain him. Breathtaking is the duel between Drona and the Panchala prince. Ah, Rajan, I am convinced that it has no equal.

Like a fire, of which his bow is the flame and his arrows the flaring sparks, Nila begins to consume the Kuru ranks like heaps of dry grass. Drona's great son Aswatthaman, who always wanted to fight Nila, cries smilingly to him, "O Nila, what honour do you gain by burning so many common soldiers with your astras? Fight me instead!"

Nila, the brightness of whose face resembles the splendour of a full-blown lotus, instantly looses a ferocious volley at Aswatthaman, whose body is like a bank of lotuses and whose eyes are like lotus-petals. Deeply and suddenly struck by Nila, Drona's son breaks his adversary's bow and cuts down his standard with three broad-headed arrows. Leaping down from his chariot, with a shield and a marvellous sword, Nila rushes at Aswatthaman wanting to pluck his head from his neck like a bird bearing away its prey in its talons. But, instead, in a gory flash, Drona's son severs Nila's handsome head, with its fine hooked nose, and long kundalas. The tall mighty Nila, whose face is bright as the full moon, and his complexion of a lotus, sprawls dead never knowing how he was killed.

Shocked and grief-stricken, the Pandava host trembles when Drona's son kills Nila of blazing tejas. The Pandava maharathas all wonder in some despair, "Ah, how will Arjuna save us when he is far away to the south locked in battle with the remnant of the Samsaptakas and the Narayana force?"'"

CANTO 29

Dronabhisheka Parva continued

"Sanjaya says, 'Bhima cannot bear to see the slaughter of his army. He attacks Balhika with sixty wrathful arrows and Karna with ten. Drona wants to kill mighty Bhima and excoriates him with twenty-six shafts of untold violence, which plunge into the very vital organs of Vayu's son like snakes of virulent poison.

Karna strikes Bhima with a dozen shafts, Aswatthaman with seven, and Duryodhana also with six more. Dauntless Bhimasena roars like five lions, and unleashes fifty burning arrows at Drona, ten at Karna, a dozen at Duryodhana, and eight thunderbolts at Drona.

Yudhishtira sees his mighty brother, his favourite brother, beset by a host of enemies who all fight reckless of their lives, in that battle where death is so easy to find; the Dharmaraja despatches a cohort of his own maharathas to Bhima's side. These tejasvin Kshatriyas, led by Nakula and Sahadeva, and others led by Satyaki, fly to Bhima's rescue. Full of battle lust, those bulls among men unitedly storm Drona's legions, protected by so many stalwart bowmen, and they are determined to tear the Acharya's forces apart.

Together now, Bhima and the others fall furiously upon Drona's host. But serene Drona, ablaze, easily checks their surging careen, holding them all at bay. The warriors of your army fight the Pandavas without a thought for their own kingdoms, without fear for their lives.

The war burns on; horsemen encounter horsemen, and maharathas other maharathas; arrows fly against arrows, swords clash against swords, and axes ring against axes. Fiercest is the battle of swords, making a terrible carnage. The elephant legions of both sides collide again in earthshaking thunder. Men plunge head first from elephant back and horseback, countless warriors, while others are struck out of their rathas dismembered by arrow showers everywhere.

In the brutal press, some lose their armour and fall to be crushed by elephants, their handsome bodies and noble heads pulped. Indeed, everywhere elephants stamp on fallen men, grinding them into flat patches of blood, flesh and bone; other great beast impale standing men on flashing tusks and fling their corpses high into the air or tear them apart after laying them on the ground. The dark and wild spirit of war possesses man and beast equally and absolutely.

Other elephants, with arrows protruding from their trunks, range madly across the field, goring and crushing men in their hundreds; while others great beasts continue to stamp fallen warriors, horses and smaller elephants cased in armour of black iron, as if these were mere reeds. Many humble and brave kings, their hour having come, lie in the last sleep on beds of pain, overlaid with vultures' feathers.

Battling from chariots, father slays son; and maddened son, also, attacks his father. The wheels of rathas are broken; banners are torn; regal parasols fall onto the earth. Dragging broken yokes, horses run everywhere. Arms still grasping swords, and heads decked with twinkling ear-rings fall continually in macabre rain. The irresistible elephants haul chariots around, then overturn them and smash them into fragments. Waylaid by elephants, horses and their riders are strewn everywhere, maimed, disfigured past recognition.

Savage pandemonium reigns; the merciless war rages on, the battle from which every shred of mercy and nobility have gone so it seems like a contention of demons.

Oh father! Oh son! Where are you, friend? Wait! Where do you go! Strike! Kill this one!—these cries and roars echo all around, as does the deranged laughter of butchery. The blood of men, horses and elephants mingle and flow together in streams, covering all the filed in scarlet. The brave exult and cowards tremble at the heart of unbridled savagery loosed upon the sacred earth.

Here a Kshatriya gets his chariot-wheel entangled with that of another, and at this intimate proximity, smashes the other's head with his mace. Why the bravest, most seasoned warriors wish for safety where there is none; they drag one another by the hair, and fight with fists, teeth and nails. Here a hero's arm upraised, sword in its hand, is hacked off at the elbow; there another's arm is lopped off at the shoulder, the hand still wielding bow, arrow or hook. Here, one roars a ringing challenge at another; and there, another turns his back on the battle and flees. Here, one cuts another's head from his throat, finding him within reach; while another rushes with loud shouts at an enemy. One soldier is filled with fear at another's roar, while another hews down another, who was a dear friend and is now an enemy.

Somewhere, a bull elephant, big as a hill, his heart pierced with an elongated shaft, falls on the field and lies like an island in a river during the summer. Elsewhere, another elephant, with sweat streaming down its body, like a mountain with rivulets flowing down its breast, also lies on the field, having crushed a glorious maharatha and his horses and charioteer when it fell.

Seeing grave and awesome warriors, masters of war, covered in blood and fighting passionately on, the timid and faint-hearted, are sombre, some even swoon. Darkness of spirit and savagery mantle Kurukshetra, as does the pall of dust raised by the teeming hosts. Suddenly, Dhrishtadyumna roars, *This is the time!* and plunges forward to assail the most vigorous and heroic enemy warriors. Riding after him the Pandavas themselves strike the Kaurava army like a storm of death and fly towards Drona's chariot like swans towards a lake.

Roars and yells of *Seize him! Stand firm! Do not run! Do not fear! Hack them to pieces!* echo close to of Drona's ratha above the rest of the tumult.

Drona, Kripa, Karna, Aswatthaman, Jayadratha, Vinda and Anuvinda of Avanti and Salya, rally to thwart the marauding Pandava Kshatriyas. They draw blood from the Panchalas and the Pandavas; but stirred by dharma and the desire for noble revenge, the attacking warriors ride on at Drona. Then Drona, enraged, looses hundreds of arrows and brings a great carnage to the Chedis, the Panchalas and the Pandavas. We hear the twanging of his bowstring and the slaps of his palms on all sides; and they are like peals of thunder and strike fear into the hearts of all.

Meanwhile, Arjuna, having killed a large number of Samsaptakas, storms up to join battle with Drona who sows death so liberally among the Pandava troops. Arjuna fords many lakes of blood, whose fierce waves and eddies are Drona's arrow gales, and arrives at the heart of the dreadful war. Suddenly he erupts on Drona's troops, Vijaya of measureless fame, Dhananjaya splendid as the Sun, flying wild Hanuman on his shining banner, whose roars terrify his enemies. Having dried up the Samsaptaka ocean with his astras, the third son of Pandu now scathes the Kurus as if he is the very Sun that rises at the end of the Yuga; as if he is like the Fire that appears then to devour all creatures.

Elephant-riders, horsemen and rathikas fall before Arjuna's lucific barrages of arrows, leaking blood onto already wet earth Some utter cries of distress while others set up loud shouts. Some struck by the shafts of Partha fall dead. Arjuna still fights the dharma yuddha—he will not shoot at those who have fallen from their mounts or in their chariots; he does not aim at those who flee the battle; he spares those that are unwilling to fight.

Deprived of their chariots and overawed, almost all the Kauravas run from the filed with piteous cries, and call out to Karna to save them. Hearing their shouts and screams, Karna roars his assurance to the Kuru troops, *Do not fear!* and he dashes up to confront Arjuna.

Karna, greatest among all the Kaurava maharathas, invokes the

Agneyastra and unleashes the weapon of fire at Arjuna. Quicker than sight, Arjuna douses it with an astra of his own, of water. Without a moment's pause he looses another elemental missile at Karna, who as swiftly quells it with another astra. A lofty and dangerous contention of devastras ensues between the two, and each is the other's equal. Then Dhrishtadyumna, Bhima and Satyaki all ride at Karna; each one striking him deep with three long and vicious barbs. Even as he fights his towering duel with Arjuna, Karna, incredibly, breaks the bows in the hands of the other three maharathas, leaving them like snakes without fangs.

They fling deadly lances at him from their chariots, with tigerish roars. The fierce and brilliant javelins hurled by mighty arms fly like snakes at Karna's ratha. Unruffled, lightning swift Karna calmly destroys those lances with three of his own, all the while covering Arjuna with arrows; Karna maharatha gives a great roar. Arjuna drills Karna with seven shafts; he kills Karna's young brother Satrunjaya with another six, and with a wedge-headed barb, strikes off Vipatha's head. Before the eyes of the Dhritarashtras and Karna, Arjuna kills Karna's three brothers.

Bhima leaps down from his ratha, fierce as another Garuda, and hacks down fifteen of Karna's followers with his huge sword. Mounting his chariot again in a trice, seizing up another bow, he strikes Karna with ten arrows and his charioteer and horses with five. Dhrishtadyumna also hefts a sword and a dazzling shield, and kills Charmavarman and Brihadkshatra, king of the Nishadas. Remounting his chariot, swooping up another bow, the Panchala prince strikes Karna with a fusillade of seventy-three arrows, and then gives a shattering roar.

Satyaki, splendid as Indra himself, also takes up a fresh bow, strikes Karna with sixty-four barbs, and he also roars like a pride of lions. In wink he severs Karna's bow in his hands and pierces his arms and chest with three shafts like serpents.

Duryodhana, Drona and Jayadratha rush forward to rescue Karna from the Satyaki-ocean, in which he is about to drown. Hundreds of your foot-soldiers, horses, chariots and elephants swarm to where Karna still terrifies his assailants. Dhrishtadyumna, Bhima, Abhimanyu, Arjuna himself, Nakula and Sahadeva dash to Satyaki's defence. The fevered battle between these archers swells towards some unthinkable crescendo.

All fight without any thought for their lives. Infantry, chariots, cavalry and elephants fight against rathas and footsoldiers, while maharathas engage with elephants and men on foot and horsemen; and rathas and infantrymen confront chariots and elephants. We see horses tilt at horses, elephants thunder at other elephants and foot-soldiers run at foot-soldiers. Thus is the horrific battle fought, marked by great bedlam, and hundreds of noble fighting men and beasts perish every moment, to the delight of the blood-drinking pisachas and carnivores that stalk Kurukshetra with burning eyes. Indeed, every moment the grisly war swells the population of Yama's kingdom.

Men, rathas, horses and elephants destroy each other in vast numbers. Elephants kill elephants and chariot-warriors with weapons raised are slain by other rathikas, horsemen by horsemen, and the massacre of foot-soldiers by other foot-soldiers is ceaseless, ubiquitous. But, also, elephants are killed by rathikas, and magnificent steeds gored or trampled by grey tuskers; horsemen mow down foot-soldiers, and cavalrymen are killed by chariot-warriors—all these against the laws of dharma yuddha, for the kali yuga has indeed dawned darkly on the world. With tongues lolling, teeth and eyes gouged out, with coats of mail and ornaments crushed into the dust, the slaughtered creatures fall in hundreds every moment.

Others who are struck or flung down onto the ground are then trampled into the earth by horses' hooves, by the mighty tread of elephants, and mangled and vivisected by heavy chariots and flying chariot wheels. Ah, how the pisachas, jackal and wild dog packs, the wolves, vultures, crows and other birds and beasts of prey delight in the vigorous, endless butchering—for the feast that will follow.

When men and beasts now beyond all count have been sacrificed to Death's maw yawned wide on Kurukshetra, the survivors bathed in blood take panting pause and look glazed-eyed at each other. The Sun sets in the western hills, and slowly both armies, O Bhaarata, retire to their encampments and tents.'"

CANTO 30

Abhimanyu-vadha Parva

"Sanjaya says, 'We look upon your warriors as defeated because the invincible Arjuna first breaks them and then Drona fails to keep his vow to capture the well-protected Yudhishtira. All of them, dusty and with rent coats of mail, cast anxious glances around. With Drona's consent they retire from the battlefield, after their flawless enemies vanquish and humiliate them; and, as they march, they hear everyone praise the countless merits of Arjuna and speak about Krishna's friendship with him. They pass the night like men under a curse, reflecting upon the course of events and in perfect silence.

Next morning, from petulance, wrath and distraught at the success of his enemy, Duryodhana, in the hearing of the troops, says to Drona, "Dvijottama, I have no doubt now that you have marked us as your enemies, that we face such defeat. You did not seize Yudhishtira today, though you had him within reach. No foe can escape you once you have him in your sights, not if the Pandavas, helped by the very gods, protect him. You granted me a boon; but now you do not honour it. The noble never betray the hopes of those devoted to them."

Drona is mortified by Duryodhana's words and, says, "You must not even think this let alone speak thus to me. I have always tried to fulfill your wishes. The three worlds with the Devas, the Asuras, the Gandharvas, the Yakshas, the Nagas and the Rakshasas cannot defeat a force that the diadem-decked Arjuna leads. Where Krishna, the Creator of the universe is, and where Arjuna leads the army, whose might can prevail against them, save the three-eyed Mahadeva's? I vow that today that I will slay a maharatha for you, one of the greatest heroes of the Pandavas. Today I will also form a vyuha that the very Devas cannot penetrate. However, Duryodhana, lure Arjuna away from the battle again, for there is nothing that he does not know or cannot achieve in war."

After this, the Samsaptakas once more challenge Arjuna to battle and draw him away to the southern side of the field. There a battle ensues place between Arjuna and Susarman's forces the likes of which has never been seen or heard of before.

Meanwhile, Rajan, the chakra vyuha that Drona forms, is magnificent, why, even hard to look at, like the sun at his zenith when he scorches everything below. At Yudhishtira's command the dashing, invincible Abhimanyu pierces the otherwise impenetrable circular formation. Once inside he kills thousands of the enemy, fighting like a god, until six great Kaurava maharathas face him together. Finally, Abhimanyu succumbs to Dusasana's son and gives up his life. This fills our side with joy and the Pandavas with black grief. After Abhimanyu dies, we withdraw our troops for the night.'

Dhritarashtra says, 'Oh Sanjaya, my heart seems to break in pieces when I hear of youthful Abhimanyu's death. Cruel and savage is Kshatriya dharma that the law-givers have laid down, when brave men, who want sovereignty have no scruples and ruthlessly butcher even a child. Tell me how so many maharathas slay that boy who, though raised in luxury, fights so fearlessly? Tell me how our warriors quell Subhadra's son of immeasurable tejas, who stormed into our chakravyuha.'

Sanjaya says, 'Rajan, I will describe the death of Subhadra's son to you in detail. Listen to how, after breaking into our midst, Abhimanyu wields his weapons even as if he were at play, and how he dismays and routs all the irresistible heroes of your army. Like the denizens of a dense forest fear a forest conflagration, Abhimanyu terrifies all the warriors of your army.'"

CANTO 31

ABHIMANYU-VADHA PARVA CONTINUED

"Sanjaya says, 'The very devas cannot oppose the five sons of Pandu and Krishna, all maharathas, as their feats in battle show. There never was and never will be another man so blessed as Yudhishtira, in dharma, karma, lineage, intelligence, achievements, fame and prosperity. Devoted to satya and dharma and with his passions under control, because of his worship of the Brahmans and other virtues, Yudhishtira always seeks and enjoys the bliss of Swarga.

We also speak of these three as being equal—the Destroyer himself at the end of the Yuga, Jamadagni's son Parasurama, and Bhimasena on his chariot, Of Arjuna, wielder of the Gandiva, who always fulfills his battle vows, I do see no equal on earth. These six qualities—reverence for elders, keeping his own counsel, humility, self-restraint, a handsome and radiant appearance and bravery—are always present in Nakula. In the knowledge of the shastras, gravity, sweetness of temper, dharma and prowess, the heroic Sahadeva is equal to the Aswins themselves.

Yet all the noble qualities that are in Krishna, and all those that the Pandavas possess, together, can be found together only in Abhimanyu.

In resolve, he is equal to Yudhishtira, in conduct to Krishna; in exploits, to Bhimasena of terrible deeds; in comeliness, in skill and in knowledge of shastras, he is the equal of Arjuna, and in humility, he is equal to Sahadeva and Nakula.'

Dhritarashtra says, 'I wish, O Suta, to hear in detail, how the invincible Abhimanyu, the son of Subhadra, is slain on the battlefield.'

Sanjaya continues, 'Be calm, Rajan, and endure your insupportable grief. I will tell you about the death of your young and incomparable kinsman.

The Acharya forms the great circular vyuha, a Chakra, and in it he positions all the kings of our side that are each equal to Indra himself. At the entrance, he stations all the princes of sun like refulgence and who have all sworn to stand by one another. They have standards decked with gold, all of them wear red robes with red ornaments, red banners and are adorned with garlands of gold and wildflowers; they are smeared with sandalwood-paste and other scented liniments.

All the renowned Kaurava archers, numbering ten thousand, face Abhimanyu in a body. They set your handsome grandson Lakshmana at their head and all of them are in consort, are comrades in joy and grief, emulate one another in feats of courage, want to excel one another and are also devoted to one another.

Surrounded by the maharathas Karna, Dusasana and Kripa, Duryodhana stands at the heart of his forces and has a white royal chatra over his head. Fanned with yak tails, he is as resplendent as the king of the Devas. At the head of your army is the senapati, Drona like the rising sun. Immovable as Meru stands the striking Jayadratha, ruler of the Sindhus. At his side and led by Aswatthaman, are your thirty sons, resembling the very gods. Also beside Jayadratha, are these maharathas—the gambler Sakuni, king of Gandhara, Salya and Bhurisravas.

The day's battle begins, fierce, breathtaking, making one's hair stand on end, both sides fighting to the death.'"

CANTO 32

ABHIMANYU-VADHA PARVA CONTINUED

"Sanjaya says, 'Led by Bhimasena the Pandava forces advance on the invincible chakravyuha created by Bharadwaja's son. All of them are seasoned and skilled warriors, wily and full of battle lust, keened for the fight—Satyaki, Chekitana, Dhrishtadyumna, the son of Prishata, Kuntibhoja of great ability, the mighty Drupada, Abhimanyu, Kshatradharman, the valiant Brihadkshatra, Dhrishtaketu, the ruler of the Chedis, the twin sons of Madri, Ghatotkacha, the powerful Yudhamanyu, the unvanquished Sikhandin, the irresistible Uttamaujas, maharatha Virata, the five sons of Draupadi, the valiant son of Sisupala, the Kaikeyas of terrific energy and the Srinjayas in their thousands. These and others, all master warriors at the head of their forces, charge roaring against Bharadwaja's son Drona.

The heroic Drona, however, coolly checks all of them with a torrid storm of arrows. Like a mighty wave striking an impregnable hill, like the surging sea restrained by its shores, Drona drives them back. The Pandavas and the Srinjayas suffer grim losses and cannot sustain their charge against the prodigious Acharya. Seeing Drona advance in fury, a frantic Yudhishtira thinks of what he can do to arrest the Brahmana warrior. Finally, in despair, Yudhishtira places the intolerable burden on the young shoulders of Abhimanyu.

Yudhishtira, who is not less than Vasudeva himself, and whose tejas is superior to Arjuna's, says to Abhimanyu, "My child, fight today so that when Arjuna returns after killing the Samsaptakas, he will not reprove us. We do not know how to break into the chakravyuha. Only you, Arjuna, Krishna, or Pradyumna can pierce the wheeling circle; there is no fifth. Abhimanyu, child, you must accomplish this thing, you must do this for us; it is your sires, your uncles, and all these troops that ask this boon of you. Take up your weapons and destroy Drona's vyuha before Arjuna returns to rebuke us all!"

Abhimanyu says, "I will breach this most difficult vyuha that Drona has formed and bring victory to my vamsa. My father has taught me how to attack and pierce the chakravyuha. However, he has yet to teach me how to come out of it once I am in, if danger overtakes me."

Yudhishtira says, "Break the vyuha once, O maharatha, and make a passage for us. In battle, you are equal to Arjuna himself. Once you break in the rest of us will follow you and protect you from all sides."

Bhima says, "I will follow you close, and Dhrishtadyumna, Satyaki, the Panchalas and the Prabhadrakas. Once you make the first breach, we will break the chakravyuha apart, and kill the greatest warriors within it."

Abhimanyu says, "I will break into Drona's impenetrable vyuha, why, like a frenzied insect flying into a flame. Today I will do what will benefit both my father and my mother's vamsas. I will make my mother and my uncles proud. Today, everyone will see the endless carnage that I, a boy by himself bring to the teeming enemy. If anyone who faces me in battle today escapes with his life, I will not call myself the son of Arjuna and Subhadra anymore. If from a single chariot I do not truncate the very race of Kshatriyas into eight slivers, I will no longer regard myself the son of Arjuna!"

Yudhishtira says, "Abhimanyu, child of splendour, glorious Kshatriya, let your strength, O son of Subhadra, increase a thousand fold to break

Drona's vyuha protected by Naravyaghras, such great and fierce bowmen, warriors that resemble the Sadhyas, the Rudras, or the Maruts, who are like the Vasus, Agni or Aditya himself in prowess!"

When Yudhishtira says this, Abhimanyu cries to his charioteer, Sumitra, "Fly at Drona's vyuha, sarathy!'""

CANTO 33

ABHIMANYU-VADHA PARVA CONTINUED

"Sanjaya says, 'Abhimanyu charges headlong at Drona's chakravyuha, roaring to his sarathy, "On! Ride on!"

The charioteer says to Abhimanyu, "Ah, you are blessed with length of days, and heavy is the burden the Pandavas have laid upon you! Think well if you are ready to engage Drona, who is an old master of war and all the great astras. While you have been reared in luxury and are new to war."

Abhimanyu replies with a laugh, "O Suta, who is Drona? What is this vast gathering of Kshatriyas? I will defy Indra himself in battle, riding his Airavata and all the devas with him. I feel no anxiety whatever about all these Kshatriyas, for they do not measure up to even a sixteen part of myself. O son of a Suta, fear will not enter my heart even if my uncle Krishna, conqueror of the universe, Vishnu himself, or my father, Arjuna confronts me in battle."

Disregarding the charioteer's advice, Abhimanyu presses on, crying, "Fly like the wind at Drona's army!"

His heart heavy, the charioteer Sumitra whips Abhimanyu's three-year old horses, caparisoned in gold, with greater speed towards Drona. Seeing him dash at them all the Kauravas led by Drona, advance to meet him, while the Pandavas follow Abhimanyu. Wearing golden armour and flying the device of a karnikara tree, Abhimanyu fearlessly attacks those warriors led by Drona, like a lion-cub a herd of elephants!

The elated warriors begin to strike Abhimanyu while he attempts to pierce their vyuha. For a moment, the disturbance there is like the one in the ocean where the Ganga flows into it. Quickly it grows frenzied and appalling; and then in a flash, under Drona's very eye, Abhimanyu breaks into the chakravyuha.

Legion elephants, cavalry, chariots and infantry surround the young hero and attack him all together. The earth resounds with the noise of diverse musical instruments, with shouts and slaps on arm-pits and roars, with yells and leonine shouts, with exclamations of *Stop! Stop!* with fierce cries *Wait! Fight me!* with repeated exclamations of *Here! I am the enemy!* With trumpeting elephants, with the chiming bells and ornaments, with bursts of laughter and the din of horses' hooves and chariot-wheels, the Kaurava warriors lay into Abhimanyu.

But that tremendous young shura, who knows all the marmas of the body, unleashes a keen hot wind of astras at his enemies, missiles that pierce all their vital organs, scorching the advancing warriors, mowing whole legions down in moments with a myriad of astras, so swiftly reducing them to helplessness. Like insects falling upon a blazing fire, they yet ride and run at Abhimanyu; he cuts off thousands of warriors' weapon-bearing arms and scatters the earth with bodies and limbs, like priests strewing the altar at a sacrifice with blades of Kusa grass.

Some of them wear corselets made of iguana skin, some hold bows and shafts, some swords or shields or iron hooks and reins; some, lances, battle axes, maces, iron balls or spears, some, rapiers, crowbars or axes. Several of them grasp short barbs, spiked maces, darts, or kampanas. Many have goads and prodigious conches; some, bearded darts and kachagrahas; a few wield mallets; several others, all manner of missiles—some nooses, some heavy clubs and some stones and bricks. Their arms are decked with amulets and laved with delightful perfumes and lotions; and with these arms dyed brightly with blood, the field of battle soon presents a startling sight, as if strewn with five-headed snakes slain by Garuda.

Abhimanyu casually scatters countless heads, graced with fine noses, faces and hair, and adorned with ear-rings. Blood flows copiously from these heads, their lips bitten with anger. Wearing gorgeous garlands, crowns, turbans, pearls and gems, and splendid as the sun or the moon, they fall like lotuses severed from their stalks. Fragrant with many perfumes, these heads could speak so pleasantly and eloquently while life was in them.

Abhimanyu destroys well-equipped and ethereal looking chariots, fitted with bamboo poles, with grand pennants flying, and their wonderfully crafted janghas, kuvaras, nemis, dasanas, wheels, standards and footboards. He breaks all the instruments of war they carry; blows away the rich cloths with which they are overlaid, and slays by thousands the warriors riding in them. Mangling everything before him with unearthly archery, rampaging Abhimanyu desiccates elephant-warriors and elephants, shredding their standards, hooks, banners, quivers, coats of mail, girths and neck-ropes blankets, bells, trunks, breaking their tusks; and also razing the foot-soldiers who protect the elephants.

We see so many horses of the Vanayu, the Hilly, the Kamboja and the Balhika breeds, with tails, ears, eyes motionless and fixed, fleet, well-trained, and ridden by accomplished warriors armed with swords and lances, lose everything, even the excellent ornaments on their lush tails. Many lie with tongues lolling out and eyes detached from their sockets, entrails and livers gouged out, the rows of bells that adorn them all ruined while the riders on their backs lie lifeless by their sides. Lying thus all over the battlefield, they delight the pisachas, rakshasas and beasts of prey, the blood-drinkers and flesh-eaters.

With the coats of mail and the other leather armour covering their limbs cut open, they lie in dung they excrete themselves. Thus slaying many great horses of your army, Abhimanyu looks splendent. Achieving the most difficult feats, alone, like the inconceivable Vibhu in days of old, Abhimanyu crushes your vast host of chariots, elephants and cavalry, like the three-eyed Mahadeva of immeasurable power crushing the terrible Asura host. Indeed, Abhimanyu, performs feats his enemies cannot match, mowing down whole divisions of your foot-soldiers everywhere.

Seeing him slaughter your army single-handedly, like Skanda the Deva-senapati did the Asuras, your warriors and sons look around vacantly, dazed. Their mouths are dry; their eyes restless; sweat covers their bodies; and their hair stands on end. Fearing complete defeat, they run for their lives. They call one another by their names and the names of their families, abandon wounded sons, fathers, brothers, kinsmen and relatives by marriage on the field, and try only to escape, goading their horses and elephants to their greatest speed.'"

CANTO 34

ABHIMANYU-VADHA PARVA CONTINUED

"Sanjaya says, 'Seeing Abhimanyu of blinding tejas put his army to flight, an angry Duryodhana takes the field against him. At this, Drona roars to all the Kaurava warriors, "Rescue the king! Look where the valiant Abhimanyu kills anyone he wants at will. Go quickly against him, and bravely protect Duryodhana."

Then many grateful, mighty warriors, who fear for Duryodhana, lay a protective ring around your son. Drona, his son, Kripa, Karna, Kritavarman, Subala's son, Brihadbala, Salya of the Madras, Bhuri, Bhurisravas, Sala, Paurava and Vrishasena loose tirades of arrows at Abhimanyu to keep Duryodhana safe. Abhimanyu attacks the maharathas, their charioteers and the horsemen with thick deluges of arrows, and roars in triumph when he makes them turn back. Hearing him roar like a hungry lion, your warriors, with Drona at their head, cannot stand it. They surround him again with a host of chariots and shoot all kinds of arrows at him.

Abhimanyu not only cuts down all their shafts before they reach him, but wounds your warriors with his own barbs, killing many. Ah, his feat is extraordinary and wonderful to behold. Scathed by his arrows like serpents, they encircle him, desperate to kill him. However, Abhimanyu singly holds off the sea of Kaurava troops, like the continent resisting the surging ocean. None among those Kshatriyas, neither Abhimanyu nor his opponents, turns away from the battle.

In that pitched and awesome encounter between a youth and an army, Duhsaha pierces Abhimanyu with nine shafts; Dusasana strikes him with a dozen; Saradwata's son Kripa, with three; Drona strikes him with seventeen arrows, each one a virulent snake; Vivimsati with seventy; Kritavarman with seven; Brihadbala with eight; Aswatthaman with seven shafts; Bhurisravas shoots him with three barbs; the king of the Madras with six, Sakuni with two, and king Duryodhana with three arrows.

The valiant Abhimanyu, however, dancing on his chariot, wounds each of these warriors with three shafts in return, quicker than seeing. Filled with rage at your sons' attempts to frighten him, he displays his wondrous prowess, inborn and honed with long practice. Borne by his marvellous steeds, fleet like Garuda or the Wind and obedient to their sarathy, he confronts the handsome heir of Asmaka, crying *Stop!* and strikes him first with ten shafts and then with ten more; he kills his horses and charioteer and cuts off his standard, his two arms, breaks his bow and severs his head; so all these fall to the ground, while Abhimanyu smiles all the while.

After Abhimanyu kills the heroic king of the Asmakas the whole of his fickle army quits the field. Then Karna, Kripa, Drona, Drona's son, the ruler of the Gandharas, Sala, Salya, Bhurisravas, Kratha, Somadatta, Vivimsati, Vrishasena, Sushena, Kundavedhin, Pratardana, Vrindaraka, Lalithya, Prabahu, Dirghalochana, and a livid Duryodhana cover the radiant Pandava prince with their arrows. Struck by the many barbs from these great bowmen, Abhimanyu responds by striking Karna deep with shafts that pierce both his armour and body. One arrow passes right through Karna's kavacha and his body and streaks down into the earth like a snake through an anthill. In agony, mighty Karna trembles like a hill during an earthquake.

Still seething, Abhimanyu kills Sushena, Dirghalochana and

Kundavedhin, all in a flash. Meanwhile, Karna recovers and pierces Abhimanyu with twenty-five shafts; and Aswatthaman strikes him with twenty, and Kritavarman with seven. Covered all over with arrows stuck into him, Arjuna's son storms all over the field in rage and your troops see him as Yama with his noose.

He attacks Salya, who happens to be near, with a burn of arrows, and raises loud shouts, frightening your men further. Struck deep in his very vital organs by Abhimanyu, Salya gives a sigh and faints on his chariot's platform. Seeing Salya collapse, all your troops flee like a herd of deer attacked by a lion, even as Drona looks on. And Abhimanyu is resplendent, like a sacrificial fire fed with ghee; and the Pitris, the Devas, Charanas and Siddhas, as well as different beings of the earth sing praises of his heroism and unworldly skill.'"

CANTO 35

ABHIMANYU-VADHA PARVA CONTINUED

"Dhritarashtra asks, 'While Abhimanyu devastates our best bowmen, which of my warriors try to check him?'

Sanjaya replies, 'Hear, Rajan, of the superb skill the youthful Abhimanyu displays while putting to rout the chariot-ranks of the Kauravas, which Drona himself leads.

Seeing Abhimanyu's volleys unman Salya, the Madra king's younger brother, filled with fury, rushes at the youthful, incredible prince, raining arrows on him. But Abhimanyu kills his charioteer, cuts down his triple bamboo-pole, smashes his seat on the ratha, his chariot-wheels, his yoke, shafts, quiver and his chariot's floorboard, his banner and every other implement of war with which the chariot is equipped; and he beheads Salya's brother as well. All this happens in the space of a thought, so swiftly that none can discern the prince's movements; they occur in another dimension where time stands still before Abhimanyu's staggering genius. Never knowing how he dies, Salya's brother, great Kshatriya, falls headless onto the ground like a hill uprooted by a tornado. His followers flee in all directions. Witnessing this feat, all men and indeed all creatures, O Bhaarata, cry out *Uttamam! Wonderful!* in their different tongues.

After Salya's brother is killed, many of his followers, wanting revenge and armed with diverse weapons, with ringing battle cries proclaiming their families, homelands and names, charge Abhimanyu; some of them on rathas, some on horses, some on elephants, while others run at him on foot. All of them are fierce warriors and they rush the son of Arjuna with the loud hum of arrows, the deep rumble of chariot-wheels, fierce whoops, shouts and yells, roars, twanging bowstrings, and the slaps of their palms, crying, *Today you will not escape us alive!*

Smiling, down those who wounded him earlier. With wonderful astras, diverse, beautiful and swifter than sight, Abhimanyu the shura fights them almost gently, using astras that he has received from Krishna and Arjuna, just as they would have.

With no thought for the great burden he has assumed, untouched by any fear, he looses his missiles in an endless stream. Such is his speed that no one can see any interval between his bending his bow, aiming and loosing his arrows; from every side, one only sees his vibrating bow drawn in a circle, like a blazing disc of the autumn sun. The twang of his bow and the slap of his palms, O Bhaarata, resound like thunder clouds.

Modest, reverential to his elders, ah, so handsome, yet ferocious and passionate in war, Abhimanyu, out of regard for these hostile heroes, merely skirmishes with them. However, beginning gently, Rajan, he soon grows fierce, like the Sun in autumn after the monsoon. Like the Sun himself blazing forth his rays, his battle rage growing by the moment, Abhimanyu soon unleashes thousands of golden-winged shafts. In the very sight of Drona, he covers the chariot-division of the Kaurava army with diverse astras—the Kshurupra, sharp as razors, the Vatsadantas, with heads like the calf's tooth, the Vipatha, a long, heavy and inflexible missile, the Naracha Ardhachandrabhai, its head a half-moon, Anjalikas with broad-heads.

Harried unbearably by Abhimanyu your army once more turns its back on the fray and runs.'""

CANTO 36

ABHIMANYU-VADHA PARVA CONTINUED

"Dhritarashtra says, 'My heart, O Sanjaya, is agitated by both shame and delight, on hearing how Subhadra's son singly curbs my son's army. Once more tell me in detail about the youthful Abhimanyu's exploits which appear to be so like Skanda's battle of old with the Asura host.'

Sanjaya says, 'I will describe to you the fearful encounter, between the radiant prince fighting alone against countless adversaries. Mounted on his chariot, Abhimanyu, with absolute daring, shoots a thick swarm of shafts at your warriors, parantapas all, full of great valour. Charging them with astounding speed, like a circle of fire, he strikes Drona, Karna, Kripa, Salya, and Drona's son, Kritavarman of the Bhoja vamsa, Brihadbala, Duryodhana, Somadatta, mighty Sakuni and various other kings, princes and their troops. As he rages around slaughtering the enemy with his remarkable weapons, Abhimanyu mahatejasvin seems, O Bhaarata, to be everywhere at once.

Seeing this, your soldiers tremble with fear, Drona, his eyes alight with joy, rides up to Kripa and says to him in Duryodhana's hearing, "There comes the youthful Abhimanyu at the head of the Parthas, enthralling his friends, and king Yudhishtira, Nakula, Sahadeva, Bhimasena, his other kinsmen, and all the rest who watch the battle as spectators, taking no part in it. I do not consider any archer on earth to be Abhimanyu's equal. If he wants, he can destroy this vast army by himself. It seems that for some reason, he does not wish it."

It is as if his words eviscerate your son. Duryodhana's eyes turn red and Drona looks at him with a faint and mocking smile. Duryodhana, his very heart on fire, says to Karna, Balhika, Dusasana, Salya and the other leading maharathas of his army, "The Acharaya of the entire Kshatriya varna, the first among all Brahmagyanis, does not want to kill this son of Arjuna. No one in battle can escape the Acharya with his life, not even the Great Destroyer himself, if Drona fights him as an enemy. What, then, to say of any mortal?

I tell you that Abhimanyu is the son of Arjuna, and Arjuna is the Acharya's beloved sishya. It is for this that Drona protects this youth, for their disciples and their sons are always dear to men of dharma, why, dearer than their own sons! Protected by Drona, the callow son of Arjuna regards himself as valorous. He is only a fool to entertain such a high opinion of himself. Ah, kill this foolish brat without delay!"

Goaded by the Kuru king, the already shamed and incensed warriors charge Abhimanyu all together. Dusasana, in particular, that tiger of the Kurus, assures Duryodhana, "Rajan, I say to you that I will kill this prince before the very eyes of the Pandavas and the Panchalas. I will consume Subhadra's son today, like Rahu swallowing Surya."

Once more addressing the Kuru king loudly, Dusasana says, "When the two vain Krishnas hear that I have killed their precious Abhimanyu, they will quit their lives and leave this world of men. Hearing of their death, the other sons of Pandu and all their friends and kinsmen will not last another day from despair. It is plain to me that if we kill this one Abhimanyu, we will kill all your enemies and victory shall be yours. Wish me well, Rajan, and I will despatch this prince swiftly to his dead sires!"

Saying this, your excited Dusasana gives a shattering roar and charges

Abhimanyu, covering him with dark arrows. Abhimanyu retaliates in wrath with twenty-six keen shafts. The battle between Dusasana, who is like an infuriated elephant, and Abhimanyu is wild and savage. Both maharathas, they wheel around each other in circles, one to the left and the other to the right. While, with their panavas, mridangas, dundubhis, krakachas, great anakas, bheris and jharjaras, your army makes deafening din, mingled with deep roars, like the very sea!'"

CANTO 37

Abhimanyu-vadha Parva continued

"Sanjaya says, 'Abhimanyu, lacerated by arrows, says smilingly to Dusasana, "It is my good fortune that I see before me the vain, cruel Kshatriya, who has abandoned dharma and lustily shouts his own praises. In the Kuru sabha, in the hearing of king Dhritarashtra, you humiliated and angered Yudhishtira Dharmaraja with your vile conduct and words. Relying on deceit at the game of dice and Sakuni's skill at cheating, and maddened by low success, you taunted great Bhima repeatedly!

You are about to reap the fruits of your arrogance that you dared anger those illustrious ones. O evil-hearted one, you are about to be punished for all your sins—for stealing what does not belong to you, for your haughty wrathfulness, your hatred of peace, your avarice, your ignorance, your enmity towards your kinsmen, for the injustice and persecution you have meted out to them, for depriving my sires, these fierce bowmen, of their kingdom and for your always vicious nature and temper.

I will punish you with my arrows today, wretched Dusasana, in the sight of your whole army. Today, I will unburden myself of the rage which I carry against you and free myself of the debt I owe the angry Krishna and my father Arjuna, who always looks for an opportunity to punish you. Kaurava, today I will free myself of the debt I owe my uncle Bhima. You will not escape me with your life today, if you do not run away from the battle."

Mahabaho Abhimanyu, razer of his enemies, invokes a shaft endued with the splendour of Yama, Agni or Vayu, an astra that will send Dusasana to the next world. Flashing straight at Dusasana's chest, the arrow strikes his shoulder-joint and plunges into his body up to its very wings. His bow drawn to its fullest stretch, Abhimanyu strikes him with twenty-five arrows more, all like fire. Struck deep and in agony, Dusasana sighs, sits down abruptly in his chariot and faints.

His charioteer swiftly bears him away senseless from the field. At this, the Pandavas, the five sons of Draupadi, Virata, the Panchalas and the Kekayas roar their approval and the elated Pandava troops blow their conches and beat their drums. Seeing Abhimanyu's spectacular feat they laugh aloud in exhilaration, especially to watch the proud and violent Dusasana humbled. The mighty sons of Draupadi, who fly banners with the images of Yama, Maruta, Sakra and the twin Aswins, Satyaki, Chekitana, Dhrishtadyumna, Sikhandin, the Kekayas, Dhrishtaketu, the Matsyas, Panchalas, the Srinjayas and the Pandavas led by Yudhishtira, are all overjoyed. They dash forward now to pierce Drona's chakravyuha, to shatter it. A dreadful battle breaks out at its rim between all these fierce heroes, all bent on victory.

Duryodhana turns to Karna and says, "Look where valiant Dusasana, who until now burned our enemies like the Sun himself, has succumbed to Abhimanyu. Look where the Pandavas, filled with war lust, come hunting us like a pride of lions to rescue Abhimanyu. Karna, do something!"

Always sensitive to Duryodhana's least concern, Karna is quick to blaze up in anger and lashes the invincible Abhimanyu with stinging torrents of arrows. Now roused, gallant Karna, as if in contempt of his young adversary, also strikes the radiant youth's followers with countless exceptional shafts. But the high-souled Abhimanyu has set his sights on Drona, and he unleashes a flurry of seventy-three arrows at Karna, drawing fonts of blood from that hero.

No maharatha of your army succeeds in obstructing Abhimanyu's charge towards Drona; indeed, Arjuna's son, Indra's grandson, brings havoc to them all, even the greatest of them. But recovering in a moment, great Karna, most honoured of all bowmen, scathes Abhimanyu with hundreds of fiery shafts, consuming the young warrior's most formidable astras; Karna bars Abhimanyu's path to Drona.

He bleeds from Karna's awesome archery, but Abhimanyu, the godlike, feels no twinge of pain! He serenely continues to break many great Kaurava heroes' bows in their hands, and also holds Karna at bay. With serpentine narachas, shot from his bow drawn into a circle, Abhimanyu destroys Karna's royal chatra, cuts slivers from his standard, and grievously hurts his sarathy and horses, ah, smiling all the while.

In froth, Karna picks up another bow and looses five immaculate arrows at Abhimanyu, who receives them fearlessly. In a wink, with a single arrow, the scintillating youth breaks both Karna's bow and flagstaff, so they fall onto the ground. Seeing Karna beset, his younger brother drawing his bow with great force, charges Subhadra's overweening son. The Parthas and their followers raise loud cheers and blow their conches and beat their drums again to celebrate the heroism of the peerless, indomitable Abhimanyu.'"

CANTO 38

Abhimanyu-vadha Parva continued

"Sanjaya says, 'Roaring, bow in hand, its string stretched full, Karna's younger brother sets himself between the two illustrious warriors. He pierces invincible Abhimanyu with ten shafts, and his chatra, standard, charioteer and horses, smiling the while. Seeing Abhimanyu, who fights with superhuman prowess even like his father and grandfather, wounded, the warriors of your army are delighted. But with a dazzling smile, Abhimanyu bends his bow and with one winged arrow cuts off his adversary's head and drops it onto the ground.

Seeing his brother defeated and slain like a karnikara tree shaken and flung down by the wind from a mountain top, Karna is stricken. Abhimanyu unleashes such a ferocious volley at him that he has to turn away from the battle; immediately, Abhimanyu attacks the other great bowmen and again demolishes the enemy elephants, cavalry, chariots and infantry. With Karna fleeing the carnage on his swift ratha, the Kaurava vyuha is shattered.

Abhimanyu's shafts shroud the sky like dark locust swarms, Rajan, and one can see nothing. All your warrior flee; other than the lone Jayadratha, king of the Sindhus. Abhimanyu, Purusharishabha, blows his conch and falls on the Bharata host like a burning brand thrown into the midst of dry grass. Gleefully, he begins to consume his enemies, charging at will through the Kaurava host. Piercing deep into their vyuha, he mangles chariots, elephants, horses and men with cataracts of shining arrows; he strews the field with headless trunks and trunkless heads. The Kaurava warriors turn tail, running down their comrades.

Arrows, loosed in an endless downpour, miraculous arrows past counting, annihilate maharathas, elephants and horses. Severed arms, decked with angadas and other golden ornaments, hands cased in leathern gloves, arrows, bows, bodies and heads adorned with chariot-rings and garlands of flowers, lie in their thousands on Kurukshetra. Covered over with upaskaras, adhishthanas, akshas, broken wheels and yokes, in thousands upon thousands, and with arrows, bows, swords, fallen standards, shields everywhere, and with the bodies of slain Kshatriyas, horses and elephants, the battlefield is quickly impassable.

Deafening is the noise the princes make, as they call out to one another while Abhimanyu slaughters them, and cowards quail at it. The din, O lord of the Bharatas, fills all the points of the compass. Abhimanyu tears into the Kaurava troops, cutting down the greatest maharathas, horses and elephants and consuming his enemies truly like a fire in the midst of a heap of dry grass. Past count are the men and beasts he kills; as he dashes everywhere at will through the heart of the Kaurava army. Surrounded by our troops and covered with dust, none of us can catch a glimpse of him as he flies joyfully killing horses, elephants and warriors, with no moment's pause. Corpses fall like rain before dreadful, inexorable Abhimanyu of sixteen summers.

Soon after, we see him flare out of the press, still burning his enemies like the meridian sun. Equal to Vasava himself in war, Abhimanyu in the midst of Duryodhana's army is beyond being merely glorious.'"

CANTO 39

ABHIMANYU-VADHA PARVA CONTINUED

"Dhritarashtra asks, 'When Abhimanyu, a mere child in years, raised in luxury's lap, proud of the strength of his arms, a wizard at war, absolutely heroic by nature, the perpetuator of his race, and heedless of his life, pierces the Kaurava army with his chariot yoked to three-years old spirited horses, does any maharatha of Yudhishtira's army follow him?'

Sanjaya says, 'Yudhishtira, Bhimasena, Sikhandin, Satyaki, Nakula and Sahadeva, Dhrishtadyumna, Virata, Drupada, Kekaya, Dhrishtaketu, and the Matsya warriors all stream fiercely behind him. Abhimanyu's sires, along with uncles, all maharathas, arrayed in battle order, come thundering in his wake, along the very path that he creates. Seeing them come in fearsome tide, your troops back away from the fight.

It is then that your son-in-law, Jayadratha of the Sindhus, his brief time of glory come, faces the Parthas and all their followers, standing at the fateful moment between them and Abhimanyu, and holding them all at bay! Like a lone elephant appeared in a bloody marsh, Vriddhakshatra's formidable son invokes great devastras to arrest the charge of the Pandavas.'

Dhritarashtra says, 'Sanjaya, the burden of Jayadratha must have been heavy, for he faced the angry Pandavas by himself, even as they stormed forward to the rescue of their beloved prince. Surely, his might and heroism are more than wonderful. Tell me about that noble Kshatriya's prowess, and how he accomplishes the incredible feat.

What dana has he given, what libations has he poured onto the sacred fire, what sacrifices has he performed, what tapasya has he undergone, that he now succeeds in holding up all the Parthas single-handed?'

Sanjaya says, 'Once, when Jayadratha tried to abduct Draupadi in the forest, Bhimasena crushed and humiliated him savagely. Utterly shamed, Jayadratha went into a deep forest and performed the most arduous tapasya. He restrained his senses, endured hunger, thirst and heat, and he emaciated his body until his veins stood out like blue snakes through his skin. Chanting the eternal mantras of the Vedas, he worshipped Mahadeva.

Finally, the illustrious Siva, who is always kindly towards his devotees, appeared in a dream and said to Jayadratha, "Ask for the boon you want. I am pleased with you, Jayadratha! What do you wish for?"

Bowing down to the Lord with folded hands, Jayadratha said, "Grant that, alone on a single chariot, I once vanquish all the sons of Pandu together, for all their terrible tejas and prowess."

This, O Bhaarata, was the boon he asked for. Mahadeva said to him, "I grant you your boon. Other than Arjuna, you will one day defeat the other four sons of Pandu in battle."

Jayadratha said to the Devadeva, "Tataasthu!" and awoke, O Rajan, from his sleep.

It was because of that boon and also through the power of his devastras that Jayadratha single-handedly arrests the entire Pandava force. The virile twanging of his bowstring and the slaps of his palms as he looses his missiles fill the enemy Kshatriyas with uncanny fear; and they delight your troops. Seeing Jayadratha's astonishing feat, the emboldened Kshatriyas of your army ride back into battle against Yudhishtira's forces."'

CANTO 40

ABHIMANYU-VADHA PARVA CONTINUED

"Sanjaya says, 'You ask me, Rajan, about the prowess of Jayadratha of the Sindhus. I will describe in detail how he opposes the Pandavas.

Great horses of the Sindhu breed, well-trained, fast as the wind and obedient to the commands of his sarathy, are harnessed to his chariot, which looks like a cloud palace in the sky. His flag that bears the device of a large silver boar is striking to behold. He shines like the moon in the firmament with his white chatra and banners, and he is fanned with yak-tails—all the emblems of sovereignty. Pearls, diamonds, rubies and gold deck his iron chariot rails and it glitters like the starry sky. Drawing his ample bow and shooting a fusillade of missiles, quick as thinking, he blocks the breach that Abhimanyu made in the chakravyuha. He pierces Satyaki with three arrows, Vrikodara with eight, Dhrishtadyumna with sixty, Drupada with five, and Sikhandin with ten.

He then draws blood from the Kaikeyas with twenty-five keen bolts. Jayadratha strikes each of the five sons of Draupadi with three arrows; he wounds Yudhishtira with seventy; pierces the other heroes of the Pandava army with thick showers of shafts: ah, a feat altogether wonderful. Rajan, then with a gleaming arrow, Yudhishtira breaks Jayadratha's bow with a smile. However, in the twinkling of an eye, the Sindhu takes up another bow and pierces Yudhishtira with ten sharp barbs and each of the others with three.

Amazed by Jayadratha's newfound dexterity, Bhima cleaves his bow, and knocks down his standard and royal parasol with three wedge-headed shafts. Jayadratha sweeps up another bow, strings it in a flash and fells Bhima's flag, bow and horses, forcing him to abandon his useless chariot. Bhima leaps onto Satyaki's ratha like a lion bounding onto a mountain. Seeing this, your troops applaud Jayadratha, and shout, "Wonderful! Wonderful!"

Indeed, they and all beings repeatedly applaud the feat of the Sindhu king who, single-handedly, holds all the Pandavas together at bay. Jayadratha bestrides and fills the path that Abhimanyu made for the Pandavas by slaughtering so many warriors and elephants. Indeed, with great effort do the mighty Matsyas, Panchalas, Kaikeyas and the Pandavas themselves manage to draw near Jayadratha; but none of them can subdue him. Jayadratha, using Mahadeva's boon, holds up every one of your enemies who tries to break into Drona's chakravyuha.'"

CANTO 41

ABHIMANYU-VADHA PARVA CONTINUED

"Sanjaya says, 'Jayadratha, king of the Sindhus, effectively halts the onrush Pandavas and the battle between them is marvellous and dreadful. First, the invincible Abhimanyu breaks into the Kaurava array and shakes it like a makara agitating the ocean. Then the principal warriors of the Kaurava army attack him in turns, each according to his rank and precedence. Fierce and bloody is the contention between these powerful maharathas on the one side and Abhimanyu alone on the other.

Surrounded on all sides by the enemy with massed chariots, the splendid prince kills Vrishasena's sarathy and demolishes his bow. He excoriates Vrishasena's horses with a brace of unerring shafts, and those horses swift as the wind bolt, bearing a helpless Vrishasena from the battle. Abhimanyu's charioteer escapes from the thick melee, whisking his young hero away to another part of the field The numerous maharathas who watch this feat are all filled with admiration and exclaim, "Uttamam! Wonderful!"

Seeing the lion Abhimanyu furiously mowing down the Kauravas like some force of nature, Vasatiya charges him and falls upon him. He pierces Abhimanyu with sixty golden-winged shafts and cries, "As long as I am alive, you will not escape with your life."

Although Vasatiya wears an iron kavacha, Abhimanyu blows his heart apart with a single arrow, and that Kshatriya falls dead out of his chariot. Incensed at this, many bulls among Kshatriyas besiege your grandson all together, Rajan, to try and overpower him. Stretching bows of diverse kinds, they assail him and another fierce battle ensues. A vengeful Abhimanyu shreds their bows and arrows, their limbs, and plucks off their heads decked with ear-rings and crowns of flowers. He lops off their arms adorned with various golden ornaments, which still hold swords, spiked maces and battle-axes in fingers cased in leather gloves.

The earth is strewn with garlands, ornaments, fine cloaks, fallen standards, coats of mail, shields, golden chains, diadems, parasols, yak-tails; with upaskaras, adhishthanas, dandakas, banduras, with crushed akshas, broken wheels, and yokes, numbering thousands; with anukarshas, banners, charioteers, horses; and also with broken chariots and felled elephants. The hallowed field spread over so liberally with slain Kshatriya shuras, rulers of different kingdoms, all come here for victory, presents a fearful sight.

When Abhimanyu angrily rides across Kurukshetra, everywhere at will, his very form becomes invisible. One sees only his coat of mail, glimmering with gold, his ornaments, bow and arrows. Indeed, he razes the enemy like the sun himself in his blazing effulgence, and no one can even look at him so bright is he.'"

CANTO 42

Abhimanyu-vadha Parva continued

"Sanjaya says, 'Abhimanyu at war resembles the Destroyer, Rudra himself claiming the lives of all creatures upon the advent of the Pralaya. His prowess like his grandsire Indra's, that prince is magnificent, ineffable! He pierces the enemy ranks like Yama and seizes Satvasravas like an angry tiger seizing a deer. Seeing this, many Maharathas, wielding all kinds of weapons, rush at him, calling out, "I will go first! Let me strike first!"

Just as a whale in the sea catches a shoal of small fish with great ease, so does Abhimanyu consume that whole division of Kshatriyas. Like rivers that never retreat as they approach the sea, none among the charging Kshatriyas draw back when they reach Abhimanyu. That legion reels like a boat tossed on the ocean where a mighty tempest rages, its crew panic-stricken by the violence of the wind.

Great Rukmaratha, son of Salya of the Madras, roars, "Kshatriyas, have no fear! When I am here, what is Abhimanyu? I will take him alive."

Riding his beautiful and well-equipped chariot, Rukmaratha dashes at Abhimanyu and bloodies him with three shafts that whistle into his torso, three into the right arm and three the left. Arjuna's son, however, breaks Rukmaratha's bow, and in a blink cuts off his arms and his head with its beautiful eyes and high-arched brows. Seeing Rukmaratha, who vowed to either kill Abhimanyu or take him alive, die gorily, a hundred of his friends, each one a heroic Kshatriya, flying gold adorned pennants, join the battle. These maharathas, stretching their bows that are full six cubits long, surround Abhimanyu and loose tornadoes of arrows at him.

Seeing him besieged by all those great princes, Duryodhana rejoices and considers Abhimanyu already a guest in Yama's halls. The princes shroud Abhimanyu with dense gusts of golden missiles, making him well nigh invisible. We quickly see Abhimanyu with his standard and his chariot covered over with barbs like a great tree with flights of locusts. His blood flowing, his ire rising, he responds like an elephant goaded with an ankusha.

O Bhaarata, he invokes the Gandharvastra and the illusions it creates. Arjuna received this astra from the Gandharva Tumburu and others through tapasya and yagnas; he gave it to his son. Now unleashing it at his enemies Abhimanyu bewilders them. He is a circle of fire and we see him sometimes as one prince, sometimes as a hundred and sometimes as a thousand. Confounding his massed adversaries with the magic illusions of that weapon, he forges ahead on his ratha and vivisects the enemy kings, sending hosts of spirits soaring into the next world while here their bodies fall onto the ground tike tops that spin no more, many cut into a hundred raw sections. He destroys their bows, horses, charioteers, standards, why, their very legions while time seems to stand still for him. He kills the hundred princes like five-year old mango-trees on the point of bearing fruit, swept down by a tempest.

Seeing Abhimanyu single-handedly massacre all these youthful princes, brought up in every luxury and resembling angry snakes, along with their rathikas, elephants, horses and foot-soldiers, fear and blind rage grip Duryodhana and the shocked Kuru king rushes roaring at Abhimanyu. The incendiary duel between them lasts only a short while, before your son, harried past endurance by the resplendent Abhimanyu, is obliged to turn away from the fight.'"

CANTO 43

ABHIMANYU-VADHA PARVA CONTINUED

"Dhritarashtra says, 'What you tell me, O Suta, about the battle between the lustrous Abhimanyu fighting alone against so many enemies, seems wonderful, why, incredible. However, I do not regard such feats as unbelievable marvels in those who have dharma for their refuge. After Duryodhana is beaten back and a hundred princes are slain, what do the warriors of my army do next against Abhimanyu?'

Sanjaya says, 'Their mouths become dry, their eyes restless; sweat covers their bodies, their hair stand on ends and they are ready to quit the field in despair. Abandoning their wounded brothers, fathers, sons, friends, and kinsmen they flee, urging their horses and elephants to their utmost speed. Seeing them broken and in full flight, Drona, Aswatthaman, Brihadbala, Kripa, Duryodhana, Karna, Kritavarman and Subala's son Sakuni come swarming to quell the invincible Abhimanyu. But your grandson, Rajan, routs all of them and only one warrior, Duryodhana's son, the noble Lakshmana, accomplished tejasvin, fearless now because his is both proud and callow, takes the field against Abhimanyu. Anxious for his son, Duryodhana turns back to follow him, as do other maharathas.

Like dark thunderheads inundating a mountain-breast with rain, all of them lash arrow showers over Abhimanyu. Abhimanyu sweeps over them the dry wind in the sky that blows in every direction scattering cloud masses. Then, like one infuriated elephant fighting another, he engages your grandson, the handsome, brave and strapping Lakshmana, who stands near his father with his bow stretched, like a prince of the Yakshas; Lakshmana who strikes Abhimanyu through his arms and his chest with robust shafts that drink his blood.

Abhimanyu Mahabaho is like a snake beaten with a stick. He cries to Lakshmana, "Look well on this world, for you will soon go to the other one. In front of all your kinsmen, I will dispatch you to Yama's realm."

He looses a broad-headed astra that resembles a snake just emerged from its slough, and dissevers Lakshmana's beautiful head, graced with a strong and noble nose, fine eye-brows and handsome curls, and with sparkling kundalas. Seeing Lakshmana killed, your troops cry out in shock and grief.

Blood leaping into his eyes to see his precious son die, Duryodhana howls long and echoingly truly like some dreadful demon, and screams at his Kshatriyas, *Kill him!*

Six maharathas—Drona, Kripa, Karna, Aswatthaman, Brihadbala and Kritavarman, son of Hridika, surround Abhimanyu. He drills each of them with his burning arrows, and beats them off like a lion might a pack of dogs. The incandescent son of Arjuna falls upon the vast forces of Jayadratha with redoubled ferocity. With their elephant-division, the Kalingas, the Nishadas and the valiant son of Kratha, all clad in gleaming mail, encircle him and block his way ahead. Another pitched battle breaks out and tameless, invincible Abhimanyu quickly melts those forces; he is at them like a hurricane.

Kratha's son showers him with deadly fire, while many other rathikas led by Drona, who returns to the field, rush at him, discharging their violent fusillades at the meridian prince. Containing their assault with some disdain, Abhimanyu looses a flash flood of arrows at Kratha's son, cutting down all his barbs, breaking his bow, severing his arms and then his head with its golden coronet. Seeing Kratha's noble, mighty and famed son, master of astras, die in the incarnadine blasts of Abhimanyu's unworldly shafts, your other maharathas quickly ride away from this terrible prince of tender years.'"

CANTO 44

ABHIMANYU-VADHA PARVA CONTINUED

"Dhritarashtra asks, 'While young and invincible Abhimanyu, who never flees a battle, strikes deep into our vyuha, so effortlessly, and achieves feats more than worthy of his lineage, which of my heroes stand up to him?'

Sanjaya answers, 'Once he breaks into the chakravyuha, Abhimanyu brings bloody mayhem to your forces and all your heroes and the kings that fight for your son turn away from Arjuna's prince, for he fights like a god and they cannot bear him. Then it is that the six maharathas surround him again—Drona, Kripa, Karna, Aswatthaman, Brihadbala and Hridika's son Kritavarman of the Yadavas.

The other warriors harry Yudhishtira, to support Jayadratha who single-handedly holds up the Pandavas, Many powerful Kshatriyas draw their six cubit long bows and shower arrows on him like rain. Abhimanyu paralyses all these great archers. He strikes Drona with fifty arrows, Brihadbala with twenty, Kritavarman with eighty, and Kripa with sixty shafts. Abhimanyu draws his bow into a circle and stabs Aswatthaman with ten gold fledged barbs, and Karna with a keen bright, bearded arrow shot with great force.

Cutting down Kripa's horses and both his Parshni charioteers, mighty Abhimanyu bloodies Kripa's chest with ten searing shafts. In the very sight of your heroic sons, he overwhelms the brave Vrindaraka, the pride of the Kurus. While Arjuna's incredible son mows down your greatest warriors, one after another, Aswatthaman strikes him with twenty-five small and clever barbs. Abhimanyu turns on Drona's son with a sizzling volley and Aswatthaman responds with sixty fierce darts. But Abhimanyu stands immovable as the Mainaka mountain.

Mahatejasvin Abhimanyu looses seventy-three gold-winged shafts in a wink at Aswatthaman so he staggers in his ratha. Drona rides to his son's rescue, striking Abhimanyu with a hundred arrows, while Aswatthaman also pierces him with sixty. From another side, Karna strikes him with twenty-two broad-headed shafts; Kritavarman with fourteen; Brihadbala with fifty and Saradwata's son, Kripa, with ten. Abhimanyu, majestic dancer in his chariot, makes each of them a home for ten missiles from his implacable bow.

Brihadbala, king of the Kosalas, drills a slender barbed shaft into Abhimanyu's chest; in a flash, that superlative prince cuts down his antagonist's horses, standard, bow and charioteer. Brihadbala seizes up a great sword and, leaping down from his ruined chariot, runs at Abhimanyu to hew his head off. With one inexorable shining shaft, Abhimanyu find Brihadbala's heart, and that great Kshatriya falls dead without a sound. Seeing this, ten thousand illustrious Kshatriyas break away from the fray and flee, cursing Duryodhana.

Having killed Brihadbala, Abhimanyu courses around the field, sowing death all around him.'"

CANTO 45

Abhimanyu-vadha Parva continued

"Sanjaya says, 'Arjuna's dazzling son again strikes Karna with a heavy barbed bolt, then quick as the mind with fifty more. Now Duryodhana pierces Abhimanyu with a relucent clutch of shafts. Covered all over by now with arrows, Abhimanyu presents a striking appearance; mad with rage, he bathes Karna in blood so that he, too, mangled by that astounding prince's archery, wears a burnished look; and both of them resemble a couple of flowering kinsukas. Without a moment's pause, amazing Abhimanyu kills six of Karna's bravest warriors, with their horses and charioteers, and shatters their chariots.

Fear lays no hand on that luminous sixteen-year-old god among men and, never pausing, he shoots the six maharathas with ten more shafts each. With six unerring barbs, he strikes off the head of the youthful Aswaketu, son of the Magadha king, in the same moment killing his four horses and charioteer; no, never pausing, he despatches the Bhoja prince of Martikavata, whose banner has an elephant emblazoned on it. Roaring like several lions, so the field echoes with his strong and youthful voice, Abhimanyu blows like a desert storm of death on Kurukshetra;

like a lion in a cattle pen is he.

Dusasana's son scathes Abhimanyu's horses with four shafts, his sarathy with one and Abhimanyu himself with ten; Abhimanyu plunges two smoking barbs into his enemy's body. Red-eyed, he cries, "Your father has fled battle like a coward. It is well that you are not like him. But you will not escape me alive today."

And Abhimanyu looses a long polished arrow at his enemy, but Drona's son cuts it down from a side with three light-like bolts.

Letting Aswatthama alone, Abhimanyu turns on Salya and shreds his chest with nine fierce barbs, vulture-feathered. The riverine arrows from his uncanny weapon break Salya's bow, kill both his Parshni charioteers, and bloody Salya himself, forcing him to quit his chariot and mount another. Tireless Abhimanyu, unchained, kills five maharathas in a blur—Satrunjaya, Chandraketu, Mahamegba, Suvarchas and Suryabhasa; he strikes Sakuni hard making him lurch in his chariot. Subala's evil son drills Abhimanyu with three barbs and says to Duryodhana, "We must attack him all together, or this boy will kill us all today. Rajan, take counsel with Drona and Kripa and think of how this horrible prince can be killed."

Karna asks Drona, "Abhimanyu crushes us all as he pleases. Tell us how we can stop him."

Drona says to all his maharathas, "You have all seen him close, this magnificent youth. Have you found any weakness in him? He careens everywhere among us all, but have any of us seen the faintest frailty in him? Ah, we can only gaze at the unearthly swiftness of this incomparable young lion, while he slaughters us, and gaze on in wonder.

We see his chariot fly among us like a streak of lightning; we see his bow always drawn in a circle; but so quickly does he aim his arrows and shoot them that it seems time is his servant. Ah, this dreadful son of Subhadra delights me, even while he razes our army, and afflicts my very prana, for he is so entirely wonderful. Our greatest maharathas are flabbergasted and I myself enchanted by the skills of Abhimanyu. Truly, I see no flaw in him, no chink to pierce so we might bring him down.

There is no difference between this youth and his father; if anything his son exceeds Arjuna! Look how he fills all the points of the horizon with his mighty shafts."

Still bleeding from Abhimanyu's arrows, Karna says between clenched teeth, "I am sorely wounded by this boy, and I fight on only because I am a true warrior. I fear that my injuries are grave, for the force of his arrows is like none I have ever known, and I fear my wounds weaken my heart."

The Acharya tells Karna, with a smile, "Abhimanyu is young, his prowess is great. His kavacha is impenetrable because I myself taught his father how to wear his coat of mail. This young parantapa surely knows that subtle science completely. Yet with shafts well shot, you can destroy his bow, bowstring, the reins of his horses, the steeds themselves and his two Parshni charioteers.

O Karna, mighty archer, do this if you can and make him turn his back on the fight; and then strike him from behind. With his bow in hand, the very Devas and the Asuras together cannot conquer Abhimanyu. If you want to kill him, first deprive him of his chariot and divest him of his bow."

Not hesitating a moment, Karna cleaves Abhimanyu's bow in his hands, even as that prince continues to vigorously burn his enemies; Kritavarman of the Bhojas kills his horses and Kripa his two Parshni charioteers. After breaking his bow, the six maharathas fall ruthlessly on the now chariot less youth, unleashing a black storm of arrows at him. Bowless and his chariot useless, but always the pure Kshatriya who never knows fear, Abhimanyu takes up a sword and shield and leaps high into the air. He hangs there, using the arcane Kausika way, going freely through the sky like Garuda, prince of all birds!

With thoughts like *He will fall upon my sword!* the maharathas, their gazes now turned up, continue to loose their arrows at the suspended prince, always wary of him striking down at them. They draw blood from Arjuna's son turned into the ultimate embodiment of a warrior.

Then, with a perfect shaft, mighty Drona breaks Abhimanyu's sword at its jewelled hilt; at the same moment Karna shatters his shield in shards. Abhimanyu falls from a height but lands unhurt on his feet. Undaunted, with never a thought for his life, he pulls a wheel free from his ratha and holding it aloft, runs roaring at the Acharya.

Ah, this world has hardly ever seen any sight equal to Abhimanyu at that moment, covered in dust, but his body shining so brightly through it, with the chariot-wheel in his hands like Krishna's very Sudarshana, and still full of fierce valour. His clothes dyed red with the blood flowing from his countless wounds, his brow knit and formidable with deep furrows, still roaring like a pride of young lions, lord Abhimanyu of immeasurable tejas, is magnificent, splendid, my king, glorious past telling or imagining on heartless Kurukshetra.'"

CANTO 46

ABHIMANYU-VADHA PARVA CONTINUED

"Sanjaya says, 'Abhimanyu, the joy of Krishna's sister, Abhimanyu the Atiratha, flaunting his wheel like the Sudarshana, is so beautiful; he is like a second Janardana. With his lambent locks flying in the wind, his body alight, and that strangest weapon, so dazzling now in his hands, the very Devas are blinded by that prince and cannot look at his splendour.

Seeing him with the chariot wheel, the unnerved maharathas tremble and, somehow, all together, cut that wheel into a hundred pieces. Peerless Abhimanyu takes up a great mace and runs at Aswatthaman. Seeing the gada aloft, and looking like Indra's Vajra, Aswatthaman, tiger among men, jumps out of his chariot and runs three loping stride to escape that blazing prince. Abhimanyu, like a flame burning brightest just before it is put out, kills Aswathaman's horses and Parshni charioteers with dreadful strokes of his mace.

Pierced all over with arrows, looking like some ethereal porcupine, he smashes Subala's son Kalikeya's head like a red melon; never stopping, never doubting himself, he fells Kalikeya's seventy-seven Gandhara followers with his supernatural mace. Next, he slaughters ten rathikas of the Brahma-Vasatiya vamsa, and then ten massive elephants! Flying then at Dusasana's son, he smashes his chariot along with its horses and pounds them down into the earth.

The indomitable son of Dusasana takes up his own gada and rushes at Abhimanyu, roaring, *Stop! Wait!* The cousins, the two young Kshatriyas heroes, begin to swing their maces at each other wildly, landing sickening blows. Both have a single thought; both *are* a single thought—to kill the other. They fight like the three-eyed Mahadeva and the Asura Andhaka in days of old. Finally, at the same instant, both land thunderous blows on each other and both fall at once onto the earth, like two uprooted yupastambas, sacrificial stakes raised in honour of Indra.

But it has been a day as long as several lives for Arjuna's matchless son. Dusasana's son, enhancer of the fame of the Kurus, is first to rise. Even as Abhimanyu begins to haul himself onto his feet, Dusasana's son swings an awful blow of his mace down squarely on the crown of noble Abhimanyu's head, shattering it. With a soft sigh, Parantapa Abhimanyu, sixteen years old, who has killed so many thousands of your greatest warriors by himself, falls dead on sacred Kurukshetra, the hint of a smile still on his bloody lips.

Thus, Rajan, many join together to finally kill this one hero, who by himself razes a vast portion of your army, like an elephant trampling lotus-stalks in a lake. And as he lies dead on the field, Abhimanyu looks like a wild elephant slain by hunters. Your troops surround the fallen Kshatriya who now resembles a raging summer conflagration extinguished after consuming a whole forest; or like a tempest divested of its fury after devastating mountain crests; like the Sun arriving at the western hills after having consumed the Bharata army; or like Soma swallowed by Rahu; or like the Ocean dried of water.

The maharathas of your army gaze at Abhimanyu whose face still has the splendour of the full moon and whose lashes black as the feathers of the raven made his eyes luminous and beautiful, Abhimanyu now lying prone on the bare earth. They are filled with joy and roar in relief and triumph again and again.

Indeed, Rajan, your troops are in transports of joy, while tears fall fast from the eyes of the Pandava heroes. Seeing Abhimanyu lying on the field of battle, like the moon fallen from the sky, diverse beings of the air lament, "Alas, he who fought alone, like an army himself, lies dead on the battlefield, murdered by six mighty maharathas of the Dhartarashtra army, led by Drona and Karna. This killing was not a deed of dharma."

Upon fall of that transplendent prince among the countless corpses he has strewn her with, the earth looks like the star-filled sky with the moon now among the fainter lights. Bhumi assumes a beautiful aspect, covered with wavelets of blood, scattered with innumerable arrows with wings of gold and spread over with the noble heads of Kshatriyas, wearing ear-rings, variegated turbans of great value, with banners, yak-tails, beautiful cloths, priceless jewel-encrusted weapons, with the bright ornaments of chariots, horses, men, elephants; sharp and well-tempered swords looking like snakes freed from their sloughs, bows, broken arrows, spears, swords, kampanas and all kinds of weapons.

The ground in many places is impassable because of the horses that lie upon her dead or dying, all weltering in blood, with their riders lying near them, felled by Subhadra's son. Kurukshetra wears a grim and terrible aspect, with iron hooks and elephants big as hills, with shields, swords and standards, lying everywhere, all cut down by Abhimanyu. Superb chariots deprived of their horses, charioteers and maharathas lie all around in death's final attitudes, some crushed flat by elephants. Ample corpses of foot-soldiers with diverse weapons lie on the bloody ground and the indescribable sight fills all faint hearts with terror.

Seeing Abhimanyu, splendent as the sun or the moon, fallen on the ground, your troops rejoice, while the Pandavas are grief-stricken. When youthful Abhimanyu of sixteen summers falls, the Pandava legions all flee in shock from the very presence of Yudhishtira. Seeing his army breaking up, Yudhishtira addresses his warriors, "The heroic Abhimanyu was killed without retreating from battle, and he has certainly risen into swarga. So stand and fear not, for we shall yet vanquish our enemies."

Endued with great energy and lustre, Dharmaraja Yudhishtira, the best of Kshatriyas, attempts to put heart into his stricken men.

He says, "Arjuna's son has given up his life after killing countless enemies princes who were like snakes of virulent poison in battle. Razing ten thousand warriors, Abhimanyu who was like Krishna or Arjuna himself, has assuredly gained the realm of Indra. He destroyed chariots, horses, men and elephants, thousands of them, and was not content with what he did. He fought as no other Kshatriya ever has, and died in battle. We should not grieve so for him for he has attained the bright regions of the righteous, realms that men acquire only through great punya karma.'""

CANTO 47

ABHIMANYU-VADHA PARVA CONTINUED

"Sanjaya says, 'And thus, on that momentous day, after killing one of their greatest warriors, after suffering untold losses and injuries at his hands, we return to our camp in the evening, covered in blood. Under the unwavering gaze of our enemy, we slowly leave the battleground, in a stupor for such have been our losses.

The wonderful twilight hour arrives. We hear inauspicious howls of jackals and the Sun, now turned the pale-red of the filaments of a lotus, sinks low on the horizon, having reached the western mountains of Astama. Surya takes with him the brilliance of our swords, arrows, blades, chariot-railings, shields and ornaments. Colouring sky and earth with the same hue, the Sun assumes his favourite form of fire.

Kurukshetra, spread over with the motionless bodies of innumerable dead elephants, looks like the crests of cloud-capped hills riven by thunder, and lying all around are their standards, hooks, and riders fallen from their backs. The earth presents an amazing spectacle with great chariots smashed to pieces, and their warriors, charioteers, ornaments, horses, standards and banners all destroyed, many past recognition. The great rathas look like living creatures whose lives the enemy has taken with his shafts. The field of battle wears a fierce and awful aspect with the legion horses and riders all lying dead, with costly trappings and coverlets of varied kinds torn and scattered about as if by some terrible storm; and tongues, teeth, entrails and eyes of men and beasts falling out of their proper places. Men wearing fine coats of mail, ornaments, bright robes and weapons, lie with dead horses, elephants and broken chariots on bare ground this twilight, although they deserve to sleep on costly beds and sheets.

Dogs, jackals, crows, cranes and other scavenging birds, and wolves, hyenas, ravens, diverse tribes of Rakshasas and sinister hosts of Pisachas arrive on the field of horror; they tear away the skins of the corpses and suck up their fat, blood and marrow, and then begin to feast greedily on their flesh and the vilest among them on all the secretions of rotted corpses. The Rakshasas laugh horribly and sing aloud, dragging dead bodies away in thousands, preventing noble Kshatriyas from having their last rites performed with honour and sanctity. The kali yuga has arrived.

A horrible river flows across the field of death, like the Vaitarani itself. Its waters are blood; chariots are its rafts; elephants its large rocks and the heads of dead men its smaller stones. It is soggy with the loosened flesh of slain steeds, elephants and men. The diverse kinds of beautiful weapons are the garlands floating on it or lying on its banks. The terrible river flows fierce through the heart of the field, bearing its dreadful cargo to the regions of the dead.

Hosts of Pisachas, their forms horrible and repugnant, rejoice as they drink and eat from that scarlet rill; wild dogs, jackals and scavenging birds, vultures, crows and the rest, partake of the same grisly feast, their ghoulish carnival. The warriors, whom death has spared on this day, gaze numbly at the field and its ghastly river, and before their eyes corpses seem to rise up and dance! Then, all those who have survived the apocalyptic day, slowly leave the field, for their eyes fill when they see Abhimanyu, who was like Sakra himself, lying there, his ornaments broken and fallen around him. Dead Abhimanyu looks like a sacrificial fire on an altar no longer fed with ghee.'"

CANTO 48

Abhimanyu-vadha Parva continued

"Sanjaya says, 'After the slaying of Abhimanyu, all the Pandava warriors leave their rathas, take off their armour, throw aside their bows, and sit surrounding Yudhishtira, all of them plunged in untold grief, their hearts fixed on one thought—dead Abhimanyu.

Upon the fall of his meteoric nephew, Yudhishtira is unmanned by sorrow and laments aloud. "Alas, Abhimanyu pierced the chakravyuha that Drona formed against me. He put so many mighty bowmen to flight, all of them masters of weapons and well-nigh invincible. He stormed our implacable enemy Dusasana and, striking him senseless, forced him to flee the field. Alas, that gallant son of Arjuna, having crossed the vast sea of Drona's army, is now a guest in Yama's halls, killed by the same Dusasana's son. Ah, how will I face Arjuna, and the blessed Subhadra who has lost her favourite son? How will I break this tragic news to Krishna and Dhananjaya? What hollow words will I speak to them? With what voice?

Wanting victory at any cost, it is I who has done this great evil to

Subhadra, Kesava and Arjuna. He who is greedy never sees his own faults. Covetousness springs from folly. Honey-gatherers do not see the fall before them; and I am like them. Alas, we set our prince who was still a child in the van of our army, while he should instead have been cossetted with fine food, carriages and chariots, rich beds and ornaments. How could our child of tender years, unskilled in battle, ride with any hope into such grave danger? Like a noble steed of proud spirit, he sacrificed himself instead of refusing to do what I asked.

Alas, today we too will lay ourselves down on the bare earth, blasted by the glances of grief that the angry Arjuna will cast on us. The very Devas applaud the feats of Arjuna, for he is mighty, handsome, liberal, intelligent, modest, forgiving, a shura who is respectful to his elders and superiors, who is heroic, beloved and devoted to truth—Arjuna of glorious achievements. This Kshatriya slew the Nivatakavachas and the Kalakeyas, Indra's enemies in Hiranyapura. In the twinkling of an eye he slew the Paulomas with all their followers. Yet he grants mercy to even his most inveterate enemies, if they but ask!

And it is his son that we could not protect from danger today. The Dhartarashtras, endued though they might be with great power and strength, will rue this day! For when he hears of Abhimanyu's death, Arjuna exterminate the Kauravas in wrath; and then, foolish Duryodhana, who has vile counsellors, who is the destroyer of his own race and friends, will give up his life in anguish. Seeing this son of Indra's son, with no remote rival in splendour and prowess, lying lifeless on the field, neither victory, sovereignty, immortality, nor living with the very Devas, can anymore fetch me the least delight!"'"

CANTO 49

ABHIMANYU-VADHA PARVA CONTINUED

"Sanjaya says, 'While Kunti's son Yudhishtira thus laments, the Maharishi Krishna-Dwaipayana Vyasa comes to him. Worshipping him duly, and offering him a seat, the grief-stricken Yudhishtira says, "Mahamuni, while he fought alone, magnificently, several great maharathas surrounded Abhimanyu and killed him treacherously. He was but a child and he fought gloriously against a whole army. I asked him to open a passage for us and he broke into Drona's chakravyuha. We wanted to follow him but Jayadratha, with Siva's boon, barred our way. A dharma yuddha is fought fairly and against an equal adversary. But here Abhimanyu was besieged by an entire army. Ah, my heart is broken when I think that I sent that child to his death, and tears leak from my eyes, and I have no peace of mind."

The illustrious Vyasa says to the distraught, shattered Yudhishtira, "Wise Yudhishtira, men like you, who are masters of yourselves and of all knowledge, never allow any calamity to overwhelm them. Having killed countless enemies, Abhimanyu has risen into swarga. Indeed, though young in years, he fought like a grown and seasoned warrior. Yudhishtira, let alone men, Death takes all Devas, Danavas and Gandharvas, without exception, and his law is inviolable."

Yudhishtira says, "Alas, these lords of earth that lie on the bare earth, slain in the midst of their forces, were all men of great prowess and valour. Some had the strength of ten thousand elephants while others were gifted with the impetuosity and force of the wind. They have all perished in battle, slain by men of their own varna.

They possessed great skills, energy and strength. Alas, the wise Kshatriyas who took daily to the field, always in the hope that they would conquer, now lie dead on Kurukshetra. The meaning of the word Death has today been amply revealed, for almost all these great lords of the earth are dead. These Kshatriyas lie motionless, bereft of vanity, having succumbed to their enemies. Many princes, themselves full of wrath, have been consumed by the fire of their enemies' fury.

A great doubt possesses me—from where comes Death? Whose son is Death? What is Death? Why does Death take away all beings? Pitamaha, O you who are like a god, tell me this."

Vyasa says, "Rajan, let me tell you this ancient story about the origin of Death that Narada once told Akampana, whilst that king suffered great and unbearable grief because his son had died. By listening to this most excellent tale, you will be freed from sorrow and the touch of affection's attachment. Listen well to this Itihasa, for it lengthens one's life, kills grief and bestows health. It is sacred, destroys hosts of enemies and is the most auspicious of all auspicious things. Indeed, this Itihasa is even like the study of the Vedas, Rajan, and every morning the best of kings, who wish for long-lived children and their own weal, should listen to it.

In olden days, there was a great and fearless king named Akampana. Once, on the battlefield, enemies surrounded and overpowered him. He had a son called Hari, equal to Narayana himself in strength. Hari was exceptionally handsome, a master of astras, gifted with great intelligence, and was like Sakra himself in battle. Surrounded by countless enemies, he shot thousands of astras at the warriors and elephants that hemmed him in. When he had achieved the most difficult feats in that battle,

Yudhishtira, they finally killed him.

Performing the obsequies for his son, king Akampana purified himself. However, he continued to grieve for his Hari day and night and could regain neither happiness nor peace of mind. Learning of his grief, the Devarishi Narada came to him.

Seeing Narada, the related everything that had happened—his defeat at the hands of his enemies and the killing of his son. Akampana said, "My son was endued with great energy, and equalled Indra or Vishnu himself in splendour. Alas they slew him, who had displayed his prowess on the field against countless enemies! O illustrious one, who is this Death? What is the measure of his energy, strength and prowess? O greatest of intelligent men, I truly wish to hear all this.'

The boon-giving lord Narada said, 'Listen, Rajan, to this long Itihasa which will destroy your grief! In the beginning, the Pitamaha Brahma created all creatures. Invested with mighty energy, he saw that his creation showed no signs of decay. So Brahma began to reflect upon the destruction of the universe but failed to find any method to achieve it. He then became angry and from his anger a fire sprang from the sky. The fire spread in all directions consuming everything in the universe, and flames filled all swarga, akasa and bhumi.

Thus Brahma began to consume the whole universe and to destroy his creatures, mobile and unmoving, terrifying all with his wrath. Then Hara, who is also called Sthanu or Siva, with matted locks on his head, the Lord of all Rakshasas and Asuras, the night-rangers, appealed to the divine Brahma, the Lord of the Devas. When Sthanu fell at Brahma's feet for the good of all creatures, the Supreme Deva said to the Mahayogin blazing with splendour, "What wish of yours can I grant, O you who deserve to have all your wishes fulfilled? O you who have been born of our wish, we will do anything that will please you! Tell me, Sthanu, what is your desire?"'"

CANTO 50

Abhimanyu-vadha Parva continued

"Siva replied, 'O Lord, you took great pains to create and nourish creatures of diverse kinds. However, you now destroy them with your fire. I am filled with pity. O illustrious one, be merciful.'

Brahma said, 'I have no wish to destroy the universe. I only want the good of the Earth, and this is why anger has possessed me. Bhumidevi suffers because of the heavy burden of creatures, and constantly urges me to destroy them. But I could not find the means to put an end to this infinite creation. At this, anger maddened me.'

Rudra said, 'Be merciful, O Lord of the universe; do not annihilate all living beings with your wrath. Let no more creatures, immobile and unmoving, perish. Through your grace, let the three-fold universe, the Future, the Past, and the Present, continue to exist. A fire has sprung from your wrath and even now it consumes rocks, trees, rivers and all kinds of plants and trees. Indeed, the fire devours all the universe and reduces it to ashes.

Be merciful, O Illustrious! Do not give way to anger. This is the boon

I seek. Your rage destroys everything that belongs even to you; appease your wrath and quench it in your own self. Look on your creatures with compassion and do good for them. Ensure that creatures with life and the power of generation do not cease to exist.

O Creator of the worlds, you have appointed me their Protector. Let not the mobile and the unmoving universe be destroyed. You are naturally inclined to grace, and it is for this that I plead with you.'

Narada continues, "Hearing what Mahadeva said, Brahma withdrew the fire of his wrath into himself and contained it there—for the weal of the world and all its creatures. Extinguishing the fire, the divine Benefactor of the world, the great Master, declared the dharma of procreation and emancipation. And while the Supreme Deity exterminated the fire born of his wrath, there emerged through the portals of his diverse senses, a young woman, dark, red and tawny, her tongue, face and eyes crimson, and decked with two brilliant ear-rings and diverse other scintillating ornaments. Issuing out of his body, she smilingly looked at the two Lords of the universe and then set out for the southern quarter.

Then Brahma, regulator of creation and destruction, named her Mrityu, and said to her, 'Slay these creatures of mine! You have been born of my wrath which I nourished for the destruction of the universe. Kill all creatures, be they fools or and seers, at my command. By doing this, you will benefit yourself.'

The lotus-devi, called Death, reflected deeply and then wept aloud and piteously in a melodious voice. The Pitamaha caught the tears she shed in his two hands.'"

CANTO 51

ABHIMANYU-VADHA PARVA CONTINUED

"Narada said, 'The compassionate young Devi repressed her sorrow and, bending with humility like a vine, with her hands folded, asked the Lord of creation, "O Lord of words, how can I, being a woman, and created by you, do what you ask when I know that it is cruel and evil? I greatly fear adharma, I fear sin. O divine Lord, be merciful. Sons, friends, brothers, fathers and husbands are always dear; if I kill them, I fear that their kin will seek to do me harm.

The thought of the tears that will fall from the eyes of grief-stricken and weeping ones, fills me with dread! I seek your protection, O greatest of Devas, I will not go to Yama's abode. O boon-giving one, with bowed head and folded hands, I beg your clemency. Pitamaha of the worlds, I beg just this one wish from you—with your leave, I want to perform tapasya. Grant me this boon, O Divine One, O Master, if you allow me, I will go to the great asrama of Dhenuka! I will undergo the severest tapasya there and worship only you. I will not be able, O Devadeva, to take the precious prana of living creatures weeping in sorrow. Protect me from sin!'

Brahma said, 'Mrityu, you have been born for achieving the destruction of creatures. Go, kill all living creatures, you need not have any scruples. It must be so. It cannot be otherwise. Do as I say and no one in the world will find fault with you.'

But she was still afraid. Looking into Brahma's face, she stood silently with joined hands. Wanting to do good to all beings, she could not bring herself to set her heart upon their destruction. Brahma also remained silent. And then, soon, the Pitamaha became pleased with himself and smiled looking upon all his creation. Thereupon, living beings were enlivened and continued to breathe as before, untouched by untimely death. When the invincible and illustrious Lord shook off his wrath, the dark and kindly girl left the presence of the wisest Deity.

Leaving Brahma, without having to destroy all creatures, Mrityu quickly went to the asrama called Dhenuka where she performed fierce tapasya and observed the sternest, most austere vratas. She stood there on one leg for sixteen billions of years, and another fifty billions, through pity for living creatures and from her wish to do them good, all the time restraining her senses from their favourite objects.

And once again, Rajan, she stood there on one leg for twenty-one times ten billions of years. And then she wandered for ten times ten thousand billions of years with the creatures of the Earth. Next, going to the sacred Nanda full of cool and pure water, she spent eight thousand years in those waters and performed a great tapasya there as well; at Nanda, she cleansed herself of all her sins.

Then, keeping her vow, she went first of all to the sacred Kausiki. Living only upon air and water, she practised tapasya there. She then went to Panchaganga and after that to Vetasa, where, by different kinds of especial austerities, that pure kanya emaciated her own body. Then she visited Ganga and from there went to great Meru, where she remained motionless like a stone, suspending her breath. Then at the summit of Himavat, where the Devas had performed their yagna in the most ancient days, the auspicious and compassionate girl remained for a billion of years standing on just her toe. Going then to Pushkara, Gokarna, Naimisa and Malaya, she emaciated her body further, practising austerities which satisfied her heart.

Without acknowledging any other God, with steady devotion only to the Pitamaha, she lived and delighted Brahma in every way.

At last, gratified with her, his heart softened and full of delight, the unchangeable Creator of the worlds said to that maiden. 'O Mrityu, why do you perform so severe a tapasya?'

Mrityu replied, 'Living beings exist in health and do not injure one another even through words. I will not be able to kill them. O Lord, I want just this boon from you. I fear sin, and this is why I am engaged in tapasya. Most blessed one, undertake to remove my fears for ever. I am a woman, in distress, and innocent. I beg you, be my protector.'

To her, the divine Brahma, knower of the past, the present and the future, said, 'You will commit no sin, O Mrityu, by killing these creatures. My words can never prove false, O amiable one! Therefore, auspicious girl, kill these creatures of the four kinds. Eternal dharma will always be yours. Yama, the Regent of the world, and the various diseases will become your helpmates. I myself and all the Devas will grant you boons, so that, freed from sin and perfectly cleansed, you will even acquire glory.'

Thus addressed, Rajan, Mrityu, joining her hands and bowing down to him, once more said, 'If, O Lord, this cannot be achieved without me, then I bow my head to your command. But I beg you, listen once more to what I say. Let covetousness, wrath, malice, jealousy, quarrel, folly and shamelessness and other violent passions rend the bodies of all embodied creatures.'

Brahma said, 'O Mrityu, it will be as you say. Meanwhile, do away with living beings appropriately and sin will not be yours, nor will I seek to injure you. Your tear drops that are in my hands will now become diseases, springing from living creatures themselves. They will kill men; and if men are killed, do not fear, for sin will not be yours. Be devoted to dharma, observe your duty, and casting off both desire and anger, take the lives of these mortal beings. This will be your eternal virtue. Sin will destroy men of evil ways. By doing my bidding you will cleanse yourself. It will be your dharma to sink them in their sins. Therefore, cast off both kama and krodha, and kill these beings endued with life.'

Seeing that Brahma persistently called her Death, she feared to do otherwise. In terror of his curse, she said, 'Yes!' Helpless not to obey, casting off desire and wrath, she began to take the lives of living creatures when the time came for their death.

It is only the living that die. Disease spring from living creatures themselves and is an abnormal condition as it causes them distress and pain. So do not indulge in fruitless grief for anyone after they are dead. The senses, after death, go with them to the other world. Achieving their respective functions, they return once more with each individual jiva when the spirit is reborn.

Thus all creatures, including the very Devas, are subject to death; they too are mortal. The awful wind, omnipresent and with infinite energy, with its terrible howl and great strength irresistibly drives the bodies of living creatures. It will not demonstrate active energy, nor will it suspend its functions; but do this naturally. Even all the Devas have the appellation of mortals attached to them.

Therefore, lion among kings, do not grieve, for your son is passing his days in perpetual happiness in swarga for he has attained those delightful regions that are reserved for Kshatriyas. Casting off all sorrows, he has gained the companionship of great souls of dharma. The Creator himself has ordained Death for all beings and when their hour comes, they are destroyed. The death of all beings arises from the creatures themselves for they are responsible for their own deaths.

Death does not kill anyone, armed with her bludgeon! Therefore, those who are wise truly know death to be inevitable because Brahma himself has ordained it. So never grieve for those who are dead; and knowing that the Supreme God has ordained this death, cast off your grief for your dead son!'

Vyasa continues, "Hearing these profound words of advice from

Narada, king Akampana said to his friend, 'O illustrious Maharishi, after hearing this Itihasa from you, my grief is gone and I am contented. I am grateful to you and I worship you.'

Hearing this, the Devarishi Narada of immeasurable soul left for the Nandana vana.

The frequent recital of this story to others, and listening to it, is said to be purifying. It leads to fame and heaven, is worthy of approbation, and also enhances the life-span. Now that you have heard this tale, cast off your grief, Yudhishtira. Reflect on the duties of a Kshatriya, and the high state of punya that can be attained by heroes. Abhimanyu, the maharathin the mahatejasvin, has attained swarga after killing numberless enemies in full view of all the mighty archers. He has fallen on the battle field, struck with sword, mace, dart and bow. Sprung from Soma Deva, he has returned into the lunar essence, cleansed of all his impurities.

Therefore, O Pandava, you and your brothers should muster all your courage and without allowing yourselves to be stupefied by sorrow, take the field again, inflamed with fury for battle.'""

CANTO 52

Abhimanyu-vadha Parva continued

"Sanjaya says, 'Hearing of the origin of Mrityu and her strange deeds, Yudhishtira humbly addresses Vyasa once more. He says, "There were many kings of dharma in blessed countries, their prowess equal to that of Indra himself. They were rajarishis, O Muni, who were sinless and spoke only truth. Once more, tell me of their feats in ancient times so that I am consoled. What was the extent of the gifts they made at yagnas? Who were these mahatmans, these royal sages of dharma? Tell me all, O illustrious one!"

Vyasa replies, "There was a king named Switya. He had a son called Srinjaya. The Rishis Narada and Parvata were his friends. One day, the two munis came to visit Srinjaya in his palace. Duly worshipped by Srinjaya, they were pleased with him, and continued to stay happily with him. Once, as Srinjaya was seated at his ease with the two rishis, his beautiful daughter came to him, smiling sweetly, and greeted him with reverence. Srinjaya blessed the delightful girl.

Seeing her, Parvata smilingly asked Srinjaya, 'Whose daughter is this girl of restless glances, who has every auspicious mark? Is she the splendour of Surya, or the flame of Agni? Or is she Sri, Hri, Kirti, Dhriti, Pushti or Siddhi, and the lambency of Soma?'

King Srinjaya answered, 'O illustrious one, this girl is my daughter. She seeks my blessings.'

Then Narada asked king Srinjaya, 'If, Rajan, you wish for great fortune for yourself, give your daughter to me as a wife.'

Delighted with the Rishi's proposal, Srinjaya said to Narada, 'I give her to you.'

At this, the other Rishi, Parvata, indignantly said to Narada 'I had in my heart chosen this girl first, but you have taken her as your wife. O Brahmana, you will not go to swarga.'

Narada replied, 'For a man to be a husband he must first give his heart and seek consent. This is followed by the solemn commitments by both parties, and the actual gift is made by the sprinkling of holy water and the recital of the mantras ordained for the taking of the bride's hand. These have been declared as the indications by which one becomes a husband. Even this ceremonial is not all. Above all is the pradakshina of seven paces by the bride circumambulating the groom. Without these your marriage is not complete. You have cursed me, and you will also not go to heaven without me.'

Having cursed each other the two Rishis continued to live there in the palace.

Meanwhile, king Srinjaya, who wanted a son, purified himself and scrupulously entertained the Brahmanas to the very best of his power, with food and clothing, and saw to their every other need and comfort. After some time, those greatest of Brahmanas became pleased with the king and wished a son for him. Together they went to Narada and said to him, 'Give this king a son of the kind he wants.'

Narada replied to them, saying, 'Tathaastu, so be it.'

Then the Devarishi said to Srinjaya, 'O Rajarishi, the Brahmanas are pleased and they wish you a son! Ask them for the boon; tell them what manner of son you want.'

With joined hands, the king asked for a son with every accomplishment, famous, of glorious feats, of great tejas and a parantapa who would vanquish all his enemies. And he further asked that the urine, the excrement, the phlegm and the sweat of that child should be gold! And in due time the king had a son born to him, who came to be named Suvarnashthivin and because of the boon, the child began to increase his father's wealth beyond all calculation.

King Srinjaya had all the objects of his desire to be wrought of gold. His houses, walls, forts, the houses of all Brahmanas within his dominions, and his beds, vehicles, plates, all manners of pots, cups, the palace that he owned, and all implements, utensils, and weapons were made of gold. And in time his fame increased.

Then some thieves heard of the prince and banded together and sought to harm the king. Some among them said, 'Let us seize the king's son for he is his father's gold mine.'

They broke into the king's palace and forcibly abducted prince Suvarnashthivin and made off with him to the forest. There those fools, urged by greed, but not knowing what to with the prince, killed him and cut his body into pieces. They did not see any gold inside him. When the prince was dead, all the rest of the gold, got through the Rishi's boon, also vanished. The thieves began to fight among themselves and killed each other, and with them perished that most wonderful prince. Those evil men plunged down into the most unimaginable and awful hell.

Seeing his son killed, king Srinjaya, in deep sorrow, began to lament piteously. Seeing the king so grief-stricken on account of his son, the Devarishi Narada appeared before him.

Listen, Yudhishtira, to what Narada said to Srinjaya. 'Srinjaya, you will have to die with your desires unfulfilled, although we Brahmavadis live in your house. Even Avikshita's son Marutta had to die.

Annoyed with Brihaspati, Marutta had Samvatta perform his great yagnas! The illustrious lord Mahadeva himself had given wealth in the shape of a golden plateau of Himavat to that royal sage. With that wealth, king Marutta performed various yagnas so that afterwards different groups of gods, the creators of the universe, with Indra himself in their company and with Brihaspati at their head, used to visit him.

All the carpets and furnishings of his yagnasala were made of gold. At his yagnas, the Munis all ate food as they pleased, food that was clean and to their taste. The milk, curds, ghee, honey and other kinds of victuals, were the very best; the robes and ornaments were enviably costly; and the Brahmanas who were masters of the Vedas were gratified.

The very Devas would serve the food in king Marutta's palace, while the Viswedevas were his courtiers. Those dwelling in swarga were happy with the libations of clarified butter and they, in their turn, increased the powerful ruler's wealth of crops with abundant rains. He always contributed to the satisfaction and joy of the Rishis, the Pitris and the Devas, by practising Brahmacharya, studying the Vedas, performing obsequial rites and giving all kinds of gifts.

Such was his immense store of wealth and gold that it was difficult to give away. And he did, in fact, give all his untold wealth away in dakshina to the Brahmanas. Sakra himself used to wish him well. He made his subjects happy by always living in dharma, and he ultimately went to those eternal realms of bliss, which he acquired through his inexhaustible punya.

With his children, counsellors, wives, descendants and kinsmen, king Marutta, in his youth, ruled his kingdom for a thousand years. When such a king died, Srinjaya, who was your superior in the four cardinal virtues—tapasya, truth, compassion and liberality—and who, being superior to you, was far greater than your son? Do not grieve saying, "O Swaitya!", for your son who performed no yagnas nor gave any dakshina at a sacrifice.'

CANTO 53

Abhimanyu-vadha Parva continued

"Narada said, 'O Srinjaya, it is said that King Suhotra also fell prey to death. He was the greatest of Kshatriyas and invincible in battle. The very Devas would come to visit him. Acquiring his kingdom through dharma, he always sought the advice of his Ritwijas, and other domestic priests and Brahmanas and followed their behests. Virtuous and liberal, familiar with the duty of protecting his subjects, king Suhotra performed yagnas, subjugated his enemies and wished to increase his wealth. He worshipped the Devas by the ordinances of the Shastras, and defeated his enemies with his astras. He brought joy to all that lived within his domains through his pure and majestic deeds.

He ruled the earth, freeing her from Mlecchas and forest-brigands. The Deva of the clouds showered gold upon him all the year around. In those times out of mind, the rivers in his kingdom flowed liquid gold and it was available to everyone. The Devas blessed his kingdom with a large number of crocodiles, crabs and fish of different species and countless objects of desire, all made of gold.

The artificial lakes in the king's dominions each measured full two yojanas. Looking at the thousands of dwarfs, humpbacks, alligators, makaras and tortoises, all made of gold, king Suhotra wondered greatly. He performed a yagna at Kurujangala and gave away the unlimited wealth of gold to Brahmanas before the completion of the sacrifice. After he had performed a thousand Aswamedha yagnas, a hundred Rajasuya yagnas, many sacred Kshatriya yagnas, at all of which he gave lavish gifts to Brahmanas, and after countless daily rituals performed for specific wants, the king ultimately obtained a most desirable end.

When, O Srinjaya, the life of such a king who was superior to you in the four cardinal virtues, had to come to an end, and who, being superior to you, was thus far greater than your son, you should not grieve saying, "Oh Swaitya, Oh, Swaitya!" for your son performed no sacrifice and made no sacrificial dakshina.'

CANTO 54

ABHIMANYU-VADHA PARVA CONTINUED

"Narada said, 'The heroic king Paurava too, O Srinjaya, fell prey to death. This king gave away a thousand times a thousand horses that were all perfectly white. Countless learned Brahmanas, all versed in the principles of Siksha, one of the six Vedangas, and Akshara, the letters of the original alphabet, came from different kingdoms to the Aswamedha yagna that royal sage performed. The king gave priceless gifts to these Brahmanas, purified by the Vedas, by gyana, and by vratas, men of liberal and gracious countenances—fine robes, houses, excellent beds, carpets, carriages and draft-cattle, and actors, dancers and singers who were marvellous exponents of their respective arts, and always entertained them.

At each of his yagnas, in due time, he gave away as sacrificial gifts ten thousand elephants of golden magnificence, with ichor trickling down their bodies, and chariots made of gold with wonderful standards and banners. He also gave away a thousand times a thousand maidens decked with ornaments of gold, chariots, horses and elephants for riding, and mansions, fields, hundreds of thousand of kine and thousands of cowherds—all decked out in gold. They who are acquainted with ancient history, sing this song about the yagna at which king Paurava gave away cows with calves with golden horns and silver hooves, brass milking pots, female slaves, male slaves, asses, camels and sheep, all countless in number, diverse kinds of gems and varied hill-like mounds of food.

Countless yagnas the king of the Angas successively performed, in the order of their merit, and according to his varna dharma, so many auspicious yagnas which yielded every possible object of desire. O Srinjaya, when such a king died, who was better that you in respect of the four cardinal virtues, and who being superior to you, was far greater than your son, you should not lament, "Oh, Swaitya, Oh, Swaitya!" and grieve for your son who performed no yagnas and gave away no dana.'

CANTO 55

Abhimanyu-vadha Parva continued

"Narada said, 'Usinara's son Sibi, too, O Srinjaya, fell prey to death. That king had, as it were, cast a leathern girdle around the Earth, making Bhumi with her mountains, islands, seas and forests resound with the clatter of his chariot. The Parantapa, king Sibi always slew his greatest enemies. He performed many yagnas and gave away gifts in profusion to the Brahmanas. That king of great prowess and intelligence had acquired enormous wealth. In battle, he won the praise of all Kshatriyas. He subjugated the whole world and performed many Aswamedha yagnas, without any impediment, giving away as sacrificial dakshina a thousand crores of golden nishkas and so many elephants, horses, deer, sheep and other animals, and hills of grain, earning him untold punya.

King Sibi also gave away the sacred Earth of diverse kinds of soil to the Brahmanas as dakshina. Indeed, Usinara's son Sibi gave away as many kine as the number of rain-drops that fall on the earth, the number of stars in the firmament, the number of sand-grains on the bed of Ganga, or the number of rocks that constitute the mountain called Meru, the number of gems or fish in the ocean.

The Creator himself had not met with and will not meet in the present or the future, another king who could bear the burdens that king Sibi carried. Many were the sacrifices with every kind of ritual that Sibi performed. In his yagnas, the sacrificial stakes, the carpets, the mansions, the walls and the arches, were all made of gold. Delicious and pure food and drink were served in profusion to the Brahmanas who went there in numbers past all count. With delicacies of every description laid out, one heard nothing but pleasing words like *Give away* and *Take*, being spoken there. Milk and curds were collected in lakes. In his yagnasala, there were rivers of drink and white hills of food. *Bathe, drink and eat as you like!* These were the only words heard there.

Gratified with his righteous karma, Rudra granted Sibi a boon, saying, "As you give away, let your wealth, devotion, fame, dharma, the love that all creatures bear you, and the heaven you attain, all be inexhaustible."

Having obtained these boons, even Sibi, when the time came, left this world for swarga. When, O Srinjaya, he who was superior to and far superior to your son had to die, you should not lament, crying, "Oh, Swaitya, Oh, Swaitya!", and grieve for your son who performed no sacrifice and gave no sacrificial gift.'

CANTO 56

ABHIMANYU-VADHA PARVA CONTINUED

"Narada said, 'Srinjaya, Rama, the son of Dasaratha, fell prey to death. His subjects were as much delighted in him, as a father is with the children of his loins. He possessed great tejas and was a home to countless virtues. Of unfading glory, at his father's command, Rama, the elder brother of Lakshmana lived for fourteen years in exile in the forest, with his wife. In Janasthana, that Bharatarishabha slew fourteen thousand Rakshasas for the protection of the munis of the vana.

The Rakshasa called Ravana who, beguiling both him and Lakshmana, abducted his wife Sita, the princess of Videha. Like the three-eyed Mahadeva killing the Asura Andhaka in the olden days, Rama in wrath slew Ravana, the offender of Pulastya's race, with all his kinsmen and followers, Ravana whom even the Devas and the Asuras together could not quell, the evil Ravana who was as a thorn to the Devas and the Brahmanas.

Because of his loving nurture of his subjects, the very Devas worshipped Rama. Filling all the Earth with his achievements, even the Devarishis lauded him. Compassionate to all beings, that king, after conquering different realms and protecting his subjects virtuously, performed a great yagna without hindrance. The lord Rama also performed a hundred Aswamedha yagnas and the mahayagna called Jaruthya. With libations of ghrita he pleased Indra. Through all these, Rama conquered hunger and thirst and all the diseases to which living creatures are subject. He possessed every accomplishment and blazed with his own tejas. Indeed, Rama, the son of Dasaratha, by far outshone all other living creatures.

When Rama ruled his kingdom, the Rishis, the Devas, and Manushyas, all lived together on the Earth, and their lives were never as full and wonderful as during Ramarajya. All life's sacred and mighty breaths, Prana, Apana, Samana, and the others, performed their functions blemishlessly. All luminous bodies shone brighter, and no calamity ever came near. All his subjects had long lives, and none died in their youth.

The dwellers of heaven were highly pleased for they received, according to the vidhis of the four Vedas, libations of clarified butter and other offerings of food made by men. Rama's realm was free from flies, gnats and other pernicious insects; and there were no beasts of prey or poisonous reptiles. There was no adharma; no one was covetous, and none ignorant. The subjects of all the four varnas engaged in acts of dharma and other worthy deeds.

When the Rakshasas in Janasthana obstructed the flow of offerings to the Pitris and the worship of the Devas, Lord Rama killed them. Men were each blessed with a thousand children, and their life-span was a thousand years. Elders had never to perform sraddhas of those younger than them. Youthful in form, with a dark-blue complexion and reddish eyes, Rama had the tread of a mighty elephant in musth. He had a lion's shoulders, untold strength, his arms reached down to his knees, and were great and handsome, and all creatures loved him. Rama ruled his kingdom for eleven thousand years and his subjects always uttered his name.

While Rama ruled his kingdom, the world was full of divine beauty and joy. Having established his own dynasty on earth, consisting of eight royal houses of the Suryavamsa, finally Rama ascended into swarga taking with him, his four kinds of subjects, all the species, men, beasts, birds, insects and plants of every kind.

O Srinjaya, even he who was vastly superior to you in the four cardinal virtues and superior to your son, died. You should not lament, crying, 'Oh, Swaitya! Oh, Swaitya!' for your son performed no yagna and gave no sacrificial dakshina.'

CANTO 57

Abhimanyu-vadha Parva continued

"Narada said, 'O Srinjaya, we hear that even king Bhagiratha died. He caused the Bhagiratha ghats of the Ganga, so named after him, to be covered with flights of steps made of gold. Surpassing all kings and all princes, he gave the Brahmanas a thousand times a thousand girls decked in ornaments of gold, riding on chariots yoked to four horses, and with a hundred kine behind each chariot, with many goats and sheep behind each cow. King Bhagiratha gave away vast gifts at his yagnas for which an immense gathering of men assembled.

The Ganga was aggrieved by her burden, so she said "Protect Me," and sat down in his lap because of which she, like the Apsara Urvasi, came to be regarded as his daughter and was named Bhagirathi after him. Having become the king's daughter, she became like a son, and thus the means of salvation to his deceased ancestors.

Soft-spoken Gandharvas of celestial splendour, gratified, sang all this in the hearing of the Rishis, the Devas and the Manavas. Thus, O Srinjaya, did the Devi, the ocean-going Ganga choose for her father king Bhagiratha, descendant of Ikshvaku, and performer of yagnas who gave lavish gifts to Brahmanas. The very Devas with Indra at their head always attended his sacrifices. The Devas used to facilitate his yagnas in every way by removing all impediments to them, in order to take their shares of the havis.

Possessed of great punya, Bhagiratha gave the Brahmanas whatever they wanted, wherever they wanted, without requiring them to move. There was nothing which he would withhold from Brahmanas. Every one received from him everything they wished for. Finally, the king ascended to the world of Brahma, through the grace of the Brahmanas. For the very object on which the Rishis who subsisted on the rays of the Sun would wait upon the Sun and the Deity of the Sun, they used to wait upon the lord Bhagiratha, the ornament of the three worlds.

O Srinjaya, when he who was superior to you as regards the four cardinal virtues, and who, being superior to you, was far superior to your son, had to die, you should not grieve, crying, "Oh, Swaitya! Oh, Swaitya!" for your son performed no yagnas and gave no sacrificial gifts.'

CANTO 58

ABHIMANYU-VADHA PARVA CONTINUED

"Narada said, 'Dilipa, the son of Havila, O Srinjaya, we hear, also fell a victim to death. Brahmanas, vested with the knowledge of Truth, devoted to the performance of yagnas, blessed with children and many grandchildren, were present during his hundreds of yagnas. King Dilipa, after performing his yagnas, gave away this very Earth filled with her treasures to those Brahmanas. At Dilipa's yagnas, the roads were all paved with gold and the very Devas, with Indra at their head, would come to visit him, equating him to Dharma himself.

The upper and lower rings of his sacrificial stake were of gold. Eating the Raga-khandavas at his yagnas, many were seen to lie down on the very streets, sated. It was exceedingly wonderful to see that while crossing water, the wheels of his chariot never sank but skimmed upon the water's surface. This never happened to other kings, Even those who witnessed king Dilipa, the indomitable, always truthful in speech, give away lavish gifts at his yagnas, ascended into swarga.

In Khattanga, the home of Dilipa, one always heard these five sounds—the sound of Vedic chanting, the twang of bows, and cries of *Drink! Enjoy!* and *Eat!*

O Srinjaya, when even he, who was superior to you in the four cardinal virtues, and therefore far superior to your son, had to die, you should not cry, "Oh, Swaitya! Oh, Swaitya!" and grieve for your son who performed no yagnas and gave no sacrificial gifts.'

CANTO 59

Abhimanyu-vadha Parva continued

"Narada continued, 'Mandhatri, the son of Yuvanaswa, O Srinjaya, fell prey to death. That king vanquished the Devas, the Asuras and Manavas. The Aswin twins brought him out of his father's belly with magical surgery.

Once upon a time, king Yuvanaswa while hunting deer in the forest became thirsty and his horses were exhausted. Attracted by a wreath of smoke, which turned out to be from a yagna fire, Yuvanaswa went and drank the sacred ghrita that he found lying there. The king, thereupon, conceived. Seeing that Yuvanaswa was advanced with child, the physicians of the Devas, the twin Aswini Kumaras, extracted the child from the king's belly.

Seeing the child of celestial splendour lying on the lap of his father, the Devas said to each other, "What sustenance will support this child?"

At this Vasava said, 'Let the child suck my fingers.'

At which, from the fingers of Indra there issued milk sweet as nectar. And since Indra, from compassion, said, "He will draw his sustenance from me", and showed him that kindness, the Deva named the child

Mandhatri. Springs of milk and divine ghee fell into the mouth of Yuvanasva's son from the hand of Indra. The boy grew up sucking nourishment from Indra's fingers. In twelve days he grew to twelve cubits in height and acquired prodigious abilities and prowess.

He conquered the whole of this Earth in a single day. Virtuous, intelligent, heroic, devoted to truth and a master of his passions, Mandhatri with his bow vanquished Sudhanwan, Jaya, Suna, Vrihadratha and Nriga. The lands lying between the mountain Udaya where the Sun rises and the Astama where it sets, are known to this day as the dominion of Mandhatri.

Rajan, after performing a hundred Aswamedha yagnas as well as a hundred Rajasuya yagnas, he gave away to Brahmanas, Rohita fish made of gold that were ten yojanas long and one yojana wide. Others, who came to his yagnas and contributed to their success, ate the mountains of savoury food of diverse kinds, but after he had entertained the Brahmanas. The vast quantities of food, drink, and mountains of rice, looked incredible and delightful where they were piled. Rivers and lakes of ghee, with different kinds of soup for their base, curds for their froth and liquid honey for their water, were beautiful to behold and, wafting honey and milk, encircled mountains of solid viands.

Devas, Asuras, Manushas, Yakshas, Gandharvas, Nagas, Pakshis, and many Brahmanas, accomplished in the Vedas and their angas, and innumerable great Rishis came to Mandhatri's yagnas. No one among those present was illiterate or less than learned.

King Mandhatri, having bestowed the Earth confined by the seas and full of wealth upon the Brahmanas, vanished like the Sun at night. Filling all the points of the compass with his fame, he left for the regions of great souls of dharma. When he, O Srinjaya, who excelled you in the four cardinal virtues and who was thus far superior to your son, had to die, you should not grieve, crying, "Oh, Swaitya! Oh, Swaitya!" for him who performed no yagna and made no sacrificial gifts.'

CANTO 60

Abhimanyu-vadha Parva continued

"Narada said, 'O Srinjaya, Yayati, the son of Nahusha, was also a victim of Mrityu. He performed a hundred Rajasuyas, a hundred Aswamedha yagnas, a thousand Pundarikas, a hundred Vajapeyas, a thousand Atiratras, innumerable Chaturmasyas, various Agnishtomas and many other kinds of yagnas, at all of which he gave away lavish dakshina and dana to great Brahmanas. Having counted it first, he gifted to Brahmanas all the wealth that existed on the Earth and was in the possession of Mlecchas and other Brahmana-haters.

When the Devas and the Asuras were arrayed for battle, king Yayati went to the Devas' help. He divided the Earth into four parts and gave it away to four great ones. Having performed various yagnas and virtuously fathered admirable offspring upon his wives Devayani, the daughter of Usanas, and Sarmishta, king Yayati, like a Deva, like a second Vasava, roamed through the Nandana vana at his own pleasure.

When Yayati, profound master of all the Vedas, found that indulging his passions did not satisfy him, he, with his wives, retired into the forest, saying, "Even all the paddy, wheat, gold, animals and women there is on Earth is not sufficient to satisfy one man. Considering this, one should cultivate contentment."

Thus abandoning all his desires and attaining true peace and satisfaction, the lord Yayati, installed his son on his throne and retired into the forest.

When he, O Srinjaya, who was superior to you in respect of the four cardinal virtues, and therefore far superior to your son, had to die, you should not cry, "Oh, Swaitya! Oh, Swaitya!", and grieve for your son who performed no yagna and made no sacrificial gifts.'

CANTO 61

ABHIMANYU-VADHA PARVA CONTINUED

"Narada continued, 'Nabhaga's son Ambarisha, O Srinjaya, we know, fell prey to death. Alone he battled a thousand kings, a thousand times. These enemies, all masters of weapons and desperately wanting victory, attacked him from all sides, with fierce war cries. With the measureless strength, vigour and skill he had acquired through long abhyasa, and his awesome astras, he destroyed his enemies' royal chatras, weapons, standards and chariots and dispelled his own apprehensions.

Throwing off their armour, these men begged him for mercy. They sought his protection, saying, "We yield ourselves to you!"

Reducing them to subjection and conquering the whole Earth, he performed a hundred yagnas of the best kind, according to the rites ordained in the shastras. At these yagnas, people of all varnas ate his pure and delicious fare and they worshipped the Brahmanas and thus greatly pleased them. The Munis ate delectable sweet-meats, purikas, puras, apupas, sashkalis and large karambhas, prithumridwikas, and diverse kinds of other dainties, and drank various kinds of soups, maireyaka, and ate ragakhandavas, and every sort of confectionary, well-prepared, soft and fragrant, as well having as nectarine ghee, honey, milk, water, sweet curds, and many kinds of exotic and succulent fruits and roots.

Those accustomed to wine, drank so many different kinds of intoxicating drinks for their pleasure, and sang and played their musical instruments. Eager revellers by the thousands, intoxicated with drink, danced and merrily sang hymns in praise of Ambarisha; while others, unable to stand, fell down. At these yagnas, king Ambarisha gave, as sacrificial gifts, the kingdoms of hundreds and thousands of kings to the ten million priests he engaged. After he had performed various yagnas the king gave to the Brahmanas, as dakshina, a number of princes and kings whose coronal locks had been washed in the sacred bath, all wearing golden armour, all having white chatras spread over their heads, all seated on golden chariots, all attired in rich robes and having large trains of followers, and all bearing their sceptres and bringing their treasuries.

Seeing this, the Maharishis were highly gratified, and said, "No one in the past has done, and none in future will be able to do, what king Ambarisha of unequalled munificence, does now."

When he, O Srinjaya, who was superior to you in the four cardinal virtues, and therefore far superior to your son, had to die, you should not cry, "Oh, Swaitya! Oh, Swaitya!" and grieve for him who performed no yagna and made no sacrificial gifts.'

CANTO 62

ABHIMANYU-VADHA PARVA CONTINUED

"Narada said, 'O Srinjaya, we hear that king Sasabindu, too, fell prey to death. He was a handsome man of great ability and intelligence and he performed a host of yagnas. The noble king had one hundred thousand wives from each of whom were born a thousand able sons. Proficient in the Vedas, these princes performed millions of yagnas, and many mahayagnas. They wore golden armour and were superlative archers. Every one of them performed Aswamedha yagnas.

Sasabindu at his own Aswamedha yagna gave away as dakshina all these sons of his to the Brahmanas! Behind each of these princes were hundreds upon hundreds of chariots, elephants and gorgeous maidens decked in ornaments of gold. With each maiden were a hundred elephants; with each elephant, a hundred chariots; with each chariot a hundred horses wearing garlands of gold. With each of these horses were a thousand kine; and with each cow were fifty goats. Such was the limitless wealth that the most blessed Sasabindu gave away to the Brahmanas.

The king caused as many sacrificial stakes of gold to be made for his great Aswamedha yagna as were ordained, and he doubled that number of the sacrificial stakes of wood in other yagnas. There were mountains of food and drink some two yojanas high. Upon the completion of his yagna, thirteen such mountains of food and drink remained untouched. His kingdom was free from evil and full of contented, well-fed and perfectly happy people.

Having ruled for many long years, Sasabindu finally ascended to swarga. When he, O Srinjaya, who was superior to you in respect of the four cardinal virtues and therefore, far superior to your son, had to die, you should not cry, "Oh, Swaitya! Oh Swaitya!", and grieve for him who performed no yagna and made no sacrificial gifts.'

CANTO 63

ABHIMANYU-VADHA PARVA CONTINUED

"Narada said, 'O Srinjaya, Gaya, the son of Amartarayas, we know, fell a victim to death. He, for a hundred years, ate nothing but the leftovers of the libations of ghee poured into the sacrificial fire. Gratified with his proof of great devotion Agni offered to grant him a boon.

Gaya said, "I wish to have a complete knowledge of the Vedas through tapasya, through the practice of brahmacharya, by observing vratas and niyamas, and through the grace of my superiors. I also want to acquire inexhaustible wealth through practice of the duties of my swadharma and without injury to others. I also wish to be able to make gifts to Brahmanas with veneration. Let me also beget sons upon wives belonging to my own varna and not upon others. Let me be able to give away food with devotion. Let my heart always delight in dharma. O Agni, supreme cleanser, let no impediment overtake me while I am engaged in sacred karma for the attainment of punya."

Saying "Tathaastu", Agni disappeared.

King Gaya got all he had asked for and also subdued his enemies in fair battle. Then, for a full hundred years, he performed a myriad yagnas with generous gifts to the Brahmanas, as well as the vratas called chaturmasyas and many others. Every year, for a century, the king gave the Brahmanas one hundred and sixty thousand kine, ten thousand horses and one crore of gold nishkas—upon rising after the completion of his yagnas. Further, he gave away as Nakshatra-dakshinas under every constellation, the gifts ordained for each of these occasions. Indeed, the king performed his many yagnas like another Soma or Angiras.

At his great Aswamedha yagna, king Gaya made a golden Earth and gave it away to the Brahmanas. His sacrificial stakes were past all calculation in value, being of gold, encrusted with such jewels and gems as fascinated and delighted all beings. Willing to fulfil every wish, Gaya gave those sacred stakes of sacrifice to delighted Brahmanas and other deserving men. He gratified all the different species of beings dwelling in the ocean, the forest, the islands, the rivers, male and female, the tanks, pools and lakes, the towns, the provinces and even in swarga, with the wealth and food distributed at his yagnas. And they all said, "No other yagna can measure up to this one of Gaya's."

The sacrificial altar of Gaya was thirty yojanas long, twenty-six yojanas wide, and twenty yojanas high. It was made entirely of gold and studded with pearls, diamonds and other precious stones. He also gave away this vedi, along with fine clothes and ornaments to the Brahmanas, as well as other gifts of the kind laid down in the shastras. Upon the completion of the yagna twenty-five hillocks of food remained untouched, and many lakes and several beautifully flowing rivulets of exquisite drink, besides many heaps of fine clothes and ornaments. Due to the merit of the great yagna, Gaya came to be renowned through the three worlds. It is because of Gaya's mahayagna that the eternal Pipal tree and the sacred Brahmasaras came into existence.

O Srinjaya, when he, who was superior to you in respect of the four cardinal virtues and, therefore, greatly superior to your son, had to die, you should not cry, "Oh, Swaitya! Oh, Swaitya!" and grieve for him who performed no yagna and made no sacrificial gifts.'

CANTO 64

ABHIMANYU-VADHA PARVA CONTINUED

"Narada said, 'Great Rantideva, too, we hear, met with death. The noble king had two hundred thousand cooks to prepare and distribute unmatched food, raw as well as cooked, dishes like amrita, to the Brahmanas who came to his palace as atithis, day and night. He gave away his wealth acquired through deeds of dharma to great Brahmanas. Having studied the Vedas, he quelled his enemies in dharma yuddha. Being of strict vows and always engaged in the performance of yagnas, countless animals, wanting to attain swarga, came to Rantideva of their own accord to become his yagnapasus, his sacrificial beasts.

So large was the number of animal yagnas in the Agnihotra that the secretions flowing from his kitchens from the heaps of skins deposited there, created a veritable river which so came to be called the Charmanwati.

He incessantly gave away thousands of nishkas of bright gold to Brahmanas, saying gently, lovingly, "I give you nishkas. I give you nishkas."

After gifting in a single day one crore of such coins, he thought that he had given away very little and would give more. Who else is there that would be able to give as much as him?

The king gave away wealth, thinking, "If I do not give wealth to the Brahmanas, I will experience great and eternal grief."

For a hundred years, every fortnight, he gave thousands of Brahmanas a golden bull each, followed by a hundred cows and eight hundred pieces of nishkas. All that was needed for his Agnihotra and other yagnas—karukas, water-pots, plates, bedsteads, carpets, carriages, mansions, houses, diverse kinds of trees and various kinds of viands—he gave away to the Rishis.

Whatever utensils and other possessions Rantideva had were of gold. Those who in ancient times saw the phenomenal affluence of Rantideva, sing this song, "We have not seen such treasures even in the abode of Kubera; what then to say of mortal men?"

People wonderingly said, "Undoubtedly, the kingdom of Rantideva is made of sacred Svarna, of gold!"

On such nights, when guests assembled in Rantideva's palace, he sacrificed twenty-thousand and one kine to feed them. Yet the royal cook, adorned with bejewelled earrings, had to cry out, "Drink as much soup as you like, for there is not as much of meat today as on other days."

Rantideva gave away even the gold that remained with him, and was his due, to the Brahmanas during one of his yagnas. In his very presence, the Devas would down come to take the libations of clarified butter poured into the fire for them, and the Pitris the food that was offered to them in Sraddhas. Rantideva was wont to fulfill all the wishes of all true and great Brahmanas.

When he, O Srinjaya, who was superior to you in the four cardinal virtues and, so, vastly superior to your son, had to die, you should not cry, "Oh, Swaitya! Oh, Swaitya!" and grieve for him who performed no yagna and gave no dakshina or sacrificial gifts.'

CANTO 65

ABHIMANYU-VADHA PARVA CONTINUED

"Narada said, 'O Srinjaya, Dushyanta's son Bharata, we know, fell a victim to death. While only a boy living in the vana, he achieved feats no other could. He was so strong that he would bring down snow-white lions, with great fangs and talons, and drag them around like little cats. He would tame tigers also, which were fiercer and more ferocious than the lions. Seizing other mighty beasts of prey, even great elephants, dyed with red arsenic and spotted with other liquid minerals, by their tusks, he would fetch them to their knees or force them to bolt from him. He would drag the mightiest of bison by their horns; he was a master of prides of hundreds of proud lions, and powerful srimaras, horned rhinoceros, and other beasts. He would bind them by their throats, beat them within an inch of their lives and then let them go.

For his feats the regenerate rishis with whom he lived, called him Sarvadamana—the controller of all. Finally, Sakuntala, his mother, forbade him to torment animals in this way.

Gifted with great ability, he performed a hundred Aswamedha yagnas on the banks of the Yamuna, three hundred on the banks of Saraswati, and four hundred on the banks of the Ganga. Having performed these sacrifices, he yet again performed a thousand Aswamedha yagnas and a hundred Rajasuyas, great yagnas in which his gifts to the Brahmanas were more than bounteous. Other yagnas, such as the Agnishtoma, the Atiratra, the Uktha and the Viswajit, he performed, together with thousands and thousands of Vajapeyas, without any impediment, and gratified the Brahmanas with vast gifts of wealth.

The renowned Bharata gave ten thousand billions of coins, made of the purest gold, to Kanwa, who had raised his mother Sakuntala as his own daughter.

The Devas with Indra at their head, accompanied by the Brahmanas, came to his yagna, to set up his sacrificial stake made entirely of gold and measuring a hundred vyamas in width. Bharata, the noblest soul, vanquisher of all his enemies, the king never defeated by anyone, gave away millions and millions of beautifully caparisoned horses, elephants, chariots, decked with gold and exceptional gemstones of all kinds as well as camels, goats, sheep, and slaves, both male and female, and wealth, grain, milch cows with calves, villages, fields, and different kinds of robes, to the Brahmanas.

O Srinjaya, when Bharata, who was superior to you in respect of the four cardinal virtues and who was far superior to your son, had to die, you should not cry, "Oh, Swaitya! Oh, Swaitya!" and grieve for your son who performed no yagna and gave no sacrificial gifts.'

CANTO 66

Abhimanyu-vadha Parva continued

"Narada said, 'O Srinjaya, Vena's son, king Prithu, we know, fell prey to death. In the Rajasuya yagna that he performed, the maharishis installed him as emperor of the world. He vanquished all and his achievements became known throughout the three worlds. For this, he came to be called Prithu, the celebrated. And because he protected all the people from injury, he became a true Kshatriya. Seeing Vena's son Prithu, all his subjects said, "We are pleased with him!"

Due to the love of his subjects, he came to be called a Rajan. During the time of Prithu, the Earth, without being cultivated, yielded crops in plenty, and cows yielded milk whenever they were touched. Every lotus was full of honey, the kusa blades were all of gold, pleasant to the touch, and otherwise delightful so that the subjects of Prithu made clothes and their beds from these grasses.

His subjects lived on fruits, which were all soft and sweet like Amrita, and none of them had ever to starve. All men were joyful, hale and robust, with all their wishes granted and with nothing to fear. They dwelt as they liked upon trees or in caves. His dominions were not divided into provinces and towns and the people lived happily and as they pleased.

When king Prithu stepped into the sea, the waves stood still. The very mountains used to yield him openings so that he might pass through them. The flagpole of his chariot never broke. Once, the tall trees of the forest, the mountains, the Devas, the Asuras, Manushas, the Nagas, the seven Rishis, the Apsaras, and the Pitris, all came to Prithu, who was seated at his ease and said to him, "You are our emperor. You are our king. You are our protector and father. You are our Lord. Therefore, O Rajan, give us the boons that we wish so that we may have gratification and joy forever."

Prithu, the son of Vena, replied, "Tathaastu".

Then taking up his bow, the Ajagava, and some dreadful astras the like of which did not exist other than with him, he reflected for a moment. He then addressed the Earth, saying, 'Come quickly, O Bhumi! Yield to them the milk they wish for. From that, blessed be you, I will give them the food they want.'

The Earth said, "You may, Shura, regard me as your daughter." And she became Prithvi.

Prithu answered, "Tathaastu"! And then the Rajarishi, his passions under perfect control, made arrangements for milking the Earth. Then the entire assembly of living beings began to milk the Earth. First of all, the tall trees of the forest rose to milk her. The Earth, full of love, stood there wanting a calf, someone to milk her, and vessels to hold the milk. The blossoming Sala tree became the calf, the Pipal became the milkman, buds became the milk and the auspicious Nyagrodha became the vessel.

Next, the mountains milked her. The Eastern mountain Udaya, where the Sun rises, became the calf; the prince of mountains, Meru, the one to milk her; the diverse gems and herbs became the milk; and the stones became the vessels to hold that milk.

Next, one of the Devas milked her, and all things that bestow tejas and urjas became the coveted milk.

The Asuras then milked the Earth, having wine for their milk and using an unbaked pot for their vessel. During this milking, Dvimurdha milked her and Virochana became the calf.

The Manavas milked the Earth for cultivation and crops. The self-created Manu became their calf and Prithu himself the milker.

Next, the Nagas milked the Earth, getting poison as milk and using a vessel made of a gourd. Dhritarashtra was the one to milk and Takshaka the calf.

The seven Rishis, who could create everything by their decree, milked the Earth, getting the Vedas as their milk. Brihaspati became the one to milk her; the Chhandas were the vessel and the excellent Soma, the calf.

The Yakshas, milking the Earth, got the power to disappear at will like the milk in an unbaked pot. Vaisravana Kubera was the one to milk her and Vrishadhvaja their calf.

The Gandharvas and the Apsaras milked all fragrant perfumes in a vessel made of a lotus-leaf. Chitraratha became their calf, and the powerful Viswaruchi the one to milk Bhumi.

The Pitris milked the Earth, getting Swaha as their milk in a vessel of silver. Yama, the son of Vivaswat, became their calf and the Destroyer Antaka the one to milk her.

Thus, the assembly of great creatures milked the Earth and all got as milk what each desired. The calves and vessels they employed exist to this day and will always exist. The powerful Prithu, the son of Vena, performed many and diverse yagnas, and gratified the desires of all creatures by gifts of whatever they wanted. He had golden images of everything found on Earth to be made and gifted them to the Brahmanas at his great Aswamedha yagna. The king caused six and sixty thousand elephants to be made of gold as well as this whole Earth to be adorned with jewels, gems and gold and gave her away as dakshina to the Brahmanas.

O Srinjaya when Prithu, who was superior to you in the four cardinal virtues and who, therefore, was far superior to your son, died, you should not, cry, "Oh, Swaitya! Oh, Swaitya!" and grieve for your son who performed no yagna and made no sacrificial gifts.'"

CANTO 67

ABHIMANYU-VADHA PARVA CONTINUED

"Narada said, 'Even Jamadagni's son Maharishi Rama, the shura worshipped by all other heroes, he of great fame, will die, without being content with length of his life. Rooting out all evils from the Earth, he ushered in the primeval Satya Yuga. He obtained unrivalled prosperity, and no one could see any fault in him.

The Kshatriyas killed his father and stole his calf, and without any boast, he slew the invincible Kartavirya, whom no enemy had ever bested. With his bow, he killed sixty-four times ten thousand Kshatriyas. In that awesome carnage were included fourteen thousand Brahmana-hating Kshatriyas of the Dantakura country. He massacred a thousand Haihayas with his short club, a thousand with his sword and a thousand by hanging them. Enraged at the murder of his father, the wise Rama killed great warriors and scattered their corpses on the battlefield, with their chariots, horses and elephants.

Rama slaughtered ten thousand Kshatriyas with his Parasu, his battle-axe, because he could not brook their arrogant ways and talk.

When many great Brahmanas called out the name of Rama of Bhrigu's race, the valiant son of Jamadagni continued against the Kashmiras, the Daradas, the Kuntis, the Kshudrakas, the Malavas, the Angas, the Vangas, the Kalingas, the Videhas, the Tamraliptakas, the Rakshovahas, the Vitahotras, the Trigartas, the Martikavatas, by the thousands, and slew them all with his astras.

Moving from kingdom to kingdom, province to province, he razed thousands of crores of Kshatriyas. Creating a deluge of blood and filling many lakes with gore as red as indragopakas or the wild fruit bandujiva and subjugating all the eighteen Dwipas of the Earth, he performed a hundred mahayagnas of great punya, all of which he completed and gave profuse dakshina to the Brahmanas.

The sacrificial altar, eighteen nalas high made entirely of gold, and wrought according to the injunctions of the shastra, full of different kinds of jewels, gems, and adorned with hundreds of standards, Kasyapa accepted as the sacrificial dakshina along with this Earth full of her animals, domestic and wild, that Rama, the son of Jamadagni, offered him. Rama also gave him many thousand prodigious elephants, all caparisoned in gold. Indeed, freeing the Earth from all thieves and brigands and filling her with honest and gracious men, Rama gave her away to Kasyapa at his great Aswamedha yagna.

Again, after he had divested the Earth of Kshatriyas twenty-one times and after performing hundreds of yagnas, that puissant Rama gave away this Bhumi to the Brahmanas. And it was Kasyapa who then accepted the Earth with her seven islands from him. Then Kasyapa said to Rama, "I command you to leave this world."

At Kasyapa's word, in obedience to the Brahmana, Rama used his arrows to make the very ocean stand aside, and going to the best of mountains called Mahendra, lived there. Even that enhancer of the fame of the Bhrigus, possessed of numberless virtues, the famed and splendid son of Jamadagni, incalculably superior to your son, will die. Do not, therefore, grieve for your prince who performed no yagna and made no sacrificial gifts. All these men, superior to you in the four cardinal virtues and also a hundred other merits, all these greatest of great men, have died, O Srinjaya, and they who are like them will also die.'"

CANTO 68

ABHIMANYU-VADHA PARVA CONTINUED

"Vyasa says, 'Hearing this sacred itihasa of sixteen kings, which can increase the listener's life, king Srinjaya remained silent. The illustrious Rishi Narada then said to the silently seated king, "O you of great majesty, have you heard these tales and understood their purport? Or, are they lost on you like a Sraddha performed by a Muni with a Sudra wife?"

Srinjaya then replied with joined hands, "O Tapodhana, after listening to these great and laudable itihasas of ancient rajarishis, all of whom performed great yagnas with lavish dakshinas to the Brahmanas, wonder has scattered all my grief, like the rays of the sun dispelling darkness. I have been cleansed of my sins, and feel no pain now. Tell me, what I should do next."

Narada said, "It is through good fortune that your grief has been dispelled. Ask any boon that you wish for and it will be granted. I never make false promises nor ever speak an untruth."

Srinjaya said, "O holy one, I am happy that you are gratified with me, for nothing is unattainable here for those with whom you are pleased."

Narada said, "I will bring back your son, whom the brigands senselessly killed like an animal slaughtered in a yagna. I will fetch him back from terrible hell."

Then Srinjaya's wonderful and magnificent son appeared, that prince resembling the son of Kubera himself, restored by the gratified Rishi to the bereaved father. King Srinjaya, united again with his son, was overjoyed. Srinjaya's son had not fulfilled the purusharthas of his life. He had performed no yagnas or given away any generous gifts upon their completion and had sired no children. He had done nothing brave and had perished miserably and not in battle. This was why he could be brought back to life.

As for Abhimanyu, he was valiant and heroic. He had fulfilled the purposes of life, for the brave son of Subhadra annihilated his enemies by the thousands before he left the world, dying on the field of battle. Your son has found even those inaccessible realms that only brahmacharya, gyana, a profound knowledge of the shastras, and the greatest of yagnas bestow.

Men of knowledge always desire swarga through their deeds of dharma. Those who live in swarga never prefer this world to it. Thus, it is not easy to bring back into this world Arjuna's son slain in battle and now dwelling in heaven; for he has no great purpose that he did not accomplish here. Your son has attained that eternal goal that yogins achieve with eyes shut in dhyana, or performers of great yagnas, or those possessed of great punya. After death, gaining a new body, he shines forth in glory like a king, with his own immortal lustre. Indeed, he has regained his own and true body of Soma rasa that all munis want.

He does not deserve your grief. Knowing this, be quiet, and slay your enemies. O sinless one, bear this with fortitude for it is the living that stand in need of our grief, and not those who have attained to paradise. Rajan, the sins increase of those for whom the living grieve. Therefore, the wise should abandon grief and strive for the good of the dead. The living man should think of the joy, the glory and the happiness of the dead.

Knowing this, the wise never indulge in grief, for grief is painful. Understand this to be the truth. Rise up! Strive to achieve your purpose. Do not grieve. You have heard of the origin of Death, and her unprecedented tapasya, and also of her impartiality towards all creatures. You have heard that prosperity is unstable and fleeting, and how the dead son of Srinjaya was revived. O wise and learned king, do not grieve. Peace be upon you. I go now, farewell!'

Having said this, the holy Vyasa, most eloquent of men, wisest of the wise, whose complexion is like that of the clouded sky, disappears before their eyes. Yudhishtira, with tejas equal to that of Indra himself, derives consolation from what he has heard about the merit and prosperity that accrued from the yagnas performed by those great kings of old, all of whom had acquired wealth by righteous means. The Dharmaraja lauds and worships those illustrious ones in his heart and is freed from grief.

However, with a melancholy heart he asks himself, "What will we tell Arjuna?""

CANTO 69

ABHIMANYU-VADHA PARVA CONTINUED

"Sanjaya says, 'When that terrible day, so full of slaughtering, comes to an end with the sunset, soothing twilight spreads itself over earth and sky. The troops of both the armies, Bharatarishabha, retire to their tents. And now the victorious vanara-bannered Arjuna makes his way back towards the Pandava camp on his triumphal chariot, after annihilating a great host of Samsaptakas with his devastras.

As he rides back, suddenly his heart clenches in a knot of grief and tears choke him. His voice low, he asks Krishna, "Why is my heart afraid, O Kesava, and why does my speech falter? I see evil omens and my limbs feel weak. Thoughts of terrible disaster fill my mind. I see everywhere, many kinds of omens and portents, which tell of some terrible tragedy. Is everything well with my brother the king, and all his companions?"

Krishna says, "It is evident that everything is well with your brother and his companions. Do not grieve; some trifling evil might have transpired."

The two shuras, Krishna and Arjuna, worship the twilight sandhya, and continue discussing the day's battle, which had claimed so many Kshatriya lives and during which they had achieved so many extraordinary feats. Finally, they arrive at the Pandava encampment.

Arjuna notices the joyless and melancholy air that hangs over the camp, a stricken pall, and again the pang of fear clutches at his heart. Trembling, he says to Krishna, "Janardana, no one blows the auspicious trumpets today, mingling its blasts with the beat of drums and the boom of conches. I hear no sweet vinanadam or the victorious slapping of palms. Our bards do not sing the auspicious songs of eulogy.

Ah, look how our warriors all turn away from me, with their heads hung down. They do not as usual tell me of the feats they have achieved. Madhava, is all well with my brothers today? Seeing our men all plunged in grief, I have no peace. Does all fare well with the lord of the Panchalas, with Virata, with all our warriors, O you of unfading glory? Alas, Subhadra's son, ever cheerful, does not come out today with his brothers, smiling radiantly to receive me as he always does."

Krishna and Arjuna enter their own quarter of the camp and find the Pandavas all plunged in deep sorrow. Seeing his brothers and sons sitting with their heads hung down, in complete silence, Arjuna is quickly distraught, full of awful fear.

Not seeing Abhimanyu there, Arjuna says, "I see that all your faces are pale, and I do not see Abhimanyu. He does not come running to embrace and welcome me as he always does. I heard that Drona formed the chakravyuha today. None among you save my son could break into that formation. I taught him myself, but I did not teach him how to break out of it again. Ah, did you make my boy enter that vyuha?

Did Subhadra's mighty son go alone into the enemy's midst? Did he kill countless maharathas there and finally fall to countless enemies combined against him? Oh, tell me how that indomitable hero of mighty arms and red eyes, born into our vamsa like a lion upon the mountain breast, Abhimanyu equal Vishnu himself, perished on the field of battle?"

Moment by moment certainty of the tragedy seizes Arjuna. His voice rises, and he cries desperately, "What warrior, whom Death deprived of his reason, dared kill Subhadra's beloved son, he who was the favourite of Draupadi and Krishna, the child whom Kunti loved most? He was equal to Krishna himself in prowess, learning and dignity; how has he been slain on the field of war? If I do not see the favourite son of the daughter of the Vrishnis, whom I loved more than my life, I will not live another moment but kill myself!"

No one makes any reply, and like one caught in a deepening nightmare, Arjuna continues, biting his lip, speaking to himself as much as to the others.

"With locks ending in soft curls, of tender years, with eyes like those of a young gazelle, with a tread like that of an elephant in musth, tall like a young Sala tree, of sweet speech, ah, such sweet smiles, quiet, ever obedient to his elders, though so young, always conducting himself like one of mature years, of untold courage and energy, his eyes like lotus-petals, always kind to those who loved him, self-restrained, never doing anything mean, always grateful, learned and wise far beyond his years, a great master of astras, never fleeing from battle, instead always delighting in fight and striking fear into his enemies, ever engaged in his kinsmen's welfare, wishing victory to his sires, never striking first, perfectly fearless in war—if I do not see that son of mine, I will follow him even now to the land of Yama."

Arjuna continues truly like a man in a dreadful dream, "He was a maharatha among maharathas; he was one and a half times the warrior I am. Of tender years, of mighty arms, so very dear to Pradyumna, Kesava and myself—if I do not see my son I must leave you and go to Yama's world.

With a beautiful nose and lofty brow, with startling, brilliant eyes, and arched lips—oh, if I do not see that face, what peace can my heart have? His voice melodious as the voice of the male kokila, enchanting and sweet as the soft, deep sounds of the vina—without hearing his voice, what peace can my heart have?

His beauty is unrivalled, rare even among the Devas. Without casting my eyes on that form, what peace can my heart have? Accomplished in greeting his elders with reverence, and always obedient to the behests of his sires—alas, if I do not see him, what peace can my heart have?

Brave in battle, accustomed to every luxury, deserving of the softest bed—alas, he sleeps today on the bare earth, as if there is none to take care of him, although he is first of those who have protectors. He was attended on by the most beautiful women, in his bed; alas, mangled with arrows, inauspicious jackals, prowling the field, will attend to him today. He who was once roused from his slumbers by singers, bards and panegyrists—alas, today he will be awakened by discordant cries of beasts of prey.

His handsome face that eminently deserves to be shaded by a royal chatra—alas, the dust of the battlefield will soil it today. O my child, unfortunate that I am, death forcibly takes you away from me, who was never sated with looking at you. Today you will illumine the palace of Yama, mansion of delight, which is always the goal of men of dharma, and your brilliance will add to is lustre. Without doubt, Yama, Varuna, Indra and Kubera, finding you their favourite guest, even now make much of you, O my heroic son."

Thus lamenting like a merchant whose vessel has sunk, grief-stricken Arjuna asks Yudhishtira, "O, Kurusthama, has he ascended into Swarga after facing their fiercest warriors in battle and slaughtering the enemy? Ah, while he single-handedly fought the greatest maharathas, countless in number, his heart must have turned towards me seeking help. While set upon by Karna, Drona, Kripa and the others with arrows of every kind, with glittering heads, my son must have repeatedly thought, 'My father will be my rescuer in this peril.'

Even while he thought of me and grieved, I feel sure that savage warriors must have felled him. Or, perhaps, as he was my son, the nephew of Krishna and born to Subhadra, he would not have uttered any lamentation. But oh, my heart is made of the adamant of the Vajra, since it does not break even though I do not see that mighty-armed shura with the red eyes.

How could these cruel maharathas shoot their deep-piercing arrows at my son of such tender years, the child who was Krishna's nephew? Every evening the noble-hearted prince would rush out to greet me when I rode home; where is he today? Terrible certainty grips me that he lies slain and bathed in his own blood on naked ground. Ah, making this bhumi beautiful with his body, my child surely lies like the sun fallen from the sky.

I grieve for Subhadra, who, when she hears of her fearless son's death in battle, will end her own life in sorrow. Missing Abhimanyu, what will she say to me? What will Draupadi say to me? Ravaged by grief as they are, what will I say to them? Surely, my heart is made of the adamantine essence of the very Vajra, since it does not break in a thousand pieces at the sight of my weeping daughter-in-law Uttaraa, impaled on her grief.

I did indeed hear the leonine shouts of the Dhritarashtras swelling with pride. Krishna also heard Yuyutsu censuring the Kshatriyas of the Dhritarashtra army saying, 'Maharathas, why do you rejoice when, unable to vanquish Arjuna, you have killed only a child? Why, having done what is intolerable to Kesava and Arjuna, why do you roar like lions in joy, when in truth it is the hour for sorrow that is come? The fruits of this horrible sin of yours will overtake you swiftly. Heinous is the crime you have perpetrated. How long can it take to bear its fruits?'

Rebuking them in these words, the noble son of Dhritarashtra by his Vaisya wife rode away, flinging aside his weapons, seized by rage and grief. O Krishna, why did you not tell me all this during the battle? I would have consumed all those heartless, bestial maharathas."

Krishna consoles the stricken Arjuna, whose eyes are bathed in tears, "Do not yield so to grief. This is the way of all brave heroes, and especially of Kshatriyas, whose dharma is battle. O Mahabuddhi, such is the goal the authors of our shastras ordain for fearless warriors in war. Death is certain for Kshatriyas who do not retreat. There is no doubt that Abhimanyu has ascended to those lofty realms that are reserved for men of the highest dharma. Bharatarishabha, all brave men wish to die in battle, facing their enemies.

As for Abhimanyu, he killed so many maharathas, before meeting with a death coveted by Kshatriyas. Do not grieve, Naravyaghra, our lawgivers of old have declared the death in battle to be the eternal punya of the Kshatriyas. Best of the Bharatas, your brothers are all forlorn, as is the king, and our friends, to see you plunged in despair. You must not sharpen their grief but comfort them by being calm and brave yourself."

Controlling himself somewhat, Arjuna, his voice still choking, says to Yudhishtira and his brothers, "Lord of the earth, tell me now how my heroic Abhimanyu fought, that shura of eyes like lotus-petals. You will see me annihilate my son's killers with their elephants, chariots, horses and all their followers and kinsmen.

Yet, my great brothers, you are all masters of arms, and you were all armed in battle. How then was Subhadra's son slain, even if it were Vajradhari Indra himself whom he fought?

Alas, if I had known that Pandavas and the Panchalas would not be able to protect my son in war, I myself would have done so. You were mounted on your chariots; you held your bows and loosed your arrows. Alas, how could the enemy kill Abhimanyu, and bring a great carnage to your ranks?

Ah, you have neither manliness nor prowess, since they killed Abhimanyu before your very eyes. Or I should blame myself, because knowing that you all are weak, cowardly and irresolute, I went away! Are your coats of mail and weapons only ornaments to embellish your bodies, and were you given words only to make fine speeches in sabhas, that you failed to protect my son, despite being clad in mail, fully armed and although you gave me your solemn word that you would safeguard my son?"

Arjuna suddenly sits down, his fists clenched around his great bow and fine sword. Indeed, no one can even look at him at that time, for he is like Death himself, repeatedly drawing deep breaths. None of his friends or kinsmen venture to look at or speak to Arjuna, as he sits there, with tears streaming down his face. No one dares address him, save Krishna or Yudhishtira. These two he reveres so much that they are free to speak to him under any circumstances, and at any time.

At last, in that deep and terrible silence, slowly, Yudhishtira speaks to Arjuna.'

CANTO 70

Abhimanyu-vadha Parva continued

'Yudhishtira says, "Mahabaho, after you rode to face the Samsaptakas, Drona did everything he could to capture me. However, we resisted the Acharya at the head of his vyuha, deploying our own forces in a powerful formation. Contained by a large number of our warriors, and I too was well protected, the infuriated Drona began to assail us with his devastras, burning up whole legions of common soldiers. We could not even look at his army, far less face it in battle.

It was then that all of us asked Abhimanyu to break Drona's vyuha! And he unquestioningly sought to fulfil our wish, dreadful though the task was. The brilliant child plunged into the chakravyuha even like Garuda into the sea. As for us, we followed Abhimanyu close, but then suddenly the wretched Jayadratha barred our way, using the boon he had from Siva. Why, by himself the vile Saindhava held all of us at bay!

And then six maharathas, Drona, Kripa, Karna, Aswatthaman, the king of the Kosalas and Kritavarman, surrounded Abhimanyu. Having encircled the child, the six, who proved more than he could contain after all the fighting and killing he had done, shattered his chariot. Abhimanyu battled on foot but finally, by great mischance, Dusasana's son struck him dead. During the day, Abhimanyu killed many thousands of men, horses and elephants; he destroyed eight thousand chariots and nine hundred elephants more, two thousand Kshatriya princes, and a vast number of warriors, all heroes if unknown to fame, and sent king Brihadbala also to heaven. Finally, through dark misfortune, your glorious son met his death.

Arjuna, that he died alone within the treacherous chakravyuha only makes our grief sharper than it might be otherwise." Yudhishtira's voice is a hoarse whisper now, "My brother, it was thus that your magnificent son, that tiger among all men, ascended to swarga!"

Arjuna moans, "Oh my son!" and heaving a great sigh, keels over on his side, swooning in agony he cannot endure. Their faces dark with sorrow, all the Pandava warriors stand around the unconscious Dhananjaya, and stare mutely at one another.

When Arjuna regains his senses, he awakes in rage that is terrible to see. Sighs like a great serpent's hisses issue from his trembling body; he draws deep shuddering breaths and tears flow in a rill down his face. He casts manic glances around him, eyes darting everywhere, like a madman, like one possessed.

In a truly dreadful voice, Arjuna says, very quietly, "I swear that tomorrow I will kill Jayadratha. If he does not forsake the Dhritarashtras from fear of death, or come to beg for our protection, or for Krishna's protection, or yours, Rajan, I will surely kill him tomorrow.

Forgetting his friendship for me, eager only to please Dhritarashtra's son, the wretch caused the death of my precious child. And tomorrow I will kill the sinner Jayadratha. Whoever faces me in battle tomorrow to protect the vile Saindhava, be it not Drona or Kripa—I will smother them with my arrows. I will kill them if they stand in my way!

O Purusharishabhas, if I do not achieve this in tomorrow's battle, let me not attain the heaven reserved for men of dharma. Why, if I do not kill Jayadratha tomorrow, let me find those hellish realms that sinners do who kill their mothers, or their fathers, or violate their guru's beds, the most vile and evil men, they who are envious of righteous men, they who speak ill of others or appropriate wealth entrusted to their care, betrayers of trusts, who speak ill of their dead wives, or who have slain Brahmanas, or sacred kine, or they who eat payasa, meat or other delicacies without having first dedicated them to the Devas. May those narakas become mine to which men who insult Brahmanas devoted to the study of the Vedas go, or speak harshly to other men worthy of respect, or to their very gurus—if I do not kill Jayadratha tomorrow!

The end that becomes theirs who lay their feet on Brahmanas or sacred fire, those who cast phlegm, excreta and urine into pure water—may even such an end be mine if I do not kill Jayadratha!

Let me find the end which is his who bathes naked in water, or his who does not hospitably entertain a guest, or he who takes bribes, speaks falsehoods and deceives and cheats others, or who offends against his own soul, or who falsely praises others, or of those low sinners who eat fine sweets in the sight of servants, sons, wives and dependents without sharing them—if I do not kill Jayadratha tomorrow!

The end of the cruel brute who does not support an obedient sishya of dharma but casts him off; the end of him who, without giving the offerings in Sraddhas to deserving neighbours, gives them instead to those who do not deserve them in the least; the end which is his who drinks wine, or insults those who are worthy of respect; or one who is ungrateful, or speaks ill of his brothers—let that end swiftly be mine if I do not kill Jayadratha!

I vow that I will immediately attain to the end of all the sinners whom I have mentioned, and also those whom I have not named, if after this night, I do not slay Jayadratha tomorrow.

And listen now to another oath of mine! If tomorrow's Sun sets without my killing that wretch, then even here will I enter a blazing fire and immolate myself! You Asuras, Devas and Manushas, you Pakshis and Nagas, you Pitris and all you Rakshasas, you Maharishis and Devarishis, O all you mobile and immobile creatures—not all of you together will succeed in protecting my enemy from me tomorrow! Even if he enters the Patalas, or rises into Akasa, or runs to the Devas in Swarga, or to the realms of the Daityas, upon the expiration of this night, I will yet with a hundred arrows, sever the head of Abhimanyu's enemy!"

Having said this, Arjuna begins to stretch the Gandiva mightily with both his arms. Echoing beyond Arjuna's voice the sound of the great bow rises and touches the very heavens. After Arjuna swears his oath, Krishna, filled with wrath, blows his conch the Panchajanya, while Arjuna blows the Devadatta. At the reverberant booming of the great Panchajanya, the rulers of the cardinal and the subsidiary points, the nether regions, why, the Lords of the whole universe tremble, as if it is the end of the Yuga. After Arjuna Mahatman has sworn his solemn oath, the sound of thousands of musical instruments and lionish warriors' roars arise from the Pandava camp.'"

CANTO 71

Abhimanyu-vadha Parva continued

"Sanjaya says, 'Duryodhana's spies quickly come to inform their masters of the cause of the great uproar raised by the Pandavas. Jayadratha is overwhelmed by terror, and feels as if he is sinking in a vortex of black despair. He sits plunged in thought for a time, numb, then slowly rises and comes into the assembly of the Dhartarashtra kings. He stands mute for a while in that conclave of those gods among men, and then breathes, "He whom Indra sired in Pandu's soil has sworn to send me to Yamaloka tomorrow! May fortune smile on you, I will return to my home for I have no wish to die. O Kshatriyarishabhas, protect me with your weapons, for Arjuna seeks to kill me. Make me fearless! Drona, Duryodhana, Kripa, Karna, Salya, Balhika, Dusasana and all you others can protect a man from Yama himself. When Phalguna alone threatens me, will these the lords of the earth not join together and protect me?

Great is my fear after hearing the Pandavas shouting loud in joy. My limbs, Bhumipalas, have turned weak like a dying man's. The Gandeevi has sworn to kill me. And that is why the Pandavas are roaring in joy at a time when they should weep! Let alone the rulers of men, the very Devas, Gandharvas, the Asuras, the Uragas and the Rakshasas cannot thwart Arjuna when he has sworn to kill me. And so, you bulls among men, blessed be you, give me leave to depart the Kuru camp for I have no wish to die. Even Arjuna cannot take my life if he does not find me here!"

Thus does the terrified Jayadratha babble in fear, but Duryodhana, always looking to achieve his own ends over everything else, says, "Do not fear, Naravyaghra! Who will dare seek to kill you when you are in the midst of all these Kshatriya tigers? Vikartana's son, Karna, Chitrasena, Vivimsati, Bhurisravas, Sala, Salya, the invincible Vrishasena, Purumitra, Jaya, Bhoja, Sudakshina of the Kambojas, Satyavrata, the Mahabaho Vikarna, Durmukha, Dusasana, Subahu of the Kalingas, and I myself, with weapons raised, Vinda and Anuvinda of Avanti, Drona, Drona's son, and Subala's son Sakuni—all these and many other kings, with their armies, will protect you on all sides. Let the fever of fear in your heart be dispelled.

You are yourself one of the greatest maharathas. O splendid Jayadratha, you are a shura, a magnificent hero. And being what you are, how can you see any cause for fear? My own eleven akshauhinis will fight just to protect you tomorrow. O king of the Sindhus, let your fears be dispelled!"

Comforted somewhat by your son, the king of the Sindhus, along with Duryodhana, goes then to meet Drona, the senapati of the Kuru army. Touching Drona's feet with reverence and taking his seat with humility, Jayadratha earnestly asks the Acharya, "Illustrious one, tell me the difference between Arjuna and myself in striking a target from a distance, in the firmness of our grips, and the force of shooting our arrows. O Acharya, I want to know accurately the difference as bowmen between Arjuna and myself! I beg you, tell me this truthfully, for only you can."

Drona says, "O son I have given both Arjuna and you the same measure of instruction. However, through yoga and because of the hard life that Arjuna has led, he is superior to you. But for no reason should you be afraid of Partha. For have no doubt that I will protect you from what you fear. The very Devas cannot prevail over him whom my arms protect. Tomorrow I will form a vyuha that Partha will not succeed in piercing!

So have no fear and observe your swadharma. O maharatha, walk in the path of your fathers and grandfathers. Having studied the Vedas, you have poured libations, according to the laws, into fire. You have performed many yagnas. Death cannot be an object of terror for you. For if you die, you will acquire the great good fortune which evil men cannot attain and you will gain all those felicitous regions in heaven that only the might of arms can bestow!

The Kauravas, the Pandavas, the Vrishnis and other men, and also my son and I, are all mortal and short-lived. Think of this. One after another, all of us, killed by Kaala which is all powerful, will go to the other world, carrying only our deeds with us—the same regions that munis acquire through severe penances and heroic Kshatriyas who observe their swadharma."

Thus, Bharadwaja's son consoles the king of the Sindhus. Banishing his fear of Partha, he sets his heart on the battle to follow. Then, Rajan, your troops also feel great delight and one hears the loud sounds of musical instruments, mingled with lusty roars."'

CANTO 72

ABHIMANYU-VADHA PARVA CONTINUED

"Sanjaya says, 'After Partha vows to kill Jayadratha, Krishna says to Arjuna, "With only your brother's consent and without consulting me, you have sworn to kill the Saindhava. You have been rash to swear this oath and taken a great burden upon yourself. Alas, how will we escape the ridicule of all men? I sent some spies into Duryodhana's camp and my men report that after you vowed to kill the king of the Sindhus, the Dhartarashtras heard our loud roaring, mingled with the sounds of our musical instruments. This terrified them and their well-wishers, and they thought these tigerish shouts could not be without good reason and waited to see what would ensue.

O Mahabaho, a clamour has arisen among the Kauravas, their elephants, horses and foot-soldiers; and we hear the terrible rattle of their chariots. After hearing of the death of Abhimanyu, they fear that you, Arjuna, will set out in the very night, raging for battle!

The Kaurava king waits ready for battle. While preparing themselves, O you of eyes like lotus-petals, they learnt of the vow that you swore to kill Jayadratha. All Duryodhana's counsellors became faint-hearted and frightened like little animals. Jayadratha, king of the Sindhus and the Sauviras, was overwhelmed by fear and hastily called his closest advisors for a consultation.

After consulting them, he went to the assembly of the allied kings and there said to Duryodhana, "Arjuna thinks of me as his son's killer and will challenge me to battle tomorrow. In the midst of his army, he has sworn to kill me. The very Devas, Gandharvas, Asuras, Uragas and Rakshasas cannot frustrate Arjuna's solemn vow. So protect me. Do not let Dhananjaya set his foot on your head, and find his mark, which is my life! Make every arrangement to safeguard me; otherwise, if you think you cannot save me from Arjuna on the field, give me leave to return to my kingdom."

Seeing Jayadratha so terrified, an unhappy Duryodhana sat with his head hung down and reflecting in silence. Seeing the Kuru king distraught, Jayadratha slowly says, "I do not see any archer here who can match Arjuna in war. Who, even if it were Satakratu himself, can stand against Arjuna who has Krishna for his sarathy, and wields the Gandiva? I hear that Partha fought Lord Maheswara himself once on the mountains of Himavat. At Indra's behest, from a single chariot he slew a thousand Danavas of Hiranyapura.

And now that the clever Vasudeva is his ally, I feel certain that Arjuna can destroy the three worlds including their very gods. I beseech you that you either grant me permission to leave Kurukshetra or ensure that the high-souled and heroic Drona with his son will assuredly protect me. I await your pleasure."

O Arjuna, hearing Jayadratha's pitiful plea, Duryodhana also added his voice to humbly beseech Drona to protect the Saindhava. And they have indeed taken every measure in their power to protect Jayadratha. They have deployed all their chariots and cavalry. Karna, Bhurisravas, Drona's son Aswatthaman, the invincible Vrishasena, Kripa, and Salya of the Madras—these six will be in Jayadratha's van. Drona will form a vyuha half of which will be a Sakata, a cart, and half a Padma, a lotus. In the midst of the leaves of that lotus will be a needle-mouthed formation, a suchimukha vyuha. At the eye of the needle, Jayadratha will take his stand, protected by those six greatest Kuru maharathas!

In the use of the bow, and every other weapon, in the ability to kill their enemies, in sheer prowess, and also in lineage, these six maharathas are well nigh without equal. Without first vanquishing these six, you will not be able to reach Jayadratha.

Think, O Arjuna, of the individual prowess of each of the six. When united they cannot be vanquished easily, if at all! And so, for our benefit and our success, we should once again take counsel with our well-wishers, who are familiar with strategy!"'

CANTO 73

ABHIMANYU-VADHA PARVA CONTINUED

"Arjuna says, 'The prowess of the six maharathas of Dhritarashtra's army whose united might you think so highly of, I believe is not equal to even half of mine! You will see, O Madhusudana, how I destroy their weapons and render them impotent, when I confront them on my way to kill Jayadratha! In the very sight of Drona and all his men, I will behead the king of the Sindhus, and Duryodhana's whole army will weep and lament.

Even if the Siddhas, the Rudras, the Vasus, with the Aswins, the Maruts, with Indra at their head, the Viswadevas with the other Gods, the Pitris, the Gandharvas, Garuda, the Ocean, the Mountains, the Firmament, Heaven, Earth, the cardinal and subsidiary points of the compass and the regents of those points, all the beasts that are domestic and all that are wild, in fact if all the mobile and the unmoving beings together become the protectors of Jayadratha, O Krishna, you will see me kill him tomorrow with my arrows! I swear by Truth; I touch my weapons and swear by them that I will, at the very outset, face the mighty Drona, who has become the protector of the sinner Jayadratha.

Duryodhana believes that this game of war hinges upon Drona. And even so, hewing my way through the very van that Drona himself commands, I will strike at Jayadratha!

Tomorrow you will see the great Acharya blown away by my arrows like the summits of a hill struck by thunder. Blood will flow in rills from the breasts of fallen men, elephants and horses, eviscerated by my showers of shafts falling heavily upon them. The astras shot from the Gandiva, fleet as the mind or the wind, will claim the lives of thousands upon thousands of men, elephants and steeds.

In tomorrow's battle, all men shall see the awesome astras that I have acquired from Yama, Kubera, Varuna, Indra and Rudra. You will witness how my Brahmastra nullifies the weapons of all those who come to protect Jayadratha.

O Krishna, tomorrow you will see the Earth strewn with the heads of kings cut off cleanly by my shafts! Tomorrow I will gratify all the thirst and hunger of all the ravening Rakshasas that stalk Kurukshetra. I will mow down the enemy and gladden my friends, and finally I will cut the head of the ruler of the Sindhus from his throat.

He is a vile and heinous sinner; he has not behaved like a relative; he is born in a sinful country and when I kill him, it will plunge dark grief through all that are his own. Krishna, tomorrow you will see the wretched Jayadratha, who was raised in every luxury, die from my inexorable arrows!

Tomorrow, Krishna, I will do that which will make Duryodhana believe that there is no bowman in the world who is Arjuna's equal. My Gandiva is a celestial bow. I, Arjuna, am the warrior. You, O Hrishikesa, are the charioteer. What can come between me and my prey, who is there that I cannot vanquish? Through your grace, O Holy one, what is there that I cannot achieve in battle? Knowing well that my power is irresistible, why, O Krishna, do you still rebuke me?

As Lakshmi is ever present in Soma, as water is ever present in the ocean, know, O Janardana, that I always accomplish what I have sworn to do. Do not think lightly of my weapons. Do not think lightly of my great bow. Do not think lightly of the might of my arms. Do not think lightly of your Dhananjaya. I will go into battle in such heart that I shall not lose but surely prevail. When I have vowed it, know that Jayadratha has already been slain. Truly, in the Brahmana is truth; in men of dharma is humility; in yagna is prosperity, and always in Narayana is victory!"

Having said these words to Krishna, having said all this to himself, as well, in a deep voice Arjuna once more addresses the Lord Kesava, saying, "Krishna, yet the task before us is grave and not easy, and you must prepare our chariot by the hour of dawn. We must ride forth at break of day and conquer!"'

CANTO 74

Abhimanyu-vadha Parva continued

"Sanjaya says, 'Stricken with sorrow and frequently sighing like two snakes, Krishna and Arjuna both get no sleep that night. Realising that Nara and Narayana are in wrath, the Devas along with Vasava grow anxious and think, "What will come of this?"

Fierce dry winds, foreboding danger, begin to blow, howling, and a headless trunk and a mace appear on the disc of the sun. And although the sky is cloudless, there are frequent peals of thunder, and flashes of lightning. The earth with her mountains, rivers and forests, shake; and the seas, the habitation of makaras, swell in agitation and crash against their shores. And the rivers flow back towards their sources, opposite to their normal course. The lips of chariot-warriors, horses, men and elephants, begin to tremble unaccountably. The animals on the field began to spray urine and dung and utter loud cries, to the delight of Rakshasas and pisachas, and foretelling a great exodus of men to the domain of Yama. Seeing these omens that make the hair stand on end, and hearing of the fierce vow of mighty Arjuna, all your warriors, Bharatarishabha, are desperately agitated.

Arjuna, the mighty-armed son of Indra, says to Krishna, "O Madhava, go and comfort your sister Subhadra, her daughter-in-law Uttaraa and her companions. Speak soothing words to her, words of deep truth and solace."

Krishna reluctantly makes his way to Arjuna's tent, and begins to console his sister grieving at the death of her son. Krishna says, "O you of Vrishni's vamsa, do not grieve, you and Uttaraa, for your son. All creatures have but one end ordained by Time. The end your son has met is the most desirable one for any Kshatriya of proud lineage. Do not grieve, for by good fortune your maharatha of great intelligence, of prowess equal to that of his father, has met with an end that all Kshatriyas covet.

After vanquishing numberless enemies and sending them to Yama's land, he himself has gone to the eternal realms of men of dharma, worlds that grant the realisation of every wish. Your son has attained the end which men of dharma attain only through tapasya, brahm, knowledge of the shastras and gyana. The mother, the wife, the daughter and a kinsman of such Kshatriyas, O Subhadra, do not grieve for a son who has obtained the supreme end.

The evil king of the Sindhus, my beautiful sister, the murderer of a child, will, with all his friends and kinsmen, find the fruit of his arrogance before the end of this day. Even if he enters Indra's domain he will not escape Arjuna. Tomorrow you will hear that his head has been cut from his neck to roll dismally on the hem of Samantapanchaka!

Abandon your sorrow and do not grieve, for your valiant son has attained the end that men of dharma who observe the svadharma of a Kshatriya fervently wish for. Your splendid, magnificent Abhimanyu has attained swarga. Drive away this fever of sorrow. Comfort your daughter-in-law, O queen, that, obedient to his fathers and his mother's kinsmen, the heroic Abhimanyu has slain thousands upon thousands of his enemies before dying a great Kshatriya's death in the field of war. Do not grieve too much, O Kshatriya woman!

Drive away your grief, gentle Subhadra, for tomorrow will bring great tidings. Arjuna will accomplish what he has sworn to do. It cannot be otherwise, for your husband never fails to do as he has sworn. Even if all Manavas, Nagas, Pisachas, Rakshasas, great Avians, and all the Devas and the Asuras come to help the king of the Sindhus, Jayadratha will still die tomorrow.'"'

CANTO 75

ABHIMANYU-VADHA PARVA CONTINUED

"Sanjaya says, 'But Subhadra cannot control her terrible grief and wails, "Oh, my son, of prowess equal to your father, O my child, how could you die? Alas, how does your face like a blue lotus, with its perfect teeth and brilliant eyes, look now covered over with battle's dust?

You were so entirely brave, your head so handsome, your neck, arms, your deep chest, your low flat belly, your splendid limbs decked with ornaments, your beautiful sparkling eyes! All creatures looked upon you as the rising moon, and now you have been mutilated, my perfect child, and fallen on the yawning field of death. Alas, your bed was always overlaid with the whitest and costliest sheets; you who deserved every luxury, how do you sleep today on the bare earth, your body mangled with arrows?

The mighty Kshatriya, whom the most beautiful women waited on, has now fallen on the field, to pass his time in the company of jackals! He whom vabdhis and magadhis daily hymned at dawn is today greeted by the savage cries and growls of Rakshasas and beasts of prey.

O my precious son, who killed you, and how, when you had the Pandavas and all the Panchalas for your protectors? Oh my son, O sinless one, I am not yet satisfied with looking at you. Wretched as I am, it is plain that I will have to go to Yama's realm now for my eyes have not seen enough of you. When will I cast my gaze again on your face with its lotus-like eyes and shining locks, the smooth radiant face from which endearing words and the most delicate fragrance constantly issued?

Fie on the strength of Bhimasena, on the archery of Partha, on the prowess of the Vrishni heroes and the might of the Panchalas! Shame on the Kaikeyas, the Chedis, the Matsyas and the Srinjayas, who could not protect you, O my shuravira! I see the Earth as being empty and hollow today, and made of just sorrow and despair. My eyes hurt and stream tears that they do not see my Abhimanyu. You were Krishna's sister's son, the son of the wielder of Gandiva, and yourself an incomparable hero and an atiratha. Alas, how will I look at you dead!

O Kshatriya, to me you were like a treasure that is briefly won and lost in a dream. Oh, everything human is as fleeting as a bubble of water on this river of time. Your young wife is overwhelmed by grief at the evil that has befallen you. And how will I, who am like a cow without her calf, comfort her? O my sweet prince, you have so untimely fled from me, even as your greatness was about to flower and bear wondrous fruit. Oh my son, can you see how my heart is breaking over and over for just a glimpse of your face! Ah, there is no doubt that not the wisest can fathom the inexorable ways of Death, since despite having Krishna for your protector you were killed as if you were quite helpless.

O son, let that end be yours which is theirs that perform yagnas, who are Brahmanas of purified souls, those who have practised brahmacharya, have bathed in all the sacred tirthas, who are grateful and charitable and devoted to the service of their gurus, and those who have given sacrificial dakshina in profusion. The end that is theirs who are intrepid and fearless in battle, or theirs who have fallen most heroically in war, after slaying their enemies—O my Abhimanyu, let that end be yours!

The auspicious end which is theirs who have given away a thousand cows, or theirs who have given lavish dana in yagnas, or theirs who give away houses and mansions, the end which is theirs who give away gems and jewels to deserving Brahmanas, or theirs who are punishers of crime—O, let that end be yours.

The end that Munis of rigid vows attain through brahmacharya, or that which women who remain faithful to one husband, attain—O son, let that end be yours.

The eternal end which kings get by their good deeds, or by those men who have cleansed themselves by leading all the four varnasramas one after another, and by duly observing their dharma, the end of men who are compassionate to the poor and the distressed, or those who equitably divide sweets among themselves and their dependants, or those who are never given to deceit and evil—O my son, let that end be yours!

O child, the end of those who observe chaste vows, or who are virtuous, devoted to the service of their gurus, or those who have never sent away a guest without entertaining them—let that end be yours.

O son, let the end of those who succeed in adversity and of those who have the most difficult trait of preserving the equanimity of their souls, however much they are burnt by the fires of grief, let that end be yours.

O son, let that end be yours which is theirs who are always devoted to the service of their fathers and mothers, or theirs who are exclusively devoted to their own wives.

O son, let that end be yours which those wise men attain who restrain themselves from the wives of others and seek the companionship of only their own wives in season.

O son, let that end be yours which is theirs that look upon all creatures with an eye of peace, or theirs that never give pain to others, or theirs that always forgive.

O son, let that end be yours which is theirs who abstain from honey, meat, wine, pride and falsehood.

Let that goal be yours which they attain who are modest, acquainted with all the shastras, content with knowledge, and have their passions under control."

While the stricken Subhadra thus laments, wildly, Draupadi accompanied by Virata's daughter Uttaraa, comes to her. All of them, in great sorrow, weep copiously and indulge in heart-rending expressions of grief. Quite lost to reason through sorrow, they faint and fall onto the earth. Then Krishna the lotus-eyed one, who stands ready with water, himself deeply affected, sprinkles water over his weeping, unconscious and trembling sister, pierced through her very heart. When she comes to her senses, he attempts to comfort her again, and the others as well.

"Grieve not, Subhadra! O Panchali, console Uttaraa! Abhimanyu, bull among Kshatriyas, has found the most laudable end for himself. O Sumukhi, you of the beautiful face, may all the other men yet alive in our race obtain the end which Abhimanyu of great fame has. We, with all our friends, together only wish to achieve in this war the feats which your son, the atiratha, achieved by himself! So do not grieve for that hero with no remote equal."

Finally, having somewhat consoled his sister, and Draupadi and Uttaraa, through his presence and grace as much as by what he says, Krishna, returns to Arjuna. Saluting the kings, friends and Arjuna himself, Kesava enters the inner apartments of Arjuna's palatial tent while the other kings return to their own tents.'"

CANTO 76

ABHIMANYU-VADHA PARVA CONTINUED

"Sanjaya says, 'Lord Kesava, of eyes like lotus petals, enters the sprawling tent, Arjuna's unrivalled mansion on Kurukshetra; he touches water, and lays out on the auspicious and even floor for Arjuna an excellent bed of kusa grasses, which are the colour of lapis lazuli. And arranging his majestic weapons around the bed, duly adorns it with garlands of flowers, fried paddy, perfumes and other auspicious things. After Partha also touches water, gentle and attentive attendants bring the nightly yagna offerings for the three-eyed Lord Mahadeva. With a serene soul, Arjuna smears Krishna with perfumes and offers him the sacred nightly offering adorned with flowers.

With a faint smile, Govinda says to Arjuna, "Bless you, Partha, lie down and sleep. I will leave you now."

Seeing that doorkeepers and well-armed guards are in their places, Krishna, followed by Daruka his charioteer, goes to his own tent. There the illustrious one of eyes like lotus petals lies on his white bed and thinks of different ways to dispel Partha's grief and anxiety and enhance his confidence and greatness. Then he, the Supreme Lord of all, Vishnu of universal fame, who always does what is for Arjuna's weal, immerses himself in yoga and dhyana.

Everyone else in the Pandava camp, Rajan, is awake, thinking, "Burning with grief at the death of his son, the Gandivi has swiftly vowed to kill the Saindhava. But how will Arjuna Parantapa accomplish his rash vow? He has sworn a difficult oath, for Jayadratha is invested with great prowess and great protection too. Oh, may Arjuna succeed in fulfilling his dire vow that he swore while he was in the grip of searing grief!

The sons of Dhritarashtra are all mighty warriors and their forces are countless. Duryodhana has assigned all of them to be just Jayadratha's protectors tomorrow. Oh, let Dhananjaya return to our encampment tomorrow after slaying the king of the Sindhus. Let him fulfil his vow. If he fails, he will surely enter the fire and immolate himself, for he never swears a false oath. If Arjuna dies, how will Dharmaputra Yudhishtira, who has reposed all his hopes of victory in Arjuna, succeed in recovering his kingdom? If we have all acquired any punya, if we have ever poured libations of ghrita into fire, let Savyasachin benefit from our punya and vanquish all his enemies!"

Speaking thus amongst themselves, and deeply anxious for the morrow, the Pandava warriors pass that long night.

In the heart of the night, Krishna awakes, remembers Arjuna's vow, and says softly, but in a terrible voice, to his charioteer, "Daruka, grief-stricken at his son's death, Arjuna has vowed, that before tomorrow's sun sets he will kill Jayadratha or take his own life. Hearing this, Duryodhana will surely take counsel with his advisors about how Partha can be prevented from fulfilling his vow. His several akshauhinis will all protect Jayadratha. Drona, too, with his son Aswatthaman, will stand watch over the Saindhava. And even Indra himself, the thousand-eyed scourge of the pride of the Daityas and Danavas, will hardly be able to kill one whom great Drona protects. And if Arjuna does not do as he has sworn he must take his own life. I mean to help Kunti's son to kill Jayadratha before the sun sets.

My wives, my kinsmen, my relatives, none among these are dearer to me than Arjuna. Daruka, I will not be able to look upon an Earth without Arjuna in it for even a single moment. I say to you, the Earth shall not be without Arjuna for I will raze them all, with their horses and elephants, by putting forth my might for Partha's sake. I will kill them all along with Karna and Duryodhana. Tomorrow let the three worlds witness my prowess when I join the fray for Arjuna's sake, and thousands of kings and hundreds of princes, with their horses, chariots and elephants, flee the battle or die from fear of me.

Daruka, you will see my wrath for I will decimate the army of kings, and the three worlds with the Devas, the Gandharvas, the Pisachas, the Nagas and the Rakshasas, will know me as a true friend of Savyasachin. Those who hate him hate me. Those who follow him, follow me. You are intelligent, Daruka, so know that Arjuna is half of myself.

When morning comes after this night ends, you, Daruka, must equip my chariot with the Kaumodaki, my Sudarshana Chakra, my Saringa and my astras, and everything else I might need, and then you must follow me discreetly into battle. O Suta, make room upon my chariot for my standard and for heroic Garuda thereon, who adorns my chatra. Yoke my horses Balahaka, Meghapushpa, Saibya and Sugriva, after having them cased in golden mail of the splendour of the Sun and Fire; and then put on your own armour and remain in the chariot vigilantly waiting.

When you hear the blast of my Panchajanya blowing the shrill Rishabha note, fly to me. In a single day, Daruka, I will dispel the wrath and the many sorrows of my cousin, the son of my aunt. I will do everything in my power to see that Arjuna kills Jayadratha in the very sight of the Dhartarashtras. Why, Daruka, I say to you that I will ensure that Dhananjaya will surely kill everyone he wants to."

Daruka says, "He, whose charioteer, O Naravyaghra, you become is certain to be victorious. Indeed, from where can defeat come to him? As for myself, I will do as you have commanded. This night will bring in its wake an auspicious morning for Arjuna's triumph and glory.""""

CANTO 77

ABHIMANYU-VADHA PARVA CONTINUED

"Sanjaya says, 'Kunti's son, Dhananjaya of inconceivable prowess, also lies thinking of ways to accomplish his vow. He recollects the mantras Vyasa had taught him and chanting them silently is soon lulled into sleep. To the Kshatriya of the Hanuman banner, his heart burning with grief even in slumber, Krishna of the Garuda banner appears in a dream. Arjuna Dharmatma always rises and advances a few steps to greet Krishna in bhakti whenever he sees him. And now in his dream as well he rises and offers Govinda a seat, while he keeps standing himself.

Krishna Mahatejasvin says to Kunti's son, "Let not your heart grieve, O Partha. Time is immutable and it forces all creatures into its inevitable course. Greatest of men, why do you grieve? Grief should never be indulged in, for it is an impediment to action. Fulfil your karma; accomplish what you have sworn to do. Dhananjaya, the grief that makes a man abandon all effort is an enemy of the warrior. By giving in to sorrow, a Kshatriya pleases his enemies and saddens his friends, while he himself is weakened. It does not become you to grieve."

The unvanquished Vijaya of deep learning says, "Grave is the vow that I have sworn, to kill Jayadratha. And tomorrow I will slay the evil one, my son's murderer. This is my solemn vow, Kesava! To frustrate me, the Dhartarashtras will keep Jayadratha at their rear, protected by all their maharathas.

Their army consists of the remnants of eleven akshauhinis of troops, still difficult to vanquish. Surrounded as he will be by all of them and by all their great maharathas besides, how will we even catch a glimpse of the vile Saindhava? O Krishna, I may not be able to fulfil my oath! And if I fail, how can I continue to live, Kesava? Ah, I fear that I will not succeed in keeping the impossible vow that I have sworn, demented as I was by Abhimanyu's death. And this is what makes me grieve.

Besides, at this time of the year, Krishna, the Sun sets early!"

Hearing this, the cause of Arjuna's grief and anxiety, Krishna gently touches water with his fingers and sits with his face turned to the east. The lotus-leaf-eyed One says to his cousin who has sworn to kill Jayadratha the next day, "Partha, there is an inexorable, supreme astra called the Pasupata. With it, the Lord Maheswara once slew all the Daityas! If you meditate upon that final weapon now, you will be able to kill Jayadratha tomorrow. If you do not know that Pasupatastra, worship Maheswara, who has the Bull for his mark. Think of the Mahadeva in your heart and fix your mind on him in dhyana, Arjuna. You are his devotee and through his grace, you will have that invaluable weapon."

Hearing Krishna's words, Arjuna now touches water and sits on the ground in deep dhyana, his thought fixed on the Lord Bhava. It is the auspicious Brahmamuhurta when Arjuna meditates on Siva. Arjuna sees himself journeying through the sky with Krishna, and travelling with the speed of the mind to the sacred foot of Himavat and the Manimat mountain replete with many brilliant gemstones, Manimat frequented by Siddhas and Charanas.

Krishna seems to hold his left arm as they course along, and Arjuna sees many wonderful sights there. Dharmatma Arjuna then finds himself at the White mountain of the north, Sweta, where, in the pleasure-gardens of Kubera, he sees the crystalline exquisite lake, the Bindusaras festooned with lotuses. He also sees the Ganga, greatest of rivers, brimful of pellucid water. Flying on, he arrives at the Mandara mountains covered with unearthly and awesome trees that are always laden with flowers and fruit.

Fine stones lie strewn everywhere in this place; all of them are the finest lucent crystals. Lions, tigers and diverse animals abound here, some truly exotic and found nowhere else, as do auspicious asramas of Munis, which echo with the sweet songs of brightly plumed birds, and also the transcendent songs of Kinnaras. Many golden and silver peaks grace this wondrous realm, and different magical herbs and plants illumine it; and Mandara trees with their gorgeous loads of flowers.

Then Arjuna comes to the mountain called Kala that looks like a great mound of antimony, and its summit Brahmatunga, and flying on, comes to many sparkling rivers and peopled realms, inhabited by men as well as unearthly beings. He comes to Satasringa, and the vana called Sharyati and sees the sacred Horse-head, the realm of Atharvana. He sees that prince of mountains called Vrishadansa, and the great Mandara, graced by Apsaras and Kinnaras.

Wandering on that mountain, Arjuna and Krishna see a place where exquisite fountains plash, a place shimmering with the rarest gold of the gods, lambent like the Moon, and with many shining cities and towns. In this fabulous zone of dreams, he also comes upon uncanny seas of marvellous shapes and diverse mines of untold wealth. And going through the sky, and over the earth, he arrives at the place known as Vishnupada. Like an arrow shot from a bow does Arjuna fly through the vaults of these skies of dream, with Krishna beside him, while below them indescribable landscapes unfold.

Soon Partha sees a mountain whose splendour equals that of the stars, the constellations, or fire. And at the summit of this lone and towering massif, he sees the Great God whose mount and emblem is the Bull. Arjuna sees Lord Siva who is always at tapasya, Mahadeva whose lustre is like that of a thousand suns fused, ah, ablaze with his own effulgence. Siva sits with trident in hand, matted jata upon his awesome head, his complexion white as snow or moonbeams, and wearing bark and deerskin.

Of tejas past telling, Maheswara's body seems to be alight with a thousand mystic eyes. He is seated with Parvati, with many creatures of fantastic and brilliant forms around him, his ganas, while his attendants sing and play musical instruments, full of joy, laughing and dancing in bliss, moving about and stretching their arms as if in waking trance, and often shouting aloud in primeval ecstasy. Divine fragrances perfume that place, and Rishis who worship the Brahman, worship Siva here with exceptional hymns of unfading glory—the God who is the Pasupati, the Lord and Protector of all creatures, who wields the great bow called the Pinaka.

Seeing Rudra, Krishna Mahatman and Arjuna prostrate and touch the earth with their heads, uttering the eternal words of the Veda. Krishna worships with speech, thought, intellect, and by what he does, the God who is the first source of the universe, himself uncreated, the Supreme Lord of unfading glory, who is the highest cause of the mind, who is Akasa and Vayu, who is the cause of all the luminous bodies in the universe, who is the cause of rain, and the Supreme, Primordial Essence of the Earth, who is the object of the adoration of the Devas, the Danavas, the Yakshas, and Manushas; who is the supreme Brahman that Yogins see and the refuge of those who know the Shastras, who is the Creator of all mobile and unmoving creatures and their Destroyer too; who is the Wrath that burns everything at the end of the Yuga; who is the Paramatman, the Supreme Soul; who is Sakra and Surya, and the origin of all the gunas.

Krishna seeks the protection of that Bhava, whom men of knowledge, wanting to attain to that which is called the sukshma and the adhyatma, seek; that Uncreated One who is the Soul of all causes. Arjuna also repeatedly worships the Great God, knowing that He is the Origin of all beings, the Cause of the past, the future and the present.

Seeing those two, Nara and Narayana, arrive, Bhava Anandatman, He of blissful soul, smilingly says, "Welcome greatest of men! Arise and let the tiredness of your journey leave you. What, O heroes, do you wish for? Tell me quickly, what brings you here? I will grant everything you want and do everything that will benefit you besides."

At these words of Siva, Krishna and Arjuna rise and then, with joined hands, the immaculate twain, both of great wisdom, praise that noblest Deity with a most resonant and excellent hymn. Krishna and Arjuna say, "We bow to Bhava, to Sarva, to Rudra, to the boon-giving Siva. We bow to the Pasupati, Lord of all creatures endued with life, to the Deva who is Ugra, fierce, to Him who is called Kapardin!

We bow to Mahadeva, to Bhimasankara, to Tryambaka, to Him who is Satchitananda. We bow to Isana, to Him who is the destroyer of Daksha's yagna.

We salute the slayer of Andhaka, the father of Kumara, to He who is Nilakantha, and the First Creator.

Our salutations to the wielder of the Pinaka, to Him who is worthy of the offering of libations of ghrita, to Him who is Truth, to Him who is All-pervading, to Him who is unvanquished, to Him who has luculent blue jata, to Him who is armed with the Trisula, to Him of celestial vision!

Our greetings to him who is Hotri, to Him who protects all, to Him who has three eyes, to Him who is disease, to Him whose hiranyaretas fell into Agni, to Him who is inconceivable, to him who is the Lord of Ambika, to Him who is adored by all the Devas!

Our salutations to Him who has the Bull for his mark, to Him who is bold, to Him who has matted dreadlocks, to Him who is a Brahmachari, to Him who stands as an ascetic in water, to him who is devoted to the Brahman, who is the Brahman, to Him who has never been conquered, to Him who is the Soul of the universe, to Him who is the Creator of the universe, to Him who lives pervading the whole universe!

We bow to You who are the object of the reverence of all, to You who are the Original Cause of all creatures, to You who are called Brahmachakra, to Sarva, Sankara, and Siva! We bow to You, the Lord of all great beings!

We bow to You who have a thousand heads, to You who have a thousand arms, to You who are called Death, to You who have a thousand eyes and a thousand feet, to You whose great deeds are innumerable!

We bow to You, Hiranyavarna, whose complexion is of gold, to You who are cased in golden kavacha, to You who are always compassionate to your devotees!

O Lord, let our wish be granted."

Having adored Mahadeva thus, Krishna and Arjuna then begin to further gratify Him to have the great Pasupatastra from the God of gods.'"

CANTO 78

ABHIMANYU-VADHA PARVA CONTINUED

"Sanjaya says, 'Partha, with a full soul and joined hands, his eyes wide with wonder, gazes at the God with the bull for his mount, He who is the home of all tejas. Partha sees the offerings that he makes every night to Krishna lying before the Three-eyed Deity. The son of Pandu worships both Krishna and Sarva in his heart, and says to Siva, "Lord, I wish to have the Pasupatastra from you."

Siva smilingly says to Vasudeva and Arjuna, "Welcome Purushottamas! I know what you want and the reason why you have come here. I will give you what you wish for. Parantapas, there is a lake full of amrita, not far from this place. In it, I left my celestial bow and astra, with which I once slew all the enemies of the Devas. Krishna, go and fetch that divine bow with the arrow fixed to it."

Hearing what Siva says, Vasudeva and Arjuna answer, "Tathaastu, so be it."

Accompanied by all the ganas of Siva, the two heroes set out for the unearthly lake replete with countless heavenly wonders, the sacred lake that can grant every object of desire. Reaching the lake, the Rishis Nara and Narayana, who are Arjuna and Krishna, go fearlessly up to the water bright as the disc of the sun, and see within it a great and terrible snake and yet another enormous, which has a thousand heads, the effulgence of fire and spews flames from all its jaws. Krishna and Partha touch the water, join their hands together, and approach the snakes, bowing in their minds to the God Siva. As they approach, the amazing Nagas, who know the Vedas, chant the hundred hymns of the Veda that praise Lord Rudra, bowing all the while with their devout souls to Bhava of immeasurable power.

Then, all at once, from their worship of Siva, the two awesome serpents abandon their snake-forms and assume the shapes of an enemy-destroying bow and arrow! Gratefully, Krishna and Arjuna seize the bow and arrow of blinding refulgence and bring them back to the illustrious Mahadeva. Now, from one side of Siva's body a Brahmacharin of tawny eyes emerges, who seems to be the very refuge of asceticism. Of blue throat and red jata, he is invested with untold might. Taking up the great bow effortlessly, the Brahmacharin places his feet in alidha, the archer's stance, fixes the brilliant arrow to the bowstring, and begins to stretch the bow.

Watching the way the Brahmacharin stands, holds the bow and draws back the string, and listening to the mantras that Siva recites, Arjuna instantly masters what he watches and hears. The mighty Brahmacharin unleashes the arrow to the same lake from which it was brought and, with a cry, flings the bow into that lake. Arjuna remembers the boon that Siva granted him in the vana when He came as a Kirata; he recalls the Vision of Himself that Siva showed him in the vana and knows that Bhava is pleased with him. Silently, Arjuna prays, "May all this bear fruit."

Understanding this to be his wish, Bhava blesses him with power over the Pasupatastra and the accomplishment of his vow to kill Jayadratha.

Thus having again obtained the Pasupata from the Devadeva, the invincible Arjuna, his hair standing on end, regards his vow as being already fulfilled. Full of joy, Arjuna and Krishna worship Mahadeva by bowing their heads deeply. Then, permitted by Bhava, the two shuras instantly return to their camp on Kurukshetra, in a transport of delight. Their joy is as great as that of Indra and Vishnu when those two Gods, wanting to slay Jambha, had Siva's blessing to kill the great Asura.

All this, Rajan, transpires in Arjuna's dream and Krishna's dhyana.'"

CANTO 79

ABHIMANYU-VADHA PARVA CONTINUED

"Sanjaya says, 'Krishna and Daruka pass the night in conversation until day dawns. Paniswanikas, Magadhas, Madhuparkikas and Sutas come to sing Yudhishtira's praises, as they do daily, and greet him with music and dance, while sweet-voiced singers sing melodious songs of praise for the Kuru vamsa. Skilled musicians play on mridangas, jharjharas, bheris, panavas, anakas, gomukhas, adambaras, sankhas, loud dundubhis and diverse other instruments. All this joyous sound, deep as the roar of clouds, touches the very heavens and they awaken Yudhishtira Dharmaraja, who lies asleep on his luxurious bed, from his slumber.

The king rises from his bed and proceeds to perform his morning ablutions. A hundred and eight freshly bathed young servants, all attired in white, approach the king with many golden jars filled to the brim with the purest water. Sitting at his ease on a royal throne, wearing a thin cloth, the king bathes in several kinds of water made fragrant with sandalwood and purified with mantras. Strong and well-trained servants wash and rub his shining body with water soaked with diverse kinds of medicinal herbs. He then washes himself with adhivasha water rendered fragrant by various exquisite scents. Yudhishtira ties a long cloth as white as the feathers of the swan, and kept loose before him, around his head to dry the water.

He smears his body with sandalwood-paste, drapes wildflower garlands around his majestic person, puts on clean clothes, and the Mahabaho sits facing the east, his hands joined together and silently says his morning prayers. Then with great humility, he enters the chamber in which the sacred fire is kept. He worships the agni by feeding it pieces of fine wood and with libations of ghee sanctified with mantras. He comes out and enters a second chamber, where many learned Brahmanas, all deep knowers of the Vedas, all self-restrained, purified by the study of the Vedas and by keeping vratas, are gathered after they have taken the ritual bath upon on the completion of the yagnas they have performed.

There are a thousand worshippers of the Sun, as well as eight thousand others of the same varna. The mighty-armed Yudhishtira presents them with honey, clarified butter, auspicious fruits of the best kind, a nishka of gold each, a hundred horses decked with ornaments, costly robes and other such gifts that they like, and in return receives their blessings in clear and distinguished voices. Yudhishtira also gives them gifts of cows that yield milk whenever touched, along with calves with their horns covered with gold and their hooves with silver; after which he circumambulates them in pradakshina. Now looking at and touching auspicious swastika symbols, which increase good fortune, nandyavartas made of gold, flower garlands, water-pots, the sacred fire, vessels full of sun-dried rice, other auspicious offerings, the yellow pigment prepared from the urine of the cow, auspicious and well-adorned virgins, curds, clarified butter, honey, auspicious birds and diverse other things held sacred, he finally comes into the outer chamber.

The attendants waiting in that chamber bring a wonderful round throne of gold, encrusted with pearls and lapis lazuli and overlaid with a priceless rug over which is spread another cloth of the finest loom. This seat is the handiwork of the Viswakarman himself. When the

Dharmaraja takes his place, the servants bring him all his invaluable, bright ornaments, which Yudhishtira puts on; and his magnificence is such as to sharpen the envy of his enemies.

The servants fan him with white golden-handled yak-tails luminous like the Moon and Yudhishtira is resplendent like a mass of clouds charged with lightning. Bards begin to sing his praises and panegyrists utter his eulogies; and other singers sing to the delighter of Kuru's vamsa, and their voices swell harmoniously and resonantly.

We then hear the rumble of chariot-wheels and the drumming of horses' hooves; and the noise mingles with the chiming of great elephants' bells, the blare of conches and the tread of numberless men, and the very Earth seems to tremble. One of the guards in charge of the doors, sheathed in armour, youthful in years, wearing brilliant ear-rings, and with his sword strapped to his side, enters the private apartment, kneels on the ground and, bending his head, salutes the Dharmaraja who deserves all worship. The young guardsman announces that Hrishikesa is waiting to enter.

Yudhishtira orders his servitors, "Get ready an excellent throne and prepare an arghya for him."

Krishna of Vrishni's race is welcomed warmly and seated on the fine throne. Greeting Madhava with the customary enquiries of welcome, Yudhishtira worships Krishna fervently.'"

CANTO 80

Abhimanyu-vadha Parva continued

"Sanjaya continues, 'Then the royal son of Kunti asks Krishna, "Have you spent the night happily, Madhusudana? Are all your faculties clear, O you of unfading glory?"

Krishna makes similar enquiries of Yudhishtira. Then the guardsman comes again and says that the other Kshatriya warriors are waiting to be announced. Commanded by the king, the man announces a roll of heroes, which consists of Virata, Bhimasena, Dhrishtadyumna, Satyaki, Dhrishtaketu, the ruler of the Chedis, the Maharathas Drupada and Sikhandin, the twins Nakula and Sahadeva, Chekitana, the king of the Kalikayas, Yuyutsu of Kuru's race, Uttamaujas of the Panchalas, Yudhamanyu, Subahu, and the five sons of Draupadi. These and many other Kshatriyas, approach Yudhsihtira Mahatman, that bull among Kshatriyas, and greeting him, sit down on the rich seats provided for them. Krishna and Satyaki sit together on the same wide throne.

Then in the hearing of them all, Yudhishtira addresses the lotus-eyed slayer of Madhu, and says humbly, "Relying on you alone, do we, like the Deva of a thousand eyes, seek victory in battle and eternal happiness.

You are aware, O Krishna, of how we were deprived of our kingdom, of our exile at the hands of the enemy, and our various sorrows in exile. O Lord of all, you who are compassionate to those who are devoted to you, the happiness and the very existence of all of us rest solely and entirely on you!

O you of Vrishni's vamsa, do that by which my heart will ever find its rest in you! Also do that, O Lord, by which Arjuna may fulfil his vow. Rescue us today from the sea of grief and rage that confronts us. Madhava, become today a ship for us who wish to cross the dreadful sea. The great maharatha who wants to kill the enemy in battle cannot do what his sarathy can, if the charioteer will exert himself subtly!

Janardana, you always save the Vrishnis from all danger and calamities, and you must save us from this looming distress! Sankhachakragadadhara, become a boat to rescue the sons of Pandu sunk in the fathomless Kuru-sagara.

I bow to you, O God of the lord of the gods, O you who are eternal, O supreme Destroyer, O Vishnu, O Jishnu, O Hari, O Krishna, O Vaikuntha, O best of friends! Narada described you as that ancient and best of Rishis called Narayana, who grants boons, who wields the Saranga, and who is the greatest of all Rishis. O Madhava, prove his words true!"

Krishna, most eloquent of all speakers, replies to Yudhishtira in a voice deep as that of clouds charged with rain, "In all the worlds, including Devaloka, there is no archer equal to Dhananjaya. Mahatejasvin, mahadhanurvan, of great prowess and untold genius, celebrated in battle, always fierce, Arjuna is the greatest of all men. Youthful in years, bull-necked and of long arms, he is endowed with measureless strength. His tread like a lion or a bull's, and divinely handsome he will kill all your enemies for you today.

As for myself, I will do what I can to help Arjuna consume the legions of Dhritarashtra's son like a great forest fire. This very day, Arjuna will despatch vile Jayadratha, sinner and murderer of Subhadra's son down the road from which no traveller returns. Today vultures, kites, ravening jackals and other carnivores will feed on the Saindhava's flesh. Yudhishtira, even if all the gods with Indra become his protectors today, Jayadratha will still leave this world for Yamaloka. And having slain the king of the Sindhus, Jishnu will return triumphantly to you in the evening. Dispel your grief and your heart's fever, Rajan, and be graced with calm and felicity.'""

CANTO 81

ABHIMANYU-VADHA PARVA CONTINUED

"Sanjaya says, 'While Yudhishtira, Krishna and the others thus converse together, Arjuna enters the auspicious chamber to meet Bharatottama Yudhishtira and also his friends and well-wishers. Solemnly, reverently he salutes his king and brother. Rising, Yudhishtira greets Arjuna with great affection, embracing him and sniffing the top of his head, blessing him warmly.

Smiling, Yudhishtira says, "Judging by your bright and cheerful countenance and from the fact that Krishna is well pleased with you, Arjuna, it is plain that complete and absolute victory awaits you in battle today!"

Now Arjuna says, "Be you blessed, Rajan, through Kesava's grace I have seen something entirely marvellous in the night."

To reassure his brothers and friends, Arjuna relates his dream of the night, and everything about his meeting with the three-eyed Lord Siva. All that listen are filled with amazement; they bend down and touch the earth with their heads to worship Mahadeva whose emblem is the Bull, and cry, "Uttamam! Wonderful!"

Then, at the command of the Dharmaputra, their hearts filled with fury against the enemy the Pandava warriors set out towards the battlefield. Saluting the king, Satyaki, Krishna and Arjuna, set out from Yudhishtira's tent; and Arjuna and Krishna ride together on the same chariot to Arjuna's tent. Arriving, Hrishikesa, like a professional charioteer, begins to prepare Arjuna's ratha, which flies the mark of the prince of the Vanaras. The wonderful chariot with the radiance of molten gold, whose rumble is like the deep roar of thunderheads, shines like the morning sun. Soon enough, Krishna, now wearing armour, comes to inform Partha, who has finished his morning prayers, that his chariot is ready. Arjuna Kiritin, clad in golden mail, his bow and magical quivers in hand, circumambulates the chariot in grave pradakshina.

Now his Brahmanas, mature in tapasya, gyana and years, always engaged in the performance of pujas and yagnas, with passions ever restrained, adore and bless Arjuna. He climbs into his great ratha, which has already been sanctified with mantras to give him victory in battle; he mounts his chariot like Surya Deva ascending the Eastern mountain. Arjuna, the greatest of all maharathas, is truly like the blazing Sun God upon the breast of Meru.

Arjuna, Satyaki and Krishna mount the chariot, like the twin Aswins riding the same chariot with Indra when they attended Saryati's yagna. Govinda, greatest of maharathas, takes the horses' reins even like Matali took the reins of Indra's steeds when he rode to slay Vritra. Mounted on that best of chariots with his two friends, Partha rides out to kill the king of the Sindhus; he goes forth like Soma rising into the sky with Budha and Sukra, to destroy the darkness of night, or like Indra going forth with Varuna and Surya to the great battle against the Asuras when the Daityas abducted Brihaspati's wife Tara.

Bards and musicians sing the praises of heroic Arjuna, as he rides forth to the sound of musical instruments and auspicious hymns of good omen. The sonorous voices of the vabdhis and magadhis uttering resonant blessings for victory and wishing for a triumphant day, mingling with the sounds of the musical instruments, are deeply gratifying to those Kshatriyas. An auspicious and fragrant breeze blows from behind Partha, vitalising him and enervating his enemies. And many propitious omens of various kinds appear, indicating victory for the Pandavas and defeat for your warriors!

Seeing these portents of victory, Arjuna says to the great archer Satyaki, now in his own chariot on the right, "Yuyudhana! Look at all the auspicious omens around us. I will surely have victory today, O bull of Sini's vamsa. I will ride straight to where Jayadratha waits, fully expecting me to send him to Yamaloka. Satyaki, today it is as much your duty to protect Yudhishtira from Drona as it is mine to ride out and kill the Saindhava. You must guard him as I myself would. I do not see anyone in the world who can vanquish you, for you are Krishna's equal in battle. The king of the Devas himself cannot defeat you. Reposing this burden on you, and on maharatha Pradyumna, I can hunt Jayadratha down with no anxiety shadowing my heart.

O Satwata, dearest friend, have no fear for me. You must wholeheartedly protect the king. Where this Krishna Mahabaho is, and where I am, together, not the slightest danger can ever befall either him or me."

Satyaki, the Parantapa replies, "Tathaastu!" He then rides to where Yudhishtira is.'"

CANTO 82

JAYADRATHA-VADHA PARVA

"Dhritarashtra says, 'On the day after Abhimanyu was killed, what did the grief-stricken Pandavas do? Who among my warriors gave them battle? Knowing, as they did, the awesome prowess Arjuna, tell me how the Kauravas, having committed such a heinous crime, could remain unafraid? How could they venture even to look at him as Arjuna Naravyaghra advanced upon them like all-destroying Death himself in fury, burning with grief at the murder of his son? Seeing the maharatha with the image of Hanuman on his banner, grieving for his dead son and brandishing his awesome bow, what did my warriors do? What, O Sanjaya, has happened to Duryodhana?

A great sorrow overwhelms us today and I no longer hear any sounds of joy. The enchanting strains of music and celebration that we once heard from Jayadratha's palace here are alas all fallen silent.

In Duryodhana's camp, we no more hear the sounds of countless vabdhis and magadhis singing my sons' praises nor the songs of musicians or the chiming of dancers' anklets. Earlier, such sounds would fall incessantly upon my ears. Alas, as they are plunged in grief, I do not any longer hear these merry noises. Previously, Sanjaya, while sitting in the home of Somadatta, who is devoted to truth, I would always such delightful sounds. Alas, how destitute of punya I am, for I hear the palaces of my sons today echoing instead with the sounds of grief and lamentations, and none full of the old life, energy and joy. In the mansions of Vivimsati, Durmukha, Chitrasena, Vikarna and my other sons, I do not hear a single sound of cheer, which they were filled with in the past.

The great archer Drona's son Aswatthaman, who is the refuge of my sons and upon whom Brahmanas, Kshatriyas, Vaisyas and a large number of disciples waited, who takes pleasure day and night, in talk, in debate and animated disputation, in the stirring music of different instruments and in various kinds of delightful songs, whom many among the Kurus, the Pandavas and the Satwatas worship—alas, his home is utterly silent today, and no singers sing there or dancers ply their sublime art.

Alas, we no longer hear the clamour of boisterous celebrations that echo in the camp of Vinda and Anuvinda every evening. Today in the camp of the Kaikeyas, we do not hear any songs or hand clapping in which their soldiers, at their music, dance and revelry, daily indulged.

Ah, we no longer hear the reverberant chanting of priests proficient in the performance of yagnas, men who are repositories of pujas, who wait upon Somadatta's son, Bhurisravas. The virile twanging of bowstrings, the sounds of Vedic chanting, the whistling of spears and the humming strokes of swords; the rumble of chariot-wheels, all of which were heard unceasingly in the abode of Drona: we hear none of these from there today. Sanjaya, today we no longer hear the swell of music from diverse kingdoms, or the rhythms and harmonies of musical instruments, which never failed to fill Drona's great and sacred home.

When Janardana of unfading glory came from Upaplavya out of his compassion for every living creature, seeking peace, O Suta, I said to the evil Duryodhana, "My son, use Krishna as the means to arrive at an amicable understanding with the Pandavas. I think it is time to make peace, so do as I say. If you spurn Krishna, who now begs you for peace and entreats you for my welfare, you will never find victory."

But Duryodhana refused Krishna, the bull among all the bowmen of Dasarha's race, Krishna who sought Duryodhana's own good. And by doing this, my foolish son embraced disaster and tragedy. Seized by Death himself, my evil-hearted prince would not obey me but followed Dusasana and Karna instead, into the jaws of doom. I did not approve of the game of dice. Nor did Vidura, Jayadratha, Bhishma, Salya, Bhurisravas, Purumitra, Jaya, Aswatthaman, Kripa or Drona, O Sanjaya! If my son had paid heed to their counsel, he would then have lived for ever in happiness and peace with his kinsmen and friends.

I said to Duryodhana: Charming and delightful in their speech, always saying what is pleasing to their kinsmen, high-born, loved by all, and wise, the sons of Pandu are sure to find success and felicity. The man, who keeps his eye on dharma always, and in all places, will find happiness and he will wins great rewards and blessings after his death. The Pandavas are noble and accomplished; they are able and deserve to enjoy half the Earth. The Earth girthed by the seven seas, is as much their ancestral possession as it is of the Kurus. Once they win back sovereignty, the Pandavas will never deviate from the path of dharma.

O child, I have kinsmen to whom the Pandavas will always listen: Salya, Somadatta, the Dharmatman Bhishma, Drona, Vikarna, Balhika, Kripa, and many others among the Bharatas who are illustrious and revered because of their years. If they speak to them on your behalf, the Pandavas will surely do what they ask. Do you think, for a moment, that anyone who is with them will counsel them otherwise? Krishna will never abandon the path of dharma and the Pandavas are all obedient to him. My words of dharma, too, those Kshatriyas will never disobey, for the Pandavas are all righteous men.

Piteously lamenting, Suta, I spoke to my son. Fool that he is, his heart full of darkness, he did not listen to me! I believe that all this is the malignant and inescapable influence of Kaala! Where Vrikodara and Arjuna are, the Vrishni hero Satyaki, Uttamaujas of the Panchalas, the invincible Yudhamanyu, the irrepressible Dhrishtadyumna, the unvanquished Sikhandin, the Asmakas, the Kekayas, Kshatradharman of the Somakas, the ruler of the Chedis, Chekitana, Vibhu, the son of the lord of the Kasis, the sons of Draupadi, Virata, the mighty maharatha Drupada, the Purushavyaghras Nakula and Sahadeva and, most of all, the slayer of Madhu, Krishna himself, is—who is there in this world, or even the next, that can fight them and expect to live?

Who else is there who would dare resist these my formidable enemies when they summon their devastras in war, save the witless Duryodhana, Karna, Sakuni the son of Subala, and Dusasana their base fourth? For I do not see a fifth who is so blind and senseless! They who have Vishnu himself driving their chariot, clad in armour and reins in his divine hands; they who have Arjuna for their warrior—they can never find defeat!

Does Duryodhana not remember my pleas and implorations now, when it is too late? You say that the invincible Bhishma has been cut down. Surely now, my sons grimly recall the prophetic words uttered by the far-seeing Vidura, and lament their folly! Seeing his army overwhelmed by Sini's grandson Satyaki and Arjuna, and seeing their countless empty chariots, my sons surely shed bitter tears today. Ah! Sanjaya, terrible Arjuna will devour my troops even like a raging fire fanned by the gusting wind consumes a heap of dry grass at the close of winter.

Sanjaya, you are a most accomplished narrator. Tell me everything that transpires in the evening after they committed the great wrong to Partha. When Abhimanyu was killed, what was their state of mind? After having grievously offended the Gandivi, my warriors cannot face him in battle. What measures do Duryodhana and Karna decide to take to contain Arjuna? What do Dusasana and Subala's son do? O Sanjaya, what has overtaken all my sons is surely because of the sins of Duryodhana, who walks the way of avarice, whose heart and mind are full of evil, whose judgment anger perverts, who blindly covets sovereignty, who is foolish besides and his reason lost to greed and anger. Tell me, O Sanjaya, what does Duryodhana do now? Are the preparations he makes and the plans he has shortsighted or well-judged?'"

CANTO 83

JAYADRATHA-VADHA PARVA CONTINUED

"Sanjaya says, 'I will tell you everything, as I saw it with my own eyes. Listen carefully, for your own guilt in this war is great. Just as an embankment is useless after the waters of the field have drained away, Rajan, your lamentations now are useless! Bharatarishabha, do not grieve. Wonderful and terrible are the decrees of Time the Destroyer, and they cannot be violated. Do not lament, for this is not a recent development. If you had restrained both Yudhishtira and your sons from the game of dice, this calamity would never have overwhelmed you. Again, if you had stopped both the sides who were inflamed by anger, this tragedy would never have occurred.

Indeed, if you had once urged the Kurus to kill the wayward Duryodhana, this disaster would never have come to you, and the Pandavas, the Panchalas, the Vrishnis and the other kings would have never had cause to blame you. Again, if you had done your duty as a father, shown Duryodhana the path of dharma, and led him to tread the way of righteousness, this misfortune would never have beset you.

You are the wisest man on earth. Forsaking sanatana dharma, how could you follow the counsels of Duryodhana, Karna and Sakuni? Therefore, Rajan, these your lamentations are in truth wedded to worldly wealth, and seem to me to be like honey mixed with poison. Time was when Krishna himself did not regard Yudhishtira or Drona, as much as he respected you. However, when, he found you to have fallen from Rajadharma, Krishna has ceased to look upon you with respect.

Your sons spoke harshly, vilely, to the sons of Pritha, and you sat silent. Nemesis for that grave sin of omission has now overwhelmed you, O Anagha, and your kingdom is in danger.

At best, you will find the shame and bitterness of ruling over a world bestowed upon you by the Pandavas. It is the virtuous Pandus who added to the kingdom and also the fame that the Kurus enjoy. These achievements, however, became fruitless and barren for them when they encountered your greed, for you deprived them of even their ancestral kingdom.

Now, Rajan, when the war has begun, you absolve yourself of all wrongdoing and censure your sons, pointing out their various faults. And this is not becoming. While they fight, Kshatriyas leave off care for their very lives, and plunge fearlessly into the Pandavas' vyuhas. Why, who but the Kauravas would dare fight and army which Krishna, Arjuna, Satyaki and Vrikodara lead? Which mortal archer is there that would dare fight them who have Arjuna for their warrior, Krishna for their adviser and Satyaki and Vrikodara for their protectors? Only your sons and their allies.

The friendly kings, full of heroism and always conscious of Kshatriya dharma, do all that they can, taking their lives in their hands. So now listen to everything that transpires in the savage war between the Naravyaghras, the Kurus and the Pandavas.'"

CANTO 84

JAYADRATHA-VADHA PARVA CONTINUED

"Sanjaya says, 'When the night ends and dawn breaks, Drona begins to array his akshauhinis for the battle of the momentous day. One hears diverse sounds, of enraged shuras' voices raised in shouts and roars, all of them eager to be at the enemy and spill blood. Some stretch their bows some strum their bowstrings and some draw deep breaths. And many of them roar in challenge, "Where is Dhananjaya?"

Many warriors throw their glinting swords high into the air and then catch them again, and brandish them, naked blades the colour of the sky, keenly honed, and with beautifully wrought hilts. One sees thousands of brave warriors, their skills perfected through years of practice, swordsmen and bowmen, all keened for battle. Some whirl their great maces decked with bells, smeared with sandalwood paste encrusted with gold and diamonds, and challengingly demand that the sons of Pandu come forth to fight. Other warriors with massive bodies and arms like pillars, intoxicated with the pride of their strength, obscure the sky with their spiked clubs that resemble a forest of great stakes raised in honour of Indra.

Still others, heroes all, wear gorgeous vanamalas, and armed with various other kinds of weapons, takes their positions across the field of fate, and they also roar, "Where is Arjuna? Where is Govinda? Where is proud Bhima? Where are their allies?"

Drona blows his conch, and urging his horses to great speed, moves everywhere with amazing celerity as he deploys all his divisions. When all the troops, every man of them ardent for battle, have taken their stations, Drona says to Jayadratha, "Somadatta's son Bhurisravas, maharatha Karna, Aswatthaman, Salya, Vrishasena and Kripa, with a hundred thousand horsemen, sixty thousand chariots, four and ten thousand elephants in musth, one and twenty thousand foot-soldiers clad in mail, will be positioned behind me to a distance of twelve krosas. You will be behind all of these. When the very gods with Vasava at their head will not be able to attack you where you are, what can the Pandavas do? Take comfort, Jayadratha, O king of the Sindhus."

Thus does Drona comfort Jayadratha who then takes himself moves to the place Drona indicates, surrounded by many Gandhara warriors and with many mail-clad foot-soldiers armed with paasas, nooses, all ready give their all in battle. Jayadratha's well-trained chariot-horses are all decked with chamari yak-tails and ornaments of gold. Seven thousand such horses and three thousand other steeds of the Sindhu breed go with him.

Your son Durmarshana, eager for combat, stations himself at the head of all the Kaurava troops today, along with a thousand five hundred infuriated elephants of awesome size, covered in mail, and all ridden by well-trained mahamatras. Your two other sons, Dusasana and Vikarna, take up their positions among the vanguard.

The vyuha that Drona forms- part sakata and part a circle is full forty-eight miles long and twenty wide, front to rear. Drona arrays that great formation with countless heroic kings, in a sea of chariots, horses, elephants and foot-soldiers. Behind the sakata vyuha, the formidable cart, is yet another impregnable legion in the form of a lotus, a Padma vyuha.

And buried deep that lotus is another dense vyuha, the suchimukha, the needle formation.

Having formed his mighty vyuha thus, Drona takes up his own station. The mouth of the needle is held by the great archer Kritavarman. Next to Kritavarman, stands the ruler of the Kambojas and Jalasandha, and then Duryodhana and Karna. Behind them thousands of dauntless Kshatriyas stand ready for fierce battle, specifically position to protect the eye of the most crucial suchimukha. Behind them all, Rajan, surrounded by a teeming force, is Jayadratha at the far end of the needle.

At the head of the Sakata, is Drona, barring the way into it; behind him the chief of the Bhojas protects Bharadwaja's son. Clad in white armour, with a superb helmet, broad chested and with mighty arms, Drona stands tall, stretching his great bow, like the Death himself in wrath. Seeing Drona's chariot graced with a beautiful standard, bearing red sacrificial altar and a black deerskin, the Kauravas are filled with joy.

Seeing the awesome vyuha Drona forms, which resembles the ocean itself in agitation, the Siddhas and the Charanas in the sky are filled with wonder and all beings think that the vast formation would devour the very Earth with her mountains, seas and forests, Bhumi abounding with life and creatures and everything else she bears. And seeing the mighty and wonderful sakata, packed dense with chariots, foot-soldiers, horses and elephants, trumpeting dreadfully, and hearing its great clamour, which could rive the hearts of his enemies, Duryodhana exults!'"

CANTO 85

Jayadratha-vadha Parva continued

"Sanjaya says, 'After the akshauhinis of the Kuru army are thus arrayed, a tumult arises from the beating of drums and mridangas, the roars and fierce shouts and the sound of different musical instruments, the blowing of conches. The awful uproar makes one's hair stand on end as the Bharata heroes eager for battle, slowly advance. Then the hour called Rudra sets in and Arjuna makes his appearance.

Many thousands of ravens and crows, O Bhaarata, sport in front of Arjuna's chariot. Various animals, giving terrible cries and inauspicious jackals begin to scream and howl on our right, as we went forward into battle. Thousands of blazing meteors fall out of a clear sky with loud noises, and all the Earth trembles on the dreadful occasion. Dry winds blow in all directions, peals of thunder crack the sky, driving gravel and gusts of little pebbles ahead of him, as Kunti's son comes to begin the days' battle.

Nakula's son Satanika, and Dhrishtadyumna, the two wise and expert warriors, array the Pandava legions into an attacking vyuha. Accompanied by a thousand chariots, a hundred elephants, three thousand Kshatriyas, and ten thousand foot-soldiers, which cover the length of fifteen hundred bows, your son Durmarshana takes up his position at the very van of all the troops, and says, "Like the continent resisting the surging sea, I will today contain the wielder of Gandiva, that irresistible Parantapa in battle today. Today let everyone witness the raging Dhananjaya collide with me, like one stone mountain against another. You maharathas eager for battle, stay back and watch me fight all the Pandavas by myself, watch me enhance my honour and fame today!"

Your noble son, the daring archer says this and stands there prepared and full of valour, surrounded by many other great bowmen.

Then, like an angry Yama, or Vajradhari Indra himself, or like Death's irresistible self armed with his cudgel and urged on by Time, or like unruffled Mahadeva armed with his trident, or like Varuna with his paasa, or the blazing fire which consumes all creation at the end of the Yuga, the slayer of the Nivatakavachas, inflamed with rage and swelling with might, the ever-victorious Vijaya, clad in mail, armed with a sword, wearing a golden coronet, adorned with garlands of white flowers, attired in white robes, his arms decked with beautiful angadas and ears with brilliant kundalas, faithful to dharma and determined to fulfil his great vow, incomparable Arjuna mounts his incomparable chariot.

The incarnate Nara, with Narayana for his sarathy, holding his Gandiva, shines as brilliantly on Kurukshetra as the risen sun. Setting his ratha, Rajan, at the very van of his army, where densest showers of arrows will fall, Dhananjaya blows an echoing, deafening gives a blast on his conch the Devadatta. Then Krishna, too, fearlessly blows with his great Panchajanya—peal after peal of booming thunder. And all your warriors quail and tremble at the massive twin sound, their hearts feel faint within them and their hair stands on end.

Just as the sound of the thunder fills living creatures with fright, even so does the chasmal booming of those conches terrify your warriors; and all their animals helplessly urinate and excrete. All your army with its animals is filled with dread, Rajan, and the limbs of your fighting men turn weak. Some among them even faint.

And then the Hanuman in his terrifying aspect on Arjuna's banner, his mouth agape, as well all the fierce spirits and creatures that surround him give vent to the most fearful and macabre sounds, further dismaying your men. But then Drona and the other maharathas of your army collect themselves, raise their conches, horns and anakas and blow resoundingly on them, and the other fighting men follow suit beating drums, clashing cymbals together, and letting out great cheers and loud yells and roars, so that the wave of terror blows away and they are emboldened again. Sounds of other instruments fill earth and sky and further defiant roaring and the loud clapping of hands and armpits. Your maharathas roar leonine challenges at their adversaries and your army is again filled with exhilaration. As that tumult rises, an uproar that raises fear in the hearts of the timid, Arjuna, the son of Pakasasana, filled with great delight, says to him of Dasarha's race, "Urge the horses, O Hrishikesa, to where Durmarshana stands. I will cut our way through his elephant legion and break into the enemy army."

Krishna flicks his reins over his gandharva horses' necks and flashes ahead at Durmarshana. Fierce and tremendous is the encounter that erupts there between one and the many, a savage encounter that destroys chariots, elephants and men. Like a cloud lashing down torrential rain on a mountain breast, Arjuna inundates his enemies with thick showers of shafts. Showing great lightness of hand, the opposing maharathas swiftly envelop Krishna and Dhananjaya in clouds of arrows.

Quickly incensed, Mahabaho Partha begins to slough off great chariot-warriors' heads at his supreme will; he strews the field with noble and handsome heads, decked with earrings and turbans, their lips bitten through, and the eyes upon their faces still dark with anger. Ah, the scattered heads are resplendent like lotuses clipped off their stems, lying everywhere.

Golden coats of mail dyed with gore lie all over the field, looking like cloud masses charged with lightning. The sound, Rajan, of severed heads falling onto the earth resembles the falling of ripened palmyra fruit. In weird pageant, headless trunks arise, some holding bows in hand and some with naked swords upraised in the very act of striking. Those valiant warriors, who swarm forward to have great Arjuna's life, never know when he strikes their heads off!

Then, quickly, the horrific and magnificent field is scattered by the absolute and sublime genius of Arjuna's incredible archery with not just the heads of great warriors but also those of horses and the trunks of elephants, while Kurukshetra rings with their screams, as well the arms, legs and other limbs of both Kshatriyas and their beasts of war. Bloody chaos sweeps your army, O king.

"This one is Partha!"

"Where is Partha? Here is Partha!"

Obsessed with just the single thought of Arjuna, these cries rise from your army. Deprived by Time of their reason and very senses, they see the whole world as being full of just Partha, innumerable Arjunas everywhere. And striking out and loosing their arrows at one another, many of your men perish. Why, some kill themselves in their delirium! With woeful cries, many heroes, not in their right minds, covered with blood and in agony, lay themselves down, calling out piteously to their friends and kinsmen.

Arms, bearing short arrows, or lances, or darts, or swords, or battle-axes, or pointed stakes, or scimitars, or bows, or spears, or other shafts, or maces, and cased in armour, and adorned with angadas and other ornaments, arms that look like large snakes, that resemble thick clubs, hacked off from trunks with mighty weapons leap from their owners, jerk and thrash about with great force, as if in separate rage of their own. Every last man who attacks Partha perishes, body pierced with the fatal shafts of that transcendent shura. While he seems to dance in his ratha, fleeting everywhere, and his bow seems always drawn in a magic circle, no adversary can find the minutest chance to strike him. The speed with which he draws, fits them to his bow, and looses them is inscrutable, a single uninterrupted blur, and fills all his enemies with wonder.

Phalguna strikes elephants and elephant-riders, horses and horsemen, rathikas and their charioteers. There is no one among his enemies, whether facing him, trying to shoot him down from a distance, or wheeling about, whom the son of Pandu does not kill. Even as the sun rising in the sky destroys a thick darkness does Arjuna annihilate Durmarshana's elephant-legion with his uncanny missiles fletched with kanka plumes.

Swiftly, the field that your troops occupy looks like the earth strewn with grey hills at the hour of the pralaya. Just as no creatures can gaze at the midday sun, Dhananjaya's enemies cannot look upon the face of Arjuna tejasvin ablaze. Stricken by Partha's arrow storms, your troops break and flee the dreadful Kshatriya.

Like a towering wind dispersing a bank of clouds, Partha rides at the Kaurava army and puts it to bloody rout, and truly none of them can even look at him as he razes them at will. Whipping and spurring their horses to greater speed, prodding them with their bows to fly faster, with threatening growls and roars at the helpless creatures, their eyes wild and full of fear, your cavalry, chariot-warriors, and your foot-soldiers as well, beset by Arjuna, flee in every direction.

Others, who ride elephants, lumber away from him by digging their sharp hooks and goads cruelly into the sides of their great mounts. Such bedlam grips the field, such panic, that many who seek to escape him run straight at Arjuna instead and are consumed by him. Awful fright, confusion and dismay seize your men entirely.'"

CANTO 86

JAYADRATHA-VADHA PARVA CONTINUED

"Dhritarashtra asks, 'When the van of my army is slaughtered by the Kiritin and falls apart and flees, who are the heroes that stand up to him? Do any of them actually fight Arjuna, or do they all abandon courage and run back into the sakata vyuha, to hide behind the fearless Drona, that immovable wall?'

Sanjaya replies, "When Indra's son breaks like a gale of death upon the frontline of your army, Rajan, many Kshatriyas are killed or run. Not one can even look at Arjuna's alight, let alone fight him.

But then, your son Dusasana, Rajan, who has watched the rout, and your men dying and fleeing, is filled with wrath and he dashes straight at Arjuna. Your fierce son, wearing a shimmering coat of golden mail, his head covered by a turban, surrounds the rampaging Partha with his own formidable elephant legion, a force that looks as if it can devour the very world. The Earth, the points of compass and the sky seem to be entirely filled with the sound of the elephant's bells, the blare of conches, the twanging of bowstrings and the deep grunts and bellows of the tuskers.

Now a pitched and ferocious battle ensues. Seeing the angry beasts, with trunks extended, thundering down on him, like winged mountains urged on with goads, Dhananjaya throws back his head and gives a shattering lion's roar. Then, in the twinkling of an eye, he begins to decimate the elephant legion. Like a makara plunging into a surging ocean, Arjuna wades into the elephant-host.

The Vijaya is like the apocalyptic Sun that rises infracting every law of direction and hour on the day of the pralaya. In moments, at his unearthly archery, men and elephants alike have their spirits broken and are deranged by the elemental force they come up against, the cosmic tempest that is Kunti's son. The sound of horses' hooves, the maddening rattle of chariot-wheels, the shouts of warriors, the twanging bowstrings, the cacophony of diverse musical instruments, and most of all the blare of the Panchajanya and the Devadatta and the deafening twang of the Gandiva serves to dement your forces even further.

And Savyasachin shreds men and elephants with his arrow that are like snakes of virulent poison, every one of them claiming a Kaurava life, man's or beast's. Thousands and thousands of deadly shafts flare from the Gandiva spraying blood everywhere, desiccating your elephant legion. Countless great grey beasts fall, shaking the sacred field, their screams echoing in the vaults of the sky; they fall like the mountain of old when Indra sheared their golden wings.

Some hulking beasts he shoots savagely through their mouths, others through their round temporal lobes, and the elephants cry out like cranes as they die. And now, Arjuna begins to clip the heads from the necks of the warriors mounted on the elephants with unerring arrows like lopping lotus flowers from their stalks. The heads shining with earrings, continually falling onto the earth, resemble a multitude of lotuses that Partha offers to his gods. While numberless elephants blunder across the field, one sees warriors hanging from their backs, stripped of armour, grievously wounded, painted in blood as if in a picture.

In some cases, he kills two or three warriors with a single arrow plumed with beautiful feathers and they plunge down to the ground. And so many elephants excoriated by long shafts, continue to fall, vomiting blood, and their riders tumble from their backs. Partha destroys standards, bows, bowstrings, yokes and shafts of the chariot-warriors that oppose him. And still no one can discern when Arjuna draws his arrows, when he fixes them to his bowstring, when he draws back the string or when he shoots them. All that they see is Partha seemingly dancing on his ratha with his bow always drawn to a circle.

Elephants fall like ranges of hills, one after the other, gored deep, immediately as they are struck, and the blood they vomit seeps across the field of dharma. In the midst of that great carnage, one continues to see innumerable headless trunks standing upright, though their arms have also been dissevered and lie about with bows in grasp, their fingers are cased in leather, some holding swords, and adorned with striking angadas and other golden ornaments.

Kurukshetra is copiously strewn with innumerable upaskaras, adhishthanas, shafts, crowns, crushed chariot-wheels, broken akshas and yokes, warriors armed with shields, bows, wildflower garlands, different sparkling ornaments, fine robes and broken standards. The Earth there assumes a most surreal aspect from the slain elephants, horses and the fallen Kshatriyas. And absolutely routed by Arjuna, Dusasana's forces turn tail. Himself direly injured and in great pain, and now stricken with such terror as he never expected, Dusasana also flees the battle and seeks shelter in the sakata vyuha behind Drona.'"

CANTO 87

Jayadratha-vadha Parva continued

"Sanjaya says, 'After annihilating Dusasana's forces, Arjuna, never pausing, sweeps on towards Drona, for his quarry Jayadratha lies beyond the Acharya and is still far. Nearing Drona at the lip of the sakata vyuha, at Krishna's behest, Arjuna folds his hands to his old master and says, "Wish me well, O Brahmana, and bless me, saying Swasti. Through your grace, I would pierce this unassailable vyuha. I tell you truly, O sinless one, you are like my father to me, or Yudhishtira, or even Krishna. Maharishi, I deserve your blessing and protection even as Aswatthaman does. And with your blessing, I want to kill Jayadratha the Saindhava today. O lord, see that my vow is accomplished."

The Acharya, smiling, replies, "Arjuna, you will not be able to strike at Jayadratha without first vanquishing me."

With this, still smiling, in a flash Drona covers Arjuna, his ratha, horses, standard and charioteer with a great burst of arrows. Arjuna cuts down the flurry of shafts, and strikes his master with nine thought-swift arrows. Drona, too, cuts down Partha's arrows in flight, and pierces both Krishna and Arjuna with clutches of venomous bolts like fire.

Then, while Arjuna is still thinking of destroying Drona's bow with his arrows, the great Brahmana, quicker than thinking, breaks the Pandava's bowstring, and draws blood from him, his horses and sarathy, and cuts slivers from his flagstaff, still with the superior smile on his lips.

Arjuna restrings his bow in a blink and shrugging off his initial hesitation unleashes a storm of six hundred blinding shafts at Drona, as if they were just a single barb; next moment, he looses another seven hundred searing arrows, and then another thousand, all in the space of a wish. He is still not done and follows these with a full ten thousand light like blazing thunderbolts, razing so many warriors of Drona's stolid vyuha, and horses and elephants as well. Maharathas fall out of their great chariots, their horses, standards, weapons and lives lost.

Elephants founder like mountain peaks, or cloud masses, or like towering palaces, loosened, dispersed and incinerated by thunder, wind and fire. Struck by Arjuna's arrows, thousands of horses collapse like swans upon the breast of Himavat struck down by the force of a sudden flashflood. Like the Sun that rises at the end of the Yuga drying up the oceans with his rays turned murderous, the son of Pandu obliterates a vast number of chariot-warriors, cavalry, elephants and foot-soldiers.

Then, like clouds covering that fulminant Sun, the Drona-cloud covers the Pandava-sun with lashing arrow showers; Drona obscures the thick swath of shafts with which Arjuna covers the great Kuru Kshatriyas of the sakata vyuha. The Acharya strikes Dhananjaya deep through his breast with a long shaft unleashed with awful ferocity, an arrow that will take the life of any adversary. Great Arjuna trembles at the force of that barb, his limbs feel faint; he shakes like a mountain during an earthquake.

But only for a moment, after which Indra's son, like whom there is no warrior, in heaven or earth, is back to himself and strikes his forbidding teacher with a volley of golden-winged missiles. Drona, unperturbed, strikes Krishna with five bolts, Arjuna with seventy-three and his standard with three. Having the better of his disciple, in a wink Drona mantles Arjuna, his chariot and sarathy entirely in a dense cloud of arrows. We see the shafts of Bharadwaja's son fly and fall in unbroken lines and his bow present the wonderful aspect of being incessantly drawn to a circle. His vicious projectiles, winged with kanka feathers, fall with the least pause on Dhananjaya and Vasudeva.

Krishna watches the soaring battle between Arjuna and Drona for a short time, then says to his warrior, "Partha we must not waste time here for Jayadratha awaits. You must ride past Drona and on towards your quarry."

Partha replies, "As you will, O Krishna!"

Now they keep Drona to their right and ride swiftly past him, which Arjuna continues to inundate with his arrows. Drona cries to Arjuna, "Where are you going, O Pandava! Is it not true that you never stop fighting until you have defeated your enemy?"

Arjuna answers, "You are my guru and not my enemy. I am your sishya and, so, like your son. There is no man in this world that can vanquish you in battle."

With this Arjuna flares on, cleaving your army, bringing death with him. The noble Panchala princes, Yudhamanyu and Uttamaujas, follow him to protect his chariot wheels.

Rajan, they find themselves facing Jaya and Kritavarman of the Satwata vamsa, and the king of the Kambojas, and Srutayus, who have ten thousand maharathas between them. Clad in glittering mail, a master of all the different forms of warfare, prepared to lose his life, the mighty and brave Abhishahas, the Surasenas, the Sibis, the Vasatis, the Mavellakas, the Lalithyas, the Kaikeyas, the Madrakas, the Narayana Gopalas and the various tribes of the Kambojas whom Karna once vanquished, all swarm recklessly at the speeding Arjuna, who comes among them in fury like the great leader of an elephant herd, eager to crush them all, to consume their entire army.

A savage battle erupts between all those heroes on the one side and Arjuna on the other, making one's hair stand on end. Like a whole host of powerful specifics resisting a raging disease, they combine to stop the inexorable Pandava flaring ahead to have Jayadratha's life.'"

CANTO 88

Jayadratha-vadha Parva continued

"Sanjaya says, 'Drona swiftly turns his chariot and rides after Arjuna, whom the others attempt to hold in some check. But the son of Pandu is like an army of dread plagues by himself and the arrows that blaze from his Gandiva like rays from the Sun razing those that come in his way. He cuts down warhorses, mauls chariots and riders, brings down elephants, cuts down royal chatras and shatters the wheels of countless rathas. Soon, your men, bloodied, their nerve broken, flee from the irresistible, unearthly storm that is Dhananjaya.

Thus does the furious contention between the massed Kuru warriors and Arjuna unfold, a gory dream in another dimension of pure war, which is shrouded in arrows and where the resplendent Vijaya harries his enemies with inspired perfect archery. Steadfastly devoted to dharma and determined to fulfill his vow, he attacks Drona who has flashed up on his ratha drawn by red horses. The Acharya strikes his disciple with twenty-five immaculate shafts that can eviscerate an enemy; Arjuna cuts them all down. Partha quickly invokes the Brahmastra and confounds Drona's deadly fusillades.

And now we witness Drona's supernal genius unbridled, for Arjuna, putting forth his own, cannot pierce the Acharya with a single shaft. Like a mass of clouds letting fall torrents of rain, Drona lashes down a ceaseless cascade of vicious barbs on the Partha-mountain. Tejasvin Arjuna receives his master's downpour by invoking the shielding Brahmastra and truncates Drona's searing shafts with his own.

The dreadful Brahmana, aroused, strikes Swetavahana with twenty-five arrows and Vasudeva with seventy, barbs that pierce their torsos and arms. Partha serenely contains his invincible Acharya, who rages like the fire at the end of the Yuga.

Nimbly avoiding Drona's brilliant and brutal onslaught, Arjuna begins to slaughter the Bhoja host. Turning away from Drona who stands immovable like the Mainaka mountain, Arjuna rides between Kritavarman and Sudakshina the Kamboja king. Kritavarman, lord of the Bhojas, calmly strikes Partha with ten scorching shafts, kanka-feathered, but Arjuna stuns the Satwata shura with a hundred and three arrows shots in the space of a thought.

Recovering quickly, the Bhojaraja, with a laugh like rolling thunder, strikes Arjuna and Krishna with twenty-five arrows each. Arjuna breaks Kritavarman's bow and stabs him with twenty-one arrows like blazing flames or angry snakes of virulent poison. Kritavarman seizes up another bow and pierces Arjuna's chest, O Bhaarata, with ten arrows swift as light; Partha bloodies his powerful antagonist's breast with nine shafts shot in a neat circle.

Again, Krishna sees his Kshatriya held up by Kritavarman, who is a Satwata fighting for Duryodhana, and cries, "Show Kritavarman no mercy! Do not think of your kinship with him. Kill him, Arjuna!"

Abandoning affection and restraint, Arjuna staggers Kritavarman with some archery for which the Bhoja has no response; Krishna dashes ahead past Kritavarman towards the Kambojas. In red-eyed fury, Kritavarman turns his frustration and ire on the two Panchala princes who guard Arjuna's rear as they follow him everywhere. The Bhoja hero strikes Yudhamanyu with three violent barbs and Uttamaujas with four. The heroic brothers instantly pierce him deep with ten shafts each, and break his bow and cut down his standard as well. Roaring, Kritavarman, son of Hridika, sweeps up another bow and rives the bows of both brothers and covers them with his scathing arrows. Yudhamanyu and Uttamaujas, quick as thinking, take up fresh bows and loose twin ferocious invectives of shafts at the Satwata.

Arjuna forges ahead, piercing deeper into the enemy army, while the Panchala princes occupy Kritavarman, who holds them up. Swetavahana attacks the akshauhinis drawn up against him but does not kill Kritavarman although he is within reach. Seeing Partha's violent progress the brave king Srutayudha rushes at him, brandishing his big bow and strikes Partha with three arrows, Janardana with seventy and Partha's standard with a razor-headed barb. Arjuna retaliates in fury, piercing his antagonist deep with ninety straight shafts, like a mahout a mighty elephant with his ankush.

Srutayudha, undimmed, finds Arjuna with seventy-seven thunderbolts but Arjuna breaks his bow, shreds his quiver, and in wrath strikes him deep through his chest with seven heavy shafts. An incensed Srutayudha takes up another bow and drills Vasava' son with nine barbs, his arms and chest. Laughing all the while, the Pandava unleashes a gale of thousands of arrows, killing his horses and charioteer. Never pausing, Arjuna bores his antagonist with seventy arrows. Leaping down from his useless chariot, valiant Srutayudha rushes roaring at Arjuna with his mace raised high.

The heroic king Srutayudha is the son of Varuna and Parnasa, the mighty river of cool, limpid waters. His mother, Rajan, once begged Varuna, "Let my son never be killed on earth."

Varuna, well pleased with her, had promised, "I will give him an ayudha, by which your son will not be killed on the ground by any enemy. No man can have immortality, O greatest of rivers, for everyone who is born must inevitably die. This child, however, will always be invincible in war through the power of this weapon. Let the fear in your heart be dispelled."

Varuna then gave Srutayudha, with mantras, a mace, and with his gada, Srutayudha became invincible on earth. However, the illustrious Lord of the waters had also said to him, "This mace should not be cast at anyone who is not actually fighting. If flung at such a one, it will fly back and fall on you, O brilliant, and take your life!"

And now, his hour to die come, Srutayudha violates that injunction. He casts his lethal mace at Krishna, who receives it upon his dark and tremendous shoulder. Like the wind failing to shake the Vindhya mountains, it has no impact on the Avatara. Instead, the occult gada flies back and fells Srutayudha himself, like a powerful spell consuming the sorcerer. Your troops see Srutayudha slain by his own mace and cries of dismay rise from your ranks.

The river Devi Parnasa's beloved son falls with his head and body shattered before the eyes of all the archers, he falls, resplendent, like a tall pipal tree with spreading branches broken by the wind. Seeing Srutayudha perish, panic grips your warriors and they flee.

Brave Sudakshina, son of the king of the Kambojas, now attacks the flashing Arjuna. Partha looses seven arrows at him that pass right through his body and burrow into the ground behind him. Though spouting blood, Sudakshina strikes Arjuna back with ten kanka-feathered shafts, Krishna with three, and Partha again with five. Arjuna severs his bow, lops off this standard and pierces him with two wedge-headed arrows.

Sudakshina stabs Partha again with three sizzling arrows, and gives an echoing roar. He looses a dread iron astra at the Pandava, a weapon decked with little bells, which blazes like a meteor, giving off sparks of fire, strikes the Vijaya squarely and fells him to his chariot floor!

Recovering in a moment, great Arjuna, now licking the corners of his mouth in anger, shoots a dazzle of fourteen barbs, drawing fonts of blood from his enemy, his horses, and charioteer, breaking his standard and bow into shards. With no instant's pause, Partha pulverises Sudakshina's chariot and then looses a mighty arrow, which blows Sudakshina's heart to shreds. With a sigh, the valiant Kamboja prince, his armour ruined, his limbs turned weak, his crown and angadas come loose, falls head first from his ratha, and his spirit departs his mangled body.

Like a beautiful Karnikara tree in the spring with handsome branches lying uprooted by the wind on a mountaintop, Sudakshina of the Kambojas lies on the bare ground lifeless, instead of on the costliest bed, wearing precious ornaments. Handsome, with coppery eyes and on his head a garland of gold, and radiant like a fire, even in death the mighty-armed Sudakshina is splendent as some wonderful mountain.

Seeing Srutayudha and Sudakshina slain, your warriors yet again take to their heels in terror.'"

CANTO 89

JAYADRATHA-VADHA PARVA CONTINUED

"Sanjaya says, "After he kills Sudakshina and Srutayudha, and when they recover their courage, your legions set on Arjuna more fiercely than ever. The Abhishahas, the Surasenas, the Sibis and the Vasatis loose storms of weapons of every kind at the Kiritin, but Arjuna responds with an awesome volley of six hundred arrows, unleashed in a moment, sprayed in all directions. Struck by panic by his archery the likes of which they have never imagined let alone seen before, your men take flight from this dreadful god come hunting them, like little animals from a great tiger.

However, they soon rally and once more surround Partha, who continues to massacre his enemies at imperious and terrifying ease; arrows flare in a constant stream from the Gandiva, hewing off heads and warriors' arms until there is no inch of the field that is not strewn with these grisly ornaments of death. The flights of crows, vultures and ravens that hover over Kurukshetra form an eerie canopy in the sky.

Seeing their men decimated, Srutayus and Achyutayus are full of belligerence and continue to fight Dhananjaya in wrath. Mighty, strong, proud, heroic, of noble lineage, the two archers, Rajan, anxious to win great fame and victory for your son, by extinguishing the elemental Arjuna, envelop him with arrows from his right and left. A thousand deadly shafts they lash down on Arjuna like two thunderheads filling a lake. Maharatha Srutayus suddenly strikes Dhananjaya with a fell spear and, deeply wounded, Arjuna Parantapa faints, to Krishna's puzzlement.

Immediately, as if to pour acid into his wound, Achyutayus from the other flank drives another javelin into Partha. In excruciating agony, Arjuna totters in the chariot and clutches at his flagstaff to support himself. And all the fighting men give a great jubilant roar, thinking that the Pandava they dread has been killed.

Krishna, grieved to see Partha swoon, soothes him with divine, comforting words. Srutayus and Achyutayus do not cease their onslaught; wheeling around the son of Indra, they mantle the Pandava's chariot with a tempest of missiles so completely that the ratha, its warrior and sarathy and its horses vanish from view. Even the banner of snarling Hanuman cannot be seen anymore.

Meanwhile, Arjuna slowly regains his senses, like someone returning from the very land of the dead. Seeing his ratha with Vasudeva overwhelmed by arrows and finding his two antagonists before him like two blazing fires, Partha the paladin invokes the Indrastra. Thousands of arrows flame forth from it, cutting down their volley in the sky and striking both their heads from their necks in scarlet bursts and they fall like two great trees brought down by the wind. This done, Arjuna ploughs on through the dense enemy, encountering many great warriors, besting them all. Shock sweeps through your ranks at the deaths of Srutayus and Achyutayus; your men stand as if they have seen the ocean dried up. Arjuna effortlessly despatches fifty maharathas who followed the two slain princes, and plunges on strewing the field with corpses of numberless great warriors. Seeing Srutayus and Achyutayus die, O Bhaarata, their sons Niyatayus and Dirghayus charge Arjuna, covering him in a gale of diverse weapons. Invincible Partha Arjuna, in an incarnadine moment, sends both princes to Yama. Arjuna thunders on through the helpless

Kuru army like some elephant trampling his way through a red lake of lotuses.

Then thousands of Angas surround Arjuna with their elephant-force. Urged on by Duryodhana, many kings of the west and the south, and many others led by the king of the Kalingas also encircle Arjuna with their great elephants. But Arjuna today is a god on Kurukshetra, and more quickly than I can tell you, Rajan, the field of death is bestrewn with thousands of heads and arms more, all richly ornamented, all struck off by the arrows than radiate endlessly from the magical Gandiva. The severed heads look like golden stones entwined by snakes. Arms lopped off from the elephant riders fall to the ground like birds dropping from trees; while the elephants, pierced by thousands of arrows and flowing blood from their wounds, look like hills in the monsoon with melted red chalk streaming down their sides.

Different kinds of Mlecchas, all variously ugly, wearing garish attire, armed with many strange and crude weapons, sit on the backs of elephants bathed in blood, while others look weirdly resplendent, as they lie prone on the field, having been killed by Arjuna. Thousands of elephants and their riders, and those on foot that urged them forward, all struck by Partha's bolts, vomit blood, scream in agony, and either fall or run in all directions.

Many of the huge beasts, terrified, lumber away from the fearsome Kshatriya and crush their own men, including countless warriors fierce as poisonous snakes. Many terrible Yavanas, Paradas, Sakas, Balhikas and Mlecchas born of the cow belonging to Vasishta, with fierce eyes, accomplished in war and looking like Yamadutas, all of them experts of the mayic powers of the Asuras, many Darvabhisaras, Daradas, Pundras in thousands of bands, and together forming a force that is beyond count, shower their missiles all together over Arjuna aflame.

The wild and skilled Mlecchas pound Arjuna with their arrows. Arjuna fluidly shoots lethal torments of shafts from the Gandiva, barbs like locust swarms which cast a deathly shadow over the Dhartarashtra troops, and mow down almost all the Mlecchas, whose heads are completely shaved or half-shaved or covered with matted locks, who are unclean in all their ways and have crooked faces.

The remaining hill dwellers flee.

In dark glees, ravens, kankas and wolves lap up the blood of elephants, horses and their Mleccha-riders lying upon the field, all felled by the Partha's burning volleys. Partha lets flow a bubbling river of blood; the slain foot-soldiers, horses, chariots and elephants are its banks; the showers of arrows, its rafts; the hair of the dead its moss and weeds and the fingers cut off from warriors' hands its little fishes—ah, river as awful as Death itself at the end of the Yuga. The bloody river flows towards the realm of Yama with the bodies of dead elephants floating on it and slowing its current.

The Earth covered with the blood of Kshatriyas, elephants, horses and their riders, has become a crimson lake, like one formed by Indra's torrential rains when they cover lands both high and low. The Kshatriya bull despatches six thousand horsemen and a thousand of the greatest rathikas into the jaws of death. Thousands of elephants, pierced all over by his arrows, lie prostrate on the field, like hills struck down by thunder and lightning.

Arjuna hurtles across Kurukshetra, an elephant in musth trampling a forest of reeds, killing horse riders, ratha-warriors and elephants with supreme ease. Just as a wind fuels a conflagration that devours a dense forest of trees, creepers, plants, dry wood and grass, Dhananjaya's fire, with shafts for its flames and fanned on by the Krishna-wind, hungrily consumes the forest of your warriors. Emptying chariots in carmine flurries, covering the ground everywhere he goes with corpses, Dhananjaya truly seems to dance, bow in hand, among teeming legions of enemies, flooding the earth with blood with his thunderous shafts.

Energized by all the killing he does, he penetrates deeper into the Bharata host and confronts Srutayudha, king the Ambashtas. Arjuna slaughters his horses with a slew of kanka-feathered arrows; he breaks that king's bow in his hands with a single unerring shaft.

The briefly shaken Ambashtha king picks up a great mace and

rushes at Arjuna's chariot and strikes Krishna a stunning blow. Arjuna's eyes turn red and he looses a vicious flight of gold-winged barbs at the Ambashtha, shrouding that hero in a small cloud, shimmering. Arjuna shatters that king's mace with another clutch of arrows, smashing the heavy weapon into dust. Quick as thinking, that king hefts another gada and, undaunted, storming the Pandava's ratha, rains a flurry of heavy blows on both Krishna and Arjuna.

Next moment, Arjuna hacks his opponent's massive arms off at their shoulders with two wedge-headed short arrows, spraying blood in the air. With another shaft, he removes Srutayudha's head from his neck in a bright ruddy blast. That Kshatriya falls like a stake raised to Indra with its ropes cut.

Hundreds of elephants and chariots beyond count surround the battling Pandava and he becomes invisible like the Sun hidden by dark clouds.'"

CANTO 90

JAYADRATHA-VADHA PARVA CONTINUED

"Sanjaya says, 'Arjuna, his heart set just on killing Jayadratha, furrows deep into the Bharata host, decimating the invincible akshauhinis of both Drona and the Bhojas; he kills prince Sudakshina of the Kambojas, as well as the valiant Srutayudha. Relentlessly he razes the Kuru army and panic takes your forces like a fever.

Seeing his army mown down at the Vijaya's will, Duryodhana rides up to Drona and cries, "Arjuna has already humbled our great army, Acharya; he has already cloven through your sakata vyuha. He brings such carnage to us, you must tell us what to do to stop him! Bless you, Acharya! You are our only refuge; do what you must to see that the Pandava does not kill Jayadratha. Like a raging fire consuming heaps of dry grass and straw, the Dhananjaya conflagration, fanned by the wind of his wrath, devours my troops.

Seeing the son of Kunti burning his way so easily through our legions, the maharathas who guard Jayadratha are full of doubt if they can stop Partha. All the kings say that Arjuna could never defeat Drona. But Pandu's son stormed disdainfully through your vyuha, most splendid one. Ah, my army must be weak indeed, why, even as if I have no warriors of any worth.

O most splendid, blessed Drona, I know that in your heart, you are devoted to the Pandavas, and that is why Arjuna has his way with us. I also seek to please you, Acharya, with everything in my power, and I cannot think of what more I can do. But you seem to disregard all that I do for you. Ah Drona, we are devoted to you but your favour lies only with the Pandavas, although you receive your livelihood from us! I did not know until now that you are a razor hidden in honey. If you had not assured that we would contain, no, even humiliate the Pandavas, I would never have prevented Jayadratha from returning to his own country. I am a fool to expect protection from you.

I assured Jayadratha that he would be safe with us and now I see him being offered up as a yagnapasu, a sacrificial animal to Yama. Any man might escape from death's very jaws, but there will be no escape for Jayadratha once he is within Dhananjaya's reach.

O you of the red horses, do whatever you must to save Jayadratha! I am deranged with anxiety. Pay no heed to my raving at you; I beg you protect the Saindhava from dreadful Arjuna!"

Drona replies, "I do not find fault with what you say. Duryodhana, I tell you truly that you are as dear to me as Aswatthaman. So do what I tell you now, Rajan! Of all charioteers, Krishna is the greatest and his horses are the best of their great pedigree. Arjuna's chariot flashes through the small gap in our forces. Do you not see the countless arrows the Kiritin unleashes from his great Gandiva that fall full two miles behind his ratha as he flies ahead, and every shaft taking a life?

I am old now, child; I cannot ride as swiftly as Pandu's son. Besides, the entire Pandava army is now close upon our van.

Arjuna has left Yudhishtira by himself, and this is my chance to seize their king, as I vowed I would before all our Kshatriyas. I cannot leave the entrance to our vyuha, and so you must fight Phalguna!

Riding with the best support, you can match Arjuna, who is alone and who only is your equal in lineage and achievements. Do not be afraid, go and fight him. You are the sovereign of the world, a great king, a famed Kshatriya and a master of quelling your enemies. O heroic subduer of enemy cities, ride swiftly and face Kunti's son yourself!"

Duryodhana says, "O Acharya, how can I fight Arjuna who passed even you, who are our greatest warrior by far? The lord of the Devas, armed with the Vajra, can be vanquished in battle but not Arjuna Purandara. He has defeated Hridika's son Kritavarman of the Bhojas and you, who are equal to a Deva. He has killed Sudakshina and king Srutayudha; he has killed both Srutayus and Achyutayus and numberless Mlecchas. How can I challenge this invincible son of Pandu, who is like an all-consuming fire? How can you think I am fit to fight Arjuna today? Ah, I am dependent on you like a slave. Protect my honour and my fame, O Drona!"

Drona says, "You rightly say, O scion of Kuru, that Dhananjaya is irresistible. Yet, today I will ensure that you will face him and contain him. Let all the archers in the world witness the wonderful feat of Arjuna being held in check by you in the very presence of Krishna. I will sheath your body in my golden kavacha in a way that no weapon will so much as graze your skin! Even if the three worlds with the Asuras, the Devas, the Yakshas, the Uragas and the Rakshasas, together with all Manavas, take the field against you today, you will still have no cause to fear them. Neither Krishna nor Arjuna, nor any other warrior, will be able to pierce your armour. Cased in this armour, ride swiftly against Arjuna today. He will not resist you!"

Then Drona, the one who knows Brahma the best, touches water, utters some powerful secret Mantras, and quickly fastens his own remarkable kavacha around Duryodhana's, astonishing everyone there, and ensuring the your son will be invincible.

Drona says, "Let the Vedas, Brahman, and the Brahmanas bless you. Let all the greater Nagas bless you, O Bhaarata!

Let Yayati, Nahusha, Dhundhumara, Bhagiratha and the other Rajarishis watch over you and do what benefits you.

Let blessings be upon you from creatures that have but one leg, and from those having many legs and from creatures that have no legs.

Let Swaha, Swadha and Sachi all be with you and help you. O sinless one, let Lakshmi, Arundhati, Asita, Devala, Viswamitra, Angiras, Vasishta and Kasyapa do what is favourable to you.

Let Dhatri, the Lord of the worlds, the points of the compass, the Lokapalas, the regents of those cardinal points, and the six-faced Kartikeya all be benign toward you.

Rajan, let the divine Vivaswat help you completely. Let the four elephants, the Diggajas of the four quarters, Bhumi, Akasa, the Navagraha, the Lord Sesha, the greatest Naga, who is below the Earth and holds her on his head, give you what fetches you weal!

O son of Gandhari, once upon a time, an Asura named Vritra, displaying his prowess, defeated the best of the Devas in battle. Those inhabitants of swarga, led by Indra and numbering thousands upon thousands, their bodies lacerated, sapped of their vitality and strength, and in terror of Vritrasura, went to Brahma and sought his protection.

The gods said, 'O best and foremost of Devas, Vritra has crushed us in battle. Be our refuge now; rescue us from this great dread.'

Addressing Vishnu beside him and the Devas led by Indra, Brahma said to the unhappy ones, these words filled with truth. 'Indeed, I will always protect the gods led by Indra, and the Brahmanas too. The tejas of Tvashtri from which Vritra has been created is invincible. Having in olden days performed tapasya for a million years, Tvashtri then created Vritra with the leave of Maheswara. This mighty enemy of yours has vanquished you through the grace of Mahadeva Siva. You must go to Sankara's abode to see him. Once you behold him, you will be able to defeat Vritra. So go without delay to the mountains of Mandara where the origin of tapasya, the destroyer of Daksha's yagna, the wielder of the Pinaka, the Lord of all creatures, the slayer of the Asura Bhaganetra, lives.'

The Devas flew to Mandara with Brahma, and saw there that mass of energy and light, that Supreme God endued with the splendour of a million suns. Seeing the Devas, Maheswara welcomed them and enquired what he could do for them. Said He, *The sight of a radiant person can never be fruitless. Let the fruition of your desires proceed from this.*

The dwellers of swarga replied, 'Vritra has deprived us of our tejas and strength. Be the refuge of the swargavasis. Look, O Lord, at our bodies battered and bruised by his blows. We seek your protection. Be our refuge, O Maheswara!'

The God of Devas, called Sarva, said, 'Devas, you well know how this originated from the fervid wish and tapasya of Tvashtri the divine artificer, whose son is Vritra. It is surely my dharma to help you dwellers of heaven. O Indra, take this lustrous armour from my body and, O king of the Devas, put it on while chanting these mantras in your mind.'

And the boon-giving Siva gave Indra the armour with the mantras to be chanted by the wearer. Protected by the armour, Indra went to battle against the army of Vritra and although they cast all kinds of astras at him, the joints of Siva's armour could not be breached. Then Indra slew Vritra, and later he gave Angiras the kavacha, whose joints are made of mantras. Angiras passed on those mantras to his son Brihaspati, who indeed has knowledge of all mantras. Brihaspati imparted that knowledge to the very intelligent Agnivesya. Agnivesya passed it down to me, and it is with those same mantras, O Duryodhana, best of kings, that I fasten this armour onto your body."

Saying this, Drona, that bull among acharyas, says again to your magnificent son, "Rajan, I sheath your body in this divine, joining its links with the Brahma mantras, even as in olden days Brahma himself fastened this kavacha to Indra's body during the Devasura yuddha sparked by the abduction of Tara. Here, I do now swathe you in the same ancient armour."

Having thus fastened the impenetrable armour onto Duryodhana with the arcane mantras of Brahma, Drona sends the king to battle Arjuna. Now wearing the armour of the Mahatman Acharya, Duryodhana rides at Arjuna's ratha with a thousand mighty war-maddened elephants, a hundred thousand horses and many maharathas. He storms forth to the sound of conches, drums and other instruments, going even like

Virochana's son Bali of yore. Then, O Bhaarata, seeing the Kuru king himself go forth a fathomless ocean, a deafening uproar of joy arises among your troops.'"

CANTO 91

Jayadratha-vadha Parva continued

"Sanjaya says, 'After Duryodhana sallies forth to hunt down Partha and Krishna, who have penetrated deep into the Kaurava army, the Pandavas, accompanied by the Somakas, charge Drona with loud shouts. A ferocious battle erupts between the Kurus and the Pandavas at the portal to the sakata vyuha, the sight of which fills all onlookers with awe and makes their hair stand on end. Rajan, the sun is in the meridian and the encounter between the two forces is truly such that we have never seen or heard of its like before.

Led by Dhrishtadyumna, the Parthas all in immaculate battle array cover Drona's legions with heavy showers of arrows. We, too, with the maharatha Drona leading us, envelop the Pandava forces under Prishata's son Dhrishtadyumna, with our missiles.

The two hosts, massed with rathas, are past magnificent, like two immense clouds in the summer sky, driven at each other by opposing winds. Locking in bloody battle, they fight wildly, recklessly, like the Ganga and Yamuna swollen with rainwater during the monsoon hurtling into confluence. Their myriad weapons are like the winds that blow before them; their legions are packed dense with elephants, horses and chariots and the maces the warriors wield their lightning that charges the awesome dark cloud formed by the Kuru host, whirled on by the Drona-tempest, and pouring incessant shafts: lashing torrents of rain that seek to quench the blazing Pandava-fire.

Like a spinning, blasting summer typhoon agitating the ocean, Drona blows at the Pandava host. The Pandavas rush towards the Acharya with terrific energy, to breach his vyuha, like a driving flood dashing against a strong embankment, to sweep it away. But Drona resists the furious Pandavas, Panchalas and Kekayas like a mountain stopping the fiercest tide. Quickly, many other avid and great kings of your army attack the Pandavas from all sides.

Then, rallying the Pandavas, Naravyaghra Dhrishtadyumna repeatedly attacks Drona, fervently trying to pierce his stolid defences. Indeed, as Drona showers his arrows on Prishata's son, so does he on Drona. With blades and swords for the winds that blow before it, richly furnished with arrows, spears and sabres, with the bowstring its lightning, and its twang its thunderclaps, the Dhrishtadyumna-cloud decants on all sides, killing many Kaurava maharathas and large number of horses, and swamps the hostile akshauhinis with his ceaseless gales of arrows.

Dhrishtadyumna stops Drona in his tracks, as the Brahmana attempts to scythe through the chariot-divisions of the Pandavas, felling their rathikas with his extraordinary thunderbolts. Although Drona struggles valiantly, his army, on encountering the fire-prince Dhrishtadyumna is truncated into three columns. One of these retreats towards Kritavarman, the Bhoja king; another towards Jalasandha; and the third, savagely set upon by the Pandavas, retreats towards Drona himself.

Drona repeatedly rallies his troops but every time Dhrishtadyumna splits them again. And the Pandavas and the Srinjayas massacre the Dhartarashtra army divided into three, like many beasts of prey a herd of cattle left unprotected by its herdsmen in a forest. Such is the slaughtering that it is as if Death himself swoops down to swallow Drona's warriors after Dhrishtadyumna first stuns them. As famine, pestilence and robbers destroy the kingdom of a weak or evil king, the Pandavas consume your army. The rays of the sun reflected by the warriors' weapons and the pall of dust raised by the fighting men blind and sting the eyes of all.

Seeing the Kaurava forces rent in three parts by Dhrishtadyumna and then butchered by the Pandavas, Drona, stirred to great wrath, begins to denude the Panchalas with his elemental astras of fire, water and wind. The Brahmana burns like the fire at the end of the Yuga. He shatters chariots, strikes down elephants, steeds and foot-soldiers, each with just a single missile. No warrior in the Pandava army can withstand Drona's grievous archery.

Scorched by the sun and blasted by the astras of Drona, the Pandava akshauhinis reel and give way on abysmal Kurukshetra. And your host, too, ravaged by Dhrishtadyumna, seems to burst into flames all around like a dry forest on fire. While both Drona and Dhrishtadyumna decimate the two vast hosts, killing untold numbers, the maharathas, the great warriors of both armies, in utter disregard for their lives, continue to fight manfully everywhere. Neither in your army, nor in that of the enemy, O Bharatarishabha, is there a single warrior who flees that hellish carnage through fear.

The brothers Vivimsati and Chitrasena and the maharatha Vikarna surround Bhimasena, while Vinda, Anuvinda of Avanti and Kshemadhurti of marvellous skill support your three sons who engage the incomparable Bhimasena.

The noble and energetic king Balhika, with his troops, fights the sons of Draupadi. Saibya, lord of the Govasanas, with a thousand of his best warriors, faces the son of the great warrior king of the Kasis and resists him. Salya, king of the Madras, surrounds Dharmaraja Yudhishtira with his legion, gentle Yudhishtira who today is a blazing fire on the abysmal harrowing field. Brave and choleric Dusasana, ably supported by his own akshauhini, as always in fury, his brow knit darkly, rides against the matchless Satyaki.

Rajan, I led my own troops, all in armour, well armed and supported by four hundred of the finest bowmen, to fight Chekitana.

Sakuni with seven hundred Gandhara warriors armed with bows, darts and swords, faces Sahadeva the son of Madri. The two great archers, Vinda and Anuvinda of Avanti, fight Virata, king of the Matsyas, with no care for their lives, fighting for their friend Duryodhana. King Balhika furiously confronts the mighty Sikhandin, son of Yajnasena. The lord of Avanti, with the Sauviras and the cruel Prabhadrakas fend off the rampaging Dhrishtadyumna of the Panchalas.

The fierce-faced Rakshasa Alambusha rushes, fangs bared, at the feral and heroic Ghatotkacha, Bhima's son who comes like Death into battle. The maharatha Kuntibhoja, with a large force, attacks the horrible Alambusha. Thus, O Bhaarata, hundreds of separate duels break out between the warriors of your army and theirs.

Meanwhile, Rajan, Jayadratha remains at the rear of the Kuru army protected by so many great archers and maharathas; among them is Kripa whose chariot wheels are guarded by Aswatthaman on his right, and Karna the Sutaputra on the left. Behind Jayadratha, protecting his rear, is a small host of heroes led by Kripa, Somadatta's son, Vrishasena, Sala and the invincible Salya, who are all masters of every aspect of warfare. After making these arrangements for the protection of Jayadratha, the Kuru army continues the tremendous battle against the Pandavas.'"

CANTO 92

JAYADRATHA-VADHA PARVA CONTINUED

"Sanjaya says, 'Listen further to that astounding encounter between the Kurus and the Pandavas. Flying straight at Drona, who stands at the lip of his great vyuha, the Pandavas put forth all their might to break into the fortress like formations. Drona and his legions fight staunchly, in rage and inspiration to keep them at bay.

Vinda and Anuvinda of Avanti, fighting for your son, unleash ten torrid shafts at Virata and a terrific battle ensues between them. Blood sprays in the sunlight and flows like water during that contention that resembles an encounter in the forest between a lion and a pair of wild elephants in musth.

The powerful son of Yajnasena strikes king Balhika with excruciating arrows piercing his innards, and Balhika drills Drupada's son with nine coruscating shafts fletched with golden wings. Indescribably brutal is the duel between those two, one that swells the delight of the brave and makes the timid wilt in terror. The dark deluges of arrows they loose over each other shroud the sky and all the points of the compass, so that darkness falls on Kurukshetra and nothing can be seen.

Saibya, king of the Govasanas, leads his fearless and wild men against the prince of the Kasis, and they lock in battle like two bull elephants.

The belligerent king of the Balhikas is glorious indeed, as he faces all five of Draupadi's sons; their unrestrained encounter is like that of the battle between the mind and the five senses! Loosing torrents of arrows from all sides Draupadi's warrior princes are like the objects of the senses constantly besieging the body.

Your son Dusasana strikes Satyaki deeply with nine keen bolts so the Vrishni almost swoons. Recovering quickly, Satyaki stabs your son deep with ten kanka-feather winged shafts. Lacerating each other, their blood flying, the two look as splendid as two kinsukas in bloom.

Mauled by the arrows of Kuntibhoja, an angry Alambusha also looks like a beautiful flowering kinsuka. The pale Rakshasa, fighting at the head of your army, begins to roar most horribly and gashes Kuntibhoja with a squall of wooden barbs. The two resemble Sakra and the Asura Jambha of old.

The two sons of Madri meanwhile find Sakuni, whom they most loathe, and a violent, hate-filled encounter erupts between them; the twins fetch carnage to Sakuni's Gandhara troops.

The fire of the Pandava's wrath, which you kindled, which Karna stoked and your sons fanned into a conflagration, blazes now as if it will surely consume the entire world. Forced to turn his back on the fight against Nakula and Sahadeva, so ferocious is their onslaught on him, Sakuni stands briefly bemused, not knowing what to do. Seeing him turn back, the fearsome twins again lash down their arrows on him like two thunderheads upon a dimmed mountain. Subala's son, overwhelmed, sorely wounded by countless powerful shafts, turns his chariot and flees towards Drona for refuge!

Magnificent, black Ghatotkacha dashes towards the vile Alambusha with gusto and the duel between the two Rakshasas is like the one between Rama and Ravana of old.

Having struck Salya of the Madras with all of five hundred arrows in a dazzle of bowmanship, Yudhishtira pierces him deep with seven more.

The duel between them swells to breathtaking proportions, and is like the one between the Asura Sambara and Indra of the Devas in olden days.

Your sons Vivimsati, Chitrasena and Vikarna, at the head of a large force, skirmish with Bhimasena.'"

CANTO 93

Jayadratha-vadha Parva continued

"Sanjaya says, 'The Pandavas wildly beset the Kauravas who have been divided into three divisions. With blood-curdling roars, Bhimasena rushes against the mighty-armed Jalasandha; Yudhishtira leads his legions against Kritavarman; and Dhrishtadyumna tears into Drona, Rajan, and his arrows flaring at the Brahmana like sunrays.

Now the individual duels cease and a great and general battle begins between all the archers of the Kuru and the Pandava armies, every man of them bright-eyed with battle lust, and an unprecedented bloodbath ensues. Great Drona looses a dense swarm of missiles at Dhrishtadyumna and his legions, and a gasp goes up from both armies. In a moment, which seems to occur in another dimension of time, Drona's virulent shafts sever the heads of some thousands of fighting men and they roll in macabre pageant on the battlefield, which then resembles a forest of ghoulish lotuses.

Fine robes, ornaments, weapons, standards and coats of mail are strewn on the ground everywhere amidst every division of the armies.

Coats of golden mail, dyed with blood, appear like clouds charged with lightning.

Other mighty maharathas, drawing great swords measuring full six cubits long, shoot down elephants, horses and men. In that frightful melee, one sees swords, shields, bows, heads and coats of mail lying scattered all around; one sees innumerable headless trunks rise up weirdly, Rajan, in the midst of the horrific battle and vultures, kankas, jackals and swarms of other carnivores rending at the flesh of fallen men, horses and elephants, drinking their blood, or dragging them by their hair, or licking up their marrow through bones bitten through, or hauling whole corpses and severed limbs, or rolling their heads on the ground.

Masters of war, seeking only fame, fight at the ends of their strength and skills. Many warriors wheel across the field, displaying various incredible maneuvers of swordsmen. The noblest men butcher one another in frenzy, with swords, darts, lances, spears, axes, maces, spiked clubs and other uncommon weapons, why they strangle each other with bare hands until tongues loll out blue, eyes roll up in their sockets and fierce spirits finally quit their manly bodies.

Maharathas fight other chariot-warriors, horsemen against horsemen, elephants other elephants and foot-soldiers fall upon foot-soldiers. The elephants present the most dramatic and gory spectacle, maddened and trumpeting shrilly, as they gore each other viciously in the manner they do in sporting arenas.

All mercy and dharma have departed Kurukshetra, on this fourth day of the kali yuga of wrath unleashed, and the greatest warriors fight like senseless beasts rather than highborn heroes. Dhrishtadyumna horses are entangled with those of Drona. Those steeds fleet as the wind, the former's white as doves and the latter's red as blood, are still so beautiful, even at the grim heart of darkness; they are like stunning clouds charged with lightning.

O Bhaarata, abruptly Prishasta's son parantapa Dhrishtadyumna sees Drona again, and in froth, flings down his bow and engages him the most difficult kind of combat—hand-to-hand, with sword and shield.

Seizing the shaft of Drona's ratha, he vaults onto it, sometimes leaping onto the middle of the yoke, sometimes on its joints and sometimes just behind the horses.

And as the fire-prince moves nimbly from place to place, even upon the very back of Drona's red horses, Drona finds no opportunity or opening to strike at him. All of us watch this in amazement! Indeed, Dhrishtadyumna's sudden attack is like the strike of a hunting hawk in the forest.

Recovering from his initial surprise, Drona first smashes Dhrishtadyumna's shield, emblazoned with a hundred moons, next his sword with ten more shafts, and finally with four and sixty arrows, kills his horses. With a few broad-headed shafts, the Brahmana fells the Panchala prince's standard, his royal chatra and then kills both his Parshni charioteers. The terrible Acharya now draws his bowstring to his ear and looses a fatal arrow straight at Dhrishtadyumna standing on his horses' necks, even like Indra casting his Vajra at an enemy.

Even as the deadly shaft flies to claim the life of the prince born to kill the grand Drona, Satyaki from a side cuts it in slivers with fourteen perfect arrows. The bull of the Sinis saves the prince of the Panchalas whom the greatest of acharyas had seized like a deer held by a lion in its jaws. Seeing Dhrishtadyumna saved, Drona in fury shoots twenty-six arrows at Satyaki, to which now the emboldened, relieved Panchala, having leapt gratefully off Drona's chariot horses, replies with precisely twenty-six of his own that thud squarely into Drona's chest in a neat round clump, even while the Brahmana turns to slaughtering the Srinjayas.

All the Panchala maharathas, agog to see the inspired Satyaki vanquish the Kuru Acharya and senapati, quickly converge and whisk their own prince Dhrishtadyumna away from immediate danger.'"

CANTO 94

JAYADRATHA-VADHA PARVA CONTINUED

"Dhritarashtra asks, 'O Sanjaya, after Satyaki saves Dhrishtadyumna's life, what does Drona do against that Naravyaghra Satyaki, the grandson of Sini?'

Sanjaya replies, 'Like a mighty Naga, with wrath for his venom, his stretched bow his yawning jaws, his sharp shafts his fangs, his eyes red as copper from the frenzy of battle, and breathing hard, Drona, his red chargers seeming to soar into the sky to scale a mountain top, turns viciously on Satyaki, covering the Vrishni who has deprived him of his most precious prey with a tempest of golden-winged arrows.

Seeing the irresistible Drona cloudburst, with the rumble of chariot-wheels its roar, the twanging of its always bent bow its thunderclaps, long arrows its lightning-flashes, the Brahmana's fury its gale winds and flying at him upon the horses that are the hurricane that impel it, Satyaki coolly rushes ahead to meet it, smilingly saying to his charioteer, 'O Suta, whip the horses to fly at this Brahmana fallen from his swadharma, this refuge of Dhritarashtra's son, the dispeller of the Kuru king's sorrows and fear, the acharya of all the princes, the warrior always so proud of his skill.'

At which, Satyaki's superb silver horses, with the speed of the wind, hurtle directly towards Drona. The two Parantapas collide, and each rains down thousands of arrows at the other, shafts that fill the firmament and obscure the ten points of the compass. Like two clouds are they, which empty themselves over the Earth at summer's end. The sun becomes invisible, the very wind ceases to blow and an endless thick pall of gloom descends on the battlefield, so that, blinded, all the other warriors on Kurukshetra are forced to stop fighting.

The thunder of the fusillades of the awesome twain is no less than that of Indra's Vajra striking. Pierced all over with long shafts, O Bhaarata, both look as if they are covered by nests of snakes. Brave warriors hear the incessant twanging of their bows and the sounds that their palms make, and to them it is just like the crash of thunder falling upon mountaintops.

The rathas of both warriors, their horses and their charioteers pierced by barbs of golden wings, are beautiful to behold. Fierce and incessant is the downpour of bright straight arrows, splendent like snakes freshly freed from their sloughs. Their canopies and their standards are shredded; their glorious bodies are bathed in blood, but spurred by the single thought of victory, they continue to strike each other with deadly shafts. With blood flowing down their limbs, they resemble a pair of elephants in musth, ichor streaming from lust rent temples.

The roars, shouts and other cries of the soldiers, the blast of conches and the beat of drums all cease, Rajan, for no one make the slightest sound. All the akshauhinis fall silent, and all their warriors stop fighting and become spectators of that single duel. Maharathas, elephant riders, horsemen and foot-soldiers surround these two bulls among men and witness their duel with unwinking eyes. The elephant-divisions, the horse-divisions, and the chariot-akshauhinis, all stand still in their ranks, like figures in a painting of war. Adorned with gems and gold, studded profusely with pearls and corals, with flags waving, with coats of shining golden mail, with triumphal banners and richly caparisoned elephants, with fine cloaks and robes, with bright and sharp weapons glinting, with the heads of horses ornamented with chamaras, yak-tails and with gold and silver, with wildflower garlands draped around the frontal lobes of elephants and shimmering rings round their tusks—the Kuru and Pandava armies look like a vast gathering of cloud banks at the close of summer, decked with rows of cranes and myriads of fire-flies under them and embellished with rainbows and flashes of lightning.

Riveted, our men as well as those of Yudhishtira watch the battle between Satyaki and the noble Drona, as do the Devas led by Brahma, Soma, the Siddhas, the Charanas, the Vidyadharas, and the great Nagas, from their invisible wondrous vimanas in the sky. All that watch are wonderstruck by the two lions among men who dash forward and fall back, striking at each other all the while.

Both of untold prowess and skill, Drona and Satyaki put their astounding genius at battle on display, and draw gushing fonts of blood from each other, always as if in sport! Satyaki cuts down a rash of Drona's powerful missiles in flight, and next moment breaks the Acharya's bow in his hands. In the twinkling of an eye, Bharadwaja's son sweeps up another and strings it, but Satyaki cleaves that one too.

Drona picks up another bow in a wink, but no sooner does he string it than Satyaki splits it; and this happens a full nine and seven times!

Watching Satyaki fight, Drona thinks, "Such prodigious archery that this greatest of the Satwatas shows may be found in Rama and Arjuna, in Kartavirya and the Purushavyaghra Bhishma! But hardly in anyone else."

In his heart he applauds the prowess of Satyaki. Seeing the Vrishni prodigy's dexterity as being equal to that of Vasava himself, Drona, greatest of all masters of weapons, is deeply stirred and gratified. So, too, are the Devas above with Indra at their head, for they have never seen another archer of such brilliance and light like swiftness of hand as Satyaki although they, the Siddhas and the Charanas are acquainted with Drona's feats.

Finally, Drona, that scourge of Kshatriyas, strings a fresh bow and launches an astra of profound maya at Satyaki. The Vrishni hero baffles that recondite weapon with a hermetic astra of his own; and then he continues to lash Drona with his arrow storms. In truth, Rajan, I have no words with which to describe the superhuman skill and unworldly feats of the two heroes, one old and the other still young. I have never before seen such a duel, which all the most knowing among both your warriors and the Pandavas' cheer and applaud. Satyaki and Drona both summon the exact same astras at the very same moments, and when they themselves become aware of this, they fight with somewhat diminished fury, as if acknowledging each other's unequalled greatness. It seems their spirits turn mild for a moment.

Then, Rajan, his wrath returning, Drona begins to invoke the most potent devastras to kill Satyaki. Seeing the dreadful foe-slaughtering Agneyastra, Satyaki invokes the Varuna. Seeing them both now summon celestial weapons, loud cries of alarm are heard and the very birds of the sky cease to fly through it. The two astras flare out at each other at the same moment and locking on high are extinguished against each other, falling away in embers and a drizzle.

Just at this time, the sun begins to sink toward the western horizon. Anxious for Satyaki, Yudhishtira, Bhimasena, Nakula, and Sahadeva charge Drona bringing the Matsyas and the Salweya troops with them. At which, thousands of Kuru princes led by Dusasana at their head, rally to protect Drona who is now surrounded by his enemies. Another pitched and tumultuous battle breaks out. The earth is quickly covered with a thick skin of dust and showers of arrows shot by both sides; and nothing is visible anymore. The battle rages on complete disregard of life and limb, of kinship and friendship.'"

CANTO 95

JAYADRATHA-VADHA PARVA CONTINUED

"Sanjaya says, 'The sun moves into his downward course towards the summit of the Asta hills, Surya turns cool, the sky is covered with dust, and the day begins to fade fast. As for the soldiers, some rest, some fight, some return to the field they have let in fear, now to vie again for victory. As the great war burns on behind them, Arjuna and Krishna fly on towards Jayadratha. With his irresistible arrows, Arjuna creates a path through the enemy forces, wide enough for his chariot and Krishna plunges his ratha along that narrow way. Awesome is the Parthasarathy's skill, quicksilver, as he flashes expertly along the narrowest openings. Your troops give way to Krishna blazing with lustre.

Arjuna's arrows, each one engraved with his name, some of bamboo, others of iron, of long range, flame from his Gandiva like the yuga fire, every last one claiming an enemy life, drinking the blood of living men and their beasts, killing scavengers and birds of prey and ill omen as well, who rend at the noble blood and swill thirstily from the river of gore flowing on Kurukshetra. Standing tall and erect upon his chariot,

Arjuna shoots his arrows full two miles ahead of him, and his chariot driven by his divine sarathy arrives where he aims even as the shafts pierce and dispatch his enemies!

Hrishikesa drives his ratha, yoked to gandharva horses swift as Garuda or the wind, with such speed that the whole universe marvels to watch him. Indeed, Rajan, the chariot of Surya himself, or those of Rudra or Vaisravana, have never gone as fast. No chariot has ever before been driven with such speed in war, as Arjuna's moving with the swiftness of a wish cherished in the mind. However, as Krishna and Arjuna race along through the enemy ranks, the superb horses begin to tire. Hunger and thirst afflict them as do the countless barbs that have pierced their sides along their careen. Yet, the wonderful beasts prance as they flash along flying over slain enemies' bodies, over dead horses, over broken chariots and even the massive corpses of fallen elephants.

Rajan, the two heroic brothers of Avanti, Vinda and Anuvinda at the head of their forces, notice that Arjuna's horses are tired, challenge him and strike him with sixty-four sizzling shafts, Janardana with seventy, and their four horses with a hundred. Infuriated, Arjuna, with his knowledge of the marmas of the body, pierces them with nine perfectly aimed barbs, striking them deep through the most critical and painful parts of their bodies. Roaring like two tigers, the brothers drown Krishna and Arjuna in a flood of arrows.

With two wedge-headed arrows Arjuna Swetavahana of the white steeds seamlessly breaks Vinda and Anuvinda's wonderful bows, and cuts down their standards bright as gold. The Avantis seize up fresh bows and resume their onslaught but great Partha easily frustrates their fire upon him. Never pausing he kills their horses, their charioteers, the two rathikas that protect their backs and the others that follow them.

Next, with another broad-headed arrow, sharp as a razor, he severs the older brother's head and Vinda falls out of his ratha like a tree broken by the wind. His eyes turning crimson to see his precious brother die, Anuvinda abandons all restraint, leaps down from his horseless chariot, mace raised high, and rushes towards Arjuna to wreak vengeance on him. He strikes Krishna on his brow, but the Avatara stands unmoved as the Mainaka mountain. In a blur of six arrows, Arjuna cuts away his legs, his arms and head and blows his wide chest apart, and Anuvinda falls onto the hallowed field like a riven hillock.

Seeing both the brothers dead, their followers, mad with grief, attack Arjuna, shooting hundreds of arrows in frenzy. Arjuna, resplendent as a fire consuming a forest at the end of winter, consumes them all in a few moments. He trundles over the fallen troops with some difficulty, shining bright like the rising sun destroying the clouds that had hidden it. Fear fills the Kauravas but seeing that he is tired and that Jayadratha is still far away, they recover quickly and surround him, shouting and roaring.

Arjuna says softly to Krishna, "Our horses are injured and tired and Jayadratha is still far away. Tell me, O Krishna, wisest of men, what should we do now? With you for their vision, the Pandavas will vanquish their enemies. I think that we should unyoke the horses and draw out luck the arrows that are stuck in them."

Kesava replies, "I too think the same, O Partha."

Arjuna then says, "I will hold the enemy forces at bay, O Kesava, while you tend to the horses."

Alighting from his chariot, Dhananjaya takes up his Gandiva, and stands fearlessly there like an immovable hill. Seeing him stand alone on the ground, the Kuru Kshatriyas, scenting victory, roar louder and surround him with a number of chariots; all of them stretch their bows and shower arrows over him. Filled with battle lust, they brandish their weapons and entirely shroud Partha with their shafts like clouds shrouding the sun. The great warriors rush impetuously at him like angry elephants attacking a lion.

And now the might of Partha that we witness is more extraordinary than ever, as he stands alone holding those countless warriors at bay. Cutting down his enemies' multitudinous shafts, he covers them all with a maelstrom of fire. The banks of shafts colliding in the sky sets the azure vaults ablaze, cascading rivers of sparks down on the field below. The air on Kurukshetra is steamy with the hot breath of Kshatriyas covered in blood, and their horses' heaving breath, and the gasping trumpeting elephants; that great crush of warriors and their beasts resounds with yells, shout, neighing, and wild roars.

That impassable, limitless, surging and implacable ocean of chariots has arrows for its tide, standards for its eddies, elephants for its crocodiles, foot-soldiers for its countless fishes, the blare of conches and the beat of drums for its roar, rathas for its surging waves, helmets for its tortoises, chatras and banners for its froth, and the bodies of slain elephants for its submarine rocks. With his arrows, Partha contains the advance of this sea like a continent.

Now Krishna says to Arjuna, "There is no well here on the field, O Arjuna, for our horses to drink from. They do not want a bath but thirst for water to drink."

Arjuna cheerfully replies, "Here it is!" And he pierces the earth with an astra and creates a wonderful lake from which the horses can drink! Swans glide on the magic lake, ducks and chakravakas; and it is wide, full of crystalline water with the finest of full-blown lotuses, and teeming with all kinds of fish. Fathomless, it is the resort of many a Rishi; and the Devarishi Narada comes there to look at Arjuna's lake of wonder. And Partha, who is capable of achieving marvels even like the celestial artificer Tvashtri himself, creates a hall of arrows there, arrows its beams and rafters, arrows its pillars, and arrows for its roof.

Smiling in joy, Krishna cries, "Uttamam! Wonderful!""

CANTO 96

JAYADRATHA-VADHA PARVA CONTINUED

"Sanjaya says, 'After the noble son of Kunti creates the lake, even while holding off the enemy, after he creates the hall of arrows, Krishna alights from the chariot and unyokes the horses lacerated by arrows. Watching this extraordinary sight, the Siddhas, the Charanas and all the Kuru warriors, too, applaud loudly.

The maharathas ranged against Arjuna cannot defend themselves against him, even when he fights on foot. It is wonderful to see that although myriads of chariots, elephants and horses attack him, Partha does not flinch but battles on as if he has juts begun his day of war, and prevails over all his enemies. The hostile kings shoot a solid swath of arrows at him, but the son of Vasava, in no anxiety whatever, seems to receive the hundreds of arrows, maces and lances cast at him as the ocean does the hundreds and hundreds of rivers flowing into it, even gladly.

Mahabaho Partha serenely receives all the weapons that the greatest of the enemy warriors loose at him in utmost fury. Fighting from the ground, he still confounds all the kings massed against him on their chariots—like that one fault, avarice, destroying a host of accomplishments!

The Kauravas, Rajan, applaud the astonishing prowess of Partha and Vasudeva, saying, "What more wonderful thing has ever been seen in this world, or will ever be than this that Partha and Govinda, in the very thick battle, have unyoked their horses? These maharathas inspire us with their energy and unshakeable assurance!"

Then Krishna, of eyes like lotus-petals, smiling as if he is in the midst of a group of women and not armed enemies, leads the horses into the hall of arrows, in the very sight of all your troops, and there takes away their fatigue, pain, their trembling and heals their wounds. At his ease, he plucks out the arrows that stick in them and, rubbing them down with his tender hands, makes them trot around slowly and coaxes them to drink. After quenching their thirst and removing their tiredness and pain, he once more carefully yokes them to the wonderful chariot. This done, Sauri, greatest of all living men, mahatejasvin Krishna, mounts the ratha again along with Arjuna and they ride back into battle, swifter then ever.

Seeing the chariot of the two Krishnas fly back into the war, its horses now refreshed, the Kauravas are crestfallen. They sigh, Rajan, like snakes whose fangs have been pulled, and say, "Oh, shame, shame on us! Partha and Krishna storm our ranks again slaughtering our troops with even like boys playing with a toy. Shame on us that, despite all our best efforts, they vanquish us with such ease and disdain."

Other warriors cry, "O brave Kauravas, kill Krishna and the Kiritin! For their horses have drunk and been refreshed and they fly closer to Jayadratha every moment, decimating us on their way."

Some great lords, Rajan, having seeing the never before witnessed sight at the very heart of a war, say among themselves, "Alas, through Duryodhana's sins, king Dhritarashtra's warriors, the other mighty Kshatriyas, and the very Earth has been plunged into calamity and are being destroyed. But ah, Duryodhana still does not understand it."

Thus speak many redoubtable Kshatriyas. Others, O Bhaarata, say, "Jayadratha has already been despatched to Yama. Let the small-minded Duryodhana, with diminished resources, prepare for the funeral obsequies of the Saindhava, his brother-in-law."

Meanwhile, Arjuna sees the sun rapidly westering and Krishna urges his heartened steeds to still greater speed. The Kuru warriors cannot impede his progress at all, as Partha furrows a bloody trail through them, menacing them all like a lion a herd of deer, killing thousands on his inexorable way, drawing nearer a quailing Jayadratha with each moment as he races the Sun to the horizon.

Krishna now whips his fabulous horses and blows a reverberant blast on his Panchajanya the colour of clouds. So swiftly do the gandharva horses fly along now that they overtake Arjuna's arrows!

Seeing danger draw nearer, many Dhartarashtra kings and other Kshatriyas group together and surround Arjuna in some frenzy. Thus confronted by them all, Arjuna has to stop for a moment and now Duryodhana races up and catches up with his lustrous cousin. Seeing the chariot whose rumble is the roar of thunderheads, the ratha that flies the terrible standard bearing Hanuman animated upon it, howling and roaring terribly at them, your forces are quickly unnerved. And when the sun is almost entirely shrouded by the dust that the armies raise, the Kuru warriors, wounded and bleeding from awesome Arjuna's onslaught can no longer bear to even look at the two blindingly splendid Krishnas.'"

CANTO 97

Jayadratha-vadha Parva continued

"Sanjaya says, 'Rajan! I watch Vasudeva and Dhananjaya penetrate deep into our forces, after overrunning many akshauhinis, with their captains running away in fear. A little later, however, the Maharathas, filled with excitement and shame, and spurred on by their innate valour, regain their composure and begin to defy Arjuna again. However, the men who now ride against Arjuna do not return, like the rivers that never return from the ocean. Seeing this, many ignoble Kshatriyas incur sin and hell by turning their backs and running away, like atheists turning away from the Vedas.

Blasting their way through the squadron of Kuru chariots, the two bulls among men finally issue out of it, looking like the Sun and the Moon freed from the jaws of Rahu. The two Krishnas, their tiredness dispelled come through the great host of enemies like two fish passing through a strong net. Truly, they look like look like Yuga-suns risen in the sky, like men who have escaped from a raging conflagration, or like two fish emerging from the jaws of a makara. And they agitate the Kuru host like a pair of antediluvian makaras agitating the ocean.

While Partha and Krishna were in the midst of Drona's division, your warriors and sons thought that they would never emerge from it. However, now seeing them blithely dash out of its confines, they no longer have hopes for Jayadratha's life. They had thought that the two Krishnas would never be able to escape Drona and Hridika's son Kritavarman. Frustrating their hopes, the two Parantapas, Rajan, slice through Drona's division, and also the impenetrable Bhoja akshauhini. Seeing them, lick their way through the formidable akshauhinis like two blazing fires, your men despair and no longer hope to save Jayadratha's life. Then the intrepid Krishna and Dhananjaya begin to discuss among themselves how they could kill Jayadratha.

Arjuna says, "Six of the very greatest maharathas among the Dhartarashtras have set Jayadratha in their midst. But today, if I only see him, he will not escape me even if Indra with all the Devas become his protectors."

Thus, do the two Krishnas talk, O Mahabaho, while constantly looking for Jayadratha. Hearing them, for they speak freely and aloud, your sons set up a loud outcry. These two Krishna look like a pair of thirsty thunderous elephants, refreshed by drinking water after having crossed a desert. Beyond death and above decay, they look like two merchants who have crossed a mountainous country infested with tigers, lions and wild elephants. Indeed, seeing them free of Drona and Kritavarman and the dreadful light on Partha and Krishna's face, your warriors set up a loud bewailing from all sides.

Having shaken off Drona who is like a deadly poisonous snake or a great fire, as well as the other lords of the Earth, Partha and Krishna are like two blazing suns. Indeed, free of Drona's ocean-like division, they are full of joy like men who have safely crossed the vast deep itself. Free from the dense showers of shafts from the Drona and Kritavarman and their legions, Kesava and Arjuna look like Indra and Agni, or Suns of blinding effulgence. Pierced by the arrows of Bharadwaja's son, and their dark bodies dripping blood, they are as glorious as two mountains covered with flowering karnikaras.

Having crossed the vast lake, of which Drona is the crocodile, numberless arrows the fierce water-snakes and makaras, and great Kshatriyas the deep waters; having emerged out of the cloud of Drona's astras, whose thunder is the twanging of bows and the lightning the flashes of maces and swords, Partha and Krishna are like the Sun and Moon liberated from an engulfing darkness.

Crossing the field which Drona's arms had barred, all beings regard the dark splendid twain as men who have forded the five rivers—the Satadru, the Vipasa, the Ravi, the Chandrabhaga and the Vitasta—, with the ocean for their sixth, all in spate during the monsoon, and full of crocodiles. Wanting to kill Jayadratha who is no longer far from them, the two heroes look like two tigers waiting to fall upon a ruru deer. Their very faces make your warriors, Rajan, think of Jayadratha as one already dead.

Krishna and Arjuna together, with red eyes, are bursting with excitement and joy, and give vent to a battery of jubilant shouts and roars at their first sight of Jayadratha. Indeed, Rajan, the splendour then of Krishna, standing with reins in hand, and of Partha armed with his bow, is like that of Surya or Agni. Free from Drona's restraint, their joy at sight of Jayadratha not far off is like that of two fierce hawks at the sight of a piece of flesh; and even like a pair of hunting hawks do they swoop down on the hapless Saindhava.

But seeing Hrishikesa and Dhananjaya rout Drona's divisions, your valiant son, the king Duryodhana, whose mystic armour Drona has fastened to his majestic form with Brahma's own mantras, dashes forward in a single chariot to protect Jayadratha. He overtakes Krishna and Partha and wheels back to face Kesava of the lotus-like eyes. Seeing this incredible happening, your troops joyfully blow on horns and conches and beat a hundred thousand drums and utter deafening roars to match. Those who stand like burning fires around Jayadratha as his final guardians are also filled with joy on seeing your son.

Seeing Duryodhana confront them, now with his followers rallied behind him, Krishna speaks softly to Arjuna.'

CANTO 98

Jayadratha-vadha Parva continued

'Krishna says, "Look Arjuna, how wonderfully Duryodhana overtook us! There is no maharatha equal to him. He is a great bowman and can shoot his arrows to a great distance. He is a master warrior, almost invincible in battle, and knows all the different arts of war. Raised in luxury, he is held in great esteem by even the most renowned maharathas. Partha, he has always hated the Pandavas and it is best that you fight him now. For upon him rests, even as on a stake at dice, victory or defeat. Arjuna, expend the venom of your wrath which you have nurtured so long against Duryodhana. He is the root of all the wrongs the Pandavas have suffered and he is now within reach of your arrows. Trust your prowess.

Why has Duryodhana come to do battle with you? Fortune has brought him to you; Dhananjaya, kill him. He was born into a great palace, and he has never known want or deprivation. O bull among men, he also does not know your true might in battle. When there is none in the three worlds of the Devas, the Asuras and Manushyas who can vanquish you in battle, what can one Duryodhana do? Partha, now that he is within range of your ratha, kill him as Purandara slew Vritra.

Duryodhana has always tried to harm you. He cheated Yudhishtira at dice, and this prince with a sinful soul has sinned in many ways against the Dharmaraja. Arjuna, have no scruple, and kill this evil, wrathful and cruel man who is the very embodiment of avarice. Remember the theft of your kingdom through vile deceit; think of your exile in the forest; remember the shame of Draupadi; and remembering all that, put forth your strength and kill this most evil prince.

He has come to bar your way to Jayadratha. Providence has fetched him to you and he is within range of your arrows. He knows that he will have to fight you and today all your purposes, even those that you have not thought of, will be crowned with success. Arjuna, destroy this wretch of his race, the son of Dhritarashtra, even as Indra did of old the Asura Jambha at the Devasura yuddha. If you kill Duryodhana, you can then easily pierce through this headless army. Cut the very root of this evil one, and perform the avabhrita snana, the final cleansing bath of this war, with his blood."

Having heard Krishna out, Arjuna says, "Tathaastu! I will do what you say. Ignore everything else and ride at Duryodhana. I will cut off the head of this devil, who has enjoyed our kingdom for too long without a qualm. Will I not succeed, O Kesava, in avenging myself against this sinner who had Draupadi dragged by her hair into the Kuru sabha when she was in her period and had done no wrong herself?"

Speaking thus among themselves, the two Krishnas are filled with exultation; they urge their great white steeds towards Duryodhana. As for your son, Bharatarishabha, as he nears Partha and Krishna, he feels no fear, even though the occasion is charged to inspire dread. The Kshatriyas of your army applaud him for his daring; indeed, the entire Kuru host roars in exhilaration to watch their king dash forward to bar Arjuna and Krishna's way.

Held up by your son with his bow upraised, Arjuna is furious, and Duryodhana, too, is no less in fury. All the fierce Kshatriyas stop to watch their duel. Duryodhana, Arjuna and Krishna, all eager for the fight, roar and the three of them together raise their conches to their lips and blow resounding blasts on them. Hearing the deep boom of the Panchajanya and the Devadatta drown Duryodhana's lesser sankha, dread quickly seizes your warriors, who are certain that your son will die; they regard him already as a libation poured into the mouth of the sacred fire.

Your warriors cry in fear, "The king is slain! Our king is slain!"

But Duryodhana roars at them, "Dispel your fears! I will send the two Krishnas to Yama." Feeling certain of victory, wearing Bramha's magic kavacha, he further cries to Arjuna, "If, Partha, you are truly Pandu's son loose all your weapons, of this world and unworldly, at me. Let me see your much vaunted manliness today that wins the praise of so many great Kshatriyas.""'

CANTO 99

JAYADRATHA-VADHA PARVA CONTINUED

"Sanjaya says, 'Roaring out his challenge, Duryodhana strikes Arjuna with three lethal shafts than can excoriate an enemy; with four more, he pierces his enemy's four horses; and with another ten searing missiles he bloodies Krishna's chest and shoots the whip out of the Blue One's hands.

Partha, calm as ever, swift as ever, looses fourteen searing barbs at Duryodhana, stone-whetted and beautifully fletched with shining feathers. They fly true to their mark but every one of them glances harmlessly off the armour that Duryodhana wears. In some surprise, Arjuna shoots another nine and five keen arrows at his hated enemy. But these, too, glance mildly off Duryodhana's kavacha.

Krishna says to Arjuna, "Ah, this is passing strange, even as if mountains moved! Your arrows, O Partha, have turned weak. Has your Gandiva lost its power? Tell me, have the might of your grip and the power of your arms grown womanish? Will this not to be your last meeting with Duryodhana? For I am amazed to watch your terrible shafts fall soft as flowers on Duryodhana. What misfortune is this that your astras filled with the power of thunder and which never fail to pierce an enemy now glance so kindly off this sinner?"

Arjuna replies, "Krishna, I feel certain that Drona has wrapped Duryodhana in his own armour, his ancient kavacha which has the powers of the three worlds, whose secret only the Acharya knows, and which he once shared with me. None of my weapons can pierce this armour; not Indra can pierce it with his Vajra.

But you know all this too well, Krishna! Then why do you berate and provoke me? You know everything that has ever happened in all the worlds, in the past, the present, and what is in the womb of future. Madhusudana, no one knows all this as you do! Duryodhana wearing Drona's armour is fearless in battle. Yet, he does not know what one wearing this kavacha should do for he wears it only like a woman.

Watch now, Janardana, the might of my arms and of my bow. Even though he wears this greatest coat of mail, I will still vanquish Duryodhana. Brahma himself gave this golden armour to Angiras, who gave it to Brihaspati. Purandara had this kavacha from Brihaspati, and Indra once showed it to me with the mantras to be chanted while putting it on. Krishna, though this armour is divine, though Brahma himself created it, it will still not protect the wretched Duryodhana from my arrows."

Saying this, Arjuna invokes an inexorable astra with potent mantras and fits it to his bowstring. But even as he draws back the string of the Gandiva, from a long way off Aswatthaman burns up Arjuna's weapon in his very hand with another astra of untold power. Seeing Aswatthaman, the Brahmavadi, consume his occult weapon from a distance, a stricken Arjuna Swetavahana says to Kesava, "Janardana, I cannot use this astra twice, for if I do it will turn itself on me and kill me and all our troops."

Meanwhile, Rajan, Duryodhana pierces each of the Krishnas with nine barbs like venom-spitting serpents, and then showers down a veritable storm of other shafts over them. Your warriors exult to see this and blow on conches and horns and beat deafening rhythms on their drums; and their roaring fills earth and sky. A fuming Partha, licking the corners of his mouth, closely examines his enemy's body but sees no part that is not covered by the impenetrable armour.

Nothing else for it, the Vijaya in a savage flash kills his adversary's horses, his two Parshni charioteers, and then cleaves Duryodhana's bow and cuts away his leather finger guards, with a perfect incredible volley. The Pandava shatters the Kaurava's chariot next and, having cut away his gloves, strikes him agonisingly through his fingers and palms!

Seeing Duryodhana stricken by Arjuna's canny brilliance, seeing him with his chariot ruined and his bow broken and wringing his hands in pain, a host of Kuru warriors rush to rescue him and surround Arjuna's chariot with thousands of rathas, elephants and horses, and also with teeming legions of foot-soldiers, so that they can no longer be seen.

Dauntless, serene Partha begins to massacre the maharathas, other warriors and elephants, in their hundreds, striking off limbs and heads at his mighty will, so they fall thick and fast on the field. Slain, or in the very moment of being killed, they all fail to reach Arjuna's chariot which stands motionless full two miles from the besieging force on every side.

Now Krishna says urgently to his warrior of light, "Draw your bow forcefully, Partha, and raze the enemy as swiftly as you can, and I will blow my conch!"

Arjuna then draws his bow Gandiva to the fullest stretch and begins to decimate the enemy horribly, in a tide of blood. Meanwhile, his face covered with dust, Krishna raises his Panchajanya to his lips and blows reverberantly on it so all Kurukshetra shakes at the sound. From the thunderous twanging of the Gandiva and the awful blast of the Panchajanya, the Kuru warriors all around, their bodies turning weak, all fall down on the ground.

Arjuna's chariot, suddenly freed from the encircling press, flashes ahead like a bright cloud driven by the wind. Seeing Arjuna flare at them, the protectors of Jayadratha and their followers, all maharathas and mighty bowmen, are shaken and shout aloud. They unleash tempests of arrows at the lone chariot descending so swiftly upon them, and fill the field of the great hunt with the whistling of their arrows, the blare of their conches and other fierce noises—all this in as much fear as wrath!

Hearing the awful uproar that your troops raise, Krishna and Arjuna blow their conches, Rajan, and the twin sound seems to fill all the Earth, with her mountains, seas, islands and the nether worlds. The blast echoes through all the points of the compass, and is echoed back by both the armies. Your maharathas are at first terrified to see Krishna and Dhananjaya but they soon recover and continue to fight. The sight of the two most blessed Krishnas charging towards them is a wonderful one!'"

CANTO 100

JAYADRATHA-VADHA PARVA CONTINUED

"Sanjaya says, 'When your greatest warriors finally see those greatest of all the heroes of the Vrishni–Andhaka and the Kuru races, they lose no time, each striving to be the first, in engaging them in battle. On their great rattling chariots, decked with gold, spread with tiger-skins, resembling blazing fires and drawn by mettlesome steeds, they charge, illumining the ten points of the compass, brandishing their bows, the backs of whose staves are chased with dazzling gold. With terrible roars, eight great chariot-warriors, Bhurisravas, Sala, Karna, Vrishasena, Jayadratha, Kripa, Salya and Aswatthaman attack as if they will devour the sky and illuminate the world around in their splendid chariots, adorned with golden moons.

Fighting inspired, on the edge of madness even, they envelop Arjuna on every side with eight gales of fire. Their shining chariots, which rumble like thunderheads, are drawn by the very best horses of different species bred in diverse countries, some in mountainous realms, some in the land of rivers, and some in that of the Sindhus. And other Kuru maharathas converge on Arjuna's chariot to protect your son Duryodhana.

These great warriors, Rajan, take up their conches and blow them, filling the sky, the earth and her seas, with their booming blare. Then Vasudeva blows his Panchajanya and Dhananjaya his Devadatta, those best of all conches on Earth. The blast of the Devadatta fills the world, the sky and the ten cardinal points; and the Panchajanya, surpassing all sounds, fills the highest heaven and the deepest earth. The awesome and appalling clamour persists, filling the timid with fear and the brave with excitement.

Thousands of great maharathas, matchless bowmen, kings from diverse realms, some fighting for the Kuru cause and other for the Pandavas, beat drums, jharjharas, cymbals and mridangas. And the Kuru heroes, filled with rage, for they cannot stand the blasting of Arjuna and Krishna's unworldly conches, also blow great conches, while their troops roar behind them in support.

Though being urged forward by the blare of conches, the chariot-warriors, elephants and horses of the Kuru army are yet full of fear, and indeed, O lord, they look ill. The booming conches of Krishna and Arjuna agitate the Kuru host and their bravest warriors seem to be like the very heavens fallen down through some vast convulsion of nature. The stunning din, Rajan, resounds all around and affrights your troops as if this is some critical moment and event at the end of the Yuga terrifying all living creatures.

Then Duryodhana and the eight great maharathas chosen to protect Jayadratha all surround Arjuna. Aswatthaman strikes Krishna with three and seventy shafts, and Arjuna with three broad-headed ones, and their standard and four horses with five others. Seeing Krishna injured, a furious Arjuna looses a hundred arrows at Drona's son. Then piercing Karna with ten arrows and Vrishasena with three, Dhananjaya destroys Salya's bow with arrows fitted to its string. Salya takes up another bow and stabs the son of Pandu with a blistering barb, while Bhurisravas cuts him sharp with three stone-whetted shafts, golden-winged.

Karna strikes Arjuna with thirty-two arrows and Vrishasena with seven. Jayadratha himself pierces Arjuna with three and seventy shafts and Kripa with ten. The king of the Madras also lacerates Arjuna with ten shafts and the son of Drona first with sixty arrows, and again with five arrows; Aswatthaman makes Krishna a home for twenty more of his scathing barbs. Unruffled, Arjuna of the white steeds, displaying supernal dexterity, and speed that is past believing, strikes Karna with a dozen shafts, Vrishasena with three, and Partha breaks Salya's bow at the grip.

Shooting the son of Somadatta with three arrows and Salya with ten, he strikes Kripa with five and twenty thunderbolts, Jayadratha with a hundred, and Drona's son with seventy: all in what seems, what is, a single moment. A battling, wrathful Bhurisravas cracks the goad in Krishna's hand, and bloodies Arjuna with three and twenty shafts. Dhananjaya retaliates with a flashflood of missiles, hundreds and hundreds of arrows, like a tempest tearing at some masses of clouds.'"

CANTO 101

JAYADRATHA-VADHA PARVA CONTINUED

"Dhritarashtra says almost abstractedly, 'Describe to me, O Sanjaya, the beautiful and resplendent standards which both the Parthas and our warriors fly.'

Sanjaya says, 'Then listen, Rajan, as I describe to you the banners that blaze on that field of death like fire and are flaunted there. They are made entirely of gold thread, or chased with strings of gold, and look like the fulvid Mount Meru. Attached to them all around are the most striking banners of different colours. Fluttering in the wind, seeming to float on the breeze, the banners of the maharathas are like exquisite women dancing in an arena of pleasure; they are magnificent like the rainbow.

Arjuna's standard, with the image of Hanuman on its main flag, the great Vanara his face snarling and a lion's tail, and also adorned with many other banners, all with strange and dreadful spirits animated upon them, which cry out and roar and screech chillingly, terrifies the Kuru host.

The lion-tail pennant atop Aswatthaman's ratha shines with the lustre of the rising sun. Decked with gold, wondrous like the rainbow, it floats and flaps in the wind high above, inspiring the greatest Kuru warriors.

The standard of Adhiratha's son Karna bears the motif of a golden elephant-rope and seems to fill the entire sky. Adorned with banners of gold and garlands, it appears to dance upon his chariot when the wind shakes it.

Kripa, son of Gotama, and the first Acharya of the Pandavas, the Brahmana given to tapasya, has for his emblem a superb bull and Kripa looks as glorious as Mahadeva the destroyer of the Tripura with his bull.

Vrishasena's pennant is always in the van of the army and his emblem is a peacock calling out, made of gold and embellished with jewels and gems. Rajan, it glows like the ratha of Skanda the celestial Senapati. Shining with his brilliant mayura and with a beautiful golden ploughshare, Vrishasena looks resplendent on his chariot, like a great flame.

Salya, the ruler of the Madras, has on his standard-top an image like Annalakshmi, the Goddess of corn, lovely and bountiful. Salya's standard also shows a huge silver elephant with golden peacocks on every side. His great graces your army like the immense white elephant Airavata adorning the host of the celestial king.

A silver boar adorns the top of Jayadratha's flagstaff, which is wound about with golden chains, and shimmers like white crystal and glorious as Surya in the battle between the Devas and the Asuras of long ago.

The standard of Somadatta's son, who is devoted to yagnas, bears the sign of a golden sacrificial stake, shining like the sun or the moon and it glitters like the lofty yupastamba erected in the greatest of sacrifices, the Rajasuya.

On king Duryodhana's towering standard chased with gold is a great black elephant encrusted with glittering jewels. Tinkling with the sound of a hundred bells, it waves on top of his chariot and, Rajan, your son, that bull among the Kurus, looks magnificent.

These nine excellent standards stand tallest among your divisions. The tenth great banner is Arjuna's, with the terrific Vanara and with it Arjuna looks like Himavat with a blazing fire on his summit.

These mighty chariot-warriors, all parantapas, take up their wonderful, bright and colossal bows to face Arjuna. Partha, too, achiever of celestial feats, raises his incomparable, enemy-destroying Gandiva—all because of your evil policy, Rajan. And because of you, so many royal warriors, rulers of men from different kingdoms called to arms by your sons, will be slain in battle and with them countless noble, blameless horses and elephants.

The maharathas led by Duryodhana on one side and the bull of the Pandavas on the other, utter loud shouts and roars and begin the encounter. And astounding and unearthly is the feat that Arjuna, with Krishna for his charioteer, achieves there by battling all your great warriors single-handed. Resplendent is the mighty-armed hero as he stretches his Gandiva, determined to vanquish all your maharathas in order to kill Jayadratha.

In a supernatural shimmer of archery, Arjuna casts a mantle of arrows, thousands upon thousands of deadly arrows, over your forces so that they become invisible. On their part, they respond with a haze of shafts loosed from every side. Seeing Arjuna engulfed, obscured, your troops set up a loud cheer.'"

CANTO 102

JAYADRATHA-VADHA PARVA CONTINUED

"Dhritarashtra asks, 'O Sanjaya, once Arjuna has Jayadratha in sight, what do Krishna and he do?'

Sanjaya says, 'It is late afternoon of the momentous day, Rajan, in the battle between the Panchalas and the Kurus, when Drona becomes the wager for which each side fights to win or lose. Intent on killing the Acharya, the Panchalas, roaring all together besiege him with multitudinous volleys. Fierce, dreadful and extraordinary as the battle of yore between the Devas and the Asuras is the encounter between the forces of Drupada and his inveterate enemy, the meridian son of Bharadwaja.

All the Panchalas with the Pandavas, finding Drona's chariot within reach, unleash many great astras in their feverish attempt to breach and destroy his vyuha. Chariot-warriors ride slowly, purposefully Drona's ratha, making the earth tremble, and loosing rivers of arrows at the master.

Brihadkshatra, the Kaikeya maharatha, attacks Drona incessantly with heavy shafts forceful as thunderbolts. The famed Kshemadhurti quickly comes between Brihadkshatra and Drona, firing scathes of razor-headed barbs at Kshemadhurti. Seeing this, the mighty Dhrishtaketu, bull among the Chedis, also swiftly assails Kshemadhurti, quite as Mahendra did the Asura Sambara. Seeing him dash forward, like the Yama himself with mouth agape, the mighty Viradhanwan confronts him.

Meanwhile, resolved to win the war by himself, Drona rides at Yudhishtira. Your son, the gifted, fearless Vikarna, confronts the marauding, potent Nakula. Parantapa Durmukha covers the onrushing Sahadeva with thousands of light-swift barbs. The heroic Vyaghradatta manfully faces Satyaki the Naravyaghra, making him repeatedly tremble with bolts like fire. Bhurisravas, son of Somadatta, stands firm against the five maharatha sons of Draupadi, he also lashing them with gales of arrows.

The sinister and powerful maharatha, the Rakshasa Alambusha, Rishyasringa's fierce son of awful mien, confronts the charging Bhimasena. That encounter between manusha and rakshasa, Rajan, resembles the mythic battle of old between Rama and Ravana.

Yudhishtira, lord of the Bharatas, strikes Drona with ninety perfectly aimed arrows in all his vital organs. The enraged Drona bloodies the Dharmaraja's chest with five and twenty excruciating shafts. In sight of all the archers, Drona looses twenty arrows at Ajatasatru's horses, charioteer and standard, but Yudhishtira, truly a majestic Kshatriya at war today, cuts them all down in flight.

Further incensed, Drona breaks Yudhishtira's bow in his hands and covers the Dharmaputra with a thousand barbs shot in a moment. Seeing the king engulfed by Drona's dark torrent, men of both armies believe that the Pandava is either dead or has fled the battle. Many Pandava warriors cry out in despair, "Oh, the Brahmana has killed our king!"

In some strife, Yudhishtira puts down the bow that Drona broke and takes up another, stronger and of exceptional brightness. Now, raising his won archery, he quite easily burns up Drona's dense tirades in the air. Rajan, the son of Dharma is altogether breathtaking to watch and, having consumed all Drona's shafts, a red-eyed Yudhishtira invokes a great astra that can rive Yudhishtira mountain. With a golden shaft, eight bells attached to it, of awesome appearance and entirely terrible, the mighty Yudhishtira raises his bow with this weapon fitted to it and gives such a roar that all the living tremble at it.

Seeing the astra that Yudhishtira holds aloft, all creatures, in accord, pray, "May Drona be saved!"

Loosed by the king, that missile like a snake just freed from its slough, flies at Drona, illumining the sky and all the directions cardinal and subsidiary, like a Nagina with a fiery mouth. Watching the Nagastra flare towards him, Drona the master invokes the Brahmastra, which flies at Yudhishtira's chariot blowing the Nagastra to dust on its way. Yudhishtira

Quicker than thinking, Yudhishtira summons his own Brahmastra and the two great ayudhas extinguish each other in the sky. Not pausing, Ajatasatru pierces Drona deep with five immaculate shafts and, with a sixth razor-faced arrow, he breaks Drona's great bow.

With a growl, Drona, the Kshatriya-grinder, flings aside his broken bow and hurls a mace like a thunderbolt at Yudhishtira. Instantly the Pandava snatches up a mace of his own and casts it at his master's gada. The two mighty weapons explode against each other showering an effusion of sparks all around Yudhishtira. His rage mounting by the moment, Drona kills Yudhishtira's horses, with four unerring deadly barbs, and with another broad-headed shaft, he breaks the king's regal bow, which is like a stake erected to worship Indra.

With another arrow, he cuts down Yudhishtira's banner and with three more, he injures the Pandava himself. Yudhishtira leaps down from his ratha and stands weaponless and with his arms raised, helpless.

O Bharatarishabha, seeing Yudhishtira without a chariot and unarmed, Drona startles his enemies, why both armies, by cleaving to the base vow he had sworn to Duryodhana and, violating every dharma of war, continues to shoots deadly showers of arrows at the Dharmaraja and charges towards him like a lion bounding at a deer.

Cries of *Oh*! and *Alas*! arise from the Pandava army.

Many cry, "Bharadwaja's son has killed our king!"

O Bhaarata, these and other loud wails go up from the Pandava forces. But before Drona can reach his brother, Sahadeva dashes up on his chariot and, mounting it with alacrity, Yudhishtira flees the field, escaping the dangerous Brahmana, who is left howling in frustration.'"

CANTO 103

Jayadratha-vadha Parva continued

"Sanjaya says, 'Kshemadhurti strikes the valorous Brihadkshatra in his chest with several arrows, and the advancing prince of the Kaikeyas strikes him back with ninety deadly straight barbs. The Kshemadhurti smashes Brihadkshatra's bow with a broad-tipped shaft and immediately stabs him deep with another longer arrow, drawing a gush of blood. Great Brihadkshatra takes up another bow and, smiling at his enemy, kills maharatha Kshemadhurti's horses, charioteer and ruins his chariot, in a flurry. Then, with another wedge-headed shafts, he cleanly dissevers his royal antagonist head, with its sparkling ear-rings, and graced with wavy locks and a crown; the noble head rolls onto the ground, shimmering like a star fallen from the sky. Having slain his enemy, the triumphant Brihadkshatra falls upon your troops with great ferocity.

The seasoned Viradhanwan flies to check Dhrishtaketu who rides intently against Drona. The two heroes lash each other with thousands of arrows. Those two Naravyaghras fight like two leaders of elephant herds in the deep jungle, both determined to kill the other, or two angry tigers in a mountain-cave, and their duel is one to be seen, O Rajan, breathtaking it is. The very Siddhas and the Charanas, in great numbers, gaze down at it raptly.

Then, with a rumbling laugh, Viradhanwan shatters Dhrishtaketu's bow with a thick and heavy arrow. Throwing down the broken bow, the king of the Chedis seizes an iron spear, its head of gold, and casts it with immense force at Viradhanwan's chariot. The lance strikes Viradhanwan squarely through his heart he falls dead, his blood spraying from both his breast and back.

After the fall of the Trigarta maharatha, the Pandavas break right through your army. Your son Durmukha looses sixty slender shafts at Sahadeva, and roars out an echoing challenge. Sahadeva, unmoved, indeed smiling, drills your son, his cousin, with a squall of arrows, flinging him back against his flagstaff. The mighty Sahadeva, roused, never pausing, gores Durmukha with nine powerful barbs, then cuts down his proud standard and fells his four horses. As his cousin stands stunned, Madri's son now beheads his sarathy, and in the same instant breaks your prince's bows in his hands grown weak.

Still not desisting, Sahadeva pierces Durmukha himself with a sizzle of five molten arrows, at which your son jumps down from his horseless chariot, and clambers onto Niramitra, prince of the Trigartas', ratha. Sahadeva kills Niramitra in the very midst of his army with a thick arrow; that prince falls headless from his chariot, plunging your army in grief. Slaying him, the mighty-armed Sahadeva looks as glorious as Dasaratha's son Rama, after he killed the feral and mighty Rakshasa Khara. O Rajan, seeing maharatha Niramitra die, loud cries of lamentation rise among the Trigarta warriors.

Nakula, in a moment, amazingly vanquishes your son, the large eyed Vikarna.

With a cloud of arrows, Vyaghradatta makes Satyaki and his horses, charioteer and standard invisible in the midst of his forces. However, Sini's mighty grandson cuts down all those missiles, and in a great scarlet eruption kills Vyaghradatta along with his horses, charioteer, felling his standard as well. At the fall of that prince, the Magadhas, fighting vigorously, surround Satyaki from all sides, covering him with their arrows and spears by the thousands, as also with mallets, thick clubs and keen lances. The invincible Satyaki, bull among men, with the greatest ease, laughing, vanquishes and annihilates almost all of them. A small remnant escapes from the field. Seeing this, your army, already distressed by Yuyudhana's fearsome shafts, breaks apart, my lord!

After slaughtering your troops, Satyaki raises his bow high and shakes it in triumph and he is resplendent. Your army shrinks from the radiant Vrishni hero and none dare approach him. Then a fuming Drona, rolling his eyes, charges the uncontainable Satyaki.'"

CANTO 104

JAYADRATHA-VADHA PARVA CONTINUED

"Sanjaya says 'The illustrious son of Somadatta strikes each of the sons of Draupadi, all great archers, with five arrows, and then seven more. Badly wounded by that fierce shura, they are dazed and for a while do not know what to do. Then Satanika, Nakula's son, strikes Somadatta's son with two searing shafts and gives a ringing roar. At once, his other brothers also resume battle and draw copious spurts of blood from Somadatta's son, each with three arrows.

That Kshatriya shoots five terrific barbs, piercing each son of Draupadi viciously. The five brothers surround him and bloody him savagely with their arrows. Arjuna's son by Draupadi despatches Saumadatti's four horses to the land of Yama, while Bhimasena's son destroys his bow, and with a loud shout transfixes his enemy with razorine barbs. The son of Yudhishtira fells his standard, while Nakula's son kills his charioteer from his ratha.

Now Sahadeva's son sees that the enemy is on the point of leaving the field and cuts off his head with a crescent-tipped shaft. The head of that illustrious warrior, decked with earrings of gold, falls on the ground and adorns the field like the burning sun that rises at the end of the Yuga. Seeing this, your troops, O Rajan, are overcome by stark terror and run in all directions.

The Rakshasa Alambusha, Rishyasringa's son, fights the mighty Bhimasena in frenzy; their contention is like Ravana's son Indrajit's encounter with Lakshmana. Seeing the Rakshasa fight the human warrior, all are enthralled and wonderstruck. An amused Bhima wounds the fiend with nine heavy arrows making the Rakshasa scream in the most hideous way. He charges Bhima with all his followers. Alambusha strikes Bhima with five thunderbolts and quickly destroys thirty rathas that support him. He blasts another four hundred of Bhima's rathas all the while lacerating Bhimasena himself with a barrage of barbarous winged missiles.

Ah, the mighty Bhima, struck deeply by the Rakshasa, swoons and sits down on the deck of his ratha. However, the son of Vayu recovers quickly and leaping up, crimson-eyed with rage, draws his tremendous bow and strikes Alambusha in every part of his body, with arrows like thunder. And the Rakshasa, who resembles a great mass of antimony, looks resplendent, O Rajan, indeed like a flowering kinsuka in full bloom.

While being struck by the shafts that fly from Bhima's bow, the Rakshasa remembers the slaying of his brother Baka by the titanic Pandava. Assuming an awful, monstrous form, he says to Bhima, "Fight a little longer, Pandava, and behold my prowess today! Evil-hearted one, the best of Rakshasas, the mighty Baka was my brother. It is true that you killed him but that was when I was away."

Saying this, Alambusha makes himself invisible with maya, and covers Bhimasena with a black storm of arrows. But Bhima, O Rajan, covers the very sky with a tremendous fusillade and forces Alambusha back to his chariot. But, next moment, the Rakshasa uses sorcery again to dive deep underground, and then once more soars high into the sky.

Alambusha assumes myriad uncanny forms, now becoming tiny and then enormous, filling earth and sky with his dreadful roaring. From above he chants many dark spells so thousands of fell arrow showers flare down on Bhima and his men, as well as kunapas, lances, spiked maces, short barbs, scimitars, swords and bolts of thunder. These eerie weapons raze Bhima's troops as well as countless elephants, horses and foot-soldiers.

Another river of blood flows, with rathas for its eddies, elephants its crocodiles, the chatras of maharathas its swans, and the flesh and marrow of animals, its mire and severed human arms its snakes. Hordes of Rakshasas, pisachas and other blood-drinkers and flesh-eaters stalk the banks of the darkling river and carry away numberless Chedis, Panchalas and Srinjayas.

Seeing Alambusha haunt the field so fearlessly, and his dark prowess, the Pandavas are full anxious; while joy fills the hearts of your troops. Amongst your army turned irrevocably to evil, hair raising sounds of musical instruments blares cacophonously, which the Pandavas cannot bear even as a snake cannot bear the clap of human palms.

Bhima, the son of the Wind-god, his eyes red as copper with rage, with glances that like fire consumes everything, invokes the astra called Tvashtri, like the divine artificer himself doing so, and millions of arrows flash out from his ratha in every direction. Bhima aroused puts your dense legions to rout, mowing them down all around him. The Tvashtrastra dissolves the maya with which Alambusha has mantled Kurukshetra; it direly wound the Rakshasa himself.

Struck violently through every part of his body, Alambusha abandons the fight and takes refuge with Drona's akshauhini. At the defeat of that prince of the Rakshasas by the noble Bhima, the Pandavas fill every point of the compass with leonine roars and joyously worship the mighty son of Marut, even like the Maruts worshipping Sakra after the defeat of Prahlada in the ancient war between Deva and Asura.'"

CANTO 105

JAYADRATHA-VADHA PARVA CONTINUED

"Sanjaya says, 'After escaping from Bhima, Alambusha fights fearfully in another part of the field, where he confronts Hidimbi's son Ghatotkacha, and harries him viciously with a spate of flaming arrows. A horrific duel breaks out between those two lions among Rakshasas. As Indra and Sambara did in olden days, they fight with deep sorcery, spells of maya, and their battle resembles that between Rama and Ravana on Lanka!

Ghatotkacha strikes Alambusha through his chest with twenty exceptionally long arrows, and repeatedly roars like a tiger. Also roaring shatteringly, and smiling to show curved fangs, Alambusha strikes back viciously. Quickly, both mighty Rakshasas, in mounting frenzy, use their powers of maya in a duel of sorcery, but neither gains any advantage so equally matched are they. Each a powerful mayavi, they create a hundred sinister spells, and bewilder the other.

Seeing Alambusha dissolve all Ghatotkacha's conjurations with his own spectres, the Pandavas are anxious and many of their foremost maharathas surround him in a protective cordon. Bhimasena and others all attack Alambusha and, hemming him in from all sides with their rathas, rain astras on him, like men in a forest cornering an elephant with blazing brands.

Annulling their arrow storms with his maya shakti, Alambusha frees himself from that press of chariots like an elephant escaping a forest fire. Drawing his terrible bow whose twang resembles Indra's Vajra striking, he pierces Bhima with twenty-five sizzling shafts, Ghatotkacha with five, Yudhishtira with three, Sahadeva with seven, Nakula with three and seventy, and each of the five sons of Draupadi with five arrows, and gives a weird and bloodcurdling scream.

Bhimasena strikes him square with arrows with the power of the wind, Sahadeva with five, Yudhishtira with a hundred, Nakula with three and Ghatotkacha with five hundred. Alambusha, unmoved, returns their fire, goring Ghatotkacha with seventy wicked barbs, and pale devil gives another horrible bellow shakes the Earth, O Rajan, with her mountains, forests, trees and waters.

Deeply wounded by those maharathas, Alambusha pierces with five arrows each, and then he swiftly covers Ghatotkacha with countless sable-hued missiles, fletched with wings of gold and whetted on stone. Every barb burns into Ghatotkacha, like angry snakes a mountain summit.

The anxious Pandavas and Ghatotkacha continue to pour on their firetides, from every side. Wounded by the Pandavas, Alambusha mortal as he is, soon does not know what to do and his chariot in flames and he himself flows blood from a thousand wounds. Seeing this, Bhima's terrific son sees time come to kill Alambusha. He leaps out of his own ratha and, rushing up to Alambusha's ratha, which now resembles a burnt mountain peak or a broken heap of antimony, seizes his dreadful enemy, snatching him down from it like Garuda snatching up a snake in his talons.

Ghatotkacha lifts Alambusha high with his mighty hands, whirls him round over his head, so like his awesome father Bhima does his enemies, and smashes him down onto the hard ground so his body is blown apart like an earthen pot flung against a rock. Such an eruption of flesh and blood, O Rajan! Roar after roar of triumph erupts from the triumphant son of Bhima, in absolute frenzy, drenched with his enemy's blood and spattered with pieces of his flesh from head to foot, and your troops tremble, whimper like small boys and many sully themselves. Alambusha, so terrible and indomitable a moment ago, lies like a tall sala tree uprooted and shattered by a wrathful wind.

Upon the slaughtering of the wanderer of the night, the Parthas are ecstatic, give vent to a vast chorus of roars, and wave their bright scarves and other cloths in the air. Your brave warriors, however, see the mighty Alambusha, prince of the Rakshasas, lying like a crushed mountain, and cry out and howl in shock and defeat. Many curious ones go up to look closely at the shattered body lying like some great piece of charcoal, no longer able to burn.

Ghatotkacha roars reverberantly like Vasava after slaying the Asura Bala. His sires and other kinsmen applaud him for felling the Rakshasa, like an alambusha fruit, and he celebrates with his friends, and there arises a loud tumult in the Pandava army of conches and arrows being rattled together. Hearing that noise the enraged Kauravas shout back in anger, filling the whole world with echoing tumult.'"

CANTO 106

JAYADRATHA-VADHA PARVA CONTINUED

"Dhritarashtra says, 'Tell me, Sanjaya, how Satyaki Yuyudhana battles Drona so valiantly. I feel a great curiosity to hear about it.'

Sanjaya says, "Listen, O wise one, to an account of the hair-raising battle between Drona and the Pandavas led by Yuyudhana. Seeing the Kuru army slaughtered by Satyaki, Drona himself attacks the brilliant Vrishni hero. Satyaki swiftly assails him with blistering ferocity with five and twenty short and savage barbs. Drona pierces Satyaki, with five perfect golden-winged shafts, which plunge through his resilient mail, and drinking his blood, enter the earth behind him like hissing serpents.

Like an elephant prodded hard with a goad, an inflamed Satyaki gores Drona with fifty long shafts that are like flames. Drona responds with fervid volleys, wounding Yuyudhana direly so the Satwata's radiant face suddenly shows anxiety, while Drona continues to loose his tide of burning arrows. Seeing Satyaki stagger in his chariot and even lower his bow, your sons and troops, O Rajan, exult and roar repeatedly.

Some way off, Yudhishtira hears that celebrant uproar and sees Satyaki in danger. He cries to all his soldiers, 'Drona is about to devour Satyaki even as Rahu does the Sun. Ride swiftly, you must save our Yuyudhana from the dreadful Acharya."

Yudhishtira cries to Dhrishtadyumna, "Why do you linger, Dhrishtadyumna? Don't you see the great peril that has already arisen from Drona? He toys with Satyaki like a cruel boy does with a bird tied with a string. Fly all of you, with Bhima, to Satyaki. I will follow with my men. Satyaki is in the very jaws of death. Do not waste a moment but go and snatch him away from the murderous Brahmana!"

And not hesitating a moment himself, Yudhishtira, with his troops behind him, charges towards Drona. Bless you, my king, but the Pandavas and the Srinjayas attack Drona all together, surrounding him, and unleash torrents of arrows at him, winged with kanka and peacock feathers shimmering in the gloom.

The Acharya receives them smiling, even like a householder welcoming honoured guests with seats and water! And he satisfies them amply with his extravagant hospitality of arrows. And none of them can even gaze at him, who is like the thousand-rayed Surya at midday who scorches all those great bowmen with lavish banks of arrows, like the Sun burning everything below him with his rays.

Struck like ten deadly storms by Drona, the Pandavas and the Srinjayas find no protector, like elephants sunk in a quagmire. And indeed the mighty arrows of the Brahmana Drona are like the scalding rays of the sun blasting everything around. In moments, he has slain five and twenty of Dhrishtadyumna's Panchala maharathas, as all the Pandava and Panchala legions are helpless onlookers. He continues to raze their greatest warriors like children before him.

After slaughtering a hundred Kekaya warriors and routing their army, Drona stands, Rajan, like Yama with maw agape, still hungry. The Brahmana vanquishes the Panchalas, the Srinjayas, the Matsyas and the Kekayas. Millions of living men suddenly breathing no more because the dreadful Acharya has hewn off their heads or blown their hearts to shreds. Their teeming troops invaded by his arrows cry out pitifully like the denizens of a forest engulfed by a conflagration. But Satyaki is rescued.

Above, riveted, the Devas, Gandharvas, and the Pitris say, "Look, the Panchalas and the Pandavas, with all their troops, are running away from Bharadwaja's son."

As Drona annihilates the Somakas, none venture to stand up to him and none succeed in wounding him in the least. While the Brahmana turned from his swadharma calmly butchers maharathas, past all count by now, Yudhishtira suddenly hears a faint tone of the great Panchajanya that Krishna blows. Such bedlam reigns on Kurukshetra, as the heroic protectors of Jayadratha fight Arjuna, and while the Dhartarashtras roar and shout before the great ratha of the two Krishna surging toward the Saindhava, that even the virile twang of the of the Gandiva is inaudible.

Yudhishtira feels faint, thinking, "Ah, Arjuna fares darkly! For I do not hear the Panchajanya anymore and the Kauravas roar so lustily and gleefully!"

Stricken with anxiety, a dazed Yudhishtira says to Satyaki, "O Yuyudhana, the time for that sanatana dharma which the mahatmans of old said that friends must do for their friends has come. Satyaki, none among all my warriors is a greater well-wisher of ours than you. Only one who is always courteous, obedient and valorous beyond all common measure should be entrusted with a grave mission in times of trouble. As Krishna is ever the refuge of the Pandavas, so are you, who are equal to him in prowess and affection.

And so I will lay a burden on you knowing that you will not frustrate my purpose. Arjuna is your brother, friend and acharya, O bull among men, so go to his help now when he is in distress, O Satwata. Mahatman, you are devoted to truth. You are a great Kshatriya. You are the dispeller of the fears of friends and celebrated in the world for your deeds and as one who is always truthful. Satyaki, he who casts away his body while fighting for friends is equal to him who gives away the Earth to Brahmanas. We have heard of many kings who are in heaven for giving away this Earth as dakshina to Brahmanas, with due rites. I beg you with folded hands, that you too attain the rewards of giving away the very Earth to Brahmanas, or something even higher, by incurring danger to yourself for Arjuna's sake.

Krishna, the dispeller of the fears of his friends, is ever willing to sacrifice himself for them. You, Satyaki, are another such. None but a hero can help another hero by fighting valorously in battle purely for fame. An ordinary man cannot do this. And now there is none but you who can protect Arjuna. Once, while lauding your many great feats, Arjuna gave me much pleasure by recounting them repeatedly. He said of you that you are gifted with unearthly dexterity of hand, and that you are a master of every manner of warfare, that you are a man of great abilities and great deeds.

My brother said, "Satyaki is endued with great wisdom, he knows every weapon thoroughly, is a true hero, and is never baffled in battle. With his powerful neck and broad chest, with mighty arms and wide face, with awesome strength and prowess, Satyaki is a maharatha among maharathas and he is the noblest of men. Yuyudhana is my disciple and my friend; I am dear to him and he is dear to me. Becoming my ally, Sini's grandson will crush the Kauravas.

Even if Krishna, Rama, and Aniruddha, the mighty Pradyumna, Gada, Sarana, Samba, with all the Vrishnis, arm themselves to fight for us, I will only appoint Satyaki, tiger among men, Satyaki of unfazed prowess, to the task, for there is none equal to him."

This is what Dhananjaya told me in the Dwaita vana while extolling your merits in an assembly of Rishis. It is only appropriate that you now live up to Arjuna's expectation, as well as Bhima's and mine! When we were on our way back from the various tirthas, I witnessed your reverence for Arjuna in Dwaraka. While we were at Upaplavya, I saw no one else who showed us as much affection as you did. You are of noble lineage and bear us both respect and love. And so, O Vrishni hero, out of your love and regard for Arjuna, who is your friend and your guru, you must do what is demanded in this critical hour by, O great bowman, your friendship, your genius, your noble lineage and truthfulness.

O Satyaki of Madhu's vamsa, Duryodhana wearing Drona's armour has gone in pursuit of Arjuna! The other great Kaurava maharathas already hunt Arjuna and I hear a great tumult in the vicinity of Arjuna's ratha. Satyaki, you must ride there like the wind for your guru is in mortal peril. Bhimasena and the rest of us will resist Drona with all our forces, if he advances against you.

Ah, look where the Kaurava troops are fleeing the battle, wailing as they run. Like the ocean at full tide agitated by a mighty tempest, Arjuna stirs the Dhartarashtra host. Look at the cloud of dust that rises and spreads across the field from the men and rathas that dash about. Ah, look where the Sindhu–Sauviras, armed with spikes, lances surround Arjuna with their horsemen.

Arjuna will never be able to kill Jayadratha without first vanquishing this host of ferocious fighters for every man of them will lay down his life for the Saindhava king before allowing Partha near him. Look at the invincible Dhartarashtra force stationed there bristling with arrows, spears, their tall standards, and teeming with cavalry and elephants. Listen to the beat of their drums and the blare of their conches, their tremendous roars, and the earthshaking rumble of their chariot-wheels. Listen to the deep grunts and trumpeting of their elephants, the heavy tread of their foot-soldiers, and the hoof-beats of their charging horses, al of which make Bhumi devi herself tremble.

Facing Arjuna is Jayadratha's akshauhini, and behind him is Drona's. The enemy is so great in numbers that it would dismay the Lord of the Devas himself. Plunged in the midst of this fathomless host, Arjuna could well lose his life. And if he is killed, how can I live on? Oh Satyaki, is this calamity to befall me when you are alive? The son of Pandu is dark-blue in colour, young in years, with wavy locks and exceptionally handsome. Vigorous in battle and familiar with every kind of warfare, the mighty-armed Arjuna penetrated the Bharata host at sunrise. The day is about to end, Satyaki, and I do not know whether he lives or not. The vast Kuru host is like the ocean and Arjuna has breached it on his own, the army which even the gods cannot overcome. My mind is clouded and Drona attacks my forces with irresistible might! You see,

O Mahabaho, how the Acharya fights.

You are discerning when several tasks present themselves at once. And it must be you who take this critical task upon yourself, none other. I am certain that going to the embattled Arjuna's help and rescuing him must be our first priority. I have no fear for Krishna of Dasarha's race because he is the Protector and the Lord of the Universe. When this Naravyaghra can vanquish the three worlds assembled together, what need be said of this insignificant Dhritarashtra host? But Krishna is sworn not to fight.

Arjuna however, Satyaki, faces the most in today's battle and may lose his life. This is what fills me with dread and grief. So go to him, mighty, Satyaki, for men like you should follow men like him, at a time like this, sent forth by one like me.

Among the greatest of the Vrishni vamsa, we regard two as Atirathas. They are the mighty-armed Pradyumna and yourself, O Satyaki great renown. In the mastery of weapons, you are equal to Narayana himself, and in strength to Sankarshana. O Naravyaghra, in courage you are equal to Dhananjaya, and exceed Bhishma and Drona and all the other greatest warriors. The wise say of you, 'There is nothing that Satyaki cannot accomplish.'

So accede to the wishes of all of us here, of myself and of Arjuna. It would not be dharma if, O Mahabaho, to refuse what we ask of you today. Reckless of your very life, ride into battle like the great hero you are. The scions of Dasarha's race never care to protect their lives in war by avoiding the most dangerous battle, or fighting from behind breast-works, or fleeing an encounter—Dasarhas never adopt the ways of cowards.

The virtuous Arjuna is your superior, and Krishna is superior to both of you. And I also say to you that I am the superior of your superiors and Arjuna agrees with me in this matter. Go then to Arjuna and, at my behest, penetrate the army of Dhritarashtra's evil son. Challenge the great maharathas who protect Jayadratha and accomplish, O Satyaki, feats you are worthy of!"""

CANTO 107

JAYADRATHA-VADHA PARVA CONTINUED

"Sanjaya says, 'Hearing these warm and loving words from Yudhishtira Dharmaraja, Satyaki, the Sini bull, says, "O you of unfading glory, I have heard you well, and what you say to me is just, delights my heart and inspires me to earn fame and honour for myself by fighting Arjuna's grave cause.

At a time like this, it is high dharma and ineluctable fate that you find me, who am devoted to you, to command at your will, as you would Arjuna himself. As for myself, I am always prepared to give my life for Arjuna, without a thought!

Lord, at your command what is there I would not do in battle let alone to Dhritarashtra's weakling army? At your command, I would go into battle against the three worlds, with the Devas, the Asuras and Manushyas massed together. Why, for your sake today I will raze Duryodhana's entire army. I vow to you, O Yudhishtira, king of kings, that I will fight my way to Arjuna and return to you only after Jayadratha is dead.

Yet, Rajan, I must also tell you of what both Krishna and Arjuna said repeatedly to me before all our warriors.

Arjuna said, "Today, O Satyaki, noble and determined in battle, protect my brother the king with your very life until I kill Jayadratha! By entrusting Yudhishtira's safety to you, or to maharatha Pradyumna, I can hunt Jayadratha down with an easy heart. You know that Drona is the greatest warrior among the Kurus. You also know the vow he has sworn to take Yudhishtira alive, which he is well capable of doing. So I charge you with his protection while I go today to kill Jayadratha.

Ensure that Drona does not succeed in seizing Yudhishtira for if that happens I will not be able to kill Jayadratha, and grief will break my heart and take my very life from me. If Drona takes my brother, we will have to return to the forest and my killing Jayadratha will be of no avail. Therefore, Mahabaho Satyaki, for my sake as well as for the success of my enterprise and my honour, protect the king today at all costs!'

You see, Rajan, Arjuna has left you to me to defend for he is in constant fear of Drona. O Dharmaraja, I myself daily see that there is none, save Rukmini's son Pradyumna, who can match Drona in battle. I am also regarded to be a match for the Brahmana. Great Yudhishtira, I find myself torn between two choices: I must either obey my master Arjuna or ride after him, leaving your side, thus obeying you and disregarding what his command!

Once he corners you, Maharajan, Acharya Drona will toy with you as a child with a little bird. If Krishna's son Pradyumna, flying the Makara on his banner were here, I could entrust you to him, for he would protect you like Arjuna himself. But I do not see him here and if I leave you who will protect you from Drona?

Rajan, do not be anxious on Arjuna's account for no burden can vanquish him. All his opponents together, the Sauvirakas and the Sindhava–Pauravas warriors, those from the north and those from the south, and those led by Karna, whom I regard as the greatest maharatha—all these together do not constitute even a sixteenth part of Arjuna. The very Earth rising up against him, with the Devas, the Asuras, and Manushyas, with all the tribes of Rakshasas with the Kinnaras, the great

Nagas, and in fact, all the mobile and the immobile beings massed together, would be no match for Arjuna. Know this, Rajan, and dispel your fears on Arjuna's account.

Wherever the two potent and inexorable Krishnas are, no obstacle can prevent them from accomplishing their mission. Think of their celestial power, their mastery over weapons, their resourcefulness, their fury in battle, their gratitude and the compassion of your brother. And think also, Rajan, of the mighty prowess of Drona, if I leave to ride out to Arjuna. The Acharya is eager to seize you for he is proud and determine to fulfill his vow, O Bhaarata!

Think first of your own safety. Who will watch over you in my absence and to whom can I entrust your protection so that I can go to Arjuna? I say to that I will not ride after Arjuna without first ensuring that you will be safe. Employ your great intelligence, O Yudhishtira Mahabuddhi; reflect on this from every angle, and then command me after deciding what is for your greatest good!"

Yudhishtira says, "It is as you say, Mahabaho! However, for all that, my heart is uneasy on Arjuna's account. I will take the greatest precaution in protecting myself; so, at my command, go without delay to Arjuna. Weighing my own safety against Arjuna's dire need, my judgment tells me that your going to Arjuna's side is the first need of the hour. Therefore, Satyaki, prepare to ride to Arjuna.

The mighty Bhima as well as Prishata's son Dhrishtadyumna, with all his brothers, our other mighty kings, and the sons of Draupadi will not fail to protect me. The five Kekaya brothers, and the Rakshasa Ghatotkacha, Virata, Drupada, and the maharatha Sikhandin, the powerful Dhrishtaketu, Kuntibhoja, Nakula and Sahadeva, the Panchalas, the Srinjayas—all of them are with me and I will be safe in their midst. Not Drona at the head of his troops, or even Kritavarman, will succeed in defeating us or harming me.

Parantapa Dhrishtadyumna will contain the raging Drona even like the continent the sea, and however he fights, Drona will never overcome our troops. Dhrishtadyumna sprang from the fire clad in mail, armed with bow, arrows and sword, and wearing unworldly ornaments; he was born just to kill Drona. Go, O grandson of Sini, with an easy heart; do not be anxious on my account. Dhrishtadyumna can always defy Drona in battle.'"

CANTO 108

Jayadratha-vadha Parva continued

"Sanjaya says, 'Satyaki still fears the censure of Arjuna if he leaves the king. However, he is certain that he will be called a coward if he disobeys Yudhishtira, and says to himself, "Let no one say that I am afraid of riding out to help Arjuna."

Reflecting repeatedly on this, that invincible Vrishni hero says to Yudhishtira, "If you think that these arrangements will suffice to keep you safe, I will do your bidding and follow Arjuna. I tell you truly that there is no one in the three worlds who is dearer to me than he, and I will follow in his wake because you command me to and because there is nothing that I will not do for you.

O best of men, the commands of my guru always weigh with me, but yours are still more important. Your brothers, Krishna and Arjuna, always do what pleases you. I too accept your command, and I will ride out for Arjuna's sake, cleaving my way through this impenetrable host of Drona, like a fish through the sea, to where Jayadratha, supported by his troops, hides in fear of Arjuna, protected by the maharathas Aswatthaman, Karna and Kripa.

O Rajan, the distance from here to where Partha forging ahead to kill Jayadratha is three yojanas, I will follow in his trail with a brave heart, and support him until Jayadratha dies. Who goes into battle without the command of his superiors? Dharmaraja, who will not fight if you command him, as I have been? I know the place where I must go, teeming as this ocean-like enemy does with ploughshares, darts, maces, shields, scimitars, swords, lances and the most potent shafts, this ocean that I will agitate today.

The enemy's elephant legion consists of a thousand elephants of the formidable Anjana breed, ridden by Mlecchas who love battle and are accomplished fighters. These musth-maddened elephants that shed their juice of rut like rain from dark clouds never retreat if goaded forward by the warriors upon their backs. They cannot be vanquished unless one kills them.

Rajan, the chariot-warriors you see, also numbering thousands, are all of royal lineage and maharathas all. They are called Rukmarathas and are all impressive warriors who fight from rathas as well as from elephant-back. They are masters of weapons as also of hand-to-hand combat. Skilled mace-fighters, they are also masters of the art of close combat, and are equally adroit with scimitars, sword, and shield.

They are brave, learned and animated by an intense spirit of rivalry and every day they vanquish a vast number of men in battle. Karna commands them and they are devoted to Dusasana; even Krishna lauds them as great maharathas. Always solicitous of Karna's welfare, they are ever obedient to him. It is at Karna's command that, after turning back from their pursuit of Arjuna, fresh as when they bean and with no trace of tiredness, these heroes, wearing impenetrable armour and armed with exceptional bows, certainly wait for me, as Duryodhana also wants. I will crush them in battle for you, Yudhishtira, and then follow in Arjuna trail.

Rajan, Kiratas ride these other seven hundred elephants that you see, all covered in armour and with ornaments, which the king of the Kiratas, fearing for his life, gifted to Arjuna together with many servitors. They were once in your employ. Behold the vicissitudes that time brings, for they now fight against you. Kiratas are sprung from the race of Agni, and they are all expert elephant warriors and they and their beast are well nigh impossible to defeat. Arjuna once quelled them all in battle and, never having forgotten the shame of that, they now stand in wait for me, under Duryodhana's command. These Kiratas, too, I will kill with my arrows and follow Arjuna as he nears Jayadratha to have the wretched Saindhava's life.

Those other hulking elephants of impenetrable hides have sprung from the race of the great elephant sire Arjuna. Caparisoned entirely in gold, with ichor running down from their rent temples and mouth, they resemble Airavata himself and are even more formidable in battle. They have come from the northern hills, and fierce bandits of mighty limbs and sinews ride them, wearing steel coats of mail. These men are great warriors, brigands though they are.

Among them are men born of the cow, the ape, diverse other creatures, as well as of humans. Look how they appear at a distance to be of a smoky hue, these terrible Mlecchas, sinners all who hail from the fastnesses of Himavat.

With these and countless great Kshatriyas, as well as Kripa and Drona, foremost of maharathas, and Karna, also, to protect him, Jayadratha thinks lightly of the Pandavas. Impelled by fate, he regards himself already crowned with success. These whom I have named will soon be within reach of my arrows. They will not escape me, O son of Kunti, even if they acquire the speed of the mind. Duryodhana, the prince who depends upon the abilities of others, regards them highly, but I say to you that when my arrows cover these warriors they will find destruction.

These other chariot-warriors with golden standards, O Rajan, whom you see, are the Kambojas. They are brave and skilled, and devoted to the astra shastra, the science of weaponry. They are close knit, firmly united and constitute a full akshauhini of furious warriors, O Bhaarata; and are on the alert, with their eyes on me and wait well protected by the Kuru heroes. I will destroy them all, like fire consuming a bale of straw.

Therefore, O Rajan, let our attendants prepare my ratha and equip it well with bows, swords, spears, arrows, quivers, every other kind of weapon and all else that I will need to take dreadful war against our enemies.

Let my chariot be furnished with weapons five times more than what acharyas of military science direct, for I will have to encounter the Kambojas and the Kiratas who are armed with diverse, and both of whom are like serpents of virulent poison, accomplished in war, and fiercely loyal to Duryodhana who has always treated them well. I will also have to fight the Sakas who are as powerful as Sakra himself, and are ferocious and difficult to extinguish as a burning forest fire. Yudhishtira, I will face many indomitable warriors today; and for this let renowned horses of the best breed with auspicious markings be yoked to my ratha, after grooming them and slaking their thirst."

Yudhishtira ensures that quivers full of arrows, all manner of weapons, and everything else that he might need are placed in Satyaki's ratha. The attendants give his four superb horses water to drink and feed them; and then after they are walked, bathed and adorned with golden chains, and the arrows stuck in them drawn out, these well-trained, fleet, docile, steeds of golden complexion are yoked again to Satyaki's ratha.

Then a tall standard with the symbol of a lion with a golden mane is mounted on the ratha embellished with gold, which carries a heavy load of weapons, and flies banners of the hue of white clouds. Then, Daruka's younger brother, who is the charioteer and the dear friend of Satyaki, comes and reports to him that the ratha is ready: like Matali reporting to Vasava himself.

Having bathed and purified himself with every auspicious ceremony, Satyaki gives nishkas of gold to a thousand Snataka Brahmanas who shower their blessings on him. With these, the radiantly handsome Satyaki, hero worthy of our worship, drinks two jars of rich, invigorating kairata and honey, and ah, he is resplendent and rolls reddened eyes in some intoxication. He touches a brazen mirror and is filled with great joy, his energy doubled, and he looks truly like a blazing fire.

Picking up his bow and strapping a quiver full of arrows across his lion's shoulders, putting on his shimmering mail and sparkling, priceless ornaments, Yuyudhana has the Rishis perform for him the profound rites of propitiation. Fair lovely young virgins honour him by showering fried paddy over him, daubing him with delicate perfume and draping vanamalas over his rippling body.

Then, with folded hands, he worships the feet of Yudhishtira, and Yudhishtira nuzzles and sniffs the top of his head in deep affection. Finally, Satyaki mounts his grand chariot. His horses, good natured, strong, swift as the wind and invincible, belong to the Sindhu breed, and bear him forward on that triumphal ratha.

Bhimasena, too, honoured by Dharmaraja Yudhishtira, reverentially salutes the king and sets out with Satyaki. Watching those two warriors advance to engage your army, your troops all stand waiting for them, with Drona at their head. When Satyaki sees Bhima cased in mail and following him, he salutes him and with every limb filled with joy, says, "O Bhima, do you protect the king for that is your first duty and I will cleave my way through this host whose hour has come. Whether now or later, the king's protection is your highest dharma. You know my ability and you wish me well, so return, O Bhima!"

Bhima replies, "Go then, and achieve your purpose, O best of men. I will protect the king."

Satyaki replies, "Go back, O Bhima! As for me, I am certain to succeed, for today all my merits are obedient to my wishes. Indeed, the omens all around tell me that I shall be victorious. After the noble Arjuna kills the sinner Jayadratha, I will embrace Dharmaraja Yudhishtira."

Saying these words to Bhima and releasing him with an embrace, the illustrious Satyaki eyes your troops like a tiger eyeing a herd of deer. Seeing his dreadful gaze, your troops tremble. And then, Satyaki dashes forward in his ratha and bursts upon your army like some dreadful plague.'"

CANTO 109

Jayadratha-vadha Parva continued

"Sanjaya says, 'O Rajan, when Satyaki attacks your troops, Yudhishtira and his forces follow him to get at Drona's ratha. The indomitable Dhrishtadyumna, the son of the Panchala king, and king Vasudana both loudly exhort the Pandava host, crying, "Come, let us be at the enemy so that Satyaki can pass easily through the Kaurava host. For many maharathas will put forth their might to vanquish him."

At this, the mighty maharathas of the Pandava army fall wildly on their enemies saying, "We will crush those that try to stop Satyaki."

Then one hears a loud pandemonium near Satyaki's ratha. Your son's host, overwhelmed by Yuyudhana's tempestuous onslaught, turns tail and runs from the terrible Yadava. With such archery as we have not yet seen, Sini's grandson truncates the united Kuru army into a hundred portions, and then straightaway beheads seven great maharathas in stunned van of Drona's vyuha. With banks of lustrous, flaming shafts, he dispatches hundreds of heroes and kings of diverse realms.

At one moment he pierces a hundred warriors with a single arrow, and at others one great maharatha with a hundred arrows. Even like Rudra devouring living beings at yuganta, Satyaki the Vrishni slaughters elephant-riders and chariot-warriors, horses and horsemen. Quickly, none among your troops dares face Satyaki, who shows blinding lightness of hand and covers them with storm clouds of fire. Panic-stricken, ravaged by the Kshatriya of long arms, all your bravest run away on seeing that radiant Kshatriya come hunting them like a god. His energy dazes them, and they see a thousand Satyakis everywhere, all come to take their lives.

The field is a horrible work of art with demolished chariots, their broken seats and wheels, with fallen canopies, standards, anukarshas, banners, with helmets decked with gold, human arms smeared with sandalwood-paste and adorned with angadas, with human thighs that resemble the trunks of elephants or the tapering bodies of great pythons, and with faces handsome as the Moon and twinkling with the kundalas of large-eyed warriors, lying all across Kurukshetra where Satyaki the Yadava holds sway.

The Earth is littered with the huge bodies of fallen elephants, cut up in diverse ways, like a plain strewn with hills. Carved by Satyaki, the carcasses of dead horses, of handsome breed and build, look striking in their traces made of burnished gold hung with rows of pearls. After razing your various troops, Satyaki of the Satwata vamsa breaches your army's ranks, agitating and routing them as he flies along unobstructed, following the very trail that Arjuna blazed.

Then Drona confronts him and, facing the son of Bharadwaja, rage flares up in Satyaki, and at first, like a tidal wave flashing past an ineffectual embankment he sweeps past the great Brahmana. Doubling back, Drona strikes him deep with five shafts like bolts of lightning. Satyaki, pausing, lacerates the Acharya with seven stone-whetted arrows, fletched with golden wings and the feathers of the kanka and peacock. Drona draws blood from the Yadava, his horses and charioteer, with six thunderous missiles.

Beside himself now, and roaring like a full pride of lions, maharatha Satyaki stabs the Brahmana with three volleys of ten, six and eight barbs, which lance agony through the Kaurava Senapati. Never pausing, glorious Yuyudhana drills Drona with ten more shafts, his charioteer with one and his four horses with four; and with another thick shafts strikes Drona's standard. Drona, his eyes crimson, envelops Satyaki, his ratha, horses, charioteer, and standard, with a locust swarm of dark arrows. Fearless Satyaki responds in kind, shrouding the Acharya in a blizzard of arrows.

Now Drona says to the Yadava, "Your master Arjuna avoids fighting me like a coward. He passed me by in fear. If you do not do the same, O grandson of Sini, you will not escape with your life!"

It is as if Drona himself tells Satyaki what he should wisely do. Satyaki says to the towering Brahmana, "I follow in Arjuna's wake at the command of Dharmaraja Yudhishtira. Bless you, O Brahmana, much as I would love to continue this battle, I will lose time if I fight you. A sishya must always follow his guru, and if Arjuna rode past you, I will do the same. Farewell, O Drona!"

Saying this, Satyaki quickly dodges past Drona and says to his sarathy, "Drona will try everything he can to stop us so go carefully and cleverly, O Suta. There you see the splendid Avanti horde and next to them the mighty army of the Southerners, and beside that, the great host of the Balhikas. Next to the Balhikas stands majestic Karna, with his powerful forces.

Suta, all these forces are dissimilar, but on the battlefield, they depend on one another for support and protection and fight as one. So guide your horses towards the open space between these divisions at a moderate speed, and aim for the place where the Balhikas stand with diverse weapons, and the countless Southerners led by the Sutaputra's division presents a serried array of elephants, cavalry and rathas and foot-soldiers from various kingdoms."

They ride on and Satyaki says again, "Now fly through the gap between those two divisions towards the Karna's fierce and mighty host!"

A wrathful Drona, however, pursues him closely, loosing countless arrows after the Vrishni shura, but the most blessed Satyaki rides on and finds no need to turn back to face the Brahmana. Smiting the great host of Karna with hurricanes of arrows, Satyaki penetrates into the vast and limitless army of the Bharatas, who flee at his advent.

A fuming incensed Kritavarman rushes up to contain Satyaki, but in a flash the inspired Yuyudhana strikes Kritavarman with six shafts and kills his four horses with four more. He unerringly finds Kritavarman's chest with four more arrows, and, all in the space of a wish, drills him with another sixteen of ferocious velocity. Kritavarman cannot bear this and, drawing his bowstring to his ear, plunges a calf-toothed astra, serpentine and swift as the wind, into Satyaki's breast drawing a geyser of blood. That weapon of beautiful feathers pierces Yuyudhana's golden kavacha, bores its way through his body and enters the ground behind him, dyed in blood.

O Rajan, heartened to see his adversary stagger in his chariot, Kritavarman unleashes a clutch of stormy arrows, and desiccates Satyaki's great bow with keen barbs fitted. In exhilaration, roaring, Kritavarman adorns Satyaki's chest with a bunch of ten thudding shafts.

Satyaki, his bow broken, hurls a spear at Kritavarman's right arm, and quickly taking up and drawing a stronger bow, he unleashes a dense cloud of fire, thousands of shafts loosed in the twinkling of an eye, and entirely shrouds Kritavarman and his ratha. With no instant's pause, he decapitates his enemy's sarathy with a wedge-headed missile so the suta falls dead from his seat. Kritavarman's horses bolt and the distraught hero is forced to take their reins and control them himself.

Yet undaunted, and bow in hand, heroic Kritavarman stands upon his chariot ready for battle again. Seeing this feat, his troops cheer deafeningly and, after drawing a few moments' breath, Kritavarman guides his fine horses and resumes fighting. Devoid of fear, he strikes fear into his enemies.

However, by this time, Satyaki has left him behind. A thwarted, frustrated Kritavarman does not pursue him anymore but instead charges Bhimasena. Blasting his scarlet way out of the legion of the Bhojas, Satyaki swoops down on the mighty Kamboja akshauhini. Many maharathas challenge him all together, and Satyaki cannot advance at all.

Meanwhile, Drona, having regrouped and arrayed his troops again, gives charge of them to Kritavarman of the Bhojas, and rides after Satyaki. Seeing Drona pursue Yuyudhana once more, the greatest Pandava warriors combine to thwart the Acharya. The Panchalas, led by Bhimasena, challenge Hridika's son Kritavarman. He displays his prowess, and holds them all up; faced with his prodigious archery, they still fight back with some vigour.

Kritavarman violently attacks his enemies' horses and elephants. However, though sorely beset by him, his valiant foemen stand firm like high-born warriors they are, resolved to vanquish the entire Bhoja akshauhini, for fame and honour.'"

CANTO 110

JAYADRATHA-VADHA PARVA CONTINUED

"Dhritarashtra says, 'O Sanjaya, our army too can boast of many outstanding attributes. Our forces are regarded as being equally superior, equally well arrayed, and equally numerous! We always treat our soldiers well, and they are always devoted to us. They are beyond count and their skill is exceptional and proven. Our men are neither too old nor very young, nor are they overly lean or corpulent. They are energetic, well built and strong, and free from disease.

They are all sheathed in excellent mail, well-armed and subject themselves to stern disciplines and arduous training. My fighters are adept in mounting and alighting from the backs of elephants, in marching, advancing, retreating, and striking with the utmost effectiveness. They have been often tested in managing elephants, horses and riding chariots. Our warriors are recruited only after passing stringent tests, and not merely because of their lineage, or from favoritism or nepotism. They are not a rabble come of their own accord, nor have they been admitted into my army without handsome payment.

My army consists of well-born and honourable men, who are

contented, well fed, and obedient. They are generously rewarded and are all famed and intelligent. They are, besides, led and protected by many of our foremost advisers and other men of dharma, all of whom are the best of men, and are like the very regents of the world. They are also led by innumerable rulers of the world, seeking to please us and who have, out of sheer goodwill and friendship, allied themselves to us with their forces and followers.

Indeed, our army is like the vast ocean filled with the waters of countless rivers flowing from all directions. It has a plenitude of horses and chariots, which, though wingless, fly like the very birds of the air. We also have an abundance of war elephants in musth. Sanjaya, only destiny can destroy such an army.

Ocean-like, the vast numbers of warriors are its interminable waters, the horses and other animals its terrible waves, the numberless swords, maces, darts, arrows and lances are the oars plied on this ocean, and the abundant standards, ornaments and the pearls and gems of the warriors represent the lotuses that adorn it, and the running horses and elephants, the winds that agitate it into fury.

Drona is the fathomless cavern of that ocean, Kritavarman its vortex, Jalasandha its mighty makara, and Karna the Moon that makes it swell in tide with pride and energy.

When Arjuna, the Pandava bull on his single chariot, has battled his way so swiftly and with such aplomb through my oceanic army, and when Satyaki has also followed him, I do not, O Sanjaya, nurture any hope that these two will leave the smallest remnant of my legions alive. Seeing that these two mahatejasvins have scythed their way through the packed van and heart of my forces, and seeing that now Jayadratha is also within reach of the shafts from the Gandiva, what measures do the Kauravas, driven by rough fate, now adopt?

What has become of my sons during this intense battle? Ah, I believe that Death himself has overcome the massed Kurus. Their prowess no longer appears to be what it once was. Krishna and Arjuna have both breached the Kuru host unharmed. There is none in our army, O

Sanjaya, who is capable of resisting them. We recruited so many of our great maharathas after a careful evaluation. We honour them with the remuneration each deserves and others with accolades. There is no one among my legions who is not rewarded and each receives his assigned payment and rations according to the extent and nature of his services. Sanjaya, there is none in my army who is unskilled in battle, none who receives payment less than what he deserves, none who does not receive any wage at all. I have acknowledged the soldiers to the best of my ability with gifts, honours and position. My sons, my kinsmen and my friends behave in the same manner towards them. Yet, Arjuna and Satyaki's mere approach has vanquished them. What can this be but Destiny ranged against us?

The protected and those who protect them all go the same way! Seeing Arjuna arrive where Jayadratha is secreted, what measures does my foolish son adopt? Seeing Satyaki also furrow a bloody path into the Kuru host, what does Duryodhana think appropriate to do? Seeing these two maharathas, who are invincible to all weapons, breach my host, what decision do my warriors take?

For myself, I must believe that the sight of both Krishna and now Satyaki engaged in Arjuna's cause, and mowing their gory way through my teeming ranks, fills my sons with shock and grief. I fear that they must be saddened and benumbed to watch their greatest maharathas flee in all directions, that they must truly despair of vanquishing the enemy. I fear they themselves must now think only of escaping with their lives.

Surely, my sons must be heartbroken to watch their thousands upon thousands of cavalry, elephants, chariots and heroic warriors run from the battle in abject fear. Surely, Duryodhana's heart must bleed to watch his great war-elephants excoriated by Arjuna's fiery tides of arrows, and turn tail, while others fall dead all around them shaking the earth.

I feel sure that, seeing Satyaki and Arjuna deprive horses of riders and warriors of rathas, and seeing Madhava and Partha rout and kill vast numbers of horses, my sons are stricken by grief.

I am certain, that seeing whole divisions of foot-soldiers flee in all directions, my sons, despairing of success, are grief-stricken.

Seeing those two heroes pass through Drona's vyuha, unvanquished, in mere moments, I am sure that my sons are full of grief.

I am shocked and aghast, O Sanjaya, to hear that Krishna and Dhananjaya, heroes of unfading glory, and Satyaki, as well, have penetrated my host. After maharatha Satyaki storms through the Bhojas, what do the Kauravas do? Tell me also, Sanjaya, about the battle where Drona disconcerts the Pandavas. Drona is imbued with immense power; he is the foremost of all warriors, and unconquerable in battle. How did the Panchalas quell this great bowman in the fight? The Panchalas and Drona are sworn enemies in Arjuna's quest for victory.

O Sanjaya, you are an eloquent raconteur; tell me everything that Arjuna does to bring death to Jayadratha.'

Sanjaya says, 'O Bharatarishabha, you should not indulge in such lamentations like an ordinary man, when you are overwhelmed by a calamity that is the result of your own sins. Years ago, many of your wise well-wishers, including Vidura, told you, 'Do not, O king, abandon the sons of Pandu.'

But at that time, you paid no heed to what they said and the man who ignores the advice of well-wishers will weep when he falls into great despair. O Rajan, he of Dasarha's vamsa came to beg you to make peace. For all that, Krishna of universal fame, could not get you to listen to his plea and the Lord of all the worlds himself realised your worthlessness, your jealousy of the Pandavas, and understood your malicious intentions towards them.

He calmly heard out your delirious protestation and then caused the flame of war to blaze forth among the Kurus. This enormous destruction has overtaken you solely because of your own guilt. It is not correct to impute the fault to Duryodhana because no merit can be attributed to you either in the beginning, the middle, or at the end in the unfolding of events. This bitter defeat is entirely due to you. Therefore, knowing as you do the truth about this world, quieten yourself and hear about the apocalyptic war on Kurukshetra, the Mahabharata yuddha that is even akin to the Devasura yuddha of time out of mind.

After the scintillating Satyaki pierces deep into your army, the Parthas led by Bhimasena also attack your troops. However, the maharatha Kritavarman, by himself, resists the Pandavas who take the furious offensive against your host. As the continent resists the surging sea, even so does Kritavarman, son of Hridika, resist the Pandava legions and he displays such wonderful skill that the united Parthas cannot defeat him.

Then the mighty-armed Bhima strikes Kritavarman with three dreadful shafts and blows his conch resoundingly, gladdening the hearts of all the Pandavas. Sahadeva strikes the Bhoja with twenty arrows, Yudhishtira with five, Nakula with a hundred, the sons of Draupadi with three and seventy, Ghatotkacha with seven, Virata and Drupada and Dhrishtadyumna each with five spiteful shafts, and Sikhandin, first with five, and again with twenty-five brutal barbs.

Seamlessly, Kritavarman strikes every one of those maharathas with five arrows, and Bhima with seven. He fells Bhima's chariot from his chariot, breaks his bow in his hands and quickly gores him with seventy barbs through his massive chest. Deeply wounded, the mighty Bhima trembles on his ratha like a mountain in an earthquake.

Seeing Bhima in danger, the Parthas led by Yudhishtira surround Kritavarman in fury, covering him in fire to protect Vayu's son. The Vayuputra recovers swiftly casts a steely spear with a golden shaft at Kritavarman's ratha. That fierce spear hurled so powerfully from Bhima's hands is like a snake freed from its slough and blazes as it flies at Kritavarman. Seeing the dart invested with the brilliance of the Yuga-fire coursing towards him, Kritavarman slices it in two as it falls onto the ground, still burning, like a meteor from the sky, illumining the ten points of the compass.

Seeing his occult lance cut down, Bhima roars in anger and, sweeping up another stronger bow, its twang like thunder, bloodies Kritavarman's chest five throbbing shafts.

All this, Rajan, is the result of your evil policy!

Kritavarman, king of the Bhojas, lacerated in every limb by Bhimasena, is resplendent like a red asoka tree covered with flowers. Roaring himself like a hunt of lions, he plunges three fervent shafts into Bhima, and slashes every maharatha ranged against him, with three passionate barbs. They strike him back with seven arrows.

Then, with a razor-tipped shaft, the battling Bhoja breaks Sikhandin's bow, but the Panchala quickly takes up a sword and a bright shield adorned with gold and a hundred moons; whirling the sword in his hands, he flings it like a dagger at Kritavarman's ratha, riving his bow with a mighty astra fitted to it, so it falls onto the earth like a star come loose from the sky, burning briefly there before dying out.

The other maharathas also cover Kritavarman with their stern shafts; upon which, casting aside the broken bow, he takes up another and strikes each of the Pandavas with three shafts like streaks of lightning. He strikes Sikhandin first with three, and then with five shafts. The illustrious Sikhandin takes up another bow, and responds with a barrage of fleet barbs fitted with heads like tortoise nails. Inflamed, Kritavarman rushes recklessly at the powerful Sikhandin, son of Yajnasena, who was the cause of a great fall in the battlefield. He dashes at Drupada's son like a tiger at an elephant.

The two parantapas, who resemble a couple of wild elephants or two blazing fires, clash in a shower of arrows. They use their best bows and shoot their arrows in hundreds, like twin suns shedding their rays and they shine in glory two suns appearing at the end of the Yuga.

Kritavarman pierces Sikhandin first with three and seventy shafts and again with seven. Deeply wounded, Sikhandin sits down in his ratha in shock and pain, drops his bow and arrows, and faints. Seeing this, your troops hail Kritavarman and wave their bright cloaks and scarves in the air. Sikhandin's charioteer quickly takes him out of the battle.

Watching this, the Parthas encircle Kritavarman with their rathas. The maharatha Kritavarman then demonstrates a feat of great wonder there, as, by himself, he holds all the Pandavas and their followers at bay. He vanquishes the Chedis, the Panchalas, the Srinjayas, and the Kekayas. The Pandava forces scatter; they cannot bear the flaming Kritavarman.

Having defeated the sons of Pandu led by Bhimasena himself, the son of Hridika shines forth like Agni himself on Kurukshetra, and all the Pandava maharathas, soundly beaten by the Bhoja's torrents of arrows, cannot find the heart to face him.'"

CANTO 111

Jayadratha-vadha Parva continued

"Sanjaya says, 'After Kritavarman, the noble son of Hridika, routs the enemy and humiliates the Parthas, your troops are jubilant. Hearing the uproar from your army, Sini's grandson Satyaki, protector of the Pandavas when they sink in that fathomless sea of distress in this awful war, quickly turns back and attacks Kritavarman who covers him with a torment of arrows. Satyaki looses a wide-tipped shaft at the Bhoja and follows this with four more terrific arrows, which kill his horses and destroy his bow. He inundates Kritavarman's charioteer and the warriors who protect his back with a deluge of shafts. They cannot withstand the lustrous Vrishni, and fall apart. The incomparable shura Yuyudhana quickly turns his chariot around and continues on his way towards his master Arjuna.

Now listen, O Rajan, to what Satyaki does to your army. After fording the sea that is Drona's division, and triumphant after vanquishing Kritavarman, he says to his charioteer, "Go with care but fearlessly."

However, he then sees your thronging army of rathas, cavalry, elephants and foot-soldiers, and says again to his sarathy, "This great legion, dark as clouds that you see on the left of Drona's vyuha, consists of a vast contingent of elephants led by Rukmaratha, and is difficult to subdue. Positioned there by Duryodhana, these warriors belong to the country of the Trigartas, are of princely birth, are great bowmen, skilled in battle, and they are all illustrious maharathas, with their standards decked with gold. All of them are prepared to die fighting. These heroes seek battle with me, so drive your horses at them swiftly! I will fight the Trigartas in the very sight of Bharadwaja's son."

His sarathy, Daruka's brother, always obedient to Satyaki, cracks his whip over his superlative steeds, white as silver or the kunda flower, swift as the mind, and the shining ratha that flies a flag bright as the sun, flies towards the elephant legion of great Rukmaratha. The elephants surround that chariot, and their riders lash down all manner of arrows over the raiding Satyaki.

Satyaki, shooting up at them, covers them in a storm-cloud of radiant fire, shredding the great beasts' flesh, felling many outright, felling their riders from their backs, all in a moment, a violent dream. Their caparisons and blankets coming loose, their very tusks cloven, their huge bodies covered in blood, their round temples split open, the flapping ears, great faces and trunks sliced in slivers, their shrill screams echoing across the grim field, the mastodons lumber away in terror from this dread god come hunting them.

The Satwata ablaze mangles the grey beasts with arrows long as spears, with calf-tooth-headed bolts, broad-headed shafts, anjalikas, razor-faced and crescent-tipped barbs, and they flee from him in perfect terror, spraying urine and dung as they go. Some of them limp away as quickly as they can for the fearsome warrior has lamed them, some just fall, and others, fleeing, are pale with tears flowing down their faces. Stricken by mighty Yuyudhana with astras that are like the sun or fire, the elephant division bolts in all directions.

When Satyaki has put Rukmaratha's elephant legion to flight, when he has slaughtered so many of the beasts, the mighty Jalasandha nonchalantly lumbers up on his elephant to confront Satyaki's ratha drawn by white horses. Wearing a golden angadas, with kundala and kirita, armed with a huge curved sword, smeared with red sandalwood-paste, his brow wreathed with a shining chain of gold, his breast covered with a brilliant kavacha, his neck also adorned with a golden chain, Jalasandha, Kshatriya of sinless soul, enthroned upon the neck of his outsized elephant, shaking his gold-inlaid bow, is as glorious as a cloud charged with lightning.

As the continent checks the surging sea, Satyaki checks the Magadha king's Jalasandha's exceptional elephant that bears down on him in fury. Finding his elephant hesitate against Satyaki's tirade of arrows, Jalasandha's eyes turn red and he strikes Yuyudhana through his chest with an angry volley. Shooting down at his adversary, the Magadhan shatters Satyaki's bow in his hands, and then drills five more serpentine shafts down into the Yadava's body.

Ah, Rajan, it is wonderful to see how the mighty-armed Satyaki hardly winces though struck so violently. Seizing up a fresh bow, and actually smiling, he makes a mess of blood on Jalasandha's wide chest with sixty shafts loosed up at his in a blink, then breaks his bow at its very grip with another razor-headed shaft, and strikes him hard with three more barbs that thud into his breast again like a single shaft.

Jalasandha flings aside his bow and hurls a terrible lance at Satyaki, which passes right through his left arm and enters the earth, like a hissing snake of gigantic proportion. Heedless of his gaping wound, the invincible Satyaki drives another thirty keen arrows deep into Jalasandha's body already covered in blood. Jalasandha takes up his sword and a large bull's hide shield embellished with a hundred moons, whirls the great blade round and casts it like summer lightning at the Satwata, demolishing his bow. The occult sword then lies upon the earth like a circle of fire.

A wrathful Satyaki takes up another bow big as a sala-offshoot, the sound of its bowstring like Indra's Vajra; drawing it in a circle he strikes Jalasandha with a heavy, ferocious arrow, stunning the Magadhan. Next moment, with two razor-sharp, crescent-headed shafts he cleanly hews off Jalasandha's ornamented arms like spiked maces at their shoulders, so they fall from the elephant's back like two thick squirming five-headed snakes falling from a mountain cliff. With a third razorine shaft Satyaki severs his antagonist's great head, with shining perfect teeth and sparkling earrings, in a carmine blast. The macabre trunk still astride the elephant dyes Jalasandha's hulking beast with gushing blood.

Rajan, Yuyudhana quickly fells the wooden warrior's frame and its rider's throne-like seat from that beast's lofty back, so that, bathed in his master's blood, Jalasandha's elephant suffers the costly seat to hang from his back, and wounded terribly by Satyaki's arrows, in absolute anguish, he blunders across the field trampling Jalasandha's own ranks to pulp, all the while trumpeting wildly in pain.

At the sight of Jalasandha slain by the Vrishni bull, wails of woe arise among your troops; and your warriors, turning their faces, flee in all directions, despairing entirely of success. Meanwhile, Drona advances again on Satyaki, on his red chargers. Many other Kuru warriors, seeing Satyaki swollen with rage and pride, furiously follow Drona. Then commences a battle, O Rajan, between the Kurus and Drona on one side and Satyaki on the other, that is yet another like the one of old between the Devas and the Asuras.'"

CANTO 112

Jayadratha-vadha Parva continued

"Sanjaya says, 'O king, shooting clouds of arrows, all these seasoned warriors cautiously advance on Satyaki. Drona strikes him with seven and seventy shafts, Durmarshana with a dozen, Dusasana with ten and Vikarna pierces him through his side as well as his chest with thirty keen kanka-feathered arrows.

Durmukha strikes him with ten shafts, Dusasana with eight, Chitrasena with two; Duryodhana and many other heroes also draw blood from Sini's sublime grandson with their dense fire. Though they surround him and lash him with their arrows, Satyaki the magnificent makes the bodies of every last one a home for his robust missiles.

He pierces Drona savagely with three, Dusasana with nine, Vikarna with five and twenty, Chitrasena with seven, Durmarshana with a dozen, Vivimsati with eight, Satyavrata with nine, and Vijaya with ten sinewy barbs. After striking Rukmangada also, Satyaki, shaking his bow, swiftly attacks Duryodhana and, in the sight of all that teem there, draws deep fonts of blood from your son. A relucent duel breaks out between the two and, each renders the other invisible with thick arrow shrouds.

Injured by the Kuru king, and blood flowing freely down his body, Satyaki soon looks like a sandalwood tree bleeding its ruddy juices. Your son too, struck often by Yuyudhana, is conspicuous, like a stake set up at a yagna, decked with gold. Then, with an imperious smile, Satyaki breaks Duryodhana's bow and strikes him with a flurry of arrows, past counting.

But Duryodhana is far from ready to concede defeat. Snatching up a fresh bow, he gashes the Vrishni hero with a hundred shafts shot like one. Stabbed deep by your mighty son's barbs, Satyaki blazes up in dreadful anger. He launches such an intense assault on your son that your other maharathas, fearing for his life, rush in to pour down opaque gales of missiles, mantling the menacing Vrishni with their fierce fire.

Satyaki pierces each of them first with five arrows, and again with seven more. He strikes Duryodhana with eight scorching arrows and serenely breaks your son's massive bow that frightens all enemies. With a few arrows more, he fells the king's standard adorned with the jewelled black elephant; and with another four arrows kills Duryodhana's four horses and then his charioteer with a razor-faced shaft. Elated by his success, Satyaki strikes Duryodhana deep with some slender missiles that pierce into his very vitals.

Rajan, wounded by Satyaki's great shafts, Duryodhana leaps out of his ratha and runs to mount Chitrasena's chariot, and arms himself with another bow. Seeing Satyaki overwhelm Duryodhana, indeed like Rahu swallowing the Moon, cries of woe arise from every part of the Kuru host. Hearing that great lament, maharatha Kritavarman quickly rides up to where Satyaki, the puissant Madhava, rules the war. Shaking his bow, crying to his charioteer, "Go! Fly at Satyaki!" comes the dauntless Kritavarman.

Seeing Kritavarman racing towards him like Death himself with jaws agape, Satyaki says to his sarathy, "Look where Kritavarman comes dashing at us. Ride to meet his charge, O Suta!"

His horses spurred to their greatest speed, Satyaki meets the king of the Bhojas, Kritavarman first among all bowmen. The two naravyaghras, both inflamed with rage, and like fire, encounter each other like two raging tigers. Kritavarman strikes Satyaki first with six and twenty whetted and keen arrows, and his sarathy with five; he stabs Satyaki's four superb steeds of the Sindhu breed with four cruel shafts. Flying a standard decked with gold, and wearing golden mail, and his arrows all golden-winged, Kritavarman, shaking his formidable bow, stops the storming Satyaki in his tracks.

Satyaki is by now more than eager to arrive at Arjuna's side. He raises his archery and plunges eight truly dreadful shafts into Kritavarman, wounding him so fiercely that invincible warrior begins to tremble like a hill during an earthquake. Fluidly, Satyaki strikes Kritavarman's four horses with three and sixty keen missiles and his sarathy with seven; he then aims another astra of golden wings that emits flames and resembles an angry snake, or the rod of Yama himself, and pierces Kritavarman with it. The flaming ayudha burns through Kritavarman's effulgent armour, his body, and enters the ground behind him.

Gravely wounded now and bathed in blood, Kritavarman, the lion-toothed hero of untold prowess, that bull among men, drops his bow and arrows and falls on his knees in his ratha. Having stopped Kritavarman who is like the thousand-armed Kartaviryarjuna of old, or the Ocean himself of immeasurable might, Satyaki dashes on once more. Mowing easily through Kritavarman's division bristling with swords, darts and bows, and thick with elephants, horses and rathas, and out of the ground mired in the blood shed by hundreds and hundreds of the best Kshatriyas, the bull of the Sinis forges on like Indra through the fell Asura legions.

Meanwhile, Kritavarman recovers, and taking up another huge bow, remains where he is, giving up his chase of Satyaki and fighting the Pandavas instead.'"

CANTO 113

JAYADRATHA-VADHA PARVA CONTINUED

"Sanjaya says, 'As Satyaki storms through the Kuru host, Drona engulfs him with a dense bank of arrows. Another pitched battle erupts between them before all the troops, even like that between Bali and Vasava in days of old.

Drona strikes Yuyudhana's forehead with three shimmering iron quarrels that are like snakes of virulent poison and Sini's grandson briefly looks like a mountain with three peaks. Drona continues to pour fire over him, shafts that roar like Indra's Vajra.

Satyaki strikes back with two beautifully winged arrows, after he cuts down all Drona's shafts in flight. Drona sees his young adversary's dexterity, and with a smile, looses thirty arrows at him in a wink, and now showing even greater speed of hand than Satyaki, in two blurred instants he strikes him first with fifty shafts and then with a hundred more. These deadly shafts spume from Drona's ratha like angry snakes boring through an anthill.

And Satyaki, not outdone, covers the Brahmana's ratha with thousands of blood-drinking missiles. None that watch the duel can mark any difference between the skills of the Acharya and the Satwata; both bulls among men, they appear to be perfectly equal.

A fiery Satyaki strikes Drona and his standard with nine straight arrows, and in Drona's sight, he berates his suta with a hundred shafts. Drona pierces Satyaki's charioteer with seventy barbs, and each of his four horses with three; with a single flawless missile he cuts down Drona's proud standard, and with another broad-headed arrow, streaked with gold, he shatters his bow.

His rage mounting by the moment, Satyaki hefts a heavy mace and hurls it like lightning at Bharadwaja's son. However, Drona smashes it to dust with an imperious volley. Satyaki picks up another bow, drills Drona with a clutch of strident shafts, and gives a deafening shout. Drona cannot bear that roar and he launches a golden-shafted lance, charged with an astra, at the Vrishni hero. But the lethal weapon passes through Satyaki's ratha never touching Sini's grandson, and plunges into the earth, and is extinguished with a loud report.

Satyaki ravages the Acharya with a still more fervid volley, drawing geysers of blood from the Brahmana, and especially his right arm. Invincible Drona once more severs Yuyudhana's great bow with one of his favoured crescent-tipped shafts and also gores his sarathy with such ferocity that the suta collapses briefly on his chariot-head.

O Rajan, what Satyaki does next is surely superhuman, for he snatches up the reins from his supine charioteer's hands, and continues to battle great Drona while guiding his own horses! Indeed, he strikes the Brahmana with a hundred arrows, and rejoices at his own marvelous feat, which even his enemies applaud. Drona unleashes five ferocious barbs at his brilliant antagonist; they pierce his armour and drink his blood.

Resorting to cunning, Satyaki looses a squall of arrows directly at Drona, absorbing him, but with a single shaft in its midst beheads the Brahmana's sarathy; Drona's already lacerated horses panic, and their reins hanging loose, careen wildly across the field, dragging the Brahmana's bright chariot in wide circles, like an unrestrained sun in chaotic motion. All the kings and princes of the Kaurava host cry out, "Quick, seize

Drona's horses!"

And leaving Satyaki, all the Kuru maharathas rush towards Drona's ratha. Your troops see this and think that they are fleeing from Satyaki and yet again their spirits plummet. Meanwhile, borne far away from Satyaki by his maddened horses, Drona, in some resignation, returns to the mouth of his vyuha. There he finds that the Pandavas and Panchalas have smashed the great cart formation; he makes no further attempt to follow Yuyudhana but employs himself in rallying his broken vyuha. Turning on the Pandava and the Panchala legions, the Drona fire, blazing up in wrath, remains there consuming all around him with dreadful astras never used against common soldiers. He burns like the uncommon Sun that rises at the end of the Yuga.'"

CANTO 114

JAYADRATHA-VADHA PARVA CONTINUED

"Sanjaya says, 'O Kurusthama, after vanquishing Drona and other warriors of your army that Hridika's son Kritavarman leads, Satyaki, the Sini bull, jocularly tells his charioteer, "O Suta, Kesava and Phalguna have already consumed our enemies, and in vanquishing them, we are merely the apparent instrument. Already slain by Nararishabha Arjuna, the son of Indra, we have but slain the dead."

Satyaki presses on, continuing to raze the Kaurava ranks all around him, arrowing on like a hawk in search of prey. Although the Kuru warriors still attack him from all sides, they cannot stop him from surging ahead, borne by his horses white as the moon or a conch, like the sun of a thousand rays. Indeed, O Bhaarata, no one can oppose the irresistible Satyaki of valour equal to that of the thousand-eyed Indra, and looking like the autumnal sun in the sky.

Then the great king maharatha Sudarshana rides at the racing Satyaki and attempts to stop him. Another calescent duel breaks out, which both your warriors and the Somakas acclaim as being like the one between Vritra and Vasava. Sudarshana looses hundreds of arrows at Satyaki from a distance, while cutting down the handful of shafts that Yuyudhana blazes at him.

But consummate Satyaki easily thwarts Sudarshana's volleys, and enraged by his enemy's disdain, fierce Sudarshana draws his bow into a circle and unleashes three exceptional astras of fire at the Vrishni hero. These burn through Satyaki's kavacha and pass through his body, momentarily fetching him up. In a flash, Sudarshana plunges four burning shafts into Satyaki's silver steeds.

But the Vrishni is as powerful as Indra himself, and, unperturbed, he slaughters Sudarshana's horses in four scarlet explosions and roars like four tigers. Next moment, he hacks off Sudarshana's sarathy's head and then, with a razor-faced arrow like the Yuga-fire, strikes off Sudarshana's own head radiant as the full moon, indeed again like Indra once did the head of the mighty Bala in that battle of long ago.

Satyaki, karmayogin, noble bull of the Yadus, is exultant after he kills prince Sudarshana and shines on Kurukshetra like the king of the Devas himself. Not pausing, he flares on along Arjuna's trail, thwarting all your troops with firetides of arrows, and filling all with amazement as he goes. All the greatest warriors gathered there, even his enemies, applaud his amazing feats, for he consumes all that come within the reach of his arrows, like a sweeping forest fire fanned by the wind.'"

CANTO 115

Jayadratha-vadha Parva continued

"Sanjaya says, 'Having killed Sudarshana, Satyaki speaks again to his charioteer, "We have forded the impassible ocean of Drona's vyuha, teeming with rathas, horsemen and elephants, whose waves are arrows and darts, its fishes swords and scimitars and its makaras maces, the great sea that roars with the songs of astras and the thunder of diverse weapons colliding, the ocean of terror, death and blood which resounds with the noise of conches and drums, whose touch is unbearable, and whose shores fierce Rakshasas and carnivores infest.

I think, beloved Suta, that now we can easily cross what remains of the vyuha, which is like a poor stream of willow water. Urge your horses on without reserve or fear, for I feel certain that I am very near Arjuna. Yes, having vanquished the invincible Drona and his legions, and the mighty Kritavarman, I do believe I cannot be too distant from my master Arjuna.

I never feel fear even if I see countless enemies before me. To me they are like a heap of straw and dry grass to a blazing conflagration in the forest. This is the path by which Arjuna Kiritin, the greatest of the

Pandavas, has gone and numberless corpses of foot-soldiers and horses, chariot-warriors and elephants have rendered the earth uneven. Look at the Kaurava army running away, routed by the noblest warrior. Look, Suta, at the brown dust the fleeing chariots, elephants and horses raise.

Yes, I am very near to the Swetavahana, Arjuna who has Krishna for his sarathy. Ah, listen! The sweet thunder of the Gandiva! From the omens I see all around me, I am certain that Arjuna will kill Jayadratha before the sun sets.

Without tiring our horses, now guide them slowly to where the warriors led by Duryodhana, their hands cased in leather gauntlets stand; and there, where the Kambojas of fierce deeds and the Yavanas with their marvellous bows; and towards the Sakas and Daradas and Barbaras and Tamraliptakas, and countless other Mlecchas, armed with diverse strange weapons. All these, with vile Duryodhana at their head, wait with their faces turned towards me, excited at the prospect of doing battle against me.

Suta, think of us as already having passed through this fierce fastness, having slain all these legions with their chariots, elephants, horses and footsoldiers."

His charioteer replies, "O you of Vrishni's vamsa, I too have no fear. Why, O indomitable one, if you face Jamadagni's son Parasurama himself in anger, or Drona, best of maharathas, or the king of the Madras, fear will not enter my heart, as long as I have the shade of your protection.

Parantapa, you have already decimated countless invincible Kambojas, invincible in battle, as many intrepid Yavanas, including Sakas, Daradas, Tamraliptakas, and many other Mlecchas armed with their myriad weapons. Never have I experienced fear in any battle. Why will I then be afraid in this miserable fray?

O you who are blessed with long life, by which route should I take you to where Dhananjaya is? With whom are you angry, and who are they that will run away from battle, when they see you demonstrate the prowess of the Destroyer himself as he appears at the end of the Yuga? O Mahabaho, who are they of whom king Vaivaswata is thinking today?"

Satyaki replies, "Like Vasava destroying the Danavas I will slay these Kamboja warriors with shaved heads and fulfil my vow. Take me there and causing a great carnage among them, I will join Arjuna. The Kauravas, with Duryodhana at their head, will see my prowess today, when I exterminate this legion of Mlecchas of shaved heads and put the whole Kaurava army to the greatest grief. Today, hearing the loud wails of the Kaurava host, mangled and broken by me in battle, Duryodhana will suffer the grief he deserves.

Today I will show my guru, the noble Swetavahana, my skill with weapons that I acquired from him. When he sees thousands of mighty warriors slain by my arrows, king Duryodhana will be plunged into great grief. The Kauravas will behold the bow in my hands to resemble a circle of fire when, light-handed, I stretch the bowstring to loose multitudes of missiles. Seeing the incessant slaughter of his troops, their bodies covered with blood and pierced all over with my arrows, Duryodhana will be filled with sorrow. While I kill the foremost Kuru warriors today, he will see not one but two Arjunas. Seeing me dispatch thousands of kings in battle, intolerable pain will fill his body and heart. Slaying those thousands of kings today, I will show my love and devotion to the noble sons of Pandu. And the Kauravas will know the measure of my might and energy, and my gratitude to the Pandavas."

The charioteer then urges his coursers of the hue of the moon to their utmost speed. The excellent steeds, swift as the wind or thought, fly forward as if to devour the very skies, and bear Satyaki to where the Yavanas are stationed. The numerous Yavanas, expert archers all, envelop the charging Satyaki with showers of arrows. The wrathful Satyaki, Rajan, destroys all their shafts and other weapons; with hosts of arrows, winged with gold and vulture's feathers he dismembers the Yavanas, striking off their heads and arms so they fall like eerie hail. Many of his shafts pass through their iron or brass coats of mail, and stick in the earth. The Mlecchas perish in hundreds; his arrows flowing in spate, a torrid river from his bow drawn to its fullest stretch, he fells five, six, seven, or eight Yavanas at a time.

Satyaki massacres thousands of Kambojas, Sakas, and Barbaras, and the great carnage makes the earth impassable with a horrible sludge of flesh and blood.

The battlefield looks exotic like a sky covered with coppery clouds, with the strewn helmets of the Mlecchas and their shaven heads, which with their long beards look like featherless birds; and the field is also covered even more thickly with headless trunks dyed in blood. Slaughtered by Satyaki, whose touch is like that of Indra's thunder, the dead Yavanas sprawl everywhere, cover the earth with their dead. The small living remnant of those warriors, Rajan, and their spirit broken, face to face with death, they whips their horses and flee in all directions, overwhelmed by the terror of Satyaki.

Thus, the insuperable Satyaki routs the invincible Kamboja host as well as the Yavana army and the large force of the Sakas, and crowned with victory, cries to his charioteer, "On! Fly!"

Seeing his indescribable feats in this battle, never achieved by anyone before, the Charanas and the Gandharvas in the sky applaud him. Indeed, O king, the Charanas, and your warriors, seeing Satyaki flying to help Arjuna, are filled with delight at his heroism.'"

CANTO 116

JAYADRATHA-VADHA PARVA CONTINUED

"Sanjaya says, 'Having vanquished the Yavanas and the Kambojas, Satyaki, most magnificent maharatha, courses on towards Arjuna, blasting his way through your terrified troops, decimating them on every side at his great will. Brandishing his glorious bow, which many moons adorn, he forges on irresistibly.

Golden angadas deck his arms; his helmet is adorned with gold; his body is covered in golden mail and his standard and bow too are embellished with gold, so that he shines like the summit of Meru. So lustrous is he, with the bow always bent into a circle, that he does resembles a second Surya in autumn. Yuyudhana, with his mighty shoulders, tread and lion's gaze, looks like a bull in a cow-pen in the midst of your troops.

Your warriors surround him again, Sini's grandson who stands so tall and proud, radiant in his chariot, like some incomparable tusker with rent temples. Indeed, after he ploughs through Drona's division, and the unfordable Bhoja division; after he wades through the sea of Jalasandha's troops as well as the host of the Kambojas; after he escapes

Kritavarman the makara, after he traverses the entire oceanic Kuru host, once more many infuriated chariot-warriors of your army attack the Yadava. Duryodhana, Chitrasena, Dusasana, Vivimsati, Sauna, Duhsaha, the youthful Durdharshana, Kratha, and many other great warriors, all difficult to defeat, wrathfully chase Satyaki as he dashes on, nearer and nearer Arjuna with each moment.

Then, O Sire, loud is the uproar that arises among your troops, like that of the ocean at full tide when lashed into fury by a tempest. Seeing all those warriors dashing at him, Satyaki smilingly says to his charioteer, "Drive slowly, Suta. Swollen with rage and pride, and swarming with elephants, horsemen, rathas and foot-soldiers, rushes towards me, filling the ten points of the compass with deep rumble of its chariots and making the earth, the sky, and the very seas to tremble.

This sea of troops, O Suta, will I contend with in a great battle, like the continent resisting the ocean risen to its height at full moon. Watch my prowess, O friend, which is equal to that of Indra himself for I will devour this hostile force with my arrows. Look at the foot-soldiers, horsemen, chariot-warriors, and elephants I slew in thousands, their bodies pierced by my fiery arrows."

While he speaks to his charioteer, the enemy host breaks upon the unassailable Satyaki. They come with a deafening din, and roars of *Kill him!* fill the field of dharma. Satyaki kills three hundred horsemen and four hundred elephants of those brave warriors in less time than it takes to tell. The exchange of arrows between the enemy bowmen and Satyaki is yet again comparable to that between the Devas and the Asuras in the days of old. Carnage rules the field; Yuyudhana's astras are like venomous snakes, not one failing to find its target and he shrouds them with his missiles in an unearthly cloudburst.

The surging sea of troops, seething with chariots rathas, elephants, cavalry and foot-soldiers, which are its waves, is stilled as soon as it comes upon the Satyaki Dwipa. Such slaughtering does he bring to them, that in no time they break ranks and flee, utterly shattered, in a daze, trembling as if struck by the icy winds of winter.

We see no foot-soldier or chariot-warrior or elephant or horseman or a horse that Yuyudhana's arrows do not strike. Not even Arjuna, O Rajan, has brought such carnage there as the dauntless Satyaki!

Then Duryodhana strikes Satyaki's charioteer with three keen arrows, his four horses with four, and Satyaki himself first with three and again with eight. Dusasana pierces him with sixteen, Sakuni with five and twenty arrows, Chitrasena with five; Dusasana drills fifteen thunderbolts into his chest. The Vrishni never flinches but proudly wounds each of them with three arrows. Yet, fiercely wounded, by enemy shafts, maharatha, mahatejasvin Satyaki flits all over the battlefield with the speed of a hawk.

He demolishes Sakuni's bow and shreds his leathern gloves, bloodies Duryodhana's chest with three shafts, Chitrasena with a hundred arrows, Duhsaha with ten, and Dusasana with twenty. Your brother-in-law Sakuni takes up another bow and strikes Satyaki first with eight arrows and again with five; Dusasana wounds him with three, Durmukha with a dozen, Duryodhana with three and seventy and then his charioteer with three keening barbs.

Satyaki excoriates each of those maharathas with five blazing shafts. He swiftly strikes Duryodhana's charioteer with a broad-headed shaft, and drops him dead on the field. At this your son's horses bolt, bearing Duryodhana madly away from the field of battle, quick as the wind. Seeing this, your other sons and warriors flee in their hundreds. Satyaki unleashes burning arrow storms after the fleeing enemy, golden-winged and shimmering.

Thus routing all your legions, thousands and thousands of men, Satyaki again courses on towards Arjuna's ratha. If truth be told, Dhritarashtra, your troops worship Satyaki, when they see him loose his gales of arrows, even while protecting his charioteer and himself. They have never before seen archery like this, or valour!'"

CANTO 117

JAYADRATHA-VADHA PARVA CONTINUED

"Dhritarashtra says, 'Seeing Satyaki fight his way towards Arjuna, smashing the large force as he went, Sanjaya, what do my shameless sons do? When he who is equal to Savyasachin himself confronts them, how can these wretches, face to face with death, feel any eagerness to fight? What do all those Kshatriyas, routed in battle, then do? Yet, how can Satyaki of renown pass through our ranks when my sons still live? Tell me all this, O Sanjaya, for I am astonished to hear about this encounter between a single hero and the many maharathas.

O Suta, fate has surely turned against my sons, that one warrior of the Satwata vamsa has killed so many mighty maharathas. Alas, my army is no match for even this one Satyaki inflamed. Let all the Pandavas hang up their weapons. Vanquishing Drona himself, Satyaki will kill all my sons, like a great lion hunting little animals. So many maharathas, Kritavarman the first among them, all fighting vigorously, cannot stop Yuyudhana. The Vrishni will surely slay my sons. Truly, Arjuna himself does not fight as the renowned Satyaki does!'

Sanjaya replies, 'All this, O Rajan, is the consequence of your evil counsels and the sins of Duryodhana. Listen attentively to what I say.

At the command of your son, the Samsaptakas now rally once more, all determined to fight to the death. Three thousand archers led by Duryodhana, with a number of Sakas, Kambojas, Balhikas, Yavanas, Paradas, Kalingas, Tanganas, Ambashtas, Pisachas, Barbaras and mountain-men—inflamed with rage and armed with stones—all rush in frenzy at Satyaki, like insects into a blazing fire. Five hundred other warriors also charge Yuyudhana. Another mighty contingent of a thousand chariots, a hundred maharathas, a thousand elephants, two thousand Kshatriyas and countless foot-soldiers also attack him. Dusasana urges all these warriors on, crying, "Surround Satyaki and cut him down like a dog!"

And then still more grand and wonderful is the fight that we see from Sini's grandson, as he fights alone against these innumerable enemies. He kills the entire body of maharathas, the elephant force, all the horsemen and the Mlecchas. Like the autumn sky spangled with stars, the battlefield is strewn with chariot-wheels his mighty weapons break apart with volleys of innumerable akshas; and reduce beautifully wrought chariot-shafts to fragments; like the star-strewn autumn sky is Kurukshetra with felled elephants and fallen standards, with coats of mail and shields scattered all around, with garlands and ornaments and fine cloaks and anukarshas, O great King!

Many hilly elephants, born of the race of Anjana or Vamana or of other noble lines, so many immense tuskers lie there on the ground, unbreathing, and their eyes shut forever. Satyaki kills the great horses of the Vanayu, the Malaya, the Kamboja and the Balhika breeds: in thousands. He razes hundreds of thousands of foot-soldiers, born in various kingdoms and belonging to diverse nations.

Even while all these men and beasts are being slaughtered, Dusasana exhorts the virile Mleccha brigands, "You warriors who know no dharma, fight now as savagely as you can! Why do you retreat? This is just one man, cut him to pieces and feed on his flesh!"

But they ignore him and just run. Now Dusasana turns to the

mountain men, the wild stone-fighters, saying, "You are masters of fighting with stones and slingshots, while Satyaki knows nothing of this way of battle. So stop this Vrishni. The Kauravas also know nothing of your method of fighting. If you rush fearlessly at Satyaki, he will be helpless against you."

Those mountain-dwelling Kshatriyas, all masters at the unusual art of fighting with stones, run towards Satyaki like ministers towards a king, with stones big as elephants' heads raised in their hands. Others, urged by your son, and wanting to kill Yuyudhana, surround him, also armed with rocks. Satyaki pulverizes the heavy cascade of rocks and stones they fling so expertly at him; he kills many of the mountain Kshatriyas, while the shattering rock fragments pierce others in hundreds blowing heads asunder, smashing open brawny chests, and countless more fall dead. Next moment, he hacks off the arms of five hundred stone-throwers, so scarlet geysers spray from their armpits, while their hands still clasp great rocks.

Never pausing, growing more fierce by the moment, Satyaki kills a thousand mountain men next, and then a whole hundred thousand, all of them never coming near him, all with their rough weapons raised above their heads, even as he strikes off those heads. It is an exceptional and incredible feat that the Yadava on fire accomplished quick as seeing.

The hordes of stone-throwers continue to rush at Satyaki in waves, for they are numerous, and he continues to kill them as they come. Many Daradas, Tanganas, Khasas, Lampakas and Pulindas fling swords and lances at him for what they believe to be a safe distance. Satyaki carves all these in flight, the rocks exploding with loud reports, which frighten horses, and elephants that flee yet again, while bedlam reigns with Satyaki its dreadful heart. The shattering fragments continue to sting and kill countless men and beasts, even as if cobras are stinging them.

The small remnant of the elephants that attacked Satyaki also flees from the Vrishni's ratha, covered with blood, their heads and frontal lobes split open. While he annihilates your legions in an unprecedented carnage, a loud and deep wailing rises from your troops, even as if the

Earth herself bellowed in agony, or the sea at full tide.

Hearing the great and dismal sound, Drona says to his charioteer, "O Suta, Satyaki fights like Yama himself enraged and annihilates our forces. Ride to where this great tumult has arisen. I have no doubt that Yuyudhana decimates the mountain men who fight with rocks and stone. And look where our maharathas also flee everywhere in terror of the Yadava. Look where they fall, the wounded and the dead, while the charioteers cannot restrain their horses."

His sarathy tells Drona, the greatest of wielders of weapons, "O you who are blessed with length of days, look at the Kaurava troops flee and all our warriors, routed by one hero, run in all directions. And here, the Panchalas and the Pandavas, united, converge on you from every side to have your life. You must decide which of these should have your first attention? Should we stay here to face the advancing Pandavas or should we find Satyaki who is so far from us?"

Even as his charioteer says this to Drona, Satyaki suddenly appears in hot pursuit of a large number of rathikas who are fleeing from him towards Drona's army. Some other chariot-warriors, Dusasana's troops, all panic-stricken, also fly towards Drona's ratha.'"

CANTO 118

JAYADRATHA-VADHA PARVA CONTINUED

"Sanjaya says, 'Seeing Dusasana's chariot near his, Drona asks him, "Why are all these rathas fleeing? Is the king not well? Is Jayadratha still alive? You are a prince, a king's brother, a maharatha. Why do you run away from battle? Hand the throne over to your brother and become the Prince Regent. You once told Draupadi, "We have won you at dice; you are our slave. Do not limit yourself to your husbands; set aside your chastity and take these robes to the king, my brother Duryodhana. Your husbands are all good as dead; they are as worthless as grains of sesame without their kernels."

And now you run away from battle? Having provoked such fierce enmity with the Panchalas and the Pandavas, why are you afraid to fight a lone Satyaki? When you took up the dice in the Kuru sabha, could you not divine that one day they would transform themselves into fierce arrows? It was you that abused the Pandavas. You are the cause of Draupadi's torment. Where is your pride now, your insolence and your brag? After stirring their wrath, now why do you run away from the Pandavas who are like terrible snakes of virulent poison?

As a brave brother of Suyodhana, you should protect the routed, panic-stricken Kaurava army with your might, instead of running like a common coward. With this dastardliness you will increase the joy of your enemies. O Parantapa, when you who are the leader of your host, flee like this, who else will stay to fight? When you, its refuge, are frightened, who in our army will not be afraid?

You run in terror from just one Satwata warrior. Kaurava, what will you do when you face Arjuna the Gandivi in battle, or Bhima, or Madri's twins? Satyaki's arrows from which you flee in terror are hardly equal to Arjuna's astras, which are like the Sun or Fire.

If you are bent on escape, let us declare peace and hand over the sovereignty of the Earth to Dharmaraja Yudhishtira. Make peace with the Pandavas before Arjuna's astras like thunderbolts enter your body. Before the noble Parthas kill your hundred brothers and wrest the Earth from you by force, make peace with the Pandavas. Before king Yudhishtira is truly enraged, and Krishna, who delights in battle, also, make peace with the sons of Pandu.

Before the Mahabaho Bhima blasts his terrible way through our vast army and seizes your brothers like a lion seizes lambs, Dusasana, make peace with the Pandavas.

Bhishma once said to your brother Duryodhana, 'The Pandavas are unconquerable in war, so make peace with them.'

Your evil brother did not listen to him. So now set your heart firmly on war and fight the Pandavas with all your might, fearless for your life. Go, coward, fly to where Satyaki is. Without you, O Bhaarata, this host will melt away. For your own sake, fly and fight the indomitable Satyaki."

Thus addressed by Drona, your son Dusasana, his heart burning with shame, says not a word in reply, feigning not to have heard him. However, taking a large force of brave Mlecchas with him, Dusasana rides at Satyaki, burning like the yuga-fire on Kurukshetra, and engages him in a pitched battle. Heartened by this, Drona turns back to attack the Pandavas and the Panchalas again.

Loudly announcing himself, that he is the great and invincible Drona, son of Bharadwaja, he plunged straight into the midst of the enemy, and begins to decimate their forces, killing thousands and thousands of fighting men. He brings another dreadful carnage to the Pandavas, the Panchalas, and the Matsyas.

The illustrious Viraketu, another son of Drupada, faces Drona boldly and strikes the Brahmana with five sizzling barbs, sticks another deep into his flagstaff and rakes his sarathy with another seven. It is an amazing sight, Rajan, to watch Drona exert himself vigorously and yet not be able to approach, let alone vanquish that Panchala prince!

The other Panchalas swoop down to surround the beleaguered Acharya, and they lash him with dense smoking gusts of fiery shafts, with whistling spears flung from all around and other powerful missiles. Cutting all these down with his own banks of astras, like the wind driving away masses of clouds in the sky, Drona is magnificent. Then he looses an astra blazing like Surya or Agni at Viraketu; the shafts of fire flames its way right through that prince and burns into the ground behind him, simmering blood. Viraketu falls dead from his ratha like a champaka tree uprooted by the wind.

The Panchalas all rush in rage at Drona—Chitraketu, Sudhanwan, Chitravarman and Chitraratha, covering him with a wrath of arrows to avenge their slain brother. Struck from all sides by these royal maharathas, the Brahmana bull summons all his energy and anger.

Drona rakes them with a hurricane of fire from his bow drawn into a circle, and they are dazed and have no reply to this awesome onslaught. Then the angry Brahmana, his lips curled in a grim smile, kills their horses and charioteers, he shatters their rathas; and before they even realise what is happening, with his favourite crescent-headed arrows he plucks their handsome heads from their throats like flowers from their stems. The Panchala princes fall out of their chariots even like the Danavas of old during the Devasura yuddha.

Roaring, Drona raises his golden-backed bow high and shakes it in triumph. He has killed five sons of his great enemy Drupada.

An anguished Dhrishtadyumna sheds tears for his brothers, who were like gods among the Panchalas; losing all control of himself, he wildly attacks Drona. So violent is the assault that a great and fearful cry goes up from your troops, for they are certain that the fire-prince, the Pandava Senapati, will have the Brahmana's life.

But Drona, smiling all the while, continues to battle, triumphant and unperturbed. Blood leaping into his eyes, Dhrishtadyumna drills a rash of terrific shafts into Drona's chest and the Acharya faints in his ratha. Seeing him swooned, Dhrishtadyumna flings down his bow and, seizing up a sword, leaps off his own chariot and running forward mounts Drona's ratha, intent on having the Brahmana's head for his trophy.

Meanwhile, Drona regains his senses, snatches up his bow and unleashes a scathing volley of special short barbs meant just for such a duel at close range at Dhrishtadyumna, wounding him deep and sharply. Dhrishtadyumna finding himself thwarted, jumps down again from Drona's chariot, runs back to his own, and again picking up a great bow once more covers Drona with savage fire.

The two duel like Indra and Prahlada once did for the sovereignty of the three worlds. Their chariots wheel and flash everywhere and torrents of arrows issue from both, cover earth, sky and all the directions, and also drawing copious blood from each other. Watching, the rest of the greatest Kshatriyas, O Rajan, and all the other warriors as well marvel at the unworldly skills of the two.

The hopeful Panchalas exclaim, "Drona fights Dhrishtadyumna who was born to kill him. The Brahmana's end is here!"

But then, like a man plucking a ripe fruit from a tree, Drona takes the head of Dhrishtadyumna's charioteer from his neck with a crescent-tipped shaft; the Panchala's horses bolt, leaving Drona to annihilate the Panchalas and the Srinjayas. After slaughtering so many of these, Drona resumes his lordly station at the heart of his own vyuha. And the Pandavas, my lord, do not venture to challenge him.'"

CANTO 119

JAYADRATHA-VADHA PARVA CONTINUED

"Sanjaya says, 'Meanwhile, Rajan, Dusasana attacks Satyaki with some vehemence. He strikes the Vrishni first with sixty arrows and then with sixteen, but fails to shake the shura who stands immovable as the Mainaka mountain. Leading a large group of rathas from various kingdoms, Dusasana fills the field with his roars deep as rumbling clouds.

Seeing the Kaurava come to battle, the mighty Satyaki flashes straight at him, covering him with arrows. Those in the van of Dusasana army all flee in terror and only your son, Rajan, remains and faces the irradiant Vrishni hero fearlessly. He pierces Satyaki's horses with aggressive shafts, his charioteer with three, and Satyaki himself with a hundred and roars yet again, challengingly. An incensed Satyaki quickly shrouds Dusasana's ratha, sarathy, banner and your son himself in a cloud of shafts, making him invisible. Yuyudhana is like a spider entangling an insect in its web.

Watching this, Duryodhana despatches a legion of Trigartas at Satyaki's ratha to bolster Dusasana. Three thousand fierce Trigarta maharathas, seasoned warriors all, surround Satyaki with their chariots, resolved to engage him and vowing not to retreat. In a trice Satyaki shoots down five hundred of their leading warriors. They fall from their rathas like tall trees from mountaintops, uprooted by a tempest.

O Rajan, Kurukshetra, strewn with mangled elephants, dead horses decked in trappings of gold and torn to shreds by Satyaki's arrows, weltering in blood and littered with fallen standards, presents a striking appearance, like a ghastly garden overgrown with flowering kinsukas. Slaughtered by Satyaki, your soldiers can find no refuge; they are as elephants sunk in mire. And all of them turn back in haste towards Drona's ratha, like mighty snakes making for their holes from fear of the hunting prince of birds. After killing those five hundred, Satyaki again makes his majestic way towards Arjuna.

As he goes, Dusasana strikes him with nine fine shafts. Turning, Satyaki pierces Dusasana with five golden-winged vulture-feathered arrows. Dusasana, smiling, shoots back three bolts, followed by another five, to which Satyaki replies with five of his own that smash your son's bow in his hands; and a smiling Yuyudhana rides on towards Arjuna. An incensed Dusasana hurls an iron spear, which Satyaki destroys with kanka-feathered shafts.

Rajan, your son takes up another bow, rakes Satyaki with a clutch of arrows and gives a lion's roar. Satyaki, aroused, turns back and plunges five arrows that burst into flames, and then eight more thick iron shafts. Dusasana, bestirred by Drona's censure, heroically lacerates the Yadava with twenty stinging shafts.

Yuyudhana, roaring now, finds Dusasana's chest with three vicious barbs; next moment, he kills Satyaki's horses. With another broad-headed arrow he cleaves your son's bow, and with five more slim missiles, shreds his leather gauntlet. Satyaki, master of weapons, severs Dusasana's standard and the wooden shafts of his chariot and kills both his Parshni charioteers in crimson eruptions.

Left without a bow, a ratha, horses and charioteer, Dusasana is rescued by the lord of the Trigartas on his ratha. O Bhaarata, Satyaki pursues him briefly and has him at his mercy, but does not kill him for he remembers the vow that Bhima swore in the Kuru sabha that he would kill all hundred of your sons. Thus, having vanquished and shamed Dusasana, Satyaki again courses ahead in Arjuna's trail.'"

CANTO 120

JAYADRATHA-VADHA PARVA CONTINUED

"Dhritarashtra says, 'O Sanjaya, are there no mighty maharathas in my army who can stop or defy Satyaki as he scythes his way towards Arjuna? Why, the Yadava's exploits are like those of Indra himself when he fought the Danavas! Perhaps, the path Satyaki rode was not defended? But no, the truth is that he has superior prowess and skills and by himself annihilates countless of our warriors. Tell me how this grandson of Sini, all alone, cleaves through the vast force facing him?'

Sanjaya replies, 'Rajan, the fierce effort and the uproar of your army, which teems with numberless chariots, elephants, horses and foot-soldiers, resembles what one sees at the end of the yuga. When your army assembles daily, it seems to me that one has never seen another such a vast gathering of men and beasts on Earth. The Devas and the Charanas who watch from above say, "This muster will be the last of its kind on Bhumi."

Truly, never has such a vyuha been formed in the past as the one that Drona has on this day of Jayadratha's killing. The din made by the vast multitude of soldiers meeting each other in battle is no less than that of the ocean lashed into fury by the tempest. In your host, as well as that of the Pandavas, are hundreds of thousands of kings. The sound these inflamed heroes of fierce deeds make while battling each other is hair-raising.

Now Bhimasena, Dhrishtadyumna, Nakula, Sahadeva and Dharmaraja Yudhishtira all cry variously, "Forward! Charge! Strike! For Krishna and Arjuna have broken into the enemy army! Do whatever we must so that they easily find Jayadratha's ratha."

Dhrishtadyumna says, "If Satyaki and Arjuna are killed, the Kurus will achieve their objective and we will be defeated. All of you unite quickly and agitate their oceanic army, like impetuous winds stirring the very deep."

And responding to their great commanders' call, the Pandava warriors surge forward in tide and, heedless of their own lives, smother the Kauravas. All of them are not merely prepared but even eager to die for their friends and lords, at either the point or the edge of the sword, expecting swarga as a reward. So also, do your warriors too crave fame and stand ready, determined to fight to the end, to kill or be killed.

In the midst of this fierce and horrible battle, Satyaki, after besting all his opponents, drives on towards Arjuna. The glare of the sun reflects from the bright armour of the warriors and dazzles all the combatants. Duryodhana, too, Rajan, pierces the mighty army of the noble Pandavas and fights dreadfully there, bringing great and dire butchery with him."

Dhritarashtra asks, 'Duryodhana must be hard-pressed while fighting the Pandava army. I hope he does not turn his back on the battle, O Suta! The contention between him and the Pandava army seems to me to be a most unequal one. Besides, Duryodhana has been raised in great luxury, in wealth and possessions and now he is a king of men. Encountering so many alone, I truly hope he does not turn back from the fight.'

Sanjaya replies, 'Listen to me, Rajan, as I describe your son's wonderful feats. Duryodhana agitates the Pandava army like an elephant stirring a bank of lotus-stalks in a lake. Seeing their forces being mown down at will by your son, the Panchalas led by Bhimasena rush at him. Duryodhana pierces Bhimasena with ten arrows, each of the twins with three, Yudhishtira with seven, Virata and Drupada with six, Sikhandin with a hundred, Dhrishtadyumna with twenty arrows and he strikes each of the five sons of Draupadi with three.

With his astras, meanwhile, he slaughters hundreds of lesser warriors, and elephants and many other maharathas, too, like an angry Yama. His bow appears to be drawn to a circle, whether while aiming or loosing his shafts. Indeed, his formidable bow, inlaid with gold, is always seen as a circle, while he destroys his enemies with it.

Then, Yudhishtira, with a brace of broad-tipped arrows, rives your son's bow and with another ten exceptional shafts strikes your son lustily. However, on touching Duryodhana's armour, Yudhishtira's arrows shatter into dust. The Parthas, filled with delight, surround Yudhishtira, like the Devas and the great Rishis in olden days surrounding Sakra when he killed Vritra. Taking up another bow, your son roars at Yudhishtira, "Stop and fight me!" and attacks him.

Seeing Duryodhana charge headlong at Yudhishtira, the Panchalas, hope of victory surging in their hearts, eagerly rush forward to meet his charge. However, Drona intercepts the onrushing Panchalas, like a mountain looming in the path of a mass of wind driven, rain-charged clouds. Brutal, O king, the ensuing bloodletting, why, like the sport of Rudra at the end of the Yuga.

Then, above every other sound in the general bedlam, there arises a spine-chilling uproar from where Arjuna is fighting.

Thus, O Mahabaho, the battle develops between Arjuna and your archers, the contention between Satyaki and your men at the heart of your army, and thus continues the bloodshed between Drona and his antagonists at the lip of his vyuha. Thus, indeed, O lord of the world, the carnage on this Earth continues, with Arjuna and Drona and Satyaki, all afire.'"

CANTO 121

Jayadratha-vadha Parva continued

"Sanjaya says, 'Beyond noon, O Rajan, another dreadful battle, marked by roars and bellows, deep as those of thunderheads, ensues between Drona and the Somakas. Drona, keened for a bloodbath, advances against the Pandavas. The pot-born magnificent son of Bharadwaja, always serving your cause, cuts down many leading enemy warriors, why, even as if he sports in battle.

Then the mighty maharatha of the Kaikeyas, irresistible Brihadkshatra, the eldest of five brothers, challenges him. Like a great cloud mass emptying itself over Gandhamadana, he lashes torrents of arrows down on Drona. Drona looses five and ten stone-whetted, golden-winged barbs at Brihadkshatra but the Kekaya prince shatter them all in flight. Drona, the Brahmana bull shoots eight whistling shafts at him; these, too, Brihadkshatra cuts down.

Your troops are filled with amazement at the prince's feat. Applauding Brihadkshatra himself, Drona invokes the Brahmastra and looses that celestial ayudha at the Kekaya prince, who, quicker than thinking, extinguishes it with a Brahmastra of his own. Immediately, he strikes the surprised Acharya with a terrific volley of sixty glittering shafts. Drona, provoked, unleashes a formidable missile at his adversary, a bolt of lightning that plunges through Brihadkshatra's armour, his body and flies on like a black cobra, hissing into the earth behind him.

Pain screaming through his every nerve, filled with rage and rolling his handsome eyes, Brihadkshatra drills Drona with seventy arrows; with another, he gores the Brahmana's sarathy through his very vitals. Lifting his archery, Drona now shoots so ferociously at the Kekaya prince that Brihadkshatra staggers in his chariot, his limbs turning weak.

In a flash, Drona kills his horses, his sarathy, cuts down that brave prince's standard and regal chatra. And then, as Brihadkshatra stands helpless, shocked by the raging Brahmana's tirade, Drona serenely blows his heart to shreds with another perfect arrow and that radiant hero falls dead.

Seeing Brihadkshatra die, Dhrishtaketu, son of the Kaikeya maharatha Sisupala whom Krishna killed at Yudhishtira's Rajasuya yagna, cries to his charioteer, "Suta, take me to where Drona stands, slaughtering the Kaikeya and the Panchala hosts!"

His charioteer turns his fleet of Kamboja horses towards Drona, and Dhrishtaketu, king of the Chedis, swelling with fury and prowess, flies at the dreadful Brahmana, like an insect towards a blazing fire to be consumed. And like a man rousing a tiger from sleep, he rakes Drona, his red chargers, his ratha and standard first with a burst of sixty shafts and again with many others. Drona the tiger responds with a razor-faced arrow winged with vulture feathers, neatly bisecting Dhrishtaketu's bow. The Chedi picks up another bow and draws blood from Drona with a flurry of shafts winged with the shiny feathers of kankas and peacocks.

Drona kills Dhrishtaketu's noble horses, strikes off his sarathy's head and wounds him direly with another five and twenty robust arrows. Dhrishtaketu jumps down from his ratha with a mace and hurls it at Drona like an angry naga. Seeing the heavy gada, hard as adamant and inlaid with gold, fly towards him like Death, Drona smashes it to dust with a thousands shafts loosed in the heart of an instant; the earth echoes with the report of that weapon being blown apart.

Now the wrathful and fearless Dhrishtaketu hurls a spear embellished with gold at the Brahmana. Drona slices the lance into slivers with five breathtaking shafts; and it falls onto the ground like a serpent mangled by Garuda. Not pausing, Drona looses another keen barb that cleaves the Chedi king's kavacha, his muscled chest and dives into the earth behind him like a swan into a lake overgrown with lotuses. And Sisupala's son keels over, dead. As a hungry blue jay seizes and devours a little insect so does Drona take the life of Dhrishtaketu.

When Dhrishtaketu dies, his enraged son, a considerable warrior himself, attacks Drona. Him Drona smilingly despatches to Yamaloka, like a great tiger in the deep vana killing a fawn.

While the Pandavas, O Bhaarata, are thus being thinned, the heroic son of Jarasandha charges Drona and covers the Acharya with such an opacity of arrows that the Brahmana is briefly invisible, like the sun hidden by black clouds. Then Drona, the scourge of the Kshatriyas, looses a hundred thousand deadly shafts at the gifted prince and kills him in the very sight of all the other great archers.

Truly, Drona is like Yama the Destroyer, jaws agape, swallowing every warrior who dares confront him. Once again roaring out his own name and his lineage in ringing proclamation and challenge, the Brahmana who has abandoned is swadharma and is far more terrible than any Kshatriya, swathes the Pandava host with millions of arrows. Each of these is engraved with his name and they massacre men, elephants and horses in thousands like the Asuras were once slain by Sakra; the Panchalas begin to tremble like a herd of cattle beset with winter's cold.

Indeed, an awful bewailing arises from the terrified Panchalas, scorched by the sun above and made ashes by Drona below. Benumbed by Drona, the greatest Panchala maharathas feel like men whose thighs have been seized by makaras.

Then, Rajan, the Chedis, the Srinjayas, the Kasis and the Kosalas band together and, with great heart attack Drona all together, roaring to one another to embolden themselves, "Drona is slain! Drona is dead!"

These Naravyaghras fall upon the illustrious Drona, bent on sending the fulminant Brahmana to Yama. But the implacable Drona annihilates those brave warriors, especially the greatest ones among the Chedis; and, struck brutally by Drona's shafts, the Panchalas quail.

They call loudly to Bhimasena and Dhrishtadyumna, crying, "This Brahmana has performed the most terrible tapasya and acquired great punya, for now, inflamed by rage, he consumes the greatest Kshatriyas. A Kshatriya's dharma is battle; a Brahmana's, mahatapasya. A Brahmana galvanized by tapasya and gyana can make ashes of anything with just his angry gaze. Here countless great Kshatriyas, O Bhaarata, have been blasted by the fire of Drona's astras. The illustrious Drona has abandoned all restraint and devours our troops as he pleases, while none can stand before him."

At this, Kshatradharman, Dhrishtadyumna's mighty son, severs Drona's bow in his hands with a crescent-tipped shaft such as the Acharya himself favours. Drona, bane of the Kshatriyas, is further incensed, and takes up another bright bow and in a blur transfixes Kshatradharman to his flagstaff with an arrow through his heart.

Now the Pandava troops quake with fear. The redoubtable Chekitana falls upon Drona and bloodies his torso with ten fulvid arrows; he pierces Drona's charioteer with four shafts and his chestnut horses with another four. The Acharya ablaze pierces Chekitana's right arm with sixteen arrows, his standard with another sixteen, and his charioteer with seven. With his charioteer killed, Chekitana's horses bolt, dragging his chariot with them, and filling the Panchalas and the Pandavas with more panic yet. And dominating, resplendent, terrifying Drona routs the united forces of the Panchalas and the Srinjayas all around him. Ah, Raja, he is beyond being merely magnificent.

The venerable Drona, full five and eighty years of age, dark in complexion and with pure white hair, dashes all over the battlefield like a youth of sixteen. Rajan, his enemies look upon him as none else than Vajradhari Indra himself come to hunt them.

Then the mighty-armed and intelligent Drupada says, "This vile and dreadful Brahmana is killing noble Kshatriyas like a hungry tiger killing small animals. The sinful Duryodhana will surely find the most vicious hell for himself in the next world. It is through his greed that countless great Kshatriyas lie dead the field like mangled bulls, weltering in their own blood and becoming food for dogs and jackals."

Saying this, O Rajan, Drupada, the lord of an akshauhini, sets the Parthas at its head, and rides with great speed towards Drona.'"

CANTO 122

Jayadratha-vadha Parva continued

"Sanjaya says, 'When the Pandava army is set upon from all sides, the Parthas, the Panchalas and the Somakas retreat to a great distance. O Bhaarata, during this harrowing battle, reminiscent of the pralaya at yuga's end, Drona, straddling the field, repeatedly roars, shaking earth and sky and continues to obliterate the Panchalas and the Pandavas.

And when Yudhishtira can find no succour in his extreme distress, he begins to wonder how the war can ever be won as long as the Brahmana, his old Acharya, is alive. Looking around him desperately for Arjuna, Yudhishtira sees neither him nor Krishna. Not finding the Naravyaghra who flies Hanuman on his banner and not hearing the twang of the Gandiva, and not seeing Satyaki anywhere either, the Dharmaraja loses all peace of mind.

Yudhishtira, fearing the world's censure, begins to think of Satyaki. "I sent the brilliant Satyaki, dispeller of the fears of friends, to follow Arjuna. Earlier I had only one source of anxiety, but now I have two. I should have some tidings of both Satyaki and Dhananjaya by now.

Having sent Satyaki to follow Arjuna, whom can I now send to follow Satyaki? If I try to find intelligence only of my brother without enquiring after Satyaki, the world will reproach me. They will say, 'Yudhishtira Dharmaputra seeks only his brother and leaves Satyaki of Vrishni's vamsa, the hero of unfailing prowess, to his fate!'

Fearing as I do the reproach of the world, I will send Bhimasena to find the noble Yuyudhana. The love I bear for the invincible Satwata is no less than the love I have for Arjuna, the Parantapa. Ah, I fear I have set the delighter of the Sinis a task more difficult than he can accomplish on his own. Yet, either at a friend's request or for honour, he has pierced deep into the Bharata army like a great Makara into the ocean. Loud is the outcry I hear from enemy heroes, fighting together against him. They appear to be too many for him and I must think quickly of rescuing him.

Bhimasena should go to the two mighty maharathas. There is nothing on earth that Vrikodara cannot face and if he fights with resolve, he is a match for all the archers in the world and with the might of his arms he can stand by himself against all his enemies. It is relying on the strength of arms of noble Bhima in the wilds that we returned from our exile and have never been vanquished in battle.

If Bhimasena joins Satyaki, both Satyaki and Arjuna will find great and real support, and I will be anxious for them anymore. Both of them are masters of weapons and Krishna protects them both. Yet, I will allay my own anxiety and send Bhima after Arjuna and Satyaki. No one can then accuse me of being carless of Yuyudhana's life."

Making up his mind, Yudhishtira tells his charioteer, "Drive me to Bhima."

His sarathy does as he is told. Typically, once he sees Bhima before him, Yudhishtira is filled with remorse, and begins to press Bhima with diverse solicitations. Finally he says, "O Bhima, I do not see Arjuna's standard—he who on a single ratha vanquished all the Devas, the Gandharvas and Asuras!"

Bhimasena replies, "Never before have I seen or heard you so agitated.

Indeed, in the past, when we were stricken with grief, it was you who were our comforter. O King of kings, stop your prevarication and command me what I should do, for there is nothing that I cannot do for you. O Kurusathama! Do not be unhappy."

Then, with a sorrowful face and his eyes bathed in tears, and sighing like a cobra, Yudhishtira says to Bhimasena, "We hear the repeated blasts on Panchajanya that Krishna wrathfully blows. Ah, I fear they are telling us that your brother Arjuna lies dead on the field and that Krishna is fighting. Our Arjuna, to whom we always turn when in trouble even as the Devas to thousand-eyed Indra, has fought his way deep into the Kuru army on his quest for Jayadratha. I know this, my Bhima, but he has not returned.

Dark in complexion, youthful in years, with wavy locks, exceedingly handsome, broad of chest and with long arms, with the tread of an angry elephant, with eyes like chakras the colour of burnished copper, the mightiest maharatha, this brother of yours, Arjuna, always terrifies his enemies. This is the cause of my grief, Parantapa! My pain increases like a fire fed with libations of ghee, because of Arjuna, as well as for Satyaki. I am dazed with sorrow for I do not see his banner emblazoned with great Hanuman.

Oh, I have no doubt that he ha been killed and that it is Krishna who now fights. Know also, Bhima, that I fear that the other tiger among men, the mighty Satyaki, is also slain. Alas! Satyaki followed in the wake of Arjuna out of his great love. Without seeing Satyaki, too, I am benumbed by grief.

O Kaunteya, if you think it your dharma to obey me, you must rush to Arjuna and Satyaki. O you who know dharma well, remember that I am your eldest brother. You should consider Satyaki dearer to you than Arjuna himself. Satyaki went forth after Arjuna for my sake, following a trail that only the noblest men can tread. Now you must follow after Yuyudhana and upon finding the two Krishnas and Satyaki of the Satwata vamsa, safe, send me a message, O son of Pandu, beloved Bhima, by giving a loud roar."

CANTO 123

Jayadratha-vadha Parva continued

Bhima replies, "The two Krishnas have gone in the ratha which once carried Brahma, Isana, Indra and Varuna to battle, so they can be in no danger. However, to obey your command, my brother, look, I too ride after them! Do not be anxious. As soon as I meet those Naravyaghras, I will send you the message you want with a roar of joy.'"

"Sanjaya says, 'Bhima prepares to set out and repeatedly entrusts Yudhishtira's care to Dhrishtadyumna and other friends, saying, "You know how Drona is always looking to seize Yudhishtira by any means. Indeed, O son of Drupada, I should never set my riding out to help Arjuna and Satyaki above my duty to protect the king. But because he has himself commanded me to go, I cannot disobey him. I will go where Jayadratha, the wretched king of the Sindhus waits in the suchimukha vyuha, at the point of death. In truth, I should only do what Arjuna and Satyaki asked me to, and remain here beside Yudhishtira. But, my dearest friend Dhrishtadyumna, I am helpless and entrust my brother's care to you. You must protect him at any cost. Of all tasks, this is your highest duty today."

To this, Dhrishtadyumna replies, "I will do as you wish. Go, O son of Kunti, without anxiety of any kind. Without killing me, Drona will never harm or take Yudhishtira. And Drona fears me more than any other warrior for he knows that his death is written at my hands."

Thus entrusting Yudhishtira to Dhrishtadyumna and saluting his elder brother, Bhimasena rides forth in search of Arjuna. Before he leaves, Yudhishtira embraces Bhimasena and sniffs his head affectionately and blesses him, for it is well known that Bhima has always been his favourite brother. After worshipping a number of Brahmanas, circumambulating them in pradakshina; after gratifying them with many gifts; after touching the eight kinds of auspicious articles and drinking potent kairataka honey, Bhimasena, the shura of all shuras, the corners of whose eyes have turned red with intoxication, feels that his natural, boundless strength has doubled.

The Brahmanas perform propitiatory ceremonies for him, various omens indicating success greet him; and seeing all this, he already feels the delight of anticipated victory. Favourable winds begin to blow to predict his success. Then, Mahabaho Bhimasena, foremost of maharathas, strongest man on earth, decked with earrings and angadas, and his hands cased in leather gauntlets, mounts his excellent ratha. His priceless armour made of black steel inlaid with gold, looks like a cloud charged with lightning. Yellow, red, black and white robes gracefully cover his great body. Also wearing a coloured cuirass that protects his neck, Bhimasena is as resplendent as a cloud ornamented with a rainbow.

Just as Bhimasena is on the point of setting out, we hear the fierce blasts of Panchajanya again, which can fill the three worlds with fear. Yudhishtira says to Bhima, "The Vrishni hero blows his conch again and fills the earth and sky with its thunder. Surely, Arjuna has fallen and Krishna now fights the Kurus. I am certain that Kunti, Draupadi and Subhadra, with their relatives and friends, have all seen inauspicious omens today. So fly to Arjuna, my brother, for all the world seems empty to my eyes that long to see Dhananjaya and Satyaki."

Bhima puts on his leather gloves, takes up his bow, calls for the drums to be beaten, blows his conch with great force and roaring like ten lions, pulls on his bowstring, shaking the field and making his enemies' hearts tremble. Assuming a dreadful form, he rides out in his great chariot yoked to horses of the finest breed, gifted with the speed of the wind or thought, their reins held by Visoka and whinnying furiously as they dash ahead into the fray.

Losing a gale of arrows, powerful as his father the Wind, be quickly begins to raze the enemy vyuha, while the valiant Panchalas and the Somakas follow him, like the Devas following Maghavat.

The brothers Dusasana, Chitrasena, Kundabhedin, Vivimsati, Durmukha, Duhsaha, Sala, Vinda, Anuvinda, Sumukha, Dirghabahu, Sudarshana, Suhasta, Sushena, Dirghalochana, Abhaya, Raudrakarman, Suvarman and Durvimochana surround him and these resplendent shuras attack him with their troops. Bhima is at them with the wild imperiousness of a lion hunting herds of deer. They loose devastras and other incandescent arrows that cover him like clouds shrouding the sun.

Blasting them out of his way, truly like some towering gale of his father Vayu, Bhima attacks Drona's elephant-force and covers them with fire. In no time, the Vayuputra demolishes that division and those that remain alive bolt in all directions. Like animals in the forest terrified at the roar of a Sarabha, the elephants all run, with frightful cries. Racing along, Bhima comes upon Drona's main host.

The Acharya checks his advance, like the continent resisting the surging sea and, smiling, strikes Bhimasena on his forehead with a shaft whereupon he looks like the sun with his rays streaming up. Drona thinks that Bhima will show him reverence as Arjuna had, and says to him, "Mighty Bhimasena, you cannot enter my vyuha without vanquishing me! Krishna, with your brother, went into my army with my consent, but you will never succeed."

Bhima, enraged, his eyes the colour of blood, red or burnished copper, replies roughly, "O wretch of a Brahmana, it cannot be that Arjuna entered this host with your consent. He is invisible and can break into an army commanded by Sakra himself. If he offered you reverence, it was only because he respects you. But know, O Drona, that I am not compassionate like Arjuna. I am Bhimasena your enemy.

We regarded you as our father, Acharya, and ourselves as your sons and so we were always humble before you. However, when you speak to us as you do today, and fight us with devastras, all that is a thing of the past. You regard yourself as our enemy, so let it be as you wish. I am Bhima and I will now show you the force of my enmity!"

And Bhima whirls a great mace, like Yama himself twirling his danda, and hurls it at Drona like lightning. Drona leaps out of his chariot in the nick of time and Bhima's massive gada shatters the Brahmana's ratha, killing his horses and sarathy in an explosion of wood and blood. Then Bhima destroys countless Kuru warriors, truly like a tempest felling trees. Your sons once more surround him while Drona, mounting another chariot, returns to the mouth of his vyuha and remains there, recovering himself, waiting for Bhima to come to him again.

The infuriated Bhima covers the chariot-division before him with showers of arrows, with force not yet seen on the field. Your sons, the maharathas, fight back manfully. Dusasana casts an iron spear at his cousin; Bhima divides it neatly, marvellously along its length as it flies towards him. With three immaculate shafts he kills your sons Kundabhedin, Sushena and Dirghanetra; he beheads your heroic son Vrindaraka, pride of the Kurus. He next despatches your sons Abhaya, Raudrakarman and Durvimochana.

Your other princes then surround Bhima, and shower fulminations of arrows over him, like lashing rain upon the mountain breast at summer's end. And like the mountain does Bhima receive those heavy salvos. Bhima feels no pain and smiling awfully sends your sons Vinda, Anuvinda and Suvarman to Yama. He does not pause and blows your son Sudarshana's chest apart, killing him instantly.

The titanic Pandava trains his wrath on the rathas of your army, and within moments overwhelms them with his fury and they flee in all directions. Like a herd of frightened deer, your sons terrified by

Bhimasena, all turn and flee from their dreadful cousin. He, however, goes coursing after their vast legion and careening everywhere as he belabours your warriors from every side. Your best soldiers spur their horses, as swiftly as they can go, away from the force of nature that is Bhima come hunting them.

Stupendous Bhimasena gives roar after shattering roar, slaps his armpits like peals of thunder, further deranging your rathikas, and flares on towards Drona's main vyuha, trampling over the corpses with which he has scattered the field.'"

CANTO 124

JAYADRATHA-VADHA PARVA CONTINUED

"Sanjaya says, 'After Bhima mows down the chariot-division, Drona, smiling, shrouds him in a downpour of arrows to stop his furious progress. However, Bhimasena confounds your army with his powers of maya and absorbs the Acharya's fusillade, while your sons attack him again. Inspired by your princes, many kings, all great archers, rush to surround him.

Bhima grins fearsomely, gives a great roar and casts a mace at them like a thunderflash, like Indra's very Vajra. Blazing with splendour, emitting streaks of lightning, that mace fills the whole world with a deafening sound and overwhelms your soldiers. It terrifies your sons and your other warriors flee again in alarm, with loud cries. Many foot-soldiers fall where they stand at the unbearable sound made by the fierce gada; many maharathas fall out of their chariots.

The occult and magical mace flies everywhere, killing hundreds; it flies back into Bhima's hands and he casts it, again and again. Slaughtered by Bhimasena's great gada, once given him by Mayaa Danava, all your warriors run away in fear, like deer attacked by a monstrous tiger. The colossal Bhima demolishes the enemy, blasting his way through their ranks in a furrow of blood. He tears his way through your army like Garuda of the beautiful feathers.

Rajan, while Bhimasena, the great leader of chariot-divisions, brings bloody carnage to your troops, Drona rushes at him again and stops him still with a supernatural volley of shining arrows; Bharadwaja's son roars in triumph and fear seizes the Pandavas. Yet another feverish duel develops between Drona and Bhima, this one also like the Devasura yuddha of yore.

Drona's luciferous astras consume brave Pandava warriors, thousands of them. Losing all control of himself, with a roar like none heard before during this war, Bhima shuts his eyes, leaps down from his chariot and runs straight at Drona's ratha, ignoring all the arrows that pierce him on his mad way like a massive bull might the rain that falls upon him.

Staggering Bhima seizes Drona's ratha by the shaft, and lifts it above his head and flings it down smashing it into shards. However, Drona nimbly jumps out of his chariot just before Bhima seizes it, and running with some celerity, quickly mounts another chariot and with his sarathy whipping his horses to great speed, the Acharya retreats, mildly dazed by Bhima, to defend the entrance to his vyuha again. Who has ever thought of a feat like the one Bhima performs, let alone seen such a thing?

Bhima quickly remounts his ratha and once more advances imperiously towards your son's army, defying all the enemy warriors like a mountain a surging sea. As he forges on, he destroys the Kshatriyas before him like a tornado uprooting rows of trees.

Bhimasena now erupts on the Bhoja troops led by Kritavarman, and flattens them. He affrights them with the very sound of clapping his huge hands; he overwhelms them like a tiger a herd of cattle. Blasting through the Bhoja division, with blood spraying all around him as he goes, and through the Kambojas as well as countless tribes of Mlecchas, he sees some way ahead of him the splendid Satyaki, fighting like an army by himself! Bhimasena flashes on relentlessly, anxious now to catch sight of Arjuna.

After he effortlessly blows his way through all your warriors, in scarcely any time at all, the gale that is Bhimasena finally sights Arjuna, fighting fervidly to reach and kill Jayadratha. And seeing his brother, Bhima gives the roar that Yudhishtira wanted of him; he roars and roars as the greatest thunderheads do during the monsoon, exhilarating his own forces and making his enemies' blood run cold.

At the heart of the raging battle, Arjuna and Krishna hear those awesome roars, and they reply with roars of their own, elated and eager to lay eyes on Vrikodara. Then, they resume their hot charge to discover Jayadratha, for their time is short. Far away, Yudhishtira clearly hears Bhima's roars and then in delight he hears Arjuna and Krishna roaring as well. In a moment, all Yudhishtira's anxiety leaves him and, a smile wreathing his noble face, he repeatedly prays for Dhananjaya's success.

While Bhima continues to bellow out his roars, to make certain that his brother has heard him above the bedlam of the war, Yudhishtira happily says to himself, "Bhima my brother, you have indeed sent me the message I asked for. You have indeed fulfilled the wish of your brother. Those who have you for their enemy can never be victorious!

It is our great good fortune that Arjuna Savyasachin is still alive and the heroic Satyaki as well.

It is my great good fortune that I hear both Vasudeva and Dhananjaya roaring as they do. Arjuna, who vanquished Sakra himself in battle and gratified Agni in the Khandava vana, still lives and my hope surges high within me again that we shall yet win this horrible war.

A benign providence has kept Arjuna Parantapa, on whose might we rely, alive.

Truly, it is kindly fate smiling on our cause that Partha, who vanquished the Nivatakavachas, whom the gods themselves could not kill, still lives.

It is through good fortune that Dhananjaya, who crushed all the Kauravas come to seize Virata's kine outside the Matsya king's city, still lives.

Ah, the Partha who slew fourteen thousand Kalakeyas, still lives—

through sheer good fortune and against all likelihood.

It is because of great destiny that the Vijaya, who for Duryodhana's sake vanquished Chitraratha, the Gandharva king in the forest, still lives.

Only providence has kept my Arjuna, always dear to me, who wears the kirita and golden garlands, who is Swetavahana of the white steeds, with Krishna himself for his sarathy, alive.

Ah, I am still anxious. Will Arjuna, burning with grief over the death of his son, succeed in his most difficult mission to kill Jayadratha? After he fulfills his vow, protected by Vasudeva, will I see Arjuna again before the sun sets?

Will the killing of Jayadratha, who is devoted to Duryodhana, break our enemies' spirit? Will they make peace with us when Jayadratha dies? Seeing his brothers all killed by Bhimasena, will he make peace with us? Seeing other great warriors lying prone on the ground in the piquant postures of death, will the dark-hearted and obdurate Suyodhana give way to remorse? Will our enmity not cease with the single sacrifice of Bhishma? Will Duryodhana make peace with us to save the remnants of what is still left to him and us?"

Diverse reflections of this kind pass through the mind of Yudhishtira, who is overwhelmed with compassion. Meanwhile, the war between the Pandavas and the Kauravas continues to rage.'"

CANTO 125

Jayadratha-vadha Parva continued

"Dhritarashtra says, 'While mighty Bhimasena roars repeatedly and loud as thunder, which of our heroes surround him? I do not know of a warrior in the three worlds, Sanjaya, who can face an angry Bhimasena armed with a gada and resembling Death himself. Not even Sakra himself can stand against our Bhima, who can destroy a ratha with a ratha and an elephant with an elephant.

Who among those devoted to Duryodhana dares to do battle with an incensed Bhimasena, ardently engaged in slaughtering my sons, like a forest fire consuming dry leaves and grass? Who are they that encircle Bhima after seeing him slay my sons one after another like Yama himself? I do not fear Arjuna, Krishna, Satyaki or the fire-born Dhrishtadyumna as much as I do Bhima. Tell me, O Sanjaya, who are the heroes that attack the conflagration that is Bhima, who devours my sons?'

Sanjaya says, 'While maharatha Bhimasena roars and roars, the great Karna cannot bear it and rushes at him with a shout. Karna bends his bow forcefully, reveals his vehement prowess, and stops Bhima's rampage like a lone great tree withstanding a hurricane. And Bhima, finding

Vikartana's son before him, flares up in wrath and charges at him, unleashing a thick torrent of arrows at the Sutaputra.

Karna serenely faces all these thunderbolts and shoots as many back at Bhima. All the other warriors, maharathas and horsemen, tremble when they hear the resounding twanging of the bowstrings of those two. Indeed, to all the great Kshatriyas there the dreadful bellowing of Bhimasena seems to fill all the earth and the sky, so both quake with it. All around him, bows clasped in the hands of warriors drop from their hands turned weak by the Pandava's terrific yells and roars. And horses and elephants, O Rajan, spray urine and dung in fear.

Various fearsome evil omens make their appearance. The sky swarms with dark flights of vultures and kankas during the remarkable duel between Bhima and Karna. Then Karna strikes Bhima with twenty arrows and quickly pierces his charioteer also with five. Mighty Bhima, with a smile, looses four and sixty sizzling shafts at Karna. Karna responds, O Rajan, with four flaming astras, which Bhima adroitly smashes into fragments. Now Karna covers him with dense showers of arrows, and Bhima breaks Karna's bow and strikes the Suta's son with ten perfect arrows.

Maharatha Karna, of terrible deeds, takes up another bow and stringing it quickly, strikes Bhima savagely with countless cruel barbs. A livid Bhima drills three straight and vigorous shafts into Karna's chest. O Bharatarishabha, with these barbs protruding from his breast, Karna looks as stunning as a mountain with three peaks; blood begins to flow from his wounds like rills of red chalk flowing down the mountain.

Wounded and bleeding, Karna is a little distraught. He strikes Bhima with one shaft of exceptional force, then assails him with hundreds, why, thousands of quicksilver barbs. Suddenly shrouded in Karna's torrid arrows, Bhima, unperturbed, almost playfully severs Karna's bowstring; then, with a broad-headed arrow, he strikes off Karna's charioteer's head in a red burst and, next moment, kills the Sutaputra's four horses. Karna, his pride sorely wounded, is forced to jump down from his chariot and hastily mount Vrishasena's ratha.

And after vanquishing Karna, the roar that erupts from Bhima is louder than any gone before; it is like booming thunder. Hearing that roar, Yudhishtira is elated knowing that Bhimasena has defeated Karna. The warriors of the Pandava army also blow their conches from all sides and your warriors, hearing this noise, shout and roar back defiantly, and sound their horns and conches. Arjuna pulls resonantly on the bowstring of the Gandiva and Krishna blows the Panchajanya. Yet, drowning all these sounds, all Kurukshetra hears the bellowing of Bhima, O Sire!

Karna and Bhima loose storms of flawless arrows at each other. While the son of Radha shoots his arrows calmly, the son of Pandu does so with great force.'"

CANTO 126

JAYADRATHA-VADHA PARVA CONTINUED

"Sanjaya says, 'After routing your army, Arjuna and Bhimasena go after Jayadratha, while your son Duryodhana rides to Drona astride his single ratha, thinking on the way about what he must say and do. His ratha endued with the speed of the wind, flies along towards Drona. His eyes red with anger, your son tells the Acharya, "O Parantapa, Arjuna, Bhimasena, the invincible Satyaki and many other maharathas have put our troops to rout and are nearing Jayadratha by the moment.

O bestower of honours, how have both Satyaki and Bhima bested you? Foremost of Brahmanas, your defeat at the hands of Satyaki, Arjuna, and of Bhimasena is like the ocean drying up: incredible to us all. All our warriors blame you and ask loudly, 'How has Drona, the greatest master of the astra shastra, been vanquished?'

When three maharathas have vanquished you in succession, it seems that I will surely lose this war. Acharya, tell me now what you have to say on what awaits us since what has happened is past and irretrievable. Think now of what remains and say quickly what we should do next to save Jayadratha's life."

Drona replies, "I have reflected upon this, Duryodhana, and listen to what I have to say. As yet only three great maharathas among the Pandavas have overwhelmed us. We have as much to fear from those behind these three, as we have to dread those that have gone ahead. Where Krishna and Dhananjaya are, our fear must be greatest. They have attacked the Bharata army, both on the front and now from behind. Surely, now protecting Jayadratha is our main task. The Sindhu is terrified of Arjuna and deserves our protection. And now the fearless Satyaki and Bhima both hunt Jayadratha. And all this is the result of the game of dice that Sakuni contrived.

Nothing of final worth was won or lost in the Kuru sabha during the game of dice. But this sport that we are engaged in now will fetch real victory or defeat. The apparently innocent die, which Sakuni cast in the Kuru sabha, have turned into deadly arrows that claim millions of lives. Today, O Rajan, Kshatriya warriors are the dice players, their lethal arrows are the long dice, and the wager is Jayadratha's life.

There is only one thing for us to do: without care for our lives, we must fight to save him from Arjuna. Today the game has become real; and here on Kurukshetra, where our greatest warriors guard Jayadratha, is where we will find final victory or defeat. So, ride with all speed to support the maharathas who are already engaged in saving his life. I myself will stay here and direct other assistance to you, while holding up the joint advance of the Pandavas and the Srinjayas."

At the Acharya's command, Duryodhana flies with his legions towards Jayadratha, now determined to accomplish the difficult task of saving him. Meanwhile, the two guardians of Arjuna's chariot-wheels, the Panchala princes Yudhamanyu and Uttamaujas, are attempting to rejoin Arjuna by skirting around the Kuru array. You may remember, O Dhritarashtra, that earlier, while Arjuna penetrated into your host, Kritavarman stopped the Panchala brothers. Now, seeing them go around his army, Duryodhana loses no time in engaging them in fierce battle.

Yudhamanyu and Uttamaujas, both known to be great maharathas, stretch their bows and attack Duryodhana fiercely. Yudhamanyu strikes Duryodhana with twenty arrows, and his horses with four shafts. But, with a single arrow, Duryodhana demolishes Yudhamanyu's standard, with another his bow, and finally with a wedge-headed arrow, fells Yudhamanyu's charioteer from his niche, stunning but not killing him. Again, he rakes Duryodhana's horses with four more arrows, and then, in ferocious inspiration, plunges thirty barbs in a blink straight into your son's chest.

Equally animated, Uttamaujas kills Duryodhana's sarathy with gold-embellished arrows. Duryodhana in rage brutally kills Uttamaujas' four horses and his two Parshni charioteers. Uttamaujas quickly jumps down from his useless ratha and clambers onto his brother Yudhamanyu's chariot. Red-eyed, he kills Duryodhana's horses.

Yudhamanyu immediately severs Duryodhana's bow and shreds his leather shooting gloves. Your son, the bull among men, leaps down roaring from his ratha with a great mace in his hand and rushes headlong at the Panchala princes. Seeing him come at them, like Yama himself with his cudgel, Yudhamanyu and Uttamaujas hastily jump out of their ratha.

Then Duryodhana, wrath incarnate, pulverizes the chariot in frenzy; with manic blow after dreadful blow he makes a pulp of blood and bone of the horses and their charioteer. Continuing to vent his blind fury, he shatters the gold-inlaid wooden ratha into fragments, which he then drives down into the earth with an uncontrolled barrage of blows. Finally spent, Duryodhana, his eyes still red as plums, climbs onto Salya's nearby chariot.

Meanwhile, those two Panchala maharathas also mount two other chariots and drive on towards Arjuna.'"

CANTO 127

Jayadratha-vadha Parva continued

"Sanjaya says, 'At the chaotic heart of the general pandemonium, Karna and Bhima duel again, like two great wild elephants in rut in the heart of a wild jungle.'

Dhritarashtra says, 'Tell me about the duel between Bhima and Karna, as they fight not far from Arjuna's chariot. Earlier Bhimasena defeated Karna, so how does the mighty Karna now fight Bhima? How does Bhima fight the Suta's son, whom so many say is the greatest maharatha on earth? Dharmaputra Yudhishtira, having prevailed over Bhishma and Drona, does not fear anybody more than he does Karna; indeed, he passes sleepless nights from fear thinking of him.

So say, O Sanjaya, how Bhima faces great Karna, who is always devoted to Brahmanas and never flees a battle? Karna now knows that he is the Pandavas' brother, and feels kindly towards them. He also remembers the solemn word he gave Kunti that he would not kill any of her sons other than Arjuna. Then how will he vanquish mighty Bhima? As for Bhima, he only remembers all that the Suta's son inflicted on him, his brothers and their beloved Panchali. Tell me how he fights Karna.

My son Duryodhana has put his faith most of all in Karna to overcome all the Pandavas in this war. How does Radheya, in whom my wretched son rests his hope of victory, fight Bhimasena of terrible deeds?

How does Bhima fight the Sutaputra, relying upon whom my sons chose to fight this war against the maharatha sons of Pandu? Burning within himself to recall all the indignity and injuries that Karna has heaped upon the Pandavas, how does Bhima contend with him?

How, indeed, does Bhima face Karna in single combat, Karna is endowed with such valour that he subjugated all this Earth on a single ratha, for Duryodhana's sake? How does Bhima fight this son of a Suta, who was born wearing blazing golden kundalas like drops of the fiery sun?

You are a masterly narrator, O Sanjaya! Tell me, therefore, in detail, how the duel unfolds between these two incomparable heroes; tell me who among them is victorious?'

Sanjaya replies, 'Maharatha Bhimasena is anxious to leave Karna behind him and join Krishna and Dhananjaya. However, the Sutaputra lashes him with relentless flights of arrows, and holds him up. The mighty son of Adhiratha, his face handsome, radiant as a full-blown lotus, and lit up with a smile, challenges Bhimasena to fight him again.

Karna says, "O Bhima, I did not in my dreams ever think that you were a coward who would show his back to a battle. But why else do you run from me in such haste to find Arjuna? O delighter of the Pandavas, this is not becoming of a son of Kunti. Stay and show me your valour, if indeed you are at all valiant. Come, loose your fiercest arrows at me!"

Bhimasena, expectedly, is cut to the quick by Karna's sneering challenge; growling, he turns his chariot around and rushes fuming at Karna. Bhima Parantapa, Pandu's choleric son who has killed so many of your princes, my lord, looses a windstorm of arrows like his father Vayu at the calm Sutaputra. The titanic Vayuputra now wants to kill Karna as quickly as he can.

O Rajan, Karna, with the tread of a royal elephant, effortlessly cuts down Bhima's frenetic torrents with just a handful of astras. With his superior knowledge of the art of war, Karna takes on the aspect of a great Acharya. He seems to mock and even toy with Bhimasena with his light-swift, feather-light touch, as the infuriated Pandava fights with great prowess but little finesse or restraint. Bhima seethes at Karna's amusement, which the many brave warriors gathered all around to watch this duel, witness.

Roaring and his eyes bulging, Bhima strikes Karna through his chest with a tempestuous clutch of calf-toothed barbs. He pierces the Suta's son, who now wears rainbow-hued armour after Indra took the golden kavacha he was born with, with three and seventy powerful shot arrows of beautiful feathers; he strikes Karna's horses sheathed in golden armour, each with five stormy barbs.

Then, in the twinkling of the eye, Karna raises his archery to a supernal level, covering Bhima, his chariot, his horses and sarathy with a network of arrows as delicate and perfect as it is violent. Next moment, with untold ferocity, the Sutaputra pierces the Pandava's impenetrable armour with sixty-four lethal barbs that plunge deep into the hulking Bhimasena's massive body.

Briefly startled, Mahabaho Vrikodara entirely disregards the onslaught, for he who once drank Nagamrita feels no pain whatever at being struck deep by Karna's missiles like serpents of virulent venom. Never flinching, Bhima rakes Karna with thirty-two flat-headed shafts, loosed with indescribable force. Mighty Karna shrugs off these arrows with the greatest disdain and again envelops Bhima in a cloud of fire.

In truth, Karna, who is beyond compare and who knows that Bhima is his brother, fights Bhima with mildness, while Bhima, his heart burning with remembering old wrongs, fights with utmost ferocity. Further incensed by Karna's cool manner, his maddening, almost tender smile for which he does not know the cause, wrathful Bhimasena unleashes a swarm of arrows at his enemy that plummet down on him like hunting falcons. Golden-winged and keen, Bhima's shafts cover the superior son of Radha like a flight of insects covering a roaring fire, and are all consumed.

Karna, still languidly, returns Bhima's fire, shaft for shaft, and Bhima cuts all these arrows down with a slew of broad-headed thunderbolts, before they can reach him. Karna, son of Vikartana, chastiser of foes, again swathes Bhimasena with some more intense volleys, indeed, now so profusely that the Pandava begins to resemble a porcupine with its quills erect.

Like the sun containing his own rays, Bhima remains unmoved by the dense clusters of golden-winged, stone-whetted barbs that protrude from him all over. With all his limbs bathed in blood, Bhimasena looks resplendent as an asoka tree in spring, bearing its flowery burden.

But he cannot countenance what Karna does, still playfully, and, rolling his eyes in rage, he strikes Karna with twenty-five great and long shafts, with all his might. At which, Karna looks like a white mountain with countless snakes hanging from its sides. And once more, Bhimasena, endowed with the skill of a Deva, pierces the undaunted Sutaputra, always ready to lay down his life for honour, with fourteen more stinging shafts.

As Karna receives these, Bhima, now smiling to himself and exerting himself truly to the fullest, breaks Karna's bow, kills his horses, his sarathy and ruptures the Sutaputra's chest with a host of elongated arrows brilliant as the sun. Those winged shafts pierce through Karna's body and into the earth, like rays of the sun piercing through the clouds.

Stricken by these arrows and with his bow destroyed, the haughty Karna's face turns red and, in considerable pain, he takes to another ratha and rides briefly away.'"

CANTO 128

Jayadratha-vadha Parva continued

"Dhritarashtra says, 'O Sanjaya, what does Duryodhana say when he sees Karna, upon whom my sons have reposed all their hopes of victory, turn away from the field? How did the mighty Bhima, arrogant of his prowess, fight on? What does Karna do after he faces Bhimasena in that fiery encounter?'

Sanjaya replies, 'Mounting another ratha that is swiftly prepared for him, Karna comes storming back to confront Bhima again; he comes with the fury of the ocean stirred by a tempest; now he comes in rage. Seeing the Sutaputra like that, his brow dark and his face set grim, your sons, Rajan, consider Bhimasena as having been already poured as a libation on the Karna fire.

Furiously pulling on his bowstring and making terrifying sounds with his palms, Karna sends scathing volleys of shafts of dire intent at Bhimasena's chariot. And once more, a pitched and awful duel erupts between the two. Both equally stirred now, both great mahabahos intent on killing the other, they glare at each other as if to consume the other with their very gaze. Their eyes are red as roses and both breathe fiercely, like a couple of snakes.

Like two fighting or two angry Sarabhas, they set upon each other, drawing gushes of blood, mangling each other. Bhima again recalls all that he endured during the game of dice, during his exile in the vana and in Virata's city; he remembers how your sons robbed the Pandavas of their kingdom full of riches; dark images of all their sufferings of the past fourteen years and before, flash before his eyes: all the numerous wrongs inflicted on his brothers and himself and Panchali by you and Karna.

Bhima remembers how you conspired to immolate Kunti and her sons in the house of lac; most of all he remembers the torment of Draupadi in the Kuru sabha. He recalls clearly, as if it were happening again before his eyes, how the bestial Dusasana dragged a wailing Panchali into the hallowed Kuru court, and what Karna said to her then rings in his ears as if all the war around them has fallen hushed: "Take another husband, for your husbands are all dead! The sons of Pritha have sunk into hell and are like sesame seeds without kernels."

Awesome Bhimasena also remembers everything your sons said to the pure Draupadi, telling her that she was now their slave and they would enjoy her as one. Bhima recalls the harsh words that Karna spoke to the sons of Pandu when, attired in deer-skins, they were about to be banished to the vana; he recalls the coarse and unbridled joy that your wrathful, envious and foolish son showed, when he himself was prosperous and the sons of Pritha were plunged in distress. The virtuous Bhima, terrible Parantapa, remembers these and indeed all the sorrows he has suffered since his very childhood, and he is beside himself in a moment, utterly reckless of his very life. He sees Karna before him and Vrikodara, wolf-belly, wants to devour him at once!

Bhima draws his gold inlaid, redoubtable bow and that tiger of Bharata's vamsa, utterly reckless of his life, bears down on Karna, covering him with shining storms of arrows, obscuring the sun. A smiling Karna destroys Bhimasena's arrow showers and pierces him with nine keen formidable bolts. Struck by these like an elephant prodded viciously with a hook, Bhima yet continues to rush at him like an angry elephant.

Blowing his conch then, whose blast is like the sound of a hundred trumpets, Karna turns his fire on Bhima's legion of elephants, horses, chariots and foot-soldiers, agitating them, like a tempest the sea. Bhima undeterred continues to attack the Suta's son with a ceaseless tirade. Now Karna artfully entangles his snow-white horses with Bhima's coloured like black bears of the Himalaya, and still envelops him with his shining river of arrows.

Seeing the traces of Bhimasena's steeds snarled with those of Karna's, loud shouts arise from your troops. Tangled together, the eight horses look like white and black clouds blown together in the sky. Watching both the heroes in their frenzied duel, the maharathas of your army begin to tremble, as the battlefield, liberally strewn all around with the corpses of men and beasts, is quickly as dreadful as Yama's dark and horrible realms.

The greatest maharathas of your army look upon that terrible duel, like spectators watching some gory sport in an arena, and they see that neither awesome warrior has any advantage over his adversary. They only see the clash of mighty weapons, all this, Rajan, I remind you again, is the fruit of the evil policy of you and your sons.

Both slayers of their foes, both gifted with wonderful strength and skill, they continue to assail each other in absolute ferocity, filling the air and sky with their arrows, razing one another's troops all around. Ah, past glorious is the duel between Karna and Bhima; the sky is alight with the lustre of their arrows like meteors, arrows that are like flights of cranes in the autumn sky.

Krishna and Arjuna also see the fearsome contention between Karna and Bhima, and think that Bhima might be in danger. All around Karna and Bhima, the arrows they loose at each other fell thousands of elephants, horses and men—bloody mayhem rules the field. Blood blows in streams, corpses cover the earth darkly.'"

CANTO 129

Jayadratha-vadha Parva continued

"Dhritarashtra says, 'Bhimasena is surely an archer of great skill if he succeeds in balking Karna, who is a greater warrior than anyone. Sanjaya, tell me why Karna, who can challenge the very Devas, with the Yakshas and Asuras, let alone men, could not vanquish Bhima. Tell me more about their duel, for I now believe that either could kill the other.

It is relying upon great Karna that Duryodhana went to war against the Pandavas and Krishna and the Satwatas. But hearing how Bhima repeatedly defeats Karna, I feel faint, O Suta; why, I fear that the Kauravas are already as good as slain because of my son's sins.'

I fear that Karna will not succeed in overcoming the sons of Pritha. In all the battles that Karna fought the sons of Pandu, they have invariably defeated him. Ah, I do believe now that not the Devas led by Indra can quell these Pandavas. Alas that my evil son Duryodhana does not know this. Having vilely robbed Yudhishtira, who is like Kubera himself, of his kingdom and his wealth, my son of little intelligence is like a honey gatherer climbing a tree overhanging a cliff. He still does not see the fall that lies ahead.

Steeped in deceit, he regards the treasures that are not rightfully his belonging to him forever; and in his delusion, he continues to provoke and insult the Pandavas and dharma itself. Sanjaya, I too am a crude soul and ruled by my blind love for my children. I also showed no scruple when I betrayed Pandu's noble sons who observe dharma. Yudhishtira, with great foresight, always wants peace but my sons foolishly think of him as being weak and despise him.

And with all the sufferings and shame they have endured at our hands, the mighty-armed Bhimasena fights Karna. Tell me, Sanjaya, how Bhima and Karna do battle, each intent on killing the other.'

Sanjaya replies, 'Then listen, Rajan, to how the battle develops between Karna and Bhima. By now in considerable rage, Karna, son of Vikartana, lifts his archery and powerfully strikes Bhima with thirty golden arrows; no longer does the Sutaputra fight with any mildness. But the wild and raging Bhima breaks Karna's bow with three exquisite arrows; with a wedge-headed shaft he fells Karna's sarathy from his seat.

In a smooth blur, Karna seizes up a magnificent spear, adorned with gold and lapis lazuli, a thing of beauty but one that is most of all a missile of death. Like Indra casting down his Vajra, Karna hurls that spear at Bhima with force enough to kill the Pandava, and then the Sutaputra roars like a pride of lions! Your sons are exultant to hear that roar; they believe Bhima will die.

However, for all his bulk, Bhima strikes down Karna's spear bright as the sun or fire, deadly as a snake that has just shed its old skin, with seven arrows too swift to see. With no moment's pause, Bhima unleashes a sizzle of splendid arrows, all golden-winged and peacock-feathered, all of which are like Yama's danda.

Mahatejasvin Karna takes up another intimidating bow, its back inlaid with gold, and, stretching it, looses a barrage of arrows at Bhima, who cuts them all down with nine true barbs and he also roars like ten lions. Roaring, and bellowing at each other like two bulls for a cow in season, or like two tigers for the same meat, they continue to loose rivers of arrows at each other, always seeking a fatal lacuna through which they can kill the other.

At times they stand still and glare at each other like bulls pawing the earth, resting briefly. Then, again, the gales of arrows from bows drawn round.

They do their utmost, Rajan, their worst; they scorch each other always with blazing anger and hatred in their eyes, for, they are pure warriors, absorbed in battle, and in the moment all else is forgotten, indeed ceases to exist. Sometimes laughing at each other, at others taunting and mocking each other, and occasionally blowing their conches, they continue to duel upon the very edge of life and death.

Then Bhima breaks Karna's bow at the grip again, and send his white horses to Yama in a crimson flurry; he fells the Sutaputra's sarathy as well. Finding himself without horses or charioteer and bleeding freely from al his limbs, Karna is plunged into swift anxiety and does not know what to do.

Seeing Karna, dearer to him than his brothers, stricken and helpless, Duryodhana blazes up in anger and commands his brother Durjaya, "Look where the beast Bhima is about to devour the son of Radha. Kill that beardless Pandava, and put heart into Karna!"

Crying "Tathaastu!" Durjaya rushes at Bhima and strikes him with nine searing shafts, his horses with eight, his charioteer with six, his standard with three, and Bhima once more with seven. Turning away from Karna with a terrible growl, red-eyed Bhima plunges a lethal volley into Durjaya's body, striking all his vital organs at once, and that brave son of yours falls, dying in agony. Seeing this, Karna, with tears flowing down his great face, circumambulates Durjaya, who, adorned with regal ornaments, lies on the earth, writhing like a snake in death's last throes.

Having destroyed Karna's chariot, Bhima, grinning awfully, covers him with arrows and makes him look like a sataghni with numberless spikes on it. Yet, Atiratha Karna, though pierced all over direly, makes no attempt to escape the preening Bhima.'"

CANTO 130

Jayadratha-vadha Parva continued

"Sanjaya says, 'The chariot-less Karna, yet again comprehensively beaten by Bhima, mounts another ratha and flies at the Pandava again. Like elephants goring each other with tusks, they strike one another with arrows shot from bows drawn to the fullest stretch. Karna scathes Bhimasena with a scorching volley, roars, then bloodies the Pandava's brawny breast.

Bhima, in return, first rakes Karna with ten deadly straight arrows and then again with twenty. Karna pierces Bhima with nine arrows and takes a substantial shard from his standard with a flat-headed shaft. The Pandava responds quick as light with three and sixty arrows, like a mahout stabbing an elephant with his goad, or a rider whipping his horse.

Bleeding profusely, Karna begins to lick the corners of his mouth, and his eyes turn redder than ever. Beside himself by now, Karna looses an extreme missile, now in deadly earnest to have his brother's life. The shaft flares from his bow, passes through Bhima, and plunges deep into the earth. Bhima, whose eyes can turn no redder, suddenly hurls a huge and heavy six-sided gilded mace, measuring full four cubits in length, and kills all four of Karna's horses.

With two razor-faced arrows, he cuts down Karna's standard and with another savage volley, kills his enemy's charioteer. Yet again, Karna must leap down from his ratha and stands bared on the ground, drawing his bow. But now the prowess that we see from Radha's son is wondrous in the extreme, as he continues to hold off the chariot-mounted Bhima.

Seeing that Karna has lost his chariot again, Duryodhana cries to his brother, "The animal Bhima has deprived Radheya of his ratha again. Take your chariot to him, my brother. Fly!"

Durmukha rushes up to support Karna and envelops Bhima with his arrows. Bhima is delighted to see your son and begins to lick the corners of his mouth. Then, even as he fends off Karna's incessant fire, he whirls his chariot round and dashes straight at Durmukha and in a flash, Rajan, slaughters him with nine irresistible shafts. Bhima, triumphant on his ratha is like the blazing sun. Seeing Durmukha sprawled dead, his powerful body blown apart by Bhima, Karna lowers his bow, stops the duel momentarily, and weeps.

Circumambulating the fallen Durmukha and leaving him there, the heroic Karna begins to draw long, hot breaths and stands dazed, not knowing what to do. Seizing the opportunity, Bhimasena strikes him deep with fourteen long barbs, vulture-feathered. Those blood-drinking shafts of golden wings, infused with great power, illuminate the ten directions of the sky as they blaze into Karna, pass right through him, drink his blood and bore their glittering way into the earth behind him.

Karna shoots back fourteen golden arrows, which pass through Bhima's right arm and dive into the earth like birds a grove of trees. Sticking in the ground, those shafts shine like the rays of the sun while he sinks towards the Asta mountains of sunset. Bhima's arm spouts blood like a mountain stream of water. Bhima, never unnerved, strikes Karna with three shafts imbued with the impetuosity of Garuda and then his charioteer with seven.

O Rajan, wounded by Bhima's might, Karna finally loses heart and that illustrious warrior abandons the battle, borne away by his fleet horses. Roaring in triumph, Atiratha Bhimasena continues to stretch his bow and radiates arrows, sowing death all around him. Like a great fire he blazes, gloriously.'"

CANTO 131

JAYADRATHA-VADHA PARVA CONTINUED

"Dhritarashtra says, 'Ah, I do believe now that destiny is supreme. Fie on men's prowess and striving, which is all in vain if Adhiratha's son Karna cannot vanquish Bhimasena, despite fighting so resolutely. Karna boasts that he can vanquish all the Parthas with Krishna. I often hear Duryodhana maintain that he has not seen another warrior like Karna in the world!

Indeed, Sanjaya, the wretched Duryodhana often told me, "Karna is no Sutaputra but a mighty Kshatriya, an unyielding archer who never feels fatigue. If I have the Vasusena for my ally, the very Devas cannot vanquish me, what then need be said of the sons of Pandu?"

So tell me what Duryodhana says when he sees Karna defeated, and flee the field like a snake that has lost its venom. Alas, mindlessly Duryodhana sends Durmukha, who has no experience of battle, alone to face Bhima, like an insect into a great fire.

O Sanjaya, even Aswatthaman, Salya and Kripa, united together, cannot stand up to Bhimasena. Even they know the terrible might of Bhima, equal to that of ten thousand elephants; they know he is endowed with the tejas of Vayu himself, as well as his brutal intentions. Why did they provoke the savage hero of cruel deeds; why did they stoke the fire of that Kshatriya who, when roused, is like Yama himself at the end of the Yuga? And then only the dauntless Karna dared fight Bhima by himself. Ah, no one can quell this son of Pandu who routed Karna in battle like Purandara vanquishing an Asura.

Who is there that can face dreadful Bhima and hope to live? Bhima who ploughs his bloody way through my army by himself, after brushing aside even Drona, Bhima who rides in quest of his brother Arjuna? Indeed who in my army, O Sanjaya, will dare to face titanic Bhimasena? Who among the Asuras will venture to face the great Indra with his thunderbolt, the Vajra, in his hand?

A man may return from the land of the dead, but no one can return alive after doing battle with Bhimasena Vayuputra! These men of little strength who senselessly rush into battle against the wrathful Bhima are truly like insects flying into a blazing fire. When I think of the gruesome oath that this Pandava swore in the Kuru sabha on the day of the game of dice that he would kill all my hundred sons, and when I hear about how he put mighty Karna to flight, I have no doubt that Duryodhana and his brothers are terrified to fight Bhima.

My evil son repeatedly bragged in our court, "Karna, Dusasana and I together will vanquish the Pandavas in battle." After seeing Bhima rout Karna thrice and deprive him of his chariot, Duryodhana is now consumed by grief not only because Draupadi rejected his suit but also to see Bhimasena butcher his brothers in battle, one after the other, as a result of his own heinous crimes.

Who that values his life will ride against Panduputra Bhima, when he straddles the field like Yama himself, burning with wrath and armed with terrible astras? A man may escape from the very jaws of the Badava fire, but I am convinced that no one can escape from Bhima. Indeed, neither Partha nor the Panchalas, nor Kesava, nor Satyaki, all excited with battle lust, shows the least care for their lives. O Suta, the lives of all my sons are in danger.'

Sanjaya replies, 'O Kaurava, you who now grieve like this after hearing of the carnage your enemies bring to your army are yourself the real root of this destruction of the world! Obedient to the sinful counsels of your sons, it is you who have yourself provoked this ghastly war. Though your well-wishers repeatedly advised you against this enormous folly, you were like a sick man who is fated to die and will not accept the only medicine that can save his life. O Rajan, best of men, having drunk the most virulent poison, now you must accept its consequences.

Your warriors all fight to the best of their abilities, putting their lives at risk. Yet, sitting here, you speak ill of them. But now listen to me and I will describe to you how the war for truth rages on.

Seeing Karna defeated by Bhimasena, five of your sons, Durmarshana, Duhsaha, Durmada, Durdhara and Jaya, all clad in beautiful armour, surround Bhimasena and shroud him with their shafts like locust swarms. Bhimasena stands smiling before these princes of celestial handsomeness. Karna dashes into battle again, losing torrents of golden-winged shafts, so that Bhima turns to face Karna, although your sons are attacking him.

Your sons continue to cover Bhimasena with showers of precise shafts. But then, with an earth-shaking roar, Bhima unleashes twenty-five lethal arrows from his massive bow and sends your five sons, with their horses and charioteers to Yama, their blood spraying in the westering sun. They fall from their rathas along with their charioteers, like large trees uprooted by a hurricane because of the weight of their variegated flowers.

And wonderful is Bhima's grisly feat for he achieves it even as he battles Karna. Attacked from every side by Bhima wheeling around him, a shocked Karna can only gaze at the massive Pandava in some disbelief that he is such an archer as well. Bhimasena, too, with eyes crimson, glowers at Karna, while stretching his awesome bow.'"

CANTO 132

JAYADRATHA-VADHA PARVA CONTINUED

"Sanjaya says, 'Seeing your sons lying dead on the field, a surge of fresh rage fills Karna. He no longer cares for his life for he considers himself responsible for the death of your sons, slain before his eyes by Bhima. Bhimasena, meanwhile, always sees images from the past of the sufferings of the Pandavas and Panchali before his mind's eye. Full of rancour, he continues to loose flaming, unerring arrows at the Sutaputra.

Smiling, or still sneering, Karna rakes Bhima first with five arrows and again with seventy razor-sharp ones with golden wings. Brushing aside the cascade of barbs that Karna pours over him, Bhima strikes him with a hundred perfect arrows, followed by five more which plunge deep into his body, and finally, with a wedge-headed arrow, he severs his bow. The dispirited Karna takes up another bow and envelops Bhimasena with some luminous archery. But indomitable Bhima gives a dreadful laugh, which rocks the field and, easily cutting down Karna's shafts in flight, yet again kills his horses, charioteer, and, with reverberant twang of his bowstring breaks great Karna's golden-backed bow once more.

Karna leaps down from his chariot with a mace in his hand that he hurls furiously at Bhima. In full view of all your troops, Rajan, Bhima blows that gada into powder with a thought-swift volley, and immediately looses a thousand arrows at Karna. Karna cuts them all down, then cuts away Bhima's armour, disjointing it neatly with some perfect shafts, and then strikes Bhima's body with twenty-five vicious short arrows.

All this, Rajan, occurs as if time has paused for the two heroes; it takes one's breath away. His fury always mounting, Bhima looses nine intense barbs at Karna, piercing his armour and his right arm and then flashing on down into the earth. Shrouded with showers of shafts from Bhimasena's bow, Karna yet again escapes by running away on foot.

Seeing this, Duryodhana tells his brothers, "Fly! Protect Karna from every side. Surround Bhima and kill him."

Your sons Chitra, Upachitra, Charuchitra, Sarasan, Chitrayudha and Chitravarman charge Bhimasena, shooting a solid swath of arrows at him. And now Bhima, showing himself to be truly the son of Vayu; Bhima who is only half-human, kills these six sons of yours, Rajan, with a single incredible arrow! And now, Karna, tears springing to his eyes again, ruefully remembers what Vidura said in dire warning fourteen years ago.

Mounting yet another ratha, Karna sweeps back into battle, to face Bhima again. The two duel feverishly, covering one another with clouds of golden missiles; they both look splendid like two cloud masses pierced by the rays of the sun.

Now Bhima cuts away Karna's armour with six and thirty flat-headed arrows shot with utmost force. The mighty-armed Karna gores Bhima with fifty immaculate barbs and, smeared with red sandalwood paste and streaming blood from all their limbs, the two resemble the newly risen sun and bronze moon. Their armour cut away, their bared bodies covered in blood, Karna and Bhima look like a couple of snakes just freed from their sloughs.

The two Naravyaghras maul each other with their shafts, like two tigers tearing into one another with fangs and talons. Circling each other in their rathas, they cover each other in ceaseless fire, drawing blood, slicing off shreds of flesh, roaring like two mythic tigers, bellowing like two massive bulls battling over a cow in season. Indeed, they are two lions from bygone times, their eyes crimson as they battle like Indra and Virochana's son Prahlada.

Bhima, thunderhead charged with lightning, mantles Karna, the mountain, with a downpour of a thousand harsh kanaka-feathered arrows. Your sons watch Bhima incredulously, for they had never imagined their cousin was such a bowman; Arjuna watches him in delight, as do Krishna and Satyaki and Yudhamanyu and Uttamaujas. Your sons are awed; they are all dismayed for it seems that the dreadful Pandava will indeed keep the vow that he swore.'"

CANTO 133

JAYADRATHA-VADHA PARVA CONTINUED

"Sanjaya says, 'Hearing the twang of Bhimasena's bow and the sound of his palms striking each other, Karna cannot bear what he sees and experiences, no more than a maddened wild elephant can the trumpeting of a rival. Turning away for a moment from Bhimasena, Karna looks with deep sorrow at the corpses of your sons whom Bhimasena has killed. Drawing hot, long breaths, he once more takes up arms against the second son of Pandu, the son of the Wind.

Eyes burning like copper, and sighing in fury like a mighty snake, Karna, as he shoots his arrows, is as resplendent as his natural father, Surya Deva, radiating his rays. Vrikodara, bristling with the shining shafts shot from Karna's bow, looks like a plant reflecting the rays of the sun. The beautiful shafts fitted with peacock-feathers penetrate every part of Bhima's majestic body, like birds entering a tree to roost there. Karna's golden winged arrows, falling incessantly, resemble an infinite flight of cranes. So numerous are they, that they seem to issue not from his bow alone but from his standard, his royal parasol, the shaft, yoke and base of his ratha! Karna shoots his sky-ranging golden shafts fitted with vulture feathers so he fills the sky with them.

Seeing him so galvanised with fury and now rushing towards him like Yama himself, Bhima still neither wavers nor feels the least trace of fear. Instead, becoming utterly reckless of his life, he strikes Karna with nine meridian missiles and stops Karna's onrush. He strikes the radiant Sutaputra, the Suryaputra, with twenty more brutal arrows. Indeed, swiftly he shrouds Karna with as many arrows as his antagonist did him a moment ago.

Seeing the prowess of Bhimasena, your warriors, as well as the Charanas on high, are filled with joy and applaud him. O Rajan, Bhurisravas, Kripa, Aswatthaman, Salya of the Madras, Uttamaujas, Yudhamanyu, Kesava, and Arjuna, all these great maharathas, among both the Kurus and the Pandavas, loudly cheer Bhima, crying, "Uttamam! Wonderful!" and they shout aloud and roar in exhilaration, friend and foe alike, for they are all noble Kshatriyas and master warriors and recognise the extraordinary archery of Bhimasena the Pandava against his redoubtable adversary.

When this pandemonium breaks out, Duryodhana tells all the kings and princes and particularly his brothers, "Bless you all, mighty ones! Ride swiftly to Karna's rescue, or Bhima will have his life today."

At this, seven of his brothers, Rajan, rush forward and surround Bhimasena, enveloping him with torrents of arrows; they assail Vrikodara like the seven planets afflicting the moon at the hour of the Pralaya. But the son of Kunti kills them all in a moment with seven luminous shafts. His lustrous shafts pass cleanly, lethally through their bodies, taking their lives with them, and soar up into the sky like birds of superb, now incarnadine plumage.

Your seven sons whom Bhima kills are Satrunjaya, Satrusaha, Chitra, Chitrayudha, Dridha, Chitrasena and Vikarna. But Bhimasena grieves bitterly for Vikarna who was dear to him. And he says in grief, his bloodshot eyes glimmering with tears, "It is only for the oath I swore that I would kill all of you in this war, O Vikarna, that I have taken your life. O Shura, you came to fight to discharge your dharma as a

Kshatriya. Otherwise, you alone among your brother always wished us well, Kaurava, and you especially loved Yudhishtira. I have kept my vow as a Kshatriya and I should not grieve but my heart does grieve, for you were noble and illustrious, my cousin!"

Having killed those seven princes, O Rajan, before Karna's very eyes, Bhimasena again gives a fulminant roar, which informs Yudhishtira at a distance that victory is his. Indeed, hearing Bhima's tremendous shout, Yudhishtira feels joy course through him in the midst of the gory battle and he responds with loud conches booming and batteries of drums being beaten. Elated to hear his brother Vrikodara's echoing message across the field, Yudhishtira, emboldened, launches an attack against Drona.

Duryodhana on the other hand, seeing one and thirty of your sons, his brothers slain, recollects the wise words of Vidura and in some anguish he thinks, "Vidura's prophecy is being realised!"

Thinking this, Duryodhana is benumbed. All that your foolish and black-hearted son, with Karna at his side, said to the princess of Panchala during the game of dice, after having Draupadi hauled roughly into the Kuru sabha, all the harsh, coarse words that Karna said to Panchali, in your presence, O Dhritarashtra, and what was said to the sons of Pandu, returns to haunt Duryodhana and paralyses him.

O Draupadi, the Pandavas are lost and have sunk into eternal hell, so choose other husbands for yourself!

Alas, my king, the bitter fruit of all that now manifests itself. On that day your despicable sons said so many vile things, calling the noble Pandavas sesame seeds without kernels. Today, Bhimasena spews forth the fire of wrath, which he has restrained for thirteen years, and massacres your haughty sons. Oh Rajan, despite his repeated pleas, his many lamentations, Vidura failed to persuade you towards peace.

O King of the Bharatas, now reap the harvest of all that you and your sons have sown. You are mature, patient, and entirely capable of foreseeing the consequences of all deeds. So it truly seems that your refusal to follow the sage counsel of your well-wishers is the result of fate.

Ah, do not grieve, O Naravyaghra! All this is your fault. In my opinion, you are yourself the cause of the destruction of your sons.

Vikarna has fallen, as has Chitrasena of great prowess. Many other maharathas and the greatest among your sons have also fallen. Yes, whichever of your sons Bhima found within range, he killed in a trice. It is for you, to narrate this horrific war to you, day after day, that I had to see our vyuha annihilated by Pandu's son Bhima!'"

CANTO 134

Jayadratha-vadha Parva continued

"Dhritarashtra says, 'O Sanjaya, I do believe that it is my evil rule that is responsible for the terrible consequences that now overtake us. I have so far thought only about the past, but what should I do now? I am calm again, so tell me how this slaughter of Kshatriyas continues.'

Sanjaya replies, 'Rajan, Karna and Bhima continue to discharge arrows at each other like two rain-charged clouds. The shafts winged with gold, whetted on stone and marked with Bhima's name, strike Karna and pierce his body, as if piercing into his very life. Similarly, Bhima is shrouded by Karna's arrows in their hundreds and thousands, each one a venomous serpent. With their arrows falling on all sides, an agitation like that of the very ocean is created among the troops. The arrows Bhima shoots from his grand bow kill countless men of your army. Bestrewn with fallen elephants and horses, and the corpses of men, Kurukshetra is like a field of trees broken by a tornado. Mown down on every side by Bhima's arrows, your warriors flee, screaming, "Ah, what is this?"

The army of the Sindhus, the Sauviras and the Kauravas are afflicted by the shafts of both Karna and Bhima, and withdraw to a great distance. The remnant of these brave soldiers, with their steeds and elephants killed, flee in all directions away from both Karna and Bhima, crying out, "Truly, the Devas are confounding us for the sake of the Pandavas, for the arrows shot by both Bhima and Karna are razing our forces!"

Your frightened troops run away beyond the range of Karna and Bhima's arrows and stand at a safe distance to watch the blazing duel. While, on Kurukshetra another river of terror flows, a river that makes heroes exult and cowards quail, a river flowing the blood of elephants, horses and men. The Earth, O Bhaarata, is weirdly resplendent covered with the lifeless forms of men, elephants and horses along with their ornaments, with flagstaffs and the bases of chariots, with broken rathas and wheels and akshas and kuveras, with bows inlaid with gold, and gold-winged arrows in millions shot by Karna and Bhima, with countless javelins, spears, swords, battleaxes, with maces and clubs all adorned with gold, with standards of diverse shapes, with darts and spiked cudgels, and with beautiful sataghnis.

The field of war looks like the sky scattered with stars, being strewn all over with earrings, necklaces of gold, bracelets loosened from wrists, rings, precious gems worn on diadems and crowns, helmets, golden ornaments of diverse kinds, coats of mail, leather gauntlets, elephants' ropes, broken chatras, Yak-tail fans, with the shredded bodies of elephants, horses and men, with blood-dyed arrows, and with diverse other objects, lying loosened from their true and living places.

Watching the inconceivable feats of those two warriors, the Charanas and the Siddhas above are full of amazement. Like a great fire, fanned by the wind, courses through a heap of dry grass, Karna engages fiercely with Bhima. Both of them shoot down countless standards and rathas, slay horses, elephants, and men: like a pair of fighting elephants trampling a forest of reeds. Your host looks like a mass of clouds, Rajan, and great is the scarlet carnage Karna and Bhima cause.'"

CANTO 135

JAYADRATHA-VADHA PARVA CONTINUED

"Sanjaya says, 'Rajan, Karna pierces Bhima with three arrows and deluges him with a relentless downpour of shafts. The mighty-armed Bhimasena stands unmoved like a mountain. In return, he rakes Karna's ear with a barbed arrow rubbed with oil and Karna's large and exquisite kundala falls from his lobe like a star from the sky.

Smiling in mockery, Vrikodara stabs Karna through his chest with another broad-headed arrow, and swiftly follows these with ten long shafts, which strike Karna's brow and pierce it like snakes entering an anthill. With these shafts protruding from his forehead, the Suta's son looks quite stunning, as if with a chaplet of blue lotuses encircling his lofty brow.

Hurt deep, Karna lurches, supports himself on the kuxara of his ratha, and shuts his eyes in a brief swoon. He soon regains consciousness and, with his face and body bathed in blood, he seems to lose all restraint and rushes roaring and wild-eyed at Bhima, unleashing a hundred vulture-winged shafts at him.

Bhima, however, ignores this tirade of shafts and looses his own scathing volley at Karna. The suddenly energised Karna strikes Bhima with nine arrows through his torso. Both Naravyaghras, roaring and growling like two tremendous tigers, continue to belabour each other with endless banks of arrows. They seek to unnerve each other by sudden bursts of thunderous hand clapping, and with uncanny missiles rarely used or seen. Then Bhima severs Karna's bow with a razor-faced arrow, and gives a bloodcurdling roar.

Throwing away the broken bow, the Suta's son seizes up another stronger one. Karna's body blazes with strange effulgence as he looks in anger at the slaughter of the Kuru, the Sauvira, and the Sindhu Kshatriyas, seeing coats of mail, standards, discarded weapons as well as the lifeless forms of elephants, foot-soldiers, horsemen and rathikas lying all around, covering the Earth. Stretching his fresh bow into a circle, he eyes Bhima wrathfully and begins to unleash his anger at him, looking like the autumn sun dazzling at mid-day.

None that watch him can see when he draws an arrow from his quiver, fits it to his bowstring, draws the string back and looses his shaft; Karna's archery is like a river in spate, his bow always drawn in a ring of fire and arrows flowing in tide from it all around him, covering the sky and dimming the sun. Karna's volleys are like flights of thousands of cranes in the sky, like locust swarms, why like a single ubiquitous missile that never stops. A raging Karna swathes Bhima with his vulture-feathered, golden-winged barbs.

And your sons, O Bhaarata, and their troops see the strength, energy, prowess and fortitude of Bhima, for with scant regard for the arrows pouring down on him, continues to attack Karna like a raging sea. Bhima stretches his bow and shoots his arrows with such ferocious speed that it seems like a second bow of Indra, his weapon also incessantly drawn to a circle. The golden shafts issuing from it form a continuous line in the sky and appear like a bright garland of gold.

Bhimasena marvellously cuts down Karna's torrents in the air, and sparks cascade down onto the field below. The sun is shrouded, the wind ceases to blow, and nothing can be seen.

Then, both atirathas raise their archery so that the very sky seems to catch fire: a conflagration on high! Karna, straining himself, unleashes a volley of golden-winged scintillating barbs at Bhima in rage, but Bhima truncates every one of them into three neat slivers and roars in jubilation.

Pandu's tremendous son afire harries his enemy with his own savage streaks of lightning. Their leather gauntlets slapping against their bowstrings, their clapping palms, their terrible roaring, the deep rumble of their chariot-wheels and the deafening twang of their bowstrings all create absolute pandemonium. All the other warriors stop fighting and stand rooted, with eyes peeled, to watch this duel that exceeds all duels. The Devarishis, Siddhas and Gandharvas applaud them, saying, "Uttamam! Wonderful!" The tribes of Vidyadharas rain flowers on them.

Cutting down Karna's incendiary shafts, Bhima lacerates his opponent with a handful of arrows. Karna, also, confounds most of Bhimasena's fire on him; he plunges nine long barbs deep into the great Pandava's vast body. Bhima, unmoved, replies with his own shafts that rake Karna sorely.

Suddenly, Bhima unleashes an astra like Yama's danda, why, like Yama himself at Karna, who with a superior smile smashes it into shards in flight with three light-like arrows. Bhima, roaring louder than ever so Kurukshetra trembles, again looses a firetide of barbs that Karna serenely douses in the air. Next moment, he shreds Bhima's quivers so the arrows fall out if them; he breaks his bow and severs the reins of his horse. Inspired, Karna kills Bhima's horses and gouges his charioteer deep with five arrows like streak lightning.

Visoka the sarathy falls out of his chariot, takes to his heels and finds refuge in Yudhamanyu's ratha. Now, smiling broadly, Karna, burning like the yuga fire, fells Bhima's flagstaff and banner.

Deprived of his bow, Bhima Mahabaho seizes up a curved dart, such as rathikas use and, whirling it round in his hand, hurls it like a meteor at Karna's ratha. Karna shatters it with ten exact arrows. Bhima picks up a shield decked with gold and a sword, but again Karna, still smiling, calmly smashes that shield into fragments with a sizzle of shafts.

In a flash a desperate Bhima flings his sword at Karna breaking his bow in his hands so it hangs limp. Cool as ever, Karna takes up another dreadful bow and unleashes a gale of a thousand arrows at the Pandava. Struck by many of these shafts, Bhima gives an agonised cry and hops about in pain. At once, Karna's soft heart melts in sorrow for his enemy who he knows is his brother.

Now sensing victory, Karna beguiles Bhima by concealing himself on the floor of his ratha. Bhima darts forward and seizes Karna's flagstaff from the ground and stands firm waiting to haul Karna out of his ratha. All the Kurus and the Charanas above applaud Bhima, who means to lay hold of Karna like Garuda snatching up a snake. His bow destroyed, his ratha ruined, Bhima stands unflinching and resolute, true to Kshatriya dharma, fearless for his life, still wanting just battle.

A livid Karna now advances against Bhima in his chariot; they rush at each other, roaring out challenges, roaring like thunderheads at the close of summer. The passage-at-arms that then takes place between the two lions among men does indeed again resemble that of old between the Devas and the Danavas.

However, Bhima's store of weapons is soon exhausted, and he is forced to turn back while Karna pursues him. Seeing the elephants that Arjuna killed slain lying near, the unarmed Bhimasena runs into their hilly midst, for Karna cannot follow him there in his chariot. And lo, the son of Pritha and Vayu actually hefts a great elephant that Arjuna slew and he waits there even like his half-brother Hanuman with the peak of Gandhamadana!

But Karna with unearthly archery shreds that great carcass in Bhima's hands. Bhima flings the pieces of flesh at his enemy, and then laying hands on anything he can find, chariot-wheels and dead horses, hurls all these at Karna. Karna carves and smashes everything that Bhima flings at him. But Bhima rushes straight at the brother he does not know, taking Karna by surprise. Bhima raises his great fists imbued with the power of thunder and then suddenly remembers that Arjuna has sworn to kill the Sutaputra and he spares Karna's life.

Karna, beside himself, now gashes Bhima with fierce bursts of arrows and finally the Pandava collapses under the onslaught and the Sutaputra has him squarely in his sights; he can kill Bhima now. Karna's rage cools quickly; he remembers his word given to Kunti that he would not kill any of her sons other than Arjuna; he remembers that the vulnerable magnificent Kshatriya now at his mercy is his brother. Instead of taking Bhima's life, he rides up to him and repeatedly prods him with the tip of his bow.

Hissing like a snake, Bhima snatches the bow from Karna's hands and strikes him a stunning blow on the head with it! Struck by Bhimasena, Karna's rage blazes up again and, his eyes burning red once more, he says to Bhima, "Beardless eunuch, ignorant fool, and glutton! You are no archer, so don't dare fight me again. You are like an overgrown child, a lout and a laggard in battle!

Pandava wretch, you should be in either a kitchen or a dining hall, not on a battlefield. Bhima, you should pass your days in the vana eating roots and flowers, keeping vratas and doing tapasya, for as a warrior you are nothing. Great is the difference between battle and the life of a muni. O Vrikodara, you are suited to a life in the forest since battle does not suit you at all.

Otherwise, glutton, you are fit to order cooks, servants and slaves, as you did in Virata's palace and reprove them when you do not like your dinner! O dimwitted one, take sannyasa and gather fruits for your insatiable appetite. Go into the forest, O son of Kunti, for you are fit to fight a war. Employ yourself in plucking fruits and roots, or in waiting upon guests, for battle does not suit you at all."

Rajan, I believe that Karna's harsh words reflect all the wrongs done to him in his youth, the shame of being spurned as a Sutaputra. As Bhima stands helpless before him, he prods Vrikodara yet again with his bow, and, laughing loudly, says again to the red-faced Pandava, "Well, if fight you must, pick on your equals not Karna! For you now see what happens to those that dare face me in battle. Go, great lout, to where the two Krishnas are so that they protect you. Or go home, for, child that you are, what place do you have on this field of heroes?"

But Bhimasena laughs in Karna's face, and says in the hearing of all, "Evil spirit, I have repeatedly beaten you! And yet you continue to boast? In this world the ancients have witnessed the victory and defeat of Indra himself. Lowborn fellow, son of a Suta, fight me with bare arms if you dare and I will kill you before all these kings even as I did the giant Kichaka."

But the intelligent Karna refuses to be provoked into such folly before all the maharathas. Instead, having deprived Bhima of his chariot and having humiliated him, Karna mocks him again in the hearing of Krishna and the noble Arjuna. Then, incited by Kesava, Arjuna looses a blazing volley of arrows from the Gandiva at Karna, golden shafts that plunge into Karna's regal frame like cranes into the Krauncha mountains. Partha drives Karna away from the imperiled Bhima. His bow broken by Bhima, and now raked by Arjuna's terrific arrows, Karna quickly rides away from Bhima on his great ratha.

Bhimasena mounts Satyaki's chariot and they hurtle after Arjuna Savyasachin. In fury Arjuna looses a dreadful astra at Karna, a missile like Yama danda, which flashes at the Sutaputra like Garuda flying at a great snake. The shafts would have killed Karna, but in that moment, from a fair distance, Aswatthaman cuts it in two, saving the Suryaputra's life. Flaring up in anger, Arjuna strikes Drona's son with sixty-four arrows, and roars at him, "Do not run away, O Aswatthaman, but stay a moment and fight me."

But, scathed by Arjuna's shafts, Drona's son quickly finds refuge in a dense division of the Kaurava army, full of maddened elephants and teeming with rathas. Pulling on the bowstring of the Gandiva, drowning every other sound on the field, Arjuna follows the hastily retreating Aswatthaman, frightening him with his shafts. As he goes after Drona's son, Partha razes hosts of men, elephants and horses with his arrows fletched with the feathers of kankas and peacocks.'"

CANTO 136

JAYADRATHA-VADHA PARVA CONTINUED

"Dhritarashtra says, 'Day by day, O Sanjaya, my once radiant glory is being tarnished. Untold numbers of my army have perished. Ah, all this is from the reversal of fortune that time inexorably brings. Arjuna, stirred by the death of his son, has broken through my legions, which Drona's son and Karna protect and which the very gods could hardly breach.

United with the two of blazing tejas, Krishna and Bhima, as well as the bull of the Sinis, Satyaki, Arjuna's powers have increased manifold. Ever since I heard of Dhananjaya's success, grief, like fire burning dry grass, consumes my heart. I see that an evil destiny has descended upon all the kings of the Earth, and Jayadratha of the Sindhus among them. Having done the Kiritin grievous wrong, if Jayadratha comes within Arjuna's reach, he will not escape with his life. Why, I already infer from the way the war swings against us, that the Saindhava, my son-in-law, is already slain.

However, relate to me exactly how the battle rages on, for you are a gifted narrator, O Sanjaya; describe to me further how the Vrishni hero

Satyaki fights. He entered my vast force alone, resolutely for Arjuna's sake, indeed like an elephant plunging into a lake overgrown with lotuses.'

Sanjaya replies, 'Seeing Bhima fight on though sorely wounded by Karna's shafts, Satyaki follows him on his ratha, drawn by silver horses, roaring like the clouds at the close of summer and blazing like the autumn sun, and begins to slaughter your son's army with his formidable bow. None of your maharathas can check his progress; indeed they tremble to see him ride at them.

Then a warrior king Alambusha, who never leaves a battle, rushes at Satyaki, greatest of the Sinis. The battle between them is one that defies description. All your warriors, and the enemy, too, stop fighting and become mere spectators of the duel between these two ornaments of war. Alambusha shoots ten arrows at Satyaki, which that bull of Sini's race destroys with his own shafts before they reach him.

Once more, Alambusha draws his bowstring to his ear and, with the force of fire or the wind, strikes Satyaki with three beautifully winged arrows that burn like fire and pierce Yuyudhana's kavacha and bore into his body. He next strikes Satyaki's four white horses, each with a vicious barb. Satyaki, endued with tejas and urjas like Kesava himself, looses four shafts to slaughter Alambusha's horses. With a broad-headed arrow, he strikes off Alambusha's head, handsome as the full moon and fierce as the Yuga-fire.

Having slain the descendant of a long line of kings, the Yadu bull forges on in Arjuna's wake, killing countless enemy warriors at will as he goes. Indeed, the Vrishni hero destroys your forces like a hurricane dispersing masses of clouds. Wherever this lion among men wants to go, his resplendent Sindhu horses, white as milk of the kunda snow, take him.

Then all the leaders of your various akshauhinis surround Satyaki and inundate him with arrows. Dusasana in particular attacks the Yadava fiercely. Satyaki, however, is undaunted and swiftly checks them all with fire tides from his impressive bow. Turning on Dusasana, he kills your son's horses. Watching him, Arjuna and Krishna are filled with joy.'"

CANTO 137

JAYADRATHA-VADHA PARVA CONTINUED

"Sanjaya says, 'Then the great archers of the Trigarta country, their banners woven with golden thread, surround the mighty-armed Satyaki, who has accomplished everything that was required of him, indeed far more, and now attacks Dusasana and his legion to lend Arjuna his support. They blockade him from all sides with a multitude of rathas and cover him with a barrage of arrows. The peerless, radiant Satyaki, having blasted his way through the Bharata army, which is like a shoreless sea, which is filled with the sound of twanging bowstrings, which bristles with swords, darts and maces, by himself vanquishes those fifty Trigarta princes.

Ah, Sini's grandson is past being merely wonderful, and so swift, effortless and light are his movements that he flits in moments from west to east, north to south, back to east to west again, as well as the other subsidiary directions, and the shura seems to dance all over the battlefield, as if he is a hundred warriors in his single self. Finding Satyaki with tread of a lion, the Trigarta warriors cannot withstand his dexterity and flee towards a greater division of their own countrymen.

Next the valiant Surasenas try to stop Satyaki, covering him with dark arrow showers. The noble Satyaki quells them in no time and then dashes against the Kalingas and, smashing his way through their mighty legions, he finally reaches Dhananjaya! Like a tired swimmer arriving ashore, the very sight of Dhananjaya, tiger among men, comforts the brilliant Satyaki.

Seeing him approach, Krishna says to Arjuna, "Here comes the grandson of Sini, following in your wake. Satyaki is your disciple and friend, and he has consumed the Kaurava warriors like straw to find you. Past all count are those that he has slain on his way here. This Satyaki comes to you, O Arjuna, after vanquishing Drona himself and Kritavarman of the Bhojas with his arrows!

Intent on achieving Yudhishtira's weal, the brave and irresistible Yuyudhana comes to you after killing countless maharathas!

Having achieved the most difficult feats in the midst of the Kaurava troops, the dashing Satyaki has come to gaze on you, O son of Pandu!

Having, from a single ratha, fought and defeated so many mighty maharathas, with Drona himself at their head, does Satyaki come to you, O Partha!

Sent by Yudhishtira, Satyaki comes to you, Arjuna, after razing a vast portion of the Kaurava army all on his own. Invincible in battle, Satyaki, whom no Kaurava warrior can match, flies to join you after decimating Duryodhana's vast legions. Look where he comes like a lion charging out of a herd of cattle.

Having strewn the earth with the heads of thousands of kings, all handsome as full-blown lotuses, does our Yuyudhana come to meet you, O Partha, after vanquishing Duryodhana himself and his brothers, and having killed Jalasandha. Having let flow a gruesome river of blood on Kurukshetra, mired with a sludge of corpses of men and beasts, ruins of rathas, look where he flashes towards you in joy!"

But Arjuna shows no great joy. He says somberly to Krishna, "I am hardly pleased to see Satyaki arrive here! I do not know how my brother Yudhishtira is. Now that he is separated from Satyaki, I doubt that he is alive. Satyaki should have protected the king. Why then, O Krishna, has he left Yudhishtira to follow in my wake, leaving the king at Drona's mercy?

I have not yet killed Jayadratha and look where Bhurisravas now attacks Satyaki. I must now protect Satyaki as well while the sun sinks lower in the sky by the moment and I have yet to kill Jayadratha. As for Satyaki, he is weary; he has exhausted his astras, and his horses and his charioteer are worn out, O Madhava! Bhurisravas, on the other hand, is not tired and he has supporters behind him. How will Satyaki defeat him?

Having crossed the very ocean of war by himself, will this bull among the Sinis not succumb? Bhurisravas is beyond doubt among the greatest Kuru warriors. Will fortune favour Satyaki against this mighty hero? O Kesava, I think Yudhishtira has erred in his judgement to send Satyaki out here to us. Forgetting his fear of the Acharya, he has sent away Satyaki from his side. Like a sky-ranging hawk after a peace of meat, Drona is always waiting for an opportunity to seize my brother. Is the king free from danger, Krishna?'""

CANTO 138

JAYADRATHA-VADHA PARVA CONTINUED

"Sanjaya says, 'Seeing Satyaki, the invincible Satwata, riding to join Arjuna, Bhurisravas swiftly advances on him and says, "It is fate that has brought you within my grasp and today I will fulfil my long-cherished wish. If you do not flee from battle, you will not escape me with your life. And by killing you who are so proud of your valour, I will gladden Duryodhana's heart. Krishna and Arjuna will see you lying dead on the field riddled with my arrows.

Hearing that I have killed you will disgrace Yudhishtira, who sent you here. Arjuna will see my prowess when he sees you lying dead on the earth, covered in blood. I have always wanted to face you in a battle, like the one between Sakra and Bali during the Devasura yuddha of old. Today, Satwata, you will feel my prowess! And then you will understand the true measure of my might and manliness.

Slain by me, Yuyudhana, you will find yourself in Yamaloka, even as Ravana's son Indrajit did when Lakshmana killed him. Today, Krishna, Partha and Dharmaraja Yudhishtira will watch you die and, grief-stricken, they will concede this war. Killing you today, O Madhava, I will bring joy to the wives of all those whom you have killed. Now that you are in my sight like a deer before a lion, you will not escape with your life."

Hearing this, Satyaki, O Rajan, laughs, "O Kurusattama, I am not frightened by my enemies' arrows and I hardly fear your words! Only he who can vanquish me at arms can kill me, and such a one will always be victorious. What use your long-winded vainglorious bragging, O Bhurisravas? Let me see your deeds not tire of your empty threats, which are like autumn cloud that fetch no rain.

Listening to you, O Kshatriya, and your hollow roars, I can only laugh. Let us fight like men and have between us the duel that you have so long wanted. My heart also longs for this battle; let us not delay! And I solemnly swear, O wretched Bhurisravas, that I will not leave this place without killing you."

And those bulls among men, both excited and charged with old animosity, unleash fiery storms of arrows at each other. Somadatta's son Bhurisravas, who has been resting while Satyaki fought his way through the entire Kuru host, draws first blood. He plunges ten pugnacious shafts into Satyaki's body, and then covers the tired Yadava in a haze of arrows.

Satyaki, summoning deep resources, invokes an astra, which quells Bhurisravas' arrow storm before it can fall on him. And then, we watch those two shuras, enhancers of the fame and honour of the Kuru and Vrishni vamsas, fight a duel that lights up the swiftly dimming sky. They mangle each other with utmost rancour and ferocity. Quickly, blood spurts richly from both in this fresh game of death, with their lives for the wager.

Like wild tigers, like great tuskers, leaders of their clans, the two heroes battle, both ardent for either victory or death, while Kurukshetra echoes with their yells and roars, while all the Dhartarashtra army watches them transfixed, the other maharathas delighted by the sublime duel. Then each one kills the other's horses and destroys the other's bow, and now they fight with swords ringing together with sparks flying brightly at each dreadful stroke.

Having taken up two great and handsome shields and two shining blue swords, they stalk each other in circles, and in parallel lines, then suddenly fly at each other striking out with fabulous skill and strength. Both master swordsmen, they put their lofty skills on display. They wheel about, make side-thrusts, rush forward abruptly, and spring high into the air to strike one another, both intent on having the other's life. And having lashed out with their blades and parried the other's strokes, they pause to rest, their gazes locked like other blades all the while.

Truly like superb dancers they are, and all the other fighting men around them their awed audience. After a brief moment's pause, the wonderful exhibition of prowess erupts again and they carve each other's beautiful shields emblazoned with a hundred moons into pieces, until both shields are useless strips, which they fling away, and their swords have been broken as well. And then they rush at each other to wrestle with bare hands.

Both wide-chested and long-armed, both equally magnificent wrestlers, they grapple. They strike each other stupendous blows and seize one another by the throat, with their arms hard as iron that resemble spiked maces. Their skills and prowess, their speed and ferocity enthrall those that watch.

Loud and fearful are their roars, yes, like thunder falling upon the mountain breast. Like two elephants goring each other with their tusks, or like two bulls locking horns, the two most illustrious Kuru and the Satwata heroes at times struggle with brawny arms entwined, at other butt heads, intertwine massive legs, now slapping their armpits in bravado, sometimes clawing each other with their nails, sometimes clasping each other in tight holds, or twining their legs round each other's waists, at others rolling on the ground locked together, sometimes advancing, sometimes retreating, sometimes rising up to their full height, and at other leaping into the air and then colliding thunderously.

Indeed, they employ all the thirty different kinds of expert tactics that characterise such encounters between masters of the art of wrestling.

When Satyaki exhausts his weapons during his duel with Bhurisravas, Krishna says to Arjuna, "Look at Satyaki, best of all archers, fighting without a chariot. He has scythed through the Bharata host, following in your wake, O son of Pandu! He has fought all the Bharata maharathas and, now in exhaustion, meets the mighty Bhurisravas, the giver of bounteous dakshina at yagnas."

The formidable Bhurisravas, excited with wrath, vigorously strikes Satyaki, Rajan, like an infuriated elephant dashing against another, blow after staggering blow. The two battle on, with Krishna and Arjuna watching.

Then Krishna says urgently to Arjuna, "Look where Satyaki, tiger of the Vrishnis and the Andhakas, is succumbing to Somadatta's son. Exhausted after his superhuman exploits, he has now lost his ratha. Arjuna, you must protect your devoted sishya otherwise Bhurisravas, of countless yagnas, will have his life. Mahabaho, you must hurry!"

But Arjuna says quite cheerfully to Krishna, "The bull of the Kurus and the best of the Vrishnis sport wonderfully with each other, like a crazed elephant and a mighty lion in the forest!"

Just then, loud cries ring out from the troops, O Bharatarishabha, for suddenly Bhurisravas unleashes a flurry of thunderous blows to Satyaki's head and face and fells him to the ground. And like a lion dragging an elephant, the mighty Bhurisravas, giver of lavish dakshina at yagnas, roughly drags the supine Satyaki around as he likes, roaring in glee as he humiliates the noble Yadava before your troops.

Then Bhurisravas draws another sword from its sheath, seizes Satyaki by his hair of his head and, setting his foot upon his chest, draws his arm back to cut the Vrishni's head, its earrings glittering, from his trunk. But, fighting to save his life, Satyaki whirls his head around a few times and with it Bhurisravas's arm that grasps his hair, even like a potter wheel being whirled along with the staff.

Seeing Bhurisravas coarsely drag Satyaki along the ground, Krishna says again to Arjuna, "Bhurisravas is about to kill Yuyudhana. The very name Satyaki means the invincible one, and that name will be proven false is the wretched Bhurisravas kills my kinsman, your disciple."

At this, Arjuna mentally salutes Bhurisravas, thinking, "I am pleased that Bhurisravas, enhancer of the fame of the Kurus, is dragging Satyaki across the ground, as if in sport, without killing him."

Silently admiring his kinsman, the Kuru tiger, Arjuna replies to Krishna, "My eyes are fixed on the Sindhus, and I cannot, O Madhava, see Satyaki. Yet, for his sake and for yours, I will achieve an impossible feat."

Then, in obedience to his Lord and charioteer, Krishna the Avatara, Arjuna, although he truly cannot see Satyaki, in a blur looses a blind shaft from the Gandiva, which, like a meteor falling from the sky, hacks off Bhurisravas's bejewelled arm with the sword in its hand in a bloody eruption.'"

CANTO 139

Jayadratha-vadha Parva continued

"Sanjaya says, 'Severed by the unseen Arjuna's sudden shaft, Bhurisravas's angada-decked arm, still grasping the sword, which was raised to hew off Satyaki's head, falls onto the ground like a five-headed snake. The Kuru warrior turns around in shock and wrathfully reproves the son of Pandu.

Bhurisravas says, "O son of Kunti, what is this cruel and heartless thing you have done, for without engaging me in battle, you cut off my arm in stealth? Will you not have to say to Yudhishtira Dharmaputra, 'I killed Bhurisravas while he fought another battle?'

Were you not taught the astra shastra by the noble Indra, by Rudra, by Drona, and by Kripa? In this world, you know the dharma of war better than anyone else does. How then have you cut off the arm of a warrior who was not fighting you? Dharma requires that one should never strike those who are unaware, those that are afraid, those who are without a chariot, those who beg for life or protection, or those who are suffering. How then, O Partha, have you done this heinous, sinful and cowardly thing that only the most lowborn, ignoble and evil wretch would do?

Dhananjaya, an upright man can easily achieve a noble feat, while a dishonourable sinful deed he can do only with great pain to himself.

A man quickly adopts the behaviour of those with whom he moves. This is surely seen in you, O Arjuna! Being of royal lineage and born especially into Kuru's race, you have forgotten the dharma of a Kshatriya, although you are known for your purity and keep stern vratas. I have no doubt that you have done this vile thing, for Satyaki's sake, at Krishna's word. Who other than a friend of Krishna's would inflict such an injury upon one who was unaware of you and fighting another battle? The Vrishnis and the Andhakas are base Kshatriyas, always engaged in sinful deeds, and are, by nature, given to disreputable conduct. Why, O noble Arjuna, have you taken them to be your models?"

Arjuna replies, "My lord Bhurisravas, it is evident from all the senseless words you utter, that with the decrepitude of the body one's intellect also becomes feeble. Although you know Hrishikesa and me well, how is it that you rebuke us like this? Knowing as I do the dharma of war and conversant as I am with the meaning of all the scriptures, I would never commit a sin in battle. You of all men know this well, and you still reproach me.

The Kshatriyas fight their foes, surrounded by their own followers, their brothers, sires, sons, relatives, kinsmen, companions, and friends. They fight, relying on the strength of their leaders. Why then should I not protect Satyaki, my disciple and dear kinsman, who is fighting for our sake without caring for his life? Invincible in battle, Satyaki is like my very right hand. In war one should not look out only for oneself, but also protect those that fight for one's cause, risking their very lives.

This is what ensures that the king is protected in the press of battle. If I had not intervened when I saw Satyaki on the point of being killed, I would have been responsible for his death and would have grievously sinned for my negligence! You know all this, then why are you angry with me for saving Satyaki?

Again, you reprimand me, O king, saying, 'Though I was fighting another, you cut off my arm without challenging me first.'

In this matter, my answer is that I erred in my judgement. Sometimes adjusting my armour; sometimes riding on my ratha, sometimes drawing my bowstring, I am at war with my enemies in the midst of a host resembling the vast deep, full of rathas, elephants, horses and foot-soldiers and echoing with fierce shouts and roars. Among friends and enemies engaged with one another, how can you say that the Satwata warrior was fighting only one warrior? Having fought many and vanquished many maharathas, Satyaki is tired, wounded and disheartened.

It is under such circumstances, and while you yourself had returned freshly to battle, that you vanquished the mighty Yuyudhana and sought to display your superiority. You were about to behead him with your sword and I could not stand by and watch that with indifference, for Satyaki is my friend and my sishya and as dear to me as my brothers. You should rather rebuke yourself that you did not take care to defend yourself while attacking another. Indeed, O Shura, I ask how, if you were in my place, how you would have behaved towards someone who depends on you as Satyaki does on me?"

Thus addressed by Arjuna, the mighty-armed and illustrious Bhurisravas, who bears the device of the sacrificial stake on his banner, leaves Satyaki, and decides to die according to the vow of praya, to starve and, here, to bleed to death. A Kshatriya distinguished by many righteous deeds, he spreads with a bed of arrows for himself with his left hand, and looking to ascend into Brahmaloka, he relinquishes his senses to the care of the deities that preside over them. Fixing his gaze on the sun, setting his cleansed heart on the moon, and meditating on the mantras in the great Upanishad, Bhurisravas sits down on the bed of arrows, yokes himself in yoga, and stops speaking.

Seeing this, your entire army, led by your sons, begins to curse Krishna and Dhananjaya and to laud Bhurisravas, bull among men. Though roundly censured, the two Krishnas speak not a word distasteful to the dying hero. Bhurisravas, also, although thus lauded, feels no joy.

Then Arjuna cannot bear to listen to the curses of your sons, and what Bhurisravas said to him. Without anger and only grief in his heart, as if to remind them all, Arjuna says, "All the kings know my solemn vow that no one will succeed in killing anybody from our army within range of my bow. Knowing this, Bhurisravas, it is not appropriate, without properly understanding the laws of dharma, for one to censure others. That I have cut off your arm while you, well armed in battle, were on the point of slaying the unarmed Satyaki is not at all contrary to dharma. But what righteous man is there that would applaud the slaughter of Abhimanyu, a mere child, unarmed, deprived of his ratha, and without his armour by six maharathas uniting against him while he stood helpless?"

Hearing this, Bhurisravas of dazzling effulgence, touches the ground with his left palm—for the right one has been lost—and remains silent, with his head hanging down.

Then Arjuna says, "O eldest brother of Sala, the love I have for you is equal to what I bear Dharmaraja Yudhishtira, Bhima, Nakula, or Sahadeva. I now say to you, as does the illustrious Krishna: *Go, O sire, to the realm of the righteous, and join Sibi, the son of Usinara, there!*

Krishna says, "You have constantly performed yagnas and agnihotras. Go straight into my pure realms that blaze with endless splendour, which the greatest deities, even Brahma, wish for, become equal to me, borne on the back of Garuda."

Meanwhile, Satyaki rises to his feet and, his eyes burning, draws his sword to cut off the noble, sinless head of Bhurisravas, who now sits in yoga with his senses withdrawn from battle, blood gushing from where Arjuna hacked away his right arm. All the maharathas cry out to Satyaki to stop: Krishna and Arjuna, as well as Bhima, Yudhamanyu and Uttamaujas, Aswatthaman, Kripa, Karna, Vrishasena and even Jayadratha. Even the other troops, watching aghast, forbid him. But Satyaki hews off Bhirusravas's head in a crimson blast even as that great Kuru sits in praya, lost in dhyana to free his soul from his body. Cries of outrage fill Kurukshetra.

The Siddhas, the Charanas, and all the fighting men, as also the Devas witness the slaying of Bhurisravas even as he sits with his eyes shut and his senses withdrawn in deep dhyana, and all of them laud that great Kuru.

Your soldiers argue the matter. "It is not Satyaki's fault; what was fated has happened. We must not yield to wrath, for anger is the root of men's sorrow. Brahma ordained that Satyaki would kill Bhurisravas in battle and there is no point in our judging what inevitably transpired."

Satyaki rages, "You sinful Kaurava wretches! You wear the outward garment of dharma, and tell me sanctimoniously that I should not have killed Bhurisravas. But where did this dharma of yours go when you slew that child, Subhadra's son Abhimanyu, while he was unarmed?

Once in a mood of pride, I vowed that I would kill anyone who flings me down alive in battle and kicks me, even if that enemy should take praya or even sannyasa. While I still struggled against Bhurisravas to stay alive, you thought me dead. This was your folly. O you Kuru bulls, the death of Bhurisravas at my hand is just and in accord with dharma!

I would have killed him anyway, but Arjuna deprived me of my glory by cutting off his arm out of his love for me and his vow to protect all that fight for Yudhishtira. Indeed, what is ordained must come to pass. Everything is destiny; fate has slain Bhurisravas in the press of battle. What sin have I committed?

Once upon a time, Valmiki sang this verse: 'You say, O Vanara, that women should not be killed. However, in all the ages, men should always and without fail do whatever brings pain to his enemies.'"

After Satyaki speaks in his ringing voice, none among the Pandavas and the Kauravas, O Rajan, say anything. However, in their hearts they are with Bhurisravas because no one there approves of Yuyudhana killing one who was like a Rishi made holy by countless yagnas, Bhurisravas who gave away incalculable gold during all his sacrifices, and who was purified beyond all common measure by the holiest mantras. The head of that hero, graced with rich blue locks and eyes red as those of a pigeon, now looks like the head of a horse decapitated at an Aswamedha yagna and placed on the sacrificial altar. Sanctified by his prowess and by the death he obtains at the edge of a weapon, the boon-giving Bhurisravas, worthy of every boon, casts off his body and ascends into swarga, sanctifying the exalted realms with his high punya.'"

CANTO 140

JAYADRATHA-VADHA PARVA CONTINUED

"Dhritarashtra says, 'Having crossed the ocean of the Kaurava army, unvanquished even by Drona, Karna, Vikarna or Kritavarman, to keep his word given to Yudhishtira, how was it that the heroic Satyaki was humiliated by Bhurisravas and flung down on the ground and almost killed?'

Sanjaya replies, 'Listen, Rajan, to the antecedents of Sini's grandson Bhurisravas. Maharishi Atri had a son called Soma, the Moon, and Soma's son was called Budha. Budha had one son, of the splendour of Indra, called Pururavas. Pururavas had a son called Ayus whose son was Nahusha. Nahusha's son was Yayati, a Rajarishi equal to a Deva. Yayati and his wife Devayani's eldest son was Yadu. In Yadu's race was born a prince of the name of Devamidha, whose son Sura was acclaimed in the three worlds. Sura's son was the greatest of men, the celebrated Vasudeva. Sura himself was the equal of Kartavirya in battle. Sini was born into Sura's vamsa, equal to Sura in tejas!

About this time, Rajan, there occurred the swayamvara of the noble Devaka's daughter Devaki, to which all the great Kshatriyas of the world came. During that swayamvara, Sini vanquished all the others and, for Vasudeva's sake, swept the princess Devaki into his chariot. Seeing Devaki in Sini's ratha, that bull among men, the mahatejasvin Somadatta could not bear the sight and he challenged Sini to a match of wrestling, which lasted half a day and was stunning and wonderful to witness. During the wrestling, Sini threw Somadatta down on the earth. Lifting up his sword and seizing him by the hair, Sini kicked his adversary before the many thousands of kings who stood as spectators all around. Finally, out of compassion, Sini spared Somadatta's life, saying in contempt, "Live!"

Humiliated by Sini, Somadatta worshipped Mahadeva for his blessings so he could avenge himself on Sini. Mahadeva, the great Lord of all boon-giving deities, was pleased with him and asked him what boon he wished. The royal Somadatta asked for his boon: "I want a son, O Divine Lord, who will strike Sini's son down in the midst of thousands of kings and kick him with his foot."

Mahadeva Siva said, "Tathaastu! So be it," and vanished from Somadatta's sight. It was from Siva's boon that the most noble and benign Bhurisravas was born as Somadatta's son. And that is also why Bhurisravas was able to fling down Sini's grandson Satyaki in battle and kick him before the eyes of the whole army.

This is the story, Rajan, and indeed, other than for Siva's boon, not the greatest of warriors can conquer the Satwata hero Yuyudhana in battle. The Vrishni heroes are all superlative archers, and masters, besides, in every other form of warfare. They are conquerors of the very Devas, the Danavas and the Gandharvas. They are never nonplussed and always fight, relying upon their own prowess and are never dependent on others. There is no one in this world equal to the Vrishnis. None, O Bharatarishabha, has been, is, or will be equal in might to the Vrishnis. They never show disrespect to their relatives and they are always obedient to the commands of their elders. When the very Devas, Asuras, Gandharvas, the Yakshas, the Uragas and the Rakshasas cannot vanquish the Vrishni heroes in battle, what need be said of men?

They never covet the possessions of those whom they help in distress.

Devoted to the Brahmanas and truthful in speech, they never display any pride although they are wealthy. The Vrishnis regard even the strong as weak and rescue them from their troubles. Always devoted to the Devas, they are self-restrained, charitable, and free from pride. This is why the abilities of the Vrishnis are never questioned. A man may uproot the mountains of Meru or swim across the ocean, but no one can defeat the Vrishnis. I believe I have cleared all your doubts, Rajan. However, O king of the Kurus, remember that all that is happening is due to your evil policy!'"

CANTO 141

JAYADRATHA-VADHA PARVA CONTINUED

"Dhritarashtra says, 'After the great Kuru warrior Bhurisravas is killed, under these extraordinary circumstances, tell me, Sanjaya, how the battle progresses.'

Sanjaya replies, 'After Bhurisravas left for the next world, Bhaarata, Mahabaho Arjuna says to Krishna, "Urge the horses, Lord, to greater speed to take me to Jayadratha, for the sun sinks swiftly towards the Asta hills. O Naravyaghra, I have yet to fulfil my vow and many maharathas still protect Jayadratha. Ah, we must fly, Krishna, racing the sun to the horizon for I must kill the Saindhava before Surya Deva sets."

Flicking his reins and whip, Krishna, greatest of all sarathies, spurs his silver horses, white as moonbeams, towards Jayadratha's chariot. At once, many great Kuru rathikas like Duryodhana, Karna, Vrishasena and, now, Jayadratha himself dash forward to stop Arjuna's careen. Finally, Arjuna sees Jayadratha before him, and glares at him fearfully, as if to burn him up with his very gaze.

Duryodhana quickly tells Karna, "O son of Vikartana, the critical hour is upon us. Now show us your true prowess, beloved friend, and ensure that Arjuna does not kill Jayadratha! The day is about to end, so cover the Pandava with clouds of arrows and slow him down! If we can protect Jayadratha until the sun sets, Arjuna would have failed to fulfil his oath, and he will take his own life by immolating himself, and then victory will be ours! For Arjuna's brothers, with all their followers, will hardly last a few moments in a world without him. And upon the death of Pandu's sons, we will enjoy the whole Earth, Karna, with her mountains, waters and forests, and without any thorn in our sides and no limit to our power!

Arjuna swore his oath in anger at his son's death; he became fate's victim for he took leave in his grief of his judgement. Karna, I have no doubt that fate favoured us at that moment, for Pandu's son, the Kiritin swore his vow to kill Jayadratha only for his own destruction.

How, when you, my great Karna, are alive, will Arjuna succeed in killing the Saindhava before the sun sets behind the Asta hills? How will he kill him when Salya of the Madras and the illustrious Kripa protect Jayadratha? How will Arjuna, who is being led to his death by fate, even reach Jayadratha when Aswatthaman, Dusasana and I protect him? Many are the heroes among us who are engaged in this battle and the sun hangs low in the sky and plummets towards the sunset mountain.

Partha will not even come near Jayadratha. So, Karna, summon your greatest determination and resolution, along with me and our other brave maharathas like Drona's son, the king of the Madras and Kripa, and resist Arjuna with all your might."

Karna replies, "Deeply has my body been injured by mighty Bhimasena, who is more of an archer that I had dreamt. I am still in battle because it is ordained that I should be here. Pain wracks my every limb from Bhima's arrows. Yet, for you I will fight with all my might. My life itself is for you and I will do everything in my power to ensure that Arjuna, greatest of the sons of Pandu, does not succeed in killing Jayadratha.

As long as I am able to fight, the ambidextrous Savyasachin, who looses his arrows with equal facility with both his hands, will not reach the king of the Sindhus. Kurusathama, all that one who bears you the great love that I do, and is always concerned for your welfare, I will do. As for victory, that depends on destiny. I will exert myself to my utmost for Jayadratha's sake and for yours. Victory, however, is dependent on fate.

Fear not, Naravyaghra, I will fight Arjuna today for you as I have never fought before. Yet, fate and fate alone will decide who wins or loses. O king of the Kurus, let all our troops witness today the fierce battle between me and Arjuna, which will make their very hair stand on end."

While Karna and your son are thus speaking together, Arjuna begins to slaughter your host again, hewing off the great arms of helpless heroes, arms like spiked clubs or the trunks of elephants. He cuts off heads, as well as actual trunks of elephants, beheads horses, and carves up the akshas of rathas all around, as well as blood-dyed horsemen armed with spears and javelins. From horses and the best of elephants, standards, royal parasols, bows, yak-tails and heads fall thick and fast on all sides. Consuming your army like a wind-fanned great fire a heap of dry grass, the invincible Arjuna covers the earth with blood, and swiftly reaches Jayadratha.

Protected by Bhimasena and Satyaki, Arjuna looks as glorious as Agni himself. Seeing Arjuna thus ablaze, the mightiest bowmen of your army, bulls among men, endowed with great energy, cannot face him at all. Then the maharathas Duryodhana, Karna, Vrishasena, Salya and Aswatthaman set Jayadratha behind them and surround Krishna and the Kiritin, who dances wildly on his ratha to the savage, reverberant music of the Gandiva's bowstring and the slap of his palms against that incomparable weapon.

Arjuna is like Death himself, with open maw, come hunting the trembling Sindhu king. The sun turns red in the sky and, wanting it to set quickly, the Kaurava warriors bend their bows with arms that resemble the tapering bodies of Nagas and cover Partha with hundreds of arrows like the very rays of the setting sun. That peerless one, however, dissects every shaft into two, three, or eight slivers, and gashes the bowmen with his raking shafts.

Aswatthaman, who flies a lion's tail on his banner, charges at Arjuna, striking him with ten whistling barbs and Krishna with seven and barring Arjuna's way to Jayadratha. Quickly, many Kurus hem Arjuna in with a mass of rathas. Stretching their bows to the fullest and shooting countless arrows, they shield Jayadratha from the Pandava, at your son's command.

And now we witness glorious Arjuna's unearthly genius; we witness the might of the Gandiva and see how his magical twin quivers well inexhaustibly with arrows. Confounding the high weapons of Aswatthaman and Kripa, he pierces all the warriors that surround him with nine bolts of thunder each. Drona's son pierces him with five and twenty arrows, Vrishasena with seven, Duryodhana with twenty, Karma and Salya with three each. And all of them roar at him and, shaking their bows, hem him in closer still and continue to strike him frequently.

They draw their rathas up in serried ranks around Arjuna and, willing the sun to set quickly, those great maharathas of the Kaurava army roar awfully at Arjuna and lash him with dense gusts of arrows. These intrepid, mighty warriors, their arms like maces, loose devastras at the battling Dhananjaya.

But the relucent Arjuna shatters all their missiles, mundane and unworldly; breaking through the encirclement of chariots he rides straight at Jayadratha. Then Karna appears as if out of nowhere, and stops Arjuna with a towering gale of arrows, in the very sight of Bhimasena and Satyaki. Arjuna cuts these arrows down and strikes Karna, before all the troops, with ten steaming shafts. Satyaki drills the Sutaputra with three stinging barbs. Bhimasena pierces him with three arrows, and Arjuna, again, with seven.

An unfazed Karna, fighting for his beloved Duryodhana to save Jayadratha's life, unleashes sixty terrific arrows, each, at Arjuna, Bhima and Satyaki. In moments, the battle between the lone Karna and his three adversaries swells to momentous proportions. Karna's skill that we then see is wondrous, as, mad with battle lust, he singly resists those three matchless maharathas.

Then Arjuna looses a torrid volley at Karna, piercing him through every limb. Bathed in blood, the Suta's son gores Arjuna with fifty lofty arrows. Arjuna breaks his bow and bloodies his chest with shafts. Seeing how the sun plunges towards the sunset mountain, Arjuna unleashes a devastra at Karna, to kill him with that single missile incandescent as the very sun. It flies inexorably towards Karna and the Dhartarashtras hold their breath for they are certain he will die. But then, from a side Drona's son Aswatthaman bisects that flaming astra and it falls tamely to the ground.

Karna takes up another bow and envelops Arjuna with a swath of thousands of arrows. Like the wind dispersing a locust swarm, Arjuna shoots them all down and covers Karna with his own arrow storms. Karna, destroyer of armies, shreds these in flight and returns Arjuna's fire, shaft for shaft. Roaring at each other like two mighty bulls, those incomparable maharathas obscure the sky with clouds of arrows. Each made invisible by the other's rain of shafts, they continue their transcendent duel, often shouting taunts at each other.

Ah, Rajan, surely unearthly is the duel between Karna and Arjuna, for each is a match of the other and they put forth their best skills and strength. All the others around stand disbelieving of what they see, lowering their own weapons and gazing at the luculent contention. Applauded by Siddhas, Charanas and Pannagas, the two fight at the limits of their prowess, entirely absorbed, each bent on killing the other.

Then Duryodhana says to his maharathas, "Do everything you can to protect Karna, for Vrisha has sworn that he will not rest until he has killed Arjuna."

With the sun plunging down every moment, Arjuna kills Karna's horses and with a broad-headed arrow, he fells Karna's charioteer from his niche in the ratha. Before Duryodhana's eyes, Arjuna Swetavahana shrouds Karna in a blizzard of arrows, overwhelming him so he stands helpless and stunned. Seeing this, Aswatthaman dashes up and, mounting Drona's son's chariot the two continue to assail Arjuna.

Salya of the Madras pierces Arjuna with thirty arrows while Kripacharya strikes Krishna with twenty telling shafts and Partha with a dozen. Still from a fair distance, joining the battle to save his life, Jayadratha now shoots the two Krishnas with four barbs each; Vrishasena also rakes them both with seven shafts. Radiant Arjuna lacerates them all in return—Aswatthaman with four and sixty tremendous arrows, Salya with a hundred, Jayadratha with ten flat-headed ones, Vrishasena with three and Saradwata's son with twenty. The lustrous Dhananjaya throws back his head and roars.

Intent on stopping the Pandava from fulfilling his vow, your warriors swarm at him from all sides. And now, terrifying the Dhartarashtras, Arjuna invokes the great Varunastra, which radiates an awesome tide of fluid arrows all around his chariot. Well aware of what is at stake and that they need only contain the godly Pandava for a brief while before the sun sets, the Kauravas withstand his occult flashflood and continue to advance upon him.

Arjuna Kiritin remains serene and intent on his single purpose; arrows of all sorts, high and plain, continue to flare from the Gandiva, darkening all the field, all the directions.

The sky, dense with shafts, is ablaze with meteors and on the ghastly ground innumerable crows alight from the sky to perch on fresh corpses, picking out eyes and swallowing them whole before setting their black beaks to work on noble steaming flesh. And Arjuna continues to provide a grisly feast for these and other birds and beasts of carrion with the Gandiva, why, like Mahadeva slaying the Asuras with his Pinaka with the tawny string. So many great Kuru maharathas, riding their best horses and elephants the inescapable Pandava sends to Yama.

Then a host of kings, taking up heavy maces and clubs of iron and swords and darts and different kinds of powerful weapons of terrible forms, rush suddenly at Partha. Bending the Gandiva Arjuna consumes them all, now uncanny laughter bubbling up in him as if at some great intuition of success; he never ceases devouring your troops with their rathas, elephants, foot-soldiers and supporting bowmen and swell the population of Yama's domain.'"

CANTO 142

JAYADRATHA-VADHA PARVA CONTINUED

"Sanjaya continues, 'Hearing the twang of Dhananjaya's bow, which is like the beckoning of Death himself, or the frightful peal of Indra's thunder, your army, Rajan, is like an ocean swept by a tempest of mountainous waves that surges up at the Yuganta. Krishna pilots Arjuna's ratha across Kurukshetra so that he seems to be in a hundred places at once, and from a hundred places apparently do his tides of arrows flare sowing death in every shaft. A hundred Gandivas afire appear all around, all bent in a constant circle, all spewing relentless, ceaseless waves of flame.

Arjuna invokes the Aindrastra, lancing terror through your legions. A hundred thousand flaming arrows issue from that fulminant celestial weapon and fetch fresh carnage to your army; so brilliant is that astra that no one can bear to look at it and then death comes for them in the twinkling of an eye. Arjuna traverses Kurukshetra at will, driven by his sarathy the Avatara, his prowess on full display, scattering the darkness that the Kauravas caused with their arrows, which no other can disperse even in imagination. But Arjuna, with his elemental devastras, summoned with ringing mantras, dispels the sinister Kaurava darkness as Surya Deva does the night when he rises over it.

Arjuna evaporates the lives of your warriors like the summer sun the waters of tanks and lakes. He mantles your legions with his shafts like the sun does the earth with his rays. With other precise arrows he enters and breaks the hearts of great enemies, even like beloved friends! He consumes your akshauhinis as a blazing fire does swarms of insects.

Devouring the lives of his enemies and their fame, Partha rides like Death embodied over Kurukshetra. He severs crowned heads, massive arms adorned with angadas, and long-lobed noble ears with earrings. He hacks away the arms of elephant-riders clutching spears to cast at him; those of horsemen with javelins clasped to fling at him; those of foot-soldiers with shields to stop his arrows; those of maharathas with mighty bows; and those of charioteers and mahouts with whips and goads. He is scintillating, a conflagration burning your army with incessant flames.

For all their resolve, the hostile Kauravas cannot even look at Arjuna, greatest of all warriors, the shura equal to Indra, the greatest bull among men. One sees him everywhere at the same time, dancing on his ratha, with no moment's pause in his apocalyptic rant of lucific astras. Ah, my lord, he is handsome, he is beautiful, and he is godly: the Kiritin like some banks of massed thunderheads adorned with many rainbows, for he is in so many places at once, in this hour that he was born for, that he learnt and suffered for.

Arjuna's immaculate inundation of devastras sees many great warriors shrink in fright, as he makes an unfordable morass upon the field of dharma and death. Strewn with elephants whose trunks or tusks have been severed, with horses that have lost hooves and heads, with rathas smashed in smithereens, eviscerated warriors with entrails hanging out, and others with legs hacked off, with corpses of men and besats lying, either still forever or convulsed in death's last throes, the vast field of Kurukshetra, which Arjuna bestraddles, resembles the coveted arena of Death, increasing the terror of the timid, or the sporting ground of Rudra when he devastated all creatures in time out of mind.

Parts of the field, strewn with the trunks of elephants cut off with razor-headed arrows, look as if scattered with thick snakes. Portions covered with the dissevered heads of warriors, look as if spread with garlands of lotuses. Variegated with beautiful head-gear, crowns, keyuras, angadas and ratha-rings with coats of mail decked with gold and with the trappings and other ornaments of elephants and horses, and scattered over with hundreds of coronets lying everywhere, the Earth looks beautiful like a new bride!

Arjuna has a gory river flow, like the Vaitarani itself and affrights the timid. The marrow and fat of men and animals forms its mire, blood its current, and limbs and bones fill it and moment by moment it grows fathomless in depth. The hairs of the dead, men and beasts, are its moss, weeds; heads and arms form the rocks and stones on its shores, and standards, and banners that brightly colour its appearance deck it. Royal parasols and bows are its wavelets and it abounds with the vast corpses of dead elephants and teems with rathas that float like countless rafts on its surface.

The carcasses of countless horses forms its banks and it is impassable because of the wheels, yokes, shafts, akshas and kuveras of rathas, and from spears, swords, darts, battle-axes and snake-like arrows. Ravens and kankas are its crocodiles, jackals, its terrible makaras, and fierce vultures, its sharks. It ripples and rings with the howls of jackals. It abounds with capering bhutas and pisachas, and thousands of other dreadful spirits that feed and drink blood from the numberless corpses of warriors that float upon it.

Seeing Arjuna's astounding prowess, the Vijaya whose visage resembles that of Yama himself, panic like never before. He obliterates all that comes before him; he seems to reveals truly himself now for what he is. His body is full of blinding light and none can even gaze upon him let alone face him in battle.

Intent on having Jayadratha's life before the sun sets, the Savyasachin demolishes all the great maharathas before him, stunning them with archery possibly never seen in this age of men. Dhananjaya, with Krishna for his charioteer, continues to blaze across Kurukshetra like streak lightning on the ground. His arrows, hundreds of thousands of them, cover the field in a cupola of endless death, his Gandiva always bent in an inscrutable circle of flames. And then blasting his bloody way through all the maharathas and other warriors arrayed in thousands before him, he finally arrives at where the terror-stricken Jayadratha is, and drills him with four and sixty deadly straight, light-swift shafts.

The Kuru warriors freeze, every one of them by now, those not dead, bleeding from Partha's arrows; they despair for Jayadratha's life. And maharatha Arjuna, greatest of victorious men, his astras blazing like pralaya fire, saturates your army with kabandhas, headless trunks of men, and fetches absolute havoc to your legions consisting of four kinds of forces.

He gashes Aswatthama with fifty thunderbolts, Vrishasena with three, mildly strikes Kripa with nine, Salya with sixteen and Karna with two and thirty. He plunges another sixty-four barbs deep into Jayadratha and gives a bloodcurdling roar. But now, actually faced with his shining hunter, Jayadratha's fear leaves him! Rage takes the place of terror, and, the Sindhu king who bears the emblem of the Varaha on his banner roars like a great tiger himself and unleashes a gale of arrows, vulture-feathered and hissing like venomous serpents, at Arjuna.

The Saindhava strikes Govinda with three shafts, Arjuna with six, Arjuna's horses with eight and his standard with one. Arjuna, unmoved, the hungry tiger, hacks away Jayadratha's sarathy's head with a wedge-tipped shaft and fells his flame like standard with another.

Meanwhile, the sun perches on the brim of the Asta mountains and Krishna tells Arjuna, "Look, Partha, they have set Jayadratha in the midst of six mighty maharathas and he waits there in fear. Bull among men, you will not be able to kill him without vanquishing the six. I will use my yoga shakti to hide the sun so everyone thinks Surya has set. They will all rejoice, thinking that, having failed to keep your vow, you will immolate yourself. Jayadratha will emerge from hiding and you must shoot him dead. Though it will seem as if night has fallen, know that the sun will not have set and kill the Saindhava!"

Arjuna replies, "Tathaastu. So be it!"

Then Krishna, the Mahatapasvin, creates darkness through his cosmic Yoga. Your warriors, O Rajan, think the sun has set and are ecstatic; they throw their heads back, including Jayadratha, gaze skywards, where the stars have appeared on high and cry out in celebration that Arjuna must now take his own life. Krishna says fiercely to Arjuna, "Look how the wretched Jayadratha look up at the sky and has lost his fear of you. Kill him now, Bhaarata. Cut off his head and fulfil your vow!"

Arjuna, in a fearsome blur, shining himself like the sun that has not truly set, strikes Kripa with twenty arrows, Karna with fifty, Salya and Duryodhana each with six, Vrishasena with eight and Jayadratha himself with sixty. Finding that he attacks them even after the sun has set, and like a great fire with its tongues of flame extended, the protectors of Jayadratha are perplexed. But they return his fire swiftly with torrents of arrows. Shrouded by their mantle of shafts, and raging, Arjuna raises his prodigious archery and creating a mesh, a great net of intertwined flaming arrows, cats it over the Kuru maharathas. Having never seen the like of this, your warriors abandon Jayadratha in fear and flee in all directions, with no two heroes going the same way.

The prowess that Arjuna now displays is uncanny, unseen ever before and will never again be witnessed. Like Rudra himself slaughtering all creatures during the pralaya, Dhananjaya butchers elephants and elephant-riders, horses and horse-riders, maharathas and charioteers. I do not see, Rajan, a single elephant, horse or warrior that is not struck with Partha's arrows. Their vision blurred by dust and darkness, your warriors cannot distinguish one another in the sudden night, and strange blackness envelops their senses and mind as well.

Urged by fate, and with their bodies cut open and lacerated by Arjuna's arrows, they begin to wander like men in a dream, to limp and fall down. Some among them are paralysed and some deathly pale. During the ensuing carnage, Arjuna the Pandava showers, drenches the earth with rills of gore, while the air clears marvellously with the blood that sprays everywhere absorbing all the raised dust and a sudden gusting wind blowing the rest away. So deep is the river of blood that the wheels of chariots are mired almost fully and thousands of terror-stricken elephants thunder about in all directions, their limbs mangled, their riders slain, trumpeting horribly and trampling your own ranks as they go.

Horses without riders and foot-soldiers, too, as well as your great warriors, Rajan, all struck by Dhananjaya's arrows, flee in abject fear, abandoning the field, their hair dishevelled, their armour cut away and blood pouring from their wounds. Some stand frozen as if crocodiles from the macabre red river have seized their legs, while some others hide behind and under the bodies of dead elephants.

Routing your army thus, Rajan, Arjuna savagely attacks the six maharatha protectors of the Sindhu king—Karna, Aswatthaman, Kripa, Salya, Vrishasena and Duryodhana. So quicksilver is his archery that in a wink he shatters Karna's and Vrishasena's bows, and fells Salya's charioteer. With dreadful storms of shafts he deeply wounds Kripa and his nephew Aswatthaman.

All of them stricken, Arjuna invokes a mahastra of the splendour of Indra's Vajra, a great weapon that he has always worshipped with incense and garlands of flowers. He summons it with the most recondite mantras and affixes it to the Gandiva and we hear loud cries from the sky for that astra is bright and fiery as the sun himself.

Krishna says again to Arjuna, "Quick, Partha, cut Jayadratha's head from his neck! The sun is about to set behind the Asta mountain, so listen to what I say to you now. Jayadratha's father Vriddhakshatra is famed the world over. It was after a long time and tapasya that Jayadratha, the Parantapa, was born to him.

At his birth, an asariri, a disembodied voice deep as rumbling clouds said to Vriddhakshatra, 'Among men in this world, in respect of blood, conduct, self-restraint and the other qualities, your son will become worthy of the two races of the Sun and the Moon. He will become one of the greatest Kshatriyas of all and will always be worshipped by heroes. However, one day in battle, a bull among all Kshatriyas, the greatest one in the world will cut off his head.'

Hearing what the asariri said, Vriddhakshatra reflected for a long while. Overwhelmed by his love for his son, he summoned all his kinsmen and said, 'The head of the man who causes my son's head to fall on the earth will burst asunder like a melon in a hundred pieces!'

Having said this, Vriddhakshatra installed Jayadratha on the throne and retired to the vana to devote himself to tapasya. Endowed with great tejas, Arjuna, he is still engaged in the observance of the austerest of penances outside this very Samantapanchaka. So, after you take Jayadratha's head, you must with the great Pasupastra ensure that the head does not fall onto the ground but flies on with the arrow and falls into Vriddhakshatra's lap! For if Jayadratha's head falls onto the ground, have no doubt that your own head will burst apart in a hundred pieces. O son of Indra, there is nothing in this world that you cannot achieve. So do this now."

Hearing this, Arjuna licks the corners of his mouth and looses the arrow he has charged with Siva's astra, which has always been worshipped with incense and garlands. The ultimate ayudha, with which once Mahadeva torched the Tripura from the sky, takes Jayadratha's head from his neck in a crimson eruption, like a hawk snatching a small bird from a tree. Arjuna follows this by shooting a dozen more shafts in a blur, arrows that carry the severed head through the sky, out to the far limits of Samantapanchaka, where your son-in-law's father, mahatejasvin Vriddhakshatra, is at his sandhya vandana, his evening worship.

Adorned with thick black hair, with sparkling kundalas, Jayadratha's bleeding head falls perfectly into Vriddhakshatra's lap, where he sits in padmasana at his twilight prayer. So deep is his dhyana that at first Vriddhakshatra does not even notice. He duly completes his worship and then slowly rises to his feet. His son's head now falls onto the earth and Vriddhakshatra's own head blows apart in a hundred pieces of flesh bone and brain, for it is he himself who has at last made his son's head fall onto the earth! And all that learn of this wonderful, terrible feat of

Arjuna laud both the Krishnas.

Rajan, after the Kiritin kills the Saindhava, Krishna withdraws the darkness, the false night that fell over Kurukshetra through his maya. As all the stars that peeped out from on high vanish, your sons and their men see that they were deceived and the sun has not yet set. And that, O Dhritarashtra, is how Arjuna kills Jayadratha and keeps his vow to avenge the death of Abhimanyu. On that day, amongst them, Arjuna, Satyaki and great Bhima slaughter eight whole akshauhinis of your army! Seeing Jayadratha killed, tears fall from the eyes of your sons that remain alive, Duryodhana weeps the most bitterly.

After Arjuna kills Jayadratha, Krishna blows a clarion blast on his Panchajanya and Arjuna raises the Devadatta to his lips and blows resoundingly on his conch. And, as if to send the message of triumph not merely to Yudhishtira but into the very heavens, Bhima fills Kurukshetra with a battery of dreadful roars drowning every other sound on the filed of dharma. Yudhishtira Dharmaputra hears these sounds across the field and knows that Arjuna has killed Jayadratha. Exultantly he has his own troops sound conches and horns and beat on drums.

And the excited, elated Yudhishtira charges at Drona to do battle with him.

By now the sun has actually set, and a most horrifying battle breaks out, by night's darkness, between Drona and the Somakas, descended from the moon. Jubilant after the killing of Jayadratha, the Pandava maharathas now attack Drona to kill him; why, they fight intoxicated with success. Having kept his vow, a celebrant Arjuna also engages many of your great chariot-warriors and now, with the great burden, upon which the very outcome of the war hinged, lifted from his shoulders, he destroys your ranks like truly the Devaputra that he is. He razes your legions like the Devas mowing down the Danavas, like the sun scattering darkness.'"

CANTO 143

JAYADRATHA-VADHA PARVA CONTINUED

"Dhritarashtra says, 'Tell me, O Sanjaya, what my warriors did after Arjuna killed the heroic Jayadratha?'

Sanjaya replies, 'After Arjuna, O sire, kills Jayadratha, an angry Kripa, son of Saradwat, confronts Arjuna and envelops him with a barrage of arrows, while a furious Aswatthaman attacks him from the rear. A tiring Arjuna bleeds from the many wounds these two maharathas inflict on him and is in considerable pain. Yet, he does not want to kill his guru, Kripa or the son of his other acharya, Drona, so he treats the encounter like some exalted lesson in archery, and instruction even.

Thwarting both Aswatthaman and Kripa, he covers both in his arrows storms, but his shafts are mild and none loosed to take either of their lives. Yet, they injure Kripa and Aswatthaman fiercely, coursing pain through their bodies while avoiding all the vital marmas that, pierced, could kill them. So swift and so many are the arrows that Arjuna unleashes that Kripa faints in his ratha. His sarathy thinks that Arjuna has killed the old Acharya and whisks him away from the field. At this, Aswatthaman also flees in fear!

Seeing his guru Kripa swoon and fall, Arjuna is overcome by great grief. His face tearful and his voice full of anguish, he says, "Vidura clearly foresaw all this long ago in his mind. When Duryodhana was born, Vidura said to Dhritarashtra, 'Have this demon born into the noble house of Kuru killed. Otherwise, unimaginable calamity will overtake the greatest Kurus.'

Ah, how true Vidura's warning has proved. It is because of Duryodhana that I see my precious Acharya Kripa lying fallen to my arrows. Fie on this unholy Kshatriya dharma! Shame on my much vaunted might and prowess! Who else will fight a Brahmana who is also his guru? Kripa is the son of a Rishi; he is my Acharya; he is also Drona's great friend and brother-in-law. Alas, now he lies sprawled on his ratha, dying from my arrows.

Krishna, I had no wish to kill him, yet that is what I have done. My heart breaks to see him like this. Even if he wounded me sorely with his arrows, I should have only looked fondly at that warrior of dazzling splendour and never attacked him in return. And now, I have sent him, my first teacher, whom I always loved and revered to Yama. I say to you Krishna, this causes me more agony that even Abhimanyu's death. Ah, look at the plight I have reduced him to; look where he lies so pitiable and dying in his chariot.

Kshatriyas who acquire knowledge from their gurus and then gift them with the dakshina that they desire, attain to Godhead. On the other hand, the lowest of men, evil ones who learn from their acharyas and then do them harm: such men go straight to naraka. And I have no doubt that I will find hell for myself having done this ghastly thing today. I have horribly wounded my Acharya Kripa with ruthless showers of arrows. While I was learning the astra shastra at his feet, Kripa once told me, 'Do not, O you of Kuru's vamsa, ever strike your acharya.'

I have not obeyed that grave command of my righteous and noble guru; on the contrary today I have struck the same Kripa, my sacred master with cruel arrows and felled him. Oh, I bow to this worshipful son of Gotama, to this inexorable shura. And everlasting shame be on me for what I have done."

While Arjuna is crying in remorse at having wounded Kripa, he thinks mortally, Karna sees that Jayadratha has been slain and rushes in fury at the victorious Pandava who has kept his vow. Seeing this, the two Panchala princes, Uttamaujas and Yudhamanyu, and Satyaki attack Karna.

Arjuna now wipes his tears and, smiling wanly at Krishna, says, "Here comes Karna, viciously attacking Satyaki. No doubt, he is incensed at the death of Bhurisravas, and the manner in which Yuyudhana killed him. Take my steeds there, O Janardana, so that Karna does not make the Satwata follow in the wake of Bhurisravas."

Krishna says, "Satyaki by himself is a match for Karna. How much more he will be with the two sons of Drupada beside him. For the time being, it is not wise for you to fight Karna. He has with him a blazing spear, like a meteor, a shakti that Indra gave him when Karna gave Sakra his golden kavacha. Parantapa, he has kept it to use against you, worshipping it with reverence. Let Karna ride against Satyaki. I know when this evil man's hour will come, and then you will dispatch him from this world, you and no one else, Arjuna."

Dhritarashtra says, 'Tell me, O Sanjaya, about the battle between Karna and Satyaki, after the fall of Bhurisravas and Jayadratha. Satyaki was without a ratha; so whose chariot does he mount? How did the guardians of the wheels of Arjuna's ratha, the two Panchala princes, fight?'

Sanjaya says, 'I will describe to you all that happens. Listen patiently, my lord, to the consequences of your own evil conduct. Before the battle, Krishna knew in his heart that Bhurisravas, who flew a banner with the insignia of a sacrificial stake, would vanquish the heroic Satyaki. Rajan, Krishna knows both the past and the future. It was for this that, the previous night, he summoned his sarathy Daruka, and said to him, "Keep my ratha ready tomorrow and wait until you hear me blow the rishabha svara on the Panchajanya."

Neither the Devas, nor the Gandharvas, nor the Yakshas, nor the Uragas, nor the Rakshasas, nor Manushyas can ever conquer the two

Krishnas. The Devas with the Pitamaha Brahma at their head, and also the Siddhas, know the incomparable prowess of these two. But listen now to the battle as it unfolds in grim reality, as if upon the edge of Yamaloka.

Seeing Satyaki without a ratha and facing Karna ready for battle, Krishna blows his conch long and loud in the rishabha note. Daruka hears what he has been waiting for, and comes flying to Krishna on his unearthly ratha with the golden standard. With Krishna's leave, Satyaki climbs into the deva ratha, driven by Daruka, which is like Surya or Agni in splendour. To that chariot are yoked the greatest of all - Saibya, Sugriva, Meghapushpa and Balahaka, all caparisoned in gold. These unearthly steeds fly anywhere at will, and now bearing Satyaki, they fly at Karna, while Yuyudhana looses a fresh torrent of shafts at the Sutaputra.

Yudhamanyu and Uttamaujas leave Dhananjaya's side and ride to help Satyaki. The duel between Karna and Satyaki is another that has hardly ever been seen on earth or in heaven, not between Devas, Gandharvas, Asuras, Uragas, or Rakshasas. Yet again, both great armies stop fighting to watch the stunning encounter; they are as awed by the superhuman skills of the two archers as they are by Daruka's wizardly chariotry, as he flies across Kurukshetra, his unearthly horses obedient to his very thought, in the most incredible manoeuvres.

The Devas, the Gandharvas and the Danavas in the sky watch the battle between Karna and Satyaki, never blinking.

The two maharathas fight one another, each for the cause of their friends. Karna, looking like a Deva now, and the brilliant Satyaki cover each other with scathing interminable volleys. Karna still has the brutal slaying of his friend Jalasandha, whom Satyaki despatched, before his eyes, and he fights the Vrishni hero in absolute rage.

Full of grief for all the Kuru maharathas that Satyaki has killed on this day, Karna glowers at Yuyudhana as if to burn him up with his eyes. The dense swarms of steaming arrows he unleashes at Sini's grandson never pause. Sinuous and powerful as two mighty tigers, the two Naravyaghras maul each other in fury.

Satyaki drills slender iron shafts into Karna's every limb, and then he fells Karna's charioteer from his ratha with a flat-headed shaft. He kills Karna's four white horses, smashes Karna's standard into a hundred pieces with a hundred arrows, and yet again Karna finds himself without a chariot in Duryodhana's sight.

All your warriors, O Rajan, are quickly dispirited. Then Karna's son Vrishasena, Salya of the Madras, and Aswatthaman surround Satyaki and a smoking fray ensues and one can see nothing anymore. When Satyaki deprives the heroic Karna of his ratha, cries of *Oh!* and *Alas!* arise from your troops. Satyaki continues to rake the already weakened Sutaputra, until Duryodhana dashes up and helps his precious friend into his chariot. Karna is distraught, hissing and sighing like a serpent now, ashamed when he thinks of how he boldly swore that he would make your son undisputed king of the world.

After he destroys Karna's ratha, the self-restrained Satyaki stops himself from killing either the Sutaputra or your sons led by Dusasana, O king, for he honours Arjuna's oath that he would kill Karna and Bhima's that he would kill all your princes. He only wrecks their chariots and wounds them sorely with his radiant archery, weakening but not killing them.

However, although all these maharathas led by Karna tried concertedly to slay the Vrishni hero, Yuyudhana shames them all. Using just one bow, he crushes Aswatthaman, Kritavarman and other maharathas, as well as hundreds of great Kshatriyas. He fights Yudhishtira Dharmaraja's cause and to attain to Swarga, and truly Parantapa Satyaki is no less than either of the two Krishnas in tejas. Always smiling, for he, the pure Kshatriya, delights in war, he puts all your troops to rout, O best of men! I say to you with conviction that, in this world, there are only three truly matchless archers—Krishna, Arjuna, and Satyaki. There is no fourth.'

Dhritarashtra says, 'Riding the invincible ratha of Krishna, with Daruka for charioteer, Satyaki, proud of the might of his arms and equal in battle to Krishna himself, destroys Karna's ratha. Did Satyaki ride any other chariot after his battle with Karna was over? I want to know this,

Sanjaya, O most gifted narrator. Truly, I believe Satyaki is endowed with enormous, superhuman prowess. Tell me everything, Sanjaya!'

Sanjaya says, 'Hear, O Rajan, what transpires on the dharmakshetra. Daruka's younger brother brings out another chariot for the battling Satyaki. It has shafts attached by chains of iron, it has gold in profusion and bands of silk; it is adorned with a thousand stars and festooned with bright banners; this ratha flies the figure of a great lion on its standard, and yoked to it are horses fleet as the wind and wearing trappings of gold; and the rumble of its wheels are like thunderheads sounding. Mounting the fresh chariot, Satyaki besieges your troops again, while Daruka goes to Krishna's side.

A new ratha is also fetched for Karna, to which are yoked pedigreed horses white as milk, caparisoned in gold. Its kaksha and standard are wrought from gold. Furnished with colourful banners and a profusion of weapons of every kind, this excellent ratha has a superb sarathy as well. Mounting that chariot, Karna also mounts an unrestrained assault on his enemies.

I have now told you all that you asked me. However, Rajan, listen once more to the extent of the horrible destruction that your evil plotting caused. Bhimasena has killed thirty-one of your sons. Led by Durmukha, they were all masters of weapons. Satyaki and Arjuna also have slain hundreds of great heroes and Bhimasena more than either of them, and so has Bhagadatta. Still, the carnage begun by your evil ways is far from over.'"

CANTO 144

Jayadratha-vadha Parva continued

"Dhritarashtra says, 'Tell me now what Bhima did, Sanjaya, at this stage of the war. Indeed, tell me everything!'

Sanjaya replies, 'After Bhimasena loses his ratha, Karna cuts him deep with his words like arrows, as Bhima stands helpless before him. Karna's acerbic words still burning him, Bhima says to Arjuna in some anger, "In your very hearing, Dhananjaya, Karna repeatedly mocked saying, 'Eunuch, fool, glutton, you are no warrior. Why have you come to fight, when you cannot bear the heat of battle? Take yourself where you belong, you overgrown child, to a kitchen or a dining table.'

I will kill any man who dares speak to me like that, Arjuna, and Karna said all this and more. You know the vows that we swore together in the Kuru sabha. Remember them now and let us fulfill both our oaths!"

Hearing this, Arjuna rides near Karna and tells him, "O false Karna, son of a Suta, you always brag and praise yourself. O evil one, listen to what I have to say to you. Heroes in battle meet with either victory or defeat, both of which are uncertain. It is no different even for Indra.

Your ratha smashed by Satyaki and standing in a daze, exposed before Yuyudhana, you were on the point of death. But Satyaki remembered that I have sworn to kill you and to honour my oath and he spared your life.

It is true that you deprived my brother Bhimasena of his ratha in fair battle. But the manner in which you taunted and abused him then was a shameful sin. No man of dharma ever humiliates an enemy after vanquishing him in battle. Your heart and mind are small, Sutaputra, as is your wisdom, and that is why you boast so loudly and speak so vilely.

Then again, the abuse that you have heaped on my brother Bhima, who is a great Kshatriya warrior and devoted to dharma, is neither true nor acceptable. In plain sight of all the troops, of Krishna, and me, how many times Bhima defeated you in battle and left you stranded without a chariot. He never once abused you, Karna. Since you have spoken harshly to Vrikodara many times, and since you were one of the six who combined to kill Abhimanyu, while I was far away, I say to you, Sutaputra, that you will find the reward for your crimes this very day. It was to call death to you, evil one, coward, that you severed Abhimanyu's bow from behind. And for that, O you of small wit, I will kill you, along with all your followers, your forces and your beasts of war.

Finish everything that you still need to do in this world, because a great misfortune will soon overtake you. I will first kill your son Vrishasena before your eyes. Then, all the other kings that ride against me I will despatch to Yama. This I swear, laying my hand on this Gandiva. You are a fool, Karna, unwise and full of vanity. I tell you that Duryodhana will soon see you lying dead on this field as carrion for vultures and jackals, and that evil prince will lament bitterly."

When Arjuna swears to kill Karna's son, a great uproar arises among the maharathas. At that very moment, when pandemonium reigns all around, the sun enters the Asta mountain.

Krishna, in the van of army, embraces Arjuna who has fulfilled his vow, and says to him, "By great good fortune, O Jishnu, you have accomplished your great vow and Vriddhakshatra has also died along with his son. Had Kumara, the Deva Senapati himself, encountered the Dhartarashtra forces, I have no doubt that he would not have prevailed. Naravyaghra, I cannot think of a single warrior in the three worlds other than you who can fight this oceanic army.

So many great maharathas of untold prowess, some equal or even superior to you, are united under Duryodhana's command. Yet, clad in armour, they cannot face you in battle when you are roused. Your tejas and urjas are equal to those of Rudra or Yama himself. No one else could have shown the prowess and genius in war that you, by yourself and alone, have done today.

And so, Arjuna, will I truly applaud and embrace you again after you kill the evil Karna and all his followers, yes, I will glorify you when you have vanquished this, your greatest, enemy."

Arjuna replies, "It is through your grace, O Madhava, that I have fulfilled my vow that even the gods might have found difficult to accomplish. And my victory is no matter of wonder for those who have you, O Krishna, for their Lord. Through your grace, Yudhishtira will regain the whole world. All this is because of your power, O Vrishni. This is your victory, O Lord! Our victory is in truth only yours; our fortune is in your care and we are your servants, O Madhusudana."

Krishna smiles slightly, and slowly drives the horses and, as they traverse the battlefield full of brutal sights, he points them out to Arjuna saying, "Having fought for victory or great fame so many heroic kings lie on the earth, struck by your arrows, their weapons and ornaments scattered, their horses, chariots and elephants mangled and their armour cloven, all of them having attained to the final sorrow. Some of them are still alive, in agony, and some dead. But look, Arjuna, even the dead still seem alive for their lustre and greatness.

Look at the field covered over with their golden-winged arrows, with their numberless other weapons, and with their dead animals. The earth is resplendent with coats of mail and necklaces of gems, with severed heads gleaming with earrings, and helmets and crowns shining with great jewels, and garlands of flowers, and kanthasutras, angadas, collars of gold and with diverse other beautiful ornaments. Strewn with anuskaras and quivers, with standards and banners, with upaskaras and adhishthanas, with shafts and crests of chariots, with broken wheels and beautiful akshas in profusion, with yokes and trappings of horses, with belts and bows and arrows, with elephants, their housings, with spiked maces and hooks of iron, with darts and short arrows, with spears and pikes, with kundas and clubs, with sataghnis and bhushandis, with scimitars and axes, with short and heavy clubs and mallets, with maces and kunapas, with whips decked with gold, with the bells and diverse other ornaments of elephants, and with rich robes, all loosened from the bodies of men and animals, the earth shines brilliantly, like the autumn sky strewn with planets and stars.

The lords of the earth, slain for the sake of earth, lie asleep on the earth clasping her like a wife. Like mountains flowing streams of liquid chalk through their caves and fissures, these elephants big as mountains, which look like Airavata himself, flow profuse streams of blood through the wounds in their bodies.

See, O Shura, where some of these vast creatures, struck by hundreds of arrows, lie spamming in death's last throes, their eyes full of pain and grief. Look where countless horses lie, their golden caparisons stained with scarlet.

Look, O Partha, at these empty chariots, which once resembled celestial vimanas of vapoury forms in the evening sky, now lying on the ground, with standards, banners, akshas and yokes cut into pieces, with broken shafts and crests, and with their warriors and charioteers slain and flung out of them. Foot-soldiers, also, holding bows and shields and slain in hundreds of thousands, lie everywhere, bathed in blood, clasping the earth with every limb and their long hair undone and smeared with dust.

Look, O Mahabaho, at all the warriors who lie unmoving, their bodies mutilated by your astras. Look at Kurukshetra scattered with yak-tails and fans, parasols, standards, steeds, chariots and elephants with diverse kinds of rich blankets, and the cut away reins of horses, and exquisite garments and the costly varuthas of the rathas. The field appears as if it is spread over with embroidered tapestry.

Many warriors fallen from the backs of elephants look like lions struck down by thunder and fallen from mountaintops. Lying among their horses and their bows, horsemen and foot-soldiers welter in blood. Ah, look how fearful this earth is to gaze upon, covered over with multitudes of slain elephants, horses, maharathas, and mired with blood, fat, and rotten flesh, on which wild dogs and wolves and pisachas and diverse fell wanderers of the night feed and around which they dance in sinister glee!

Only you, O Arjuna, or Indra himself, could have accomplished such a feat and fetched such carnage."

Thus showing the Kiritin the grisly field of devastation, Krishna raises his Panchajanya and blows triumphal thunder on it and the joyful soldiers of the Pandava army respond by blowing their conches too. And Janardana drives his chariot swiftly towards Yudhishtira Ajatasatru and brings him news of the killing of Jayadratha.'"

CANTO 145

JAYADRATHA-VADHA PARVA CONTINUED

"Sanjaya says, 'After Arjuna kills Jayadratha, Krishna drives to Yudhishtira, worships him with a glad heart and says, "Through good fortune, Rajan, your prosperity increases and you have killed your enemy. By great good luck, your brother has fulfilled his vow."

Yudhishtira, the subjugator of hostile towns, is overjoyed and climbs down from his ratha! His eyes fill with tears of joy and he embraces the two Krishnas and then, wiping his bright and lotus-like face, he says to Kesava and Arjuna, "Mighty Maharathas, it is destiny that I see both of you now after you have accomplished your mission. It is indeed great good fortune that you have killed the sinner Jayadratha.

You Krishnas have filled me with untellable joy, and plunged our enemies into an ocean of grief. You are the sovereign Lord of all the worlds, Krishna, O Madhusudana! In the three worlds, there is nothing that those who have you for their lord and master cannot achieve.

Through your grace, O Govinda, we will conquer our enemies, as Indra did the Danavas in olden times. Be it the conquest of the world, or be it the conquest of the three worlds, everything is assured for those with whom you are pleased. They can be stained by no sin, nor can they meet with defeat in battle, O Lord of all the gods!

It is through your grace, Hrishikesa, that Indra became the king of the Devas. It is through your benevolence that he won the sovereignty of the three worlds on the field of battle. It is through your kindness, O Devadeva, that he gained immortality and enjoys the eternal regions of bliss. Having slain thousands of Daityas with powers acquired by your grace did Indra win lordship over the Devas.

It is through your grace, Hrishikesa, that the mobile and immobile universe, without swerving from its ordained course, is engaged in prayers and homa. In the beginning, this universe, enveloped in darkness, was one vast expanse of water, the Ekarnava. Through your grace, O Mahabaho, the universe became manifest! You are the Creator of all the worlds, you are the Supreme Soul, and you are immutable.

Those who see you, O Hrishikesa, are never mystified. You are the Supreme God, you are the God of the gods, and you are Ananta. Those who seek refuge with you, O Lord of the Devas, are never lost. Without beginning and without death, you are Divine; you are the Creator of all the brahmandas, and Absolute. Those who are devoted to you, O Hrishikesa, always tide over every difficulty. You are Supreme, the Ancient One, the Divine Being, and that which is the Highest of the high. He who attains your Supreme Self obtains the highest felicity.

You are sung in the four Vedas and the four Vedas sing of you. By seeking your protection, O noblest one, I will enjoy unrivalled prosperity. You are the Supreme God, you are the God of the highest gods, you are the lord of winged creatures, and the lord of all humans. You are the Supreme Lord of everything. I bow to you, O Best of beings!

You are the Lord, the Lord of lords, O Omnipotent One! Prosperity to you, O Madhava! O you of the louts eyes, O Universal Soul, You are the origin of all things.

He, who is a friend of Arjuna or is devoted to Arjuna's welfare, finds you who are the Guru of Dhananjaya and attain ultimate bliss."

Thus addressed by him, Kesava and Arjuna cheerfully say to Yudhishtira, "The fire of your wrath has consumed the sinful Jayadratha, O puissant one. Although the Dhartarashtra host is vast and swells in pride, yet it daily faces death and diminution; the Kaurava host is being annihilated. It is because of your wrath that the Kauravas are being destroyed. Having angered you, most gentle and patient soul, who can kill with just your gaze, the evil Duryodhana with all his friends and kinsmen will have to lay down his life in battle. Already slain because of your ire, and struck down by the gods themselves, the invincible Bhishma, Pitamaha of the Kurus, now lies on a bed of arrows.

O Parantapa, victory in battle is impossible, and death waits for those who have you for their enemy. Kingdom, life, dear ones, children, and all kinds of bliss will soon be lost by him with whom you are angry. I look upon the Kauravas as having already lost their sons and kinsmen, when you, who observe, why, embody Rajadharma, are wroth with them."

Then Bhima, O king, and Satyaki, both lacerated and bleeding by arrows past count, come and pay their salutations to Yudhishtira. Those two mighty bowmen then sit on the ground surrounded by the Panchalas. Seeing the two heroes brimming with joy and waiting with folded hands, Yudhishtira embraces them both and cries, "It is through good fortune that I see you both before me, O Shuras, see you after you have escaped with your lives from the raging sea of enemy legions, the sea in which Drona is an invincible crocodile and Kritavarman, the son of Hridika, a ravening shark. It is destiny that you two have vanquished all the greatest kings of the earth.

It is by good fortune that I see both of you victorious in battle. It is by good fortune that you have defeated Drona as well as the mighty Kritavarman. It is by providence that you have defeated Karna in battle with your barbed shafts. It is by good fortune that Salya was forced away from the field by you both, O you bulls among men. By good fortune, I see you both returned from battle safe, you who are the greatest of all maharathas and masters of war!

It is my good fortune that I see you heroes again, who have forded that sea of enemy troops at my command, you who went into battle to honour me! You are true and pure Kshatriya heroes who revel in battle. You are dear to me like my own life. Ah, it is through great good fortune that I see you both again alive!'

Having said this, Yudhishtira embraces Satyaki and Bhima, the Naravyaghras, again, and tears of joy flow down his noble face. Then, the entire Pandava army is full of good cheer and a tide of joy surges through all the warriors. All of them are once more determined to give battle and win this war to end all wars.'"

CANTO 146

JAYADRATHA-VADHA PARVA CONTINUED

"Sanjaya says, 'Upon the fall, O Rajan, of Jayadratha, your son Duryodhana, his face bedewed with tears, breathing hot sighs like a snake whose fangs have been drawn, this offender against the whole world, experiences bitter sorrow. Seeing the terrible slaughter of his troops that Arjuna, Bhimasena and Satyaki have wrought, he becomes pale and dejected. He begins to believe that no warrior on earth can compare with Arjuna.

"Neither Drona, Karna, Aswatthaman, nor Kripa can stand up to Arjuna when he is provoked," Duryodhana says to himself, "After defeating all the maharathas of my army, Arjuna has kept his vow and killed Jayadratha. No one can resist him and the Pandavas have almost exterminated my once vast army. Ah, no one can protect my army, no, not even Purandara himself. He, upon whom I relied most in this war, Karna, has been defeated and Jayadratha slain. I believed so much in Karna's prowess that I thought of even Krishna, who came to me to sue for peace, as being but a straw in gale; and now, Karna has been vanquished in battle."

Grieving thus, his dark and powerful spirit all but broken, Duryodhana comes to see Drona. He informs the Acharya of the immense slaughtering of the Kurus, the victory of his enemies, and the grim catastrophe that faces the Dhartarashtras.

Duryodhana says fervidly, "Look, Acharya, at this vast carnage of kings. Setting the invincible Bhishma at our head, I came to war. Having cut the Pitamaha down, Sikhandin, his aspirations fulfilled, leads his troops, surrounded by all the Panchalas and seeking another triumph. Another disciple of yours, the invincible Savyasachin, decimated seven akshauhinis of troops and has despatched Jayadratha to Yama. How, Acharya, will I ever free myself of the debt that I owe those allies of mine who, fighting this war for my sake, have lost their lives? Ah, those lords of the earth now lie prone and lifeless upon the earth, having lost their kingdoms, possessions and prosperity.

Alas, it is true that I am a coward! Having caused such a massacre of my friends, I dare not believe that I can purify myself with even a hundred Aswamedha yagnas. I am covetous, sinful and a transgressor of dharma. Because of my greed and envy, and nothing else, these lords of the earth, in their quest for victory, have gone to Yama's halls. Why, in presence of all these kings, does the kindly Earth not yield me a hole through which I can sink, for I am the greatest sinner ever and the sole fomenter of this horrible war between cousins? Alas, what will the Pitamaha of bloodshot eyes, the invincible shura who has conquered the other world, say to me in the midst of all the great kings when he meets me?

There lies the mighty bowman Jalasandha, killed by Satyaki. How proudly he came to fight, ready to lay his life down for me. Looking at the dead king Kambojas, as well as Alambusha and so many, many other allies of mine, all slain, what reason can I have to continue living? Ah, all of them died savage deaths, even as they put forth their great valour to vanquish my enemies.

Acharya, today I will give my all in battle to free myself from the debt that I owe them and then gratify then with oblations of water by going to the Yamuna. O greatest of warriors, I tell you truly and swear by all the punya I have ever done, by the prowess and skill that I possess, and on my sons' heads, that I will kill all the Panchalas along with the Pandavas, and find peace of mind, or, killed by them in battle I will go to the realms where my friends and allies have gone while fighting my cause during this war.

Seeing that we are not able to protect them, our allies that still live no longer wish to stand by us, Mahabaho, and they now regard the Pandavas as being preferable to us. And you, Acharya, have fetched doom upon us by showing your favourite sishya Arjuna softness and leniency in battle. This is why all these heroes, who endeavoured to secure victory for us, have been slain. It seems that only Karna now truly wishes us victory. A man of weak understanding, who without properly examining another, accepts him for a friend, and enlists him in matters that require true friends for their achievement, is certain to suffer disappointment. You, upon whom I so relied, have brought dreadful disappointment and defeat to me, O Drona.

I am inordinately covetous, sinful, crooked, and avaricious! Alas, Dussala's husband Jayadratha has been killed, and Somadatta's son Bhurisravas of great tejas, and the Abhishahas, the Surasenas, the Sibis, and the Vasatis. And I myself mean to leave this world today and join those bulls among men, whom Arjuna slaughtered while they fought for me. With them gone, I have no wish to live on. O Acharya of the sons of Pandu, let me have your leave to die fighting.'""

CANTO 147

JAYADRATHA-VADHA PARVA CONTINUED

"Dhritarashtra says, 'After Savyasachin kills the king of the Sindhus, after the death of Bhurisravas, what was the state of mind of our army? After Duryodhana passionately addressed Drona in the midst of the Kurus, what did the Acharya say to him? Tell me, Sanjaya!'

Sanjaya says, 'Loud wails arise among your troops, O Bhaarata, after the killing of Bhurisravas and Jayadratha. Now all of them show scant regard for the command and policy of Duryodhana, based on which hundreds of great maharathas have died.

As for Drona, he listens to what your son says and is full of grief. Reflecting for a short while, Rajan, he says in anguish, "Duryodhana, why do you pierce me so with your wordy shafts? I have already told you that no one can defeat Arjuna in battle. Protected by Kiritin, Sikhandin cut Bhishma down. This feat by itself, O Kuruttama, should have convinced you of the invincible prowess of Arjuna. For myself, I was certain on that day, seeing Bhishma, whom the Devas and the Danavas could not vanquish, felled, that this Bharata army is doomed. After the fall of

Bhishma, whom we all looked upon as the greatest Kshatriya in the three worlds, whom else can we rely upon now?

The loaded dice that Sakuni spun in the Kuru sabha were not dice but keen arrows that would claim countless lives. The same arrows, unleashed now by Jaya, are now decimating us. Though Vidura said this even then, you did not understand him or chose not to. With tears in his eyes, he begged you to make peace with the Pandavas, but you did not listen to him. The calamity that he foretold has come to pass.

This horrible carnage, Duryodhana, is the result of your defiance of Vidura's sage counsel. The foolish man who disregards the precious advice of true and trusted friends, and follows only his own lusts, falls swiftly into deep trouble and distress. O son of Gandhari, you had Draupadi dragged into the Kuru court before us all, while she was in her period and wore but a single cloth. How did you dare do this to one as pure as her, she who owns every virtue, she who was born from the sacred fire?

Yet, know Duryodhana that all this is as nothing, for in the next world you will be visited with retribution before which this carnage will seem pale. Beating the Pandavas at dice by deceit, you sent them into the forest, wearing deerskins. Which other Brahmana in this world, other then I, would seek to harm the sons of Pandu, Kshatriyas of dharma, who are like my own sons. In the Kuru sabha, with your father Dhritarashtra's approval, you, with Sakuni for your collaborator, provoked the ire of the Pandavas. Together with Dusasana, Karna then fanned that wrath. Disdaining Vidura's wisdom, you repeatedly stoked that fire yourself.

With great determination and resolve, all of you surrounded Arjuna, to save Jayadratha. Why, then, have you all been vanquished and why has Jayadratha been killed? Why, when you, Karna, Kripa, Salya and Aswatthaman are alive, O Kauravya, has the king of the Sindhus been killed? All the mighty kings who fight this war for you spared no effort to save his life; how was Jayadratha beheaded in their very midst? Relying on me, Jayadratha thought he would be saved from Arjuna. He did not find the rescue he expected.

Suyodhana, I too do not see any safety for myself. Until I succeed in killing the Panchalas with Sikhandin, I always feel like one sinking deeper in the mire that is the fire prince Dhrishtadyumna. Having failed to save Jayadratha's life, why do you pierce me with your words like arrows of fire, when you plainly see that I too burn with grief?

No more do you see Kurukshetra adorned with the golden standards of Bhishma, who knew no tiredness in battle, whom no warrior could face. How, then, can you have any hope for victory? When the king of the Sindhus and Bhurisravas have been slain in the very midst of so many mighty maharathas, do you still not see how this war must inevitably end?

Kripa, well nigh impossible to defeat, is still alive, Rajan! He did not follow Jayadratha out of this world, and I applaud him. When I saw Bhishma himself, whom not the Devas led by Indra, could vanquish in battle, felled before your very eyes, I thought that the Earth had abandoned you.

Look where the troops of the Pandavas and the Srinjayas, united, come rushing at me. To bring you victory, I swear that I will not remove my armour until I have killed all the Panchalas. Rajan, go and tell my son Aswatthaman that even at the risk of his life he must attack the Somakas without let.

Say to him and yourself follow what I tell you now: Observe all the teachings you have received from your father. Be firm in deeds of humility, in self-restraint, in satya and dharma. Observe dharma, artha, and kama, but, most of all, you must always follow the way of dharma. You must always gratify the Brahmanas with gifts. All of them deserve your worship. You must never do anything to hurt them. They are like flames. As for myself, I will break into the enemy army, O Parantapa, for a great battle, for you have pierced me with words sharper than arrows. If you can, Suyodhana, go and protect the troops. Both the Kurus and the Srinjayas are full of rage. They will fight even during the night."

Saying this to Duryodhana, Drona rides against the Pandavas. He, the Brahmana warrior, goes forth to eclipse the tejas of the Kshatriya like the sun dimming the light of the stars.'"

CANTO 148

JAYADRATHA-VADHA PARVA CONTINUED

"Sanjaya says, 'Duryodhana, a being of absolute rage now, sets his heart on battle: to kill or be slain. He says to Karna, "Look how the Kiritin son of Pandu, with only Krishna going with him, penetrated three vyuhas of Drona, formations that the Devas themselves could not pierce and, in the very sight of the illustrious Acharya and all our other maharathas, killed Jayadratha.

Look, Karna, at the countless great kings lying dead on the earth, killed by Arjuna, like a host of little creatures by a single great lion, despite Drona and I doing our utmost to stop Arjuna. The son of Indra has reduced my army to a small remnant of what it was. How could Arjuna have kept his impossible vow unless Drona himself allowed it? Ah, truly, Arjuna always was and still is exceedingly dear to our illustrious Acharya! And for this he allowed Arjuna into the great Sakata vyuha, without properly fighting him.

My friend, look at my misfortune! Having first assured Jayadratha of his protection, Drona let Arjuna into our army like a tiger into a calf-pen. If the Brahmana had allowed Jayadratha to return to his kingdom, as the Saindhava so dearly wanted to, this day's unimaginable carnage would never have occurred and our army would not have been reduced to a mere fraction of its great size. Ah, I was a fool to believe Drona when he swore to protect Jayadratha! I should have let Dussala's husband return to his kingdom. And for my foolishness, today so many of my brothers, led by mighty Chitrasena, have perished before our very eyes."

Karna says, "Do not blame the Acharya, for he is giving his all in battle, and without a care for his very life. If Arjuna broke into our army, no fault attaches to Drona. Arjuna is a great maharatha, and he is young compared to the Acharya; the Pandava is renowned for his speed. Armed with devastras and mounted on his ratha that flies the Hanuman banner, with the reins of his horses in the hands of Krishna, cased in impenetrable armour and wielding the celestial Gandiva, Arjuna bested Drona, who is old now. There is nothing to wonder at this and certainly nothing to blame Drona for. He has not betrayed you in any way, only that his age slows him and tires him quickly, and, most of all, Arjuna has Krishna for his sarathy!

For myself, I believe that whatever Fate had ordained will come to pass, for while Arjuna swept his way deep into our vyuhas and slew Jayadratha, Drona, for all his prowess, could not vanquish the Pandavas and take Yudhishtira captive. Despite all our concerted efforts, despite all of us giving our all in battle, Arjuna yet succeeded in killing Jayadratha and fulfilling his impossible vow. Surely, this could only have happened because Fate did not smile on us.

Duryodhana, the truth is that we have always tried to harm the Pandavas, resorting to both deceit and strength. Whatever a man crossed by Fate attempts is undone by Fate, however the man himself may strive to achieve his end. Whatever a persevering man should do, he must do fearlessly, without caring for the outcome of his exertions. Success and failure depend on destiny!

We have wronged the sons of Pandu. We first tried to poison them, and then immolate them in the house of lac. Finally, we vanquished them deceitfully at the game of dice; we humiliated them and banished them to the forest. Fate seemed to be with us at that time and now seems to have turned against us. It appears, Duryodhana, that now you must reverse the present course of fate as well as fight the Pandavas. Fight resolutely, fight with all your might and valour and only then can you still possibly prevail. Fight without doubt and fear and the side which excels the other will triumph.

The Pandavas have used no superior intelligence or strategy in this war, and neither have your methods been inferior or wanting. I say to you again that inscrutable Fate alone decides the outcome of all karma, wise or unwise. Fate, ever intent on its own purposes, is awake when all else sleeps. Vast was your army, and your warriors numberless, when the battle began. Though their host was smaller, it would seem that their warriors were more effective in battle and we find ourselves terribly reduced. I fear it is the work of Fate that has frustrated our efforts."

Rajan, while Karna and Duryodhana thus confer, the Pandava akshauhini comes into view, eager for fight. Another fevered battle breaks out between your legions and theirs, with chariots, horsemen and elephants flying at each other.

Remember, O Dhritarashtra, that your evil policy towards the Pandavas is the single root and cause of all this bloodshed!'"

CANTO 149

GHATOTKACHA-VADHA PARVA

"Sanjaya says, 'Your elephant force, Rajan, burgeoning with might, fights everywhere, prevailing over the Pandava forces. Determined either to find the next world or to triumph, the Panchalas and the Kauravas fight for admission into the swelling domains of Yama. Fearless warriors face valiant rivals, drawing geysers of blood with arrows, spears and darts and despatch one another to Yama's abode in thick streams. Dreadful and savage is the battle between the maharathas who cause blood to flow furiously across Kurukshetra.

Infuriated elephants gore each another deep with great curved tusks. Horsemen, seeking glory, cut one another down in the terrific melee with lances, arrows and battle-axes. Foot-soldiers too, in hundreds, repeatedly attack one another with resolute ferocity! So great is the bedlam, that the Panchalas and the Kurus can only be distinguished from the tribal, family and personal names they shout as battle cries. Horrible and relentless is the carnage everywhere, and darkness mantles the filed of death for by now the sun has set. Deranged with wrath at the slaying of Jayadratha, and more than willing to lay down his life, Duryodhana charges straight into the midst of the Pandavas. Filling the earth with the rumble of his chariot-wheels and making Bhumi tremble, your son and his forces attack the Pandava host headlong and terrific is the battle between the two forces and blood runs in frothing streams on the ground.

Like the meridian sun that burns everything with his rays at midday, the blazing Suyodhana scathes the enemy forces with relentless flights of arrows so that the Pandavas cannot even look at him. Indeed, so terribly and gloriously does he fight, that the sons of Pandu and their legions despair of defeating the Kauravas and, slaughtered by your lustrous son, his tides of gold-winged arrowheads ablaze, the Panchalas flee in all directions.

Duryodhana mows down the Pandava legions as he pleases, heads and severed arms falling like rain onto the gory ground. Truly, Rajan, none among the Pandavas has achieved the feats that Duryodhana now does on the darkling field. He ravages the enemy like great Surya and Vayu wilting a pool of lotuses with their searing rays and arid winds.

He strikes the Panchalas and Bhimasena with ten shafts, each of the sons of Madri with three, Virata and Drupada each with six, Sikhandin with a hundred, Dhrishtadyumna with seventy, Yudhishtira with seven, Satwata with five, each of the five sons of Draupadi with three, Ghatotkacha also with many barbs, and the Kaikeyas and the Chedis with innumerable keen arrows, and then roars like a mythic lion from time out of mind. Annihilating hundreds of other warriors as well as elephants and horses with his fierce shafts, he is like Rudra devouring the creatures at the pralaya.

Then Yudhishtira rives his bow in three with two immaculate broad-headed arrows. He strikes Duryodhana with ten potent shafts loosed in an unbroken line that pass clean through Duryodhana's limbs and pierce the earth behind him. The Pandava troops surround Yudhishtira, as the Devas did Purandara when he killed Vritra.

Another mighty shaft from Yudhishtira fells Suyodhana onto his knees in his great ratha. Thereupon, the Panchala troops roar in jubilation, "Duryodhana is slain!"

Now we hear a great and wild buzzing of countless arrows, like many swarms of bees, O Bhaarata, and Drona appears, holding up the enemy with a firestorm of arrows that light up the early night. Meanwhile, Duryodhana recovers, seizes up a fresh bow and charges Yudhishtira, roaring, "Stop and fight!" Sensing victory, the Panchalas charge Drona, who, unruffled, implacable, has rushed to the rescue of your son and now beats back the Panchalas and decimates their troops spraying blood copiously everywhere. Yet another pitched and lethal battle erupts and rills of blood flow glimmering in the soft and dreadful dark.'"

CANTO 150

GHATOTKACHA-VADHA PARVA CONTINUED

"Dhritarashtra says, 'When the mighty Drona breaks through the Pandava ranks and rides his ratha all over the battlefield, how do the Pandavas stop him? Who protects the right wheel and who the left wheel of his chariot as he slaughters the enemy? Who are the brave warriors who follow him and protect his back? Who are those who confront the maharatha? When that the greatest of all warriors, dancing in his chariot scythes his way into the Pandava host, his enemies must feel an unseasonable cold in their very bones. They must tremble like cattle exposed to wintry blasts. How does the bull among rathikas, who consumes all the Panchala troops like a raging conflagration, meet his death?'

Sanjaya says, "After killing Jayadratha at the twilight hour, Arjuna meets Yudhishtira and Satyaki, and then rides at Drona, as do Yudhishtira and Bhimasena, each with an akshauhini of troops. The intelligent Nakula, the invincible Sahadeva, and Dhrishtadyumna, with their divisions, Virata, and the king of the Salwas with a large force, also advance against Drona. Dhrishtadyumna's father, king Drupada, leads the Panchalas against the Acharya as do the sons of Draupadi and the Rakshasa Ghatotkacha with his feral army. The Prabhadraka–Panchalas, too, six thousand strong and all great fighters led by Sikhandin, advance against Drona. Other leading Kshatriyas and maharathas among the Pandavas unite and take the field against Drona.

As these heroic warriors, O Bharatarishabha, fly into battle, the night by now is pitch dark, increasing the terrors of the timid. During this hour of darkness, Rajan, numberless warriors, elephants, horses and foot-soldiers die and jackals howling all around create great fear with their blazing mouths and predatory owls with lamp like eyes perch on the standards of the Kauravas and hoot abysmally, foretelling further murdering.

A grim and resounding uproar arises everywhere from the troops, mingling with the loud beating of drums and cymbals clashing, deep grunts of elephants, neighing of horses, and stamping of horses' hooves and a truly dreadful battle ensues between Drona and all the Srinjayas. The world is enveloped in utter darkness; the sky is obscured by the dust raised by the combatants and nothing can be seen. The blood of men, horses and elephants flow freely together with palls of dust and disappears into the thirsty earth and all of us are overwhelmed by dejection and panic.

During this grimmest night, we hear weapons clashing, which sound like a burning forest of bamboos upon a mountain. With the sounds of drums like mridangas, anakas, vallakis and patahas, with the shouting and neighing, horrific pandemonium rules the dark. No one can tell friend from foe and madness possesses all in the night. The showers of blood everywhere quickly settle the dust arisen, O Bharatarishabha, and the golden coats of mail and the bright ornaments of the warriors glint some light through the gloom.

When the blood-drenched dust settles, the air clears and the Bharata host adorned with gems and gold and wielding spears and standards looks like the sky strewn with dim twinkling stars. Kurukshetra resounds with the howls of jackals, the cawing of crows, the grunts of elephants, and the shouts, roars and screams of warriors. All these sounds mingle into a hair-raising din and fill all the points of the compass like the report of Indra's thunder.

At dead of night, the Bharata host is illumined by the angadas, earrings, cuirasses, and the other weapons of the fighting men. The elephants and chariots, adorned with gold, look like clouds charged with lightning. Swords, arrows, maces, scimitars, clubs, lances and axes, as they fall, are dazzling flashes of fire. Duryodhana is the gust of wind that is the precursor of the two tempestuous armies. Chariots and elephants are its dry clouds and the loud noise of drums and other instruments form the peals of its thunder and the bright standards and bows its lightning flashes.

Drona and the Pandavas are its rainclouds, while swords, darts and maces are its thunder, arrows are its downpour, and ceaseless flights of every other kind of weapon are its blasting winds. Hot are these deadly storms that blow, or agonisingly cold, as they claim lives past all count. There is nothing that can protect the warriors from death's night gale. Brave men who still lust after battle enter into the frightful fray on this dread night that echoes with horrifying sounds, which sharpen the fears of the timid and swell the joy of heroes.

As the war at night swells, the Pandus and the Srinjayas unite and attack Drona. However, Rajan, all who advance against the illustrious Drona are either forced to turn back or despatched to the halls of Yama. Indeed, on this appalling night, Drona by himself cuts down thousands of elephants, tens of thousands of chariots, and millions of foot-soldiers and horses.'"

CANTO 151

GHATOTKACHA-VADHA PARVA CONTINUED

"Dhritarashtra asks, 'As the invincible Drona Mahatejasvin, his wrath stirred by Jayadratha's death, wreaks havoc upon the Srinjayas, what do my sons and the rest of you feel? After the death of Jayadratha and of the great Bhurisravas, and after the Acharya says what he did to my recalcitrant Duryodhana, when that maharatha Brahmana breaks viciously on the Panchalas by night, scattering them, what does Arjuna do? What does Duryodhana think that he should do now? Who follows the boon-giving hero, the foremost of Brahmana warriors, and stands behind him while he fights so dreadfully, like all the spirits of darkness embodied, and who fights in his van? Ah, Suta, as you speak I can feel upon my very skin the fear and devastation that Drona brings to the Pandava host; I feel them tremble like cows under a wintry sky.

After he breaks into the midst of the Panchala forces, how does this Parantapa, the Naravyaghra, meet with his death? When on that night all the troops unite and all the great Pandava maharathas combine and Drona still rules the dark disdainfully, imperiously, which of our best warriors stand and face him?

You also say that my troops are either being slain or huddle together, and that my maharathas have lost their chariots having had them shattered by the sons of Pandu. While the Pandavas fetch terror and death to our forces, how do they withstand those shuras in the gruesome dark? You say that the Pandavas are heartened and full of hope for victory, while my troops are dejected and panic-stricken. How, O Sanjaya, do you perceive this distinction between the Kurus and the advancing Parthas? Tell me all, old friend, and in every detail.'

Sanjaya says, 'As the red and black night deepens, Rajan, the Pandavas and the Somakas all attack Drona. As if he sees through the dark as clearly as by daylight, Drona kills all the Kaikeyas and the sons of Dhrishtadyumna, as well as many other maharathas. At this, king Sibi, master archer, challenges the heroic son of Bharadwaja, and seeing this great hero riding at him, maharatha Drona strikes him with ten thick iron barbs. Sibi drills Drona with thirty arrows, fitted with kanka feathers; smiling fiercely, he fells Drona's charioteer with a broad-headed shaft. Drona kills the illustrious Sibi's horses and his charioteer and, quicker than it takes to tell, hacks off Sibi's head, with its crown and helmet.

Duryodhana sends a charioteer out to Drona and as soon as this sarathy takes up the Brahmana's reins, the Acharya resumes his savage decimation of his enemies.

Full of rage at Bhima having slain his father, the Kalinga king, supported by his troops, attacks Bhimasena. He first strikes Bhima with five arrows and again with seven more; rakes Bhima's sarathy Visoka with three perfect shafts and cuts a wedge from his proud standard with another. Roaring, Vrikodara leaps off his chariot straight onto his adversary's ratha, kills the Kalinga with his bare hands, tears him limb from limb, and strews black Kurukshetra with the pieces of his body!

Karna, the brother of the slain prince and others cannot bear to watch the brutal deed and looses narachas like venomous serpents at the giant Pandava. Jumping down from Kalinga's ratha, Bhima, covered in gore, runs to the chariot of Dhruva, the brother of the king whom he has just dismembered, and strikes that Kalinga prince a single blow with his fist that shatters his royal head like a melon and Dhruva dies.

Bhimasena, now roaring like a king lion in great fury, runs to the chariot of Jayarata, and dragging Jayarata down onto the ground with his left hand, kills him with a slap of his right, which blasts his head off his neck and inundates Bhima with his blood as well. All this he does before Karna's eyes and Karna casts a golden spear like a gash of lightning at him. But, smiling hideously, the Pandava seizes the golden lance and hurls it back at Karna! In the very nick of time, Sakuni divides that lance before it can reach Karna.

Having killed these three Kalingas, Bhima returns to his own chariot in some satisfaction, dripping scarlet, and charges your troops again, mowing them down before him like Yama himself enraged. Your sons steel themselves to stand firm against the advent of the horrible apparition and cover the hulking Pandava with ceaseless showers of arrows.

Grinning fiendishly, Bhima unleashes a gust of arrows at Durmada's charioteer and horses, sending them in a wink to Yama. Durmada quickly mounts Dushkarna's chariot and together they charge Bhima, even like Varuna and Surya rushing against Taraka, that best of Daityas. They pierce Bhima with a hundred arrows. However, in the very sight of Karna, Aswatthaman, Duryodhana, Kripa, Somadatta and Balhika, Bhima stamps his great foot with such violence that the wheels of Dushkarna's ratha sink into the earth. In a flash, Bhima is upon them, striking them wildly with inexorable blows of his prodigious fists, beating both into a pulp of blood, bone and flesh so they are a single mangled corpse. Horrified wails arise from your watching troops.

Their kings look at Bhima and say, "That is Rudra who fights from Bhima's body. This is Rudra come among the Dhartarashtras." And deranged by the titan's awful ferocity, they all flee in all directions whipping their horses to their greatest speed. Indeed, no two of them can be seen fleeing together such is their absolute panic in the hellish night.

Many kings applaud Vrikodara when he brings bloody havoc to your army in the night. His eyes as beautiful as full-blown lotuses, he goes to

Yudhishtira and pays his respects to his brother. Nakula and Sahadeva, Drupada, Virata, the Kaikeyas, and Yudhishtira are overjoyed and honour Vrikodara just as the Devas did Mahadeva after he had killed Andhaka.

Then your sons, all equal to the sons of Varuna, and fulminant with wrath, ride with the awesome Drona and a large force of chariots, foot-soldiers, and elephants, and they surround Bhima, intent on putting an end to him. On this terrible night, Rajan, when everything is enveloped in darkness as if by a black thunderhead, another dreadful battle erupts between those illustrious warriors, an unbridled contention that pleases the ravening hearts of wolves, crows and vultures.'"

CANTO 152

GHATOTKACHA-VADHA PARVA CONTINUED

"Sanjaya says, 'After Satyaki kills his son Bhurisravas, while he sat in praya, an outraged Somadatta says to Yuyudhana, "Why, O Satwata, have you abandoned the Kshatriya dharma that the great Gods ordained and taken to the ways of base bandits? Why would one who observes Kshatriya dharma and possesses wisdom strike a man who turns his back on battle, or one who has become helpless, or one who has laid down his weapons, or one who begs for quarter? Two among the Vrishnis are reputed to be the best of great maharathas —Pradyumna of mighty tejas and you, Satyaki! Why then did you act so cruelly and sinfully towards one who sat on praya and who had, besides, his arm hewn off by Partha?

Now reap the fruit of what you did to my son, sinner! For I mean to cut your head off with a winged and powerful astra. I swear by my two sons who are dear to me and by all my deeds of punya, that if I do not kill you before this night passes, you who are so proud of your heroism, with your sons and younger brothers, unless Pritha's son Arjuna protects you, then let me sink into terrible hell, O wretch of the Vrishnis!"

Saying this, and demented with grief, the mighty Somadatta blows his conch and gives a leonine roar. Satyaki, with eyes like lotus-petals and teeth like a lion's, says angrily to Somadatta, "O you of Kuru's race, whether fighting you, or any other, no trace of fear enters my heart. Even if you fight me protected by all your troops, I will have no complaint! I always observe Kshatriya dharma and you cannot frighten me with brave, brash words or with insults. If you want to fight me today, strike me with arrows and I will do the same.

Your son, the maharatha Bhurisravas, Rajan, I have slain; and Sala, and Vrishasena, I have vanquished. And I will kill you as well today with all your sons and kinsmen. Fight with resolve for you, Kaurava, are endowed with great strength. Yet Somadatta, you are already dead for you fight against mahatejasvin Yudhishtira Dharmaraja, of the drum banner, in whom there is always charity, self-restraint, purity of heart, compassion, modesty, intelligence, forgiveness, and all else that is indestructible. You will die along with Karna and Subala's son Sakuni. I swear by Krishna's feet and by all my punya that I will kill you and your sons. You will save yourself only if you flee from battle.

After addressing each other thus, their eyes red with fury, the two great Kshatriyas begin to fight with arrows. Then with a thousand rathas and ten thousand horsemen, Duryodhana casts a defensive circle around Somadatta, as does Sakuni armed with every kind of astra and supported by his sons, grandsons and brothers: why, a power to equal Indra's. Your brother-in-law, Rajan, young in years and his body hard as the Vajra, and canny and wise, has a hundred thousand brave horsemen with him with which force he defends Somadatta. Protected by these powerful ones, Somadatta shrouds Satyaki with clouds of arrows.

Seeing Satyaki so besieged, Dhrishtadyumna rushes up to protect him with a large force, and the two vast legions collide with a sound like that of many oceans lashed into fury by tearing hurricanes. Somadatta pierces Satyaki with nine arrows; Yuyudhana strikes him back also with nine shafts of such power that Somadatta staggers and sits down abruptly in his chariot, fainted. His sarathy whisks him away from the battle. Drona sees this and arrives swiftly to face the Yadu hero.

Seeing the Acharya attack him, many Pandava warriors led by Yudhishtira come to Satyaki's rescue. Then commences a battle between Drona and the Pandavas, like that between Bali and the Devas for the sovereignty of the three worlds. Drona covers the Pandava host with a barrage of arrows and sharply wounds Yudhishtira. He strikes Satyaki with ten barbed shafts, Dhrishtadyumna with twenty, Bhimasena with nine, Nakula with five, Sahadeva with eight, Sikhandin with a hundred, and each of the five sons of Draupadi with five. Next, he shoots Virata with eight arrows, Drupada with ten, Yudhamanyu with three and Uttamaujas with six. And piercing many other warriors, he rushes towards Yudhishtira whose troops run in all directions wailing.

Seeing Drona slaughter his forces, an incensed Arjuna quickly rides up to contain the Acharya. Now Yudhishtira's army rallies to support him and, again, the fierce battle between Drona and the Pandavas ensues. Drona, supported by your sons, begins to consume the Pandava host like a fire devouring a heap of cotton. He is radiant like the sun at dead of night, and like a blazing fire he looses his ray-like arrows without any moment's lapse from his bow, which is always drawn into a circle. Like the sun he scorches everything around him and consumes his enemies, and there is none in that army who can stop him.

Drona's shafts hack away the heads of all who venture to confront him before burrowing into the earth. Butchered by the illustrious Brahmana, the Pandava host once more turns tail and flees in the very presence of Arjuna. Seeing the rout that Drona perpetrates, at Arjuna's instance, Krishna guides his ratha harnessed to horses white as silver, or milk, or the kunda flower, or the moon, towards Drona's chariot. Bhimasena, too, seeing Phalguna ride at Drona, says to his charioteer, "Take me towards Drona's legion."

Visoka urges his horses down Arjuna's wake. Seeing the two brothers ride towards Drona's akshauhini, the greatest maharathas among the Panchalas, the Srinjayas, the Matsyas, the Chedis, the Karushas, the Kosalas, and the Kaikeyas, all follow them. Then, Rajan, a hair-raising battle breaks out as two mighty squadrons of rathas led by Arjuna and Bhima attack your host; the former on the right and the latter in the van. Seeing them dimly in the night lit by flaming astras, Dhrishtadyumna and Satyaki rush to support them.

The two hosts come together with a sound that is like the noise made by many seas lashed into fury by many tempests. Spying Satyaki in the battle, Aswatthaman, wroth at the killing of Bhurisravas, rides furiously against him. However, Bhimasena's Rakshasa son, the towering Ghatotkacha, riding on a massive chariot of black iron covered with bear-skins, which is twelve thousand cubits tall and wide, swoops down on Drona's son, coming like another night himself.

The eerie creatures yoked to it are neither horses nor elephants, but strange beasts big as elephants. On its lofty flagstaff is perched a prince of vultures with outstretched wings and outspread talons, with glaring, unwinking eyes, and shrieking dreadfully. The immense ratha is festooned with red flags, decked with the entrails of various animals and fitted with eight wheels. Riding on it, is a full akshauhini of the most ferile and macabre Rakshasas armed with spears, great clubs, rocks and trees, all surrounding their prince Ghatotkacha.

Seeing Ghatotkacha come to battle at night, the time when his kind are at their strongest, the enemy kings are struck with fear. He, the prince of Rakshasas, looms like some great black hill of terrible aspect, altogether frightful, with terrible fangs bared and his visage fierce, with arrowhead-like ears and high cheek-bones, stiff hair rising straight up from his head, glittering eyes, a sunken belly, a blazing mouth yawned wide as a chasm, and a crown on his head, darkly splendid, and waves of terror sweep your son's army even like the current of the Ganga agitated by the wind.

At his dreadful roars, elephants spray urine and dung and the kings tremble. Then the Rakshasas, whose day is night, cover the field with a shower of stones, with wheeling chakras, bhundis, darts, lances, spears, sataghnis and axes. Rajan, all your sons and Karna flee from that ghastly phalanx. Only Drona's proud son Aswatthaman, ever arrogant of his valour, stands fearlessly and quickly dispels the mayic illusions that Ghatotkacha creates.

His rage mounting, Ghatotkacha looses a tirade of arrows at Aswatthaman, which pass through his body, emerging dyed with his blood and streak into the earth like snakes into an anthill. However, an inspired Aswatthaman does not flinch but wounds Ghatotkacha deeply in all his marmas with ten arrows that lance agony through the great Rakshasas so he throws back his head and howls abysmally. Bhima's son takes up a chakra with a thousand spokes and an edge sharp as a razor, shining like the rising sun and adorned with diamonds, and hurls it at Aswatthaman. As the wheel flies spinning towards Drona's son, he shatters it into fragments with a tremendous volley and it falls onto the earth, like the cherished hopes of an ill-fated man.

Ghatotkacha swiftly mantles Aswatthaman with a torrent of thunderbolts, even like Rahu swallowing the Sun. Meanwhile, Ghatotkacha's splendid son Anjanaparvan, looking like a mass of shining antimony, checks the Brahmana warrior like Meru, king of the mountains, checking the coursing wind. Beleaguered and bleeding profusely from the recalescent arrows of Bhimasena's grandson, Aswatthaman looks like Sumeru receiving a lashing of rain from a mighty cloud.

By the moment battle fury mounts in Aswatthaman, who is no less than Rudra, of whom he is often called an amsa, or Upendra in prowess, and with one shaft he smashes Anjanaparvan's standard, with two more kills his two charioteers, and with three others, his trivenuka. Next, with a single astounding shaft he destroys his bow and slaughters his horses with four more thick barbs. His ratha rendered useless, Anjanaparvan picks up a sword engraved with golden stars but Aswatthaman breaks it in two in his hands with a single arrow.

Hidimba's grandson hefts a gold-chased mace and, whirling it over his head casts it like fell lightning at Aswatthama, who calmly smashes it into dust even as it flares at him. Now, Anjanaparvan flies up high into the air, snatching up some trees as he goes! Roaring like a thunderhead from above, he hurls the trees down over Aswatthaman like thunderbolts.

Adroitly avoiding these, Drona's son covers Anjanaparvan, the mayavi hanging in the sky, with an upward storm of shafts.

The Rakshasa descends again on to his gold-decked chariot, still looking like a high and beautiful hill of antimony running rillets of blood. And finally, Aswatthaman kills Anjanaparvan, cased in a heavy iron coat of mail, even like Mahadeva killed the Asura Andhaka in olden days. Seeing his mighty son slain, Ghatotkacha's roars erupt like peals of thunder across dark Kurukshetra; he rides up to Drona's son who now consumes the Pandava troops like a raging forest-fire, and cries: "Stop and fight me, O son of Drona! You will not escape me alive! I will kill you today like Agni's son did Krauncha."

Aswatthaman replies, "Go, child, and fight others, O you who have the power of a Deva. It is not proper, O son of Hidimbi, that I should have battle with one who is like a son to me. I have no grudge against you! Yet, when one's ire is roused, one may even kill one's own self."

Ghatotkacha, stricken at the death of his son, and his eyes red as copper, tells Aswatthaman, "Am I a coward, O son of Drona, that you try, like some vulgar fellow, to frighten me with this talk? Your words do not become you. I have been sired by Bhima in the celebrated Kuru vamsa and I am a son of the Pandavas, the heroes who never retreat from battle. I am also the king of the Rakshasas, equal to the ten-headed Ravana in prowess. Stop, Stop, O son of Drona! Brahmana, I will remove your very wish for battle and you will not escape me alive today!"

With that, Ghatotkacha, son of Bhima, attacks Aswatthaman like a lion a prince of elephants. He unleashes a gale of arrows of the measure of akshas at the Brahmana bull among maharathas. Aswatthaman consummately cuts down the furious shafts before they can reach him. The night sky is lit up bright with the astras the two loose at each other, and the sparks that flow down in cascades from the unearthly weapons locked together are like vast swarms of fireflies.

Ghatotkacha uses fluent sorcery, maya, against Drona's son, who, however, is particularly adept at dispelling such illusions and proud of his prowess at this. Ghatotkacha quickly makes himself invisible with maya and again suddenly assumes the towering form of a great mountain appeared out of nowhere, crowded with cliffs, trees and fountains from which spears, lances, swords and heavy clubs flow in a cataract. Aswatthaman remains unmoved and invokes the Vajrastra, imbued with the force of thunder, which blasts the mayic mountain into the stuff of dreams of which it is made.

Now the Rakshasa becomes a mass of deep blue clouds in the sky, decked with a rainbow, and begins to hurl down storms of stones and rocks on Drona's son. Then summoning the Vayavyastra, Aswatthaman blows away the sorcerous cloud mass. Seamlessly, he turns his attention back to the ground and the battlefield plunged in night and now using every devastra at his command, without the least restraint, covers all the points of the compass with his flaming arrows and, in moments, kills a hundred thousand maharathas.

He sees Ghatotkacha riding fearlessly at him, with bent bow and a large cohort of tigerish Rakshasas, some riding elephants, some on dark chariots and some on enormous horses, all followers of the son of Hidimbi, their faces fearsome, their heads and necks great and outlandish. These Rakshasas are from the strains of both Paulastyas and Yatudhanas, their powers equal to that of Indra, and they carry large and exotic weapons and wear diverse kinds of mail not seen among human warriors. So terrible are they and so obviously hard to quell, and swollen with rage, that Duryodhana looks at them and is plunged into swift dejection.

Aswatthaman tells him, "Stop, O Duryodhana! You need have no fear. Stand aside with your brothers and these lords of earth, powerful as Indra. I swear that I will kill all your enemies and you will not face defeat. Meanwhile, reassure your troops of this."

Duryodhana replies, "I do not find what you say surprising for your heart is great, O son of Drona, and your love for us greater."

Then he says to Sakuni, "Arjuna fights supported by a hundred thousand maharathas of untold valour. Ride against him, Matulan, with sixty thousand rathas, while Karna, Vrishasena, Kripa, Nila, Kritavarman, the sons of Purumitra, Dusasana, Nikumbha, Kundabhedin, Puranjaya,

Dridharatha, Hemakampana, Salya, Aruni, Indrasena, Sanjaya, Vijaya, Jaya, Purakrathin, Jayavarman, Sudarshana, and the Northerners will follow you with sixty thousand foot-soldiers. O my uncle, kill Bhima, the twins and Dharmaputra Yudhishtira, as Indra did the Asuras. You are my hope of victory. Drona's son has already grievously wounded them, mauling all their limbs; so now kill the sons of Kunti, O Sakuni, like Kartikeya slaying the Asuras."

Sakuni hears this and, without hesitating a moment, rides forth to have the Pandavas' lives, filling your son's heart with delight. Meanwhile, Rajan, a fearsome battle is underway between the Rakshasas and Aswatthaman, truly like that between Sakra and Prahlada in days of yore. A raging Ghatotkacha strikes Drona's son in the chest with ten powerful shafts, fierce as poison or fire, and Aswatthaman trembles on his ratha like a tall tree shaken by a storm. With a broad-headed arrow, Bhima's son severs the bright bow in Aswatthaman's hands.

Aswatthaman sweeps up another mighty bow and looses an occult, spreading torrent of shafts at all the Rakshasas. These shafts draw gushes of blood from the great Rakshasa legion and they are like a herd of elephants harried by a pride of lions. Drona's son overwhelms Ghatotkacha's Rakshasas with their horses, charioteers and elephants, and blazes forth like Agni consuming all the living at the end of the Yuga.

With astras of recondite fire, he incinerates a full akshauhini of Rakshasa troops, and looks as magnificent as the divine Maheswara in Swarga after the Lord torched the triad city of Tripura from the sky. Aswatthaman shines forth on dark Kurukshetra like the apocalypse of the pralaya after it has cremated every creature.

A wild Ghatotkacha roars at his vast Rakshasa force, "Slay the son of Drona!"

Their fangs curved and bright like diamonds, their faces great and frightful, their mouths agape with long tongues lolling out, and their eyes burning in the darkness like ominous slitted flames, the night-rangers fill the world with their devastating roars; armed with strange and glinting weapons, they rush headlong at Aswatthaman, attacking him ferociously with thousands of sleek lances, sataghnis, spiked maces, asanis, axes, scimitars, maces, short arrows, heavy clubs, thick spears, swords, polished kampanas, kunapas, hulas, strange keening rockets, stones, vats of hot oil, thunas of black iron, and massive mallets, all dreadful and eerie.

Seeing this downpour of weapons fall upon the head of Drona's son, your warriors are shaken. Aswatthaman, however, nervelessly destroys the entire lot of ayudhas, looming in magnificence like a golden cloud rising by dark. Never pausing, he yet again razes entire hordes of the demons. The skill that Aswatthaman displays is wondrous, my lord, incomparable.

Alone and unsupported, an expert with great and mighty weapons, he consumes the seething Rakshasa army with his blazing astras in the very presence of Ghatotkacha, so they turn into pillars of ashes, which the wind scatters. Drona's son is irradiant in the night as the Samvartaka fire.

Indeed, Rajan, there is no warrior among all the thousands of great kings and Kshatriyas on that chasmal field that can face Aswatthaman as he devours the Pandava host as he pleases, none except Bhima's son Ghatotkacha. His coppery eyes by now rolling in wrath, biting his lips until they bleed, Ghatotkacha says in deathly quiet to his sarathy, "Take me to the son of Drona."

Riding on the formidable chariot that flies banners of victory, Bhima's son by Hidimbi rides again at Aswatthaman ablaze. With a roar to drown all gone before, he whirls a grave asani, an iron mace of celestial craft fitted with eight golden bells, and flings it like a thunder flash at Drona's son. But in a blink, Aswatthaman leaps high in his chariot, seizes the lethal weapon in his hands and casts it right back at the Brahmana! Now Ghatotkacha hurls himself out of his ratha and the incandescent asani explodes on his massive chariot, turning it to a heap of ashes along with its horses, charioteers and standard, and then lies still smouldering on the ground before subsiding in a reverberant susurrus.

Everyone applauds this feat of Drona's son. Ghatotkacha now runs to Dhrishtadyumna's chariot, takes up a bow as great as that of Indra himself, and shoots again at Aswatthaman. Dhrishtadyumna, too, pierces Aswatthaman's chest with many gold-winged shafts, all vicious as serpents.

Drona's son retaliates with burning arrows by the thousands, which Ghatotkacha and Dhrishtadyumna repel with their own shafts of fire. The battle that swells between Ghatotkacha and Aswatthaman is awesome, terrible and it enthralls all the warriors around them, O Bharatarishabha!

Then, with thousands of rathas, three hundred elephants, and six thousand horsemen, Bhimasena arrives there. With unflagging zeal, Aswatthaman continues to fight Ghatotkacha and Dhrishtadyumna with his forces. Wondrous, past describing is the genius that Drona's son displays; why, one might well say that no one else could match his valour. In the flash of an eye, he slaughters a full akshauhini of Rakshasa troops with horses, charioteers, rathas and elephants, in the presence of Bhimasena, Ghatotkacha, Dhrishtadyumna, the twins, Yudhishtira, Arjuna and Krishna.

Struck deep by Aswatthaman's arrows, elephants fall on elephants like crestless mountains. Strewn all around with the still convulsing trunks of elephants lopped off, Kurukshetra looks as if it is overspread with writhing snakes. The field is resplendent with golden staves and royal parasols, like the sky at the end of the Yuga, shining with planets, stars, and many moons and suns. He lets flow a river of the blood of elephants, horses and warriors. Tall standards are its great frogs; drums its large tortoises; white royal parasols its rows of swans; yak-tails its kankas, vultures, and crocodiles; weapons its fish; elephants the rocks on its banks; horses, its sharks; chariots, its broad and shifting banks; and banners, its rows of fine trees. With arrows for its smaller fish, the frightful river has spears, darts and swords for snakes; marrow and flesh for its mire, and trunkless bodies floating on it for its rafts. It is choked with the hair of men and beasts, which are its moss and it filled the timid with fear. We see bloody waves on its surface and it is frightful because of the corpses of foot-soldiers that fill it. Yama's world is the ocean towards which this river flows.

After killing the Rakshasas, Aswatthaman now turns his supernatural archery on Ghatotkacha. He also lacerates the mighty Parthas, Vrikodara, the sons of Dhrishtadyumna and hacks away the head of Suratha, one of Drupada's sons. He kills Suratha's younger brother Satrunjaya, and then Valanika, followed by Jayanika and Jaya. He beheads Prishadhra with a roar, and next the proud Chandrasena and, with ten exact arrows, despatches Kuntibhoja's ten sons.

Then, Rajan, he sends Srutayus to Yama, the Lord of Death. Now Aswatthaman, the terrible, affixes a devastra to his bowstring, draws it to his ear and unleashes that celestial weapon, like the very Yama danda, the rod of death, at Ghatotkacha. The astra blasts through Ghatotkacha's chest and bores into the ground behind him. Bhima's son collapses in his chariot.

Believing him dead, maharatha Dhrishtadyumna spirits him away and sets him on another chariot. And, Rajan, Yudhishtira's chariot legion flees the battle from Drona's invincible son, who throws back his head and gives a triumphant roar that shakes the earth, while all your sons and your army cry out his name and hail his feat. The earth, strewn all around with the fallen, hilly bodies of dead rakshasas, mangled and shredded by thousands of arrows, presents the face of an indescribable nightmare. The Siddhas, Gandharvas, Pisachas, Nagas, Pitris, black ravens, large numbers of pisachas, bhutas, Apsaras and Devas, all laud Aswatthaman, the son of Drona.'"

CANTO 153

GHATOTKACHA-VADHA PARVA CONTINUED

"Sanjaya says, 'On finding the sons of Drupada, Kuntibhoja and the Rakshasas, in their thousands, killed by Aswatthaman, Yudhishtira, Bhimasena, Dhrishtadyumna and Satyaki converge on him together, determined to stop him.

Somadatta sees Satyaki and rage surges up again in him and he looses a cataract of arrows at Yuyudhana. A bloody and thrilling battle breaks out again between your army and the enemy, Seeing Satyaki beset, Bhima attacks the Kaurava hero Somadatta, raking him with ten searing arrows. Somadatta replies with hundred frenzied shafts.

Then an angry Satyaki looses ten razor like thunderbolts at the grand old warrior, grieving over the death of his son Bhurisravas—Somadatta blessed with every estimable virtue, who is even like Yayati, the son of Nahusha. Yuyudhana strikes him again with seven excruciating shafts, while Bhimasena casts a dreadful adamantine parigha at the ancient. Satyaki gores Somadatta's chest with an exceptional astra fierce as fire. The parigha and the fire shaft, both strike him at once and fell the heroic Somadatta.

Seeing his son fallen into a swoon, Balhika rushes at Satyaki, covering him with arrows as a cloud does a mountain during the monsoon. Bhima, defending Satyaki, strikes the illustrious Bahlika with nine arrows, at which the mighty-armed son of Pratipa casts a javelin like Indra's Vajra at Bhima's great chest. Struck squarely, mighty Bhima trembles on his ratha and faints for a moment.

Recovering quickly, with a shattering roar, the titanic Pandava hurls a mace at Balhika, which strikes his head off in a scarlet explosion and that aged shura falls like an old and great tree struck by lightning. Upon his death, your sons Nagadatta, Dridharatha, Virabahu, Ayobhuja, Dridha, Suhasta, Viragas, Pramatha and Ugrayayin, each equal in prowess to Dasaratha's son Rama, rush at Bhima, their bows streaming deadly fire. Seeing them, Bhimasena's eyes light up and with nine marvellous arrows, loosed in a single moment, he kills them all, either taking their heads or blowing their hearts to shreds.

After killing your nine sons, Bhima shrouds Karna's favourite son in a swathe of arrows. The vaunted Vrikaratha, Karna's brother, strikes Bhima with a slew of powerful shafts but growling, the mighty Pandava takes his head from his neck with a wide-headed arrow. Next, O Bhaarata, he slays seven maharathas of Sakuni's forces, and strikes Satachandra down and rides over him with his chariot, crushing him into the earth. Unable to bear watching this savagery, Sakuni's brothers, five mighty Kshatriyas, Gavaksha, Sarabha, Vibhu, Subhaga and Bhanudatta rush at Bhimasena showering arrows at him. A calm Bhima gladly kills all five with five heavy shafts. Seeing those heroes killed, many other great Kshatriyas feel the touch of fear upon them and waver.

Showing uncommon fury, now Yudhishtira attacks your troops and begins to raze them as he pleases, in full view of Drona and your sons. He despatches the Ambashtas, the Malavas, the brave Trigartas, the Sibis, the Abhishahas, the Surasenas, the Bahlikas and the Vasatis, turning the earth soggy with flesh and blood. Turning in another direction, with ferocity so unexpected of the Ajatasatru, he sends the Yaudheyas and a large host of the Madrakas to Yama.

Now a loud tumult arises around Yudhishtira's chariot, and we hear roars and cries of, "Kill!" "Hack him to pieces!" "Seize him!"

Seeing the Dharmaraja raze your troops, Drona, urged on by your desperate son, unleashes the Vayavyastra at Yudhishtira. But the son of Pandu counters the astra of the Wind with his own weapon of Vayu. Inflamed by this, Drona looses a clutch of unearthly astras at the Dharmaputra—the Varuna astra, the Yamya astra, the Agneya astra, the Tvashtra astra and the Savitra astra. But amazingly the gentle Yudhishtira, now turned into a pure Kshatriya warrior, easily negates every unworldly weapon that his Acharya aims at him.

Drona, determined to keep his vow to Duryodhana, invokes the Aindra and the Prajapatya astras to kill the son of Dharma. However, Kuruttama Yudhishtira, with the gait of an elephant or lion, of broad chest, large red eyes and endowed with tejas hardly less than that of Drona, summons the Mahendrastra to confound all Drona's celestial ayudhas. The Mahendra extinguishes Drona's entire volley. A livid Drona, his eyes aflame to kill the Pandava, his disciple, summons the Brahmastra so the dark filed is suddenly illumined as if by another blinding sun and all that watch are terror-stricken.

Seeing the Brahmastra invoked, Yudhishtira summons his own Brahmastra and the two great weapons extinguish each other. All the great maharathas there applaud both Drona and Yudhishtira.

In frustration, in great rage, his eyes turning the colour of copper, Drona turns away from Yudhishtira and begins to annihilate Drupada's akshauhini with the Vayavyastra. Before the very eyes of Bhimasena and Arjuna, the Panchala forces flee from the Acharya. Arjuna and Bhima check the flight of their troops and attack the enemy with two large divisions of rathas. Arjuna assails the right and Bhima the left, and they confront Bharadwaja's son with two veritable tornadoes of arrows. The Kaikeyas, the Srinjayas, and the vigorous Panchalas again follow the two brothers, Rajan, as do the Matsyas and the Satwatas.

And now Arjuna Kiritin brings such devastation to your army, already besieged by exhaustion and sleep, that they break ranks and flee. Drona and Duryodhana try to rally them but they cannot check their troops in their flight.'"

CANTO 154

GHATOTKACHA-VADHA PARVA CONTINUED

"Sanjaya says, 'Looking at the vast, seething army of the Pandavas your son Duryodhana now thinks it impossible to withstand the enemy. He says to Karna, "Loyal friend, the hour has come when your friends need you most. O Karna, save us! Our army is encircled by the Panchalas, the Kaikeyas, the Matsyas, and their maharathas, all full of rage and like hissing snakes. There, the Pandavas, sure of victory, shout for joy. The teeming chariot-force of the Panchalas is now as powerful as Indra himself."

Karna replies, "If Purandara himself comes here to save Arjuna, I will vanquish even the Deva king before I kill that son of Pandu. Believe me that this is the truth. Be of good cheer, O Bhaarata! I will kill Arjuna and all the Panchalas and bring you victory even as Pavaka's son gave Vasava. I will achieve whatever you need to win this war.

Among all the Pandavas, Arjuna is most powerful and I will use Indra's shakti against him. Upon his death, his brothers will either surrender themselves to you or retire once more to the forest. As long as I am alive, O Kauravya, never yield to grief or despair. I will vanquish the united forces of the Pandavas, the Panchalas, the Kaikeyas, and the Vrishnis. I will make porcupines of them with my arrows and I will give you the Earth and everything in it."

At this, Kripa, who is near enough to hear what Karna says, tells him with a sardonic smile, "Your speech is fair indeed, Karna! If fine words could fetch victory, surely with you for his protector, this Bharatarishabha Duryodhana would be thought to have abundant protection. But you boast so much in the presence of the Kuru king, but we seldom see you prove yourself with deeds to match.

Many times we have seen you fight the sons of Pandu, and on every occasion, O Suta's son, they have beaten you soundly. When the Gandharvas captured Duryodhana, all the men fought except you, who were the first to run away. Outside Virata's city, Arjuna defeated all the Kauravas including you and your younger brother. You are no match for even one of the sons of Pandu in battle; how can you expect to vanquish all of them together led by Krishna?

Karna, you brag too much! Sutaputra, good men, men of true worth, do not talk they prove themselves with their deeds. You, on the other hand, are always thundering like the dry clouds of autumn, and you have shown yourself to be a man of no substance. Sadly, Duryodhana does not seem to understand this.

You rant and roar, Karna, as long as you do not see Arjuna. And, as soon as you see him near, you fall silent. Indeed, you roar as long as you are out of range of Arjuna's arrows and your bragging is stanched the moment Partha's thunderbolts strike you. Kshatriyas prove themselves by their feats of arms; Brahmanas, by their wise and sacred speech; Arjuna proves himself with his bow, but Karna only by the castles he builds in the air.

Fool, who is there that can stand up to Pandu's son Partha who pleases Rudra himself?"

Thus railed at by Saradwat's son, Karna answers, "Heroes always boom like the clouds of the monsoon, and just like seeds planted in fertile soil, quickly sprout. I do not see any fault in heroes who accept great loads on their shoulders before making boastful speeches on the field of battle. When a man mentally resolves to bear a burden, Destiny itself helps him in its execution. Wishing in my heart to accept a great responsibility, I am always firm and resolved. If before killing the sons of Pandu with Krishna and Satwatas, I do proclaim what I will do, what is it to you, O Brahmana? True heroes never roar fruitlessly like autumn clouds. Conscious of their own might, only the wise dare tell of it.

In my heart I am determined to vanquish Krishna and Partha today! It is for this that I declare myself, O son of Gotama! Now behold the fruit of my roars, Brahmana. Slaying the son of Pandu with all their followers, Krishna and the Satwatas, I will bestow this whole Earth on Duryodhana without a thorn in it."

Kripa replies, "I do not give much credence, Sutaputra, to your delirious boasting, for they are mere words not deeds. You always deprecate the two Krishnas and Dharmaraja Yudhishtira. But Karna, Yudhishtira will have victory for he has the two Krishnas on his side. I tell you, the Devas, the Gandharvas, the Yakshas, Manavas, the Nagas, and the Garudas cannot defeat Krishna and Arjuna.

Yudhishtira Dharmaputra is devoted to the Brahmanas, truthful in speech and self-controlled. He reveres the Pitris and the Devas, is devoted to the practice of satya and dharma, is a master of weapons, possesses great intelligence, and he is also grateful. His brothers are endowed with great strength and are masters of war. They are devoted to the service of their elders, possess wisdom and fame, and practise dharma. Their kinsmen are all powerful as Indra and great warriors, and they are all exceptionally devoted to the Pandavas. Dhrishtadyumna, Sikhandin, Janamejaya, the son of Durmukha, Chandrasena, Madrasena, Kritavarman, Dhruva, Dhara, Vasuchandra, Sutejana, the sons of Drupada, and Drupada himself, all maharathas and owners of devastras, and the king of the Matsyas with his younger brothers, all fight resolutely for Yudhishtira's cause.

Gajanika, Virabhadra, Sudarshana, Srutadhwaja, Balanika, Jayanika, Jayapirya, Vijaya, Labhalaksha, Jayaswa, Kamaratha, the handsome brothers of Virata, and the twins Nakula and Sahadeva, the five sons of Draupadi and the Rakshasa Ghatotkacha all fight for the Pandavas. The sons of Pandu cannot be destroyed. Why, Bhima and Phalguna with their cosmic weapons can annihilate the entire universe, with the Devas, Asuras, and Manavas, with all the tribes of Yakshas and Rakshasas and with all the Gajas and Nagas, and all other creatures.

As for Yudhishtira, he can consume the whole world with just an angry look from his pure eyes. How, Karna, can you vanquish these enemies for whom Krishna of immeasurable might has donned armour? This intention of yours, Sutaputra, is just your folly, that you dare contend with Sauri himself, who is the Lord of the universe."

Karna replies, smiling, "O Brahmana, whatever you say about the Pandavas is true. All the virtues you see in them, and many more besides, can be found in the sons of Pandu. It is true also that even the Devas led by Vasava, the Daityas, the Yakshas, and the Rakshasas cannot vanquish the Parthas. For all that, I, Karna, will defeat the Parthas using the inexorable astra given me by Indra. With that shakti, I will kill Arjuna and when he dies, all his brothers, and Krishna too will never enjoy sovereignty over the Earth, not without Arjuna. They will all perish. And then, this Bhumi, with her seas, will belong undisputedly to Suyodhana.

In this world, one can achieve anything one wants, as long as one plans carefully for it. This I know well, and that is why I venture to proclaim what I will do, O Kripa. As for you, you are old, a Brahmana by birth, and no Kshatriya. You bear too much love for the Pandavas and that is why you repeatedly belittle me. I have been patient, but if you speak mockingly to me again, I will cut out your tongue, O wretch!

You want to praise the Pandavas to frighten all our troops and the Kauravas. Listen to what I say now. Duryodhana, Drona, Sakuni, Durmukha, Jaya, Dusasana, Vrishasena, Salya, you, Somadatta, Drona's son and Vivimsati—all these maharathas are here with us, clad in armour. Which enemy, even if he has the power of Indra, can vanquish you all? All that I have named are great warriors, knowers of dharma, and have earned their place in Swarga. They can match the very gods in battle, and they have taken the field to kill the Pandavas for Duryodhana's sake.

I regard victory and defeat to depend on destiny, even in the case of the greatest maharathas. When Mahabaho Bhishma himself lies pierced with a hundred arrows, and Vikarna, Jayadratha, Bhurisravas, Jaya, Jalasandha, Sudakshina, Sala the great, Bhagadatta mahatejasvin and many others equal to them, heroes all and mightier than the Pandavas, lie on Kurukshetra, killed by the Pandavas, what can you think, O wretched Brahmana, except that all this is the result of destiny?

As for the enemies of Duryodhana, whom you so adore, their brave warriors, too, have been slaughtered in thousands. The armies of both the Kurus and the Pandavas diminish with every passing moment; I do not see in this the prowess of the Pandavas! For Duryodhana's sake, O lowest of men, I will challenge the sons of Pandu with all my heart and all my might. As for victory, that depends on destiny.'""

CANTO 155

Ghatotkacha-vadha Parva continued

"Sanjaya says, 'Aswatthaman is at hand and, hearing his uncle Kripa spoken to so harshly and contemptuously by Karna, Drona's son draws his sword and, in the very presence of Duryodhana, rushes roaring at Karna.

Aswatthaman says, "Vile of men, Kripa speaks of the virtues that Arjuna truly has. And you dare rebuke him from being evil-minded and malicious. Your pride and insolence make you brag without a sane care for any of the world's great bowmen! Where was your great prowess when, after chasing you away like a dog, the Gandivi slew Jayadratha in your very sight? Vainly, O wretch of a Suta, do you carry in your mind the hope of beating him who once fought Mahadeva himself.

The very Devas and the Asuras united, and with Indra at their head, failed to vanquish Arjuna, with only Krishna for his ally. How then do you, Sutaputra, hope to defeat the greatest shura in the world, the unconquered Arjuna? But look now, vile Karna, what I, Aswatthaman, do to you today. Lowest of men, dimwitted, evil-minded Karna, I will cut your head from your neck!"

And Aswatthaman rushes furiously at Karna but Duryodhana and Kripa seize him together and firmly restrain him.

Then Karna says, "This dark-hearted dog of a Brahmana thinks he is great and boasts of his strength. Set him free, Duryodhana, and let him feel the might of Karna."

Aswatthaman replies, "Son of a Suta, O you with an evil mind, we may pardon you, but Phalguna will quell your rising pride."

Duryodhana intervenes and says, "Aswatthaman, control your anger. You must forgive, Anagha, and not be angry with Karna. Upon you, him, Kripa, Drona, Salya and Sakuni a great burden rests. Drive away your wrath, O best of Brahmanas! Look where all the Pandava troops advance to attack Karna. Indeed, here they come, challenging us all."

Pacified by the king, Aswatthaman, the noble son of Drona, suppresses his fury and forgives Karna. Then the quiet and mild Acharya Kripa says to Karna, "Dark-hearted Sutaputra, we forgive you, but Arjuna will quell your pride."

Meanwhile, the Pandavas and the Panchalas charge your army unitedly, with reverberant roars. Mahatejasvin Karna maharatha, leading many great Kuru warriors and looking like Indra in the midst of the Devas, waits, his bow drawn. As if each battle that erupts is more frightful and deafening than the ones gone before, so is the one that now breaks out between the Pandavas and the Panchalas and Karna and his forces.

The enemy warriors roar, *There stands Kana in his ratha!* and *Evil one, come fight us now!* Others, with eyes bulging in rage, cry, "Let our great Kshatriyas kill this arrogant wretch of little discernment, this son of a Suta. He must not live. This sinner is the Pandavas' worst enemy. Loyal to Duryodhana, he is the root of all these evils that we have seen on Kurukshetra. Kill him!"

With these and other cries, and exhorted by Yudhishtira, many great Pandava and Panchala maharathas rush at Karna, unleashing a cataract of arrows at him. But the Sutaputra is supremely unmoved; no trace of fear lays its fingers on his heart and a mocking smile curves his fine lips. Seeing that sea of troops, Karna, like Death himself, begins to mow them down with clouds of arrows.

The Pandavas respond with arrows from their lakhs of bows; they fight Radha's son as the Daityas of old fighting with Indra. Indeed, so evenly matched are the two vast forces that the gory, magnificent contention between them is like the Devasura yuddha of old.

Karna's archery is wonderful, for not all his enemies combining against him can find a home in his body for a single arrow. He cut down all the barbs that streak at him in flight and responds by severing royal parasols, smashing chariots and killing enemy horses—all with arrows that bear his name upon them, every one. Harried by Karna so they quickly lose all assurance, the Pandava Kshatriyas begin to wander across the field like a herd of cattle stricken by bitter cold.

Struck by Karna's transcendent, godlike volleys, countless horses, elephants and maharathas fall dead and yet again the entire field is strewn with the severed heads and limbs of noble Kshatriyas. With the dead, the dying, and the wailing of wounded warriors, Kurukshetra by night truly resembles Yama's realm.

Duryodhana watches Karna at his splendid best, goes to Aswatthaman and tells him proudly, "Look where Karna torments and routs all the enemies massed against him! Why, he overwhelms them as Kartikeya did against the Asura host. And look where Arjuna now rides to kill him. Aswatthaman, my friend, you must protect Karna!"

Aswatthaman, Kripa, Salya and the great maharatha Kritavarman, son of Hridika, all ride against against Partha dashing towards them like Sakra against the Daitya host. They go gladly to support the heroic Karna. However, Rajan, Arjuna surrounded by the Panchalas presses on against Karna, like Purandara against the Asura Vritra.'

Dhritarashtra asks, 'Finding Phalguna advancing like Rudra himself, as he appears at the end of the Yuga, what does Karna do? Maharatha Karna, son of Vikartana, has always challenged Partha and always maintained that he can defeat the invincible Arjuna. What then, O Suta, does he do when he is suddenly face to face with his inveterate enemy?'

Sanjaya says, 'Seeing Arjuna rushing towards him like an elephant towards a rival elephant, Karna stands fearlessly up to him. Partha covers Karna with showers of shafts with wings of gold, and Karna envelops Vijaya with his arrows. Clouds of golden-winged, uncanny barbs they exchange, until, his rage boiling up, Karna strikes Arjuna with three deadly missiles. Arjuna can hardly bear to watch his adversary's virtuosity and looses a swath of thirty shafts at him, all with burning heads.

Arjuna strikes Karna through his left wrist with another long arrow, smiling, and forcing Karna to drop his bow. But Karna recovers in a flash, picks up his bow again and once more covers Arjuna with gales of wondrous fire, now showing his true unearthly skill. Not to be outdone, Dhananjaya cuts down Karna's arrow storms with his own.

Approaching each other quite close, these two greatest of all archers, fighting for honour, fighting at the outer limits of their incomparable prowess, continue to shoot at each other in an astounding display of genius, which makes one's hair stand on end.

Arjuna, inspired by his antagonist's prowess and swiftness of hand, lifts his archery and breaks Karna's bow at the very grip, kills his four horses with a scathe of wedge-headed shafts, and decapitates Karna's charioteer. As Karna stands vulnerable, Partha drills him with deadly volleys, so blood spouts from the golden Sutaputra. Karna leaps down from his useless ratha and quickly finds sanctuary in Kripa's chariot. Seeing Karna beaten again, your warriors run in all directions.

Duryodhana roars to them to stop. "Shuras, do not turn your backs on the battle. You bulls among Kshatriyas, stop! I will kill Partha myself, and all the Panchalas. When I fight the Gandivi today, he will see that my prowess is as that of Rudra at the end of the yuga. Today the Pandavas will find my arrows among them like locust swarms, like the torrents of rain that fall at summer's end.

Today I will put the proud Arjuna to rout and remove your fear of him. Arjuna will not withstand me today, brave heroes, even as the ocean can only dash helplessly against the continents."

His eyes red, Suyodhana rides at Arjuna, taking a teeming host with him. Seeing this, Kripa tells Aswatthaman, "Look, where Duryodhana, made mad by anger, goes to fight Arjuna, like an insect flying into a blazing fire. Stop him before this great king loses his life, in our very sight. He will certainly die if comes within range of Partha's arrows. My son, stop the king before Arjuna's astras make ashes of him. While we are still here and alive, it is a crime for the king to go into battle himself as if he has no one to fight for him. And if he engages Arjuna, his life will be good as lost!"

Aswatthaman rides quickly to the canny Duryodhana and says to him, "When I who love you am alive, O son of Gandhari, you must not go into battle yourself! Do not be anxious about vanquishing Arjuna, for I will stop him for you. Stay here, O Suyodhana, and watch me fight the son of Pandu."

Duryodhana replies, "Drona always protects the sons of Pandu, as if they are his own sons. You, also, either do not put forth your true prowess against the Pandavas or it is my fate that your awesome might wanes as soon as you are faced with Kunti's sons. Perhaps, you bear Yudhishtira or Draupadi some exceptional love for otherwise I cannot fathom why you do not fight the Pandavas as you do our other enemies.

Ah, shame on me for my bottomless greed, for whose sake all my dearest friends, who dearly want to please me, find themselves vanquished and shamed on the field and plunged into great grief! But you, Aswatthaman, who are Mahadeva's very equal and can destroy the enemy, will not do it. O son of my Acharya, I beg you, be pleased with me and vanquish my enemies!

Neither the Devas nor the Danavas can stand your astras, O son of Drona. For my sake, for all our sakes, kill the Panchalas and the Somakas with all their followers. The rest, with your protection, we ourselves will slay. Look, O Brahmana, where the famed Somakas and the Panchalas blaze among my troops like a great forest fire. Douse them, Aswatthaman, as only you can, and the Kalikeyas; otherwise, led by Arjuna, they will annihilate us all.

O Aswatthaman, Parantapa, ride there in haste. Whether you achieve it now or later, you must accomplish this feat and fetch us victory. The

Rishis have all said that you have been born for the destruction of the Panchalas and that you will remove them from this world. It will be as they have predicted. O Naravyaghra, fulfil your destiny and kill the Panchalas with all their forces. When even the Devas with Indra at their head cannot face your astras, what can these Parthas and Panchalas do?

I speak truly when I say that the Pandavas united with the Somakas are no match for you. Ride, O Mahabaho! Do not delay another instant for look, where stricken by Arjuna's tides of arrows, our army breaks up and flees. Use your celestial tejas, my friend, for you can bring ruin to the enemy by yourself!'"'

CANTO 156

GHATOTKACHA-VADHA PARVA CONTINUED

"Sanjaya says, 'After Duryodhana speaks to him, Aswatthaman the insuperable is determined to annihilate the enemy. He tells your son, "It is as you say, O Kuruttama! The Pandavas are always dear to both my father and to me just as both of us are precious to them. But not in battle. We fight fearlessly, to the best of our abilities, and reckless of our lives. Karna, Salya, Kripa, Kritavarman and I could destroy the Pandava host in the twinkling of an eye just as the Pandavas could destroy the Kaurava host, if we were not here.

We fight the Pandavas to the best of our might, and they too fight us with their best strengths. Power, encountering power, is neutralised, O Bhaarata! I say to you, the Pandava army cannot be overcome as long as the sons of Pandu themselves are alive. The Pandavas are born with unworldly prowess and they are fighting in their own interest. Why, Duryodhana, should they not be able to kill your troops?

However, you are covetous and deceitful, Rajan, beyond all measure. You are vainglorious and suspicious of everything, which is why you suspect even us. I also think that you are evil, mean-spirited, selfish, why, an embodiment of sin, that you question us after everything that we do for you, day after harrowing day.

As for myself, I fight with determination for your sake, always prepared to lay down my life for you. I will return to battle now, O Kuruttama, and will fight and kill a great host of your enemy. I will do battle with the Panchalas, the Somakas, the Kaikeyas, and the Pandavas as well, only to please you. Seared by my arrows today, the Chedis, the Panchalas and the Somakas will scatter like a herd of cattle hunted by a lion. Today, seeing my prowess, the Dharmaputra with all the Somakas will find the whole world filled with Aswatthamans. Yudhishtira will be heartbroken to watch me slaughter the Panchalas and Somakas.

I will, O Bhaarata, slay all who dare come near me and no one will escape me alive today."

Saying this to your son, the mahabaho Aswatthaman charges the enemy, his arrows flaring in all directions. He cries to the Panchalas and the Kaikeyas, "Great maharathas, strike me! Show me your prowess."

At this, all the enemy warriors shower their shafts upon Drona's son. Easily cutting down all their arrows, Aswatthaman kills ten brave warriors among them, in the very sight of Dhrishtadyumna and the sons of Pandu. The Panchalas and the Somakas abandon the fight and flee. Dhrishtadyumna rides into the fray surrounded by a hundred unflinching maharathas in their chariots, the rattle of whose wheels is like the thunder of rain-charged clouds.

Looking at this, Dhrishtadyumna says to Aswatthaman, "O foolish son of Drona, of what use is killing common warriors? If you are a hero, then fight me. I will kill you, wretched Brahman. Stop and fight me for a moment without fleeing."

He shoots the Acharya's son countless savage barbs, which fly in an unbroken line and pierce Aswatthaman's body like honey bees entering a flowering tree. Deeply wounded and swelling with rage like a snake trodden upon, Aswatthaman, astra in hand, says, "Dhrishtadyumna, stop for a moment and I will send to straight to Yama!"

With astonishing dexterity, bending his arrows in flight at impossible trajectories, he covers Dhrishtadyumna from every side with a cascade of gold-winged shafts. Dhrishtadyumna says, "You know nothing of my birth, evil Brahmana, or of my vow. I will not kill you today when Drona himself is still alive. After this night passes and day dawns, I will first kill your father and then send you to your ancestors. This is my purpose today.

So, until then display the hatred you bear towards the Parthas, and the devotion you cherish for the Kurus. Come morning and you shall not escape me with your life. The Brahmana who abandons his svadharma and takes to the dharma of a Kshatriya can be killed by any Kshatriya, O lowest of men. So I will break no law by killing both your father and you."

So harshly does Dhrishtadyumna speak, as if to a servant, insulting the finest of Brahmanas, that, mustering all his choler, Aswatthaman answers him, saying, "Stop! Stop and fight, you Panchala wretch!" And he glares at him as if to burn him up with his eyes.

Sighing with rage like a snake, Aswatthaman looses a scorching volley at Dhrishtadyumna, striking him squarely and drawing blood. Dhrishtadyumna hardly winces but returns the fire with his own torrid salvo. The two are matched so evenly that no arrow separates them, one from the other. The duel escalates and each one kills hundreds of the other's common soldiers on every side even as they fight one another. Such is that marvellous contention between Drona's son and Dhrishtadyumna that the Siddhas, Charanas and other sky-ranging beings applaud them from above.

Filling the sky and all the points of the compass with veritable cloudbursts and covering the dim stars therewith, the two great warriors continue to duel and none can see them or where their arrows fly, land or claim countless lives in pitch darkness. As if dancing with their bows drawn into circles, intently trying to kill each other, those mahabahos fight so remarkably that even the greatest maharathas around them tremble in wonder, while others are terrified. Indeed, loud cheers and handclapping breaks out among both armies and every true warrior is filled with elation to watch that duel among duels. We hear loud shouts and so many combatants blow their conches, and begin to sound thousands of musical instruments.

This duel blazes equally but for a brief while. Then, darting forward suddenly, Aswatthaman cleaves Dhrishtadyumna's bow, standard, royal parasol, and kills his two Parshni charioteers, the principal sarathy, and his four horses. Roaring aloud, he then massacres the unprotected Panchalas in thousands! The Pandava host quakes with fear, for Drona's son is no less than Indra himself in the night.

In the very sight of Dhrishtadyumna and Arjuna, Aswatthaman slays a hundred Panchalas that face him with a hundred arrows, including three maharathas with three thunderbolts. The Panchalas and the Srinjayas turn tail with their banners torn. Having vanquished his enemies, Drona's son give a roar like stormclouds thundering at summer's end. He is as resplendent as the blazing fire at the end of the Yuga, after it has consumed all living creatures. Cheered deafeningly by all the Kauravas after he kills thousands of enemies, the valiant Aswatthaman shines in splendour, like the king of the Devas himself after vanquishing his enemies.'"

CANTO 157

Ghatotkacha-vadha Parva continued

"Sanjaya says, 'Now Yudhishtira and Bhimasena besiege Aswatthaman. Seeing this, Duryodhana and Drona ride against the Pandavas and a tumultuary battle ensues, to make the timorous tremble. A furious Yudhishtira despatches vast numbers of Ambashtas, Malavas, Vangas, Sibis and Trigartas to the land of the dead. Bhima, too, mauls the Abhishahas, the Surasenas and other mighty Kshatriyas, and makes the earth a swamp of blood.

Then, Rajan, Kiritin Swetavahana sends the Yaudheyas, the Madrakas, the Malavas and the Mountain-men to the regions of Yama. Struck by arrows shot with terrific force, elephants fall onto the earth like twin-peaked hills. Strewn with the lopped-off trunks of elephants that still writhe in convulsions, the field again looks as if covered with wriggling snakes. Kurukshetra is horribly magnificent, covered with the fallen golden chatras of kings; it looks like the firmament at the end of the Yuga, spangled with suns, moons and stars beyond count.

At this very time, there is an uproar near Drona's chariot, in which one can hear the words, "Kill!", "Strike!", "Hack!", "Pierce!", "Cut him to pieces!" Drona swiftly summons the Vayavyastra and begins to decimate the enemies that surround him, like a mighty tornado destroying gathering masses of clouds, and the Panchalas run away from fear, while Bhimasena and the noble Partha look on. However, they soon check the flight of their troops and lead a large force of chariots against the equally vast force of Drona. Arjuna attacking the right and Vrikodara the left, they lash Bharadwaja's son with two heavy torrents of arrows.

The maharathas among the Srinjayas and the Panchalas, with the Matsyas and the Somakas, Rajan, follow the two against Drona. While, many maharathas loyal to your son, bringing a great host with them, rush forward to support Drona. However, swiftly slaughtered by Arjuna and overcome by the turgid darkness, your Bharata host falls apart. Your son and Drona try to rally them but to no avail. Indeed, razed mercilessly by the arrows of the incomparable Arjuna, your army takes to its heels in all directions in that hour when the world is plunged in night. Abandoning the animals and chariots they ride, many great kings flee, Rajan, overwhelmed with fear of the hunting Kiritin.'"

CANTO 158

GHATOTKACHA-VADHA PARVA CONTINUED

"Sanjaya says, 'Finding Somadatta brandishing his massive bow, Satyaki tells his charioteer, "Drive me towards Somadatta. I tell you truly, O Suta, I will not return from battle today without killing that worst of the Kurus, the son of Balhika."

The sarathy whips his fleet horses of the Sindhu breed, white as conch shells, and strong, so they fly at Somadatta, bearing Satyaki towards him even as the steeds of Indra bore him in the olden days against the Danavas. Seeing the Satwata hero coming like a storm, Somadatta turns fearlessly turns towards him and shrouds Yuyudhana in a cloudburst of shafts.

Satyaki, who knows no fear ever, returns Somadatta's calescent fire, and two gales of flaming shafts light up the thick darkness of Kurukshetra. Somadatta strikes Satyaki's chest with sixty shafts, while Satyaki draws blood all over Somadatta's body with arrows like streaks of lightning. Lacerated by each other the two look magnificent, like a couple of flowering kinsukas in spring. Dyed all over with blood, those illustrious warriors of the Kuru and the Vrishni races glare at each other as if they will ignite the darkness and each other with their eyes.

Riding on their chariots, these maharathas of terrible countenances circle each other, glowering like two baleful planets. Their bodies torn all over by arrows that still protrude from them, Rajan, they are like two porcupines. Pierced with countless golden-winged shafts, the two warriors glitter like a pair of tall trees covered with fireflies. Their bodies bright with the blazing arrows planted in them, the two maharathas look like two angry elephants caparisoned with burning torches. Then, Rajan, all at once, with a crescent-tipped arrow, Somadatta cleaves Satyaki's bow and, with dazzling swiftness, strikes him with thirty thunder flashes loosed quick as a thought.

Satyaki snatches up another bow, pierces Somadatta with five iron shafts and, with another broad-headed arrow smilingly rives his golden standard. Somadatta drills Satyaki with five and twenty shafts and in rage, with a razor-faced arrow, Satyaki breaks Somadatta's bow and savages him with a hundred straight gold-winged barbs, reducing him to the state of a snake without fangs.

However, Somadatta picks up another bow and looses banks and banks of arrows at Satyaki, who responds in kind. Somadatta continues to assail Satyaki without let. Then Bhima joins the fight to support Satyaki and gashes Somadatta with ten arrows and the great Kuru strikes back with many fanged shafts of his own properly inflamed Satyaki aims a terrible parigha at Somadatta's chest, an astra with a golden shaft and hard as the Vajra itself. However, smiling the while, Somadatta slices the dreadful astra as it flashes toward him, and riven in two, it falls to the earth like some mountain peak cloven by lightning.

With a broad-headed arrow, Yuyudhana severs Somadatta's bow again, and with another five arrows, cuts the leather gauntlet that covers his fingers into shreds. Never pausing, he cuts down Somadatta's four great horses, and with another immaculate shaft, beheads his sarathy. He now draws a stone-whetted, oil-slicked, gold-winged and occult arrow, a most exceptional shaft, and unleashes it at his hated enemy with such ferocity that it ignites into blinding light and flame as it falls like a hawk upon the old Kuru warrior, plunges into his chest, blows his heart into pieces and maharatha Somadatta, the hitherto invincible Kuru Kshatriya, falls dead without a murmur.

Seeing maharatha Somadatta killed, your warriors attack Satyaki with a force of rathas. Meanwhile, the Pandavas also, Rajan, with all the Prabhadrakas, and a large legion, tear into Drona's army. Yudhishtira leads this attack and puts Drona's forces to rout, killing hundreds of brave soldiers in his Acharya's very presence. Drona rushes in to defend his troops and strikes Yudhishtira deep with seven keen arrows. Yudhishtira responds by goring his master with five whistling shafts. Bleeding profusely, Drona licks the corners of his mouth and cuts down Yudhishtira's standard and breaks the bow in his hands.

Quicker than seeing, when speed is of the essence, Yudhishtira sweeps up another bow and covers Drona, his horses, charioteer, standard, and grand chariot with a thousand arrows! And all are spellbound with amazement, for they can hardly believe that this is the gentle, patient Dharmaraja they are watching.

Wounded and in great pain, Drona, the bull among Brahmanas, sits down for a while on the floor of his chariot. Then, recovering, sighing like a snake and full of rage, the Acharya invokes the Vayavyastra. However, Yudhishtira calmly summons a weapon of the Wind himself and nullifies Drona's astra; in the same moment, he breaks the Acharya's bow in two. Drona takes up another bow, which Yudhishtira again breaks.

Now Krishna says to Yudhishtira, speaking into his heart from afar, "Listen to me, O Mahabaho. Do not fight Drona anymore for he means to take you his captive. He who has been born to kill Drona will slay him; that task is not yours. Leave the Acharya and fight Duryodhana, for kings should battle kings, and not others. Surround yourself with elephants, horses and chariots and come where Dhananjaya and I, and Naravyaghra Bhima are fighting the Kurus with but a small force."

Yudhishtira reflects for a moment and then goes to that part of the field where Bhima, fighting in fury, is slaughtering your troops like Death himself with maw agape. Making the earth resound with the rumble of his chariot, like the roar of thunderheads at the end of summer, Yudhishtira forms the flank of Bhima's forces. Meanwhile, Drona, too, in the horrible night, turns away and begins to destroy his most detested enemies, the Panchalas.'"

CANTO 159

Ghatotkacha-vadha Parva continued

"Sanjaya says, 'While the dreadful war is being fought, when the world is enveloped in darkness and dust, the warriors on the field cannot see each other; they battle with sheer instinct and by calling out names to discern friend from foe. O Bharatarishabha, during this unmentionable carnage of maharathas, elephants, horses and foot-soldiers, Drona, Karna, Kripa, Bhima, Dhrishtadyumna and Satyaki wreak havoc on one another's troops. The common soldiers of both armies, demoralised all around by these great maharathas in the hour of darkness, break and flee in all directions. Even as they run, they are massacred and thousands of leading maharathas slaughter one another, while they are blind in the dark and full of fear.

All this is the result of the evil counsels of your son. Indeed, at the hour when the world is shrouded in darkness, all creatures, even the greatest Kshatriyas, are overcome with panic, and quite lose their minds.'

Dhritarashtra asks, 'What is the state of mind of the troops when, in the dark, all of you are sapped of your courage and sorely pressed by the Pandavas? O Sanjaya, when everything is swathed in darkness how do the Pandava and my troops become visible again?'

Sanjaya replies, 'Drona somehow masses again in a compact array the remnants of the army of the Kauravas, under their leaders. He sets himself in the van, Salya at the rear, Aswatthaman and Sakuni on the right and the left flanks. Duryodhana on this most dreadful night busies himself with protecting all his legions. The king, your son, puts heart into the foot-soldiers, Rajan, and tells them, "Lay aside your weapons and take up torches and lamps in your hands instead. Let the maharathas alone continue to fight."

The foot-soldiers gladly take up burning lamps and the Devas, Rishis, Gandharvas, Deva-rishis, the diverse tribes of Vidyadharas and Apsaras, Nagas, Yakshas, Uragas, Kinnaras, looking on from the heavens, also joyfully take up blazing celestial lanterns. We see many wondrous floating lamps, filled with sweet-scented oil, fall from the Regents of the principal and the subsidiary directions. For Duryodhana's sake, we see many come down especially from Narada and Parvata, lighting up the stagnant darkness so full of death. Now arrayed in a compact vyuha, the Kaurava army looks dazzling with the light of the marvellous lamps shining on their costly ornaments and the Devastras blazing as they are shot or hurled. On each chariot five lamps are set, three on each maddened elephant and on each horse one large lamp. Thus, the Kuru warriors light up the field and the army, revealing now the true extent of the massacre that has occurred by darkness.

Set in their places quickly, these lamps light up your army wonderfully. All the great Kshatriyas, made radiant by the foot-soldiers with oil-fed lamps in their hands, are as handsome as clouds in the night sky illumined by flashes of lightning. When the Kuru host has been thus lit up, Drona, of the effulgence of fire, scorching everything around, looks as radiant Rajan, in his golden armour as the midday sun. The light of the lamps reflects from the golden ornaments, the bright cuirasses, the bows and the other polished weapons of the warriors, from their maces twined with strings, from the bright parighas, their chariots, arrows and javelins, as they fly in scintillating arcs and streaks.

The royal parasols, yak-tails, swords, blazing brands and necklaces of gold, as they are whirled or moved, mirror the lamplight and the spectacle of Kurukshetra is now entirely beautiful. Your army burns with soft splendour that no artist has beheld or captured. Ornaments, beautifully wrought weapons, red with blood and whirled by heroes, create a glowing effulgence like dim flashes of lightning in the sky at the end of summer.

The faces of warriors, impetuously pursuing foes to strike them down and themselves trembling in the ardour of battle, are altogether breathtaking. As the sun is fierce when a forest is on fire, in the same manner, the terrible night grows in grandeur both from the fighting and the now lamplit host.

Seeing our army illuminated, the Parthas too with great alacrity exhort the foot-soldiers throughout their army to imitate what ours have done. On each elephant, they place seven lamps; on each chariot, ten; and on the back of each horse, two; and on the flanks and rear of their rathas as well as on their flagpoles, they place multiple lamps. Also, on the flanks of their army, at the rear, in the van, all around and within, they light numberless lamps. And now, both armies are strangely and gloriously lit up in the fleeting night of all horrors.

Throughout your army, foot-soldiers carrying lamps mingle with elephants and chariots and cavalry. The army of Pandu's son is also illuminated by foot-soldiers with blazing torches in their hands. The twin hosts are refulgent as fire and sun when they burn together. As more and more lamps are lit, the splendour of both armies seems to illumine not just the field of war but the very sky and all the directions. Both armies are clearly visible and distinguishable from each other.

Awakened by the light that reaches into the sky, the Devas, the Gandharvas, the Yakshas, the Rishis, other Mahatapasvins and the Apsaras all gather directly above Kurukshetra. Thronged with Devas, Gandharvas, Yakshas, Maharishis, Apsaras, and the spirits of slain warriors about to enter the celestial realms, the battlefield looks like a second Swarga. Teeming with chariots, horses and elephants, by now brilliantly illumined with a million lamps, with wild warriors either lying in the poses of death or wandering bemused across the field like madmen, and horses slain or roaming dazed, the immense hosts resemble the vyuhas of the Devas and the Asuras in days of old when they fought.

The dense swish of shafts form the fierce winds; great rathas, the clouds; the neighing and trumpeting of horses and elephants, the thunder; the lash of arrows landing and the spraying, gushing blood of warriors and animals is the flood of the tempestuous nocturnal encounter between all those godlike men.

In the very midst of the battle, the greatest of Brahmanas, the noble Aswatthaman, scorching the Pandavas with flames from his bow, is the midday sun at the end of the season of rains, burning everything with his fierce rays.'"

CANTO 160

GHATOTKACHA-VADHA PARVA CONTINUED

"Sanjaya says, 'When the battlefield which had been plunged in darkness is illumined, great warriors, maharathas, again attack each other ferociously. With so many thousands of lamps burning all around and with the unearthly lanterns of the Devas and the Gandharvas now set on golden stands decked with jewels, and fed with fragrant oil, Kurukshetra, O Bhaarata, is wonderfully resplendent, bright as the earth lit by the lesser flames of the pralaya! With every side scintillating with lamps, of this world and the one above, the field of death looks like a forest covered over by fireflies on a monsoon evening.

At your son's command, maharathas engage with other maharathas, elephants with elephants, horsemen with horsemen, all filled with joy on this fiercest night. Terrible and now plainly visible is the war between the Kaurava army and that of the Pandavas without the sun above.

Then Arjuna begins to annihilate the Kaurava ranks with unprecedented ferocity and swiftness, weakening the position of all the kings who fight for you.'

Dhritarashtra says, 'When the invincible Arjuna breaks into the ranks of my son's army, what is the state of their minds? Indeed, what do our soldiers feel and think? What steps does Duryodhana take to contain Partha?

Who challenges the Kiritin? When Swetavahana breaks into our army, who protects Drona? Who guards the right wheel, who the left wheel and who the rear of Drona's ratha? Who are they that fight in his van? The mighty Drona battles his way into the midst of the Panchalas, dancing on his ratha, and shatters a huge number of Panchala chariots with his arrows; alas, how does the Acharya meet with his death?

You always speak of my enemies as cool, unvanquished, cheerful and swelling with might. However, you do not speak of my men in such words. On the other hand, you describe them to be dead, pale, and beaten, and you speak of my maharathas as always deprived of their chariots in all the battles they fight!'

Sanjaya replies, 'Understanding the wishes of Drona who is determined to give his all in the war at night, Duryodhana says to his brothers Vikarna, Chitrasena, Suparsva, Durdharsha, Dirghabahu, and all the men who follow them, "You heroes of great valour, fight with resolve and protect Drona's rear. Kritavarman will protect his right and Sala his left flanks."

Saying this, your son sets these brothers of his in the van of his forces, and then himself advances with the remnant of the Trigarta maharathas, saying, "The Acharya is merciful! The Pandavas fight with great resolution, so unite and protect him well. Drona is mighty; he is endued with great agility and valour. He can vanquish the very Devas; what need then be said of the Pandavas and the Somakas? All of you, however, must remain united and support the invincible Acharya against the dangerous maharatha Dhrishtadyumna. Other than Drupada's fire-born prince, I do not see the man among all the Pandava warriors who can vanquish Drona. And so, we must, with all our souls, guard the son of Bharadwaja against the Panchala prince.

Protected by us, Drona will massacre the Somakas and the Srinjayas, one after another. After the slaughter of all the Srinjayas at the head of the Pandava army, Aswatthaman will kill Dhrishtadyumna, and Karna will vanquish Arjuna maharatha. As for Bhimasena and the other sons of Pandu, I myself will kill them all. After that, our army will easily raze what remains of the Pandava forces. It is all plain to me now. And when we have won the war, my victory will last forever, and I will rule the earth unopposed, with all of you beside me.

I have given you the reasons. Now go forth, taking courage in both hands and, at all costs, protect Acharya Drona."

Saying this, Duryodhana charges headlong into the fray with his best troops around and behind him. The two armies collide again, each side intent on securing victory. Arjuna continues to inflict heavy losses on the Kauravas, and now the massed Kauravas begin to trouble Arjuna with diverse kinds of weapons.

Aswatthaman attacks Drupada of the Panchalas, while Drona covers Srinjaya with multitudes of deadly straight shafts. And as the Pandava and the Panchala troops on the one side and the Kaurava troops on the other, O Bhaarata, are engaged in butchering each other, absolute bedlam and bloody mayhem hold sway over lamplit Kurukshetra, field of truth. The war by night is more brutal than it has ever been. Great spirits of darkness crowd the field, unseen.'"

CANTO 161

Ghatotkacha-vadha Parva continued

"Sanjaya says, 'During the ghastly bloodbath by night, Yudhishtira exhorts the Pandavas, the Panchalas and the Somakas to destroy men, rathas and elephants without mercy, and cries to them, "Attack Drona! Kill the Acharya!"

At this command, Rajan, the Panchalas and the Somakas rush at Drona with terrifying roars. We, on our part, are equally energised, and roaring dreadfully in return, rush to confront the enemy to the utmost limits of our prowess, courage and might.

Kritavarman, son of Hridika, challenges Yudhishtira, as the Dharmaraja charges towards Drona, like an infuriated elephant against another. The great Kuru warrior Bhuri bars the way of Satyaki, who comes flying into the thick of battle, spraying arrows all around with incredible power and swiftness. Karna faces Sahadeva, as Madri's brilliant son rides at Drona, and Duryodhana himself faces the stupendous Bhimasena, riding on his chariot like the Great Destroyer.

Sakuni, son of Subala, stands firm against maharatha Nakula, who is an adept at every kind of battle. Kripa, son of Saradwat, sets himself in the way of Sikhandin, while Dusasana contends vigorously with Prativindhya whose chariot is yoked to steeds coloured like peacocks, their skins glistening marvellously by the now glaring lamplight! Aswatthaman defies Ghatotkacha, master of maya, a hundred different kinds of sorcery and illusion. Vrishasena quells the mighty Drupada with his troops as the Panchala king aims to cut Drona down. Salya, king of the Madras, holds up Virata, as the Matsya king also rushes towards Drona. Chitrasena forcefully holds up Nakula's son Satanika with a thousand shafts, as that prince also rides at Drona. Alambusha, the Rakshasa prince, defies Arjuna, and Dhrishtadyumna gladly contains Drona as the seemingly demented Acharya devours the Pandava forces with devastras, making no distinction between great warrior and common foot-soldier.

As for the maharathas of the Pandavas who advance against Drona, other maharathas of your army attack them ferociously. Elephant riders meet elephant riders in this frightful battle by lamplight, and grind each other down in their thousands. In the dead of night, as bright horses charge each other recklessly, they look like winged hills. Horsemen encounter horsemen, armed with lances, darts and swords and give vent to loud roars. Vast numbers of bold foot-soldiers slaughter one another, with corpses heaping up, with maces, short clubs and diverse other weapons.

Kritavarman fights Yudhishtira in rage, like a continent, a great dwipa, resisting the surging sea. Yudhishtira first pierces Kritavarman with five arrows and then with twenty more, and roars, "Stop! Stop and fight."

Kritavarman breaks Yudhishtira's bow with a wedge-headed arrow and draws blood from him with seven more. Yudhishtira picks up a fresh bow and gashes his adversary's arms and chest with ten arrows, making him tremble and retort with seven veritable thunderbolts. At which, Yudhishtira demolishes his bow, shreds his leather gauntlet and pierces him fiercely with five long shafts that rip through his gold-inlaid armour, his body and dive into the ground like snakes into an ant-hill.

In a wink, Kritavarman takes up another bow and blasts the son of Pandu first with sixty arrows and then with ten more. Yudhishtira puts down his bow and casts a serpentine javelin that passes through Kritavarman's right arm and into the earth. Taking up his formidable bow again Yudhishtira covers Kritavarman in a lashing downpour of exact barbs, making him cry out in pain.

In swift rage, the mighty Bhoja kills Yudhishtira's horses and charioteer and makes a wreck of his chariot. The Pandava hefts a sword and shield only to have them instantly shattered by the maharatha of the Madhu vamsa. Yudhishtira sweeps up a spear with a golden staff and hurls it like light at the illustrious son of Hridika; smiling arrogantly, Kritavarman neatly slices the missile along its length as it flashes at him.

He then shrouds Yudhishtira with a hundred arrows and, utterly roused by now, disjoints the Dharmaputra's golden armour so it falls from his body like a cluster of stars from the sky. His chariot in shambles, his armour cut away and bleeding from Kritavarman's hail of arrows, Yudhishtira quickly retreats from battle. Having vanquished the Dharmaputra, the mighty Kritavarman returns to once more protect the right wheel of Drona's chariot.'"

CANTO 162

Ghatotkacha-vadha Parva continued

"Sanjaya says, 'Bhuri, Rajan, stands in the way of Sini's grandson Satyaki who comes charging like an elephant towards a lake full of water. An angry Satyaki makes five springs of blood spurt from Bhuri's body. The Kuru warrior retaliates with great speed and pierces splendid Satyaki with ten arrows through his chest. Drawing their bows to their fullest stretch and with eyes red, these two begin to maul each other. Their cascades of lethal arrows are like rays of the sun; their duel is as if Death has taken two forms to do battle against himself. For a while, the battle is perfectly even. Until, with a terrible smile, Satyaki breaks Bhuri's bow and plunges nine arrows deep into his breast, and gives a terrible roar.

Bhuri quickly picks up another bow and strikes the Satwata with three light like barbs, and then, he also smiling, splits his antagonist's bow a wide-headed shaft. Beside himself, Satyaki flings a mighty javelin right into Bhuri's heart, and that great Kuru warrior, covered in blood, falls dead out of his chariot, like the sun from the sky when he sets.

Seeing Bhuri slain, Aswatthaman charges Satyaki recklessly. He shouts,

"Stop! Stop and fight!" at Yuyudhana and covers him with a blistering flight of arrows, like clouds lashing Meru's crown with a torrential rain.

Seeing the grim Aswatthaman rush towards Satyaki, Ghatotkacha gives a roar that makes all of Kurukshetra cringe; he says to Drona's son in the most dreadful voice, "Stop, O son of Drona! You will not escape me with your life and I will kill you like the six-faced Karttikeya did the Asura Mahisha. Stay and fight me, for today I will purge your heart of all desire for battle."

And the coppery-eyed Rakshasa, Bhima's tremendous son, attacks Aswatthaman like a prince of elephants, unleashing indescribable shafts at him, each the size of a chariot's axle-rod! Quicker than thinking, Aswatthaman smashes those massive arrows into dust and pierces Ghatotkacha deep with hundreds of keen barbs.

The handsome Rakshasa resembles an incredible porcupine with quills all erect! Unmoved, Bhima's son looses a terrific tirade of shafts at Aswatthaman, missiles that fly roaring like thunder at Drona's son, crashing into the Brahmana's shining body, making him stagger in his ratha. Ghatotkacha does not pause but looses volley after volley of different arrows over Aswatthaman; some have razor like heads; others are crescent-tipped; some have elongated points; some are frog-faced; other have heads like boar's ears; some are barbed, and there are others as well.

Drona's son remains immaculately calm throughout this onslaught and with hands moving quicker than thoughts, like the wind scattering large cloud masses, he consumes every shaft shot by Ghatotkacha, common and strange, with the handful of devastras that he invokes. And when Ghatotkacha also discharges his own unworldly astras, the dark sky is lit up by other suns where his astras and Aswatthaman's fuse and hang until falling away in showers of sparks. Ah, the firmament is exquisitely lit up, as if with a swarm of fireflies at twilight.

Aswatthaman fills all the points of the compass with his arrows and envelops Ghatotkacha in his storm of shafts—for the sake of your sons. The duel that develops between the two is like the one of yore between Indra and Prahlada. Ghatotkacha pierces Aswatthaman's chest with ten arrows that burn like the yuga fire, and the Brahmana trembles like a tall tree shaken by the wind. He supports himself briefly by clinging to his flagstaff, then collapses. There is an outcry of woe from yours troops who think him slain, while the Panchalas and the Srinjayas shout in glee.

However, maharatha Aswatthaman recovers quickly and, drawing his bowstring to his ear in a blur, looses a torrid astra at Ghatotkacha, a shaft like Yama's danda. The arrow with golden wings ploughs right through the Rakshasa's chest and enters the earth behind him. Gored savagely through, spouting blood, the prince of Rakshasas sits down in his ratha and his eyes glaze over. Seeing this, his charioteer spirits him away from the field. Having wounded Ghatotkacha grievously and driven him from the fray, Aswatthaman gives a ringing roar of triumph. Your sons and all your warriors cheer him deafeningly, O Bhaarata, and Aswatthaman's body blazes like the midday sun.

Looking at Bhimasena who battles like ten maharathas in front of Drona's chariot, Duryodhana strikes him with a fierce and heartfelt volley of utmost hatred. Bhima pierces him in return with nine arrows and Duryodhana strikes back with twenty. Quickly mantled over by each other's arrows, the two magnificent maharathas look like the sun and the moon covered by clouds in the sky. Then Duryodhana pierces Bhima deeply with five gold-winged thunderbolts and roars, "Stop! Stop and fight!"

In a flash, Bhima shatters Suyodhana's bow, cuts down his standard and strikes him in a dazzle with full ninety barbs. Duryodhana takes up an even more formidable bow and returns his cousin's fire so that blood flowers sprout all over the Pandava's vast body, in full view of all the other maharathas. Destroying many of Duryodhana's shafts in flight, Bhima pierces him with five and twenty short, heavy arrows. Duryodhana smashes Bhimasena's bow with a razor-faced arrow and pierces him with ten more.

Bhimasena snatches up another bow and rakes your son with seven violent shafts. Displaying great lightness of hand, Suyodhana cuts Bhima's bow in two. The second, third, fourth and the fifth bows that Bhima picks up, also, Suyodhana demolishes. Indeed, Rajan, full of self-assurance and feverish eagerness to kill the cousin whom he has always detested the most, your son breaks every bow that Bhima picks up immediately as he does so.

Finding his bows repeatedly broken, Bhima hurls an iron spear at Duryodhana, hard as diamonds, which ignites in the air as it flies at your son, which resembles Yama's sister Mrityu. Before all the watching warriors, Suyodhana cuts the lance into three pieces, even as it flares at him through the sky straight as the parting in a woman's hair. Bhima now picks up a heavy mace alight, and casts it like doom at Duryodhana's chariot and that weapon kills your son's horses, charioteer and blows his chariot apart.

Now afraid of dreadful Bhima, your son uses the anima siddhi to make himself little and hastily climbs into the illustrious Nandaka's chariot. In the half-light of the lamplit night, Bhima thinks he has killed Duryodhana and gives an earthshaking triumphant roar, challenging the Kaurava host. Your warriors also believe their king dead, and dismal cries echo across Kurukshetra.

Yudhishtira hears Bhima's repeated roaring and the howls of your terrified warriors, Yudhishtira also thinks that Duryodhana has been killed, and rushes to Bhima. The Panchalas, the Srinjayas, the Matsyas, the Kaikeyas, and the Chedis turn their chariots and charge Drona all together, and another horrible battle erupts between Drona and the enemy, during which thousands on both sides die scarlet deaths.'"

CANTO 163

GHATOTKACHA-VADHA PARVA CONTINUED

"Sanjaya says, 'Karna, son of Vikartana, Rajan, faces the mighty maharatha Sahadeva, who is closing in dangerously on Drona. In a flash, Sahadeva strikes Karna with nine sizzling arrows and then another nine in a blink. Karna returns his fire with a full hundred storming shafts; he severs Sahadeva's bowstring. Sahadeva takes up another bow and strikes Karna squarely with twenty arrows, a wonderful feat. Karna, roused, despatches Sahadeva's horses with a flock of perfect arrows and his sarathy with a single wedge-headed one. Without a ratha, Sahadeva picks up a sword and shield, which Karna shatters with a lofty smile.

Sahadeva flings a heavy mace of power at Karna, a dread weapon adorned with gold; Karna demolishes that, too, with a rash of incredible arrows. His mace shattered, Sahadeva casts a whistling spear at Karna, which that greatest bowman slices in two along its length. Madri's red-eyed son leaps down from his chariot, pulls a wheel free from his ruined ratha and hurls it spinning at the brother he does not know. Karna, still with the mocking, maddening smile, looses a thousand arrows in a moment and smashes that chariot wheel flying at him like Death's very chakra.

In a frenzy, the desperate Sahadeva pulls off the yokes, shafts and other parts of his chariot, the traces of his horses, and casts all these like deadly weapons at the Sutaputra. Karna disdainfully shoots them all down. Now Sahadeva picks up whatever he finds lying around him—the limbs of elephants, horses and even dead men—and hurls these at his enemy. Karna's speed artistry as he shreds all these in flight is amazing to behold, my lord. Deprived of all his weapons and fairly mangled by Karna's barrage of shafts, Sahadeva quits the unequal duel and leaves the field.

Karna pursues him for a while and, with the same smile, now turned so mysterious, mocks him, "Kshatriya, do not fight your superiors. Seek out your equals to do battle with, O son of Madri! Listen to me, what I say is for your own good!"

Karna then prods Sahadeva with the tip of his bow, and says, "Look where your great brother Arjuna fights so resolutely against the Kurus. Go to him or, if you prefer, go back home!" And he laughs at Sahadeva, a sound more cruel than any arrow.

Thus, Karna, when he could have done so, does not kill Madri's son, remembering his word given to Kunti before the war. Instead, he now rides away against the troops of the king of the Panchalas. A dispirited Sahadeva, wounded equally by Karna's arrows and by his words, is humiliated, crestfallen, even wishes for death, proud Kshatriya that he is. He sadly climbs into the Panchala prince Janamejaya's chariot.'"

CANTO 164

GHATOTKACHA-VADHA PARVA CONTINUED

"Sanjaya says, 'Salya, king of the Madras, holds up Virata and his troops, with clouds of missiles as they advance to attack Drona. The duel between Salya and Madra is like the one between Bala and Vasava of old. Salya strikes Virata, who commands a large akshauhini, with a hundred immaculate shafts. Virata, in return, pierces him first with nine sharp arrows, then with three and seventy, and again with a hundred. Salya kills the four horses yoked to Virata's chariot and cuts down his royal parasol and standard.

Virata jumps down from his useless ratha and, standing on the ground, continues to loose storms of arrows at Salya with undimmed ferocity. Seeing his brother exposed on the ground, Satanika rides swiftly to rescue him. With a flurry of lethal barbs, Salya sends the advancing Satanika to Yama. At the fall of Satanika, his brother Virata climbs into the fallen hero's chariot, and his prowess fuelled, doubled by his rage, glares his eyes wide at Salya and mantles the Madra and his ratha with a cloudburst of arrows.

But the mighty Salya responds in strength and strikes Virata squarely through his chest with a hundred slender shafts, forcing the Matsya king to sit down in a swoon. His charioteer quickly takes his king away from the field, and, its spirit broken, the vast Matsya force flees, pursued, O Bhaarata, by the thousands of arrows that Salya, that ornament of battle, shoots after them. Seeing their troops run, Krishna and Arjuna come dashing up to confront Salya.

Now, Rajan, the Rakshasa prince Alambusha appears, looming on an altogether macabre and wondrous chariot of black iron, harnessed to eight awful pisachas with equine faces, flying blood-red banners, festooned with wildflower garlands, covered with bear-skins and mounted with a lofty standard atop over which a fierce-looking and incessantly shrieking vulture with spotted wings and gaping eyes perches. The Rakshasa looks like a heap of antimony; and he stands up to the advancing Arjuna like Meru withstanding a tempest, and rains down showers of arrows on Arjuna's head. Ah, pitched and intense is the ensuing battle between the Rakshasa and the human warrior; it fills all that watch with awe and it adds to the glee of the vultures, crows, ravens, owls, kanakas and jackals that patrol death's abysmal field.

Arjuna strikes Alambusha with six bolts of lightning and cuts off his standard with ten more. He beheads his strange demon sarathy in a burst of slimy green blood, severs his weirdly shining bow in his hands and kills the equine pisachas with four occult barbs. Alambusha takes up another sinister bow, but that too Arjuna rives. Bharatarishabha, Partha strikes that vile prince of Rakshasas with four such formidable shafts that Alambusha takes to his heels.

Having vanquished the fiend of darkness, Arjuna rides swiftly towards Drona, on his way slaughtering innumerable men, elephants and horses that fall like trees laid low by a storm, while the remaining soldiers run away like a frightened herd of deer.'"

CANTO 165

Ghatotkacha-vadha Parva continued

"Sanjaya says, 'Your son Chitrasena, O Bhaarata, confronts Nakula's son Satanika who is consuming your army with his missiles. Satanika strikes Chitrasena with five arrows and your prince responds with ten whetted shafts. Chitrasena gashes Satanika with nine bolts, at which the son of Nakula responds with a fusillade of arrows that rip Chitrasena's armour from his body: a wonderful feat. Without his armour, your son looks remarkable, like a snake that has just cast off his slough. Satanika cuts down the struggling Chitrasena's standard, and then breaks his bow.

The beleaguered Chitrasena seizes up another powerful dhanusha and plunges countless arrows at Satanika. His fury mounting, Satanika kills Chitrasena's horses and his charioteer, at which his powerful opponent jumps down from his ratha and drills Satanika with five and twenty arrows. Satanika destroys Chitrasena's gold-decked bow with a crescent-tipped arrow. Deprived of his bow, chariot, horses and charioteer, Chitrasena quickly runs to Kritavarman's chariot and climbs aboard.

Karna's son Vrishasena leads his legion against maharatha Drupada, spraying multitudinous arrows at the Panchala king, who is closing rapidly on Drona. Yajnasena challenges the son of Karna and plunges sixty barbs into his arms and chest. The doughty Vrishasena responds with astounding speed and draws spouts of blood from Drupada's chest. These two, as well, with each other's arrows protruding from their bodies, look startlingly like a couple of huge porcupines with quills erect. Bathed in blood from wounds taken from golden-winged arrows, they are especially striking during their wrathful duel. Indeed, the spectacle they present is as that of a pair of radiant Kalpa vrikshas or of two kinsukas laden with blood flowers.

Vrishasena strikes Drupada with nine arrows, then with seventy more and again with another three. Loosing a gale of arrows, Karna's son, Rajan, makes a resplendent spectacle. An inflamed Drupada splits Vrishasena's bow in two with a broad-headed arrow. Vrishasena picks up another gold chased bow, invokes a great astra and, taking careful aim at Drupada, while he ignores the slew of barbs that the Panchala king looses at him, unleashes the blazing thing at the Acharya, filling all the Somakas with fear. The astras plunge straight through Yagnasena's chest and he collapses onto the floor of his chariot. His sarathy whisks him away from the field. Seeing the great Panchala maharatha leave the battle in a faint, the Kaurava army fervidly attacks Drupada's troops.

The lamps fallen from the hands of slain warriors light up the earth all around so Kurukshetra looks even like the firmament lit by stars and planets. The ground sparkles with the angadas of fallen heroes, like a great cloud mass during the monsoon, in which streaks of lightning flash. From fear of Karna's son, the Panchalas flee on all sides, as the Danavas did from terror of Indra during the great Devasura yuddha.

Thus stricken by Vrishasena, the Panchalas and the Somakas, illumined by lamps, present an unusual and arresting sight. Having vanquished them, Vrishasena looks like the sun, O Bharata, when he reaches his zenith. Among all those thousands of kings on your side and theirs, the valiant Vrishasena seems to be the only resplendent luminary. Having vanquished many heroes and all the great maharathas among the

Somakas, Karna's son races on towards the Pandava king Yudhishtira.

Your son Dusasana rides against the mighty Prativindhya, who charges at Drona who unabatedly devours the enemy troops with his devastras. The duel that erupts between them is like the contention between Mercury and Venus, Budha and Sukra, in a cloudless sky. Dusasana pierces Prativindhya, who is accomplishing fierce feats, with three arrows shot straight into his forehead. Gushing blood from the wounds Prativindhya looks like a three crested hill with streams of red chalk flowing down.

Prativindhya strikes back in fury, first piercing Dusasana with three arrows and again with seven. Now your son achieves a difficult feat. He first fells Prativindhya's horses with a dense volley, then, with one broad-headed shaft, kills his sarathy and then cuts down his standard. Dusasana then smashes Prativindhya's chariot under him into a thousand pieces, shreds his banner, his quivers, bowstrings and the traces of his ratha.

Deprived of his chariot, the virtuous Prativindhya stands, bow in hand, and contends with your son, shooting an opacity of arrows at him, until Dusasana, showing marvellous dexterity, breaks his adversary's bow and then lacerates him with ten brutal arrows. Seeing Prativindhya's plight, his brothers, maharathas all, come dashing forward with a large force to protect him. Prativindhya climbs onto Sutasoma's splendid chariot and, taking up another bow, continues to shoot at your son. A strong force of your warriors arrives swiftly to support Dusasana.

Another dreadful battle ensues between your troops and theirs, O Bhaarata, at the midnight hour, and swells the population of Yama's domain.'"

CANTO 166

Ghatotkacha-vadha Parva continued

"Sanjaya says, 'Roaring "Stop! Stop!" Subala's son Sakuni in sudden fury attacks Nakula, who is decimating your forces. Bows drawn in circles, both show the same measure of skill, lashing each other with arrows. Soon, these two also resemble strange porcupines. Their armour cut away and each bathed in blood, they resemble two beautiful and brilliant Kalpa vrikshas, or flowering kinsukas, or Salmali trees with prickly thorns on them.

Eyes red and bulging with rage, they cast sidelong glowers at each other, as if to kill the other with their gazes. Then, with a fiendish grin, Sakuni pierces Nakula's chest with a barbed arrow and Madri's son swoons in his chariot. Sakuni roars as loud as the clouds at the end of summer.

Nakula recovers quickly and attacks his vile enemy again, now like the Destroyer himself with jaws agape; Nakula drills him first with sixty arrows and again with a hundred long shafts right through his chest. He breaks Sakuni's bow, and fells his haughty standard. He plunges an arrow shot with all his might deep into Sakuni's thigh and drops him onto the floor of his chariot, clasping his flagstaff like an amorous man his mistress.

Seeing your brother-in-law felled and fainted, his charioteer quickly rides away from the van of the battle. At this, the Parthas and all their followers give a loud and triumphal shout.

Nakula, the Parantapa, says to his sarathy, "Take me towards the forces that Drona commands." The man does as he is commanded. Seeing Nakula ride against Drona, Kripa rides to stop him but a smiling Sikhandin pierces Kripa with nine arrows from a flank. Turning, Kripa strikes Sikhandin first with five arrows, and then with twenty more. The duel that breaks out between the two is hair-raising, my lord, even like the one between Sambara and the king of the Devas in the war of antiquity between the Devas and the Asuras.

Both maharathas cover the heavens with their missiles, like clouds at the end of summer. The night is full of terror and evokes all sorts of fears in the warriors. Then Sikhandin splits Kripa's large bow with a crescent-headed arrow and ravages him with a flurry of other shafts. The infuriated Kripa casts a polished golden spear at the Panchala prince, which Sikhandin shatters in flight with ten immaculate arrows.

Kripa takes up a fresh bow and looses such a rage of arrows at the prince who was once a princess that Sikhandin collapses onto the floor of his ratha. Kripa continues to strafe him with many more shafts, trying to kill him, but his charioteer bears Sikhandin away to safety.

The Panchalas and the Somakas see the mighty maharatha son of Yajnasena retreat from battle, and rush to his rescue, while your sons surround Kripa, best of Brahmanas, with a large force to support him. Another ferocious battle ensues; a great tumult arises, full of roars and screams, and the thunder of horses' hooves and lumbering elephants, filling the hour past midnight like massed thunderheads. The earth trembles with the tread of running foot-soldiers, why like a woman shaking with fear.

Maharathas dash manically at one another, in their thousands, slaughtering numberless common soldiers as they go. Great elephants, with ichor flowing down their bodies, rush at other mastodons, and fight furiously with trunks and curved, glinting tusks that are soon dyed in red. Horsemen and foot-soldiers, too, fight without any vestige of restraint or sanity.

In the heart of night, the sound of troops attacking and retreating is deafening and bizarre. The blazing lamps placed on chariots, elephants and horses are like meteors fallen from the sky and smouldering still. Lit by these, the night, O lord of the Bharatas, is a strangest day. As the sun dispels the darkness of every night, do the blazing lamps the turgid darkness of the war.

Indeed, the sky, the earth, the cardinal and the subsidiary points of the world, enveloped by dust and darkness, are all illuminated by the lamplight, which is increased many times over by being reflected by splendid weapons, coats of mail and the jewels of famed Kshatriyas. Yet, during the tumultuary war at night, few of the fighters, O Bhaarata, can distinguish ally from enemy and father kills son, son kills father, friend slays friend, relatives slay relatives, uncles kill sisters' sons, countless warriors kill other warriors of their own side.

Absolute brutal chaos and madness rule everywhere, and all that appears to matter is to kill or be killed, regardless of who kills and who is slain.'"

CANTO 167

GHATOTKACHA-VADHA PARVA CONTINUED

"Sanjaya says, 'Dhrishtadyumna, fire-prince of the Panchalas faces Drona in this night. His formidable bow raised and repeatedly twanging its string, Drupada's meridian son, supported by his own troops and those of the Pandavas, charges toward Drona's gold-bedecked ratha. Seeing the great Acharya thus assailed, your son resolutely protects Drona on all sides and the two hosts collide again in vast numbers, even like two awesome seas lashed into fury by a tempest surging into each other, with all their marine creatures frantically agitated.

Dhrishtadyumna pierces Drona's torso with five arrows and gives a roar of triumph. Drona strikes his most feared enemy with five and twenty arrows and, with another broad-headed shaft, severs his bright bow. Dhrishtadyumna casts aside his broken bow, bites his lip in rage and, picking up another awesome weapon, drawing its string to his ear in a flash, looses an astra that can have Drona's life. The missile illuminates the whole army like another sun. Seeing the incandescent astra, the Devas, the Gandharvas and the Danavas pray: "May Drona live!"

At that moment, from a far flank, Karna, showing godlike genius, shatters the fulminant astra into a dozen pieces even as it flies inexorable towards the Acharya; extinguished, the astra falls onto the earth like a snake that has lost its fangs and venom. Karna inundates Dhrishtadyumna with a torrent of arrows. Maharatha Aswatthaman strikes him with five singing barbs, Drona with another five, Salya with nine, Dusasana with three, Duryodhana with twenty and Sakuni with five of his own. Thus, seven mighty maharathas come quickly to Drona's rescue and vigorously assault the burning prince of the Panchalas.

He, however, draws blood from every one of them: Drona, Karna, Drona's son and your son with three arrows each. Their roaring, Rajan, all this while, is truly horrible, as they combine to wildly beset Dhrishtadyumna. Then Drumasena wounds the fire-prince deep with a gold-winged shaft, and again with another three, shouting, "Stop! Stop and fight me!"

Dhrishtadyumna strikes back with three deadly accurate arrows, fletched with wings of gold and shining slick with oil; with another crescent-headed arrow he blasts Drumasena's head from his neck, and its earrings sparkle red as the grisly thing falls onto the ground, a final cry frozen on its lips curled in fury still. The head of that hero falls like a ripe palmyra fruit blown from its stalk by a powerful gust of wind.

Dhrishtadyumna, the irradiant, sprays fire all around him despatching thousands to Yamaloka; with a wedge headed arrow he splits Karna's bow in two. Karna cannot abide this; he is like a some wild lion that has its tail cut off! He takes up another bow, and with eyes red as plums and breathing hard, envelops mighty Dhrishtadyumna with riptides of arrows. Seeing Karna in this mood, your six other maharathas quickly surround the prince of the Panchalas, determined to kill him.

Seeing their Senapati facing the six greatest warriors of your army, all your troops consider him as being already delivered into the jaws of death. But then, Satyaki of the Dasarha vamsa arrives to support the embattled Dhrishtadyumna; the Satwata hero comes loosing a tide of arrows before him. Karna greets him with ten arrows. Before the watching maharathas, Satyaki responds with ten thunderbolts and cries tauntingly, "Do not run away again, Karna! Stay and fight me."

And once more, the blazing duel that ensues between mighty Satyaki and the redoubtable Karna resembles, O Rajan, that between Bali and Vasava in the days of old. Satyaki, bull among Kshatriyas, terrifies all your warriors with the rumble of his ratha, and he strikes the lotus-eyed Karna deep with countless arrows. Making the earth shudder with the twang of his bow, the majestic Sutaputra covers the relucent Satyaki with a barrage of long, barbed, tall-toothed and razor-headed arrows and diverse other missiles. Satyaki of the Vrishnis also shrouds Karna in a mantle of fire.

For a time, that duel is magnificent and equal. Then, your sons, keeping Karna at their head, shoot at Satyaki from every side. Fending them all off, including Karna, with his own astras, Satyaki abruptly strikes the valiant Vrishasena through his chest so that he falls down in his chariot, casting aside his bow.

Believing his son, the maharatha Vrishasena, dead, shock plunges through Karna and he attacks Satyaki in reckless frenzy. Satyaki serenely pierces Karna with many strong shafts. He first strikes the Sutaputra with ten arrows, then Vrishasena, who has arisen again, with five, and finally shreds the leather gloves and severs the bows of both father and son. Stringing fresh bows, father and son assail Satyaki from two sides and lacerate him with countless arrows.

During the course of the war by night that kills so many heroes, we hear the loud twang of the Gandiva, O Rajan, over every other sound. Hearing the rumble of Arjuna's ratha as well as reverberant Gandiva, Karna tells Duryodhana, "Arjuna strums his great bow after slaughtering our leading warriors, so many great archers among the Kauravas, and, indeed much of our entire army. The thunder you hear is the rumble of his ratha. It is plain that this son of Pandu tonight achieves feats truly worthy of him and that he will swiftly raze all our forces.

Many of our troops already flee ad no one dares stand up to Arjuna as he scatters our legions as the mighty wind may a rising mass of clouds. Encountering Arjuna, our soldiers all capsize like small skiffs on the raging ocean. You hear the wails, Duryodhana, of our best warriors as they run from the field, or fall to the arrows loosed in great waves from the Gandiva.

Listen, O tiger among maharathas, to the sound of drums and cymbals being beaten near Arjuna's ratha at dead of night like the deep roll of thunder in the sky. Listen to the screams of wounded soldiers and the tremendous roars and victorious shouts around Arjuna's chariot.

However, here Satyaki, the greatest of the Satwata vamsa, holds us all up. If Yuyudhana can be brought down, we might conquer all our enemies. Also, Dhrishtadyumna battles Acharya Drona, and many of our best rathikas encircle those two. If we can kill Satyaki and Dhrishtadyumna, victory will certainly be ours. So let us surround these two shuras even as we did Abhimanyu in the chakravyuha and kill them both. Arjuna already turns his chariot toward Drona's chariot, for he knows that Satyaki holds up so many of our Kuru maharathas. Let another goodly number of our greatest warriors ride to prevent Partha from coming to the beleaguered Satyaki's rescue. And let those that remain attack Satyaki all together, putting forth their fiercest prowess so that Yuyudhana of Madhu's race is despatched swiftly to Yama's abode."

Duryodhana concurs with Karna's view and, like the illustrious Indra requesting Vishnu, says to his uncle Sakuni, "Matulan, ride against Arjuna with ten thousand elephants and ten thousand chariots. Dusasana, Durvishaha, Subahu and Dushpradharshana will follow you with an akshauhini of foot-soldiers. Kill the two Krishnas; kill Yudhishtira, Nakula, Sahadeva and Bhima. My hope of victory rests in you, as that of the gods on their lord Indra. O Sakuni, slay the sons of Kunti, like Kartikeya slaying the Asuras."

Clad in armour and taking your sons and a large host with him, Sakuni rides against the Parthas to have their lives. Another great and general battle begins between the warriors of your army and the enemy. When Subala's son Sakuni advances against the Pandavas, Karna leads a teeming force against Satyaki, unleashing a gale of arrows. Your warriors all combine and surround Satyaki. Then, Bharatarishabha, Drona advances against Dhrishtadyumna's ratha and fights a wonderful and bloody night battle against the Panchalas.'"

CANTO 168

Ghatotkacha-vadha Parva continued

"Sanjaya says, 'All the indomitable kings of your army besiege Satyaki's ratha in fury, to put an end to his lustrous and terrible exploits. Mounted on their fine chariots decked with gold and encrusted with jewels, and accompanied by cavalry and elephants, they surround the Satwata hero and, roaring an earthshaking challenge at him, cover him with their arrows. Even as they come at him, Sini's grandson snips off countless heads even as if he were plucking flowers from their stems. With his razor-faced arrows, he hacks away the trunks of so many elephants, the necks of numerous horses and the arms of countless warriors, wearing sparkling angadas.

The field of dreadful dharma is covered over by fallen chamaras and white chatras, O Bhaarata, and resembles the sky with stars in it. The screams of the host slaughtered Satyaki is as awful as those of shrieking ghosts in hell. The world is filled by the horrible uproar and the night becomes still more brutal and appalling. Seeing Yuyudhana desiccate your army, hearing the incredible bloodcurdling din at dead of night, your mighty Duryodhana cries to his sarathy, "Ride to where this dreadful sound comes from."

Duryodhana, master archer, rides at Satyaki, who greets him with a dozen blood-drinking arrows shot from his bow drawn to its fullest stretch. A maddened Duryodhana gashes Yuyudhana with ten shafts like streaks of lightning. Meanwhile, the battle that rages between the Panchalas and your troops presents an exceptionally wonderful sight. Satyaki bores Duryodhana's brawny breast with eighty arrows, then despatches his horses to Yama's realm and fells his charioteer from his ratha.

Your son, Rajan, remains standing on his immobile chariot and looses a brilliant arrow storm at Satyaki, the Satwata cuts down with luculent skill. Then, with a broad-headed shaft, Satyaki breaks your son's formidable bow. Deprived of both his ratha and bow, Suyodhana, powerful ruler of men, quickly mounts Kritavarman's bright chariot and rides away. After Duryodhana's retreat, Satyaki harries and routs your army all around.

Meanwhile, surrounding Arjuna on all sides with thousands of rathas, elephants and horses, Sakuni lays violent siege to the glorious Pandava. Many of the Kuru maharathas loose devastras of great power at Arjuna. Indeed, these Kshatriyas fight Arjuna, accepting the certitude of death. An inspired Arjuna single-handedly arrests the progress of the thousands of chariots, elephants and horses; he is awesome, he is a god on the darkling field, and he forces them all to turn back. His eyes glittering coppery with rage, Sakuni strikes Arjuna powerfully with twenty shafts, drawing fonts of blood; with another hundred vicious barbs, he halts the sweeping advance of Partha's great chariot.

Arjuna first strikes Sakuni with twenty arrows and then each of the maharathas who ride with him with three. Stopping all of them with his scintillating volleys, Arjuna razes your army's warriors at will, with arrows shot with the force of striking thunder. Strewn with corpses of man and beasts, and arrows cut down, the earth looks as if it is covered with morbid yet fascinating flowers. Spread over with the heads of Kshatriyas, heads wearing crowns, their faces with noble noses, noble ears with beautiful earrings, lower lips bitten through in rage and pain, and staring eyes; covered by these heads graced with rich collars and crowned with gemstones, and lips that spoke sweet, eloquent words when life was in them, the earth looks splendent as if with hillocks covered with champaka flowers.

Having perpetrated this carnage, Arjuna pierces Sakuni once more, strikes his son Uluka with an arrow, and gives a roar that fills the world. He smashes Sakuni's bow and sends his four horses to Yama's realm. Sakuni, O Bharatarishabha, jumps down from his chariot and clambers into Uluka's ratha. Riding on the same chariot, the maharatha father and son shower arrows over Partha like twin clouds lashing a mountain with rain. Arjuna rakes both with ferocious shafts and scuttles your troops so violently that they run in their thousands. Like a vast cloud mass dispersed on all sides by an irresistible wind, your army runs in all directions, in full view of their commanders. In the sinister night, many abandon the beasts they are riding; others urge their horses to their greatest speed and flee. Having put your forces to complete rout, Krishna and Arjuna sound their conches echoingly.

Dhrishtadyumna stabs Drona with three arrows, and severs the Acharya's bowstring. Throwing down that bow, Drona, the Kshatriya grinder, takes up another and, quicker than seeing, strikes Dhrishtadyumna with five arrows, and his charioteer with another five. Holding the Brahmana up, Dhrishtadyumna begins to destroy the Kaurava host like Maghavat annihilating the Asura army. He lets flow a ghastly, frothing river of blood, which glimmers in the lamplight. It runs between the two hosts, and bears away men, horses and elephants on its current! It resembles, O Rajan, the Vaitarani that flows down to the domain of Yama.

Harrying and decimating your army, the valiant Dhrishtadyumna blazes with tejas as Indra in the midst of the Devas. Then Dhrishtadyumna and Sikhandin blow their great conchs, as do the twins, Nakula and Sahadeva, and Bhima as well. Thus, O Dhritarashtra, do these inexorable maharathas vanquish thousands of your illustrious kings before the eyes of Duryodhana, Karna, Drona and Aswatthaman!'"

CANTO 169

Ghatotkacha-vadha Parva continued

"Sanjaya says, 'Seeing his army being massacred by the illustrious enemy maharathas, your son, O Rajan, rides up in fury to Karna and Drona and says to them, "You two started this battle in resentment, after Arjuna killed Jayadratha. And now you watch with indifference as the Pandavas decimate my army although you are both entirely able to vanquish them. If you intend to abandon me now, you should have warned me before we went to war.

'Together we will vanquish the sons of Pandu,' is what you said to me then. Listening to you, I went to war. If you had said otherwise, I would never have provoked hostilities with the Parthas, this dreadful battle that is killing our heroes past all count. If I do not deserve to be abandoned by you two, then fight as you truly can, O you bulls among men!"

Prodded by the shrewd Duryodhana with his goad of words, Karna and Drona attack the enemy again, like two snakes prodded with sticks. These two greatest maharathas in the world rush forward against the Parthas led by Satyaki and others. And uniting, the Parthas, with all their troops advance against these two shuras, who now repeatedly roar their ringing challenges at the Pandava forces.

Great Drona, master of all weapons, pierces Satyaki, bull of the Sinis, with ten arrows while Karna strikes him with ten, your son with seven, Vrishasena with ten, and Sakuni with seven. They join the unbreachable wall of Kauravas built around the Satwata. Seeing Drona mow down the Pandava army with his astras, the Somakas cover him from every side with dense showers of arrows. Drona continues to annihilate the Pandava Kshatriyas around him, Rajan, as the sun destroys darkness with his rays.

We then hear an uproar among the Panchalas, who call out pitifully to one another, while Drona the Brahmana butchers them. Some abandoning sons, some fathers, some brothers, some uncles, some their sister's sons, some other relatives and kinsmen, all run to save their own lives. Many are so panic-stricken that they run straight at Drona himself. Ah, past all count are the common Pandava soldiers and great Kshatriyas that the incendiary Acharya sends to Yama. Set upon in the night by the blazing master, the Pandava host flings down its weapon and runs from the terrible Acharya in full view of Bhimasena, Arjuna, Krishna, the twins, Yudhishtira and Dhrishtadyumna.

The world being plunged in darkness, one might otherwise see nothing; but by the light of the lamps from the Kaurava troops, one sees the flight of the enemy. Drona and Karna pursue your legions, killing countless men from behind with ruthless volleys of arrows and devastras too.

Seeing the Panchalas thus butchered, Krishna tells Arjuna and the rest of the Pandavas, "Dhrishtadyumna and Satyaki, with the Panchalas, have confronted Drona and Karna. But they have been soundly beaten and the Brahmana and the Sutaputra have put our vast to flight and not all our persuasions will fetch the men back to fight.

Yet have no fear, O sons of Pandu, for the two Krishnas will now descend upon Drona and Karna like doom!"

Krishna sees Bhima riding up, and says again to Arjuna, to put heart into him, "There comes Bhima, leading the Somakas and the Pandavas, to confront Drona and Karna. O Pandava, fight now for the morale of all your troops, supported by Bhima and the rest of the many maharathas we have with us!"

The two Naravyaghras, the two Krishnas, ride to the van of their forces and advance on Drona and Karna. Now, Yudhishtira's army returns to the battle again, to the place where Drona and Karna are decimating their forces. Another horrific battle erupts between the two hosts, like two oceans swollen at moonrise and surging into each other in tide. And now, the warriors of your army throw away the burning lamps they hold and, with the world plunged in darkness again, they rush at the Pandava soldiers again, guided only by the names they call out.

We hear the names that the kings fighting there proclaim, O Rajan, as if they are being announced at a swayamvara. Suddenly, a grim silence spreads over the field and lasts for a moment. Then, once more, we hear the bedlam raised by the roars and cries of the fighting men, both victors and vanquished. The heroes rush to where they see lamps still burning, like insects to a blazing fire. One by one, the lamps all die down and, as the Pandavas and the Kauravas wage bloodthirsty war between them, the darkness of the night thickens around them.'"

CANTO 170

Ghatotkacha-vadha Parva continued

"Sanjaya says, 'Karna, slayer of enemy Kshatriyas, sees Dhrishtadyumna and strikes him powerfully through his chest with ten excoriating arrows. Dhrishtadyumna swiftly returns Karna's fire with five searing arrows and shouts, "Halt! Stop and fight!"

They shroud each other in arrow clouds shot from bows drawn into circles. Then Karna kills Dhrishtadyumna's four horses; Karna destroys his enemy's best bow and, with a broad-headed shaft, fells the Panchala prince's sarathy from his niche in the chariot. Dhrishtadyumna jumps down from his chariot with a mace in hand. Though continuously gashed by Karna's arrows, he runs at him, clubs his horses so their heads are crushed, and then running back climbs nimbly into Arjuna's chariot. From there, Dhrishtadyumna wants to continue his duel with Karna but Yudhishtira stops him.

Mahatejasvin Karna, whose leonine roars mingling with the resounding twang of his bow, pauses, raises his conch to his lips and blows a blast on it like age-ending thunder. Seeing Dhrishtadyumna beaten, the Panchalas and the Somakas, mighty maharathas all, attack

Karna all together, intent on killing him and with no care for their lives. Meanwhile, Karna's charioteer has great Sindhu horses, white as moonbeams and fleet as thoughts, attached to his ratha.

Karna resumes battle with great energy, harrying the Panchala maharathas with a torrent of blazing arrows. The Panchala soldiers flee in terror, like some little does frightened by a lion. O Rajan, we see horsemen fall from their horses all around, elephant-riders from their elephants and maharathas from their chariots, all slain by Karna's supernal archery. In this battle being fought surely in a zone of hell, Karna lops off the arms of fleeing warriors with razor-faced shafts, their heads decked with chariot-rings, the thighs of others that are seated on elephants, or on horseback, or stand upon the earth. So sharp are his arrows that many of these fleeing maharathas do not realise for a while that they have lost their limbs or their mounts.

Killed by the Sutaputra's terrible shafts, the Panchalas and the Srinjayas are so seized by fear that they begin to see Karna everywhere; they imagine that the wind stirring a blade of grass for that awesome, superhuman maharatha. Why, they lose their wits to the extent that they see Karna in the forms of their friends and comrades and flee from them in terror. Karna pursues the broken and retreating army, his arrows flaring everywhere as he mows down the hapless enemy at his great will.

Others run away when Drona just looks at them. Seeing his army turn tail, Yudhishtira thinks it would be advisable for them all to retreat, and says to Arjuna, "Look where mighty Karna stands like Rudra himself with his Pinaka. In the dead of night, look how he scorches everything around him like Surya himself. All we hear are the helpless screams of those whom Karna tears apart with his arrows. So swiftly does he aim and loose his shafts that it appears to be an unbroken movement. He will annihilate all our friends, so quickly do whatever you must to kill Karna, for his time may have come."

Hearing this, Partha says to Krishna, "The Dharmaputra is frightened today by Karna's great skill. His legions repeatedly overwhelm ours and our men are fleeing. The rest of our army is already in shreds from the

Acharya's arrows. Slaughtered and terrified by these two, we cannot seem to make a stand against them. I see Karna ride fearlessly everywhere and our best maharathas fleeing from him.

He unleashes his fervid tirade as he likes and I cannot bear to watch this anymore than a trodden-upon serpent. O tiger of Vrishni's vamsa, let us ride at mighty Karna. I will either kill him, or let him kill me."

Krishna says, "Naravyaghra, this superhuman warrior rides across the field at will sowing death all around him, and he is like Indra himself. Arjuna, no one can challenge the Sutaputra other than you or Ghatotkacha. I do not think that the time has come for you to face the Suta's son. He still has the astra given him by Indra, which he has kept carefully to use against you. It has now assumed a terrible form.

Ghatotkacha is devoted to you and wishes to serve you, so let the great Rakshasa ride against Karna. Bhima is his father and Ghatotkacha is as powerful as a Deva. He has the astras of the Devas as well as those used by Rakshasas."

They send for Ghatotkacha and he appears before them, Rajan, clad in black armour and armed with a sword, a bow and arrows. Saluting Krishna and Arjuna, he proudly says, "Here I am, command me!"

Krishna says to Hidimbi's Rakshasa son of the blazing mouth and fiery eyes, his body the hue of clouds, "Listen, O Ghatotkacha, to what I have to say. The time has come for you, and none else, to display your prowess. Become the raft in this battle to save the sinking Pandavas. You have a myriad of weapons, and many kinds of Rakshasa maya. Look where Karna decimates the Pandava army as if it were a herd of cattle before him. Karna, mahabuddhi, mahatejasvin, consumes our greatest Kshatriyas in the flames of his astras as if offering them as havis to the gods.

The Pandava warriors cannot withstand him; burnt and shredded by the Sutaputra's arrows, the Panchalas also run from him like deer chased by a lion. You are the only one who can face him in battle, Ghatotkacha. Your time for glory has come. O Mahabaho, do what is worthy of your mother's race, as well as that of your sires. Men wish for sons to be delivered by them from strife. You must rescue your kinsmen tonight, Ghatotkacha, at this hour of your great strength.

Fathers wish for sons in order to accomplish their own objectives. Sons are the source of everything good, and are expected to save their fathers both here and in the hereafter. Illustrious you are and your might is dreadful and unrivalled; there is no one to equal you in battle. Become tonight the ship in which the Pandavas, whom the terrible Karna routs with his astras, and who are sinking in the Dhartarashtra ocean, safely come ashore. By night, all Rakshasas are infused with limitless powers, great might and untold courage. At this hour, they turn into invincible warriors of matchless valour. Using your maya shakti and all your astras, slay Karna in this heart of the night. The Parthas, with Dhrishtadyumna, will then easily do away with Drona."

Arjuna adds, "Ghatotkacha, the long-armed Satyaki, Bhimasena and you are, in my judgment, our greatest warriors. Go and fight Karna tonight in single combat. Satyaki will protect your rear and, with his help, kill the brave Karna, as Indra did, with Skanda's, the Deva senapati's help, the Asura Taraka."

Ghatotkacha replies, "I am a match for Karna, and for Drona, O Bhaarata, or for any great Kshatriya maharatha. This night I will fight such a duel with the Suta's son that it will be spoken of as long as the world lasts. Tonight, I will spare neither the brave nor the timid, nor even those who, with joined hands, pray for quarter. Following Rakshasa dharma, I will kill all that come before me."

Saying these words, Hidimbi's Parantapa son, does not tarry a moment but rushes at Karna, attacking him with such ferocity that your troops are terrified. The Sutaputra, the Naravyaghra, smilingly meets the Rakshasa warrior of the blazing mouth and wild flaming locks down to his shoulders. And there is no doubt, O tiger among kings, that the battle between Karna and Ghatotkacha resembles the one between Indra and Prahlada in the old days.'"

CANTO 171

GHATOTKACHA-VADHA PARVA CONTINUED

"Sanjaya says, 'Seeing the mighty-armed Ghatotkacha attack Karna's chariot in frenzy, Duryodhana says to Dusasana, "Stop the dangerous Rakshasa! Take a strong force with you and ride to Karna's help. Put forth all your prowess, my brother, and ensure that the terrible demon does kill Karna out of our heedlessness."

Meanwhile, Jatasura's mighty son, Alambusha, comes to Duryodhana and says, "O Suyodhana, I seek consent to go into battle. I mean to kill your celebrated enemies, the mighty Pandavas and all their followers. The despicable sons of Pritha killed my father Jatasura, greatest of all Rakshasas, by using some occult mantras. O king of men, I wish to worship my dead sire by offering him the blood of his enemies, and their flesh as tarpana and pinda! It is only just that you allow me this."

Duryodhana is delighted and says to that vile and powerful one, "I can vanquish my enemies with the might of Drona, Karna and others. However, you may, O Rakshasa, go and kill the monstrous Ghatotkacha, this Rakshasa who is always devoted to the Pandavas and now kills our elephants, horses and maharathas from the sky. Go, O Alambusha, and send Bhima's bestial son to Yamaloka."

Saying, "Tathaastu, so be it," Alambusha roars an echoing challenge to Ghatotkacha and attacks him furiously with diverse kinds of missiles. However, Hidimbi and Bhima's prodigious son blows in indescribable fury at Alambusha, Karna and the vast Kuru host like some unprecedented tempest banishing a mass of clouds. Seeing the power of Ghatotkacha's maya, his dreadful sorcery, Alambusha strikes Ghatotkacha with a slew of different kinds of arrows; he then ravages the Pandava army with many strange and sinister astras, which consume whole legions with dark fires, in the twinkling of an eye. The Pandava troops break and flee from the tameless Rakshasa.

Mangled by Ghatotkacha's missiles, your troops also flee in their thousands, throwing down their torches as they go. Alambusha strikes Bhimasena's rampaging son with countless volleys. Ghatotkacha shatters Alambusha's chariot, kills his weird sarathy and incinerates all his weapons, then laughing frightfully, Bhima's son unleashes a cataract of seething barbs down on Karna, Alambusha and all the Kurus, like a cloudburst over the mountains of Meru. Hunted mercilessly by the staggering Ghatotkacha, unearthly panic and terror seize the Kuru host of the four kinds of forces, and in their haste to flee the awful Rakshasa, who is sometimes in the air and at others on the ground, your soldiers push, shove, trample and ride over one another in absolute pandemonium.

Without a chariot or a charioteer, Alambusha leaps at Ghatotkacha and fetches him several blows like thunder with his fists. Ghatotkacha trembles like a mountain with its trees, creepers and grasses struck by an earthquake; his eyes the colour of sunset, he raises his own arm like a spiked mace and strikes Jatasura's son a stupendous blow that fells him onto the ground. He kneels on his back and grinds Alambusha into the earth. Alambusha frees himself and, springing up, attacks Ghatotkacha wildly, trips him and throws him down. Now he kneels on the supine son of Bhima and batters him in fury.

Awful and bloodcurdling is the hand-to-hand battle between the two Rakshasas, their fangs glinting in the night. They fight like Indra and

Virochana's son Bali; now they begin to use maya, dark sorcery, as they fight. Turning into fire and water, then into Garuda and Takshaka, then into a cloud and a tempest, and after that into thunder and a mountain, then two elephants and then Rahu and the Sun, they employ a hundred different kinds of illusions to kill each other.

Alambusha and Ghatotkacha strike each other with clubs, maces, lances, mallets, axes, short cudgels and crags. Riding on horseback or on elephants, fighting on foot or from chariots, the great Rakshasas, both gifted with ample powers of magic, fight on bewildering and mystifying those that watch them. Then, Ghatotkacha leaps down again from his ratha in a flash, like a hunting hawk, gives a horrible roar and, seizing the gigantic Alambusha, he flings him down on the earth, like Vishnu slaying the Asura Maya. With a gleaming stroke of a magnificent curved and serrated scimitar, he hews off his ferile enemy's head in an eruption of gore, even as Alambusha is still roaring hideously. The head roars on even after its has been cut from its neck.

Holding the blood-dyed head by its long red hair, Ghatotkacha runs to Duryodhana's chariot and, with a smile, flings Alambusha's frightful head down at your son's feet. With a roar deep as clouds during the rains, he says to Duryodhana, "Here is the head of your monster on whom you relied! I will bring you your precious Karna's head next, and then take yours, vile Duryodhana! One who observes dharma, artha and kama never visits a king, a Brahmana, or a woman with empty hands. Take this head as my tribute to you, O king of evil. And live happily still, until I bring you Karna's head."

Duryodhana stands frozen in shock, and Ghatotkacha lopes away into the night, mounts his chariot and rides straight at Karna, loosing a hundred arrows at his head. A duel breaks out between the two that is altogether wonderful and well nigh indescribable.'"

CANTO 172

Ghatotkacha-vadha Parva continued

"Dhritarashtra says, 'Tell me about this battle in the middle of the night between Karna and Ghatotkacha. Describe the form of the Rakshasa to me. What kind of chariot does he ride and what is the nature of his horses and his weapons? How big are his horses, the standard on his chariot and his bow? What kind of armour and what type of casque does he wear? Describe all this to me, O Sanjaya, for you are a marvellous narrator!'

Sanjaya says, 'The gigantic Ghatotkacha has eyes the colour of blood, a face the colour of copper; his belly is low and sunken and the bristles on his body all point upwards. His head is green, his ears are like arrowheads, his cheekbones are high, and his mouth is wide, extending from ear to ear. His teeth are sharp, with four of them high and curved fangs; his tongue is long and his lips are heavy, both coppery. His brows are long and thick, his nose is heavy, his body is blue and his neck is red. Tall as a hill, he is terrible to behold and has strength to match his massive frame. By the standards of men he might be called ugly, yet he is striking, O king. His limbs are as tough as tree-trunks or rocks; the hair on his head is tied up in topknot of a fearful shape. His hips are large and his navel is deep. Although he is enormous, he is muscular and lithe.

The ornaments on his arms are both dark and bright, rough and beautiful. He wears heavy angadas and a corselet on his torso like a circle of fire upon the breast of a mountain. On his head is a brilliant golden crown, exquisitely wrought, and rising over his lofty brow in an arch. His earrings are as bright as the morning sun, and his garlands are made of gold and also scintillating. Apart from the cuirass, he wears a great and heavy coat of polished brass armour of great effulgence.

His chariot is decked with a hundred tinkling bells, and on his flagstaff flutter numerous blood-red banners. Of prodigious proportions, and of the measure of a nalwa, the ratha is covered with bearskins. Carrying all kinds of mighty weapons, it has a tree-tall standard, eight wheels, is adorned with every kind of wildflower garland, and its rumble is like the roar of the clouds. His horses are immense, of unknowable breed; they are like infuriated elephants and they have red eyes that shine in the night; of utterly terrible appearance, they are variegated in hue and, for all their bulk, are gifted with great speed as well as strength. Untiring, with long manes and neighing repeatedly in voices that horrify, they bear the Rakshasa hero into battle. A rakshasa of sinister eyes, with a fiery mouth and earrings like circles of flame, is his charioteer, holding reins bright as the rays of the sun in his claw like yet elegant hands. With this charioteer, Ghatotkacha comes to battle, like Surya with his legless sarathy Aruna.

He looks like a small mountain encircled by a mighty cloud; the standard he flies seems actually to scrape the skies. A carnivorous vulture, its feathers also the hue of blood, perches on top of the flagstaff. Bhima's son comes into battle drawing his bow with a sound like Indra's Vajra; his bowstring is hard as diamonds and sparkles; his bow is twelve cubits long and one cubit wide. Filling all the points of the sky with missiles the length of the aksha of a chariot, the Rakshasa attacks Karna, on this night that has already destroyed so many heroes.

The Rakshasa stands looming and erect, proudly on his chariot, and his bow roars as he stretches it. O Bhaarata, your troops tremble like an agitated sea when they see Hidimbi's son ride toward them. However, Karna gazes calmly at the fearsome apparition advancing wrathfully on him. A smile curving his haughty lips, the Sutaputra stands unmoved and does battle with the monstrous one, at close quarters, like one great tusker against another, or a hilly bull against another lord of a great herd. The duel between the two cannot be described as being any less than that between the one of yore between Indra and Sambara.

Each wields a formidable bow, its twanging like thunder, and lays unbridled siege to the other with arrows of untold power. The shafts shot from the bows drawn to their fullest stretch, pierce brazen armour and draw geysers of blood. With these, with spears as long as akshas, they maul each other like tigers with fang and talon. Ah, searing one another with arrow storms they are peerless, resplendent.

Their limbs pierced and gashed, bathed in blood, they look like two hills of chalk, with crimson rillets running down their breasts. Neither can make the other flinch, Rajan. For a long while, the duel by night between Kara and Ghatotkacha is even, nothing separates the twain.

The reverberations of Ghatotkacha's bow fill both friends and foes with fear. Karna cannot prevail over the Rakshasa with common arrows and he invoke devastras and discharges these at Ghatotkacha; at which, Ghatotkacha promptly begins to uses maya, the sorcery of illusions. He appears as if surrounded by a teeming akshauhini of frightful Rakshasas armed with lances, great rocks, hillocks and cudgels. Seeing Ghatotkacha himself advance towards Karna with a mighty and bizarre weapon raised in his hands, like the Destroyer himself armed with his club, all the kings there pierced through with fear and panic.

Terrified by Ghatotkacha's horrible roars, the elephants spray urine and dung, and all the warriors tremble with fright. Then a thick rain of rocks and stones falls everywhere, flung incessantly by all the Rakshasas, for their strength swells many times at the midnight hour. Iron wheels, bhusundis, strange darts, lances, spears, sataghnis and axes also fall in torrent. At this, all the kings of your army, as well as your sons and the rest of their soldiers flee. Only one stands unmoved, a grim smile still curving his handsome lips; Karna stands quite unmoved, like a god upon dark Kurukshetra.

Why, he dispels every illusion of dread that Ghatotkacha creates. Seeing his sorcery dispersed, an infuriated Ghatotkacha once more aims deadly astras at the radiant Sutaputra. These bolts of lightning, fire, wind and water plough right through Karna's body and, covered in blood, flash into the ground hissing like angry snakes. The Suta's son looses ten excruciating barbs at Ghatotkacha, which plunge into his very marmas. Agony screams through the Rakshasa's blood, yet never wavering, he summons an unworldly chakra from patala, thousand spoked, sharper than razors, brilliant as the morning sun, shimmering with dark and resonant gemstones, and he hurls that wheel of death at Karna.

But Karna blows the wheel of death, spinning at him like a hurricane, into dust with his superhuman archery; the dazzling and eerie chakra falls as powder on to the ground, dashed like the hopes and plans of an unfortunate man.

His fury mounting by the moment, Ghatotkacha envelops Karna with lashing showers of shafts, like Rahu covering the Sun. However, invested with the skill of Rudra or of Indra's younger brother or of Indra, Karna shrouds Ghatotkacha's chariot in a darkness of arrows. Ghatotkacha whirls a golden mace and casts it ardently at Karna, who demolishes that exceptional weapon as well.

The titanic Rakshasa flies up into the sky and, roaring deep like a mass of thunderheads, rains down a shower of occult golden trees, their leaves like swords, over the Sutaputra. Karna desiccates these and strikes the mayavi poised above him so that now his blood rains down over the Sutaputra's ratha; ah, Radha's son is truly like Surya piercing ominous cloud with his ineluctable rays. Slaughtering Ghatotkacha's horses, smashing his chariot into a hundred pieces, Karna assaults him with arrows like streak lightning, blinding astras.

Quickly, Ghatotkacha is so covered by Karna's shafts that stick quivering in his body that nowhere upon him can even two finger widths of space be found that are arrowless. The Rakshasa resembles the most astounding porcupine with quills erect. So entirely is he covered with arrows that we no longer see Ghatotkacha or his dead horses, his broken chariot or even his lofty standard with the sinister vulture on top.

Ghatotkacha repels and destroys Karna's devastras with his own astras. Showers of dark shafts fall from an invisible source in the sky, O Bhaarata, and he assumes a terrifying form that chills the blood of the Kauravas. With maya, he assumes many ferocious and grim heads and faces, and he consumes all Karna's devastras. Then, all of a sudden, the enormous Rakshasa, bleeding from a hundred wounds on his body, lays down on the field, as if life has left him. Thinking him dead, the Kauravas erupt in joy.

However, next moment, Ghatotkacha appears everywhere! He runs all across Kurukshetra, changing shapes every moment, until he again looms over the field in a giant form with a hundred heads and a hundred bellies, and looking like the Mainaka Mountain. He next becomes minuscule, about the measure of a thumb, and flits about on the ground and through the air. He burrows down into the earth, then soars up into the sky, then dives down into the pools and lakes of blood, dyeing himself in scarlet.

We see him near us one moment, then far away the next. With his maya, we see him blaze across earth and sky and all the directions, and then again standing mountainous wearing his brazen armour on a massive golden chariot. His pendulous kundalas waving about, the Rakshasa comes right up to Karna's chariot and fearlessly says to the Sutaputra, "Stop a while, O Suta's son. Where will you go tonight? You will not escape me alive. For tonight, I mean to quench forever your consuming thirst for battle by killing you, O Karna!"

Saying this and laughing like thunder, the coppery-eyed Ghatotkacha once more soars steeply up into the sky, from where he lashes down a downpour of arrows over Karna, all of them big as akshas, the axle-rods of chariots. The unruffled Karna fluently destroys the heavy cascade before it comes anywhere near him.

Ghatotkacha uses maya again and makes himself invisible. Then he turns into a mountain with many summits and covered with tall trees. From that black mountain, streams of spears, swords and clubs issue incessantly. Karna remains unmoved and, still smiling, invokes a great devastra, which consumes the barrage of weapons and blows the mountain of illusion apart.

Ghatotkacha turns himself into a blue cloud with a glimmering rainbow in the sky and begins to pelt the Suta's son with a storm of hard stones. Vikartana's son Karna, also called Vrisha, the greatest of all men that know of weapons, invokes a Vayavyastra and destroys the cloud. Ghatotkacha casts down another weapon like a bolt of lightning at him; Karna douses this with a weapon of water. The mighty son of Bhimasena laughs uproariously, shaking earth and sky; he conjures up an all-powerful illusion against the mighty Karna.

Karna sees Ghatotkacha advance wildly on him, surrounded by a host of Rakshasas who resemble lions and tigers and infuriated elephants; some ride on elephants, some on chariots, and some on horseback; all are armed with diverse, uncanny weapons and clad in diverse kinds of armour and wear sundry kinds of ornaments. Seeing Ghatotkacha with his fiends like Indra surrounded by the Maruts, Karna gives him violent battle.

Ghatotkacha pierces Karna with five arrows and gives a roar that again terrifies all the kings and maharathas. He looses an Anjalikastra and shatters the bow in Karna's hands, as well as all the shafts that the Sutaputra has shot at him. Karna takes up another bow as big and mighty as Indra's dhanusha, draws its bowstring back powerfully and unleashes a lethal volley of golden-winged arrows at the sky-ranging Rakshasas. Ravaged by these shafts, the host of wide-chested Rakshasas is as agitated as a herd of wild elephants chased by a kingly lion. Karna devours all the Rakshasas in the air and upon the ground, along with their elephants and other extraordinary mounts; the Sutaputra, Suryaputra looks like apocalyptic Agni burning all creatures at the pralaya.

Having destroyed the Rakshasa army, the Suta's son is as resplendent as the Lord Maheswara when he once razed the triad city of the Asuras, the Tripura in the sky. Among the thousands of kings on the Pandava side, O sire, there is not one who can match Karna then, save Ghatotkacha, prince of Rakshasas, invested with unearthly strength and who, inflamed with battlelust and fury, looks like Yama himself. The Rakshasa's eyes seem to spew flames, even like burning drops of oil from two blazing brands. Striking palm against palm like thunderclaps, biting his lower lip, we see the Rakshasa again mounted on a chariot wrought from maya to which are yoked a number of macabre fanged green donkeys, which as big as elephants and have the faces of Pisachas.

He says to his charioteer, "Take me to the Suta's son."

Riding at Karna again on his fearful ratha, Ghatotkacha hurls an asani of Rudra's workmanship, dreadful and furnished with eight wheels at the Suta's son. Throwing down his bow, Karna jumps down onto the ground, seizes the asani in his hands and hurls it back at Ghatotkacha. The Rakshasa also leaps out of his chariot before the dreadfully blazing weapon burns the dark chariot to ashes in a flash of fire, taking with it horses, charioteer and standard, and then plunges down into the earth and deep into its very bowels, filling even the Devas with wonder. All who see Karna's incredible feat applaud him.

Karna climbs back into his ratha and once more unleashes a tirade of arrows. Indeed, O Maharajan, there is none among all living creatures who could have done what Karna does during his battle with Bhima's awesome son. Struck by Karna's missiles, like a mountain lashed by torrents of rain, Ghatotkacha vanishes again from the field with maya.

Fighting with sorcery, the great Rakshasa destroys Karna's lustrous devastras with his maya. Karna is not intimidated but battles on splendidly. The mighty son of Bhimasena divides his body into many sorcerous forms, frightening all the maharathas of the Kuru army. There bound onto the field of war lions, tigers, hyenas, snakes with fiery tongues, and birds with iron beaks.

Whenever Karna strikes him deep with mighty arrows and astras, the Rakshasa, looming large as Himavat, vanishes using his maya. Immediately, many Rakshasas, Pisachas, Yatudhanas, teeming wolf packs, and leopards of frightful aspect rush towards Karna to devour him. They run at the Suta's son, with fierce roars and howls to frighten him. Karna strikes each of the mayic beasts and apparitions with golden-winged arrows that drink their unnatural blood; finally, with a Gandharvastra he dissipates all the Rakshasa's illusions.

Karna never pauses but looses a brutal volley at Ghatotkacha's freshly appeared horses so they buckle and fall before the Rakshasa's eyes, their bodies mangled, their backs torn open by the Sutaputra's virile shafts. Seeing his maya dispelled, Hidimbi's son vanishes again, warning Karna, "I will be back soon to kill you, Sutaputra!"'

CANTO 173

Ghatotkacha-vadha Parva continued

"Sanjaya says, 'As Karna and Ghatotkacha battle luciferously, the valiant and grotesque Rakshasa appears on the field, leading a large force of fiends, and approaches Duryodhana. Thousands of sinister Rakshasas, of diverse forms and endowed with great heroism, come with him. He has come because of his old animosity for the Pandavas. Bhima had killed all his kinsmen—the great Baka, who ate Brahmanas, as well as the powerful Kirmira—and his friend Hidimba.

Alayudha has waited for a long time, brooding over his old enmity. Learning now that a nocturnal battle rages, he arrives like an angry elephant or a provoked snake, driven by the wish to kill Bhima.

The awful Alayudha says to Duryodhana, "You know how Bhima killed my kinsmen, Baka, Kirmira and Hidimba. He deflowered the virgin Hidimbi, dishonoring us Rakshasas. I am here to kill Bhima with all his followers, horses, chariots and elephants, as well as the son of Hidimbi and his warriors. I will slaughter all the sons of Kunti today, and Krishna and all that walk before them. I will devour them with all their followers. Command all your troops to desist from battle for we will fight the Pandavas."

Duryodhana, surrounded by his brothers, is delighted! He tells the Rakshasas, "I will place you in the van of army but my own troops will not stand by as spectators for their enmity has not cooled."

Alayudha, bull among Rakshasas, saying, "Tathaastu, so be it!" to the king, and sweeps at Bhima with his horrible army. He has a blazing form, and rides a chariot bright as the sun and very like Ghatotkacha's ratha. The rumble of Alayudha's huge chariot is as deep as Ghatotkacha's and it too is covered with bearskins and measures a full nalwa. His horses, like those of Ghatotkacha, are swift as thoughts, are as big as elephants, have faces like pisachas and bray like donkeys. They live on warm flesh and blood, and a hundred of these gigantic creatures are yoked to Alayudha's black chariot. Truly, Rajan, the sound of Alayudha's chariot is just as loud as Ghatotkacha's and his bowstring too is hard and strong as diamonds. His arrows, winged with gold and whetted on stone, are as big as Ghatotkacha's, measuring as much as an aksha.

Alayudha is as mighty-armed as Ghatotkacha, and the banner of his ratha is fiery and has the splendour of the sun, and like Ghatotkacha's, vultures and great ravens perch on it. In form, he is more handsome than Ghatotkacha, and his face blazes in wrath. With dazzling angadas, shining coronet and wildflower garlands, a glittering helmet, a great curved sword, a mace, bhusundis, short clubs, ploughshare weapons and bows and arrows, his skin black, and thick and hard as an elephant's, riding on the magnificent chariot, the dreadful Alayudha looks indeed like some great storm cloud gashed by flashes of lightning.

The greatest Pandava kings and maharathas joyfully ride forward to meet Alayudha the Rakshasa's onrush. Yet another battle that makes one's hair stand on end breaks out between the demons and the Pandava forces, at dead of night.'"

CANTO 174

GHATOTKACHA-VADHA PARVA CONTINUED

"Sanjaya says, 'The advent of Alayudha puts heart into your sons; also knowing that Duryodhana himself leads them now, they are in high spirits, like men wanting to cross the ocean when they find a raft. The surviving kings and maharathas of the Kuru army regard themselves having obtained a new lease of life and all of them accord a respectful welcome to Alayudha, who is such a vile Rakshasa that Bhishma would never have allowed him near his army as long as he had command. But now, the Kali yuga has risen over the world and this is the war at night, the soul of darkness.

The preternatural battle between Karna and Ghatotkacha's Rakshasa, which though savage and horrible is yet magnificent, holds the Panchalas and all the other Kshatriyas who watch it spellbound in irresistible fascination. Meanwhile, your soldiers, though protected on all sides by Drona, Aswatthaman, Kripa and the others, are all seized by absolute terror and we hear loud wails everywhere, dismal cries of "All is lost!"

Having watched his unimaginable feats on Kurukshetra, your warriors are all frantic with fear of Ghatotkacha, frightened out of their very wits.

Your troops give up all hope of Karna surviving the duel with Bhima's son.

Seeing his precious Karna in grave distress, Duryodhana summons Alayudha and says to him, "Look where Karna battles Hidimbi's son by himself. Look at the corpses of the thousand great kings that lie askew upon the ground, all slain by Bhima's monstrous son with his dark and bright astras; ah, look where they lie like trees struck by lightning or uprooted by an elephant in rage. If you agree, mighty Alayudha, from this moment, among all my warriors, let it become your sole mission to slay Bhima's horrible son. My friend, you must see that Ghatotkacha does not take Karna's life on this night, using his maya shakti, or our cause will be lost and the war. And all who have died for our sake will have sacrificed their lives in vain. Grave and great is the mission with which I entrust you, noble Alayudha; I know you will not disappoint me."

Alayudha says "Tathaastu—so be it," and attacks Ghatotkacha. Turning away from Karna, Ghatotkacha greets Alayudha with a terrific volley. An epic battle ensues between the two night rangers. Karna turns his attention to Bhima, riding his chariot of solar effulgence. Bheema sees Alayudha locked in battle with Ghatotkacha and, troubled like the great bull of a herd facing a lion, Vrikodara ignores Karna charging at him and dashes instead at Alayudha, covering him with gusts of arrows.

At this, Alayudha abandons Ghatotkacha and turns to face Bhima. Bhima, the Rakshasa slayer, lays violent siege to him and Alayudha too shrouds the Pandava in clouds of arrows. All Alayudha's dreadful Rakshasas turn on Bhima, for it is him that they have come to kill and avenge Hidimba, Kirmira, Baka and the others that the son of Pandu despatched. Bhima Mahabaho strikes each fiend deep with five scalding arrows at which they scream horribly and flee.

Seeing Bhima drive away his Rakshasas like some dogs, Alayudha assails the Pandava ever more fiercely. Bhimasena also shoots back at him with great violence, but the Rakshasa cuts down Vrikodara's shafts in flight and some he even catches with his hands. Bhima pauses, gazes for a long moment at his enemy and casts a mace like a thunderbolt at him. Alayudha smashes that weapon with a mace of his own.

Kunti's son again unleashes squalls of arrows at the Rakshasa prince and Alayudha cuts these down with his own arrow storms. Seeing their lord Alayudha contain Bhima by himself, the Rakshasas who fled in fear return to battle and begin to slaughter Bhima's elephants; they also harry the Panchalas, the Srinjayas and the horses of Bhima's army, considerably disconcerting them.

Watching the battle between Bhima and Alayudha, Krishna says to Arjuna, "Bhima is succumbing to this prince of Rakshasas. We must leave everything else and protect Bhima. Let Dhrishtadyumna, Sikhandin, Yudhamanyu and Uttamaujas, along with the sons of Draupadi, ride against Karna. Let Nakula, Sahadeva and Satyaki kill Alayudha's Rakshasas! As for you, O Mahabaho, face this akshauhini led by Drona for great is the danger that threatens us now."

At Krishna's command, the Pandava and Panchala maharathas ride against Karna and the Rakshasas that fight for the Kurus.

Alayudha draws his bow into a circle and looses some astras like venom spitting cobras at Bhima, breaking his bow. The mighty Rakshasa kills Bhima's horses and charioteer, so Bhima leaps down from his ratha. With an echoing roar, Vrikodara casts a mace heavy as a hill at his adversary. Alayudha shatters that gada with one of his own and the report deafens all the war by night; the Rakshasa gives a bloodcurdling roar. Bhimasena seizes up another massive mace, and the battle that now erupts between the human prince and the Rakshasa makes brave men tremble.

They swing their maces at each other with such violence that the very earth trembles and both are covered in brilliant showers of sparks. When the maces shatter, they cast them aside and fight with bare arms and fists: with blows that echo like spring thunder. In frenzy they fight, soon with chariot wheel, yokes, akshas, adhishthanas, upaskaras, and indeed with anything that comes to hand. Both are covered in blood and present such a magnificent spectacle, O Rajan!

Then, Krishna sends Hidimbi's son Ghatotkacha to protect Bhimasena.'"

CANTO 175

GHATOTKACHA-VADHA PARVA CONTINUED

"Sanjaya says, 'Seeing Bhima sorely tried and wounded by Alayudha, Krishna rids to Ghatotkacha and says to him, "O Mahabaho, look where the Rakshasa violently besets Bhima in front of all the troops and you. Leave Karna for now and kill Alayudha. You can despatch Karna later."

Ghatotkacha immediately abandons his duel with Karna and confronts Alayudha. The battle between them is intolerably ferocious, O Bhaarata. Meanwhile, the mighty Yuyudhana, with Nakula and Sahadeva, looses a firetide of blazing shafts at Alayudha's terrible-looking and heroic Rakshasas. Spraying arrows all around him Arjuna Kiritin claims the lives of many great Kshatriyas.

Karna continues to harangue so many kings and maharathas amongst the Panchalas led by Dhrishtadyumna, Sikhandin and others. Bhima rushes at Karna, covering the Sutaputra with a tempest of arrows. Having slain Alayudha's Rakshasas, Nakula, Sahadeva and Satyaki ride at Karna, while the Panchalas confront Drona.

The raging Alayudha strikes Ghatotkacha on his head with a huge parigha, making him swoon and forces him to sit in his chariot, where he remains still. Bhima's son recovers soon and hurls a golden gada, with a hundred little bells, at his enemy with untold force. This mace of power kills Alayudha's steeds, his charioteer, and shatters his loud ratha. Using sorcery, Alayudha jumps down from his smashed chariot and decants a copious shower of blood. The sky appears overspread with a mass of black clouds adorned with flashes of lightning. We hear a booming thunderstorm with the strangest peals of thunder on high, all created by Alayudha's maya.

Ghatotkacha soars up from his chariot and dispels this threatening illusion. Alayudha now rains down a storm of smooth hard pebbles over Ghatotkacha, who blows the stones into smithereens with his astras. The two inundate each other with cascades and cataracts of iron parighas, spears, maces, short clubs, mallets, pinakas, swords, lances, long spears, kampanas, keen shafts, both long and flat-headed arrows, quoits, battle-axes, ayogudas, short-arrows, weapons with heads like those of cattle and ulukhalas.

Tearing up great sami, pilu, karira, champaka, ingudi, badari, the flowering kovidara, the arimeda, plaksha, banyan and peepul trees, they batter each other with these; they tear mountain peaks and hurl these at each other and large crags and balls of iron. Kurukshetra quakes with the sound of these weapons crashing against each other and the battle between Alayudha and Bhima's son is like the one between Vali and Sugriva, the two Vanara princes of old.

They hew and smite each other with other missiles, with countless powerful spells, and with glinting swords curved like half moons. The two titanic Rakshasas pause often to wrestle and strike one another with their bare hands, as blood and sweat run profusely down their great bodies; they seize each other by their locks of wild hair. Finally, Ghatotkacha darts low and bodily hefts Alayudha over his head. Whirling him around, he dashes that Rakshasa down onto the ground so Alayudha briefly faints. Before he awakes, Ghatotkacha, quick as light cuts his grisly head from its thick neck with a sweeping arc of his great sword. Hidimbi's half-human son throws back his head and roar after echoing roar erupts from him.

The Pandavas and Panchalas also roar out their relief and exhilaration at seeing the great Alayudha slain; they blow ten thousand conches and beat a thousand batteries of drums. Lamps are lit again everywhere. Victory clearly belongs to the Pandavas and the grim night is bright and magnificent with the din of celebration that your enemies raise. Once more, Ghatotkacha lopes up to Duryodhana's chariot and flings Alayudha's still warm and bleeding head down at his feet.

Duryodhana is stricken with dread for his troops. Alayudha had come to Duryodhana on his own, wanting to avenge his kinsmen whom Bhima had killed, and Duryodhana had rejoiced thinking that this great demon would surely kill his most hated cousin. Suyodhana had thought that Bhima's death would break the spirits of the other sons of Pandu and that victory would then be his. Besides, with Bhima killed, he had thought that his own brothers' lives would be safe.

Now with Alayudha killed by Ghatotkacha, Duryodhana hangs his head and feels instead that Bhima's vow is already as good as fulfilled and he, Duryodhana, and his brothers are as good as slain by Pandu's second son who blows everywhere on Kurukshetra, irresistibly as a hurricane of his father Vayu the Wind.'"

CANTO 176

Ghatotkacha-vadha Parva continued

"Sanjaya says, 'After killing Alayudha, the Rakshasa Ghatotkacha is overjoyed and, standing in front of the army, he gives all kinds of shouts and roars. Hearing these inhuman sounds that make elephants tremble, a great fear, O Rajan, lays hold of your warriors. Karna, apparently unmoved, attacks the Panchalas. He draws blood from Dhrishtadyumna and Sikhandin with ten strong and perfect arrows, each; with a flurry of other powerful barbs, he makes Yudhamanyu, Uttamaujas and even the great Satyaki shudder as the shafts crash into their great bodies. These warriors, too, draw their bows into circles and shoot at Karna from all sides.

During the war by night, the twanging of their bowstrings and the rumble of their chariot-wheels are loud and deep as the thunder of clouds massed at the end of summer. Their arrows are streaks of lightning; they are the driving deadly rain. Standing immovable like a hill, a prince of the mountains, Parantapa Karna cuts down every arrow shot at him. With speed that defies imagination, he strikes his enemies viciously with javelins flung with the force of thunder and with arrows that have golden wings.

He destroys the standards of some maharathas and mauls the bodies of others, deprives some of their charioteers, and some of their horses. Unable to withstand the Suryaputra, thousands flee from him and seek refuge with Yudhishtira's force.

Seeing them thus broken and fleeing, Ghatotkacha who has just killed Alayudha, gives a roar more dreadful than any heard before, and rushes towards Karna unleashing a torrent of savage shafts, big as axle rods. Locking quickly into another frenetic duel, both loose barbed bolts, cloth-yard shafts, frog-faced arrows, nalikas, dandas, asanis, arrows with heads like the calf's tooth or the boar's ear, broad-headed arrows, those pointed like bulls' horns, and others with heads like razors. All these have golden wings and as they fly through the air they seem to drape a garland of unworldly lotuses around the throat of the sky.

Evenly matched, they loose blazing devastras at each other and astra consumes astra lighting up the night sky with many small suns. No one can see the slightest difference between the two, in speed or prowess, and the scintillating duel between the son of Surya and the son of Bhima presents a breathtaking spectacle even like the contention between the Sun and Rahu in the firmament.

Rajan, when Ghatotkacha finds that he cannot prevail over Karna, he invokes an astra with which he first kills Karna's horses and then his charioteer, after which he vanishes.'

Dhritarashtra asks, 'When the Rakshasa, fighting deceitfully, vanishes, tell me, O Sanjaya, what the warriors of my army think.'

Sanjaya says, 'Seeing the Rakshasa disappear, all the Kauravas cry, "The Rakshasa with reappear as suddenly as he has disappeared and he will kill Karna."

Karna Mahabuddhi is aware of the danger and covers all the directions with dense showers of shafts darkening earth and sky so everything becomes invisible. So great is the lightness of hand Karna displays that no one can discern when he touches his quiver, when he fits his arrows to his bowstring and when he aims and shoots them. The whole sky is shrouded by his shafts.

In the sky, the Rakshasa creates a profound and deadly illusion of maya in the firmament. We see above us what appears to be a mass of red clouds blazing like fire. From this cloud issue flashes of lightning, and many burning brands, O Kuru king! Frightful roars also emanate from there, like the sound of thousands of drums beaten at once. From it fall, all around, countless golden-winged shafts, darts, lances, weighty clubs, battle-axes, scimitars washed with oil, axes with blazing edges, short spears, long spears with keen points, spiked maces emitting strange bright rays of light, beautiful maces of iron, others of solid gold and twined about with silver string and sataghnis. Huge crags fall from it, and thousands of thunderbolts with deafening reports, and hundreds of chakras and razor sharp blades, brilliant as the fire.

Karna's missiles cannot destroy all that thick and blazing deluge. Loud is the sound of falling horses killed by the wizardly weapons pouring down, mighty elephants struck with thunder, and great maharathas slain. Ravaged by Ghatotkacha, Duryodhana's host wanders demented and in agony all over the battlefield. With piteous cries, even as those of women, your hoist drifts lost and aimless, on the point of being annihilated.

Only their leaders, great Kshatriyas noble of heart, do not turn their faces from the battle but stand steadfast waiting for death. Seeing the carnage Ghatotkacha fetches upon their host, terror and dismay grip your sons. Hundreds of jackal packs, with tongues blazing like fire and terrible voices, begin to howl, further petrifying the Kaurava warriors. The Rakshasas that tread air on high, with fiery tongues and burning mouths, fangs like thick needles and forms big as hills, lash down arrows over your hapless forces. Struck by shafts, darts, lances, maces and spiked clubs, by thunderbolts, pinakas, asanis, chakras and sataghnis, the Kaurava troops are on the very verge of complete collapse and surrender. The maya Rakshasas further assail them with sthunas made of black iron and twined about with strings of jute.

All your combatants are in a nightmarish stupor. The bravest warriors have their weapons broken, or their heads hewn off, or limbs fractured and fall like grass being mown, while falling rocks crush horses, elephants and rathas. The Yatudhanas of terrible forms that Ghatotkacha creates with maya spare neither those who are terrified nor those who cry for mercy. During the brutal carnage of Kuru heroes, and the extermination of majestic Kshatriyas brought on by Death himself, the Kaurava warriors break ranks and flee all together, crying, "Fly, you Kauravas! All is lost! The Devas with Indra at their head are killing us for the sake of the Pandavas!"

And at this horrible juncture, there is not a soul that can rescue the Bharata troops. During the mayhem, no one can distinguish friend from foe; all run any way they can from the horror with which Ghatotkacha visits them in that very soul of darkness. All your warriors and soldiers having fled, Kurukshetra seems eerily empty as if no living man is anywhere near the gruesome field of fate.

We see only Karna, Rajan, shining by himself, drowning in the awful shower of weapons that falls incessantly from above.

Karna covers the sky with his missiles, resisting the unworldly sorcery of the Rakshasa. In truth, we see that he is endowed with deep humility, which enables him to achieve the most difficult and noble feats; Karna remains calm, unmoved by the horrors that flare down from the sky. All the Saindhavas and Balhikas are frightened and look just to Karna for protection. They worship him in their thoughts, while Ghatotkacha continues to wreak havoc upon them.

Ghatotkacha casts down a sataghni of a hundred fire, fitted with scything chakras, and kills Karna's four horses simultaneously and they fall dead on their knees. Jumping down from his horseless chariot and seeing the Kauravas run away, and finding his own devastra nullified by the Rakshasa's maya, Karna still remains calm and turns his thought inward in dhyana to reflect on what he should do next.

Watching Karna and the infernal Rakshasa maya that Ghatotkacha uses, all the Kauravas and your sons cry out in despair, "Karna, kill the Rakshasa with your shakti or he will kill us all tonight! What will Bhima and Arjuna do to us? Slay this wretched Rakshasa or he will consume us all. Only those who escape from this monster tonight will live to fight the Parthas. Karna, you must use the shakti you had from Indra and slay Ghatotkacha. Karna, there is no other way. You must kill Bhima's dreadful son or we will lose everything within the hour."

Karna seeing the Rakshasa ablaze at dead of night, and the Kuru army struck with terror; hears the piteous entreaties of the Kauravas and knows he has no choice but to use Indra's shakti. Quivering all over his mighty form like some mythic lion, magnificent Karna summons Indra's shakti, which he has kept so carefully and worshipped for years so that, when the time came, he could kill Arjuna with it. But now, he summons the awesome weapon that looks like the very tongue of Death lolling out to drink copious blood, or Yama's sister Mrityu herself descended on dark Kurukshetra being laid waste by Ghatotkacha.

Karna invokes that burning weapon called Naikartana and casts it at Bhima's son. Seeing that inexorable shakti in the Sutaputra's hands, Ghatotkacha in a flash assumes a body as big as the foot of the Vindhya mountain! Bhima's Rakshasa son tries to flee. Seeing that apocalyptic shakti all creatures, visible and hidden, human, divine and all the rest, on the ground and in the air, cry out in fear.

Fierce winds begin to blow, and thunderclaps resound as if to break the very sky into shards. Indra's fulminant shakti consumes all of Ghatotkacha's mighty maya in a wink. It then courses straight through the Rakshasa's massive breast, flares on upwards and flies into a constellation deep in the heavens, leaving a flaring trail in its wake! Sky shaking roars erupt from great Ghatotkacha and he keels over dead. Indra's shakti claims the life of Bhima and Hidimbi's son who had razed so many great heroes, both human and demonic, who had by himself devoured a vast portion of your army by night.

Rajan, listen to a final astounding feat that Ghatotkacha accomplishes even as he falls dead. He shines like a sun and having assumed a form as great as the Vindhya mountain, falls in death upon a teeming akshauhini of your army, crushing thousands of your men with his stupendous body. Even as life quits him, out of his fathomless love for the Pandavas, he obliterates a full akshauhini of your troops.

A bedlam of triumphant sounds erupts from your sons and their forces—lion's roars, blaring conches, the thunder of drums and cymbals. Unbridled is the joy of the Kauravas when they see Ghatotkacha's maya cloven and the Rakshasa himself slain. Idolised, worshipped, eulogised by the Kurus even as Sakra had been by the Maruts after he slew Vritra, a smiling Karna climbs into your son Duryodhana's chariot and, watched by all, joins the Kuru host.'"

CANTO 177

Ghatotkacha-vadha Parva continued

"Sanjaya says, 'Meanwhile, the Pandavas are pierced through by savage grief when they see Ghatotkacha die; they see him lying on Kurukshetra like a cloven mountain and weep bitter tears. But Krishna seems in a transport of delight! He roars as jubilantly as the Kauravas and embraces Arjuna fervently. Tying up his horses, he leaps down from his chariot and dances in ecstasy, still giving vent to joyous shouts and roars. He embraces Arjuna yet again, and repeatedly slapping his own armpits, the Krishna Mahabuddhi climbs back onto his ratha and continues to roar in some unnatural rapture.

The Pandavas and their troops are shocked to watch this display.

His heart bursting with grief, Arjuna cries at Krishna in anguish, "Madhusudana, how are you so delighted at this hour of tragedy when Bhima's precious son has died? Our troops flee in all direction to see Ghatotkacha slain and we too are filled with anxiety. Yet, you are so full of joy! There must be some great cause for your celebration, Krishna. If it is not a secret, you must share the reason for your strange delight with me. Tell me why you appear to have lost your very mind and rejoice when the rest of us grieve. Ah, you terrify me, Krishna, for looking at your levity I feel as if Meru has moved from his proper place or as if the ocean has dried up!"

Krishna replies, "Great is the joy I feel. Listen to me, Dhananjaya, and what I say to you will dispel your sorrow and infuse delight into your heart as well. Understand clearly what has happened—Karna has used his inexorable astra against Ghatotkacha and for that Karna is already as good as dead. Hear me well, O Pandava. There is no man in this world, including you, who could have vanquished Karna, who straddled Kurukshetra like Kartikeya himself, in battle as long as he had Indra's shakti with him.

He would have been invincible anyway, but through good fortune the kavacha and kundalas that he was born with were both taken from him. Now, again through fate, his infallible astra has also been lost to him. You do not know who Karna is. I say to you that, wearing his golden armour and earrings, Karna could vanquish the three worlds by himself and the very gods. Not Indra, Varuna or Yama could withstand mighty Karna. If this bull among men had his natural armour and earrings, neither you, bending the Gandiva, nor I with my Sudarshana chakra, could kill him.

For your weal, your father Indra took Karna's golden kavacha and kundalas away from him. And even knowing the reason why Indra went to him as a Brahmana to ask him for these as a gift at the hour of his noonday prayer, the noble Karna cut them from his body and gave them away. And for that is he known as Vaikartana.

Now having exhausted the shakti he had from Indra in exchange for the armour and earrings, Karna is like a virulent serpent that has lost his venom; he is like an inextinguishable fire whose flames have turned mild. As long as he had Indra's astra, which he kept just to kill you, Karna always knew that you were as good as dead!"

Krishna pauses, then continues gravely, "But listen well to me Arjuna, even without his kavacha, kundalas and the shakti of Sakra, there is no man on earth, or any warrior in heaven, who can kill great Karna other than you. It is because he is devoted to Brahmanas, is always truthful in speech, engages himself in tapasya, observes his vratas and is kind even to his enemies, that Karna is called Vrisha. He is heroism embodied; there is no archer in the world like Karna; his bow is always ready and he is the lion in the jungle that takes his pride from great lords of elephants. Karna is he who strips the greatest maharathas of their pride on the filed of battle. He blazes like the midday sun at his zenith, at whom no one can gaze.

Fighting all the most illustrious warriors of your army, O Naravyaghra, Karna, shooting his arrows, looks like the autumn sun with his thousand rays. The Sutaputra is like a great cloud that rains devastras. Not the Devas can quell him; he could carve them up so their divine flesh and blood fell copiously onto the earth. But deprived of his armour and his earrings, and now without the astra given him by Vasava, Karna is like a mere mortal and no longer like a god.

You will find an opportunity to kill him when his chariot-wheels sink into the earth. You must not hesitate or let pity rule at that moment. I will give you a sign when the moment arrives and you must act instantly and kill this hero like whom there is no other.

The vanquisher of Bala himself, Indra wielding his Vajra, cannot kill invincible Karna while he stands with a weapon in his hand. Indeed, Arjuna, for your benefit, using different stratagems I have killed, one after the other, Jarasandha, Sisupala of the Chedis and the mahabaho Nishada Ekalavya. Other great Rakshasas among which Hidimba, Kirmira, Baka were the greatest, as well as Alayudha, grinder of hostile troops, and Ghatotkacha, crusher of his foes and warrior of fierce deeds, have all been killed.'"

CANTO 178

GHATOTKACHA-VADHA PARVA CONTINUED

'Arjuna asks, "How, O Janardana, for our sake, and by what stratagems, were these lords of the earth, Jarasandha and the others, killed?"

Krishna says, "If Jarasandha, Sisupala of the Chedis, and Ekalavya, the peerless son of the Nishada king, had not been slain, they would have become terrible. Duryodhana would have had these maharathas to fight for him. They have always been hostile to us, and they would all have supported the Kauravas. They were all heroes and mighty archers, accomplished in weaponry and resolute. Like Devas they would have protected Dhritarashtra's sons. Indeed, if Karna, Jarasandha, Sisupala and Ekalavya had been with Duryodhana, he would have conquered the whole world.

Listen, Dhananjaya, to how they were killed. Without using strategy, the very gods could not have slain them. Each of them, O Partha, could fight the entire celestial host protected by the Lokapalas, regents of the world.

Once, when Balarama attacked him, a livid Jarasandha hurled a gada that could destroy any creature at our city from his own city of Girivraja. With the splendour of fire, the mace flew towards us dividing the sky like the line on her head that parts the tresses of a woman; it blazed at us like Sakra's Vajra. Seeing the mace fly at us, Rohini's son Balarama loosed the astra called Sthunakarna at Jarasandha's mace. Its vigour destroyed by the energy of Balarama's weapon, that mace fell onto the earth, splitting her open with its force and making the very mountains tremble.

There once lived a terrible Rakshasa called Jara, gifted with great powers. She joined together the infant Jarasandha, who had been born as a child cloven in two halves. For this, that mighty king was called Jarasandha, joined by Jara. Jarasandha's mace, when it plunged down into the earth along with the Sthunakarnastra, killed Jara in her subterranean cave home and her son and kinsmen. Later, it was in your presence and mine that Bhima killed Jarasandha by tearing his body along its length, where once the Rakshasi Jara had joined it. If Jarasandha had stood armed with his mace, the very Devas led by Indra could not have quelled him.

O best of men, It was for your sake that Drona, whom Ekalavya worshipped from afar as his Acharya, asked for the Nishada's thumb as his guru dakshina. Ekalavya was no less an archer than Rama of Ayodhya himself! With all his digits, he too was invincible even to the Devas, the Danavas, the Rakshasas and the Uragas all together. Even without his thumb, he was far greater than any mere mortal. I killed Ekalavya on another field of battle, to protect you, Arjuna.

I killed Sisupala, king of the Chedis, before your very eyes during the Rajasuya yagna. Him, also, the Devas and the Asuras together could not overwhelm. I was born to kill him, as well as the other enemies of the Devas, and so were you. O Naravyaghra, for the weal of the world Bhimasena killed Hidimba, Baka and Kirmira. All these Rakshasas were as powerful as Ravana and all of them were destroyers of Brahmanas and yagnas.

Ghatotkacha killed Alayudha who possessed awesome powers of maya. And Ghatotkacha I sacrificed through strategy, using Karna and his astra. If Karna had not killed Ghatotkacha, I myself would have had to kill Bhima's son. I did not kill him earlier, only for your sake. Much as he loved you and your brothers, the Rakshasa was inimical to Brahmanas and yagnas and he had to be slain. He would have grown altogether too powerful in this world if he had been left alive.

O sinless one, with Ghatotkacha's death Indra's shakti can no longer be used against you. I have come to this world to establish dharma and I will kill all those who are destroyers of dharma, for I have sworn a solemn vow to establish righteousness on earth. Wherever the Vedas, truth, self-restraint, purity, dharma, modesty, prosperity, wisdom and forgiveness need to be maintained, there I will always be.

Now you have no need to fear great Karna, for I will tell you how and when to kill him. And Bhima will kill Duryodhana. I will also tell you how that final death shall be achieved. Meanwhile, listen, the uproar of the hostile army swells by the moment. Your troops are fleeing on all sides. Having killed Ghatotkacha, the triumphant Kauravas are mowing down your troops at will. Ah, look where Drona, the terrible Brahmana, devours our men with blazing astras, burning whole legion to ashes.'""

CANTO 179

Ghatotkacha-vadha Parva continued

"Dhritarashtra says, 'When Karna had an astra with which he could kill any one warrior, why did he not use it against Arjuna? If he had killed Partha with the Naikartana, all the Srinjayas and the Pandavas would have been as good as dead. If Arjuna had died, nothing could have stood between us and victory. Arjuna had sworn a vow that he would never refuse to accept a challenge to fight. The Sutaputra's son should have challenged Dhananjaya and killed him with Indra's Naikartana. Oh, why did he not do this? Truly, my son Suyodhana is without both intelligence and proper counsellors!

When the wretched sinner is constantly confounded by the enemy, how can he ever hope to defeat them? Ah, how cunningly Krishna had Karna use the one weapon that could have won the war for us against Ghatotkacha! Why, he snatched it right out of Karna's hands like a fruit from the withered hand of a cripple.

In a fight between a boar and a dog, upon the death of either, the hunter is the one profited. So, too, Krishna is the one benefited by the battle between Karna and Hidimba's son. If Ghatotkacha had killed

Karna, that would have been a great gain for the Pandavas. If, as has happened, Karna killed Ghatotkacha, that also would have favoured the sons of Pandu for then the Naikartana would have been lost anyway.

Krishna is the only real lion among all men and, in his great wisdom, he saw this clearly and had Karna kill Ghatotkacha with Indra's astra, while shielding Arjuna from the Suta's son. How canny this Yadava is, Sanjaya—he contrived a subtle battle that he could not lose!'

Sanjaya says, 'Knowing that Karna had Indra's astra and that he was saving it to kill Arjuna, Krishna knowingly sent Ghatotkacha into battle against the Suryaputra, for he also knew that Karna would be obliged to exhaust the Naikartana against Bhima's mighty son.

Rajan, do not forget that all this is the fruit of your evil rule! We would certainly have achieved victory, O Kuruttama, if Krishna had not saved Arjuna's life by sacrificing Ghatotkacha's. Karna would have consumed Arjuna along with his horses, standard, and chariot, if the Master, the Lord of yogins, Krishna had not saved him. Without Krishna's grace upon him, Arjuna would have been blasted like a tree struck by lightning.'

Dhritarashtra says, 'My son is addicted to violence, his advisers are foolish and he is vain about his own intelligence of which he has dire little. It is for this that the only weapon with which Arjuna could be killed has been lost to us. O Sanjaya, why did Duryodhana not command Karna to cast the fatal astra at Dhananjaya? O son of Gavalgana, you who are so wise, why did you also forget to remind Karna of what he should have done?'

Sanjaya says, 'Indeed, O Rajan, this was the subject of deliberation between Duryodhana, Sakuni, Dusasana and me every single night. We would tell Karna, "Forget every other warrior, O Karna, and kill Arjuna. With Arjuna slain, we can keep the Pandavas and the Panchalas for your slaves. If at Partha's death, Krishna exalts another son of Pandu in his place, we must kill Krishna himself. Krishna is the very root of the great Pandava tree, and Arjuna is its trunk. The other sons of Pritha are its branches, while the Panchalas are just its leaves.

The Pandavas have Krishna for their protection, Krishna for their might and Krishna for their Lord. Indeed, Krishna is their essential support even as the Moon is of the constellations. Therefore, O Sutaputra, ignore the leaves, branches and trunk, and kill Krishna who is everywhere and is always the root and foundation of the Pandavas."

If Karna had killed the dark lion of the Dasarha vamsa, the delighter of the Yadavas, there is no doubt that all the world would have belonged just to you and your sons. Have no doubt that if this illustrious Krishna could be slain, Rajan, all this Bhumi, with her mountains and forests would have accepted your sovereignty.

Although we would rise every morning resolved to eliminate the Lord of the very gods, Hrishikesa of immeasurable tejas, uncannily once the fighting began, we would forget our resolve. Kesava always protected Arjuna and never allowed Arjuna to face Karna as long as the Suta's son had Indra's astra. Indeed, Krishna would always turn his chariot away from Karna and set some other great maharatha to fight him, intent on making Karna use his Naikartana, intent on saving Arjuna's life. O Rajan, when the noble Krishna protected Arjuna thus from Karna, how would Arjuna, greatest of all warriors, not protect Krishna? I have reflected deeply on all this and concluded that there is no one in the three worlds who can even dream of vanquishing this Parantapa, Janardana Krishna, the hero who wields the Sudarshana Chakra!

Why, Satyaki, the invincible tiger among maharathas asked Krishna, "Janardana, Karna is resolved to kill Arjuna with Indra's weapon. Why, then, does he not do so?"

Vasudeva replied, "Dusasana, Karna, Sakuni and Jayadratha, all led by Duryodhana, have frequently discussed this very matter. They would say to the Sutaputra, 'O Karna, matchless bowman, O you of immeasurable prowess, O foremost of all victors in battle, you must not even think of casting this astra at anyone other than Kunti's son Dhananjaya. He is the greatest among the enemy; he is like Vasava amongst the Devas. If he dies, all the other Pandavas and the Srinjayas will be broken in spirit and might, even as the Devas without Agni to fuel and feed them!'

Karna agreed to this, saying 'Tathaastu—so be it!'

O Satyaki, bull of the Sinis, the wish to kill the Gandivi was always in Karna's heart. However, I would subtly bewilder and distract his mind and he would forget to cast the Naikartana at Arjuna! As long as I could not remove the dire threat to Phalguna's life, I had neither sleep nor joy in my heart. But today, seeing the Naikartana spent against Ghatotkacha, I know that Dhananjaya has been saved from the jaws of Death.

Satyaki, I do not view my father, my mother, my brothers, you, or my own life as being as precious as Arjuna's. If there is anything more valuable than the sovereignty of the three worlds, I do not want to have it without Dhananjaya to share it with me. That is why, Yuyudhana, that seeing Arjuna saved from Karna's astra and a certain death, I am in a transport of delight. And this is the reason I sent Ghatotkacha into battle against Karna. No one else could defy the Sutaputra at night. Only Ghatotkacha could try Karna so gravely that he would be forced to use the Naikartana against Bhima's son."

This is what Devaki's son Krishna, who is for ever devoted to Arjuna, told Satyaki.'"

CANTO 180

GHATOTKACHA-VADHA PARVA CONTINUED

"Dhritarashtra asks, 'I see clearly that what Karna, Duryodhana and Sakuni and you did was against the dictates of all good sense and strategy. Indeed, when you knew that the astra could always slay only one warrior, and that it could not be either contained or confounded by the very Devas led by Vasava, why then, O Sanjaya, did Karna not cast it against Arjuna or Krishna whenever he fought them earlier?'

Sanjaya says, 'As I told you, Rajan, we would return from battle every day and all of us would confer about this very thing, and we would say to Karna, "Tomorrow morning, Karna, you must cast the Naikartana against either Arjuna or Krishna."

However, when the morning came, either through fate or Krishna's subtle power, both Karna and the rest of us would completely forget this resolve. Surely, fate reigns supreme, for Karna did not kill either Krishna or Arjuna, although he faced them repeatedly on the field. I have no doubt that the gods themselves clouded his mind, and destiny conspired against us that time and again, whenever he had ample opportunity, he did not yet cast the astra against either of the two Krishnas!'

Dhritarashtra says, 'Destiny, your own lack of understanding, and Krishna destroyed you! Indra's astra is gone, having effected the death of Ghatotkacha who was as insignificant as a straw. To my mind, through this single act of folly, Karna, my sons and all the other kings have already entered the halls of Yama.

Tell me now how the battle continues between the Kurus and the Pandavas after the fall of Hidimbi's son Ghatotkacha. How do the Srinjaya and the Panchalas fight great Drona? How do the Pandus and Srinjayas defy the battling Acharya when he attacks them in fury, agitated at the death of Bhurisravas and Jayadratha, reckless of his own life and like some tiger from antique times or Rudra himself with jaws agape? What do Aswatthaman, Karna, Kripa and the others led by Duryodhana do to protect the Acharya?

Tell me, O Sanjaya, how my warriors contain Dhananjaya and Vrikodara who are intent on killing Drona. Frantic as they are with anger, how do they fight the battle by night, for some have been moved to wrath by the death of Jayadratha, and others at the death of Ghatotkacha, and both sides cannot abide their loss?'

Sanjaya says, 'After Karna kills Ghatotkacha, your troops are exuberant and roar and shout with joy. In the darkness, they fall wildly upon the Pandava troops and begin to slaughter them. Yudhishtira is crestfallen to see this; besides, Ghatotkacha was always his most favourite nephew.

He tells Bhimasena, "I am dazed by my child Ghatotkacha's death. Bhima, Mahabaho, go and confront Dhritarashtra's army. Lead our men into battle, for my head spins and my body is weak with grief."

Having said this to Bhima, Yudhishtira sits down in his ratha with a tearful face, sighing repeatedly and utterly afraid and dejected by Karna's awesome archery. Seeing him suffering, Krishna consoles him, "O son of Kunti, do not grieve so much. It does not become you, as it may an ordinary man. Arise, fight and bear the heavy burden that is your! If you, our king and lord, are plunged in gloom, how will we win this war?"

Yudhishtira wipes his eyes, and says to Krishna, "O mighty one, the golden path of dharma is not unknown to me. The dire consequences of Brahmahatya, killing a Brahmana, visit those who forget the services he receives at another's hands. Janardana, while we lived in the forest, Hidimbi's noble son Ghatotkacha, although he was then a mere child, did us so many services!

When he learnt that Arjuna had gone to acquire the devastras, Ghatotkacha came to me in the Kamyaka vana and lived with us until Dhananjaya returned. When we journeyed through inaccessible regions of the world, he carried the tired Draupadi on his back. The feats he achieved on the war showed that he was a great and unequalled warrior. Ah, that noble child accomplished so many difficult tasks for my sake. My love for Ghatotkacha is twice that I bear for Sahadeva. The Rakshasa mahabaho was devoted to me; I was dear to him and he was precious to me. This is why I am numb with grief, burning with it.

Look, O Madhava, where our troops are being routed and butchered by the Kauravas. Look where now, in this abysmal night, Drona and Karna fight in earnest. Look as the Pandava host being crushed this night, like some light woods by two musth maddened elephants. Listen to the terrible celebrant roaring of Drona, Karna and Duryodhana, even as they annihilate our hapless fighting men.

How, O Krishna, when we Pandavas are still alive and you as well, could the Sutaputra kill Bhima's son? Karna fetched untold carnage to our legions and then, as if to crown his dreadful achievements, he slew our precious nephew in the very presence of Arjuna. Arjuna was far away when the evil Dhartarashtras killed Abhimanyu; at that time, Jayadratha used his boon from Lord Siva to keep the rest of us from breaking into the chakravyuha.

Drona and his son Aswatthaman perpetrated that dastardly deed. The Acharya himself told Karna how to kill Abhimanyu. While Abhimanyu fought with his sword, it was the Acharya himself who destroyed the weapon. And while he was in lonely distress, Kritavarman ruthlessly killed his horses and his Parshni charioteers. And then other Kaurava maharathas brought down our splendid child like a throng of huntsmen a golden stag.

For his small enough offence, O Krishna, Arjuna killed Jayadratha. I found no great joy in that killing. If it is our dharma to kill our enemies, then Drona and Karna should have died first. O Lord, these two are the root of Duryodhana's confidence and of all our sorrows. Arjuna should have despatched Drona or Karna to Yama, instead he chose to kill the insignificant Jayadratha, whose role in Abhimanyu's death was hardly direct."

Suddenly, a great rage takes hold of Yudhishtira. His frame shudders in anger, his eyes turn red as plums, and he says, "Bhima now fights against Drona's legion. So I will myself fight and kill the Suta's son. Yes, Karna shall die at my hands today!"

Yudhishtira raises his bow, blows resoundingly on his conch and dashes at Karna. Leading a combined force of Panchalas and Prabhadrakas numbering a thousand rathas, three hundred elephants and five thousand horses, Sikhandin swiftly follows the wake of the king. Now, with some heart restored, the mail-clad Panchalas and the Pandavas led by Yudhishtira all beat their drums and blow their conchs.

Krishna says urgently to Arjuna, "Look where Yudhishtira, beside himself with grief and anger, rides against Karna. You must not allow him to do this or his life will be in danger!"

And Krishna also rides quick as the wind after the distraught Dharmaraja, who by now has gone some way.

In his mind's eye, Vyasa sees Yudhishtira, deranged by grief, rushing recklessly at Karna. Vyasa appears before the eldest Pandava and says, "Through Krishna's wisdom and good fortune, Arjuna still lives. Krishna kept him from facing the Sutaputra in single combat when Karna still had his Naikartana that he had kept to use against your brother. If Karna had killed Arjuna, then truly great would your grief have been, O Yudhishtira.

O bestower of honours, it is your great good fortune that Ghatotkacha has sacrificed himself for Arjuna's sake. Why, Death himself has taken Ghatotkacha using the Vasava astra as merely an instrument. It is for your good, O Pandava, that the Rakshasa has died. Do not yield to anger, and do not grieve, Yudhishtira. This war is war to end all others and a new and evil age has risen over the earth. Unite with your brothers and all the illustrious kings that are with you and dharma, and fight the Kauravas!

O Naravyaghra, on the fifth day from today, the earth will be yours, so set your mind on dharma. Set aside this mad sorrow and rage. With a serene heart, practise karunya to all creatures, and tapasya, daana, kshama and dharma. Jaya is where dharma is."

Having said these words to the son of Pandu, Vyasa vanishes before Yudhishtira's eyes.'"

CANTO 181

DRONA-VADHA PARVA

"Sanjaya says, 'His holy grandsire, the profound Maharishi, arrests Yudhishtira's insane careen; the Dharmaputra's blind fury leaves him and he stops himself from riding ahead to fight the dangerous Karna, the older brother he does not know. However, grief still wracks the Pandava king from of the death of Ghatotkacha.

Yudhishtira looks at Bhima containing your still vast army; he turns to Dhrishtadyumna and says, "Ride against the pot-born Drona! O Parantapa, you were born a full-grown youth from the sacred fire, wearing armour and armed with a sword, bow and arrows. You were born to kill Drona! So go confidently into battle; you need have no fear. Let Janamejaya, Sikhandin, Durmukha's son and Yasodhara attack Drona from every side. Let Nakula, Sahadeva, the sons of Draupadi, the Prabhadrakas, Drupada, and Virata with their sons and brothers, Satyaki, the Kaikeyas, the Pandavas and Dhananjaya all attack him together. Let all our maharathas, all our elephants, our cavalry and foot-soldiers join forces to bring down the implacable Acharya who burns up the very night!"

Thus commanded by the illustrious son of Pandu, all of them launch a combined attack against Drona, determined to put an end to the Brahmana ablaze. Drona, however, meets their onslaught with such a fusillade of arrows and astras! He hold them all up. Anxious for Drona's life, Duryodhana rushes to his support with all his forces, might and resolve. A general battle now breaks out between the Kurus and the Pandavas, all of them shouting and roaring at one another.

By now, the animals of both armies as well as the warriors are all exhausted. The greatest maharathas find they can hardly keep their eyes open or move their limbs, and feel helpless and worn. This horrific night of nine hours appears to have no end. While they mutilate and slaughter one another in droves by darkness, and while sleep sits heavy on their eyelids, it is past midnight. All the Kshatriyas are miserable and the soldiers of both armies have no weapons or arrows left. Yet, the warriors of both the armies do not quit the fight; they keep their svadharma and, summoning the very dregs of the reserves of strength they still possess, battle on.

Others, blind with sleep, lay aside their weapons and lie down, some on the backs of elephants, some on chariots, some on horseback and some on the ground. And when they fall into helpless slumber, other warriors who are awake despatch them to Yama's abode. Others, senseless with fatigue, and in a waking dream, kill their own comrades as well as their enemies. Indeed, they fight giving vent to weird cries and exclamations. Many warriors of our army who still want battle stand half awake but unable to fight on, their eyes half shut. However, some exceptional Kshatriyas, during the terrible night, although exhausted and being dragged down by drowsiness, continue to glide superbly across the field killing one another. Many among the enemy, stupefied by slumber, are slain without their being aware of the strokes and barbs that send them into eternity.

Seeing this state of the troops, Arjuna cries out in a loud voice, "All of you, and your animals, are exhausted; you are plunged in darkness and dust and sleep overcomes you all. So let us all agree to call a halt to the battle and sleep awhile. When the moon rises, Kurus and Pandavas, awake again and do battle once more to find victory or heaven."

The tired men of both armies gladly agree. The Kaurava troops shout all together, "O Karna, O Duryodhana, stop the fighting. The Pandava army has ceased to attack us."

At Arjuna's word, the Pandava army as well as yours, O Bhaarata, refrain from battle. Indeed, the Devas and the noble Rishis all applaud Partha's noble thought and all the worn out Kshatriyas lie down to sleep like some sea subsiding among all the corpses that are strewn everywhere, of man and beast. Your army blesses Arjuna, "In you, great Arjuna, the Vedas and all the astras truly dwell together. In you are intelligence and supernal ability. In you are dharma and compassion for all creatures, O sinless Partha. And since you have comforted us, we wish you well, O Dhananjaya. Let prosperity be yours. May you soon have, O hero, all that is dear to your heart!"

Blessing him thus, the great Kuru maharathas fall silent and sleep comes swiftly over them. Many lie down to sleep with their weapons—maces, swords, battleaxes, lances and with their armour still strapped on. Elephants, heavy with sleep, make the earth cool with their breath that passes through their snake-like trunks stained with dust. Surely, the great elephants, as they breathe on the ground, and sleep standing, look as serene and beautiful as hills scattered across the field of battle over which giant snakes hiss.

Horses in trappings of gold and with manes entwined with their yokes and stamping their hooves, make the ground uneven. Thus, every warrior sleeps there with the animal they ride. The slumbering host, plunged in unconsciousness, looks like a wonderful picture drawn on canvas by the most gifted artists.

The more youthful Kshatriyas, their kundalas gleaming softly, their limbs lacerated by arrows and swords, have laid themselves down on the round heads of their elephants, and look as if they lie in the embraces of beautiful women.

Then, the Moon, the delighter of the eye and lord of the lotuses, white as the fair cheeks of a virgin, rises in the East, adorning the direction presided over by Indra. Indeed, like a lion of the Udaya hills, its rays his mane of brilliant yellow, he issues out of his cave in the east, shredding the blackness of the night. The lover of all lotuses and lilies in the world, bright as the body of Mahadeva's Bull, full-arched and radiant as Kama's bow, enticing as the smile on the lips of a bashful bride, Soma Deva begins to bloom in the firmament.

Soon, however, the divine lord with the hare for his sign shows himself more fully, shedding brighter rays. Soma Deva gradually emanates a bright halo of far-reaching light with the splendour of amber-gold. Quickly, his lustre, dispelling the darkness entirely, spreads over all the quarters, the sky and the earth. The world is illuminated and the unspeakable darkness that had hidden everything melts away. When the world is lit up in silver, among creatures that wander the night some continue to roam while others retire to their hides, caves and holes.

The sea of troops, Rajan, is awakened by the light of the Moon and they arise like a great lake of lotuses blossoming or like the ocean surging up in tide at moonrise. Then, Rajan, the war commences again on earth, for the destruction of the race of warriors, between men who wish to attain heaven.'"

CANTO 182

DRONA-VADHA PARVA CONTINUED

"Sanjaya says, 'An excited and rested Duryodhana approaches Drona and, to encourage him and provoke his ire, says to him, "You should have shown no mercy to our enemies while they were downcast after Ghatotkacha's death and exhausted, especially when they are all deadly archers. To satisfy your noble wish, Acharya, we showed them misplaced kindness by allowing a cessation in a battle we were winning. Having rested and slept, the Pandavas are stronger now.

As for ourselves, we loose energy and strength in every way, hour by hour, while the Pandavas, whom you so lovingly protect, gain ground and success. All the Devastras and Brahmastras dwell in you. I say to you, O Drona, if you put forth your true prowess, neither the Pandavas nor we, nor any other bowmen in the world are a match for you on the field of battle.

O Mahamuni, you are a consummate master of every manner of weapon and warfare, the teacher of us all. With your devastras, you can destroy the three worlds with the Devas, the Asuras and the Gandharvas. The Pandavas are all afraid of you and yet, time and again, you spare them, remembering fondly that they were your students. Or, perhaps, this is all because of my ill luck and the stars turning against me."

Thus chided by your son, Drona wrathfully tells Duryodhana, "Although I am old, Suyodhana, I still exert myself to the utmost in this war. All these men are hardly acquainted with the weapons of which I do indeed possess mastery. So, if, from a desire for victory, I become responsible for the death of such common soldiers, there can be no more ignoble deed. However, now, O Kaurava, I will at your evil command, do what you have in your dark heart, be it good or bad. It will not be otherwise. Duryodhana, I will not remove my kavacha from my body until I have killed all the Panchalas. I swear this to you.

You think that Kunti's son Arjuna is worn out by the war? Listen to me carefully, and I will truly tell you about his prowess. If Savyasachin is truly roused, not the Gandharvas, the Yakshas or the Rakshasas can hope to stand up to him. In the Khandava vana, he encountered the Lord Indra himself in battle. Arjuna confounded a raging Indra with his arrows. He killed the Yakshas, Nagas, Daityas, and all rest, so proud of their might in that forest when it burned, so none escaped.

And when you went to mock the Pandavas in the forest and were humiliated and taken captive by Chitrasena and his people, it was Arjuna that vanquished the Gandharvas and set you free, while the unearthly ones had you bound firmly in a net. This is the hero who quelled the Nivatakavachas, who not the Devas could resist or conquer in battle.

Naravyaghra Partha vanquished the thousands of Danavas who dwelt in Hiranyapura. How can you be so foolish to imagine for a moment that mere human warriors can withstand him? You saw with your own eyes, Duryodhana, how Arjuna razed your army on his way to kill Jayadratha. Is your mind so clouded with darkness that you have forgotten that so quickly?"

Duryodhana replies in anger to hear Arjuna being extolled, "Dusasana, Karna, Sakuni, and I will divide this Bharata army into two akshauhinis. We will take one host with us and kill Arjuna today."

Drona laughs and says sardonically, "My blessings go with you! But which Kshatriya among you will kill this bull among all Kshatriyas, the immortal bearer of the Gandiva, the hero who blazes forth with divine tejas? Not Kubera, Lord of treasures, not Indra or Yama, not the Asuras, the Uragas and the Rakshasas can face an armed Arjuna in battle. Only fools will speak such nonsense as you just have, Duryodhana! Who can return with his life after facing Arjuna in battle? As for you, you are sinful, cruel and suspicious of everyone. You are always ready to rebuke even those who risk their lives to fight for you.

Yes, go and give battle to the son of Kunti, for you are a well-born Kshatriya who seeks combat. But why cause all these other unoffending Kshatriyas to be slain? You are the root of this enmity and this war, so go and fight Arjuna yourself. Your uncle Sakuni has wisdom and observes Kshatriya dharma. Let Sakuni the great gambler take the field against Arjuna. He is skilled in dice, wedded to deception, addicted to gambling, and a master of cunning and subterfuge. Surely, this great man will vanquish the Pandavas in battle!

With Karna in your company, you often boasted foolishly in the hearing of Dhritarashtra, "O father, we three, Karna, Dusasana and I will kill all the sons of Pandu in battle."

We heard this brag of yours at every conclave in the Kuru sabha. Do what you said you would now; show that your boasts were neither hollow nor idle. Look, there before you is your mortal enemy, Arjuna, son of Pandu. Observe Kshatriya dharma and fight him. Your death at the hands of the Vijaya shall be worthy of our every praise. You have practised charity, you have eaten everything that you ever wished, you have gained as much wealth as you wanted, more than any other man, and you leave no debts. You have done all that a prince should do. So have no regrets or fears. Go and fight the son of Pandu."

Then, the battle begins.'"

CANTO 183

DRONA-VADHA PARVA CONTINUED

"Sanjaya says, 'When three yaamas of the night have worn away, Rajan, the battle between the Kurus and the Pandavas resumes and both sides are exhilarant, born warriors that they are! Soon after, Surya's sarathy, the legless Aruna, weakening the splendour of the moon, appears upon the Udaya mountain, turning the sky a coppery hue. The east is soon lit with the crimson rays of the Sun, who, rising, resembles a circular plate of gold. All the warriors of the Kuru and the Pandava armies alight from their chariots, horses and palanquins, stand with joined hands, facing Surya Deva, and recite the Gayatri Mantra appropriate to greet the first sandhya of the day, the golden dawn.

The Kuru army is divided into two parts. Drona, with Duryodhana going before him with one of the hosts, advances with the other one against the Somakas, the Pandavas and the Panchalas. Seeing the Kuru army thus divided, Krishna says to Arjuna, "Keep your cousins to your left, and the division commanded by Drona to your right."

Arjuna moves to the left of the mighty Drona and Karna.

Understanding Krishna's intention, Bhimasena says to Partha who is at the van of the army, "Arjuna, Bibhatsu, listen to me. The time has come to fulfil the purpose for which Kshatriya women bear sons. If you fight for victory now, you will demean your birth. The moment has come to pay the debt you owe Truth, Prosperity, Virtue and Fame. O greatest of warriors, keep this akshauhini to your left and destroy it."

When Bhima and Krishna urge him on, Arjuna truly puts his unrivalled prowess on display and, dominating Drona and Karna, begins to raze the Kaurava forces all around him. Many great Kshatriyas among the Kurus do their best but cannot stop the Kiritin as he sweeps over them like a raging conflagration, consuming them all. Duryodhana, Karna and Sakuni shoot tremendous volleys at Kunti's son. Defending himself with light like swiftness, he cuts down every arrow loosed at him, and then strikes each of the three with ten deep barbs.

The dust and thick arrow showers darken the sky as if night has returned, and a great din arises everywhere. The sky, the earth and all the directions are obscured. Blinded by the swirling dust, and yet again no one can tell friend from foe, ally from enemy. Once more, the kings and warriors loudly call out their own names, and fight the war for dharma by instinct and approximation.

Maharathas losing their chariots run headlong into one another and are tangled together in chaos. Their horses killed and charioteers slain, many remain petrified, sitting or standing perfectly still to save their lives. Dead horses and their riders lie on felled elephants as if stretched out on mountain summits.

Drona then rides away from the general melee towards the north and takes up his station there, like a smokeless fire, resplendent, magnificent and blazing with energy. Seeing him, the Pandava troops tremble; they turn pale and falter on the field, O Bhaarata. From seeming like an elephant in rut, the enemy loses its nerve entirely, terrified as the Danavas when they fought Vasava. Some among them are broken in spirit, while other, bolder ones are enraged. Others are filled with wonder, and some, though they would try, are unequal to the challenge of the refulgent

Acharya. Some of the Pandava kings wring their hands, and some are beside themselves with anger and bite through their lips in that wrath. A few brandish their weapons, others rub their arms; and some who possess truly great tejas and whose souls are under complete control, attack Drona. The domineering Brahmana mauls the Panchalas in particular with arrows mundane and unworldly; mangled, burnt and bleeding, and in agony, they yet continue to contend with him.

Then Drupada and Virata take the field against Drona who by now rages unchecked all across Kurukshetra sowing death wherever he rides like some storm of another furious world. Drupada's three grandsons also ride against Drona, as do the mighty Chedi archers. Seeing them come, in a flash, Drona beheads all three Panchala princes, who are no remote match for him. He next routs the Chedis, the Kaikeyas, the Srinjayas and all the Matsyas.

In rage past enduring, Drupada and Virata unleash gales and hurricanes of arrows at the dreadful Brahmana. The scourge of the Kshatriyas swathes both Drupada and Virata with harrowing gusts of shafts, and they, also, strike him back ardently. Drona, roused, looses two of his favoured crescent-tipped shafts and breaks both Drupada and Virata's bows at the same moment.

Virata flings ten spears at Drona, desperate to have his life, while Drupada, great Kshatriya, casts a blazing astra of iron and gold inlaid with lapis lazuli, a weapon like a gleaming serpent, at him. Drona cuts all these weapons down with a lordly and serene display of superhuman archery. Next moment, with a long roar, with two perfect arrows, he sends both those great and aged kings to the world of Yama, cutting one's head from his throat and blowing the other's heart to shreds. A terrible wail rises from the armies of the Panchalas and the Matsyas.

Dhrishtadyumna watches Drona kill his father Drupada, his own sons, and Virata; he watches him slaughter the Kaikeyas, the Chedis, the Matsyas and the Panchalas; he sees him kill Drupada's three grandsons and the fire-prince is filled with grief and swears an oath in rage before all the maharathas: "Let me lose all the punya of all the dharma that I have done, as well as my Kshatriya and Brahma tejas if Drona escapes me today with his life, or if he succeeds in vanquishing me!"

With this, taking his own division with him, the Panchala prince rides at Drona. The Panchalas then fall upon Drona from one side and Arjuna from the other. Duryodhana, his brothers, Karna and Sakuni defend Drona against the attack and, though the Panchalas fight with fury and vigour, your sons and their allies prevent the dead Drupada's sons and warriors from so much as catching a proper look at the Acharya.

Bhimasena is furious with Dhrishtadyumna and berates him, "What Kshatriya is the warrior born into great Drupada's vamsa, and who is besides the greatest warrior of all born from the fire, who can only look at his enemy standing before him? What true man, who has seen his father and his son slain before his eyes, and who has sworn to have revenge on their killer, stands listless and helpless before his enemy? There stands Drona like a fire blazing high with its own energy and, with his bows and arrows for fuel, consumes all our Kshatriyas that come before him like mere straws. Why, he will annihilate all the Pandava army by himself in a brief hour if he is not extinguished.

If you will not fight, be spectators and watch me as I fight Drona. I do not fear this vile Brahmana. I do not revere him."

With this, the fuming Vrikodara rips into Drona's vyuha and begins to decimate that host. In a moment, Dhrishtadyumna follows Bhima and quickly the two of them engage Drona in a fiery battle as the sun rises and bathes the holy field of Kurukshetra in dawn's light. By first light of day, we see the enormity of the night's carnage—the rathas entangled with one another, and the dead scattered in their thousands and thousands, men and beasts, all over the field. And again, the war resumes between the two armies, more bloodthirsty than ever. Some, while riding towards another part of the field are waylaid and butchered; others, who are fleeing, are struck in their backs, or through their sides like beasts on a hunt.

The general engagement, the war from which every vestige of a dharma yuddha has fled, continues to rage as the morning sun rises higher.'"

CANTO 184

DRONA-VADHA PARVA CONTINUED

"Sanjaya says, 'The warriors, however, Rajan, do pause briefly to worship the thousand-rayed Aditya, as he ascends the field of battle on this morning. When they have paid their daily homage to God of day, they fight again exactly as they did by night.

Bharatarishabha, horsemen fight maharathas, elephants confront horsemen, foot-soldiers battle elephants and horsemen other horsemen. Sometimes united and sometimes separately, the warriors lay into each other, and many, having fought through the night and slept only briefly, are tired, weak with hunger and thirsty and they fall unconscious. The uproar made by the blare of conches, the beating of drums, the trumpeting of elephants and the twanging of bowstrings drawn and released with force, reaches the very heavens.

So, too, is the clangour of charging infantry, weapons falling, horses neighing, chariots thundering along, and the roaring, shouting and yelling of the warriors earthshaking; it, too, swells by the moment and echoes in the realms of the gods. The screams, groans and wails of pain, of falling and fallen foot-soldiers, rathikas and elephants multiply by the moment; they wash across the field in a piteous, horrifying wave.

Men and animals fall like leaves in autumn blown down by a strong wind. Hurled from Kshatriyas' hands at other warriors and elephants, we see swords heaping themselves on the ground, many bloody, like heaps of cloth on a washing ghat. The sound of falling swords resembles that of clothes being beaten to wash them well. Rajan, though we should now be inured to the horror after the grisly night, the battle by daylight continues to be appalling.

A river runs again towards the land of the dead. The blood of elephants, horses and men are its current, weapons its fish in profusion, blood and flesh its mire, the cries of grief and pain its roar, and proud banners cut down and other bloodied cloths are its froth.

Pierced all over by arrows and spears, elephants and horses stand perfectly motionless on Kurukshetra, worn out with exertion, spent with the grim toil of the night, and utterly exhausted so they cannot move. With their arms in graceful attitudes, their beautiful coats of mail, with their turbaned and crowned heads decked with sparkling kundalas, even on this ghastly morning the warriors bearing the instruments of war look magnificent.

Meanwhile, the chariots find passage across the field difficult indeed, for all the dead, the dying and the scavenging carnivores that cover the ground of death. Stricken by arrows and worn out by their exertions, steeds of the noblest breed and high mettle, of gigantic size and strength, tremble with effort as they attempt to draw the chariots whose wheels have been mired deep in the blood swamped earth. Terror and only terror holds every warriors of both armies in its cold, benumbing clasp, O Bhaarata, with the exception of only Drona and Arjuna. These two become the refuge, the saviours of the warriors of their respective legions. Others who encounter these two are swiftly sent to Yama's abode.

Entwined, enmeshed, even like the great bodies of unimaginable and violent lovers in the throes of lethal lust, the armies of the Kurus and the Panchalas are no longer distinguishable. During this carnage where Kshatriyas turn Kurukshetra into an endless smasana, a cremation ground, nothing and no one is plainly visible—not Karna, Drona, Arjuna, Yudhishtira, Bhimasena, the twins, the Panchala fire-prince, Satyaki, Dusasana, Drona's son, Duryodhana, Subala's son, Kripa, Salya, Kritavarman, all the great others, nor the earth, nor the points of the compass, nor I, can be seen as clouds of dusts shroud all the heroes, their chariots and beats and the thousands of foot-soldiers.

As the war burgeons by the moment, it seems that another night has fallen over the filed for the pall of dust that rises and billows, and the swarms of arrows and other weapons, which cover the sky, hiding the sun. You cannot tell Kaurava from Panchala, or Panchala from Pandava; all is a single haze, which rings hellishly with roars and screams. The warriors, possessed absolutely by the spirit of murdering, by now kill friend and enemy alike, making no more distinction, for to kill is all that matters regardless of who kills and who is slain.

Then, suddenly, strong winds arise and, blowing powerfully from all directions like the breath of a many faced God, blows away the single vast cloud of dust. Now there is a unique rain of blood everywhere, Rajan! Elephants, horses, maharathas and foot-soldiers, all bathed in crimson, look as wondrous as the celestial forest of Parijata flowers.

The four Kaurava maharathas Duryodhana, Karna, Drona and Dusasana attack the Pandava host with renewed ferocity. Duryodhana and his brothers fight Nakula and Sahadeva, while Karna battles Vrikodara Bhima, Arjuna confronts Drona, and all the troops from every side stand still and gaze at these scintillating duels. Why, even the maharathas of both armies pause and quietly watch the superhuman engagement between those greatest among all Kshatriyas.

The interminable and deadly rain of arrows and other weapons pours on. The great maharathas, bulls among all men, riding their chariots of solar effulgence, still look as stunning as dark and golden clouds in the autumn sky. Avid of blood, thirsty for revenge and killing, this handful of the greatest warriors on earth engage one another like infuriated leaders of elephant herds.

In truth, Rajan, death does not ever come until its hour is come, and not all the warriors on Kurukshetra perish all together in the battle. Strewn with lopped off arms, legs, heads with dazzling earrings, bows and arrows, lances, swords, battleaxes, nalihas, razor-headed arrows, cloth-yard shafts, darts, diverse kinds of exquisite armour, splendid rathas broken into pieces, slain elephants, other huge chariots without standards broken like cities, yet others being dragged here and there by frightened horses without a charioteer to control them, by hosts of grandly adorned warriors of immeasurable courage, fallen chamaras and coats of mail and standards, scattered ornaments, robes and fragrant bloodied garlands, chains of gold, diadems, crowns, helmets, rows of bells, jewels worn on breasts, cuirasses, collars, and with gems that adorn coronets, the field of battle looks as marvellous as the endless firmament spangled with countless stars.

Now there ensues a duel between a furious Duryodhana, voracious for revenge, and Nakula full of the same hunger. Madri's son shoots hundreds of arrows at your son on his right, and is loudly cheered by the Pandava soldiers. Duryodhana responds with vehemence and passion. Nakula wheels away to the left, and now attacks your son from that side. However, your son is not to be bested on this day and, with incandescent archery, forces Nakula to turn back. All the troops applaud Suyodhana's feat, while Nakula recalls every indignity of the past and roars at your incensed son, "Stop! Stop and fight, you wretched sinner!"'"

CANTO 185

DRONA-VADHA PARVA CONTINUED

"Sanjaya says, 'An angry Dusasana pushes fiercely towards Sahadeva, making the earth shiver with the speed of his chariot. But, in a flash, with a wedge-headed arrow, Sahadeva strikes off the head of your son's sarathy, helmet and all. So swiftly does Sahadeva do this that neither Dusasana nor any of the troops even notices that the charioteer has been decapitated, until their reins hanging loose, Dusasana's horses careen wildly away.

Being a master charioteer himself, Dusasana quickly takes the reins up himself and fetches the horses under control. Friend and foe alike acclaim his feat, for now driving the chariot himself, he moves effortlessly and fearlessly across the field, attacking Sahadeva again. Sahadeva pierces your son's horses now with a volley of vicious arrows and, flowing blood, whinnying in pain, they bolt once more, for as soon as Dusasana picks up his bow to fight Sahadeva he loses control of his agonised steeds again.

The relentless Sahadeva drills him with a score of hate-filled arrows. Karna comes dashing to rescue your son, when, taking careful aim, Bhima strikes the Sutaputra deep through his arms and chest with three shafts like thunderbolts shot from his bow drawn into a circle. Struck by these arrows like a snake with a stick, Karna stops and faces Bhimasena in wrath, unleashing a terrific volley of slender deadly shafts at him.

Another fervid duel breaks out between Bhima and Karna, both roaring like bulls and their eyes dilated with rage. Both find themselves too close to each other and cannot shoot their arrows with any freedom. Thereupon, they fight with maces and Bhimasena quickly smashes the kuvara of Karna's ratha, a feat to watch. Then Karna hurls his gada in fury at Bhima's chariot; Bhima strikes it aside with his own mace. Bhima sweeps up another mace and hurls it with titanic force at Karna; Karna shoots the heavy thing with an astonishing golden-winged volley, which turns the massive gada right back at Bhima, like a snake charmed by mantras! The mace strikes Bhima's immense flagpole, which breaks, falls and strikes his charioteer senseless.

His brows knit, Bhima, with the greatest care, rives Karna's standards, his bow and shreds his leather gauntlet. Radheya takes up another gold-decked bow and in a blur kills Bhima's horses the colour of bears, and his two charioteers. Bhima quickly jumps into Nakula's chariot like a lion bounding down a mountain summit.

Meanwhile, Drona and Arjuna, the two greatest maharathas, Acharya and sishya, duel, stunning all that watch with their mastery over the astras, the sureness of their aim, and with the manoeuvres of their chariots. Watching that battle, the like of which they have never seen, the other warriors stop fighting and stand with hair standing on end, quivering with equal parts of awe and fear.

Both Arjuna and his master display immaculate tactics, while trying always to keep the adversary to his right. The plane on which these two make sublime war is such that all the other maharathas can only gaze in wonder. That duel is like one between a pair of eagles in the sky fighting over a piece of meat. Whatever Drona does to have the better of his favourite pupil, Arjuna matches.

When Drona can find no edge over his younger rival with common shafts or lesser astras, the Brahmana invokes into the Aindra, the Tvashtra, the Vayavya and the Yamya astras. No sooner do these issue from Drona's bow, Dhananjaya extinguishes them with his own astras. At this, Drona looses the very greatest astras at Arjuna, but even these Partha nullifies. Seeing Arjuna negate all his weapons, even the highest celestial ones, Drona applauds his disciple in his heart and is full of secret joy.

Since the days when Arjuna was his pupil, the Acharya has regarded himself as the greatest master of weapons in the world. Now, equalled by his sishya in the midst of all those most illustrious and discerning warriors on earth, Drona continues to attack and to defend himself energetically, marvelling all the while at the genius of his opponent.

We plainly see the Devas, Gandharvas in their thousands, Rishis and bodies of Siddhas, everywhere in the sky. Filled with these as well as with Apsaras, Yakshas and Rakshasas, it once more seems as if gathering clouds fill the vaults of the firmament. We hear a reverberant asariri, a disembodied voice from above, repeatedly sweep through the sky, end to end, full of praise for the mighty Drona and the noble Partha.

From the flames and lustre of the astras that Drona and Partha loose at each other, all creation seems to blaze with light, and the Siddhas and the Rishis on high say, "This is not a Manava, an Asura, a Rakshasa, a Deva or a Gandharva yuddha. Without doubt, this is a transcendent Brahma yuddha!"

And indeed so it is, the unmatched, spectacular contention, the like of which we have never even heard before let alone seen. As we all stand transfixed, now the Acharya prevails over Arjuna, and then the son of Pandu over Drona, and no one can find any difference between them. Only if Rudra, dividing himself into two parts fought against himself, could there be a battle to match this one. The astra shastra, focused, embodied, dwells in the Acharya on one side; so, too, does it, on the other, in the resplendent and profound Arjuna, along with deep substance. Virata, heroism, in one place, dwells absolutely in Drona; on the other side, heroism and strength are in the son of Pandu. Neither of these warriors can be challenged by enemies in battle. It is the opinion of all the invisible and visible beings, who watch the sacred conflict, that either of them can destroy the very universe with all the gods, if they wish.

Drona now invokes the Brahmastra against Arjuna and the all invisible ones above and below, and the Earth with her mountains and waters and trees tremble. Howling winds begin to blow, the seas rise up, and the warriors of the Kuru and Pandava armies, as well as all other living creatures are struck through with fear, when Drona raises that astra. Arjuna, O king, summons his own Brahmastra and like two other suns risen into the bright sky, their weapons extinguish each other. All agitated Nature is pacified again.

Finally, acknowledging that neither can vanquish the other, the two armies engage each other, generally, once more. Widespread havoc occupies Kurukshetra again. And mayhem, pandemonium and darkness engulf the battlefield all around. The sky is obscured with dark swarms of arrows, as if with masses of heavy clouds, and the creatures that fly through the air can no longer find a passage through the element.'"

CANTO 186

DRONA-VADHA PARVA CONTINUED

"Sanjaya says, 'During the carnage of men, horses and elephants, Dusasana, O Rajan, meets Dhrishtadyumna in battle. Dusasana ravages the fire-prince mounted on his golden chariot; in fury, Dhrishtadyumna covers your son, his chariot, horses and sarathy in an opacity of arrows so they become invisible. Dusasana is forced to turn away from the Pandava senapati and Dhrishtadyumna forges on toward his main enemy, Drona, the one he must kill. As he goes, he showers arrows all around him, claiming a thousand lives each moment.

Kritavarman, with three of his Bhoja brothers, challenges dead Drupada's son, but Nakula and Sahadeva, who are following Dhrishtadyumna while he makes his way like a blazing fire towards Drona, are at hand to keep these heroes at bay. All of them, fighting now on the very brink of death, attack one another in perfect fury, determined to kill or be killed. Of pure souls and pure conduct, and with swarga in mind, they fight according to the noble tenets of dharma. Of impeccable lineage, un-stained deeds and gifted with great intelligence, these lords of men fight righteously and with Kshatriya dharma, using no vile weapons that might be regarded as unfair.

None of them use either cruelly barbed arrows, those called nalikas, poisoned ones, those with heads made of horns, those with many pointed heads, ones made of the bones of bulls and elephants, those having two heads, ones with rusty heads, or those that do not fly straight. All of them use simple and direct weapons and wish to win both fame and heaven and the region of great blessedness, by fighting justly. Yet, the battle between the four warriors of your army and the three from the Pandava side is fearsome, O king.

Meanwhile, Dhrishtadyumna seeing Nakula and Sahadeva successfully contain your mighty maharathas, surges on toward Drona. Held up by the tigerish twins of Madri, your warriors fight them like the wind assailing two mountains.

Seeing the Panchala fire-prince ride like another wind at Drona and the four heroes of his own army obstructed by the twins, Duryodhana dashes against the dangerous Dhrishtadyumna, loosing thunderous volleys of blood-drinking arrows at him. At which, Satyaki rides up, quick as a wish, to stop him. These two Naravyaghras, descendants of Kuru and Madhu, fall wildly upon each other. Then the strangest thing, Rajan—both recall with pleasure and affection the days of their boyhood, when they had been loving friends and, even as they fight savagely, they look at each other with some love and smile repeatedly!

Indeed, so moved is your son that, with tears standing in his eyes, guilt and sorrow laying their touch upon his heart, he says to his ever dear Satyaki, "Shame on anger, my precious friend, and shame on revenge! Shame on Kshatriya dharma and shame on valour and prowess, for today you aim your astras at me and I also loose my shafts at you. In those days when we were young, you were dearer to me than life itself, and you felt the same for me. Alas, where have that love and those childhood memories gone now? They mean nothing on this field of war. Alas, O Satwata, moved by greed and hatred, we are here today fighting each other to kill or die!"

Hearing this, Satyaki draws a clutch of sharp arrows from his quiver, and replies with a smile, "This is no sabha, O prince, nor the home of our Acharya, where we once played together."

Duryodhana says, "Where have those games of our childhood gone, O bull of Sini's race, and how has this battle come upon us now? It seems that the influence of Time is irresistible. Urged though we are by the desire for wealth, what use is the wealth for which you and I meet to fight, moved only by avarice."

Satyaki replies, "This has always been the way of the Kshatriyas that they must fight even against their acharyas. If I am dear to you, Suyodhana my friend, then kill me quickly. Let me find the realm of the righteous by your hand. Nothing would make me happier. I cannot bear this loving talk. Put forth your best valour and let us do battle like the Kshatriyas that we are. For to speak of the past and our friendship is far more cruel than to fight with arrows."

With this, and not without tears in his own eyes, Satyaki rides at Duryodhana with his bow raised. Seeing him come, your son cascades a blithe shower of deadly shafts on his old and beloved friend, and a pitched and mighty duel breaks out between those scions of the races of Kuru and Madhu, like one between an elephant and a lion. Drawing his bow round, Duryodhana strikes the invincible Satyaki with a blizzard of vicious shafts and Yuyudhana of the Satwatas responds with first fifty, then with twenty, and once more with ten keening arrows.

Duryodhana, still smiling, his eyes still moist, rakes Satyaki with thirty arrows shot from his bowstring drawn to his ear; then, with a razor-headed arrow, he breaks Satyaki's bow. Quicker than thinking, Sini's grandson picks up another bow and covers Duryodhana with a marvellous unbroken straight line of burning barbs. With wonderful skill, Suyodhana cuts every shafts into pieces, at which your army cheers him loudly.

Duryodhana lacerates Satyaki with three and seventy shafts, with wings of gold, dipped in oil and shot from his bow drawn to its fullest stretch. In a flash, the explosive Yuyudhana cleaves your son's bow in his hands and gores him with a hundred barbs, which draw fonts of blood from Duryodhana and course agony through his body. Duryodhana swiftly seeks refuge in another chariot. Having rested awhile, he rides once more against Satyaki, shooting blazing salvos of arrows at the Satwata hero's chariot. Always smiling, Rajan, Satyaki continues to pour an endless river of arrows at his childhood friend, his enemy.

The immaculate shafts of both Kshatriyas meet in the sky, in small explosions and fall broken on every side, sounding like a raging fire consuming a great forest. The thousands of arrows that they both shoot densely cover earth and sky. Then, Karna sees that Satyaki is surely beginning to prevail over Duryodhana and rides up swiftly to rescue your son. However, Bhima is quick to see this and races up to cut Karna off. He unleashes powerful heavy volleys at the Sutaputra who, with great grace and ease, cuts down Bhima's wall of fire, severs his bow, and maims his charioteer.

Bhima hefts a mace and, running headlong at Karna, smashes his bow, standard, one of his chariot wheels and his charioteer with a flurry of sickening blows like thunder. But Karna stands on his broken chariot, immovable as Meru, the king of all mountains. His horses continue to draw his wonderful ratha with only a single wheel, even like Surya's one-wheeled chariot, drawn by the Sun God's seven celestial steeds.

Karna finds Bhima's irrepressible prowess intolerable; he continues to fight the titan with storms of arrows and diverse astras as well. An incited Bhima matches Karna's shaft for shaft, astra for astra.

Then the battle spreads, when Yudhishtira says to all the leading warriors among the Panchalas and the Matsyas, "Those who are our very life, who are our heads, who are powerful bulls among men are all fighting the Dhartarashtras. How then do you all stand here, as if stupefied and deprived of your very senses? Fly to those great maharathas of my army. Drive out your fears and fight. Hold your Kshatriya dharma high, for with that, regardless of victory or death, you will attain swarga. If you prove to be victors, you will perform great yagnas with lavish dakshina to the Brahmanas. If, instead, you are killed, you will become equals to the Devas, and win many realms of felicity and bliss."

Thus exhorted by the king, the rest of the maharathas of the Pandava army charge into battle, the Panchalas attacking Drona from one side, while Bhimasena leads the others from another.

Bhima, Nakula and Sahadeva are the most ardent and active warriors for the Pandavas. They also read the battle the best at this time. They cry to Arjuna, "Dhananjaya, brother, drive the Kurus away from Drona's side. If the Acharya loses his defenders, then the Panchalas can kill him."

At this, Partha rides swiftly against the Kauravas, while Drona continues to battle the Panchalas led by Dhrishtadyumna. On the fifth day of Drona's command, O Bhaarata, Bharadwaja's implacable son slaughters the enemy with unearthly archery and inhuman ruthlessness.'"

CANTO 187

DRONA-VADHA PARVA CONTINUED

"Sanjaya says, 'Drona razes the Panchala legions even as Indra did the Danavas of old. Though he sends gales of fire and wind swirling at them, and countless numbers of their troops are consumed by the matchless, apparently deranged Acharya, the great Pandava maharathas remain unmoved and continue to advance and to fight. In fact, Rajan, the Panchalas and the Srinjayas rush all together at Drona with fierce yells and surround the dreadful Brahmana. He, however, burns and mows them down at will.

Seeing the lustrous Drona putting the Panchalas to rout with unworldly astras, to which they have no defence, fear grips the hearts of the Pandavas and they despair of having victory and tell one another, "Ah, it is plain that Drona will consume us with his astras like a forest fire does a heap of straw in spring. We have no one who can so much as look at him in battle. Arjuna is possibly the only one who can face this apocalyptic Brahmana, and he will not fight him, for he does not consider it dharma to fight his Acharya."

Finding the sons of Kunti sorely pressed, bleeding and now truly frightened, from Drona's many fires, the omniscient Krishna says to Arjuna and his brothers, "Not the Devas with Vasava at their head can vanquish this Brahmana in battle. He can only be killed if he were to lay down his weapons himself. You must set aside your lofty dharma, you sons of Pandu, and use some cunning stratagem to kill Drona. Otherwise, from the golden ratha, the Brahmana will kill us all."

He pauses and, seeing he has their attention, says quietly, "Drona loves his son more than his life. I think if Aswatthaman were to die, Drona would abandon the war and lay down his weapons. So, let someone go and tell the Acharya that his son Aswatthaman has been killed."

Arjuna looks at Krishna in some shock and does not approve of this counsel. The others, seeing the havoc from hell that Drona sows all around him, and knowing very well that the war would indeed be swiftly lost if he was not stopped, quickly concur with Krishna. Yudhishtira thinks a long while and then, unwillingly, accepts what Krishna says. Rajan, then Mahabaho Bhima armed with his mace goes and kills a dangerous elephant whose name is also Aswatthaman and which belongs to his own army, to Indravarman, the king of the Malavas.

Riding upto Drona, with some reluctance in his heart and shame, Bhima begins to roar aloud, "Aswatthaman has been killed. Aswatthaman is dead!"

Bhima proclaims this white lie for it is not the Acharya's son who has died. Drona hears what Bhima says and feels all his limbs turn weak as if they have dissolved like sand in water. Then, he remembers the invincible prowess of his son and quickly concludes that Bhima is lying. Strength floods back into his mighty body. He knows that his son wears a secret jewel that makes him invincible to his enemies; Drona knows that his beloved Aswatthaman could not be dead.

Drona bears down hotly on Dhrishtadyumna, who he wants to kill above all else, for he knows that the Panchala prince is destined to kill him, indeed born just for that. He covers Dhrishtadyumna with a thousand keen kanka-feathered arrows. At this, full twenty thousand powerful Panchala maharathas inundate him with their barbs even as he dashes across Kurukshetra as he likes leaving spasming corpses all around him.

Completely shrouded by Panchala arrows, we no longer see the Acharya; he is as the sun hidden by rainclouds during the monsoon.

But no Panchala arrow finds its home in Drona's body, for he invokes the Brahmastra to protect himself and to ravage them. Drona is like a smokeless, blazing fire and he is invested with celestial grandeur as he slaughters the Somakas. He fells heads and cuts off massive arms like spiked maces decked with golden ornaments; these fall in a veritable rain. Massacred by Bharadwaja's meridian son, the Panchala Kshatriyas fall everywhere like trees uprooted by a tempest.

Yet again, the field of death becomes impassable for fallen elephants and horses, O Bhaarata, and the thick sludge of flesh and blood. Having killed all twenty thousand Panchala maharathas, Drona shines forth gloriously, truly like a smokeless fire. The inexorable son of Bharadwaja then beheads Vasudana with a broad-headed arrow, and then he kills five hundred Matsyas, six thousand elephants and ten thousand horsemen, in less time than it takes me to tell you of it.

Seeing Drona annihilating the very race of Kshatriyas on chasmic Kurukshetra deeper than death, the Rishis Viswamitra, Jamadagni, Bharadwaja, Gautama, Vasishta, Kasyapa, Atri, and the Srikatas, the Prisnis, Garga, the Balakhilyas, the Marichis, the descendants of Bhrigu and Angiras, and diverse other sages of subtle forms, gather there quickly, with Agni, the bearer of sacrificial libations at their head. They want to fetch Drona to Brahma, the Grandsire. They say to Drona, the ornament of battle, "You are fighting sinfully, without dharma. The hour of your death has come, O Brahmana. Lay down your weapons, Drona. Look, we are here and, after seeing us, you must no longer perpetrate such cruel violence.

You are well versed in the Vedas and their angas. You are devoted to dharma, especially because you are a Brahmana. Such brutal deeds do not become you. Lay down your weapons, drive away the film of darkness that blinds your heart and your eyes and cleave fast again to the sanatana dharma. The time that you had to spend in this world of men is now full.

You have consumed ordinary soldiers with the Brahmastra, burnt men who know nothing of the divine weapons to ashes. What you have done, O Muni, is in no way dharma. O blessed Drona, put aside your weapons without delay, and do not remain an hour longer on earth. Sin no more! You have done enough grievous harm."

Drona hears what the great Rishis say; he remembers again what Bhima had declared, that Aswatthaman was dead; he sees Dhrishtadyumna advancing upon him and a great pang, verily of death, clenches his heart. Burning with grief and plunged into sudden dejection, while he burned with energy and wrath a moment ago, Drona rides up to the one man that he trusts completely. He goes to the always truthful Yudhishtira Dharmaraja and asks him if his son Aswatthaman has indeed been killed.

Drona firmly believes that Yudhishtira would never tell a lie, not for the sovereignty over the three worlds. This is why he asks the question of Yudhishtira and nobody else. He had always looked for and found perfect truth in Yudhishtira from that Pandava's very boyhood.

Meanwhile, Krishna, knower of all things, is anxious for he knows that the indomitable Acharya can indeed devour all the Pandavas with his astras; he knows that Drona cannot be killed unless he lays down his weapons. Addressing Yudhishtira he says, "If Drona fights as he does now for half a day more, he will have exterminated all your army and ourselves. Save us, Yudhishtira, from the terrible Brahmana. In dire circumstances, falsehood is advocated if it saves lives. There is no sin in a lie spoken to women, or in marriages, or to save kings, or to rescue a Brahmana's life."

Bhima says, "As soon as I heard of the only way by which Drona can be slain, I killed a mighty elephant, like the elephant of Sakra himself, which belonged to Indravarman, the king of the Malavas, a great beast that stood within our army. I then went to Drona and told him, 'Aswatthaman has been killed, O Brahmana. Lay down your weapons and stop fighting!'

However, the Acharya does not believe that I spoke the truth. If you want to save us all and win this war, Yudhishtira, do as Krishna says and tell Drona that Aswatthaman, the son of Saradwat's daughter, is indeed dead. The Brahmana bull will never doubt what you say to him, for it is known that you are the most truthful one in all the worlds."

Hearing what Bhima says, persuaded by what Krishna also says, and bowing also to inevitable destiny, Yudhishtira decides to go along with what they want him to do. Yet, fearing to tell an outright lie Yudhishtira clearly says that Aswatthaman is dead, but adds under his breath, "the elephant Aswatthaman". Until that moment, Yudhishtira's chariot and horses were always suspended at a height of four fingers' breadth from the ground, for his immaculate dharma and honesty. No sooner does he tell this white lie than his ratha and steeds descend and then on ride along the earth as any other man's! When Yudhishtira says that his son is dead, Drona's already faltering spirit breaks. Having heard what the unworldly Rishis said to him, he suddenly sees himself as a most heinous sinner, and particularly against the noble Pandavas who always trod the path of dharma. At this critical juncture, he sees Dhrishtadyumna drawn dangerously close to him, and finds that his arms have grown weak and that he can no longer fight as he did before.'"

CANTO 188

DRONA-VADHA PARVA CONTINUED

"Sanjaya says, 'Dhrishtadyumna sees Drona stricken before him and charges at him with doubled celerity. As we know, king Drupada received Dhrishtadyumna from Agni Deva at a great yagna, and the fire-prince was born for Drupada to have revenge against Drona who had humiliated him. Dhrishtadyumna had been born just to kill Drona.

Wanting to kill Drona, to accomplish the final purpose of his birth, the Panchala prince picks up an unearthly bow, a weapon with few rivals. He fits an arrow on it, a shaft like a serpent of the most virulent venom, and that arrows glow with a fierce flame within the circle of his bow, and is like the splendent autumn sun within a radiant disc. Seeing Prishata's son bend that blazing bow, all the troops think that the last hour of the world has come.

Seeing the arrow aimed at him, Drona, son of Bharadwaja, also thinks that the last moment of his body has come. The Acharya prepares to parry the shaft. However, his astras, O Rajan, no longer appear at his bidding, although he has not exhausted them despite shooting them ceaselessly for four days and one night. Yet, when the third part of the fifth day is past, his shafts are all exhausted. Seeing that his arrows have all been spent, broken with grief believing that his son is dead and finding that the Devastras no longer appear at his bidding, he is overcome by a wish rising from the very depths of his being to lay aside his weapons as the Rishis asked him to.

Though still full of great tejas, he cannot fight as before. But, being the master he is and tameless, he takes up another celestial bow given him by Angiras, and some arrows that are like a Brahmana's curse; with his last vestiges of strength, the Acharya continues to battle Dhrishtadyumna!

Suddenly renewed, like a flame that blazes most brightly before it dies, Drona covers the Panchala prince with a steaming fusillade, which strike his adversary heavily, drawing fonts of blood from Dhrishtadyumna. Drona shatters the Panchala prince's shafts into dust; he cuts down the Pandava senapati's standard, severs his bow and beheads his sarathy: all in a flash. Dhrishtadyumna, still smiling, takes up another bow and drills a long violent shaft deep into Drona's torso.

Deeply wounded by that staggering shaft, losing his self-possession, Drona roars dreadfully and again rives Dhrishtadyumna's bow. As the Panchala prince seizes up more bows, the Acharya, apparently undimmed, destroys all of them, Rajan, leaving him only his mace and sword. He strikes the enraged, roaring Dhrishtadyumna with nine shafts such as would kill any enemy. But maharatha Dhrishtadyumna, of immeasurable soul, invokes the protective Brahmastra, and with light like speed and adroitness entangles his own horses with the Brahmana's, steeds red and dove coloured. Their whinnying is like the raging of stormclouds during the season of rains, and their shimmering skins flash like lightning.

The unrelenting Dvija shatters the shaft-joints, the wheel-joints, and all the other joints of Dhrishtadyumna's chariot so it collapses under that hero. Deprived of his bow, ratha, horses and sarathy, Dhrishtadyumna, in great distress, grasps up a mace. In a wink, Drona splits that weapon into slivers just before it is hurled at him. Dhrishtadyumna, Naravyaghra, picks up a gleaming sword and a bright shield decked with a hundred moons. Despite every reversal, the Panchala prince remains absorbed in his single intention: to kill Acharya Drona.

At times sheltering low in his chariot, at others leaping onto his chariot-head, the fire-prince remains in constant motion, brandishing his sword and whirling his bright shield, perhaps foolishly, still wanting to achieve his impossible task of despatching the Brahmana, who has him at his mercy. Now he leaps onto the very yoke of Drona's ratha, then dives under his chestnut horses and hides himself briefly beneath their haunches. With such mercurial speed does he move, that the troops all around break into spontaneous applause. And indeed, O Dhritarashtra, he is an incredible marvel to watch darting about as quickly as the very mind, denying Drona any opportunity to strike him down. Both of them strangely resemble, in their different roles, hawks flying after a piece of flesh or a smaller bird—both are hawk and both are quarry.

Expertly now, Drona spears his antagonist's white horses, one after another, without touching his own red ones tangled with them. Dhrishtadyumna's horses die, freeing Drona's red horses from the traces of Dhrishtadyumna's chariot. Seeing his horses killed, Dhrishtadyumna, the best of all swordsmen, springs at Drona with his sword, even like Vinata's son Garuda swooping upon a snake. The appearance, Rajan, of Dhrishtadyumna resembles Vishnu's when he was on the point of slaying Hiranyakasipu. He performs many elegant flourishes with his sword, including the well-known twenty-one different kinds of movements. With sword and shield in hand, he wheels about whirling his sword above his head, makes side thrusts, rushes forward, runs sideways, leaps high, attacks his antagonist's flanks, retreats, closes with his enemy, and presses him hard. Having practised them thoroughly, he also shows the manoeuvres called the Bharata, the Kausika and the Satwata, as he prepares to kill Drona. Seeing Dhrishtadyumna's striking display as he charges about the field, sword and shield in hand, all the warriors, as well as the Devas assembled there, are full of wonder.

Drona shoots a thousand arrows in the thick of the fray and destroys Dhrishtadyumna's sword as well as his shield of a hundred moons. The arrows that Drona uses are special short ones, used only in close combat. No one other than Kripa, Partha, Aswatthaman, Karna, Pradyumna and Yuyudhana own or know how to use these; Abhimanyu also had such arrows. Now the Acharya wants to kill his helpless disciple, who is like his own son, and affixes a deathly shaft to his bowstring. Just then, from a way off, the splendid Satyaki shatters that lethal arrow with ten whistling barbs, in the very sight of your son and the noble Karna, and rescues Dhrishtadyumna who would not otherwise have escaped with his life.

Krishna and Arjuna cry joyfully, "Uttamam! Uttamam!" and loudly applaud Satyaki of unfading glory, who continually destroys the devastras of all the enemy maharathas. Then Kesava and Dhananjaya charge towards the Kurus.

Dhananjaya says, "Look Krishna, how Satyaki, the joy of the Madhu vamsa, sports before the Acharya and the other maharathas and gladdens the twins, Bhima, Yudhishtira and me. With skill acquired through long abhyasa and deep humility, Yuyudhana toys with these mightiest warriors."

All the troops and the Siddhas in the sky look at the invincible grandson of Sini, are filled with joy and wonder and laud him, saying, "Wonderful, Wonderful!" Indeed, Rajan, all the warriors of both armies show their appreciation of the Satwata hero's stunning feats.'"

CANTO 189

Drona-vadha Parva continued

"Sanjaya says, 'Seeing what Satyaki does, an angry Duryodhana and others quickly surround him. Kripa and Karna join them, loosing towering gales of arrows at the Satwata hero. Swiftly, Yudhishtira, the twin sons of Madri and the stupendous Bhimasena arrive to support Satyaki. Karna, Kripa, Duryodhana and many others attack Satyaki viciously, all of them at once. But Yuyudhana is equal to them all; he cuts down all their arrows and incinerates the devastras that flare at him from all around.

So bloody and brutal is the war now that Kurukshetra resembles a scene from antiquity when Rudra, filled with rage, destroyed all creatures. Human arms, heads, royal parasols cut down, and yak-tails are seen lying in heaps on the field of dharma where dharma itself has all but perished. The earth is strewn thickly with broken wheels and rathas, massive arms lopped off from trunks and brave horsemen deprived abruptly of their lives, many of them headless. Thousands of valiant men, mangled by cruel shafts and lances, roll and writhe on the ground in agony, in the spasms of death. What doubt can there be, Rajan, that the Mahabharata yuddha fought on Kurukshetra is like the Devasura yuddha of old fought on the filed of swarga?

Dharmaraja Yudhishtira says to his warriors, "O Maharathas, attack Drona the pot-born with all your might! Look where Dhrishtadyumna, the heroic son of Prishata, is doing his utmost to slay the son of Bharadwaja. Looking at him, I feel certain that he will not fail today. But the Acharya is formidable and you must support him if he is to succeed. So unite and fight Drona!"

At Yudhishtira's command, the maharathas of the Srinjayas all rush forward feverishly to attack the still battling son of Bharadwaja; he sees them come at him and knows that his end is near. He does not pause but continues to fight back like some deranged god. Suddenly, the earth trembles unaccountably, fierce winds blow, meteors fall in showers out of the sky, seemingly issuing from the Sun, blazing fiercely, foreboding great terrors; the omens send waves of terror and panic through your army.

The weapons of Drona seem to blaze more lividly than ever; the chariots on the field rumble louder and the horses all seem to weep. Drona, then, appears to rapidly lose his tejas and his left eye and hand begin to twitch. He sees Dhrishtadyumna before him again and, he hears the words of the Devarishis echo in his mind, saying that the time had come for him to leave the world. Drona feels a tide of despair and resolves to give up his life but after burning fiercely again in battle.

Surrounded on all sides by the troops of Drupada's son, Drona begins to range across the field, massacring countless Kshatriyas with his astras. After he first annihilates four and twenty thousand Kshatriyas, he despatches another hundred thousand, with his unearthly ayudhas. He stands upon Kurukshetra like a smokeless fire and, then, decides that he will exterminate the very Kshatriya race with the Brahmastra.

The mighty Bhima races up to help Dhrishtadyumna who, without a chariot or weapons, still defiantly assails Drona with his bare hands and with whatever he can retrieve from the bloody mire around his feet. Bhima takes the Panchala prince into his ratha and says to him, "Only you can kill the dreadful Brahmana. The task of killing him rests with you; Dhrishtadyumna, hurry or he will finish us all!"

Dhrishtadyumna quickly seizes up a fresh, marvellous bow and once more covers Drona with a tornado of arrows. Both invoke the Brahmastra and many other Devastras. Gradually Dhrishtadyumna destroys and somewhat depletes the arsenal of Bharadwaja's son; having done this, the Panchala prince begins to mow down the Vasatis, the Sibis, the Balhikas and the Kurus, all those who are protecting Drona.

The incandescent Acharya continues to summon and unleash fusillades of elemental arrows on all sides, while Dhrishtadyumna too is resplendent as the sun with his millions of rays. Then, once more, Drona breaks the bow in the Panchala prince's hands and bores him deep with fierce clutches of shafts that pierce his very marmas and fling him back in Bhima's ratha.

At this, Rajan, Bhima loses his temper completely. Besides himself with fury, the Vayuputra leaps out of his chariot, seizes Drona's red horses by their bits, and cries reverberantly to the Acharya, "If the vilest wretches among Brahmanas, discontented with their swadharma but well-versed in the use of arms, did not fight, the Kshatriya varna would not have been exterminated. Refraining from injury to all creatures, non-violence, the highest of all virtues and the Brahmana is the root of that virtue. As for you, you are the greatest of all knowers of the Brahman. These Mlecchas and other warriors are all engaged in their own swadharma and are motivated by ignorance and folly, and by the desire for wealth for their sons and wives. But you, O despicable and lowly Brahmana, commit genocide for the sake of an only son. Are you not ashamed? Unknown to you, Aswatthaman for whom you have taken up weapons, and for whom you live, lies dead today on the field. Yudhishtira himself has told you this, and do you still doubt it?"

With such fervour does the great son of the Wind speak that the already heartsick Drona lays down his bow and all his other weapons as well. The invincible Brahmana says aloud in his lion's voice, "O Karna, Karna maharatha, O Kripa, O Duryodhana, I say to you again, be careful how you fight the Pandavas otherwise they will kill you all. As for myself,

I am laying down my weapons now. My time has come."

And then he repeatedly, dementedly calls out Aswatthaman's name in absolute grief. Having finally laid down his weapons, he sits on the floor of his chariot, and takes up a Yogic posture to reassure all the warriors, why all living creatures and to dispel their abject terror of him. Seeing his chance, Dhrishtadyumna gathers all his strength and courage. Laying aside his own bow and grasping up a sword, he lean down from Bhima's ratha and runs towards Drona. All men, all the unearthly ones who watch from the sky cry out in distress.

Drona, having abandoned his weapons, is in a supremely tranquil state. Having called out the name of his son, he fixes his mind in dhyana, concentrating on attaining Yoga, communion with the Brahman. Endued with great radiance by years of tapasya, he fixes his heart on that Supreme, Ancient and Eternal Being, the Lord Vishnu. Bending his head down, thrusting his chest out a little, closing his eyes, yoking himself now to the sattva guna, giving his heart and soul up to the most profound meditation, focused on the Pranava, the single syllable AUM that is the Brahman, the ultimate, his heart flying like an arrow toward the puissant and indestructible God of gods, with great punya acquired through tapasya, the Acharya of the Kurus and the Pandavas soars into Swarga, which even the pious find so difficult to attain.

When Drona's spirit ascends into Swarga, the sky is lit by two suns, until the soul of Bharadwaja's incomparable son dims and vanishes. We hear strange cries of joy from the delighted celestial ones above, Devarishi, Gandharva, Charana, Apsara, Vidyadhara, Deva and others as well.

When Drona leaves his body thus, Dhrishtadyumna stands beside him, unconscious of what has happened. Only we five among men, Arjuna, Aswatthaman, Krishna, Yudhishtira and I see the noble Drona engrossed in Yoga ascend to the highest realm of blessedness. Nobody else, O Rajan, sees the lustre or magnificence of the wise Drona, devoted to Yoga, when he leaves this world. Indeed, all present know nothing of it, or that, after setting aside his weapons, Drona has attained to supreme Brahmaloka, a region mysterious to the very gods, in the company of the greatest Rishis, leaving his body lacerated by arrows and bathed in blood.

Dhrishtadyumna knows nothing of it either and he roughly seizes the Acharya's lifeless body and, coarsely dragging it around on the floor of the golden chariot, hacks off the Acharya's head with his sword in an eruption of blood, while the already departed one makes no sound. Having beheaded him, Dhrishtadyumna gives a tremendous shout of joy, and whirls his sword around in triumph.

Dark of complexion, with white locks hanging down to his ears, that Brahmana of five and eighty years ranged over the battlefield with the vigour of a youth of sixteen: only for your sake, O Rajan! Before Dhrishtadyumna has his way with Drona, Arjuna cries to him, "Take the Acharya alive, do not kill him. He should not be slain!"

All the troops also cried out similar pleas; Arjuna, in particular, melts with pity, and cries out repeatedly. However, Dhrishtadyumna disregards all those cries and kills Drona on the floor of his ratha. Covered with the Brahmana's blood, Dhrishtadyumna jumps down from the chariot, red as the sun and as fierce. This is how your troops and the Pandavas' witness Drona killed in the battle. Though we five saw how Drona, called by the Sages of Swarga, attained to a transcendent realm before Dhrishtadyumna apparently slew him, fulfilling his destiny.

Then the exultant Panchala fire-prince flings down Drona's leonine, majestic head, flowing blood from its throat, before the warriors of your army, roaring terribly all the while. Your soldiers flee in all directions.

Meanwhile, Drona courses up through the firmament along the path of the stars. Through the grace of the Rishi Krishna Dwaipayana, the son of Satyavati, I was a witness, Rajan, to the true circumstances of the death of Bharadwaja's great son. I saw the illustrious one going, after he ascended the sky, like a smokeless brand of blinding splendour.

Shocked and panic-stricken by the death of Drona, the Kurus, the Pandavas and the Srinjayas, all run from the battle. As your army breaks up and flees, many are killed and many wounded. Your warriors seem as if they have lost all will to continue fighting; they seem already vanquished, dead, and fear rips through them. The Kurus think of themselves as having lost both worlds and lose all self-control.

The kings of your army seek out Drona's body, Rajan, on the field covered over with thousands of headless trunks, and they cannot find it. With Drona slain, the Pandavas celebrate, twanging their bows, blowing their conches and beating their drums. Bhimasena and Dhrishtadyumna embrace each other in the midst of the Pandava host and Bhima says, "I will embrace you again, O son of Prishata, as a senapati who has won the war, when the wretch of a Suta's son Karna, and the other wretch Duryodhana have been slain!"

After he says this, Bhimasena, in a transport of joy, makes the earth tremble by deafeningly slapping his cavernous armpits. Terrified by that sound, the remainder of your troops run from the battlefield, forgetting Kshatriya dharma and intent on saving their lives. The Pandavas, O king, are overjoyed, for, a short while ago, it had truly seemed that Drona by himself would annihilate them and win the war by himself.'"

CANTO 190

Drona-vadha Parva continued

"Sanjaya says, 'Upon the fall of Drona the Kurus, beaten, broken, wounded and now leaderless, are listless, desperate and sapped of all will and energy to continue the battle. They mourn with loud wailing and lamentations and, seeing their enemies, the Pandavas, prevail over them all around, cutting them down at will, they quake with fear. Their eyes fill with tears, their hearts are afraid, and they become melancholic and gather forlorn around your son. Covered with dust and grime, they cast glazed and vacant looks all around, and with their very breaths choked with terror, they resemble the Daityas after the fall of Hiranyaksha in the olden days.

Surrounded by them, as if by small terrified animals, Duryodhana cannot bear to remain in their sorry midst and moves away. Hungry, thirsty and scorched by the sun, your warriors, O Bhaarata, are entirely demoralised. For them the fall of Bharadwaja's son Drona is as if the sun fell onto the earth, or the ocean dried up, or Meru was moved from his true place, or Indra vanquished and slain. Losing all composure and dignity they scatter with anxiety lending them great celerity.

Sakuni, king of the Gandharas, watches Drona of the golden chariot killed, and he too runs away with the maharathas of his division, with even greater speed than any of the others. Even Karna flees in shock, taking with him his own vast division, with all its standards flapping in the hot wind that blows across Kurukshetra.

Salya of the Madras casts vacant looks all around him; he, too, escapes with his akshauhini, with all his chariots, elephants and horses.

Saradwat's son, Kripa, too, flees crying aloud, "Alas! Alas!" at the fall of his brother-in-law, and takes with him his akshauhini of elephants and foot-soldiers, the greater part of which have by now been killed.

Kritavarman also takes flight, borne by his swift horses, and surrounded by the remnants of his Bhoja, Kalinga, Aratta, and Balhika troops.

Uluka, O Rajan, seeing Drona slain, is terror-stricken and runs away, with his teeming cohort of foot-soldiers.

Handsome, youthful and reputed for his bravery, Dusasana, also, turns his back on the battle with alacrity, surrounded by his elephant division.

Vrishasena also flees at the sight of Drona's beheading, along with his ten thousand chariots and three thousand elephants.

With his elephants, horses, chariots and foot-soldiers, even your otherwise fearless son, the mighty Duryodhana also rides away in panic, Rajan, as do the remnants of the Samsaptakas whom Arjuna has not yet slaughtered. Seeing Drona die, Susarman flees.

Riding on their elephants, chariots and horses, all the warriors of the Kaurava army run from the field of battle; some call out to their fathers to flee, some to their brothers, some to their uncles, some to their sons and some to their friends. Others cry out to their brothers in arms, their sisters' sons or other kinsmen, and everyone bolts in all directions. With dishevelled hair, and clothes come loose, they all run so that no two men can bee seen to be fleeing together with any composure. It is every man for himself and each of them believes that the war is lost and the Kuru army has been entirely destroyed. Others among your troops flee,

Rajan, throwing off their armour so they can go faster.

A very few of the warriors and soldiers cry out to the others, "Stop! Do not run!" And then they themselves flee. Abandoning their fine chariots, and their bright ornaments flashing, they flee on horseback or on foot.

Only Drona's son Aswatthaman, like a great crocodile swimming against the current of a river, does not run but bears down on his enemies instead. A fierce battle breaks out between him and the many warriors led by Sikhandin, the Prabhadrakas, the Panchalas, the Chedis and the Kaikeyas. Even while cutting down vast numbers of the enemy, this Brahmana hero, with the tread of an infuriated elephant, sees the Kaurava host running from battle, bent just upon escape.

Aswatthaman rides up to Duryodhana and says, "Why, O Bhaarata, do our men flee as if in some great dread? Why do you not rally them? Rajan, you seem dazed and not yourself. Which of our maharathas has been killed that our men flee in such terror? O Kaurava, Karna himself leads those who run away. Never before have I seen such a sight. What dire evil has befallen your troops, O Suyodhana?"

Duryodhana cannot bear to tell him. Your son seems to sink deeper into an ocean of grief, like a foundering boat; he looks at Aswatthaman and tears flow down his face. Full of shame, your son finally says, "Blessed are you that you ask before any other why our army runs like frightened boys."

Then, Saradwat's son Kripa, in great anguish, tells Drona's son how his father had been killed. He says, "We set Drona, greatest of all maharathas, at the head of our troops and began to fight the Panchalas. The Kurus and the Somakas closed with each other with a roar as of spring thunder and we fought closely, with swords and bare hands. As the battle progressed, the Dhartarashtras were being swiftly thinned and, seeing this, your august father was filled with rage and invoked a Brahmastra, which incinerated thousands of the enemy, great warriors and common soldiers alike. Any man of the Pandavas, Kaikeyas, Matsyas or Panchalas, O Aswatthaman, who came near Drona's ratha, died. With his Brahmastra, Drona sent a thousand maharathas and two thousand elephants to the land of Yama.

Dark, with gray locks hanging down to his ears, and full five and eighty years old, the aged Drona would ride into battle like a youth of sixteen. While he razed the enemy troops and slew so many of their kings and maharathas, the Panchalas, though desperate to have revenge on him, ran from the fight in disorder. Invoking Devastras and unleashing them without discrimination, Drona burned like the sun. Your father, radiating arrows as Surya does his rays, was like the star at his zenith at whom no one can gaze. He scorched his enemies; he incinerated them or sapped them of their energy and will.

Seeing Drona devour their troops, Krishna said to Arjuna, 'Truly, not Indra who slew great Vritrasura can vanquish this Brahman in battle. O you sons of Pandu, set aside your dharma and look for victory, otherwise Drona of the golden chariot will slaughter all of you this very day. We must use stratagem against him for only thus can he be killed. I believe that if he hears that Aswatthaman is dead he will not fight on. Only if Drona lays down his weapons can he be killed. Someone must say to him that his son had been slain. That will break his heart and his will not only to fight but to live.'

Arjuna did not approve of what Krishna said but the others all agreed, even Yudhishtira although after struggling with his conscience. Then, Bhimasena killed a great elephant called Aswatthaman, which belonged to the Malava lord Indravarman; his heart full of shame, he then went to your sire and said, 'Aswatthaman has been killed.'

But your father did not believe Bhima and he asked Yudhishtira is this was true. Afraid of telling a lie, but knowing that the war would be lost otherwise, and wanting victory, Yudhishtira said to the Acharya, 'He for whom you wield weapons, he for whom you live, your beloved son Aswatthaman has been slain. He lies unbreathing on the ground like a young lion killed in his prime.'

Knowing well the consequences of telling a lie, Yudhishtira added under his breath 'the elephant Aswatthaman'. Hearing this from the

Dharmarajan, whom he did not doubt for a moment, the stricken Drona wailed aloud, his limbs turned weak and he did not fight as he did before. Seeing him almost senseless with shock and anxiety, Drupada's son, the cruel Dhrishtadyumna, rushed towards him.

Seeing the prince who had been born to kill him, Drona, knower of all things, knower of fate and its inexorable ways, cast aside his weapons and sat down in his chariot in praya. Dhrishtadyumna bounded onto that ratha, seized Drona by the hair with his left hand and, ignoring the loud admonitions of all the heroes around him, struck off the Acharya's head with his sword.

'Drona must not be killed!' These were the words that echoed from all sides. Arjuna, too, jumped down from his chariot and ran towards Prishata's son with arms upraised and repeatedly cried to him, 'O you who know the ways of dharma, do not kill the Acharya but take him alive!'

Though the Kauravas and Arjuna forbade him, Dhrishtadyumna brutally killed your father even as he sat with his eyes shut in dhyana. And now, our terrified troops run in all directions as if they have themselves been beheaded. Aswatthaman, Anagha, I and my brothers are also plunged in grief and fear, and we are also fleeing the field."

When he hears this, Aswatthaman's hisses like a serpent trodden upon; rage like a fire fed with ample fuel blazes up in him. He wrings his hands, grinds his teeth, breathes like a snake and his eyes turn red as blood.'"

CANTO 191

DRONA-VADHA PARVA CONTINUED

"Dhritarashtra says, 'When he hears about how his father Drona was killed, what does Aswatthaman say, O Sanjaya? He in whom the Manava, Varuna, Agneya, Brahma, Aindra and Narayana astras reside always, what does he say when he hears that Dhrishtadyumna has, sinfully and eschewing dharma killed the virtuous Acharya in battle?

Having learnt the astra shastra, the science of weapons, from Parasurama himself, including all the Devastras, Drona had imparted all his knowledge to his son, wanting to see him invested with all the accomplishments of a great warrior. In this world, there is only one person, and none else, whom even the greatest men wish to see become superior to themselves and that is the son.

All the noblest, greatest teachers have this characteristic and they impart all the mysteries of their science to either their sons or devoted disciples whom they think of as being their own sons. Becoming his father's disciple, and obtaining all those mysteries in every nuance and detail, Aswatthaman became a veritable second Drona. Aswatthaman is equal to Karna in the knowledge of weapons, to Purandara in war, to Kartavirya in might, Brihaspati in gyana, a mountain in fortitude, in tejas to Agni, in depth to an ocean, and in wrath and virulence to the venom of a great serpent.

He is the best of all maharathas in war, accomplished and indefatigable. In speed, he is equal to the wind and he tears about in the thick of a battle, like Yama in a rage. The very Earth shakes when he shoots his arrows. With prowess that cannot be confounded, this Brahmana hero is remorseless as well.

Purified by the Vedas and by his vratas, he is a perfect master of the science of arms, why, even like Dasaratha's son Rama. Like the ocean, he is imperturbable.

Hearing that Dhrishtadyumna has killed his father Drona, with adharma, what did Aswatthaman say? Even as Yagnasena's son was born to become the slayer of Drona, so too was Aswatthaman born to avenge his father's death and to kill Dhrishtadyumna. What does Aswatthaman say, hearing that the ruthless Dhrishtadyumna has beheaded his sire, the Acharya?'"

CANTO 192

DRONA-VADHA PARVA CONTINUED

"Sanjaya says. 'Aswatthaman is filled with grief and rage in equal parts, O Rajan, on hearing how Dhrishtadyumna slaughtered his father like some animal. His body blazes forth with wrath like that of the Destroyer while he consumes all the creatures at the end of the Yuga. Repeatedly wiping his tears, and breathing hot sighs in anger, he says to Duryodhana, "Ah, Yudhishtira is the greatest hypocrite that he bears the standard of dharma, always sanctimoniously preaches the virtue of truth but then lies so vilely himself. No one could have vanquished my father unless he first set his weapons down and he would have consumed the Pandavas and their entire army with the fires of his astras. Now, he has been killed by a lie and in the most treacherous and cowardly way even while he sat in praya. So this is the great dharma of Dharma's own son!

Men who fight a war must inevitably find either victory or defeat. Death in battle is always commended and the sages have declared that the death of a warrior fighting in the cause of dharma is never to be mourned. My father met with a noble death and he has, beyond doubt, found the loftiest realm of felicity. I should not mourn him. But the utter shame of being crudely seized by his white hair before all the troops, even as he fought a dhama yuddha, burns and rends the very core of my heart. If my father could thus be seized by his silver locks and be beheaded while he sat in dhyana, why then should any sonless man ever want to have a son?

Moved by lust, wrath, folly, hatred or levity, men perpetrate deeds of grave adharma and humiliate the noblest souls. The cruel and evil son of Prishata has committed this unforgivable sin but he forgot that this Aswatthaman is not dead but alive! He will pay with his life, and savagely, for what he did to Drona; the lying Yudhishtira will pay for the lie he told my father that made him lay down his weapons. Drona trusted Yudhishtira absolutely and the Pandava betrayed his trust to have his life and win this war.

This very day, the earth will drink the blood of this false Dharmaraja. Besides this, I swear by the Truth, O Kauravya, as also by all my religious karma, that I will not continue to live unless I annihilate all the Panchalas for what their prince did to my father. I swear that I will kill the sinner Dhrishtadyumna, even as brutally as he did my father. Let the means be any, mild or violent, but I will not rest in peace until I have wrought the destruction of all the Panchalas.

O Kaurava, Naravyaghra, men wish for sons so that they may be saved from great fears both here and in the hereafter. Yet, my father met a disgraceful death, like a friendless creature, although I, his son and disciple, am alive, and like a mountain in strength. Shame on my devastras, fie on my weaponry, shame on my prowess, for Drona, although he had a son in me, had his gray locks seized by the Panchala and his head hewn off!

O Duryodhana, king of the Bharatas, I will now do what will free me from the debt I owe my sire who has left this world. A superior man never praises himself. But I cannot bear the sinful slaying of my father and today I will speak of my prowess. Let the Pandavas, with Krishna among them, behold my tejas today as I consume all their troops even as Rudra does when the yuga ends.

Not the Devas, the Gandharvas, the Asuras, the Uragas, the Rakshasas, nor all the greatest Manavas shall contain me in battle today. There is none in the world to equal Arjuna or me in the knowledge of weapons. Today I will break into the Pandava army, shining like the Sun himself with his blazing rays, and I will incinerate the enemy with my devastras. Endless arrows will spume forth from my bow and devour them all. Today the warriors of our army will see all the points of the compass, O Rajan, obscured by my arrows, as if with dark torrents of rain. Today I will mow them all down like a great tempest does trees, great and small, that stand in its way. Not Arjuna, Janardana, Bhimasena, Nakula, Sahadeva, Yudhishtira, Drupada's evil son Dhrishtadyumna, Sikhandin or Satyaki possess the astras that I have, for my father gave me more than he did any of them.

Once, assuming the form of a Brahmana, Narayana himself came to my father and, after bowing down to him, my father made his offerings to Him. Taking them in his own hands, the divine Lord offered to give him a boon. My father asked for the supreme weapon, the Narayanastra.

The Devadeva said to my sire, 'No man will ever be your equal in battle. However, O Brahmana, you must never use this weapon lightly or in haste, for it never returns without destroying the enemy at whom you loose it. There is no one whom it cannot slay! Indeed, the Narayanastra would consume even the immortals. Therefore, it should be used only after the greatest deliberation and to serve the gravest cause. This astra, O Parantapa, should never be cast against men who abandon their chariots or weapons in battle, at those who seek quarter or those that concede defeat. Also, he who seeks to injure the Immortal One with it will himself be severely afflicted by this supreme weapon!'

My sire humbly received the Narayanastra. Then Lord Narayana said to me, 'With this Narayanastra, you will also be able to unleash other astras beyond count in battle and blaze with tejas.'

Having said these words, the divine Lord vanished before our eyes and ascended into Swarga. This is the tale of how I came to possess the ineluctable Narayanastra. Today, I will put it to good use and annihilate the Pandavas, the Panchalas, the Matsyas and the Kaikeyas, even as Sachi's lord razed the Asuras. My arrows, O Bhaarata, will fall upon my enemies in the very forms that I wish them to assume; they shall be without count or end and they will not cease falling upon the enemy until their last warrior is dead. I am a Parantapa, O Duryodhana, a blazing scourge of my enemies, and today you will see me destroy the Pandavas and all who fight their cause. As for that cur of the Panchalas, Dhrishtadyumna, who is an offender of friends, Brahmanas and of his own Acharya, who is a deceitful and ignoble wretch, he will not escape me with his life today."

Hearing what Aswatthaman says, the Kuru army takes heart and rallies. Many great warriors are delighted and blow their gigantic conches; the troops beat their drums and dindimas by the thousands. The earth resounds with the hooves of charging horses and the racing wheels of chariots; the sky echoes with the great sounds. Hearing this uproar, deep as rolling thunder, the Pandava maharathas take counsel together.

Meanwhile, after he has spoken, Drona's son, O Bhaarata, touches holy water and invokes the devastra called the Narayana.'"

CANTO 193

Drona-vadha Parva continued

"Sanjaya says, 'No sooner does Aswatthaman invoke the Narayanastra than violent winds begin to blow with lashing showers of rain, and we hear peals of thunder although there is not a cloud in the sky. The earth trembles and the seas swell up in great agitation. The rivers begin to run back towards their sources in terror; mountain peaks cleave themselves and giant crags come loose of their own accord and crash down sheer precipices; diverse beasts of the earth all run in panic, keeping the Pandavas ever to their right.

Darkness sets in. The sun is obscured and all manner of birds of prey and beasts of carrion alight on the field in joy of a further fresh feast to come. The Devas, the Danavas and the Gandharvas, Rajan, are all petrified. Seeing this tremendous upheaval in nature, all the men begin to cry out loudly to one another about its cause. A terrible wave of anguish, both bodily and spiritual, courses through all the kings and maharathas when Drona's son summons the Narayanastra.'

Dhritarashtra asks, 'O Sanjaya, tell me what strategy the Pandavas adopt to protect Dhrishtadyumna when they see the Kauravas advance again into battle, rallied by Drona's son seared by grief at the murder of his sire?'

Sanjaya continues, 'Having seen the Dhartarashtras turn tail earlier, and now finding them prepared for a furious battle, Yudhishtira asks Arjuna, "Dhananjaya, after Dhrishtadyumna slew the Acharya even as Indra did Vritrasura, the Kurus' spirit was broken and they fled in fear. Some kings dashed away on chariots along uneven paths without Parshni drivers, without standards, banners, chatras and with their kuvaras broken, and all their weapons awry.

Others, losing their wits with fear, whipped and kicked their horses and fled in frenzy. Many, riding on chariots with broken yokes, wheels and akshas, flew in absolute fear. Several on horseback were borne away, almost unseated and clinging on for dear life. Some warriors were dislodged from their lofty seats and transfixed by arrows to the necks of their elephants, while the great creatures lumbered away in equal terror. Elephants, mangled with hundred of barbs, trod on other fighting men, crushing them to pulp.

Having lost their weapons and armour, great fighting men fell down upon the earth from their chariots and animals. Chariot-wheels cut others in two, or they were crushed by horses. Others, calling loudly after their sires and sons, also fled in fear, without recognising one another, all their courage and energy gone from shock and grief at the death of Drona. Some, setting their dead sons, fathers, friends and brothers on their chariots and taking off their armour, were seen dementedly washing them with water. After the slaying of Drona, the Kuru army had fallen into utter despair and chaos and scattered in every direction. Who, then, has rallied it now? Tell me, Arjuna, if you know.

We hear neighing horses and trumpeting elephants, their cries resounding once more with the rumble of chariot-wheels. These fierce sounds from the Kuru ocean swell in tide and make my troops tremble. This spine-chilling uproar that we now hear, it would seem, will swallow the three worlds with Indra at their head. Why, I feel as if the Vajradhari himself makes this terrible din. Arjuna, I feel certain that Indra himself comes to fight us at the fall of Acharya Drona; I do fear that the gods themselves have taken the field against us and will fight for the Kauravas.

My hair stands on end; our greatest maharathas are all full of anxiety. O Dhananjaya, tell me who rallies the Kurus against us that they return to battle so fiercely and full of courage again?"

His eyes full of angry tears, Arjuna replies with some passion, "He, relying upon whose tejas, the Kauravas are determined to accomplish fierce deeds, and blow their conches in blaring challenge; who roars so loudly, having rallied the Dhartarashtras after the fall of the Acharya; who is endued with modesty, possesses mighty weapons, has the tread of an enraged elephant, a face like a tiger's, always accomplishes fierce deeds and dispels the fears of the Kurus; he upon whose birth Drona gave away a thousand heads of the finest cattle to the worthiest Brahmanas; he, Rajan, who bellows like Nandin himself is Aswatthaman.

As soon as he was born, this hero neighed like Indra's steed Ucchaisravas and made the three worlds tremble at the sound. Hearing that sound, an asariri spoke resonantly out of the sky and called him Aswatthaman, the horse-voiced. Aswatthaman is the shura who roars today as if he means to end the world.

Drupada's son Dhrishtadyumna took Drona's life brutally today, hacking off his head while the Acharya sat in praya. He killed him as if he was never his guru. Because Dhrishtadyumna seized his father, our Acharya, by his hair, the proud Aswatthaman will never forgive him.

You told your Acharya a lie for the sake of a kingdom! Although you know dharma better than anyone, yet you committed this grave sin. Your infamy will resound through the three worlds for the death of great Drona, and it shall be eternal, Yudhishtira, even as Rama's is because of the way in which he slew Vali the Vanara, treacherously.

Of you Drona thought, 'The son of Pandu possesses every virtue; besides, he is my sishya. He will never lie to me.'

And believing this he never doubted you when you told him that Aswatthaman was dead. You added 'the elephant' under your breath, but what you swore to your Acharya was still a lie and a terrible sin.

Believing what you said, our Acharya laid down his weapons and grew indifferent to the war. His heart was broken and he was senseless with grief. He sat down on the floor of his ratha, shut his eyes and gave himself up to dhyana.

And it was at such a time that a sishya, Dhrishtadyumna, abandoning dharma, killed his own acharya. Having caused to lay down his weapons with your lie and thus be savagely killed, now protect Dhrishtadyumna if you can, with all your allies and counsellors. All of us together will not be able to protect Drupada's son today from the grief and wrath of Drona's son Aswatthaman.

Aswatthaman is no mere mortal warrior; the knowing say that he is an amsa of Siva himself. This superhuman Brahmana, who is given to showing affection and friendship towards all, is in the grip of righteous anger and no one will save us from his ire today. Aswatthaman will consume us all for the manner in which we slew his great father.

Although I cried repeatedly at the very top of my voice to save the Acharya's life, yet ignoring me and abandoning dharma, a sishya, Dhrishtadyumna, took the life of his own acharya in the vilest, most brutal manner imaginable. All of us have passed the greater part of our lives and the days that remain to us are limited. This sin that we have committed will darken the rest of our lives. For the deep love he bore towards us, he was like a father to us. According to the dictates of the scriptures too, he is a sire to us for he was our guru. Yet we killed our acharya for the sake of a short-lived, meaningless kingdom.

Dhritarashtra, Rajan, gave Bhishma and Drona all the Earth, and what is more precious, all his children. Though thus honoured by our uncle, our enemy, and though he had gained untold wealth from him, the Acharya still loved us as his own children. Of unfading tejas and prowess, Drona was killed only because, persuaded by your lie to him, he set aside his weapons. As long as he fought, he was invincible and not even Indra could kill him. Our Acharya was venerable in years and always devoted to our welfare. Yet sinners that we are, we had no scruple in sending him to his death. The sin that we have committed is inconceivably heinous and cowardly, for moved by the desire of enjoying the pleasures of sovereignty, we have murdered great Drona.

My Acharya always believed of me that, because of my love for him, I would gladly abandon my father, brothers, children, wife and life itself for his sake. And yet, moved by the lust for a kingdom, I did not intervene when he was about to be killed. I did not stop Dhrishtadyumna with an arrow when I well could have. For this crime, Rajan, I am overwhelmed with shame and I have already plunged into hell. For the sake of a kingdom, I caused the death of one who was a Brahmana, who was venerable in years, who was my Acharya, who had laid down his weapons, and who was at the time devoted, like a great ascetic, to yoga.

Ah, death has become preferable to me over life!'""

CANTO 194

Drona-vadha Parva continued

"Sanjaya says, 'Hearing what Arjuna says, the maharathas present there say not a single word to him, O Rajan, good or bad.

Then, an angry Bhimasena, his brow dark, upbraids Arjuna sharply, "You preach the truths of dharma like a sannyasi living in the vana or a Brahmana of rigid vratas and his senses under complete control. But a man is called a Kshatriya because he saves others from danger and harm. Being such, he must save himself from hurt and injury as well. Showing forgiveness towards the three that are good—the Devas, the Brahmanas and an Acharya—a Kshatriya, by performing his svadharma, soon wins the earth and also piety, fame and prosperity. O perpetuator of your race, you possess every attribute of a Kshatriya. Therefore, it does not look well for you to speak like an ignorant lout. O son of Kunti, your prowess is as that of Sachi's lord, Sakra himself. You do not break the bounds of dharma, like the ocean that never transgresses its continents. Who is there that will not worship you, seeing that you seek dharma, having abandoned the anger you cherished for thirteen years?

Fortunately, today your heart follows the path of dharma. O you of unfading glory, providentially, your intellect is disposed towards compassion. However, though you are inclined to tread the path of dharma, your kingdom was taken from you most sinfully. Dragging Draupadi to the Kuru sabha, your enemies insulted and shamed her. Clad in barks of trees and skins of animals, all of us were banished to the vana. Though we did not deserve it, our enemies compelled us to endure our exile for thirteen years. O sinless one, you have forgiven all these circumstances, every one of which demands the demonstration of our anger. Wedded as you are to Kshatriya dharma, you quietly bore these trials and tribulations.

I, however, remember all those sins committed against us and I came here with you for revenge. But when I see that you are so indifferent, why, I myself will kill these low wretches that stripped us of our kingdom. You once said, 'We will fight the war to the utmost of our abilities.'

Today, you reproach us and you now seek dharma. So what you said earlier must be untrue. We are already stricken with fear and you sow doubt and weakness in the very core of our hearts with your words, O Parantapa, like one pouring acid into open wounds. My heart is breaking to listen to you preach. You are virtuous, Arjuna, but you do not know what dharma truly consists of, since you laud neither yourself nor us, though all of us are worthy of praise for our deeds on the field of battle.

When Krishna himself told us how to kill Drona, how can you praise the son of Drona, a warrior who does not measure up to even a sixteenth part of yourself, Dhananjaya? Do you not feel ashamed confessing your own faults like some weakling?

I can rend asunder this earth in anger, or split the very mountains with my gada decked with gold. Like a tempest of my natural sire, I can tear down trees tall as hills. Partha, with my arrows, I can rout all the Devas with Indra at their head, together with all the Rakshasas, the Asuras, the Uragas and Manushas. Knowing me, your brother, to be such, O bull among men, it is not fitting that you should entertain any fear about Drona's son. Otherwise, stand here with all these heroes,

Bibhatsu, while, alone and unsupported, armed with my gada, I vanquish this fellow of no great worth in a duel."

When Bhima has finished, Dhrishtadyumna rounds on Arjuna, and says in a tone as terrible as the one Hiranyakashyapu used when he once addressed Vishnu, "O Bibhatsu, the sages have ordained that assisting in yagnas, performance of yagnas, teaching, giving away alms, receiving gifts, and study to be the six duties of Brahmanas. To which of these six duties was Drona, whom I have slain, devoted? Fallen from the dharma of his own varna and practising those of the Kshatriya varna, this doer of evil deeds burned us and our common soldiers with his devastras. Professing himself to be a Brahmana, he used irresistible maya against us as well.

Today he has been killed with maya, an illusion. O Partha, what is reprehensible in this? If Drona's griefstricken and enraged son roars threats at us after I punished Drona, what do you lose by it? I myself believe that, after rallying the Kauravas back to battle, Aswatthaman, who roars so loudly, will find himself unable to protect them and will be the cause of their being killed instead.

You know dharma well. Why then do you say that I am a slayer of my Acharya? It is for this very task that I was born as a son to the king of the Panchalas, having sprung from a yagna fire. How, O Dhananjaya, can you call him a Brahmana or Kshatriya, to whom, while waging war, all actions, righteous and utterly sinful, are the same? O best of men, why should he who, losing his mind in anger, used the Brahmastra to kill even those who knew nothing of the astras, our common troops, not be killed by any means?

He who lives by sin is considered by men of dharma to be like poison. Knowing this, why do you, Arjuna, who know all the truths of dharma, reproach me?

I seized and killed the ruthless and cruel maharatha. I have done nothing that is worthy of reproach. Why then, O Bibhatsu, do you not congratulate me? O Partha, I cut off the terrible head of Drona that was like the blazing sun, virulent poison or the all-destroying Yuga fire.

Why do you not approve a deed that is worthy of the highest praise? He has killed only my father and kinsmen and not those of anyone else. I say that by having only beheaded him, the fever of my heart has not cooled. My heart is in anguish that I did not fling Drona's head among the Nishadas, like that of Jayadratha!

I have heard, O Arjuna, that one incurs sin by not killing one's enemies. The dharma of a Kshatriya is to slay or be slain. Drona was my enemy. I have killed him in battle, O Pandava, exactly as you killed the brave Bhagadatta, who was your friend. Having cut down your own grandsire Bhishma in battle, you still speak of dharma! How, after that, do you dare say I sinned by killing my wretched and inveterate enemy?

Because of our relationship, O Partha, I cannot raise my head in your presence and am like a prostrate elephant with a ladder against his body for helping puny creatures to climb on its back. So do not reproach me, it does not become you.

For the sake of my sister Draupadi and her children, and no other reason, I forgive you what you have dared say to me today. It is well known that my enmity with the Acharya has come down from sire to son. Everybody in this world knows it. You sons of Pandu, husbands of my sister, are you not acquainted with it? The eldest son of Pandu has not lied. I myself, O Arjuna, have not sinned. The wretched Drona was a hater of his disciples. Stop whining like a witless boy and fight now. Victory will be yours.""'

CANTO 195

DRONA-VADHA PARVA CONTINUED

"Dhritarashtra says, 'The illustrious Drona, who had studied the Vedas with all their angas; he in whom the entire science of arms and modesty dwelt; the Brahmana through whose grace so many of the greatest still achieve superhuman feats that the very gods perform with difficulty—alas, when the Maharishi Bharadwaja's invincible son was humiliated and beheaded by the base and sinful Dhrishtadyumna, slayer of his own Acharya while all men watched, was there no Kshatriya who felt called upon to display his anger? Shame on the Kshatriya varna and fie on wrath itself!

Tell me, O Sanjaya, what the sons of Pritha, and all the other royal archers of the world, say to the prince of Panchala after he murdered his guru Drona.'

Sanjaya replies, 'All that are present there remain perfectly silent, O Rajan, when they hear what Drupada's dishonest son says. Arjuna, however, casting oblique glances at Dhrishtadyumna, seems to reproach him with tears and sighs, which say, "Shame! Shame!", while Yudhishtira, Bhima, the twins, Krishna and the others stand there saying nothing.

But Satyaki says clearly, "Is there no man here who will at once kill this sinful creature, this lowest of men, who speaks so evilly? The Pandavas all condemn you for your sinful deed, like Brahmanas condemning a Chandala. Having committed such a heinous crime, and incurring the censure of all honest men, are you not ashamed to open your mouth and speak in the midst of such an honourable gathering of Kshatriyas? Despicable wretch, why did your head not burst apart into a hundred pieces when you were about to slay your own Acharya? Why does your tongue not spilt into slivers when you now defend what you did? Why does your sin not strike you down even now, vile Dhrishtadyumna?

You not only commit an unmentionable sin but you applaud and congratulate yourself in the midst of noble men. Panchala, I swear that you incur the censure of the Parthas, all the Andhakas and the Vrishnis. Having perpetrated atrocity, you still loudly declare your rancour and hatred for the one that taught you everything you know. And for this you deserve death at our hands. You should not be left alive for even a moment. Who other than you, O filthy wretch, would dare seize our great Acharya by his silver locks as he sat in yoga and cut his head from his neck?

Having got you for part of their great vamsa, vile man, your ancestors for seven generations and your descendants for seven generations, deprived of honour and fame, have sunk into hell. You dare charge Arjuna, bull among men, with the killing of Bhishma. But the truth is that Bhishma sought and brought about his own fall, for no other could bring him down. And in truth, wretched Panchala, it is your own brother Sikhandin, greatest of sinners, who was the cause of Bhishma's fall.

I say that there are no greater sinners in this world than the sons of the Panchala king. Your father created Sikhandin for Bhishma's destruction, and you to kill Drona in the most depraved manner. As for Arjuna, he only protected Sikhandin while your brother shot Bhishma down with his arrows because the noble Bhishma would not defend himself against one whom he regarded to be a woman.

Having you, whom all righteous men condemn, and your eunuch

brother born into their clan, the Panchalas have fallen from dharma and, stained with malice, have all become haters of friends and acharyas. Dhrishtadyumna, if you say what you have again in my presence, I will then smash your head with my mace that is like Indra's Vajra.

Anyone who so much as looks at you, O Brahmana slayer, marked with the guilt of the direst sin of Brahmahatya, must look up at the sun to purify himself for having set eyes on such a sinner. You dog of a Panchala, evil man, do you feel no shame casting aspersions first on my guru Arjuna and then on my guru's guru the great Drona himself?

Stop, and have done, you lowly thing! Bear but one stroke of my mace and I myself will bear many blow of yours."

Harshly rebuked by the Satwata hero, Prishata's son Dhrishtadyumna, filled with rage, says to Satyaki with a superior, mocking smile, "I have heard you, O you of Madhu's race, but I forgive you. Being a sinner and an adharmi yourself, you now wish to censure honest men of dharma? The quality of forgiveness is acclaimed in the world while sin like yours deserves none. He who has a sinful soul regards the forgiving man as being weak. You are evil in your conduct, your soul is dark with sin, and you are wedded to adharma. You are culpable in every way, from the tips of your toes to the ends of your hair. And you, base Satwata, still speak ill of others?

What can be more sinful than what you did when you murdered the armless Bhurisravas, while he sat in praya, and you were unleashing devastras. Yes, Drona had laid aside his weapons and I killed him. Crooked hypocrite, what did I do that was wrong? How can you, O foolish Satyaki, blame me for what I did, when you did exactly the same, and that, too, after Arjuna saved your worthless life by cutting off Bhurisarvas' arm? This valiant Kuru enemy of yours displayed his prowess by throwing you down onto the earth and stamping on you with his foot. Why did you not kill him then, and show your manliness? No, vile Satyaki, you killed great Bhurisravas only after Arjuna had hewn away his arm and when he sat in dhyana.

And now you dare preach dharma to me? When Drona was

annihilating the forces of the Pandavas, I fought him with thousands of arrows. But having yourself behaved like a Chandala and become worthy of censure, how do you now reproach me so harshly? You are the evil one and not I, O wretch of the Vrishni vamsa! You are the home of all sins, so it is better that you remain silent and not point your crooked finger at me again in blame.

Don't dare speak to me again. This is the reply I give you with my lips. But if, from folly, you say anything more, I will send you to Yama before you have finished talking.

Through dharma alone, O fool, one cannot vanquish great enemies. If you have forgotten, listen to all the adharma the Kurus committed against the sons of Pandu, which caused this war. Pandu's son Yudhishtira Dharmaraja was deceived with rank adharma at the game of dice. O Satyaki, the sons of Dhritarashtra and the sinner Karna coarsely humiliated my sister Draupadi in the hallowed Kuru sabha. The Pandavas, with Panchali, were then exiled and robbed of their all, O foolish Satwata. Was that, according to you, dharma?

With cunning, the enemy deprived us of a valuable ally, Salya of the Madras. Subhadra's son was trapped in the chakravyuha by your great Acharya and cut down by six maharathas. Do you call that dharma, O Yuyudhana, fool?

On our side, it was though adharma that Bhishma, the Kuru grandsire, was brought down and with adharma that you slew Bhurisravas. This is how both the enemy, as well as the Pandavas, have fought this war. They are all valiant and mighty; they are all knowers of dharma; yet, they have all sinned in order to have victory in this ghastly war. O glib Satwata, true dharma and adharma as well are difficult to comprehend, and vary according to circumstances.

I say to you, stop this talk now and now fight the Kauravas, without turning back to the home of your fathers!"

Dhrishtadyumna speaks with contempt and vituperation, and the radiant Satyaki begins to tremble from head to foot in anger. His eyes turn the hue of copper. Sighing like a snake, he leaves his bow in his ratha, grasps his mace and rushes at the prince of the Panchalas, and cries, "I will not speak to you anymore, but kill you as you deserve!"

Seeing Satyaki rushing at the Panchala prince, like one Yama at another, Bhima, urged by Krishna, jumps down from his chariot and clasps Yuyudhana firmly in his mighty arms. Satyaki, who is strong himself, still manages to take five steps forward, dragging Bhima with him. Then, Bhima plants his massive feet firmly and stops the bull of Sini's race at the sixth step.

With Bhima restraining the red-eyed Satwata, Sahadeva leaps down from his chariot, and mollifies Satyaki, "O Naravyaghra, we have no friends dearer to us than the Andhakas, the Vrishnis and the Panchalas. So, also, the Andhakas and the Vrishnis, particularly Krishna, have no friends dearer to them than us. The Panchalas, too, even if they comb the whole world to the confines of the sea, have no friends dearer to them than the Pandavas and the Vrishnis. You are such a friend to this prince Dhrishtadyumna; and he is a similar friend to you. You all are to us even as we are to you. Knowing dharma as you do, think now of the dharma that you owe your friends. Restrain your anger and be calm, O best of Sini's race! Forgive Dhrishtadyumna, and let him also forgive you. We, too, will forgive all that has been said in anger. What is there, Yuyudhana, that is better than forgiveness?"

Even as Sahadeva is attempting to pacify the furious Satyaki, Dhrishtadyumna, smiling arrogantly, says, "O Bhima, release Sini's grandson who is so proud of his prowess in battle. Let him come to me like the wind assailing the mountains and I will quell his anger and lust of battle. I will have his life with my arrows.

Look, where the Kauravas advance on us. After killing this fool Satyaki, I will burn all Duryodhana's troops with my astras, or let Arjuna do so if he chooses to. But now I mean to cut this vile Satwata's head from his neck. He thinks I am like the armless Bhurisravas. He will find he is sadly mistaken. Either I will kill him or he will kill me today."

Satyaki wriggles like an angry snake to get free from Bhima's clasp. Both Dhrishtadyumna and he bellow at each other like a pair of bulls.

Finally, Krishna and Yudhishtira, with some effort, succeed in calming the two. Having placated those maharathas, whose eyes had turned the colour of blood, all the Kshatriyas of the Pandava army take the field against the Kaurava warriors to do battle again.'"

CANTO 196

DRONA-VADHA PARVA CONTINUED

"Sanjaya says, 'Then Drona's son Aswatthaman inflicts great carnage among his enemies like the Destroyer himself at the end of the Yuga. Killing them with banks of broad-headed missiles, he soon heaps a mountain of dead on the battlefield. The banners of chariots form its trees; weapons are its pointed peaks; lifeless elephants are its large boulders; dead horses and their riders are its Kimpurushas, half man and half equine; bows are its creepers and plants; and it resounds with the cries of birds of prey and carrion, its feathered population, and the spirits that walk there are its Yakshas.

Aswatthaman repeats his dreadful vow in the hearing of your son Duryodhana: "Since Kunti's son Yudhishtira, who wears only the false outer garb of dharma, lied to my father, who fought righteously, to lay aside his weapons and be slain, I will, in his very sight, destroy his entire army and then kill Dhrishtadyumna, sinful prince of the Panchalas. Rally your troops, O Suyodhana, for I swear to you that I will annihilate them all if they dare face me in battle!"

Dispelling the fears of his men with a booming bellow, your son gathers his troops. The battle between the Kurus and Pandavas resembles two seas in high tide surging into each other. The Kauravas are now emboldened by Drona's son, and the Pandus and the Panchalas are inspired by Drona's death. Indescribable mayhem and bloodshed rule Kurukshetra again and all who fight have battle lust and no trace of fear coursing through them.

Truly, Maharajan, the collision between the Kurus and the Pandavas is like one mountain striking another, or an ocean another ocean.

Full of spirit and bravado, the Kuru and the Pandava warriors beat thousands of drums and the ear-splitting bedlam that arises from the troops resembles that of the Kshirasagara when it was churned in days of old by the Devas and the Danavas when they sought the Amrita.

And now Aswatthaman invokes the Narayanastra and unleashes it at the Pandava and Panchala host. Thousands of serpentine arrows with blazing mouths appear in the sky, and rain down on the Pandavas. Like rays of the sun, in a moment these shafts shroud all the directions of the sky and engulf all the enemy legions. Innumerable iron balls appear like resplendent luminaries in the clear firmament. Sataghnis, some with four and some with two wheels, innumerable maces, and discs with edges sharp as razors and shining like lightning, also appear from the Narayanastra. Seeing all the sky covered by these uncanny weapons, O Bharatarishabha, the Pandavas, the Panchalas and the Srinjayas are absolutely terror-stricken. Most of all, wherever the Pandava maharathas offer resistance to the awesome astra of the Lord Vishnu, it only increases in power and ferocity. Devoured everywhere by the Narayanastra, as a heap of dry grass by some raging forest fire in summer, the Pandava warriors have no answer to Aswatthaman's ultimate ayudha and it consumes them rabidly on all sides.

Yudhishtira watches his men being incinerated and mown down in their thousands every moment, standing stupefied or flying blindly in all directions, and Arjuna doing nothing to stop the carnage, a panic-stricken Yudhishtira cries, "Dhrishtadyumna, escape with your Panchala troops! Satyaki, run with the Vrishnis and the Andhakas. Krishna will save himself. He can counsel the whole world so what need to tell him what he should do? We will not fight any more. This is my command.

As for myself, my brothers and I will climb onto a funeral pyre. Having crossed the Bhishma and the Drona oceans in this war, can I sink with all my followers in a cow's hoof print that is Drona's son? Let what Duryodhana wants be crowned with success today, for today I have killed our Acharya, who always loved us well, Drona who had the child Abhimanyu slaughtered by six maharathas and a host of warriors besides in the chakravyuha; the Acharya who sat indifferent with his son in the Kuru sabha, without answering Draupadi when she was dragged into that ancient court of dharma and asked him for truth and justice; Drona who wrapped an impenetrable kavacha around Duryodhana when Dhritarashtra's son wanted to kill Arjuna and sent him to protect Jayadratha; Drona who did not hesitate to turn Satyajit and his warriors into ashes with the Brahmastra while they protected my life; the Acharya, who, while we were being wrongfully exiled from our kingdom, gladly told us to go into the vana although our friends all asked him not to take sides with the Kauravas. Alas, it is this great friend of ours that has been slain! And for his sake today, I will, with my brothers and friends, lay down my life."

When Kunti's son, Yudhishtira says this with some fervour, Krishna makes a sign to the troops not to flee and says, "Be quick and lay down your weapons, all of you, and alight from your chariots. This is the only way, declared by the Lord Narayana himself, to render his great astra powerless. All of you come down onto the ground from your elephants, horses and chariots. If you stand weaponless on the earth, this astra will not touch you, while if you seek to fight it, it will only grow stronger and more devastating. The Narayanastra does not kill those who throw down their weapons and alight from their rathas, while those who even think of resisting it will be consumed, even if they seek refuge in the deepest Patala."

At what Krishna says, all the warriors of the Pandava army fling down their weapons and drive out every thought of violence from their hearts.

But seeing this, Bhimasena roars, "No one should lay down his weapons here. I will face and extinguish Aswatthaman's astra. With this golden mace of mine, I will range across the field and quell the Narayanastra on my own!

There is no man here equal to me in strength, even as there is no luminary in the firmament equal to the Sun. Look at these arms of mine like the trunks of mighty elephants, which can tear down the very peaks of Himavat. I possess the might of a thousand elephants. I have no peer for strength among men, even as Indra has none among the Devas. Let all men witness today the might of these arms and my chest as I smash down Aswatthaman's Narayanastra. If there is no one else who can face this weapon, I, Bhima, do so alone before all the Kurus and the Pandavas. O Arjuna, Bibhatsu, if you lay the Gandiva aside, a stain will attach to you like the one on the Moon."

Arjuna says, "Bhima, I have vowed that my Gandiva will not be used against the Narayanastra, cows and Brahmanas."

Hearing this, Bhima, roaring, riding his chariot of solar effulgence, whose rumble is like that of massed thunderheads, dashes off alone against Aswatthaman. With awesome prowess and lightness of hand, in the twinkling of an eye he covers Drona's wrathful son in a cloud of arrows. Smiling at Bhima's folly, Aswatthaman looses a storm of astras at him, each blazing like a small sun. Shrouded by these shafts that vomit fire and resemble snakes with mouth afire, as if covered with sparks of gold, Bhimasena looks like a mountain in the evening burning with many fires in the dry summer.

The Narayanastra now focuses it fury on just Bhimasena and, by the moment, swells in ferocity like a fire fanned by an angry wind. Watching this, further dread and panic seize the hearts of all the Pandava warriors other than Bhima. All the others, to the last man, throw down their weapons and alight from their mounts and chariots; now, that the rest supplicate themselves before it, the fulminant astra rages just at Bhima.

A great lament goes up from the Pandavas, for the dreadful Narayanastra swiftly overwhelms the defiant son of the Wind.'"

CANTO 197

DRONA-VADHA PARVA CONTINUED

"Sanjaya says, 'Seeing Bhimasena overwhelmed and being set on fire by the Narayanastra, Arjuna envelops him with a Varuna astra to douse its flames. So swiftly does Arjuna do this that no one can see the watery cupola that covers Vrikodara. Still enveloped by Aswatthaman's Narayanastra, Bhima, his horses, charioteer and ratha are like a great flame at the heart of a raging fire.

Even as at close of night, O Rajan, all the luminaries drop towards the Asta hill, the fiery arrows of Aswatthaman all fall on just Bhimasena's ratha, and he, his chariot, horses, and charioteer seem to be on fire. As the Yuga fire consumes the entire universe with all its creatures when Pralaya comes and finally re-enters the mouth of the Creator, even so does Aswatthaman's astra begins to enter the body of the fearless and brash Bhimasena.

Just as one cannot see a fire if it falls into the sun or the sun if it enters into Agni, no one can see the blinding energy that suffuses Bhima's body. Seeing the astra invading Bhima, and seeing Drona's son swelling with tejas, and being without an opponent to face him; seeing that all the warriors of the Pandava army have laid down their weapons and that all the maharathas of the Yudhishtira's army have turned their faces from the enemy, Arjuna and Krishna, leap out of their chariot and run towards Bhima; using maya shakti, they dive straight into the fires of the Narayanastra. The flames of the Lord's own weapon does not burn for, unlike Bhima, they have laid down their weapons, and also because of the Varuna astra and their own tejas.

Then, to pacify the Narayanastra, ancient Nara and Narayana forcibly lay hold of Bhima and wrest all his weapons away from him, at which the son of Vayu begins to roar in anger like a pride of lions being attacked! As he resists Krishna and Arjuna, the terrific astra grows even more ferocious.

Krishna says to Bhima in an irresistible voice, "How is it, O son of Pandu, that after being warned by us, you still continue to fight? If the Kurus could be vanquished now, while the Narayanastra hangs above us like the pralaya, we and all our maharathas would surely have fought as well. Look, all the warriors of your army have left their chariots. And you must do the same if you do not want to die!"

Krishna's tone will brook no refusal, and Bhima allows him to be hauled out of his flaming chariot, his eyes still crimson with rage, and sighing like some unimaginable serpent. As soon as he is pulled out of his chariot and made to lay down his weapons, the Narayanastra is pacified and grows cool. It drifts away in the sky, now a clear azure again, from above Kurukshetra.

All the directions and points of the firmament, cardinal and subsidiary, became clear. Sweet breezes begin to blow and the birds and animals are all calm again. The horses, elephants as well as all the warriors are enlivened once more, O ruler of men. Indeed, when the dreadful urjas of the Narayanastra is stilled, Bhima shines resplendent as the morning sun! With the passing of the threat from the Narayanastra, the remnant of the Pandava army once more stands ready to fight your sons.

Duryodhana says urgently to Aswatthaman, "Quick, use this astra again, for the Panchalas have taken up their weapons again and stand ready for battle!"

Aswatthaman sighs and says sadly, "The Narayanastra, O king, cannot be brought back and used again. If it is summoned again, it will have the life of the one that invokes it. Krishna knew the only way in which the Lord's own astra could be overcome, and he saved them all. But defeat and death are the same, Duryodhana. In fact, defeat is worse than death. Look at the enemy, vanquished and forced to lay down their weapons and prostrate before our Narayanastra. They are full of shame and even look as if they have lost their lives!" Duryodhana says, "Aswatthaman, if this weapon cannot be used twice, let these murderers of their Acharya be slain with other weapons! In you all the Devastras dwell, even as they do in the three-eyed Siva of immeasurable tejas. Even a raging Purandara cannot escape you."'

Dhritarashtra says, 'After Drona was killed with deceit and the Narayana weapon foiled, what does Drona's son, incited by Duryodhana, do, when he finds the Parthas ready for battle again and leading their troops at our army?'

Sanjaya says, 'Aswatthaman thinks of how his father was killed and rage fills him again. Casting aside all fear, flying the device of a lion's tail on his banner, he rides furiously at Dhrishtadyumna. Racing towards him, he pierces the Panchala prince with five and twenty small thunderbolts. Dhrishtadyumna retaliates with sixty-four searing shafts that rake Drona's son, strikes his charioteer with twenty golden-winged arrows whetted on stone, and his four horses with four long keen barbs that make them whinny in pain.

Repeatedly striking Aswatthaman with endless flights of arrows, and making the earth tremble with his thunderous shouts, a murderous Dhrishtadyumna appears intent on taking the lives of all the creatures of the world. Making death itself his only goal, the mighty son of Drupada, a great master of weapons and gifted with unerring aim, charges Drona's son pouring a deluge of arrows upon his head.

A roaring covers the angry Panchala prince with endless volleys. Always remembering the killing of his father, he pierces Drupada's son with lightning bolts and cuts down Dhrishtadyumna's standard and breaks his bow with two perfect shafts with razor heads. Never pausing his assault, he deprives his adversary of his horses, charioteer and chariot, and envelops all his followers with dense showers of sizzling shafts. Mauled by Aswatthaman, the Panchala troops, Rajan, flee.

Finding the troops turning away from battle and Dhrishtadyumna in dire trouble, Satyaki dashes at Aswatthaman and drills him first with eight straight, slender arrows and again stabs the roaring Brahman with twenty shafts of diverse kinds. Yuyudhana is a blur of fluid movement, as he then pierces Aswatthaman's sarathy with four barbs and his horses with another four. Without a moment's pause, displaying wonderful adroitness, he breaks Aswatthaman's bow and standard, and then shatters his gold-decked chariot, killing his horses as well in the same insant. Finally, he plunges thirty violent barbs into Aswatthaman's chest.

Beset by the resplendent Satyaki, bleeding profusely from his arrows, the mighty Aswatthaman founders, he does not know what to do. Seeing Drona's son in grave peril, Duryodhana, Kripa, Karna and others begin to cascade arrows over the radiant Satwata hero. They besiege Satyaki from every direction; Duryodhana pierces him with twenty stunning shafts, Acharya Kripa with three, Kritavarman with ten, Karna with fifty, Dusasana with a hundred and Vrishasena with seven. However, the marvellous Satyaki whirling around in his ratha, quickly demolishes the chariots of all these great heroes and they have to run from him on foot.

Meanwhile, Aswatthaman regains consciousness and, sighing repeatedly in pain and grief, thinks of what he should do. Mounting another chariot, he challenges Satyaki, shooting hundreds of arrows at the Satwata. Seeing him come to battle again, Satyaki, quick as a thought, destroys his ratha again and forces him to turn back. The Pandavas blow their conches with great force and give tremendous shouts. Having deprived Aswatthaman of his chariot, the invincible, scintillant Satyaki kills three thousand great maharathas of Vrishasena's akshauhini, slaughters fifteen thousand elephants of Kripa's division and fifty thousand horsemen of Sakuni's army.

Aswatthaman, riding another chariot and beside himself with rage at Satyaki, sets upon him, determined to kill him. Satyaki, nemesis of his enemies, instantly gores him with diverse kinds of arrows, fiercer than he had used earlier. Although deeply injured by these variegated shafts that Yuyudhana shoots, Aswatthaman still says, with his superior smile, to his enemy, "O grandson of Sini, I know your affection for Dhrishtadyumna, killer of his Acharya, but you will not be able to save him or yourself from me. I swear to you, Satyaki, by truth and by my tapasya, that I will know no peace until I kill all the Panchalas. You may unite the Pandava and Vrishni forces together and attack me, but I will still rid the world of the Somakas."

Saying this, the son of Drona shoots an astra with the effulgence of the sun at Satyaki, just as Indra in days of old cast his Vajra at the Asura Vritra. That astra flashes right through Yuyudhana's armour, passes through his body and dives into the earth like a hissing snake into its hole. Like an elephant deeply struck with a hook, the Satwata hero is bathed in the blood that gushes from his yawning wound. His bow, with an arrow fitted to its string, come looses from his mighty grasp and he sits down weakly on the floor of his chariot, while the blood continues to flow copiously, covering his magnificent body. Quickly, his sarathy whisks him away from the deadly Aswatthaman.

Immediately, Aswatthaman turns and strikes Dhrishtadyumna right between his eyebrows with another perfect arrow. Already sorely wounded, the Panchala prince, senapati of Yudhishtira army is flung back against his flagstaff and clutches onto it to prevent himself from falling. Seeing Dhrishtadyumna in distress and danger, like a weakened elephant attacked by a great lion, five Pandava maharathas—Kiritin, Bhimasena, Brihadkshatra of the Puru vamsa, a youthful prince of the Chedis and Sudarshana, lord of the Malavas, rush to defend him.

In moments, they surround Aswatthaman and, advancing twenty paces, all of them strike him simultaneously with five and twenty arrows. Pivoting on his heels, Drona's son cuts all twenty-five blistering shafts down with five and twenty barbs of his own that are like virulent snakes;

so swift is he that he appears to achieve this feat in the heart of a single instant. Aswatthaman then draws seven fonts of blood from the Paurava prince, three from the Malavas' chieftain, one from Partha, and six from Vrikodara, once more, it seems, at the same moment.

Now Rajan, those maharathas attack Drona's son, both united and separately, with storms of arrows whetted on stone and fletched with wings of gold. The youthful prince of the Chedis drills him with twenty barbs and Arjuna pierces him with three. Aswatthaman strikes Arjuna with six arrows, Krishna with six, Bhima with five, and each of the other two, the Malava and the Paurava, with two arrows. Then gouging Bhima's charioteer with six thunderbolts, Aswatthaman destroys Bhimasena's bow and standard with another two heavy, precise shafts of iron. Drona's stalwart son covers Arjuna once more with a dense and furious volley, and the Brahmana hero gives a deep and echoing shout.

Aswatthaman covers the earth, the sky, all the directions, cardinal and subsidiary, with his arrows so they are shrouded in darkness. Fierce is his tejas and his skill equal to Indra's; with three exact arrow he hacks off Sudarshana's arms like yupastambas and his head. He shatters the Paurava's chariot, then lops off his sandalwood seared arms and noble young head as well. Next moment, with a blaze of burning shafts he send the mighty Chedi prince, dark as a blue lotus, to Yama, along with his charioteer and horses.

Seeing the Malava lord, the scion of Puru and the youthful prince of the Chedis killed in front of his eyes by Aswatthaman, rage blazes up in Bhima and he swathes Drona's son with hundreds of serpentine narachas. But Aswatthaman destroys these showers of fiery shafts and strikes Bhima deep with his own thundering missiles. The dauntless Bhima rives Aswatthaman's bow with a wedge-headed arrow and pierces him deep with a smoking iron barb, heavy as a mace.

Throwing away his broken bow, Aswatthaman takes up another and rakes Bhima again with countless shafts. Locking into a duel, the two scathe each other with gales of arrows, like two masses of rain-clouds. Gold-winged arrows, whetted on stone and engraved with Bhima's name cover Drona's son, and thousands of powerful shafts shot by Drona's son enfold Bhima. Though wounded and bleeding profusely, it is wonderful that Bhima feels no pain, O Rajan!

Mahabaho Bhimasena looses ten shimmering gold-decked arrows up into the sky, from where they fall squarely on Aswatthaman, truly like streaks of lightning. Aswatthaman shuts his eyes and supports himself by gripping his flagstaff. He recovers his composure in a moment and, bathed in blood, musters all his valour and strength and races towards Bhimasena's chariot. From his bow drawn to its fullest stretch, he unleashes a hundred electrifying arrows at the hulking Pandava. Bhima merely shakes these off and responds with another burning volley.

As the battle continues, Drona's raging, magnificent son once more cleaves Bhimasena's bow in his hands and then gores his chest with a clutch of vicious shafts. The imperturbable Vrikodara merely picks up another bow and gashes Aswatthaman deep with five smouldering shafts. Once more, shooting ceaselessly at each other the two red-eyed heroes completely swathe one another with their banks upon banks of formidable missiles. Attempting to frighten each other by roaring and slapping their armpits echoingly, they fight on and there is nothing to choose between them.

Bending his massive bow, chased with gold, Aswatthaman gazes steadily at Bhima who continues to inundate him with shafts of fire, and, shooting back at Bhima, Drona's son looks like the meridian sun radiating his rays on an autumn day. So quicksilver is Aswatthaman's archery that no one can distinguish when he pulls an arrow from his quiver, when he fixes it to his bowstring, when he draws back the string, and when he looses his shaft. His bow, Rajan, seems always to be drawn into a circle of fire. And the terrible golden shafts, in their hundreds of thousands course like a river through the sky, like a swarm of locusts at Bhima's chariot.

We then see, O Bhaarata, an extraordinary demonstration of Bhimasena's skill, his strength, energy and spirit, for he shrugs off the riptides of Aswatthaman's arrows as if they were no more than gentle rain falling on him. Bhima, awesome, dreadful Bhima lets loose a typhoon of arrows at Drona's son, even as his father Vayu does at sea. Bhima's prodigious golden-backed bow also appears drawn into a constant circle; it is as lustrous as another bow of Indra and, spewing forth arrows past counting, shrouds Aswatthaman, that jewel of the war, so no one can see him or his chariot anymore. So thick and dense are their volleys that the very wind finds it difficult to flow through them.

Aswatthaman looses countless golden arrows, their points slick with oil, at Bhima. Bhimasena truncates each one into three segments before they can reach him. Bhima, with a roar, covers Drona's son in fierce rash of shafts. Aswatthaman shatters these in flight, then breaks Bhima's bow and pierces him with burning volleys.

Bhima casts a spear like a gash of lightning at the Brahmana; he divides it along its length as it flies burning at him.

Vrikodara the terrible takes up another massive bow and covers Aswatthaman in fire; Aswatthaman strikes Bhima's sarathy through his brow with a lean shaft and the charioteers swoons, drops his reins and his panicked horses bolt before all the watching warriors. Seeing Bhima borne helplessly from the field, the undefeated Aswatthaman blows a deep and echoing blast on his huge conch and all the Panchalas abandon Dhrishtadyumna and flee. Drona's son, unleashing torrid gusts of arrows pursues the fleeing Panchalas and cuts them down as he likes. Screaming, dying in droves, they never look back but continue their flight, and now many of the Pandava warriors join them.

Seeing the Panchala force broken and running, as also his own men, Arjuna quickly takes the field against Aswatthaman. The troops rally behind Krishna and Arjuna and remain on the field. Supported by the Somakas and the Matsyas, Arjuna lays dreadful siege to the Kauravas and stops them in their tracks.

The two Krishna ride up to Aswatthaman, and Arjuna says to him, "Now show me your prowess, your knowledge of the astras and your manliness, as well as your love for the Dhartarashtras and your hatred for us. Show me your fortitude and determination. I say to you that I will quell your pride today. Come now and face this Dhananjaya, who burns like the Yuga fire and Rudra himself, with Krishna for his sarathy. You have shown us your hubris in battle, Aswatthaman, but I will quell your arrogance."

Dhritarashtra asks, 'O Sanjaya, Aswatthaman is noble, mighty and worthy of our respect. He loves Dhananjaya dearly and the noble Arjuna loves him in return. Partha has never addressed Drona's son in this way before. Why then did the son of Kunti speak so roughly to his friend?'

Sanjaya says, 'Seeing the death of the youthful prince of the Chedis, of Brihadkshatra of the Puru vamsa, and of Sudarshana, the lord of the Malavas, who were all great warriors, and watching the defeat of Dhrishtadyumna, Satyaki and Bhima, Arjuna feels great sorrow. He is also touched to the quick by what Yudhishtira said to him. Most of all, all the wrongs of the past rise up in Arjuna in tide, and with it, suddenly, wrath the like of which he had never felt before. This was why he rounded on Aswatthaman, who is indeed worthy of our regard, and spoke in rage to him, like any lowborn man, in a crude, indecent, bitter, and harsh manner. Hearing those coarse and cruel words so unexpectedly from Arjuna, Aswatthaman is furious and especially with Krishna, whom he blames for influencing Arjuna and the Pandavas and for the death of his father.

Standing resolute in his chariot, Aswatthaman touches water and invokes the Agneyastra, which the very gods cannot resist. Aiming the weapon of the Fire god at Arjuna and indeed all his enemies, he breathes a mantra into the ayudha incandescent as smokeless fire and looses it at the Pandavas and their allies. It spumes up into the sky and, hanging there, erupts into thousands of flaming missiles that flare down crackling over Arjuna's chariot. Many of these fly at that ratha in uncanny trajectories, from every side. Meteors blaze down from the firmament and a thick gloom descends the Pandava host and envelops all the directions.

Rakshasas and Pisachas, thronging together, utter fierce cries. Inauspicious winds blow like simooms of the desert and the sun no longer exudes any warmth; a dreadful chill falls on Kurukshetra. Ravens caw raucously everywhere, and strange crimson clouds shower a rain of blood from the sky. Birds, beasts, kine and rishis with souls under perfect control, all grow distraught. The Panchamahabhutas, the very elements, appear to be in upheaval; the sun seems to spin like a top and the entire universe, scorched by the heat of the weapon of fire, to be in a fever.

Seared by the fiery energy of that astra, great elephants and other beasts of the world lose their wits in terror and dash about, panting and desperate for salvation from the weapon made of the flames that consume the world when the yuga ends. Seas, lakes, river, pools and tanks begin to steam and bubble, and the fish and other creatures living in them are scalded and perish in agony. From all the points of the sky, from the highest firmament and from the very bowels of earth, cataracts of fiery arrows erupt out of the ground, as if released with the force of Garuda or Vayu himself. Struck and burnt to cinders by these, the enemy warriors are made ashes like trees devoured by a raging conflagration.

The biggest elephants, leviathans, are incinerated by the Agneyastra and fall in great mounds of whispering ashes, while others of their kind thunder about everywhere in absolute panic, trumpeting in terror. Everywhere, thousands of horses and chariots burn like the tops of trees in a forest-fire. Indeed, O Bhaarata, it is as if the divine lord Agni has come down to burn the Pandava army, like the Samvarta fire consuming everything at the end of the Yuga.

Your soldiers, Rajan, are elated and give vent to loud shouts. Sensing victory, your troops blow thousands of conches and trumpets as they watch the Pandava army being devoured by the flames of the astra of fire. Darkness and smoke wrap the world and neither any part of the Pandava army nor Arjuna can be seen at all. The war has not yet seen the like of this weapon which Drona's son unleashes.

Then, Arjuna invokes the Brahmastra, which belongs to the Lotus-born Brahma himself and which can confound every other astra. Within a moment, all the darkness is dispelled, cool winds begin to blow, and all the directions of the sky become clear and bright; and now the wondrous and dreadful sight of a full akshauhini of the Pandava army having being turned to ashes becomes visible. Some of the dead men, chariots and beasts of war stand as pillars formed of ash, like the most delicate sculptures, while all the rest have been entirely consumed and lie in grey heaps or blow in the dry wind that sweeps Kurukshetra.

Emerged from the darkness, we see Krishna and Arjuna again, like the Sun and the Moon. And, Rajan, there is not a wound, not even the merest scratch of burn upon them from Aswatthaman's astra. The ratha, which strikes such terror into your warriors' hearts, shines resplendent on the field, its great banner with Hanuman flapping free in the wind, its gandharva horses white and shining like great lotuses, and with all the mighty astras in it untouched and still unsummoned by the invincible Dhananjaya.

Now the remnant of the Pandava host erupts in joyful sounds, with roars and laughter of great relief, with booming conches and drumrolls. Both hosts had thought that Krishna and Arjuna had perished, but finding them alive and shine forth again after the darkness has been dispelled, all the Pandavas are filled with absolute joy, and the Kauravas with wonder.

Unharmed and cheerful, the two heroes blow their wonderful conches, the Panchajanya and the Devadatta, and Kurukshetra trembles in delight at their melodious thunder. Your troops, however, are crestfallen, as is Aswatthaman who had also believed that he had slain the two Krishnas. For a moment, my lord, he reflects on what has happened and he is filled with dismay and lancing anxiety; he breathes long, hot sighs and is plunged into an abyss of dejection.

Aswatthaman flings aside his bow, alights from his chariot, cries in utter despair, "Shame, O shame! Everything is lost, everything is a lie, all is adharma!" and like one gone mad he runs away from the battle, waving his arms wildly.

On the way, he meets the impeccant Krishna Dwaipayana, Maharishi Vyasa dark as thunderheads, compiler of the Vedas, home of the Shastras, the abode of Saraswati. Seeing him standing in his path, Aswatthaman prostrates before him and, in a voice choked with grief and frustration, asks, "O Sire, Mahamuni, is this an illusion or a whim of the Agneyastra? I do not know how my astra proved ineffectual. What flaw was there in its invocation? Is this my fault, something supernatural, or have the two Krishnas achieved victory over Nature herself and Agni that they are still alive?

Ah, it seems that Kaala is irresistible. The Agneyastra that I unleashed at the Pandava army, the Asuras, Gandharvas, Pisachas, Rakshasas, Uragas, Yakshas, Pakshis and Manavas cannot ever hope to confound, the blazing ayudha which must devour all that stand before it, was doused after killing just one akshauhini of troops. Why did it not kill Kesava and Arjuna, both of whom are human? O Holy one, O Mahamuni, answer me truly and in detail."

Vyasa replies, "What you ask is grave and significant, so listen well to what I have to tell you. He who is called Narayana is older than the very oldest ones. To fulfil a great mission in the world, the Creator of the universe was once born as the son of Dharma. He undertook the most arduous tapasya, the atikatora, upon the Himavat mountan.

Imbued with infinite tejas, and like fire or the sun in splendour, he stood there with arms raised to the skies. His eyes like lotus-petals, he emaciated himself there for sixty-six thousand years, subsisting all the while only on air. When this was over, he resumed his tapasya, now of another king, and this time for twice as many years as the first. He filled the space between earth and heaven with his boundless energy. When, through those tapasyas, he became like Brahma himself, he then beheld the Master, the Origin, and the Guardian of the Universe, the Lord of all the gods, the Supreme Deity, who it is well nigh impossible to gaze upon, who is more minute than the most minute thing, and greater than the greatest; who is called Rudra, who is the Lord of all the Superior Ones, who is called Hara and Sambhu, who wears matted jata on his head, who is the infuser of life into every living being, who is the First Cause of all things, mobile and unmoving; who is irresistible and of frightful aspect, who is fierce in anger and the Final Great Soul, who is the All-destroyer, and whose heart is as vast, loving and merciful as all eternity; who wields the celestial bow, the Pinaka, and wears two inexhaustible quivers, who wears golden kavacha and whose energy is infinite; who holds a blazing Trisula, the battle axe, a mace and a huge sword; whose eyebrows are fair, whose locks are always matted, who wields the heavy cudgel, who has the Moon on his brow, who is clad in tiger-skin; who is decked with beautiful angadas, who has snakes for his sacred thread, and who is surrounded by diverse creatures of the universe and by numerous ghosts and spirits; who is the One, who is the abode of ascetic austerities, and who is adored by those of venerable age; who is Water, Heaven, Sky, Earth, Sun, Moon, Wind and Fire, and who is the measure of the duration of the universe.

Sinners can never obtain a sight of the Un-born One, the slayer of all haters of Brahmanas, the giver of Mukti. Only Brahmanas of dharma, when cleansed of all their sins and freed from the control of grief, see him with their mind's eye. As a result of his two unequalled tapasyas, Narayana obtained a sight of the Unfading One, Siva the embodiment of dharma, the Adorable One, the Being whose Form is the universe. Seeing that Supreme Abode of all splendour, the God with a garland of akshas around his neck, Narayana Vasudeva, his soul gratified, was filled with rapture, and he sought to express it through words, with his heart, understanding and body. Narayana worshipped the Divine Lord Siva, the First Cause of the universe, the giver of boons, the Puissant One who is always at love with the fair-limbed Parvati, the Noblest Being surrounded by large bands of bhutas, pramathas, the Unborn Aja, the Supreme Lord, the Embodiment of the Unmanifest Brahman, the Essence of all causes, the One of unfading power and glory.

Having saluted Rudra, destroyer of the Asura Andhaka, the lotus-eyed Narayana, his heart full of love, began to praise the Three-eyed One: 'O Adorable one, O First of all the gods, Creator of the Prajapatis who are the regents of the world, who having entered the Earth, your first work, O Lord, protected it once, all, all have sprung from you.

The Devas, Asuras, Nagas, Rakshasas, Pisachas, Manavas, Pakshis, Gandharvas, Yakshas and all other creatures, along with the entire universe, we know, have all sprung from you.

Everything done to worship and propitiate Indra, Yama, Varuna, Kubera, the Pitris, Tvashtri and Soma, is really offered to you.

Form and light, sound and sky, wind and touch, taste and water, scent and earth, time, Brahma himself, the Vedas, the Brahmanas and all these moving beings have sprung from you.

Vapours rising from diverse bodies of water, become raindrops, which falling upon the earth, are separated from one another. When the time of the Mahapralaya, the Universal Dissolution comes, these individual water drops, separated from one another, once more unite together and make the Earth one vast expanse of water. Thus observing the origin and the destruction of all things, the learned man understands your Oneness.

You have created everything—the two birds Iswara and Jiva, four Aswatthas with their wordy branches the Vedas, the seven guardians, which are constituted by the five Panchamahabhutas, the elements, the heart, the understanding, and the ten senses that constitute the body. But you are separate from and independent of them.

The Past, the Future, and the Present, over each of which none can have any sway, are from you, as also the seven worlds and this universe. I am your devoted adorer, Lord, be kind to me. Do not injure me by causing evil thoughts to enter my heart.

You are the Soul of souls, incapable of being known. He who knows you as the Universal Seed, attains Brahman. Wishing to offer you reverence, I do praise you, endeavoring to ascertain your true nature,

O you whom the very gods cannot fathom, I worship you fervently, so grant me the boons I want that are difficult to acquire. Do not hide yourself in your maya.'

The blue-throated God of inconceivable Soul, the wielder of the Pinaka, the divine Lord forever praised by the Rishis, then gave boons to the deserving Narayana.

Mahadeva said, 'O Narayana, through my grace, you will be of immeasurable might and soul among Manushas, Devas and Gandharvas. Neither Devas, Asuras, great Uragas, Pisachas, Gandharvas, Rakshasas,

Manavas, Garudas, Nagas, nor any creature in the Universe will ever be able to withstand you. None among even the Devas will be able to vanquish you in war. Through my grace, no one will ever be able to cause you the least injury, not even with the Vajra or with any weapon that is wet or dry, or with anything mobile or unmoving. You will even be superior to me if you ever go to battle against me.'

This is how Narayana acquired boons in the past. Even that Narayana now walks the Earth as Krishna, beguiling the universe with his maya. From Narayana's tapasya a great Muni of the name of Nara was born, and he was equal to Narayana himself. Know that Arjuna is none other than that same Nara. These two Rishis, said to be older than the oldest gods, are born in every Yuga to serve the mysterious purposes and designs of the universe. You, too, O you of great heart, have been born as an amsa of Rudra, by virtue of all your punya of past lives and as a result of your stern and lofty tapasya, and you are endowed with Rudra's own energy and wrath. You were, in a former life, imbued with great wisdom and were equal to a Deva.

Thinking of the universe as consisting only of Mahadeva Siva, you once emaciated yourself through diverse vratas from a wish to gratify this God. Assuming the form of a very superior person who blazes fourth with splendour, you worshipped the Great God with mantras, with homa, and with offerings. Thus adored by you in your past life, Siva was gratified with you, and granted you many boons, everything that your heart wanted. Like Kesava's and Arjuna's, your punya karma and tapasya were also exalted and superior. Like them, in your worship, you have, in every Yuga, worshipped Mahadeva as Linga, his phallic form.

Krishna is that devoted worshipper of Rudra who has sprung from Rudra himself. Kesava always worships the Lord Siva, believing his sacred Linga to be the origin of the universe. That supreme knowledge, which allows him to see the identity of Brahman with the universe, as well as that other trikaalagyana by which he sees the Past, the Present and the Future, the near and the remote, as if all are before his divine eyes, dwell in dark Krishna. The Devas, the Siddhas and the great Rishis worship

Krishna to acquire that highest object in the universe, which is Siva Mahadeva. Krishna is the creator of everything. The Eternal Krishna must be worshipped with sacrifices. The Lord Kesava always worships Siva as Linga as the origin of all creatures. The God, with the bull for his mark, cherishes greater regard for Krishna than for anyone else."

Having heard what Vyasa says, Aswatthaman bows to Rudra and now looks upon Krishna as worthy of the highest reverence. Having fetched his soul under complete control, he is filled with bliss, the marks of which communion with Brahman appear on his body. Bowing to the great Rishi, Aswatthaman turns back to the unhappy Kuru army and withdraws them from the field for the night. The Pandavas also, Rajan, follow.

Having fought for five days and caused immeasurable carnage, thus does great Drona, the Brahmana who knew the Veda in its entirety, leaves this world and attains to Brahmaloka!'"

CANTO 198

Drona-vadha Parva continued

"Dhritarashtra says, 'After the killing of Atiratha Drona by Drupada's son Dhrishtadyumna, what do my sons and the Pandavas do?'

Sanjaya says, 'After the rout of the Kuru army and the death of Drona, Arjuna, who saw something wonderful during the great battle, asks his grandsire Vyasa, who arrives in Kurukshetra during his wanderings.

Arjuna says, "O Maharishi, while I loosed a river of arrows at the enemy, I always saw before me, always going before my chariot, a shining, resplendent being, one who had the effulgence of fire. Wherever he went with his spear raised, all the enemy warriors fell before him. While everyone thought that I vanquished the enemy, in truth they died at the hands of this mysterious being. I merely followed I his wake and only put down those that he had already destroyed.

Holy one, tell me who is this greatest one that I saw, armed with a spear, and shining like the Sun himself in tejas? He did not touch the earth with his feet, nor did he cast his spear even once. Yet, through his energy, thousands of spears, why, millions of spears issued out of the single one that he held."

Vyasa replies, "Arjuna, you have seen Sankara, the First Cause[1] from which the Prajapatis have sprung; you saw the omnipotent One of infinite tejas, He who is the embodiment of Swarga, Bhumi and Akasa, the Divine Lord, the protector of the universe, the great Master, the giver of boons, who is also called Isana. O Arjuna, seek the protection of this boon-giving Deity, the Lord of the universe. He is called Mahadeva, the Supreme Deity, of Supreme Soul, the One and only Lord, with matted jata, Siva the abode of auspiciousness. With three eyes and mighty arms, with his locks tied in the shape of a crown, and his body clad in skins, He is called Rudra.

This Lord of the universe, the Supreme God, is also called Hara and Sthanu. He is the Best of every being in the universe; He cannot be vanquished, He is the delighter of the akhanda and its Supreme Sovereign. He is the First Cause, the light and refuge of the universe, and ever victorious. He is the Soul and the Creator of the Brahmanda with the Brahmanda for his form, and He possesses eternal fame.

The Lord of the universe and its great Ruler, this powerful One, is also the master of all karma, of every deed. Also called Sambhu, He is Self-born; He is the Lord of all creatures and the Origin of the Past, the Future and the Present.

He is Yoga and the Lord of Yoga; He is called Sarva, and is the King of all the worlds. He is superior to everything. The best of everything in the universe, and the highest of all, He is also called Paramesthin.

The Ordainer of the three worlds, He is their sole refuge. Invincible, He is the protector of the universe, and the cause of birth, decay and death. The Soul of knowledge, incapable of being grasped by knowledge, and the highest of all knowledge, He is unknowable.

Through his grace, He gives his worshippers the blessings they desire. This Lord has for his companions celestial beings, Ganas, of various

---

[1]This passage is based on Siva's sacred names, each a holy mantra, found in the Sata Raudriya and the Koti Rudra.

forms, some of whom are dwarfs, some have matted locks, some are bald, some have short necks, some protuberant bellies, some huge bodies, some long ears and some possess great strength. All of them, O Partha, have deformed faces and mouths and legs and wear strange attire. These Siva Ganas are his nearest, greatest followers and they worship this Supreme God called Mahadeva.

It is this same Siva, O son, who, through his kindness and love, rides in front of you. Partha, who other than the divine Maheswara, the greatest of all archers, can even in imagination venture to vanquish a host led by maharathas like Aswatthaman, Karna and Kripa? No one can face the warrior who has Maheswara going before him. There is no being in the three worlds that is equal to Rudra. The very scent of an enraged Mahadeva causes men in battle, to tremble and fall senseless and in their thousands. It is for this that the Devas in Swarga worship and bow to Him. The men in this world and these other men of pious conduct, that devoutly worship the boon-giving, divine and auspicious Siva, find happiness here and attain to the highest state in the hereafter.

O son of Kunti, bow down to Him who is peace, to Him who is called Rudra or Nilakanta, to Him who is the Subtlest and of great refulgence and is also Kapardin, the skull-bearer.

Bow down to him who is terrible, who has tawny eyes, who is boon-giving; bow to the Great Ordainer of red locks and righteous conduct; to Him who always performs and enables auspicious deeds; to Him who is the final object of desire; to Him who is called Sthanu; who is called Purusha; who has tawny hair; who is without fear, who is subtler than all that is sukshma and of absolute radiance; bow to Him who is Light and the giver of light; who is the embodiment of all sacred tirthas and waters; to He who is the God of gods, and who is also endued with great impetuosity.

Bow down to him who is of manifest form; who is called Sarva; who wears truly agreeable attire; who wears a wonderful crown, who is handsomeness itself; who has the mountains for his dwelling; who is Peace; who is the Protector; who wears valkala, tree bark; he whose arms are decked with ornaments of gold; who is Ugra, fierce, who is the Lord of all the directions; he who is the Lord of the clouds and of all created beings: He who is the Lord of all trees and of all kine, He whose body is shrouded by trees.

Bow down to him who is the celestial Senapati; who inspires all thought; who holds the yagna ladle in his hand; who is ablaze; who wields the great bow; who is Rama's very self; who has diverse forms; who is the Lord of the universe; who is attired in munja grass; who has a thousand heads, a thousand eyes, a thousand arms, and a thousand legs.

O son of Kunti, seek the protection of this boon-giving Lord of the universe, the Lord of Uma, the God with three eyes, the destroyer of Daksha's sacrifice, the Guardian of all created things, who is always blissful, the Protector of all beings, the God of unfading glory; the One with jata; the Mover of all superior beings, the One whose navel is like that of a bull and who has the bull for his symbol; the one who is proud like the bull, who is the Lord of bulls; who is represented by the horns of the bull; and who is the Bull of bulls: He who has the image of the bull on his banner.

Seek the protection of him who is liberal to all the righteous; who can be approached only through Yoga; and whose eyes are like those of a bull; who owns the highest weapons: who has Vishnu himself for his astra; who is the embodiment of dharma; who is called Maheswara; who is of infinite belly and body; who sits on a leopard's skin; who is the Lord of the worlds; who is devoted to Brahman and who loves Brahmanas; who is armed with a trident; who is boon-giving; who wields the sword and the shield and who is the Auspicious One, who wields the bow called Pinaka, who gave away his battle axe to Parasurama, and who is the Protector and Lord of the universe.

I place myself in the hands of this divine Lord, the grantor of protection, the God clad in deer-skins.

Salutations to this Lord of the celestials who has Vaisravana for his friend.

Salutations to Him of great vows; to Him who has the mightiest archers for his companions; to Him who himself wields the bow; to the God with whom the bow is a favourite weapon; who is himself the shaft shot by the bow; who is the bowstring and the bow; who is the Acharya of acharyas who teach the use of the bow.

Salutations to the God whose weapons are fierce and who is the greatest of all the gods.

Salutations to Him of diverse forms, to him who is surrounded by many bowmen.

Salutations to Him who is called Sthanu and who has an immense host of great archers for companions.

Salutations to Him who destroyed the triple city of Tripura.

Salutations to Him who slew the Asura Bhaga.

Salutations to Him who is the Lord of trees and of men.

Salutations to Him who is the Lord of the Devas, the Mothers, and of those tribes of spirits known as Ganas.

Salutations to Him who is the Lord of kine and of sacrifices.

Salutations to Him who is the Lord of the waters and the Lord of the gods, who broke Surya's teeth, who has three eyes, who is the grantor of boons; who is called Hara, who is blue-throated, and who is of golden dreadlocks.

I will now tell you, as best I know, all the divine deeds of Mahadeva of Supreme Wisdom. If Mahadeva becomes angry, neither the Devas, the Asuras, the Gandharvas or the Rakshasas, even if they hide themselves in the deepest oceans, can find peace.

In olden days, Brahma's son, the Prajapati Daksha undertook a great sacrifice and insulted Siva by not inviting him to attend, not offering him a share in the havis. Daksha's daughter, Rudra's wife Sati, killed herself at her father's yagna and Mahadeva destroyed the sacrifice in wrath. He was truly fearsome on that occasion and roared most horribly and shouted in anger so earth and sky shook. The Devas were terrified then. Indeed, at Mahadeva's fury, Yagna himself fled and the gods were beside themselves for fear at the twanging of Mahadeva's bow and the sound of his palms.

The Devas and Asuras fled all together. All the waters, great and small rose up in agitation and the Earth trembled. The mountains split, all the points of the sky wavered, and the Nagas were petrified. The universe was enveloped in a thick darkness and could no longer be seen. The splendour of all the stars and of the Sun grew dim. The Rishis, filled with fear, were distraught and, wanting to save themselves as well as all creatures, performed propitiatory rites, with Surya being given the principal oblation to eat. Smilingly, Sankara approached him and tore out his teeth.

The humbled gods then fled as one. Once more, Mahadeva aimed a shower of arrows like the flames of the pralaya at the Devas, astras like densely smoking fire, or clouds with lightning. Seeing the luciferous volley, all the Devas prostrated again to Maheswara, and to Him a substantial share in yagnas. In fright, the gods, O prince, sought Rudra's protection. His wrath having been dispelled, for He is easily pleased, the great God then restored the yagna. The gods that had fled came back, but to this day they are afraid of Maheswara.

Once, the great and valiant Asuras had three cities in the sky, the Tripura. Each of these was vast and wonderful. One was made of iron, another of silver, and the third of gold. The golden city belonged to Kamalaksha, the silver city to Tarakaksha, and the third, made of iron, to Vidyunmalin. With all his weapons, Indra Maghavat Indra could not breach or make any impression on those triad cities. Troubled by the Asuras, the Devas sought the protection of Rudra.

Approaching Siva, all the gods with Indra at their head, pleaded, 'These terrible dwellers of the Tripura have blessings from Brahma. Filled with pride because of these boons, they are wreaking havoc upon the universe. O Devadeva, no one save you can stop them. O Mahadeva, slay these enemies of the Devas. O Rudra, creatures sacrificed in every yagna will then be yours.'

Thus implored by the gods, Siva was moved by the desire to help them. He agreed and said, 'I will overthrow the Asuras.'

Then Hara made the two mountains Gandhamadana and Vindhya the two poles of his chariot; He made the Earth with her oceans and forests his ratha. The three-eyed Lord made Sesha, that prince of snakes, the aksha, of that chariot. That God of gods, the wielder of Pinaka, then made the Moon and the Sun his two chariot wheels, and the Lord made Elapatra and Pushpadanta, the two pins of its yoke. Mahadeva made the Malaya mountains the yoke, and the great Takshaka, the rope that bound the yoke to the poles, and the ganas about him the traces of the horses.

Maheswara made the four Vedas his four horses and made the Vedangas the bridle-bits. Mahadeva made Gayatri and Savitri the reins, Om the whip, and Brahma was the charioteer. Making the Mandara mountains his great bow, Vasuki the bowstring, Vishnu his awesome astra, Agni the arrow-head, and Vayu the two wings of that missile, Yama the feathers in its tail, lightning its whetting stone, and Meru his standard, Siva, riding on that magnificent chariot which was wrought from all the celestial forces, went forth to destroy the Tripura, the three sky cities of the Asuras.

O Partha, then Sthanu of incalculable prowess, worshipped by the Devas and by Rishis, He of untold tapodhana, formed an unrivalled vyuha named after Himself, and stood unmoving for a thousand years. Finally, when the three cities came together in the firmament, the Lord Mahadeva struck them through with his that awesome astra of three knots. The Danavas could not look at the shaft made of the Yuga-fire and composed of Vishnu and Soma.

When the Tripura began to burn, the Devi Parvati went there to see the sight. She had on her lap a child with a bald head with five clumps of hair on it. The Goddess asked the Devas who the child was. Sakra, through malice, tried to strike that child with his thunderbolt. The divine lord Mahadeva, for the child was none other than He, smilingly paralysed the arm of the enraged Indra. Sakra, with all the celestials, flew went to the Lord Brahma of unfading glory and, bowing their heads to him, they said to him with joined hands, 'Some wonderful Being, O Brahma, lies on the lap of Parvati, in the form of a child. We saw but did not pay him reverence and he has vanquished us all. We ask you, Pitamaha, who the child may be, who, without fighting, has with the greatest ease vanquished us all with Purandara at our head.'

Hearing this, Brahma the greatest of all the Gods, knower of the Brahman, reflected for a moment and knew that boy of immeasurable energy was none other the divine Sambhu. He said to all the Devas with Indra at their head, 'That child is the divine Hara, Lord of the mobile and unmoving universe. There is nothing superior to Maheswara. That Being of immeasurable splendour whom you all saw with Uma, the Divine Lord, had assumed the form of a child for Uma's sake. Let us all go to him. That illustrious One is the Supreme Sovereign of the worlds. O Devas, you could not recognise the Master of the universe!'

All the Devas with the Grandsire went to that child, of the radiance of the morning Sun. Beholding Maheswara, and knowing that he is the Supreme Being, the Pitamaha Brahma worshipped him: 'You are Sacrifice, O Lord, you are the stay and refuge of the universe. You are Bhava, you are Mahadeva, you are the abode of all things and you are the highest refuge. This whole universe, with its mobile and rooted beings is pervaded by you. O Holy One, O Lord of the past and the future, O Lord of the world, O Protector of the universe, show your mercy to Indra whom you have paralysed.'

Hearing these words of the Lotus-born Brahma, Maheswara was gratified; He laughed aloud, a wondrous sound so full of grace. The Devas then eulogised both Uma and Rudra and paid them great reverence. Indra's arm was free again when The Greatest God Maheswara, the destroyer of Daksha's sacrifice, the Divine Lord with the Bull for his emblem, grew benign towards Indra and his Devas.

He is Rudra, He is Siva, He is Agni, He is Sarva, and He has knowledge of everything. He is Indra, He is Vayu, He is the Aswin twins, and He is the lighting. He is Bhava, He is Parjanya, He is Mahadeva, He is sinless. He is the Moon, He is Isana, He is Surya, He is Varuna. He is Kala, he is Antaka, He is Mrityu, He is Yama.

He is the day, and He is the night. He is the fortnight, He is the month, He is the seasons. He is the morning and evening sandhyas, He is the year. He is Dhatri, He is Vidhatri, He is the Soul of the universe, and He is the doer of all karma in the universe. Though bodiless, He is also the Great God embodied. Endowed with the Splendour beyond all splendour, He is worshipped and praised by all the gods. He is One, He is Many; He is a hundred, a thousand and beyond all count.

Brahmanas versed in the Vedas say that He has two forms, the terrible, Ugra, and the auspicious, Siva. These two forms, again, are multifarious. His auspicious forms are water, light, and the moon. Whatever is most recondite and mysterious in the several angas of the Vedas, in the Upanishads, in the Puranas, and in the Atmavidyas, the sciences that deal with the Soul, dwells the Lord Maheswara.

O Arjuna, Mahadeva is Aja, Un-born. All the attributes of this God not even I can begin to enumerate, not if I were to describe them with out pause for a thousand years. Even to those who are afflicted by all the evil planets, even to those who are stained with every sin, this great Protector grants salvation, if only they seek him, and He becomes pleased with them. He grants and takes away life, health, prosperity, wealth and all the diverse kinds of objects of desire.

The prosperity seen in Indra and other gods is his. He is ever engaged in the good and evil of men in this world. As a result of his supremacy, He can always have whatever He wishes for. He is called Maheswara and is the Lord of even the Supreme ones. In many forms, of many kinds, He pervades the universe. The mouth of that God is in the deepest ocean. It is well-known that, assuming the form of a mare's head, this mouth drinks the sacrificial libation in the form of water.

This Siva always dwells in smasanas, burning ghats. Men worship this Supreme Lord in that place where none but the courageous can go. Many are the blazing and terrible forms of this God that men speak of and worship in the world. Many also are the true names of this Deity in all the worlds. These names are based upon his supremacy, his omnipotence, and his divine and unequalled deeds. In the Vedas, the marvellous and sacred hymn called the Sata Rudriya has been sung in honour of this great God, the infinite Rudra.

This God is the Lord of all wishes that are human and heavenly.

He is omnipotent, and He is the supreme master. Indeed, He pervades the infinite universe. The Brahmanas and the Munis describe him as the First-born of all creatures. He is the First of all the gods; from his mouth was born Vayu the wind.

Since he always protects the creatures of the universe and plays with them, and since he is the Lord of all creatures, he called Pasupati.

Since his Linga is always in the observance of the vow of Brahmacharya, and since He always gladdens the world, He is called Maheswara. The Rishis, the Devas, the Gandharvas and Apsaras ever worship his Lingam, which stand eternally upright. This worship pleases Maheswara and makes him joyful.

With regard to the past, the future, and the present, Siva has many forms, and for that he is known as Bahurupa. Possessing one eye, he blazes forth in effulgence; He is otherwise known to have infinite eyes on every part of his body.

Since He possesses the worlds He is called Sarva.

Since his form is like that of smoke He is called Dhurjjati.

Since the Viswedevas dwell in him, He is called Viswarupa.

Since three Goddesses, Heaven, Water and Earth adore and depend on the Lord of the universe, he is called Tryambaka.

Since he always increases all kinds of wealth and wishes the good of mankind in all their actions, He is called Siva, the Auspicious One.

He has a thousand eyes, ten thousand eyes, and they gaze in all directions. And because He protects this vast universe, He is called Mahadeva.

Since He is Great and Ancient and is the Source of life and of its continuance, and since his Lingam is everlasting, He is called Sthanu.

Since the rays of the Sun and the Moon that appear in the world are spoken of as the hair on the Three-eyed One, He is called Vyomakesa.

Since, from Kalpa to Kalpa, He destroys every Brahma, Indra, Varuna, Yama, Kubera, and the rest, He is called Hara.

Since, He is the Past, the Future and the Present, and everything in the universe, and since He is the Origin of the past, the future, and the present, He is for that reason called Bhava.

Kapi means Supreme, and Vrisha is said to mean righteousness. The illustrious God of gods, is hence called Vrishakapi.

Since Maheswara, with his two eyes shut in dhyana, created through sheer force of will a third eye on his forehead, He is called Trinetra.

Whatever sickness there is in the bodies of living creatures and whatever health is in them represent that God. He is the Wind, the vital airs called Prana, Apana and the others in the bodies of all creatures, including those that are diseased. Those who worship any image of the Sivalinga, always obtains great felicity.

He is fiery below his waist, and the upper half of his body that is cool and auspicious is Soma the Moon. So too, half his Soul is Agni and the other half Soma. His auspicious form, full of tejas, blazes more brightly that than the forms of all the gods together. Among men, his burning and dreadful form is called Agni. With his cool and auspicious form, He practises Brahmacharya.

With the other terrible form He is the Supreme Lord who devours everything. Since He burns, since he is fierce, since he is endued with great prowess and devours flesh, blood and marrow, he is called Rudra.

O Partha, this is the Deity called Mahadeva, armed with the Pinaka, whom you saw going before your chariot and killing your enemies. After you vowed to kill the king of the Sindhus, O sinless one, Krishna showed you this God, in your dream, sitting on the top of Kailasa, the holiest mountain. This illustrious God goes before you in battle. It is He who gave you the weapons with which you brought carnage to the Danavas.

O Arjuna, I have now told you of the Sata-Rudriya, contained in the Veda, which is the hymn that describes and praises the God of gods, and enumerates some of his endless names, each one a potent and holy mantra. This hymn of four divisions, with which every objective is achieved, is perfectly sacred, destroys all sins removes all stains and destroys all sorrows and all fears. Men that always listen to this Sata-Rudriya, Siva's hundred names, will vanquish all their enemies and be highly regarded in the land of Rudra.

The person who always attentively reads or listens to this auspicious account of how Siva went before Arjuna's chariot and annihilated his enemies, and devoutly worships that illustrious Lord of the universe, will obtain all the objects of his desire as a result of the Three-eyed God being pleased with him. Go and fight, O son of Kunti! Defeat is not for you, who have Krishna on your side for your advisor and protector."

O Bhaarata, having spoken thus to Arjuna, Maharishi Vyasa, the son of Parasara, vanishes and returns to his asrama from whence he had come.'

CANTO 199

Drona-vadha Parva continued

"Sanjaya says, 'Having fought savagely for five days, Rajan, the Brahmana Drona fell and ascended into blessed Brahmaloka. The very benefits that accrue from a study of the Vedas arise from a study of this Drona Parva. The great feats of the most intrepid and majestic Kshatriyas have been described here. He who reads or listens to the recitation of this Parva every day is freed from the most heinous sins and the most atrocious crimes. Brahmanas will always obtain the fruits of yagnas from here. From this Parva, Kshatriyas will have victory in the fiercest battles. The other varnas, Vaisyas and Sudras, can acquire desirable sons and grandsons and all objects of desire!'"

The End of Drona Parva